Fifth Edition

Introduction to Computers & Information Systems

The Internet Edition

Larry Long & Nancy Long

 Prentice Hall, Upper Saddle River, NJ 07458

Library of Congress Cataloging-in-Publication Data

Long, Larry E.
    Introduction to Computers & Information Systems/Larry Long &
Nancy Long.—5th ed., the Internet ed.
    416 pp.   cm.
    Rev. ed. of: Introduction to Computers and Information systems.
4th ed. c1994.
    Includes index.
    ISBN 0-13-255639-1 (pbk.)
    1. Electronic digital computers   2. Electronic data processing.
    I. Long, Nancy.   II. Long, Larry E. Introduction to computers
and information systems.   III. Title
QA76.5.L655   1996
004—dc20   96-31703
                                                          CIP

Editor-in-Chief: Rich Wohl
Senior Acquisitions Editor: Jo-Ann DeLuca
Production Editor: Anne Graydon
Managing Editor: Katherine Evancie
Senior Designer: Sue Behnke
Interior Design: Jill Little
Design Director: Pat Wosczyk
Cover Designer: Maureen Eide
Cover Illustrator: Don Baker
Executive Marketing Manager: Nancy Evans
Senior Manufacturing Supervisor: Paul Smolenski
Manufacturing Manager: Vincent Scelta
Assistant Editor: Audrey Reagan
Editorial Assistant: Marc Oliver
Production Coordinator: Renee Pelletier
Director of Manufacturing and Production: Joanne Jay

© 1997, 1994, 1991, 1988, 1985 by Prentice Hall, Inc.
A Simon & Schuster Company
Upper Saddle River, New Jersey 07458

Printed in the United States of America
10 9 8 7 6 5 4 3 2

ISBN 0-13-255639-1

Prentice Hall International (UK) Limited, London
Prentice Hall of Australia Pty. Limited, Sydney
Prentice Hall of Canada Inc., Toronto
Prentice Hall Hispanoamericano, S.A., Mexico
Prentice Hall of India Private Limited, New Delhi
Prentice Hall of Japan, Inc., Tokyo
Simon & Schuster Asia Pte. Ltd., Singapore
Editora Prentice-Hall do Brasil, Ltda., Rio de Janiero

● *To the instructors whose dedication
to the principles of education
have enabled thousands to enter
the age of information with confidence.*

● *To the students with the will
to accept challenge and the foresight
to seize opportunity.*

CONTENTS OVERVIEW

CONTENTS

CORE Module

ADDITIONAL TOPICS Module

SPECIAL INTEREST SIDEBARS

PREFACE TO THE STUDENT

Welcome to the computer revolution. You've taken the first step toward computer competency, the bridge to an amazing realm of adventure and discovery. Once you have read and understood the material in this text and have acquired some hands-on experience with computers, you will be poised to play an active role in this revolution.

- You'll be an intelligent consumer of PCs and related products.
- You'll be better prepared to travel the rapidly expanding information superhighway and you'll know where to exit to get the information or services you need.
- You'll become a participant when conversations at work and school turn to computers and technology.
- You'll be better able to relate your information processing needs to those who can help you.
- You'll know about a wide variety of software and services that can improve your productivity at work and at home, give you much needed information, expand your intellectual and cultural horizons, amaze you, your family, and your friends, and give you endless hours of enjoyment.

Achieving computer competency is the first step in a lifelong journey toward greater knowledge and interaction with more and better applications of information technology (IT). Computer competency is your ticket to ride. Where you go, how fast you get there, and what you do when you arrive is up to you.

LEARNING AIDS

Introduction to Computers and Information Systems: The Internet Edition is supported by a comprehensive learning assistance package that includes these helpful learning aids.

- **Long and Long INTERNET BRIDGE.** The *Long and Long INTERNET BRIDGE* <http://www.prenhall.com/~longlong> is designed to help you make the transition between textbook learning and real-world understanding. This Internet World Wide Web site invites you to go online and explore the wonders of the Internet through a compre-

hensive set of Internet exercises. The exercises challenge you to learn more about the topics in this book and to do some "serendipitous surfing." The Internet Bridge icons in the margins throughout the book relate material in the book to applicable exercises on the *INTERNET BRIDGE.*

- **IT Works CD-ROM: Courseware for Information Technology**. *IT Works* is a CD-ROM-based multimedia learning tool that interactively demonstrates many important computer concepts and applications. The IT Works icons in the margins throughout the book relate material in the book to applicable modules in *IT Works*. (ISBN: 0-13-366766-9)
- *Interactive Study Guide to accompany Introduction to Computers and Information Systems: The Internet Edition, fifth edition.* The PC-based *Interactive Study Guide* contains chapter summaries, practice exams, graphical exercises, and essay/short answer exercises. Hints and a glossary are available at the click of a mouse. (ISBN: 0-13-287400-8)
- *Study Guide to accompany Introduction to Computers and Information Systems: The Internet Edition, fifth edition* The *Study Guide* contains chapter summaries, practice exams, chapter checkups (essay/short answer), and graphical exercises. (ISBN:0-13-273228-9)

YOU, COMPUTERS, AND THE FUTURE

Whether you are pursuing a career as an economist, a social worker, an attorney, a dancer, an accountant, a computer specialist, a sales manager, or virtually any other career from shop supervisor to politician, the knowledge you gain from this course ultimately will prove beneficial. Keep your course notes and this book; they will prove to be valuable references in other courses and in your career.

Even though computers are all around us, we are seeing only the tip of the computer-applications iceberg. You are entering the computer era in its infancy. Each class you attend and each page you turn will present a learning experience to help you advance one step closer to an understanding of how computers are making the world a better place in which to live and work.

PREFACE TO THE INSTRUCTOR

THE PARADIGM SHIFT

It happened during the first few months of 1996. Corporate executives, university administrators, medical personnel, and others who follow technological progress began to realize that all the rules are changing. The criteria by which they make decisions, the way they do things, and even what they do will change—dramatically. The explosion of the Internet, a rapidly expanding worldwide network of computers, coupled with increased interest in personal computing has resulted in an acceleration in the pace of change. You can look at almost any organization and envision the changes. For example, Wal-Mart, the world's largest retailer now lets you browse the aisles of their Supercenters from your PC. You select what you want, send in your order, and your order is delivered to your doorstep. The Internet provides a worldwide forum for those seeking children to adopt and those seeking parents. Many universities and colleges offer online courses that are administered entirely over the Internet. Publishers are producing material to support this new era of education—online distance learning.

We designed *Introduction to Computers and Information Systems: The Internet Edition* to give students a power boost up the learning curve. Throughout *Introduction to Computers and Information Systems: The Internet Edition*, we play to the student's sense of exhilaration by projecting the excitement of the age of information. Every page contains something that will tickle their senses and inspire them to read on. Eventually anxieties and fears fade away as students recognize the dawning of a new era in their life, an era bursting with opportunity.

THE INTRO COURSE

The introductory computer course poses tremendous teaching challenges. To be effective, we must continually change our lecture style. Sometimes we are historians. Much of the time we are scientists presenting technical material. On occasion we are sociologists commenting on social issues. In the same course we now toggle between lecture and lab. Moreover, we are teaching an ever-increasing amount of material to students with a wide range of career objectives. We and Prentice Hall have done everything we can to help you meet this challenge.

Opportunity, challenge, and competition are forcing all of us to become computer competent and to prepare ourselves for a more interconnected world. *Introducrion to Computers and Information Systems: The Internet Edition* and its ancillary materials provide a launch pad toward these objectives. The target course for this text and its teaching/learning system

- *Provides overview coverage of computing concepts and applications for a wide variety of introductory courses. The* Right PHit *custom binding solution allows you to select only those modules required to meet your course's educational objectives.*
- *Accommodates students from a broad spectrum of disciplines and interests.*
- *May or may not include a laboratory component. The* Right PHit *offers an extensive array of optional hands-on laboratory materials. (See the Right PHit section that follows on p.* **x**.)

THE INTERNET EDITION

Books have been the foundation learning resource for centuries. The Internet has opened the door for change. This Internet Edition is designed to help you learn *about the Internet* and *from the Internet*. It does this by offering the following.

- *Extensive coverage of Internet applications and concepts.* Students are given an opportunity to take an extended trip on the information superhighway. Internet and general online capabilities and concepts are covered in detail.
- *Internet exercises in the margins throughout the book.* These in-book Internet exercises give students a feeling for the scope of the Internet, whether they log on or not. Should they wish to log on, they can navigate directly to an interesting and informative Internet site.
- *The Long and Long INTERNET BRIDGE icons.* The Long and Long INTERNET BRIDGE is designed and maintained to complement this and other Long and Long books. The INTERNET BRIDGE icons in the margins throughout the books direct the student to an applicable topic on the Long and Long INTERNET BRIDGE <http://www.prenhall.com/~longlong>.

- *The Long and Long INTERNET BRIDGE Monthly Technology Updates.* Each month we compile a chapter-by-chapter summary of important changes and happenings in the world of computing. These summaries are intended to help you keep the student's learning experience current with a rampaging technology.

THE RIGHT PHit: PRENTICE HALL'S CUSTOM BINDING SOLUTION

Prentice Hall's custom binding program offers the Right PHit for everyone. The Right PHit program allows you to create the book that is right for your course, curriculum, and college. *Introduction to computers and Information Systems: The Internet Edition* is organized into two modules that can also be ordered as part of our custom binding program.

The Right PHit custom binding program offers a complete solution for introductory computer courses, from *concepts* to *applications.* Any component of the Grauer and Barber *Exploring Windows 95 Series* can be bound with one or both modules of *Introduction to Computers and Informations Systems: The Internet Edition.* The Windows 95 series includes *Exploring MS Office Professional 3.1; Office Professional 95, Vol. I and Vol. II; Brief Office Professional 95; Exploring MS Word 7.0 for Windows; Exploring MS Excel 7.0; Exploring MS Powerpoint 7.0; Exploring Windows 95 and Essential Computing Skills; Exploring the Internet; Exploring Netscape; Essentials of Word 7.0; Essentials of Excel 7.0; Essentials of Access 7.0; Essentials of Powerpoint 7.0; Essentials of Windows 95; Essentials of the internet; and Essentials of Netscape.* The Grauer and Barber series are part of the most extensive array of hands-on laboratory materials offered by any textbook publisher. Your Prentice Hall representative will be happy to work with you to identify that combination of student support materials that best meets the needs of your lab environment.

POPULAR FEATURES RETAINED IN THE FIFTH EDITION

- *Applications-oriented.* The continuing theme throughout the text is applications. Hundreds of applications are presented from online universities to telemedicine to robotics.
- *Readability.* All elements (photos, figures, sidebars, and so on) are integrated with the textual material to complement and reinforce learning.
- *Presentation style.* The text and all supplements are written in a style that remains pedagogically sound while communicating the energy and excitement of computers and computing to the student.
- *Currency-plus.* The material actually anticipates the emergence and implementation of computer technology. Included is coverage of digital convergence, Unicode, workgroup computing, software agents, the P6 processor, compact disk-recordable (CD-R), hydra printers, modern telephony, hypertext, wireless communications links, Web browsers, animation, morphing, and Java.
- *Flexibility.* The text and its teaching/learning system are organized to permit maximum flexibility in course design and in the selection, assignment, and presentation of material.
- *Analogies.* Analogies are used throughout the book to relate information technology concepts students are learning to concepts they already understand, such as airplanes (computer systems), CDs (random processing), and cars/parking lots (files/disks).
- *Chapter pedagogy.* Chapter organization and pedagogy are consistent throughout the text. Each chapter is prefaced by a Let's Talk (an introduction to terms in the chapter), a Chapter Outline, and Student Learning Objectives. In the body of the chapter, all major headings are numbered (1-1, 1-2, and so on) to facilitate selective assignment and to provide an easy cross-reference to all related material in the supplements. Important terms and phrases are highlighted in boldface type. Words and phrases to be emphasized appear in italics. Informative boxed features, photos, and "Memory Bits" (outlines of key points) are positioned strategically to complement the running text. Each chapter concludes with a Summary Outline and Important Terms, Review Exercises (concepts, discussion and problem solving), and a Self-Test.

NEW FEATURES IN THE FIFTH EDITION

- *The Right PHit.* The fifth edition of *Introduction to Computers and Information Systems: The Internet Edition,* is available in one or two modules:

    Core Chapters 1–7 introduce students to the world of computing, concepts relating to interaction with computers, and fundamental hardware, software, communications concepts, and going online (the Internet, online information services). This module also includes a Windows 95 appendix.

Additional Topics This module (Chapters 8–11) includes two personal computing chapters that introduce students to the most popular personal computing applications (word processing, desktop publishing, spreadsheet, database, graphics, and multimedia). Another chapter introduces students to the various types of information systems (MIS, DSS, expert systems, software agents, and so on). The last chapter discusses computing in context with society, addressing the many issues raised by the coming of the information age.

■ *A new pedagogical philosophy.* The fifth edition of *Introduction to Computers and Information Systems* begins quickly with a fast-paced and exciting introduction to computing, building to a technical crescendo in Chapter 2. These chapters act as a springboard to learning. By Chapter 2 students understand the essential terminology and concepts. From here, they can learn subsequent material more quickly with a better understanding of its relevance to their computer education.

■ *Reorganized for better flow.* The chapters have been reorganized for better flow and to reflect changes in the technology, in student awareness, and in curriculums. Even though the fifth edition has three fewer chapters than its predecessor, it covers the entire gamut of introductory computer education.

■ *An entirely new art program.* Virtually all of the figures in the book are either new or have been substantially revised since the fourth edition of *Introduction to Computers and Information Systems.*

■ *Two new pedagogical features.* A *Let's Talk* "conversation" opens each chapter. Let's Talk introduces many of the terms in the chapter within the context of an everyday conversation. *Issues in Computing* boxes provide opportunities for lively in-class discussions.

■ *Walk-through illustrations.* Every attempt was made to minimize conceptual navigation between the running text and figures. This was done by including relevant information within the figures in easy-to-follow numbered walk-throughs.

■ *IT Works CD-ROM: Courseware for Information Technology.* Accompanying *Introduction to Computers and Information Systems: The Internet Edition* is the most comprehensive and exciting multimedia courseware ever produced for introductory computing education. Cross-references to multimedia Explorations and Challenges are included in the margins throughout the book.

■ *Three colorful new Image Banks. Image Banks* combine dynamic photos with in-depth discussions of topics that are of interest to students: how chips are made, how to buy a PC, and the history of computers.

THE *INTRODUCTION TO COMPUTERS AND INFORMATION SYSTEMS: THE INTERNET EDITION* TEACHING/LEARNING SYSTEM

The fifth edition of *Introduction to Computers and Information Systems* continues the Long and Long tradition of having the most comprehensive, innovative, and effective support package on the market. The teaching/learning system includes the following components.

Long and Long INTERNET BRIDGE <http://www.prenhall.com/~longlong> The Long and Long INTERNET BRIDGE is designed to help students studying Long and Long resources make the transition between textbook learning and real-world understanding. The Internet exercises are the foundation of the INTERNET BRIDGE. To use this resource, the student goes online, navigates to the INTERNET BRIDGE, clicks on the *Computers and Information Systems:*

The Internet Edition image, and selects a specific chapter to begin an online adventure that will take him or her around and into the exciting world of computing. The student's journey will include many stops that can increase his or her understanding and appreciation of the technologies that change and embellish our lives.

Each chapter has from 1 to 7 topics (printers, telecommuting, computer monitoring, newsgroups), at least one of which is Serendipitous Surfing. Each topic has from 3 to 7 Internet exercises. For each exercise, the student: 1) reads the exercise; 2) navigates to the applicable Internet site(s); 3) notes the source(s), title(s), and URL(s); 4) finds the requested information; and 5) returns to the topic page and enters the requested information in the response box. When all Internet exercises are completed for a given topic, the student clicks the "Submit Answers" button to e-mail the responses to his or her instructor/grader.

The Long and Long INTERNET BRIDGE also offers monthly technology updates, all of which are keyed to the book, a comprehensive search engine, a student/faculty resource center, student/faculty forums, and much more.

IT Works CD-ROM: Courseware for Information Technology Prentice Hall has made a significant commitment and contribution to introductory computer education with the release of the *IT Works CD-ROM*. The IT (Information Technology) Works CD-ROM represents a new generation in college-level courseware. IT Works is an innovative multimedia educational tool that can work one-on-one with students to demonstrate interactively many important computer concepts and applications. This extremely visual and interactive courseware employs sound, motion video, colorful high-resolution graphics, and animation. Plan on students spending many informative and fun-filled hours with IT Works.

The initial version sports four modules, each of which contains the following main menu options: *Exploration* (teaches important concepts and applications); *Challenge* (tests the student's knowledge of the subject);*Review* (multiple-choice and true/false questions); *Video* (video vignettes); and *Glossary*. The IT Works CD-ROM has four Explorer modules.

Peripherals Explorer This Peripherals Explorer activity introduces common input/output devices, storage devices, and storage media that might be configured with a PC.

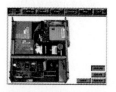

Inside the Computer Explorer. This explorer examines the system unit, inside and out (front and rear). The student simply drags the cursor over a component to learn more about it.

Going On-line Explorer. This explorer simulates going online. The student can "log on" and learn to navigate the Internet, America Online, and a BBS.

Applications Explorer. The applications explorer gives the student a better vision of what software is available. Students can explore various applications in four software categories: productivity (word processing, spreadsheets, database, graphics, and so on), multiuser applications, home/personal, and system software.

IT Works, like the technology, is dynamic—ever changing and growing. As your needs change, so will IT Works.

Long and Long Presentation Manager CD-ROM The Presentation Manager is a truly user-friendly PC-compatible presentation program that enables you to integrate Prentice Hall-supplied resources with your own for vibrant multimedia lectures. The Long and Long Presentation Manager CD-ROM contains hundreds of images and many videos that can be organized to meet your presentation needs. The CD-ROM contains all of the figures in the text and over a hundred photo images from the book and elsewhere, plus hundreds of CIS PowerPoint images and a variety of video vignettes. All of these resources are organized by chapter for your convenience. Should you wish to modify the resources for a chapter, simply use the key word search and preview feature to find exactly what you need. You can also integrate images of your own; and the software enables you to include (or modify) notes for each image or video.

Interactive Study Guide The diskette-based *Interactive Study Guide* (ISG), which is installed on a PC, helps the student learn and retain concepts presented in the text. For each chapter in the text the *ISG* has a Vocabulary Study (online definitions of boldface terms), Interactive Review (fill-in-the-blanks within a summary presentation of concepts), Practice Exam (multiple choice, true/false, and matching), Practice Exam Review (review of missed questions), Chapter Checkup (descriptive and cognitive exercises that can be selectively printed to be handed in), GUI (graphics-based exercises), and Glossary. Students get immediate feedback in the form of hints.

Study Guide The *Study Guide*, coauthored with Henry Rowe, is a supplementary book designed to support the student learning objectives in the text. It contains summaries, practice exams, chapter checkups (essay/short answer), and graphical exercises.

PH Custom Test. PH Custom Test is an integrated PC–compatible test-generation and classroom-management software package. The package permits instructors to design and create tests, to maintain student records, and to provide online practice testing for students.

Test Item File The *Test Item File* contains thousands of multiple-choice, true/false, essay, and matching questions. The questions are listed by numbered section head. The *Test Item File* diskettes are distributed for use with PH Custom Test software.

Instructor's Resource Manual (IRM) The *IRM* contains teaching hints, references to other resources, lecture notes, key terms with definitions, solutions to review exercises, and more.

Color Transparency Acetates Over one hundred color transparency acetates, which support material in the text, are provided to facilitate in-class explanation.

PowerPoint Slides Over two hundred colorful and illustrative PowerPoint slides are available for use with Microsoft PowerPoint. The PowerPoint slides are distributed as topical files so they can be integrated into your multimedia presentations.

The Prentice Hall/*New York Times* Supplement Prentice Hall, in cooperation with one of the world's premier newspapers, brings you and your students the Contemporary View Program. The program involves the periodic distribution of a *New York Times* supplement to you and your students. The supplement is the compilation of pertinent and timely *New York Times* articles on computers and automation.

"Computer Chronicles" Video Library Prentice Hall and "Computer Chronicles" have joined forces to provide you with a video library that offers a variety of documentary and feature-style stories on computers and applications of information technology.

Author Hotline If you have questions about the text, its package, or course planning, call us on the hotline (see the *IRM* for number) or contact the authors via the Internet (textwriter@aol.com).

ACKNOWLEDGMENTS

The production of *Introduction to Computers and Information Systems: The Internet Edition* is a team effort. The authors supply the content, but many talented people are needed to bring it to the book shelf. We wish to extend our sincere appreciation to the entire team, for it is their book, too.

Once again, the Long and Long team at Prentice Hall proves why their company remains the biggest and best college textbook publisher in the world. The team members include Jo-Ann DeLuca, Rich Wohl, Audrey Regan, and Marc Oliver in Editorial; Steve Deitmer in Development; Nancy Evans in Marketing; Anne Graydon, Joanne Jay, Katherine Evancie, Sue Behnke, Pat Wosczyk, Paul Smolenski, and Richard Bretan in Production; and John DeLara, Phyllis Bregman, Thom San Filippo, Karen McLean, and Grace Walkus in New Media.

Many of our academic colleagues joined the team to provide valuable insight during the conceptualization and writing stages of the project. For this edition, they include

- Suzanne Baker, Lakeland Community College
- Amanda Bounds, Florida Community College at Jacksonville
- Don Cartlidge, New Mexico State University (emeritus)
- Stephanie Chenault, The College of Charleston
- Eli Cohen, Wichita State University
- William Cornette, Southwest Missouri State University
- Paul Dietz, University of Mary
- Timothy Gottleber, North Lake College
- Vernon Griffin, Austin Community College
- Sandra Brown, Finger Lakes Community College
- Mike Michaelson, Palomar College
- Domingo Molina, Texas Southmost College
- Joseph Morrell, Metropolitan State College of Denver
- Patricia Nettnin, Finger Lakes Community College
- Anthony Nowakowski, State University of New York College at Buffalo
- Anne Parker, Manatee Community College
- Michael Padbury, Arapahoe Community College
- Carl Uebelacker, Cincinnatti State Technical and Community College

For previous editions, they include

1st Edition: Fred Scott, Broward Community College, Ft. Lauderdale; Pete Kokoros, Broward Community College, Pompano Beach; Jacques Vail, Burlington County College; Lance Eliot, California State University—Dominguez Hills; Grazina Metter, Catonsville Community College; Seth A. Hock, Columbus Technical Institute; Maria Kolatis, County College of Morris; Allan Escher, DeVry Institute of Technology, Irving TX; Ed Nemeth, DeVry Institute of Technology, Atlanta, GA; A. Peter Nardis, DeVry Institute of Technology, Tucker, GA; David Wen, Diablo Valley Community College; W. Leon Pearce, Drake University; Richard Kerns, East Carolina University; Leonard Meyer, Eastern Illinois University; J. Liskey, El Paso Community College; George Vlahakis, Evergreen Valley College; William L. Bonney, Hudson Valley Community College; Elaine Rhodes, Illinois Central College; John G. Williams, Jr., Indiana University/Purdue University; Thomas Cunningham, Indiana University of Pennsylvania; James Payne, Kellogg Community College; Mary Rasley, Lehigh County Community College; Lincoln Andrews, Miami Dade Community College; John Dineen, Middlesex County College; Michelle Jones, Missouri Institute of Technology; John Loyd, Montgomery College; Ralph Szweda, Monroe Community College; Nancy Chilson Grzesik, National Education Corporation, Newport Beach; Norman Williamson, North Carolina State University; Donnavae Hughs, North Harris County College; Roy Martin Richards, North Texas State University; Jeff Slater, North Shore Community College; Victor B. Godin, Northeastern University, Boston; Dan Simon, Northampton County Area Community College; Carol Grimm, Palm Beach Junior College; Ronald Teichman, Pennsylvania State University; Phil Raymond, Peripheral Vision Co., Maynard, MA; Peter Irwin, Richland College; Linda Rice, Saddleback Community College; Carla Hall, St. Louis Community College at Florissant Valley; Richard Matson, Schoolcraft College; Alton Roe Dillaha, Tarrant County Junior College; Tom Scharnberg, Tarrant County Junior College; Steve Murtha, Tulsa Junior College; Richard Austing, University of Maryland; Sumit Sircar, University of Texas at Arlington; Robert Lacey, Valencia Community College; John Grose, Villanova University.

2ND EDITION: Wayne Bowen, Black Hawk College; Geoffrey Cadby, Jr., Baton Rouge Vocational Tech; Ralph Cioppa, Saint Thomas Aquinas College; Roger L. Cutler, Real-Word Learning Company; Thomas E. Gorecki, Charles County Community College; Fred L. Head, Cypress College; Jim G. Ingram, Amarillo College; Peter L. Irwin, Richland College; SusanK. Johnson, Ball State University; Kai Siak Koong, Virginia Commonwealth University; Thomas Kuczkowski, Wordwright's Office; L. Gail Lefevre, Florida Junior College at Jacksonville; Steve Murtha, Tulsa Junior College; Mary E. Rasley, Lehigh County Community College; Frank Relotta, DeVry Technical Institute; Elizabeth L. Ross, Clarion University of Pennsylvania; Connie Wilson, Langston University; Margaret Zinky, Phoenix College.

3RD EDITION: Sarah Rothenberg, Hartwick College; Maribeth King, Kilgore College; Larry Buch, Milwaukee Area Technical College; Alex Ephrem, Monroe Business Institute; Don Cartlidge, New Mexico State University; Jeffrey Corcoran, Nichols College; Vernon Case, Penn Valley Community College; Gary Nunn, Radford University; Paul Dietz, The University of Mary; Gary Hyslop, The University of Rhode Island.

4TH EDITION: Lillian Beauchemin, Springfield Technical Community College; Mary A Burnell, Fairmont State College; Dr. William R. Cornette, Southwest Missouri State University; Jerry Elam, St. Petersburg Junior College; Maryangela R. Gadikian, State University of New York College at Buffalo; Dr. Fred Charles Homeyer, Angelo State University; Juliann G. Orvis, Hillsborough Community College; E. Bernard Straub, Trident Technical College; Fred L. Wells, Dekalb College

Over one hundred companies have contributed resources (information, photos, software, images) to this book and its supplements. We thank them, one and all.

We would like to extend a special thank you to those who created key ancillaries for *Introduction to Computers and Information Systems: The Internet Edition*: Henry Rowe (*Study Guide, Interactive Study Guide, Test Item File, and Instructor's Resource Manual*), Lewis Hershey (transparencies and PowerPoint slides), Matthew Hightower (teaching notes to accompany the transparencies and slides), and the people of G3 Systems (*IT Works CD-ROM*).

Finally, we wish to thank the hundreds of here unnamed instructors, administrators, and students who have provided feedback on previous editions of *Introduction to Computers and Information Systems*. Their input, also, has been invaluable to the evolution of this fifth edition.

LARRY LONG, PH. D.   NANCY LONG, PH.D.

ABOUT THE AUTHORS

Drs. Larry Long and Nancy Long have written more than 30 books, which have been used in over 600 colleges throughout the world. Larry is a lecturer, author, consultant, and educator in the computer and information services fields. He has served as a consultant to all levels of management in virtually every major type of industry. He has over 25 years combined of classroom experience at IBM, the University of Oklahoma, Lehigh University, and the University of Arkansas. Nancy has teaching and administrative experience at all levels of education: elementary, secondary, college, and continuing education. Both play tennis and coach soccer.

CHAPTER 1

The World of Computers

Courtesy of International Business Machines Corporation

Let's Talk

The following conversation introduces many of the terms in this chapter. Read it now, then again after you have read the chapter.

The Scene:
The car pool arrives at Frank's house, the last stop on a 40-minute commute into the city.

Frank: Good morning, all. I need some help—and quick!

Jill: What's up, Frank?

Frank: Got an **e-mail** last night from my boss. He wants me to put together some demographic information for our regional sales manager in Portland. And, he wants it yesterday! Any ideas?

Maria: You know, while I was cruising **the Internet** this weekend I found an **online** version of *The World Fact Book*. It might have what you need.

Spike: I think we can help, Frank. Here, Jill, let's plug my new **notebook PC** into your cellular phone. Where did you find that **information**, Maria?

Maria: On the CIA's **Internet** site. Just search on "CIA."

Spike (after about a minute): OK, we're **online** to the CIA site and here's the **data.**

Frank (looking at Spike's PC): Fantastic, Spike! That's exactly what the boss wants. Can you **download** the **data** for Washington, Oregon, and Idaho? Say, your new **PC's monitor** has great **resolution.**

Spike: Thanks, it's got a top-of-the-line **processor** with loads of **RAM.** And, when I need **hard copy**, I've got this one-pound **printer.** Do you want to e-mail your boss while I've got this **communications** link?

Frank: Sure. Send this to j_rossi@amicorp.com. Subject: Demographic data. Message: Jim, I'll have the data you requested on your desk by nine.

Spike (handing him a diskette): Frank, here's a diskette containing the file.

Frank: Thanks, I owe you guys.

Jill: Hey, what are friends for? But next time, how about greeting us with coffee and donuts instead!

STUDENT LEARNING OBJECTIVES

▶ *To grasp the scope of computer understanding needed by someone living in an information society.*

▶ *To describe the implications of computer networks on organizations and on society.*

▶ *To demonstrate awareness of the relative size, scope, uses, and variety of available computer systems.*

▶ *To describe the fundamental components and the operational capabilities of a computer system.*

▶ *To identify and describe uses of the computer.*

We live in an **information society** where **knowledge workers** channel their energies to provide a cornucopia of information services. The knowledge worker's job function revolves around the use, manipulation, and dissemination of information. This book will help you cope with and understand today's technology so you can take your place in the information society.

The Computer Revolution

In an information society, the focus of commerce becomes the generation and distribution of information. A technological revolution is changing our way of life: the way we live, work, and play. The cornerstone of this revolution, the *computer,* is transforming the way we communicate, do business, and learn. An explosion of technological advances is accelerating this change.

▶ Already, you need go no further than your home computer to get the best deal on a new car, send your congressperson a message, order tickets to the theater, or play chess with a Russian master.

▶ Millions of people can be "at work" wherever they are as long as they have their portable **personal computers**—at a client's office, in an airplane, or at home. The *mobile worker's* personal computer enables electronic links to a vast array of information and to clients and corporate colleagues.

▶ Personal computers, or **PCs,** offer a vast array of *enabling technologies* from road maps that help mobile workers navigate the streets of the world to presentation tools that help them make their point.

▶ Increasingly, the computer is the vehicle by which we communicate, whether with our colleagues at work through **electronic mail (e-mail)** or with our cyberfriends through **bulletin-board systems (BBSs).** Both electronic mail and BBSs allow us to send/receive information via computer-to-computer hookups.

That's *today. Tomorrow,* a new wave of enabling technologies will emerge that will continue to cause radical changes in our lives. For example, if you're in the market for a new home, you will spend less time in the seat of a realtor's car. From the comfort of your home you will be able to "visit" any home for sale in the country via computer. All you will need to do is select a city and enter your criteria to take advantage of the ultimate real estate multilist. The electronic realtor will then list those houses that meet your criteria, provide you with detailed information on the house and surrounding area, then offer to take you on a tour of the house—inside and out. After the electronic tour, you will be able to "drive" through the neighborhood, looking left and right as you would in your automobile. If such systems seem a bit futuristic, think again. Online real estate listings are under active development!

Each day new applications, such as a national multilist for real estate, as well as thousands of companies, schools, and individuals are being added to the **National Information Infrastructure (NII).** The NII, which is also called the **information superhighway,** refers to a network of electronic links that eventually will connect virtually every facet of our society, both public (perhaps the local supermarket) and private (perhaps to Aunt Minnie's daily schedule).

Looking Back a Few Years

To put the emerging information society into perspective, let's flash back a half century and look at the evolution of computing.

▶ *Fifty years ago,* our parents and grandparents built ships, did accounting, and performed surgery, all without the aid of computers. Indeed, everything they did was without computers. There were no *computers!*

This surreal scene is all the more remarkable for the way the computer artist has used graphics techniques to model light, shadow, and reflections, mimicking a photograph's realism.   Courtesy of Pixar, Inc.

Computer History

The industrial society evolved in a world without computers. The advent of computers and automation has changed and will continue to change the way we do our jobs. In the automobile industry, those assembly line workers who used to perform repetitive and hazardous jobs now program and maintain industrial robots to do these jobs.   GM Assembly Division, Warren, Michigan/Courtesy of Ford Motor Company

▶ *In the 1960s,* mammoth multimillion-dollar computers processed data for those large companies that could afford them. These computers, the domain of highly specialized technical gurus, remained behind locked doors. In "the old days," business computer systems were designed so a computer professional served as an intermediary between the **user**—someone who uses a computer—and the computer system. Users are blue- and white-collar workers who use the computer to help them do their jobs better.

▶ *In the mid-1970s,* computers became smaller and more accessible. This trend resulted in the introduction of commercially viable personal computers. During the 1980s, millions of people from all walks of life purchased these miniature miracles. Suddenly, computers were for everyone!

▶ *Today,* one in four Americans has a general-purpose computer more powerful than those that processed data for large banks during the 1960s. The widespread availability of computers has prompted an explosion of applications. At the individual level, we can use our PCs to go on an electronic fantasy adventure or hold an electronic reunion with our scattered family. At the corporate level, virtually every business has embraced **information technology (IT),** the integration of computing technology and information processing. Companies in every area of business are using IT to offer better services and gain a competitive advantage. For example, AT&T now offers you a phone number for life. These numbers have a "500" area code. Should you elect to subscribe to this service, your number will follow you wherever you go.

Data: Foundation for the Information Society

Information as we now know it is a relatively new concept. Just 50 short years ago, *information* was the telephone operator who provided directory assistance. Around 1950, people began to view information as something that could be collected, sorted, summarized, exchanged, and processed. But only during the last decade have people begun to tap the potential of information. To fully appreciate information, we must also examine its origin—*data.* **Data** (the plural of *datum*) are the raw materials from which information is derived. **Information** is data that have been collected and processed into a meaningful form. Said in another way, information is the meaning we give to accumulated facts (data). Data are all around us. We, as members of the information society, generate an enormous amount of data.

Computers are very good at digesting facts and producing information. For example, when you call a mail-order merchandiser, the data you give the sales representative (name, address, product number) are entered directly to the computer. When you make a long-distance telephone call, your number, the number you call, the date, and the length of the conversation are entered into a computer system. When you run short of cash and stop at an automatic teller machine, all data you enter, including that on the magnetic stripe of your bank card, are processed immediately by the bank's computer system. A computer system eventually manipulates your *data* to produce *information*. The information could be an invoice from a mail-order house or a summary of last month's long-distance telephone calls.

Traditionally, we have thought of data in terms of numbers (account balance) and letters (customer name), but recent advances in information technology have opened the door to data in other formats. For example, dermatologists (physicians who specialize in skin disorders) use digital cameras to take close-up pictures of patients' skin disorders. Each patient's **record** (information about the patient) on the computer-based **master file** (all patient records) is then updated to include the digital image. During each visit, the dermatologist recalls the patient record, which includes color images of the skin during previous visits. Data can also be found in the form of sound. For example, data collected during noise-level testing of automobiles include digitized versions of the actual sounds.

The relationship of data to a computer system is best explained by an analogy to gasoline and an automobile. Data are to a computer system as gas is to a car. Data provide the fuel for a computer system. A computer system without data is like a car with an empty gas tank: No gas, no go; no data, no information.

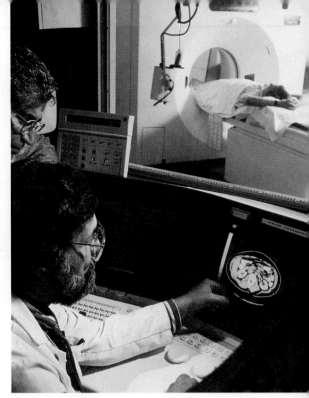

Today, we belong to an information society where we are "knowledge workers," as well as doctors, engineers, and accountants. Here physicians at the UCLA Medical Center in California examine a CAT scan. Computers help these doctors gather and analyze images of a patient's tissue structure. The higher levels of accuracy and resolution made possible by computer-based imaging have greatly improved medical diagnosis. Courtesy of Harris Corporation

℞ for Cyberphobia: Computer Competency

Not too long ago, people who pursued careers in almost any facet of business, education, or government were content to leave computers to computer professionals. Not so today. In less than a generation, **computer competency** has emerged in virtually any career from a *nice-to-have skill* to a *job-critical skill.*

By the time you complete this course, you will achieve computer competency. If you've got **cyberphobia,** the fear of computers, computer competency is a sure cure. Computer competency will allow you to be an active and effective participant in the emerging information society. You and other computer-competent people will:

1. *Feel comfortable using and operating a computer system.*
2. *Be able to make the computer work for you.* The computer-competent person can use the computer to solve an endless stream of life's problems, from how to pass away a couple of idle hours to how to increase company revenues.
3. *Be able to interact with the computer—that is, generate input to the computer and interpret output from it.* **Input** is data entered to a computer system for processing. **Output** is the presentation of the results of processing (for example, a printed résumé or a tax return).
4. *Understand the impact of computers on society, now and in the future.*
5. *Be an intelligent consumer of computers and computer equipment, collectively called* **hardware.** Expenditures for computers and related products have emerged as the third most important purchase behind homes and automobiles. For those who rent and do not own a car, it may be *the* most important purchase.
6. *Be an intelligent consumer of software and other nonhardware-related computer products and services.* **Software** refers collectively to a set of instructions, called **pro-**

Have you ever wondered where you are or how to get to where you are going? The Rockwell PathMaster™ route guidance and information system tells you exactly where you are (anywhere in the world) and provides turn-by-turn visual and voice-prompted directions to get you to your destination. The system relies on a global positioning system (GPS) and map matching to ensure accurate vehicle positioning at all times. The PathMaster is being installed in rental cars, service fleets, emergency vehicles, real estate vehicles, and many other destination-oriented markets. In a few years it may be standard equipment on your car. Rockwell Automotive

grams, that can be interpreted by a computer. The programs cause the computer to perform desired functions, such as flight simulation (a computer game), the generation of business graphics, or word processing.

7. *Be conversant in* **computerese,** *the language of computers and information technology.* In this book, you will learn those terms and phrases that not only are the foundation of computer terminology but are very much a part of everyday conversation at school, home, and work.

This Course: Your Ticket to the Computer Adventure

You are about to embark on an emotional and intellectual *journey* that will stimulate your imagination, challenge your every resource from physical dexterity to intellect, and, perhaps, alter your sense of perspective on technology. Learning about computers is more than just education. It's an adventure!

Gaining computer competency is just the beginning. This computer adventure lasts a lifetime. Information technology is changing every minute of the day. Every year, hundreds of IT-related buzz words, concepts, applications, and hardware devices will confront you. Fortunately, you will have established a base of IT knowledge (computer competency) upon which you can build and continue your learning adventure.

The Global Village

1–2 NETWORKING: BRINGING PEOPLE TOGETHER

In this section we discuss the global village and how *the Internet* and *information services* have helped to create this global village.

The Global Village

Three decades ago, Marshall McLuhan said, "The new electronic interdependence recreates the world in the image of a global village." His insightful declaration is now clearly a matter of fact. At present, we live in a *global village* in which computers and people are linked within companies and between countries (see Figure 1–1). The global village is an outgrowth of the computer network. Most existing computers are part of a **computer network;** that is, they are linked electronically to one or more computers to share resources and information. When we tap into networked computers, we can hold electronic meetings with widely dispersed colleagues, retrieve information from the corporate database, make hotel reservations, and much, much more.

On a more global scale, computer networks enable worldwide airline reservation data to be entered in the Bahamas and American insurance claims to be processed in Ireland. Securities are traded simultaneously on the New York Stock Exchange by people in Hong Kong, Los Angeles, and Berlin. A Japanese automobile assembled in Canada might include American electronics and Korean steel. Computer networks are the vehicles for coordination of the international logistics and communication needed to make a multinational automobile.

Thanks to computer networks, we are all part of a global economy, in which businesses find partners, customers, suppliers, and competitors around the world. The advent of this global economy is changing society across the board, often in subtle ways. For example, customer service may continue to improve as companies realize how

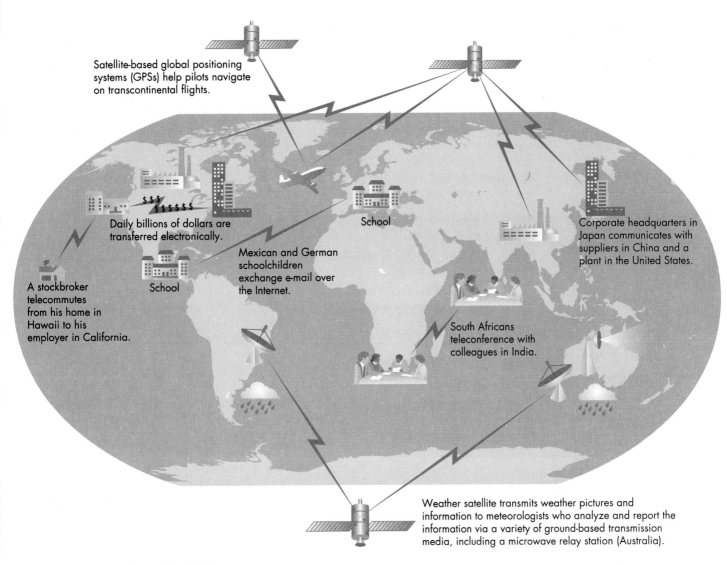

FIGURE 1–1 The Global Village
Computer-based communication is turning the world into a global village. We can communicate electronically with people on the other side of the world as easily as we might have a conversation with a neighbor.

quickly a dissatisfied customer can spread the word about flaws in products and services. An irate customer can broadcast messages vilifying a company or a particular product to thousands of potential customers over regional, national, and international bulletin boards. This is particularly true of computers, related hardware, and software products. If a product does not stand up to advertised capabilities, the computing community will quickly expose its shortcomings to literally millions of potential buyers. This same level of scrutiny will ultimately be applied to other products and services. For example, there are hundreds of bulletin boards devoted exclusively to discussions of restaurants in various cities and counties. In these cities and counties, you can be sure that frequent diners know which restaurants offer good food and value and which ones do not. Frequently, these and thousands of other special-topic bulletin boards can be found on the Internet. **The Internet** is a worldwide network of millions of computers that has emerged as the enabling technology in our migration to a global village.

The Internet and Information Services: Going Online

The Internet (**the Net**) connects more than 40,000 networks, millions of large multiuser computers, and tens of millions of users in almost every country. The Internet can be accessed by people in organizations with established links to the Internet and by individuals with PCs. Most colleges are on the Net; that is, they have an Internet account. A growing number of corporations are also becoming authorized Internet users. If you have access to a computer at work or go to college, you're probably "on the Net." If not, you can link your PC to a computer at an organization with an Internet account. As an alternative, you can subscribe to a commercial **information service,** such as America Online (see Figure 1–2), CompuServe, or Prodigy (see Figure 1–3). These and other commercial information services have one or several large computer systems that offer a wide range of information services, including up-to-the minute news and weather, electronic shopping, e-mail, and much, much more. The services provided by information services are **online;** that is, once the user has established a communications link via his or her PC, the user becomes part of the information network. When online, the user interacts directly with the computers in the information network to obtain desired services. When the user terminates the link, the user goes **offline.**

The Internet emerged from a government-sponsored project to promote the interchange of scientific information. This spirit of sharing continues as the overriding theme over the Internet. For example, aspiring writers having difficulty getting read or published can make their writing available to thousands of readers, including agents and publishers, in a matter of minutes. Unknown musicians also use the Internet to gain recognition. *Surfers* on the Internet (Internet users) desiring to read a story or listen to a song, **download** the text or a digitized version of a song (like those on an audio CD) to their personal computer, then read it or play it through their personal computer. Downloading is simply transmitting information from a remote computer (in this

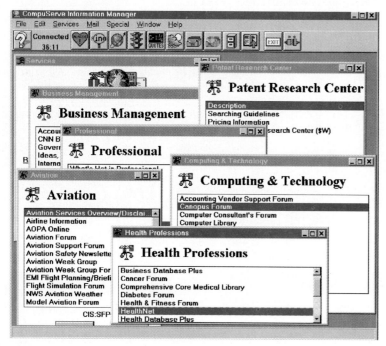

FIGURE 1–2 Help at Work over CompuServe
A wealth of information for people in all professions is available over the Internet.

case, an Internet-based computer) to a local computer (in most cases a PC). Information (perhaps a story or a song) transmitted from a local computer to a remote computer is said to be **uploaded.** Some writers and musicians have not only won the acclaim of fellow surfers, but have gone on to commercial success as well.

This spirit of sharing has prompted people all over the world to make available large databases on a wide variety of topics. This wonderful distribution and information sharing vehicle is, of course, too good to be overlooked by commercial enterprises. In time, more and more businesses will use the Internet to generate revenue. Already, scores of newspapers, magazines, and database services give Internet users access to their information, but for a fee. In contrast, commercial information services, like telephone and insurance companies, offer a valuable service and hope to make a profit.

Services and capabilities of the Internet and commercial information services are growing daily. For example, a hungry traveler on the Internet can now order a pizza via PizzaNet. The customer sends the order over the Internet to a Pizza Hut computer in Wichita, Kansas, where it is interpreted and rerouted to the customer's nearest Pizza Hut. Of course, the actual pizza is delivered in the traditional manner. Already you can order almost any consumer item from tulips to trucks through the electronic malls of information services (see Figure 1–3). Like the Internet, information services continue to provide increased services. For example, information services now offer subscribers the opportunity to interact directly with famous people, from world leaders to rock stars. The Internet and other information services are important forces in the shaping of our information society; therefore, we'll discuss both in considerable detail throughout the book.

FIGURE 1–3 Shopping on Prodigy
You can shop the electronic malls of the information superhighway to get bargains on everything from pasta makers to high fashion.

1–3 COMPUTERS: THE ESSENTIALS

Anyone who lives in the information society has a basic understanding of what a computer is and what it can do. This book is designed to add depth to this basic understanding. The best way to tackle computer concepts is incrementally, a little at a time. In the remaining sections of this chapter, we'll define the computer, identify its basic components, illustrate how it works, talk about its fundamental capabilities, list its strengths (as compared to the human computer), and talk briefly about the ways it is used. This section addresses the essentials.

Conversational Computerese: Basic Terms and Definitions

The **computer** is *an electronic device that can interpret and execute programmed commands for input, output, computation, and logic operations.* Computers may be technically complex, but they are conceptually simple. The computer, also called a **processor,** is the "intelligence" of a **computer system.** It performs all *computation* and *logic* operations. A computer system has four fundamental components: *input, processing, output,* and

Federal Express, the overnight courier service, uses a worldwide computer network to track millions of parcels from source to destination. Couriers use handheld data collection devices to enter status information directly from their vans to a central database.   Courtesy of Federal Express Corporation. All rights reserved

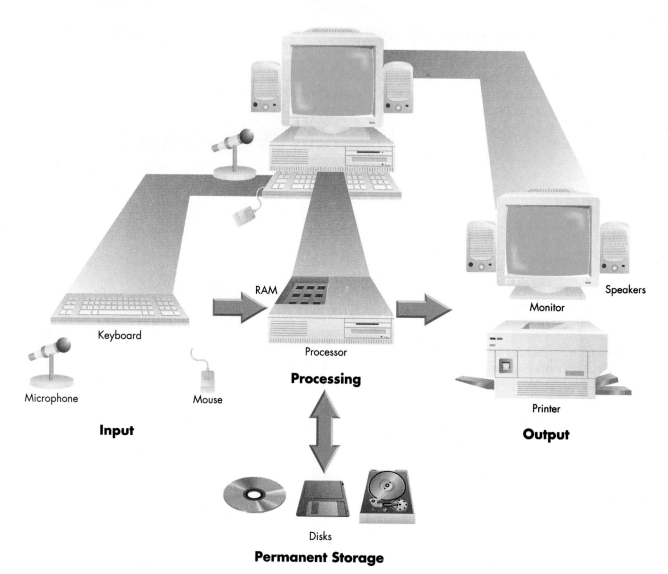

RAM

Processor

Processing

Keyboard

Microphone

Mouse

Input

Monitor

Speakers

Printer

Output

Disks

Permanent Storage

FIGURE 1–4 The Four Fundamental Components of a Personal Computer System
In a personal computer system, the storage and processing components are often contained
in the same physical unit. In the illustration, the disk storage medium is inserted into the
unit that contains the processor.

storage. Note that a computer system (not a computer) is made up of the four components. When the processor is combined with the other three components, it forms a *computer system* (see Figure 1–4).

Each of the components in a computer system can take on a variety of forms. For example, *output* (the results of processing) can be routed to a television-like **monitor,** audio speakers (like those on your stereo system), or a **printer** (see Figure 1–4). The output on a monitor is temporary and is called **soft copy.** Printers produce **hard copy,** or printed output. Data can be entered to a computer system for processing (input) via a **keyboard** (one character at a time), a microphone (for voice and sound input), or a point-and-draw device, such as a **mouse** (see Figure 1–4).

Storage of data and software in a computer system is either *temporary* or *permanent.* **Random-access memory (RAM)** provides temporary storage of data and programs during processing within solid state **integrated circuits.** Integrated circuits, or **chips,** are tiny (about .5 inch square) silicon chips into which thousands of electronic components are etched. The PC's processor is also a chip. Permanently installed and interchangeable **disks** provide permanent storage for data and programs (see Figure 1–4).

Computer Systems: Commuters to Wide-Bodies

The differences in the various categories of computers are very much a matter of scale. A good analogy can be made between airplanes and computers. Try thinking of a *wide-body jet* as a *supercomputer,* the most powerful computer, and a *commuter plane* as a *personal computer.* Both types of airplanes have the same fundamental capability: to carry passengers from one location to another. Wide-bodies, which fly at close to the speed of sound, can carry hundreds of passengers. In contrast, commuter planes travel much slower and carry about 30 passengers. Wide-bodies travel between large international airports, across countries, and between continents. Commuter planes travel short distances between regional airports. The commuter plane, with its small crew, can land, unload, load, and be on its way to another destination in 15 to 20 minutes. The wide-body may take 30 minutes just to unload. A PC is much like the commuter plane in that one person can get it up and running in just a few minutes. All aspects of the PC are controlled by one person. The supercomputer is like the wide-body in that a number of specialists are needed to keep it operational. No matter what their size, airplanes carry passengers and computers process data and produce information.

Computers can be found in a variety of shapes, from cube-shaped to U-shaped to cylindrical to notebook-shaped. However, the most distinguishing characteristic of any computer system is its *size*—not its physical size, but its *computing capacity.* Loosely speaking, size, or computer capacity, is the amount of processing that can be accomplished by a computer system per unit of time. **Mainframe computers** have greater computing capacities than do personal computers, which are also called **microcomputers** (or **micros**). Mainframe computers vary greatly in size from midsized mainframes serving small companies to large mainframes serving thousands of people. And **supercomputers,** packing the most power, have greater computing capacities than do mainframe computers. Depending on its sophistication, a **workstation's** computing capacity falls somewhere between that of a PC and a midsized mainframe. Some vendors are not content with pigeonholing their products into one of these four major categories, so they have created new niches, such as *desktop mainframes.* In this book, we will limit our discussion to these four major categories (see Figure 1–5).

All computers, no matter how small or large, have the same fundamental capabilities—*input, processing, output,* and *storage.* Keep this in mind as you encounter the computer systems shown in Figure 1–5 in this book, at school, and at work. It should be emphasized that these categories are relative. What people call a personal computer system today may be called a workstation at some time in the future. In keeping with conversational computerese, we will drop the word *system* when discussing the categories of computer systems. Keep in mind, however, that a reference to any of these categories (for example, supercomputer) implies a reference to the entire computer system.

PCs, workstations, mainframes, and supercomputers are computer systems. Each offers many **input/output,** or **I/O,** alternatives—ways to enter data to the system and to present information generated by the system. Besides obvious differences in size and capabilities, the various types of computers differ mostly in the manner in which they are used. Discussions in the following section should give you insight into when and where a particular system might be used.

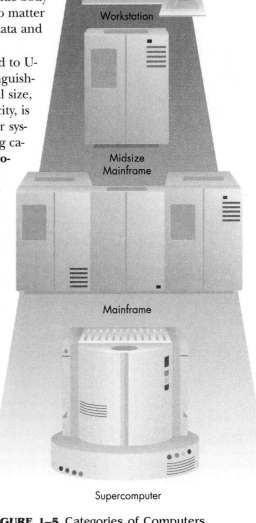

FIGURE 1–5 Categories of Computers

INTERNET BRIDGE

Personal Computers

Every 10 hours, more computers are sold than existed in the entire world 25 years ago (about 50,000). Back then, computers came in one size—big. Today, computers come in a variety of sizes. In this section we discuss the capabilities and uses of the four basic categories of computers: personal computers, workstations, mainframes, and supercomputers.

Microcomputers: Getting Personal

Most micros are used by one user at a time. You will be the person who turns on the micro, selects the software to be run, enters the data, and requests the information. The micro, like other computers, is very versatile and has been used for everything from communicating with business colleagues to controlling household appliances. Because the micro, or PC, will likely be the center of your computing experience, it and its applications are discussed in more detail in this and other chapters. Throughout the book, we will discuss PC applications of a personal nature and those that involve the shared resources of a computer network. Remember, all computers perform essentially the same functions. Any PC concept you learn can be applied to the other types of computers. Note that the terms *personal computer, PC, microcomputer,* and *micro* are used interchangeably throughout the book, as they are in practice.

The PC Family: Pockets, Laptops, Desktops, and Towers   Personal computers come in four different physical sizes: **pocket PCs, laptop PCs, desktop PCs,** and **tower PCs.** The pocket and laptop PCs are light (a few ounces to about 10 pounds), compact, and can operate without an external power source. They earn the "portable" label. The pocket PC, sometimes called a **palmtop PC,** literally can fit in a coat pocket or a handbag. Any hand-held PC falls into the pocket PC category. Laptops, which weigh from four to eight pounds, are often called **notebook PCs** because they are about the size of a one-inch thick notebook. Desktop PCs and tower PCs are not designed for frequent movement and, therefore, are not considered portable. Typically, the desktop PC's monitor is positioned on top of the processing component. The processing component of the tower PC is designed to rest on the floor, usually beside or under a desk. The tower PC resembles the processing component of a desktop PC placed on end.

The power of a PC is not necessarily directly related to its size. A few laptop PCs can run circles around some desktop PCs. Some user conveniences, however, must be sacrificed to achieve portability. For instance, input devices, such as keyboards and point-and-draw devices, are given less space and may be more cumbersome to use. This is particularly true of pocket PCs, where miniaturized keyboards make data entry and interaction with the computer difficult and slow. The display screen on many portable PCs is monochrome (as opposed to color) and may be difficult to read under certain lighting situations. Portable computers take up less space and, therefore, have a smaller capacity for permanent storage of data and programs. However, the number one concern of those who use portable PCs, especially notebooks, is insufficient battery life, which can be as little as a couple of hours for older models to 20 hours for state-of-the-art rechargeable lithium batteries. The battery-life problem will probably be resolved with the introduction of the next generation of portable PCs. The rechargeable batteries of the near future are expected to offer a full workweek of usage on a single battery. This should suffice for even the most demanding mobile knowledge worker.

The word *portable* invites abuse. We as consumers assume that luggage, automobiles, or anything that is moved frequently is indestructible. Manufacturers recognize that notebooks and attaché cases must navigate the same treacherous obstacle course

The PC Family

When searching for a personal computer, this executive identified portability and flexibility as her primary criteria. She chose a docking station for the office that she uses in conjunction with her IBM Thinkpad notebook PC.   Courtesy of International Business Machines Corporation

This real estate appraiser uses an Apple Powerbook notebook PC in conjunction with a digital camera (foreground) to prepare appraisals. She inserts digital photographs of the property directly into an electronic document, which is then printed and given to her client.   Courtesy of Apple Computer, Inc.

This executive's day-timer is just one of many applications on his pen-based PC.   Photo provided by GRiD Systems Corporation

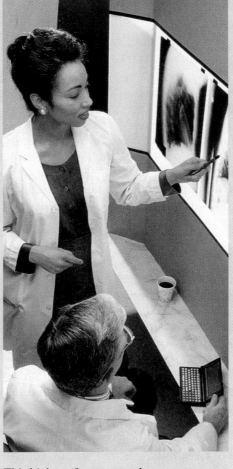

Students use an Apple Newton, a PDA, to take notes for a presentation. Courtesy of Apple Computer, Inc.

Each year millions of people purchase desktop PCs, like this Compaq Presario, for their homes.   Reprinted with permission of Compaq Computer Corporation. All Rights Reserved.

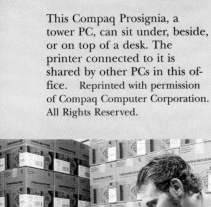

This Compaq Prosignia, a tower PC, can sit under, beside, or on top of a desk. The printer connected to it is shared by other PCs in this office.   Reprinted with permission of Compaq Computer Corporation. All Rights Reserved.

This high-performance palmtop computer being used by these doctors can run the same applications as its desktop cousin. Photo courtesy of Hewlett-Packard Company

Workers at McKesson Corporation wear their PCs. The wearable PCs weigh 13 ounces, fit over the hand and forearm, contain a small screen and key pad, and can scan bar codes. This receiving clerk can read bar codes and enter data while keeping both hands free to lift and move shipping containers.   Photo courtesy of McKesson Corporation

(coffee spills, overhead storage on airplanes, being dropped). One company has designed the notebook to resist rain, extreme temperatures, and even fungus. The market for this PC is expected to be the military, law enforcement, utility workers, and other mobile employees. It sounds like a good match for college students as well.

A recent innovation is the 2-in-1 PC that can be used as both a notebook and a desktop PC. The PC is in two parts: a fully functional *notebook PC* and a **docking station.** The docking station can be *configured* with a high-capacity disk, several interchangeable disk options, a magnetic tape backup unit, an easy-to-see monitor, greater memory, and other features that may not fit within a notebook. A computer system's **configuration** describes its internal components (for example, size of RAM and special features) and its **peripheral devices** (printer, various disk storage devices, monitor, and so on). Two-in-one PCs have a configuration that allows users to enjoy the best of both worlds: portability and the expanded features of a desktop. The notebook, which supplies the processor, is simply inserted into or removed from the docking station, depending on the needs of the user.

Pen-based Computers Mobile workers in increasing numbers are using portable **pen-based PCs.** Pen-based PCs use electronic pens instead of keyboards. Users select options, enter data, and draw with the pen. United Parcel Service (UPS) uses pen-based PCs. UPS couriers ask you to sign for packages on a pressure-sensitive display screen with an electronic stylus.

Pen-based computers are poised to make an entry into the world of mobile professionals who cannot or will not use keyboard-based portables. Many professionals cannot type, and in meetings, colleagues find the click-clack of a portable's keyboard an annoying distraction. In other situations, typing on a laptop is simply impractical. Insurance agents and claims adjusters who need to work at accident or disaster scenes have found pen-based computers more suitable to their working environment.

Peripherals Explorer

Personal Digital Assistants Personal digital assistants (**PDAs**) are hand-held personal computers, like palmtop and pen-based computers, that take on many forms. Like Apple Computer Company's Newton, most PDAs are pen-based. They can include a built-in cellular phone. The cellular phone enables the wireless sending/ receiving of faxes and wireless sending/receiving of electronic mail and voice mail. PDAs, which have also been labeled as *personal communicators,* can be carried in pockets, purses, and attaché cases, or they can be strapped to parts of the body (a hand, an arm, a leg, or around the waist). Generally, PDAs support a variety of personal information systems, such as scheduling, phone number administration, to-do lists, tickler files, diaries, and so on. Of course, they can support a variety of PC-type applications. A beverage distributor equips its salespeople with PDAs, which enable them to better manage their territories. Technicians rely on their PDAs when they need information on how to make a particular repair. PDAs can store the equivalent of thousands of pages of technical manuals. Forecasters predict that some form of PDA may replace what we now know as textbooks.

Configuring a PC: Putting the Pieces Together Normally, computer professionals are called upon to select, configure, and install the hardware associated with mainframe computers. But for PCs, the user typically selects, configures, and installs his or her own system; therefore, it is important that you know what makes up a personal computer system and how it fits together. The configuration of a microcomputer or what you put into and attach to your computer can vary enormously. Common configuration options are shown in Figure 1–6.

Nowadays, the typical off-the-shelf PC is configured to run multimedia applications. **Multimedia applications** combine text, sound, graphics, motion video, and/or animation. Computer-based encyclopedias provide a good example of multimedia applications. They can take you back to July 20, 1969, and let you see motion video of the Apollo 11 lunar module *Eagle* landing on the moon at the Sea of Tranquility. If you wish, you can listen to Commander Neil Armstrong step onto the moon and pro-

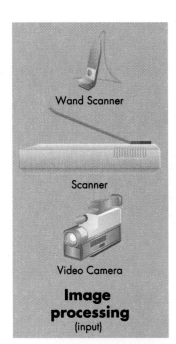

Wand Scanner

Scanner

Video Camera

Image processing
(input)

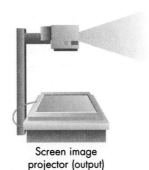

Screen image projector (output)

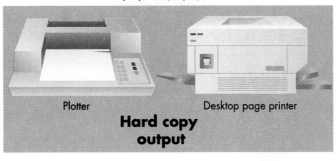

Plotter

Desktop page printer

Hard copy output

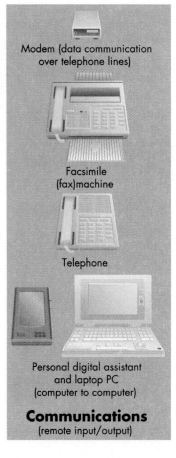

Modem (data communication over telephone lines)

Facsimile (fax)machine

Telephone

Personal digital assistant and laptop PC (computer to computer)

Communications
(remote input/output)

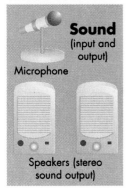

Sound
(input and output)

Microphone

Speakers (stereo sound output)

Monitor (input/output)

Touch screen (input)

Keyboard (input)

Uninterruptible power supply (UPS) to enable clean, steady power

Point and draw devices
(input)

Mouse   Trackball

Digitizer tablet and crosshair

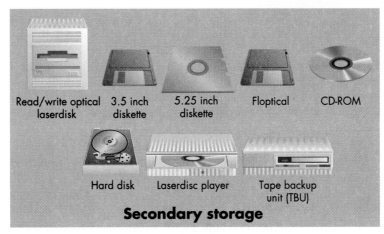

Read/write optical laserdisk

3.5 inch diskette

5.25 inch diskette

Floptical

CD-ROM

Hard disk   Laserdisc player   Tape backup unit (TBU)

Secondary storage

FIGURE 1–6 The Personal Computer and Common Peripheral Devices
A wide range of peripheral devices can be connected to a PC. Those shown here and others are discussed in detail in later chapters.

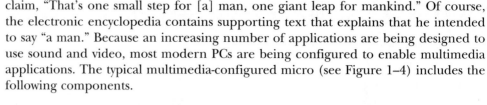

INTERNET BRIDGE

Work Stations

This plant design engineer uses a Hewlett-Packard Apollo workstation. Because his workstation is on a network with other similar workstations, all plant design project team members can follow the progress of the design effort. Photo courtesy of Hewlett-Packard Company

claim, "That's one small step for [a] man, one giant leap for mankind." Of course, the electronic encyclopedia contains supporting text that explains that he intended to say "a man." Because an increasing number of applications are being designed to use sound and video, most modern PCs are being configured to enable multimedia applications. The typical multimedia-configured micro (see Figure 1–4) includes the following components.

1. A microcomputer (the processor)
2. A keyboard for input
3. A point-and-draw device for input (usually a mouse)
4. A monitor for *soft-copy* (temporary) output
5. A printer for *hard-copy* (printed) output
6. A permanently installed high-capacity **hard disk drive** for permanent storage of data and programs
7. A low-capacity **floppy disk drive** into which an interchangeable **floppy diskette** is inserted.
8. A **CD-ROM drive** into which an interchangeable **CD-ROM,** which looks like an audio CD, is inserted.
9. A microphone (audio input)
10. A set of speakers (audio output)

In desktop and tower microcomputer systems, these components generally are purchased as separate physical units and then linked together. Notebook PCs may include all but the printer in a *single unit*. Virtually all micros give users the flexibility to configure the system with a variety of peripheral devices (input/output and storage). A component stereo system provides a good analogy with which to illustrate the concept of flexibility in PC configuration. In a stereo system, the tuner is the central component to which equalizers, tape decks, compact disk players, speakers, and so on can be attached. A microcomputer system is configured by linking any of a wide variety of peripheral devices to the processor component. Figure 1–6 shows the more common peripheral devices that can be configured with a PC. Many other peripherals can be linked to a PC. For example, if you enjoy following the weather, you can link devices directly to your PC that will give you a continuous display of wind direction and velocity, temperature, humidity, rainfall, and barometric pressure. Notice that PCs can be linked to facsimile (fax) machines, video cameras, telephones, and other computers.

Workstations: The Hot Rods of Computing

What looks like a PC but isn't? It's a *workstation* and it's very fast. Speed, or computing capacity, is one of the characteristics that distinguishes workstations from micros. In fact, some people talk of workstations as "souped-up" PCs. The PC was fine for word processing, spreadsheets, and games, but for real "power users"—engineers doing **computer-aided design,** or **CAD** (using the computer in the design process), scientists, and other "number crunchers"—the PC fell short. Power users needed the speed of a mainframe at a fraction of the cost. The workstation, introduced in the early 1980s, filled this gap. Today's high-end workstations have processing capabilities similar to that of mainframe computers serving as many as 2000 terminals.

The workstation's input/output devices also set it apart from a PC. A typical workstation will sport a large-screen color monitor capable of displaying high-resolution graphics. **Resolution** refers to the clarity of the image on the monitor's display. For pointing and drawing, the workstation user can call on a variety of specialized point-and-draw devices that combine the precision of a gunsight with the convenience of a mouse. Add-on keypads can expand the number of specialized function keys available to the user.

The clean lines of this mainframe computer system (in the background) hide the thousands of integrated circuits, miles of wire, and even gold that make up its inner workings. This data center provides information processing support for hundreds of end users. Photo courtesy of Hewlett-Packard Company

The capabilities of today's high-end PCs are very similar to those of low-end workstations. In a few years, the garden variety PC will have workstation capabilities. As the distinction between the two narrows, the two will become one. Time will tell whether we call it a PC, a workstation, or something else.

Mainframe Computers: Corporate Workhorses

The two larger multiuser computers, with their expanded processing capabilities, provide a computing resource that can be shared by many people. Mainframe computers are usually associated with **enterprise-wide systems;** that is computer-based systems that service entities throughout the company. For example, human resource management, accounting, and inventory management tasks are usually enterprise-wide systems handled by mainframe-based networks. Users communicate with a centralized mainframe, called a **host computer,** through their **video display terminal (VDT)** or their PCs. Like the PC, the VDT, or simply **terminal,** has a keyboard for input and a monitor for output. Depending on the size of the organization, a dozen people or 10,000 people can share system resources by interacting with their VDTs or PCs.

Until the late 1960s, all computers were mainframe computers, and they were expensive—too expensive for all but the larger companies. Large companies shelled out $1.5 million and more for mainframe computers with less power than today's one thousand-dollar PCs. In the late 1960s, computer vendors introduced smaller, slightly "watered down" computers that were more affordable for smaller companies. The industry dubbed these small computers **minicomputers,** or simply **minis.** The term was used until recently, when the distinction between minis and mainframe began to blur. Today the term is seldom used. Smaller mainframes are called midsized computers.

Mainframe computers are *designed specifically* for the multiuser environment, in contrast to PCs and workstations, which are frequently used as stand-alone computers. Mainframes are oriented to **input/output-bound** applications; that is, the amount of work that can be performed by the computer system is limited primarily by the speeds of the I/O and storage devices. Administrative data processing jobs, such as generating monthly statements for checking accounts at a bank, require relatively little cal-

Mainframe Computers

We've now entered the era of affordable supercomputing. This CRAY J916 sells in the six-figure range. Just a few years ago, low-end supercomputers sold for millions of dollars.   Courtesy of Cray Research, Inc.

INTERNET BRIDGE

Supercomputers

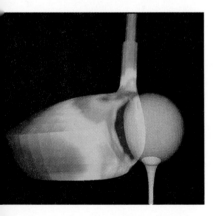

MacGregor Golf Company turned to a Cray Research supercomputer to design its titanium-head club. A supercomputer model "hits" the ball, collects and analyzes data, and makes design recommendations. The result was a club with added airfoils that yields the average duffer an extra seven to ten yards per drive.   Courtesy of Cray Research, Inc.

culation and a great deal of input and output. In I/O-bound applications, the computer is often waiting for data to be entered or for an output device to complete its current task.

It is unlikely that you would find two mainframe computers configured in exactly the same way. For example, a large municipal government generates a tremendous amount of *external output* (output that is directed to persons not affiliated with city government, such as utility bills and tax notices) and would require several high-speed page printers. In contrast, a software development company might enter and process all data from terminals with relatively little hard-copy output.

Supercomputers: Processing Giants

During the early 1970s, administrative data processing dominated computer applications. Bankers, college administrators, and advertising executives were amazed by the blinding speed at which million-dollar mainframes processed their data. Engineers and scientists were grateful for this tremendous technological achievement, but they were far from satisfied. When business executives talked about unlimited capability, engineers and scientists knew they would have to wait for future enhancements before they could use computers to address truly complex problems. Automotive engineers were still not able to build three-dimensional prototypes of automobiles inside a computer. Physicists could not explore the activities of an atom during a nuclear explosion. The engineering and scientific communities had a desperate need for more powerful computers. In response to that need, computer designers began work on what are now known as supercomputers.

Supercomputers primarily address applications that are **processor-bound.** Processor-bound applications, which are helpful to engineers and scientists, require little in the way of input or output. In processor-bound applications, the amount of work that can be done by the computer system is limited primarily by the speed of the computer. In contrast, mainframe computers are oriented to *input/output-bound* applications. A typical scientific job involves the manipulation of a complex mathematical model, often requiring trillions of operations to resolve. During the early 1970s some complex processor-bound scientific jobs would tie up large mainframe computers at major universities for days at a time. This, of course, was unacceptable.

Supercomputers are known as much for their applications as they are for their speed or computing capacity, which may be 10 times that of a large mainframe computer. These are representative supercomputer applications:

▶ Supercomputers enable the simulation of airflow around an airplane at different speeds and altitudes.

▶ Auto manufacturers use supercomputers to simulate auto accidents on video screens. (It is less expensive, more revealing, and safer than crashing the real thing.)

▶ Meteorologists employ supercomputers to study the formation of tornadoes.

▶ Hollywood production studios use advanced graphics to create special effects for movies like *Jurassic Park* and TV commercials.

▶ Supercomputers sort through and analyze mountains of seismic data gathered during oil-seeking explorations.

▶ Physicists use supercomputers to study the results of explosions of nuclear weapons.

All of these applications are impractical, if not impossible, on mainframes.

In this section we illustrate how a computer system works by looking at how it does processing for a payroll system. Also, we discuss what a computer can and cannot do.

Processing Payroll: Payday

One computer-based system makes us happy each and every payday. It's called a *payroll system*. We'll use this popular system to illustrate how a computer system works. Just about every organization that has employees and a computer maintains a computer-based payroll system. The payroll system enables input and processing of pertinent payroll-related data to produce payroll checks and a variety of reports. The payroll system walkthrough in Figure 1–7 illustrates how data are entered into a network

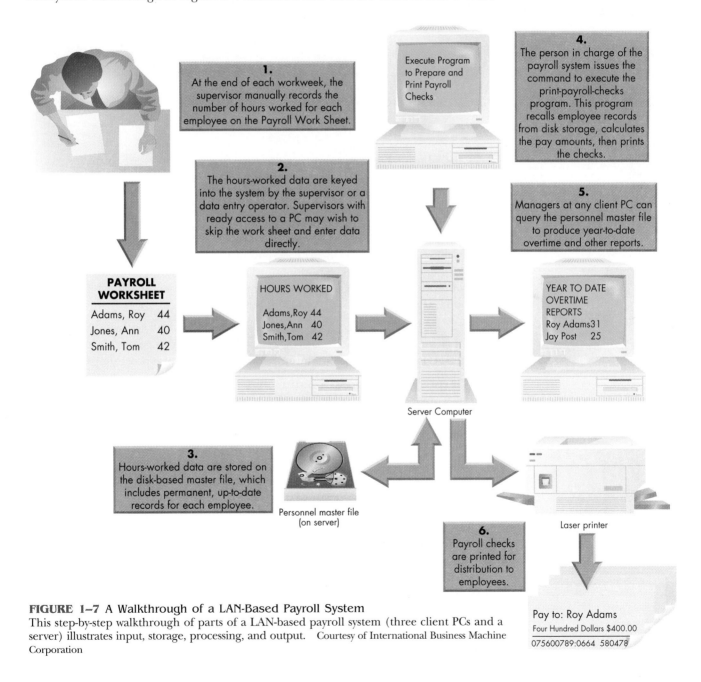

1. At the end of each workweek, the supervisor manually records the number of hours worked for each employee on the Payroll Work Sheet.

2. The hours-worked data are keyed into the system by the supervisor or a data entry operator. Supervisors with ready access to a PC may wish to skip the work sheet and enter data directly.

3. Hours-worked data are stored on the disk-based master file, which includes permanent, up-to-date records for each employee.

Execute Program to Prepare and Print Payroll Checks

4. The person in charge of the payroll system issues the command to execute the print-payroll-checks program. This program recalls employee records from disk storage, calculates the pay amounts, then prints the checks.

5. Managers at any client PC can query the personnel master file to produce year-to-date overtime and other reports.

6. Payroll checks are printed for distribution to employees.

PAYROLL WORKSHEET

Adams, Roy 44
Jones, Ann 40
Smith, Tom 42

HOURS WORKED

Adams,Roy 44
Jones,Ann 40
Smith,Tom 42

Server Computer

Personnel master file (on server)

YEAR TO DATE OVERTIME REPORTS
Roy Adams31
Jay Post   25

Laser printer

Pay to: Roy Adams
Four Hundred Dollars $400.00
075600789:0664 580478

FIGURE 1–7 A Walkthrough of a LAN-Based Payroll System
This step-by-step walkthrough of parts of a LAN-based payroll system (three client PCs and a server) illustrates input, storage, processing, and output.   Courtesy of International Business Machine Corporation

Issues in Computing

Monitoring of E-mail

Many organizations monitor both e-mail and telephone conversations of their employees. These organizations cite productivity and quality control as justification. People who used to chat at the water cooler or snack counter do so now over office e-mail. Monitored e-mail is just as likely to surface "meet you at the gym after work" as "meet you in the conference room."

Realistically, e-mail is monitored to discourage nonbusiness messages and to keep employees focused on job-related activities. We now know that e-mail, when used responsibly, can boost productivity. We also know that, if abused, e-mail can be counterproductive.

Once an organization decides to monitor e-mail, it can do so in several ways. Individuals can scan e-mail archives for inappropriate transmissions, often a time-consuming process. In large organizations, computers scan e-mail archives for key words (baseball, party, boss, and so on) and kick out messages with questionable content. A couple of employees were fired after making negative comments about the company's president. Many others have been fired or disciplined for abusing e-mail.

Employees feel that monitoring of e-mail is an invasion of personal privacy. The issue is being argued in the courts.

Discussion: Does an employer's right to know outweigh the employee's right to privacy?

of personal computer systems and how the four system components (input, processing, output, and storage) interact to produce payroll checks and information (a year-to-date overtime report).

In the walkthrough of Figure 1–7, the payroll system and other company systems are supported on a **local area network (LAN).** A LAN connects PCs or workstations in close proximity, such as in a suite of offices or a building. In most LANs, one PC, called a **server computer,** performs a variety of functions for the other PCs on the LAN, called **client computers.** The functions include the storage of data and applications software. In Figure 1–7, client PCs throughout the company are linked to a server computer (a tower PC in the example).

What Can a Computer Do?

Computers perform two operations: input/output operations and processing operations.

Input/Output Operations: Readin' and 'Ritin' Computers perform input/output (I/O) operations (see Figure 1–7). The computer *reads* from input and storage devices. The computer *writes* to output and storage devices. Before data can be processed, they must be "read" from an input device or data storage device. Input data can be entered directly by end users or by professional data entry operators. Typically, data are entered on a VDT or a PC keyboard or they are retrieved from data storage, such as a magnetic disk. Once data have been processed, they are "written" to a magnetic disk or to an output device, such as a printer.

Input/output (I/O) operations are illustrated in the payroll-system walkthrough example shown in Figure 1–7. Hours-worked data are entered, or "read," into the computer system (Activity 2). These data are "written" to magnetic disk storage for recall later (Activity 3). Data are "read" from the personnel master file on magnetic disk, processed (Activity 4), and "written" to the printer to produce the payroll checks (Activity 6).

Processing Operations: Doing Math and Making Decisions The computer is totally objective. Any two computers instructed to perform the same operation will arrive at the same result. This is because the computer can perform only *computation* and *logic operations*.

Computation operations. Computers can add (+), subtract (−), multiply (*), divide (/), and do exponentiation (^). In the payroll-system example of Figure 1–7, an instruction in a computer program tells the computer to calculate the gross pay for each employee in a computation operation. For example, these calculations would be needed to compute gross pay for Ann Jones, who worked 40 hours this week and makes $15 per hour.

Pay = 40 hours worked * $15/hour = $600

The actual program instruction that performs the above calculation might look like this:

PAY = HOURS_WORKED * PAY_RATE

The values for HOURS_WORKED and PAY_RATE are recalled from the personnel master file. PAY is calculated.

Logic operations. The computer's logic capability enables comparisons between numbers and between words. Based on the result of a comparison, the computer performs appropriate functions. In the example of Figure 1–7, Tom Smith and Roy Adams had overtime hours because they worked more than 40 hours (the normal workweek). The computer must use its *logic capability* to decide if an employee is due overtime pay. To do this, hours worked are compared to 40.

Are hours worked > (greater than) 40?

For Roy Adams, who worked 44 hours, the comparison is true (44 is greater than 40). A comparison that is true causes the difference (4 hours) to be credited as overtime and paid at time and a half. The actual instruction that would perform the logical operation might look like this.

IF HOURS_WORKED > 40 THEN PAY_OVERTIME

The Computer's Strengths

In a nutshell, computers are fast, accurate, consistent, and reliable; they don't forget anything; and they don't complain.

Speed: 186 Miles/Millisecond Computers perform various activities by executing instructions, such as those discussed in the previous section. These operations are measured in **milliseconds, microseconds, nanoseconds,** and **picoseconds** (one thousandth, one millionth, one billionth, and one trillionth of a second, respectively). To place computer speeds in perspective, consider that a beam of light travels down the length of this page in about one nanosecond. A millisecond can be sliced into a thousand microseconds, and a microsecond can be sliced into a thousand nanoseconds.

Accuracy: Zero Errors Computers are not only accurate, but their accuracy reflects great *precision*. Computations are accurate within a penny, a micron, a picosecond, or whatever level of precision is required. Errors do occur in computer-based information systems, but precious few can be directly attributed to the computer system itself. The vast majority can be traced to a program logic error, a procedural error, or erroneous data. These are *human errors*.

At the New York Stock Exchange, literally billions of dollars' worth of securities are routinely bought and sold with nary a penny lost, a testament to the accuracy of computers.   Courtesy of the New York Stock Exchange

Consistency: All Strikes   Human baseball pitchers try to throw strikes, but often end up throwing balls. Computers always do what they are programmed to do—nothing more, nothing less. If we ask them to throw strikes, they throw nothing but strikes. This ability to produce consistent results gives us the confidence we need to allow computers to process mission-critical information.

Reliability: No Downtime   Computer systems are particularly adept at repetitive tasks. They don't take sick days and coffee breaks, and they seldom complain. Anything below 99.9% **uptime,** the time when the computer system is in operation, is usually unacceptable. For some companies, any **downtime** is unacceptable. These companies provide **backup** computers that take over automatically should the main computers fail.

Memory Capability: Virtually Unlimited   Computer systems have total and instant recall of data and an almost unlimited capacity to store these data. A typical mainframe computer system will have trillions of characters and millions of images stored and available for instant recall. High-end PCs have immediate access to two or three billion characters of data and thousands of images. To give you a benchmark for comparison, this book contains approximately 1.25 million characters and about 350 images.

Serendipitous Surfing: The Movies

1–6   HOW DO WE USE COMPUTERS?

The uses of computers are like the number of melodies available to a songwriter—limitless. If you can imagine it, there is a good chance that computers can help you do it. This section provides an overview of potential computer applications. This presentation should give you a feel for how computers are affecting your life. These applications, however, are but a few of the many applications presented throughout the book.

Information Systems

The bulk of existing computer power is dedicated to **information systems.** This includes all uses of computers that support the administrative aspects of an organization, such as airline reservation systems, student registration systems, hospital patient-billing systems, and countless others. We combine *hardware, software, people, procedures,* and *data* to create an information system. A computer-based information system provides an organization with *data processing* capabilities and the knowledge workers in the organization with the *information* they need to make better, more informed decisions.

Personal Computing

The growth of **personal computing,** an environment in which one person controls the PC, has surpassed even the most adventurous forecasts of a decade ago. It's not uncommon for companies to have more personal computers than telephones.

A variety of domestic and business applications form the foundation of personal computing. Domestic applications include everything from personal finance to education to entertainment. Microcomputer software is available to support thousands of common and not-so-common business applications.

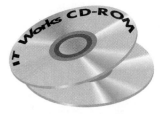

Applications Explorer

Retailers have worked hard to create information systems and automate the checkout process. Now they are poised for the next step in automation—self-checkout. Already most of us are comfortable with the convenience of the automatic teller machine (ATM). Perhaps we will embrace the automated checkout machine (ACM) as well. The move to self-checkout in supermarkets is gaining momentum. Shoppers scan their own groceries and receive visual and verbal confirmation of each purchase from the monitor. With ACMs, checkout is faster and less expensive. Monetary transactions are handled electronically. The coming of the ACM in grocery and eventually other retail businesses moves us one step closer to the cashless society.   CheckRobot Automated Checkout Machines/Courtesy of International Business Machines Corporation

Emerging Technology

Going Grocery Shopping: Let Your Fingers Do the Walking

How would you like to do a week's worth of grocery shopping in 10 minutes? Rather than loading the kids into the minivan on shopping day, you can send them out to play and do your shopping from the comfort of your home. Thousands of busy people have traded their shopping carts for keyboards. Rather than fight the crowds in the Chicago and San Francisco areas, they log on to the Peapod, an online shopping and delivery service.

The Peapod system has made life easier for a great many people. It has also saved them time and money. Working parents gladly trade shopping time for more time with the kids. Some people enjoy saving big on coupons and baby-sitting costs. Just about everyone saves money because the system encourages you to buy the product with the best per unit price.

People who haven't set foot in a grocery store for months say their families are eating better than ever.

Peapod is giving us a glimpse into the future of retailing—the *virtual store*. Peapod is a pioneer in a rapidly expanding industry that is dedicated to enabling us to buy almost anything from a PC. Peapod subscribers go shopping at the virtual grocery store by logging on to a system that lets them interactively shop for grocery items, including fresh produce, deli, bakery, meat, and frozen products. Rather than running from aisle to aisle, you simply point and click around the screen for the items you want. Once online you can

- Choose from over 20,000 items
- Compare prices instantly to find the best deal
- Check your subtotal at any time to stay within your budget
- Create personal shopping lists to save time
- View images of products
- Check out store specials
- View nutritional labels for products
- Sort like products instantly by nutritional content
- Choose a delivery time that fits your schedule

Peapod's online shopping system is linked directly to its partner stores' computer systems (Safeway in San Francisco and Jewel in Chicago). When you send your shopping list to Peapod, an order is transmitted to the nearest partner store. A professionally trained shopper takes your order, grabs a shopping cart, and does your shopping for you. The professional shopper takes a fraction of the time you would take because the list is ordered by aisle and the shopper knows exactly what to get. You can redeem your coupons when the shopper/delivery person arrives with your food. Food is delivered in temperature-controlled containers.

Grocery shoppers now have another option—going online. The Peapod system lets subscribers point and click their way around a virtual supermarket.

A growing family of productivity software is the foundation of personal computing in the home and in the business world. These are some of the most popular productivity tools.

▶ *Word processing.* **Word processing software** enables users to enter and edit text in documents in preparation for output (printed, faxed, or sent via e-mail). Word processing documents can include graphic images.

▶ *Desktop publishing.* **Desktop publishing software** allows users to produce near-typeset-quality copy for newsletters, advertisements, and many other printing needs, all from the confines of a desktop.

▶ *Spreadsheet.* **Spreadsheet software** permits users to work with the rows and columns of a matrix (or spreadsheet) of data.

▶ *Database.* **Database software** permits users to create and maintain a database and to extract information from the database.

Shopping online means never having to leave your home.

items be arranged alphabetically by brand, by price per unit, by package size, or, we can even request a listing by nutritional value.

In the minds of the busy people who shop online, the cost of the service (approximately $11 on a $100 order) is easily offset by the savings in dollars (better prices, less spent on travel, and so on). These savings do not consider the extra personal time shoppers recover by shopping online.

Online shopping is here to stay. Since linking up with Peapod, the grocery store partners have experienced an 8% increase in sales. Already, online shopping accounts for over 15% of the sales volume at the partner stores. Such success has not gone unnoticed by other entrepreneurs. Shoppers Express has teamed up with grocery and pharmacy stores throughout the United States to offer an online shopping service over the information service America Online. Apparently a growing number of people are willing to give up the smell of fresh bread to avoid the long lines at the checkout counter.

The virtual supermarket is sure to change the way we shop. This interactive online approach helps take the hassle and the mystery out of grocery shopping. We can view items by category (snack foods), by item (cookies), or by brand (Keebler). We can even peruse the items on sale. We can request that

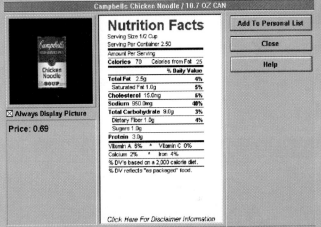

Online grocery shoppers can request nutritional facts on grocery items. They can also compare nutritional value between like products.

▶ *Graphics.* **Graphics software** facilitates the creation and management of computer-based images, such as pie graphs, line drawings, company logos, maps, clip art, blueprints, and just about anything else that can be drawn in the traditional manner.

▶ *Communications.* **Communications software** lets users send e-mail and faxes, tap the Internet, log on to an information service, or link their PC with a remote computer.

Communication

Computers are communications tools that give us the flexibility to communicate electronically with one another and with other computers. For example, we can set up our computers to send e-mail birthday greetings to our friends and relatives automatically. We can log on to a commercial information service (like Prodigy or CompuServe) to "talk" online with one person or a group of people. Communications applications and concepts are discussed in detail throughout the book.

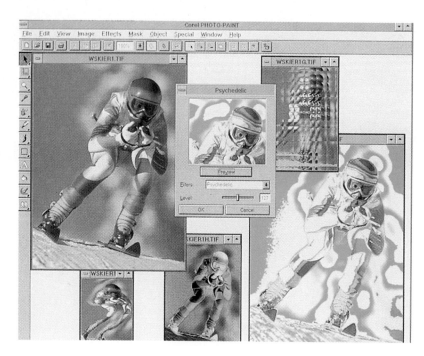

Graphics software is the newest member of the PC productivity software family. A wide range of graphics software enables you to create and work with computer-based images. Corel's Photo-Paint, shown here, allows you to edit (change) photographs. Here, the original photo (upper left) is given a psychedelic effect (lower right), warped (lower left), and recolored (bottom center).   Courtesy of Corel Corporation

Science, Research, and Engineering

Engineers and scientists routinely use the computer as a tool in *experimentation, design,* and *development*. There are at least as many science and research applications for the computer as there are scientists and engineers.

Emerson Electric Company's Advanced Motor Technology Center in St. Louis supports the company's product engineering and development in electric motors. A new variable-speed furnace blower motor is shown undergoing acoustic and vibration tests to improve sound characteristics.   Courtesy of Emerson Electric Company

As we witnessed firsthand in the 1995 O. J. Simpson "trial of the century," multimedia presentations are beginning to revolutionize courtroom litigation techniques. This law firm uses a multimedia system to capture video, audio, and text information. Once captured, the system assists lawyers in mixing video depositions, animated simulations, graphs, and other physical evidence into a multimedia package for courtroom presentations.   Courtesy of Dynatech Corporation

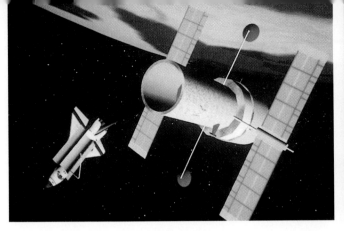

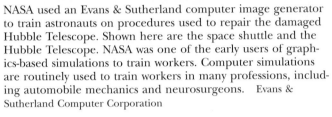

NASA used an Evans & Sutherland computer image generator to train astronauts on procedures used to repair the damaged Hubble Telescope. Shown here are the space shuttle and the Hubble Telescope. NASA was one of the early users of graphics-based simulations to train workers. Computer simulations are routinely used to train workers in many professions, including automobile mechanics and neurosurgeons.   Evans & Sutherland Computer Corporation

Computer-aided design (CAD) has revolutionized the way in which engineers and scientists design, draft, and document a product. With CAD, most of the "bugs" can be worked out of a design before a prototype is built.   Courtesy of International Business Machines Corporation

Education and Reference

Computers can interact with students to enhance the learning process. Relatively inexpensive hardware capable of multidimensional communication (sound, print, graphics, and color) has resulted in the phenomenal growth of the computer as an educational tool in the home, in the classroom, and in business. Computer-based education will not replace teachers, but educators agree that **computer-based training (CBT)** is having a profound impact on traditional modes of education. Available CBT programs can help you learn keyboarding skills, increase your vocabulary, study algebra, learn about the makeup of the atom, and practice your Russian. These are just the tip of the CBT iceberg.

Computer-Aided Design

Computer-aided design (CAD) is using the computer in the design process. CAD systems enable the creation and manipulation of an on-screen graphic image. CAD systems provide a sophisticated array of tools enabling designers to create three-dimensional objects that can be flipped, rotated, resized, viewed in detail, examined internally or externally, and much more. Photographs in this chapter and throughout the book illustrate a variety of CAD applications.

It's never a rainy day on the PC. Electronic golfers can play the finest golf courses in the world without paying the greens fee, including Pinehurst Country Club shown here. Electronic golfers are confronted with the same challenges as outdoor golfers—wind, club selection, water hazards, and so on. However, the electronic golfer swings with the finger tips rather than with arms and legs.   Courtesy of Microsoft Corporation

Entertainment and Edutainment

More applications are being created that tickle our fancy and entertain us. You can play electronic golf. You can buy a computer chess opponent in the form of a board, chess pieces, and a miniature robotic arm that moves the pieces (you have to move your own pieces). You can "pilot" an airplane to Paris and battle Zorbitrons in cyberspace. The debonair thief, Carmen Sandiego, of computer games and television fame, thrills children with the chase to find her and her accomplices, while teaching them history and geography. Software, such as Carmen Sandiego, that combines *edu*cation and enter*tainment* has been dubbed **edutainment software.**

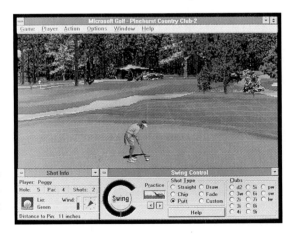

The amount of computing capacity in the world is doubling every two years. The number and sophistication of applications are growing rapidly with the increase in the number of computers and their capabilities. Tomorrow, there will be applications that are unheard of today.

IMPORTANT TERMS AND SUMMARY OUTLINE

1–1 THE INFORMATION SOCIETY In an **information society, knowledge workers** focus their energies on providing a myriad of information services. The knowledge worker's job function revolves around the use, manipulation, and dissemination of information.

The computer revolution is transforming the way we communicate, do business, and learn. This technological revolution is having a profound impact on the business community and on our private and professional lives. For example, increasingly, we communicate with our colleagues at work through **electronic mail (e-mail)** or with our online friends through **bulletin-board systems (BBSs).**

After the turn of the century we can anticipate traveling the **information superhighway,** a network of high-speed data communications links that eventually will connect virtually every facet of our society (also called the **National Information Infrastructure** or **NII**). Today, millions of people have a **personal computer (PC).** This widespread availability has resulted in an explosion of applications for computers.

Through the 1970s, **users** related their information needs to computer professionals who would then work with the computer system to generate the necessary information. Today, users work directly with their PCs, to obtain the information they need.

Data, which all of us create and use every day, are the raw materials from which information is derived. **Information** consists of data collected and processed into a meaningful form. The data in a computer-based system are stored on the **master file,** which is made up of **records.**

Computer competency is emerging as a universal goal in the information society. Computer-competent people know how to purchase, use, and operate a computer system, and how to make it work for them. The computer-competent person is also aware of the computer's impact on society and is conversant in **computerese.** Computer competency is a cure for **cyberphobia.**

Software refers collectively to a set of machine-readable instructions, called **programs,** that cause the computer to perform desired functions. Computers and computer equipment, which accept **input** and provide **output,** are called **hardware.**

Learning about computers is an adventure that will last a lifetime because **information technology (IT),** the integration of computing technology and information processing, is changing daily.

1–2 NETWORKING: BRINGING PEOPLE TO-GETHER We now live in a global village in which computers and people are linked within companies and between countries. Most existing computers are part of a **computer network** that shares resources and information.

The Internet links tens of millions of users in a global network. **The Net** can be accessed by people in organizations with established links to the Internet and by individuals with PCs. Commercial **information services** offer a wide range of information services, including up-to-the-minute news and weather, electronic shopping, e-mail, and much more. The services provided by information services are **online.** When the user terminates the link, the user goes **offline.** Internet users can **download** text or a digitized version of a song to their computer, then read it or play it through their personal computer. Information is **uploaded** from a local computer to a remote computer.

1–3 COMPUTERS: THE ESSENTIALS The **computer,** or **processor,** is an electronic device capable of interpreting and executing programmed commands for input, output, computation, and logic operations.

Output on a computer can be routed to a **monitor** or a **printer.** The output on a monitor is temporary and is called **soft copy.** Printers produce **hard-copy** output. Data can be entered via a **keyboard** or a **mouse,** a point-and-draw device.

Random-access memory (RAM) provides temporary storage of data and programs during processing within solid state **integrated circuits,** or **chips.** Permanently installed and interchangeable **disks** provide permanent storage for data and programs.

The differences in the various categories of computers are very much a matter of scale. **Mainframe comput-** ers have greater computing capacities than PCs, or **microcomputers (micros).** And **supercomputers** have greater computing capacities than mainframe computers. Depending on its sophistication, a **workstation's** computing capacity falls somewhere between that of a PC and a midsized mainframe. All **computer systems,** no matter how small or large, have the same fundamental capabilities—*processing, storage, input,* and *output.* Each offers many **input/output** or **I/O** alternatives.

1–4 MICROS TO SUPERCOMPUTERS: CAPABILITIES AND USES Personal computers come in four different physical sizes: **pocket PCs (palmtops), laptop PCs** (also called **notebook PCs), desktop PCs,** and **tower PCs.** Pocket and laptop PCs are considered portable. A 2-in-1 PC that can be used as both a notebook and a desktop is in two parts: a fully functional *notebook PC* and a **docking station.** Two-in-one PCs have a **configuration** that allows users to enjoy the best of both worlds: portability and the expanded features of a desktop. **Pen-based PCs** use electronic pens instead of keyboards. **Personal digital assistants (PDAs)** are hand-held personal computers that support a variety of personal information systems.

Multimedia applications combine text, sound, graphics, motion video, and/or animation. The typical multimedia-configured micro includes a microcomputer; a keyboard and a point-and-draw device for input; a monitor and a printer for output; a **hard disk drive** and a **floppy disk drive** into which an interchangeable **floppy diskette** is inserted; a **CD-ROM drive** into which an interchangeable **CD-ROM** is inserted; and a microphone and a set of speakers for audio I/O. Micros are designed to give users the flexibility to configure the system with a variety of **peripheral devices.**

The workstation's speed and input/output devices set it apart from a PC. A typical workstation will have a high-**resolution** monitor and a variety of specialized point-and-draw devices. The most common use of workstations is for **computer-aided design (CAD).**

Mainframe computers are usually associated with **enterprise-wide systems;** that is, computer-based systems that service entities throughout the company. Users communicate with a centralized mainframe, called a **host computer,** through their **video display terminals (VDTs),** or simply **terminals.** The term **minicomputer,** or simply **mini,** was used until recently, when the distinction between minis and mainframes began to blur. Mainframes are oriented to **input/output-bound** applications. Supercomputers primarily address applications that are **processor-bound.**

1–5 A COMPUTER SYSTEM AT WORK A **local area network (LAN)** connects PCs in close proximity. The LAN's **server computer** performs a variety of functions for the other PCs on the LAN, called **client computers.**

Computers perform input/ouput (I/O) operations by reading from input and storage devices and writing to output devices.

Computer system capabilities are either input/output or processing. Processing capabilities are subdivided into computation and logic operations.

The computer is fast, accurate, consistent, and reliable, and has an enormous memory capacity. Computer operations are measured in **milliseconds, microseconds, nanoseconds,** and **picoseconds.** For some companies, any **downtime** (versus **uptime**) is unacceptable. These companies provide **backup** computers that take over automatically should the main computers fail.

1–6 HOW DO WE USE COMPUTERS? There are many applications of computers, including the following:

■ *Information systems.* The computer is used to process data and produce business information. Hardware, software, people, procedures, and data are combined to create an **information system.**

■ *Personal computing.* The micro is used for **personal computing** by individuals for a variety of business and domestic applications, including such productivity tools as **word processing software, desktop publishing software, spreadsheet software,** **database software, graphics software,** and **communications software.**

■ *Communication.* Computers are communications tools that give us the flexibility to communicate electronically with one another and with other computers.

■ *Science, research, and engineering.* The computer is used as a tool in experimentation, design, and development.

■ *Education and reference.* The computer interacts with students to enhance the learning process. **Computer-based training (CBT)** is having a profound impact on traditional modes of education.

■ *Computer-aided design.* Computer-aided design (CAD) is using the computer in the design process.

■ *Entertainment and edutainment.* Every day, computer applications are being designed and created just to entertain us. Software that combines *educ*ation and enter*tainment* has been dubbed **edutainment software.**

 ## REVIEW EXERCISES

Concepts

1. What are the four fundamental components of a computer system?
2. Which component of a computer system executes the program?
3. Associate the following with one of the application areas for computers discussed in Section 1–6: experimentation, home use, CBT, architectural design, the Internet, and business information systems.
4. What global network links millions of computers throughout the world?
5. Compare the information processing capabilities of human beings to those of computers with respect to speed, accuracy, reliability, consistency, and memory capability.
6. In terms of physical size, how are PCs categorized?
7. Describe the relationship between data and information.
8. Within the context of a computer system, what is meant by *read* and *write*?
9. Name five microcomputer productivity tools.
10. Which microcomputer productivity tool would be most helpful in writing a term paper? Explain.
11. List at least three services provided by a commercial information service.

12. The operational capabilities of a computer system include what two types of processing operations? Give an example of each.
13. What term is used to describe the integration of computers and information processing?
14. What do we call mail that is sent electronically?

Discussion and Problem Solving

15. The computer has had far-reaching effects on our lives. How has the computer affected your life?
16. What is your concept of computer competency? In what ways do you think achieving computer competency will affect your domestic life? Your business life?
17. At what age should computer-competency education begin?
18. Discuss how the complexion of jobs will change as we evolve from an industrial society into an information society. Give several examples.
19. The use of computers tends to stifle creativity. Argue for or against this statement.
20. Comment on how computers are changing our traditional patterns of personal communication.
21. Comment on how computers are changing our traditional patterns of recreation.

1–1 a. To be computer-competent, you must be able to write computer programs. (T/F)

b. A person whose job revolves around the use, manipulation, and dissemination of information is called: (a) a computerphobe, (b) a knowledge worker, or (c) a data expert?

c. _____ are the raw materials from which _____ is derived.

d. _____ is data entered to a computer system for processing, and _____ is the presentation of the results of processing.

1–2 a. A _____ integrates computer systems, terminals, and communication links.

b. When the user terminates the link with a commercial information service, the user goes: (a) offline, (b) on-log, or (c) online?

c. Uploading on the Internet is transmitting information from an Internet-based host computer to a local computer PC. (T/F)

1–3 a. A printer is an example of which of the four computer system components?

b. Output on a monitor is soft copy and output on a printer is hard copy. (T/F)

c. Integrated circuits are also called: (a) slivers, (b) chips, or (c) flakes?

1–4 a. The power of a PC is directly proportional to its physical size. (T/F)

b. The four size categories of personal computers are miniature, portable, notebook, and business. (T/F)

c. A 2-in-1 PC is in two parts: a fully functional _____ PC and a _____ station.

d. What is the name given those applications that combine text, sound, graphics, motion video, and/or animation: (a) videoscapes, (b) motionware, or (c) multimedia?

e. The workstation was introduced in the early 1980s. (T/F)

f. The _____ _____ _____ (VDT) is a terminal link to a host computer.

g. Supercomputers are oriented to _____-bound applications.

1–5 a. The two types of processing operations performed by computers are _____ and _____.

b. A microsecond is 1000 times longer than a nanosecond. (T/F)

1–6 a. Desktop publishing refers to the capability of producing _____ copy from the confines of a desktop.

b. The greatest amount of available computing capacity is dedicated to the information systems application of computer usage. (T/F)

c. The microcomputer productivity tool that manipulates data organized in a tabular structure of rows and columns is called a _____.

d. _____ software combines education and entertainment.

Self-test Answers. **1–1 (a)** F; **(b)** b; **(c)** Data, information; **(d)** Input, output. **1–2 (a)** computer network, **(b)** a; **(c)** F. **1–3 (a)** output; **(b)** T; **(c)** b. **1–4 (a)** F; **(b)** F; **(c)** notebook, docking; **(d)** c; **(e)** T; **(f)** video display terminal; **(g)** processor. **1–5 (a)** computation, logic; **(b)** T. **1–6 (a)** near-typeset-quality; **(b)** T; **(c)** spreadsheet; **(d)** edutainment.

IMAGE BANK

The History of Computing: An Overview

The history of computers and computing is of special significance to us, because many of its most important events have occurred within our lifetime. Historians divide the history of the modern computer into generations, beginning with the introduction of the UNIVAC I, the first commercially viable computer, in 1951. But the quest for a mechanical servant—one that could free people from the more boring aspects of thinking—is centuries old. Why did it take so long to develop the computer? Some of the "credit" goes to human foibles. Too often brilliant insights were not recognized or given adequate support during an inventor's lifetime. Instead, these insights would lay dormant for as long as 100 years until someone else rediscovered—or reinvented—them. Some of the "credit" has to go to workers, too, who sabotaged labor-saving devices that threatened to put them out of work. The rest of the "credit" goes to technology; some insights were simply ahead of their time's technology. Here, then, is an abbreviated history of the stops and starts that have given us this marvel of the modern age, the computer.

Computer History

1623–1662: Blaise Pascal
Although inventor, painter, and sculptor Leonardo da Vinci (1425–1519) sketched ideas for a mechanical adding machine, it was another 150 years before French mathematician and philosopher Blaise Pascal finally invented and built the "Pascaline" in 1642 to help his father, a tax collector. Although Pascal was praised throughout Europe, his invention was a financial failure. The hand-built machines were expensive and delicate; moreover, Pascal was the only person who could repair them. Because human labor was actually cheaper, the Pascaline was abandoned as impractical.
Courtesy of International Business Machines Corporation

3000 B.C.: The Abacus   The abacus is probably considered the original mechanical counting device (it has been traced back 5000 years). It is still used in education to demonstrate the principles of counting and arithmetic and in business for speedy calculations.
The Computer Museum, Boston, MA

1642: The Pascaline
The Pascaline used a counting-wheel design: Numbers for each digit were arranged on wheels so that a single revolution of one wheel would engage gears that turned the wheel one tenth of a revolution to its immediate left. Although the Pascaline was abandoned as impractical, its counting-wheel design was used by all mechanical calculators until the mid-1960s, when they were made obsolete by electronic calculators.
Courtesy of International Business Machines Corporation

1793–1871: Charles Babbage

Everyone from bankers to navigators depended on mathematical tables during the bustling Industrial Revolution. However, these hand-calculated tables were usually full of errors. After discovering that his own tables were riddled with mistakes, Charles Babbage envisioned a steam-powered "differential engine" and then an "analytical engine" that would perform tedious calculations accurately. Although Babbage never perfected his devices, they introduced many of the concepts used in today's general-purpose computer. Courtesy of International Business Machines Corporation

1801: Jacquard's Loom

A practicing weaver, Frenchman Joseph-Marie Jacquard (1753–1871) spent what little spare time he had trying to improve the lot of his fellow weavers. (They worked 16-hour days, with no days off!) His solution, the Jacquard loom, was created in 1801. Holes strategically punched in a card directed the movement of needles, thread, and fabric, creating the elaborate patterns still known as Jacquard weaves. Jacquard's weaving loom is considered the first significant use of binary automation. The loom was an immediate success with mill owners because they could hire cheaper and less skilled workers. But weavers, fearing unemployment, rioted and called Jacquard a traitor. Courtesy of International Business Machines Corporation

1842: Babbage's Difference Engine and the Analytical Engine

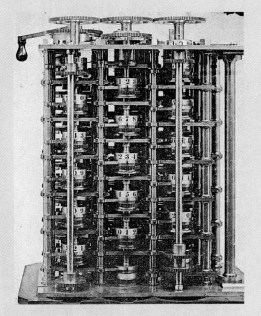

Convinced his machine would benefit England, Babbage applied for—and received—one of the first government grants to build the difference engine. Hampered by nineteenth-century machine technology, cost overruns, and the possibility his chief engineer was padding the bills, Babbage completed only a portion of the difference engine (shown here) before the government withdrew its support in 1842, deeming the project "worthless to science." Meanwhile, Babbage had conceived of the idea of a more advanced "analytical engine." In essence, this was a general-purpose computer that could add, subtract, multiply, and divide in automatic sequence at a rate of 60 additions per second. His 1833 design, which called for thousands of gears and drives, would cover the area of a football field and be powered by a locomotive engine. Babbage worked on this project until his death. In 1991 London's Science Museum spent $600,000 to build a working model of the difference engine, using Babbage's original plans. The result stands 6 feet high, 10 feet long, contains 4000 parts, and weighs 3 tons. New York Public Library Picture Collection

1816–1852: Lady Ada Augusta Lovelace   The daughter of poet Lord Byron, Lady Ada Augusta Lovelace became a mentor to Babbage and translated his works, adding her own extensive footnotes. Her suggestion that punched cards could be prepared to instruct Babbage's engine to repeat certain operations has led some people to call her the first programmer. Ada, the programming language adopted by the Department of Defense as a standard, is named for Lady Ada Lovelace.   The Bettmann Archive/BBC Hulton

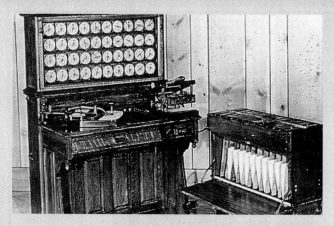

1890: Hollerith's Tabulating Machine   Hollerith's punched-card tabulating machine had three parts. Clerks at the U.S. Bureau of the Census used a hand punch to enter data into cards a little larger than a dollar bill. Cards were then read and sorted by a 24-bin sorter box (right) and summarized on numbered tabulating dials (left), which were connected electrically to the sorter box. Ironically, Hollerith's idea for the punched card came not from Jacquard or Babbage but from "punch photography." Railroads of the day issued tickets with physical descriptions of a passenger's hair and eye color. Conductors punched holes in the ticket to indicate that a passenger's hair and eye color matched those of the ticket owner. From this, Hollerith got the idea of making a punched "photograph" of every person to be tabulated.   Courtesy of International Business Machines Corporation

1860–1929: Herman Hollerith   With the help of a professor, Herman Hollerith got a job as a special agent helping the U.S. Bureau of the Census tabulate the head count for the 1880 census—a process that took almost eight years. To speed up the 1890 census, Hollerith devised a punched-card tabulating machine. When his machine outperformed two other systems, Hollerith won a contract to tabulate the

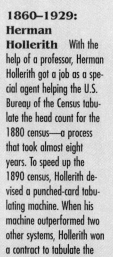

1890 census. Hollerith earned a handsome income leasing his machinery to the governments of the United States, Canada, Austria, Russia, and others; he charged 65 cents for every 1000 people counted. (During the 1890 U.S. census alone, he earned more than $40,000—a fortune in those days.) Hollerith may have earned even more selling the single-use punched cards. But the price was worth it. The bureau completed the census in just 2½ years and saved more than $5 million.
Courtesy of International Business Machines Corporation

1924: IBM'S First Headquarters Building   In 1896 Herman Hollerith founded the Tabulating Machine Company which, in 1911, merged with several other companies to form the Computing-Tabulating-Recording Company. In 1924 the company's general manager, Thomas J. Watson, changed its name to International Business Machines Corporation and moved into this building. Watson ran IBM until a few months before his death at age 82 in 1956. His son, Thomas J. Watson, Jr., lead IBM into the age of computers.   Courtesy of International Business Machines Corporation

1920s–1950s: The EAM Era   From the 1920s throughout the mid-1950s, punched-card technology improved with the addition of more punched-card devices and more sophisticated capabilities. The *electromechanical accounting machine (EAM)* family of punched-card devices includes the card punch, verifier, reproducer, summary punch, interpreter, sorter, collator, and accounting machine. Most of the devices in the 1940s machine room were "programmed" to perform a particular operation by the insertion of a prewired control panel. A machine-room operator in a punched-card installation had the physically challenging job of moving heavy boxes of punched cards and printed output from one device to the next on hand trucks.   Courtesy of International Business Machines Corporation

1904– : Dr. John V. Atanasoff   In 1939 Dr. John V. Atanasoff, a professor at Iowa State University, and graduate student Clifford E. Berry assembled a prototype of the ABC (for *Atanasoff Berry Computer*) to cut the time physics students spent mak-

ing complicated calculations. A working model was finished in 1942. Atanasoff's decisions—to use an electronic medium with vacuum tubes, the base-2 numbering system, and memory and logic circuits—set the direction for the modern computer. Ironically, Iowa State failed to patent the device and IBM, when contacted about the ABC, airily responded, "IBM will never be interested in an electronic computing machine." A 1973 federal court ruling officially credited Atanasoff with the invention of the automatic electronic digital computer. Courtesy of Iowa State University

1942: The First Computer, The ABC   During the years 1935 through 1938, Dr. Atanasoff had begun to think about a machine that could reduce the time it took for him and his physics students to make long, complicated mathematical calculations. The ABC was, in fact, born of frustration. Dr. Atanasoff later explained that one night in the winter of 1937, "nothing was happening" with respect to creating an electronic device that could help solve physics problems. His "despair grew," so he got in his car and drove for several hours across the state of Iowa and then across the Mississippi River. Finally, he stopped at an Illinois roadhouse for a drink. It was in this roadhouse that Dr. Atanasoff overcame his creative block and conceived ideas that would lay the foundation for the evolution of the modern computer.   Courtesy of Iowa State University

IMAGE BANK: THE HISTORY OF COMPUTING   **35 CORE**

1944: The Electromechanical Mark I Computer   The first electromechanical computer, the *Mark I*, was completed by Harvard University professor Howard Aiken in 1944 under the sponsorship of IBM. A monstrous 51 feet long and 8 feet high, the MARK I was essentially a serial collection of electromechanical calculators and was in many ways similar to Babbage's analytical machine. (Aiken was unaware of Babbage's work, though.) The Mark I was a significant improvement, but IBM's management still felt electromechanical computers would never replace punched-card equipment.   Courtesy of International Business Machines Corporation

1951: The UNIVAC I and the First Generation of Computers   The first generation of computers (1951–1959), characterized by the use of vacuum tubes, is generally thought to have begun with the introduction of the first commercially viable electronic digital computer. The Universal Automatic Computer (*UNIVAC I* for short), developed by Mauchly and Eckert for the Remington-Rand Corporation, was installed in the U.S. Bureau of the Census in 1951. Later that year, CBS News gave the UNIVAC I national exposure when it correctly predicted Dwight Eisenhower's victory over Adlai Stevenson in the presidential election with only 5% of the votes counted. Mr. Eckert is shown here instructing news anchor Walter Cronkite in the use of the UNIVAC I.
Courtesy of Unisys Corporation

1946: The Electronic ENIAC Computer   Dr. John W. Mauchly (middle) collaborated with J. Presper Eckert, Jr. (foreground) at the University of Pennsylvania to develop a machine that would compute trajectory tables for the U.S. Army. (This was sorely needed; during World War II, only 20% of all bombs came within *1000 feet* of their targets.) The end product, the first fully operational electronic computer, was completed in 1946 and named the *ENIAC* (Electronic Numerical Integrator and Computer). A thousand times faster than its electromechanical predecessors, it occupied 15,000 square feet of floor space and weighed 30 tons. The ENIAC could do 5000 additions per minute and 500 multiplications per minute. Unlike computers of today that operate in binary, it operated in decimal and required 10 vacuum tubes to represent one decimal digit.

    The ENIAC's use of vacuum tubes signaled a major breakthrough. (Legend has it that the ENIAC's 18,000 vacuum tubes dimmed the lights of Philadelphia whenever it was activated.) Even before the ENIAC was finished, it was used in the secret research that went into building the first atomic bomb at Los Alamos.   United Press International Photo

1954: The IBM 650   Not until the success of the UNIVAC I did IBM make a commitment to develop and market computers. IBM's first entry into the commercial computer market was the *IBM 701* in 1953. However, the *IBM 650* (shown here), introduced in 1954, is probably the reason IBM enjoys such a healthy share of today's computer market. Unlike some of its competitors, the IBM 650 was designed as a logical upgrade to existing punched-card machines. IBM management went out on a limb and estimated sales of 50—a figure greater than the number of installed computers in the entire nation at that time. IBM actually installed 1000. The rest is history.   Courtesy of International Business Machines Corporation

1907–1992: "Amazing" Grace Murray Hopper

Dubbed "Amazing Grace" by her many admirers, Dr. Grace Hopper was widely respected as the driving force behind COBOL, the most popular programming language, and a champion of standardized programming languages that are hardware-independent. In 1959 Dr. Hopper led an effort that laid the foundation for the development of COBOL. She also created a compiler that enabled COBOL to run on many types of computers. Her reason: "Why start from scratch with every program you write when a computer could be developed to do a lot of the basic work for you over and over again?"

To Dr. Hopper's long list of honors, awards, and accomplishments, add the fact that she found the first "bug" in a computer—a real one. She repaired the Mark II by removing a moth that was caught in Relay Number II. From that day on, every programmer has *debugged* software by ferreting out its *bugs*, or errors, in programming syntax or logic. Official U.S. Navy photo

1963: The PDP-8 Minicomputer

During the 1950s and early 1960s, only the largest companies could afford the six- and seven-digit price tags of *mainframe* computers. In 1963 Digital Equipment Corporation introduced the *PDP-8* (shown here). It is generally considered the first successful *minicomputer* (a nod, some claim, to the playful spirit behind the 1960s miniskirt). At a mere $18,000, the transistor-based PDP-8 was an instant hit. It confirmed the tremendous demand for small computers for business and scientific applications. By 1971 more than 25 firms were manufacturing minicomputers, although Digital and Data General Corporation took an early lead in their sale and manufacture. Courtesy of Digital Equipment Corporation

1959: The Honeywell 400 and the Second Generation of Computers

The invention of the transistor signaled the start of the second generation of computers (1959–1964). Transistorized computers were more powerful, more reliable, less expensive, and cooler to operate than their vacuum-tubed predecessors. Honeywell (its *Honeywell 400* is shown here) established itself as a major player in the second generation of computers. Burroughs, Univac, NCR, CDC, and Honeywell—IBM's biggest competitors during the 1960s and early 1970s—became known as the BUNCH (the first initial of each name). Courtesy of Honeywell, Inc.

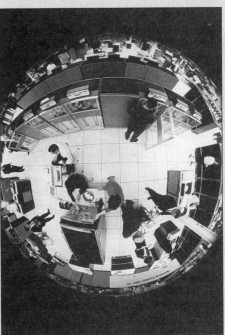

1964: The IBM System 360 and the Third Generation of Computers

The third generation was characterized by computers built around integrated circuits. Of these, some historians consider IBM's *System 360* line of computers, introduced in 1964, the single most important innovation in the history of computers. System 360 was conceived as a family of computers with *upward compatibility*; when a company outgrew one model it could move up to the next model without worrying about converting its data. System 360 and other lines built around integrated circuits made all previous computers obsolete, but the advantages were so great that most users wrote the costs of conversion off as the price of progress. Courtesy of International Business Machines Corporation

1964: BASIC—More than a Beginner's Programming Language
In the early 1960s, Dr. Thomas Kurtz and Dr. John Kemeny of Dartmouth College began developing a programming language that a beginner could learn and use quickly. Their work culminated in 1964 with BASIC. Over the years, BASIC gained widespread popularity and evolved from a teaching language into a versatile and powerful language for both business and scientific applications. From micros to mainframes, BASIC is supported on more computers than any other language. Courtesy of True BASIC, Inc.

1975: Microsoft and Bill Gates
In 1968, seventh grader Bill Gates and ninth grader Paul Allen were teaching the computer to play monopoly and commanding it to play millions of games to discover gaming strategies. Seven years later, in 1975, they were to set a course which would revolutionize the computer industry. While at Harvard, Gates and Allen developed a BASIC programming language for the first commercially available microcomputer, the MITS Altair. After successful completion of the project, the two formed Microsoft Corporation, now the largest and most influential software company in the world. Microsoft was given an enormous boost when its operating system software, MS-DOS, was selected for use by the IBM PC. Gates, now the richest man in America, provides the company's vision on new product ideas and technologies. Courtesy of Microsoft Corporation

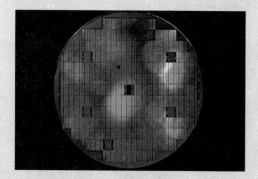

1971: Integrated Circuits and the Fourth Generation of Computers
Although most computer vendors would classify their computers as fourth generation, most people pinpoint 1971 as the generation's beginning. That was the year large-scale integration of circuitry (more circuits per unit of space) was introduced. The base technology, though, is still the integrated circuit. This is not to say that two decades have passed without significant innovations. In truth, the computer industry has experienced a mind-boggling succession of advances in the further miniaturization of circuitry, data communications, and the design of computer hardware and software. Courtesy of International Business Machines Corporation

1977: The Apple II
Not until 1975 and the introduction of the Altair 8800 personal computer was computing made available to individuals and very small companies. This event has forever changed how society perceives computers. One prominent entrepreneurial venture during the early years of personal computers was the Apple II computer (shown here). Two young computer enthusiasts, Steven Jobs and Steve Wozniak (then 21 and 26 years of age, respectively), collaborated to create and build their Apple II computer on a makeshift production line in Jobs' garage. Seven years later, Apple Computer earned a spot on the Fortune 500, a list of the 500 largest corporations in the United States. Courtesy of Apple Computer, Inc.

1984: The Macintosh and Graphical User Interfaces

In 1984 Apple Computer introduced the Macintosh desktop computer with a very "friendly" graphical user interface—proof that computers can be easy and fun to use. Graphical user interfaces (GUIs) began to change the complexion of the software industry. They have changed the interaction between human and computer from a short, character-oriented exchange modeled on the teletypewriter to the now familiar WIMP interface—Windows, Icons, Menus, and Pointing devices.   Courtesy of Apple Computer, Inc.

1981: The IBM PC

In 1981, IBM tossed its hat into the personal computer ring with its announcement of the IBM Personal Computer, or IBM PC. By the end of 1982, 835,000 had been sold. When software vendors began to orient their products to the IBM PC, many companies began offering IBM-PC compatibles or clones. Today, the IBM PC and its clones have become a powerful standard for the microcomputer industry.

Courtesy of International Business Machines Corporation

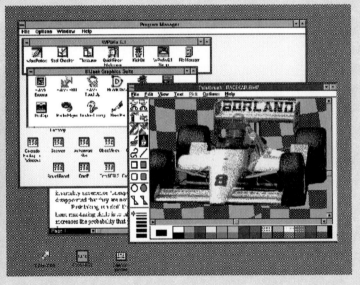

1985: Microsoft Windows

Microsoft introduced Windows, a GUI for IBM-PC—compatible computers in 1985; however, Windows did not enjoy widespread acceptance until 1990 with the release of Windows 3.0. Windows 3.0 gave a huge boost to the software industry because larger, more complex programs could now be run on IBM-PC compatibles.

1982: Mitchell Kapor Designs Lotus 1-2-3

Mitchell Kapor is one of the major forces behind the microcomputer boom in the 1980s. In 1982, Kapor founded Lotus Development Company, now one of the largest applications software companies in the world. Kapor and the company introduced an electronic spreadsheet product that gave IBM's recently introduced IBM PC (1981) credibility in the business marketplace. Sales of the IBM PC and the electronic spreadsheet, Lotus 1-2-3, soared.

CHAPTER 2

Inside the Computer

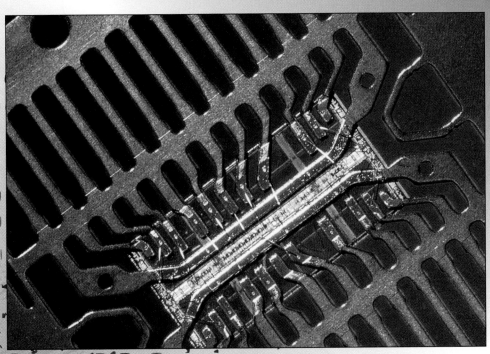

Courtesy of International Business Machines Corporation

Let's Talk

The following conversation introduces many of the terms in this chapter. Read it now, then again after you have read the chapter.

The Scene:
Travis is visiting a high school friend, Deb, at her house.

Travis (entering Deb's game room): What are doing, Deb?

Deb: Yo, Trav. I'm taking the cover off my PC.

Travis: How come?

Deb: It's a long story, but here's the short version. I just bought the new Intergalactic Invaders game, but my **motherboard** didn't meet the system requirements.

Travis: Why? What does it need?

Deb: Well, my **Pentium microprocessor**'s got the umph at 100 **MHz** and plenty of **cache memory,** but I'm short on **RAM.** Invader's needs 12 **megabytes,** so I bought 4 **MB** of **SIMMs** to get me up to speed *(inserting the SIMMs on the motherboard).*

Travis: What's that **expansion card** over there?

Deb: It's a new 28.8-**kilobit fax modem.** Since I paid for the SIMMs, I appealed to my parents to pay for the fax modem.

Travis: Wow! Are they always this generous?

Deb: No, but they wanted the fax modem so they could get America Online. Let's put it right here in the last **PCI local bus expansion slot** on my **system board** *(inserting it carefully in the only available slot).*

Travis: All right! Let's put the cover on and take off!

STUDENT LEARNING OBJECTIVES

▶ *To describe how data are stored in a computer system.*

▶ *To demonstrate the relationships between bits, bytes, characters, and encoding systems.*

▶ *To understand the translation of alphanumeric data into a format for internal computer representation.*

▶ *To explain and illustrate the principles of computer operations.*

▶ *To distinguish processors by their word size, speed, and memory capacity.*

▶ *To identify and describe the relationships between the internal components of a personal computer.*

2-1   DATA STORAGE: A BIT ABOUT THE BIT

The computer's capabilities seem limitless. It can transform itself into an entertainment center with hundreds of interactive games. It's a virtual school or university providing interactive instruction and testing in everything from anthropology to zoology. It's a painter's canvas. It's a video telephone. It's a CD player. It's a home or office library giving ready access to the complete works of Shakespeare or interactive versions of corporate procedures manuals. It's a television. It's the biggest marketplace in the world. It's a direct link with millions of people all over the world. It's a medical in-

strument capable of monitoring vital signs. It's a home meteorological center giving you periodic updates on weather information. It's an expert in thousands of disciplines capable of talking with you about anything from investment strategies to medical diagnosis. It's the family photo album. It's a print shop. It's a wind tunnel that can test experimental airplane designs. It's a voting booth. It's a calculator. It's a calendar with a to-do list. It's a recorder. It's an alarm clock that can remind you to pick up the kids. It's a set of encyclopedias. It can perform hundreds of specialty functions that require specialized skills: preparing taxes, editing text, drafting legal documents, counseling suicidal patients, and much more.

Digital sound information is stored temporarily in the RAM chips on this circuit board (center) which enables stereo sound output from a PC. Sound information can be stored permanently on magnetic disk or optical laser disk (left).   ATI Technologies Inc.

The computer has proven time and again to be the most versatile, enabling device ever invented. Ironically, the foundation of its versatility is its simplicity. In all of these applications, the computer deals with everything in digitized format—ultimately, in strings of 1s and 0s. To make the most effective use of computers and automation, everything is *going digital.*

Going Digital

Electronic signals come in two flavors—**analog** and **digital.** Electronically, analog signals are continuous wave forms that can be used to represent such things as sound, temperature, and velocity. Our audiocassette tapes store and transmit analog signals that can be interpreted and played as music. In contrast, our audio compact disks (CDs) store and transmit music in digital format, that is, in strings of 1s and 0s.

Computers are digital and, therefore, require digital data. A by-product of the computer revolution is a trend toward "going digital" whenever possible. Two good examples are the telephone system and recorded music. The emergence of the global village has prompted telephone companies to replace antiquated analog lines with ones capable of digital transmission. Another high-profile (and very audible) example of this transformation is the movement to digital recording on CD, away from analog recordings. Analog signals cannot be reproduced exactly. If you have ever duplicated an audio or VHS video tape (both being analog), you know that the copy is never as good as the source tape. In contrast, digital CDs can be copied over and over without deterioration. When CDs are duplicated, each is an exact copy of the original.

So how do you go digital? The music industry **digitizes** the natural analog signals that result from recording sessions, then stores the digital version on CDs (see Figure 2–1). To digitize means to convert data, analog signals, images, and other things into

This optical device uses solid-state laser technology to convert analog signals to digital signals, and vice versa.
Courtesy of E-Systems, Inc.

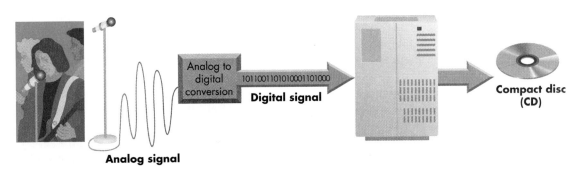

FIGURE 2–1 Going Digital with Compact Discs
The recording industry has gone digital. To create a master CD, analog signals are converted to digital signals that can be manipulated by a computer and written to a master CD. The master is duplicated and the copies are sold through retail channels.

the discrete format (1s and 0s) that can be interpreted by computers. Images such as photographs are scanned with a scanner to create a digitized version of the image. The photos you see in this book were scanned, entered into the computer, and integrated with other computer-based text and images. We can capture the shape of two-dimensional images by tracing on a special digitizing tablet. Digital cameras record digital representations of images, both still and motion. A mechanical arm can be moved on and around a 3-D object, such as a car, to create a digital representation of its shape. Once digitized, the music recording, data, image, shape, and so on can be manipulated by the computer. For example, old recordings of artists from Enrico Caruso to the Beatles have been digitized and then digitally reconstructed on computers to eliminate unwanted distortion and static. Some of these reconstructed CDs are actually better than the originals!

Binary Digits: On-Bits and Off-Bits

It's amazing, but the seemingly endless potential of computers is based on only two electronic states—*on* and *off.* The electronic nature of the computer makes it possible to combine these two electronic states to represent letters, numbers, colors, sounds, images, shapes, and much more—even odors. An "on" or "off" electronic state is represented by a **bit,** short for *b*inary dig*it.* In the **binary** numbering system (base 2), the *on-bit* is a 1 and the *off-bit* is a 0.

Vacuum tubes, transistors, and integrated circuits characterize the generations of computers. Each of these technologies enables computers to distinguish between on and off and, therefore, to use binary logic. Physically, these states are achieved in a variety of ways.

- In RAM, the two electronic states often are represented by the presence or absence of an electrical charge.
- In disk storage, the two states are made possible by the magnetic arrangement of the surface coating on magnetic tapes and disks (see Figure 2–2).
- In CDs and CD-ROMs, digital data are stored permanently as microscopic pits.
- In fiber optic cable, binary data flows through as pulses of light.

Bits may be fine for computers, but human beings are more comfortable with letters and decimal numbers (the base-10 numerals 0 through 9). We like to see colors and hear sounds. Therefore, the letters, decimal numbers, colors, and sounds that we input into a computer system while doing word processing, graphics, and other applications must be translated into 1s and 0s for processing and storage. The computer translates the bits back into letters, decimal numbers, colors, and sounds for output on monitors, printers, speakers, and so on.

Data in a Computer

To manipulate stored data within a computer system, we must have a way of storing and retrieving this raw material. It is easy to understand data storage in a manual system. For example, when a customer's address changes, we pull the customer's manila folder from the file cabinet, erase the old address, and write in the new one. We can see and easily interpret data that are kept manually. We cannot see or easily interpret data stored in a computer. Data are represented and stored in a computer system to take advantage of the physical characteristics of electronics and computer hardware, not human beings.

Data are stored *temporarily* during processing in random-access memory (RAM). RAM is also referred to as **primary storage.** Data are stored *permanently* on **secondary storage** devices such as magnetic tape and disk drives. We discuss primary storage (RAM) in detail in this chapter, as well as how data are represented electronically in a computer system and on the internal workings of a computer.

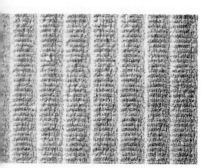

FIGURE 2–2 Bits on the Surface of a Magnetic Disk This highly magnified area of a magnetic disk-face surface shows elongated information bits recorded serially along 8 of the disk's 1774 concentric tracks. One square inch of this disk's surface can hold 22 million bits of information. Courtesy of International Business Machines Corporation

FIGURE 2–3 Encoding When you tap the B key on the keyboard, a binary representation of that *B* is sent to the processor. The processor sends the encoded *B* to the monitor which interprets and displays a **B.**

Character	ASCII Code
A	100 0001
B	100 0010
C	100 0011
D	100 0100
E	100 0101
F	100 0110
G	100 0111
H	100 1000
I	100 1001
J	100 1010
K	100 1011
L	100 1100
M	100 1101
N	100 1110
O	100 1111
P	101 0000
Q	101 0001
R	101 0010
S	101 0011
T	101 0100
U	101 0101
V	101 0110
W	101 0111
X	101 1000
Y	101 1001
Z	101 1010
0	011 0000
1	011 0001
2	011 0010
3	011 0011
4	011 0100
5	011 0101
6	011 0110
7	011 0111
8	011 1000
9	011 1001
Space	010 0000
.	010 1110
(	010 1000
+	010 1011
&	010 0110
$	010 0100
*	010 1010
)	010 1001
;	011 1011
,	010 1100
-	101 1111
?	011 1111
:	011 1010
=	011 1101

2–2 ENCODING SYSTEMS: BITS AND BYTES

Computers do not speak to one another in English, Spanish, or French. They have their own languages that are better suited to electronic communication. In these languages, bits are combined according to an **encoding system** to represent letters (**alpha** characters), numbers (**numeric** characters), and special characters (such as *, $, + , and &).

ASCII and ANSI

The seven-bit **ASCII** encoding system (*American Standard Code for Information Interchange*—pronounced *"AS-key"*) is the most popular encoding system for PCs and data communication. In ASCII, a B and a 3 are represented digitally in a computer by 1000010 and 0110011, respectively. Letters, numbers, and special characters are collectively referred to as **alphanumeric** characters. Alphanumeric characters are *encoded* into a bit configuration on input so that the computer can interpret them. When you tap the letter *B* on a PC keyboard, the *B* is transmitted to the processor as a coded string of binary digits (for example, 1000010 in ASCII) as shown in Figure 2–3. The characters are *decoded* on output so we can interpret them. This coding, based on a particular encoding system, equates a unique series of bits and no-bits with a specific character. Just as the words *mother* and *father* are arbitrary English-language character strings that refer to our parents, 1011010 is an arbitrary ASCII code that refers to the letter Z. The combination of bits used to represent a character is called a **byte** (pronounced *bite*). Figure 2–4 shows the binary value (the actual bit configuration) of commonly used characters in ASCII.

The seven-bit ASCII code can represent up to 128 characters (2*2*2*2*2*2*2 or 2^7). Although the English language has considerably fewer than 128 *printable* characters, the extra bit configurations are needed to represent a variety of common and not-so-common special characters (such as - [hyphen]; @ [at]; | [a broken vertical bar]; and ~ [tilde]) and to signal a variety of activities to the computer (such as ringing a bell or telling the computer to accept a piece of datum).

ASCII is a seven-bit code, but the microcomputer byte is eight bits. There are 256 (2^8) possible bit configurations in an 8-bit byte. Hardware and software vendors accept the 128 standard codes and use the extra 128 bit configurations to represent control characters or noncharacter images to complement their hardware or software product. For example, the IBM-PC version of **extended ASCII** contains the characters of many foreign languages (such as *ä* [umlaut] and *é* [acute]) and a wide variety of graphic images that can be combined on a text screen to produce larger images (for example, the box around a window on a display screen).

Microsoft Windows uses the 8-bit **ANSI** encoding system, a standard developed by the American National Standards Institute, to enable the sharing of text between

FIGURE 2–4 ASCII Codes This figure shows the ASCII codes for upper-case letters, numbers, and several special characters. The ASCII codes for upper-case and lower-case letters are similar. Replace the second binary digit with a 1 to get the lower-case equivalent (*A* is 1000010 and *a* is 1100010).

Creating text for a video display calls for a technology called "character generation." An 8-bit encoding system, with its 256 unique bit configurations, is more than adequate to represent all of the alphanumeric characters used in the English language. The Chinese, however, need a 16-bit encoding system, like Unicode, to represent their 13,000 characters.   Courtesy of Dynatech Corporation

Windows applications. Like IBM extended ASCII, the first 128 ANSI codes are the same as the ASCII codes, but the next 128 are defined to meet the needs of Windows applications.

Unicode: 65,536 Possibilities

A consortium of heavyweight computer industry companies, such as IBM, Microsoft, and Sun Microsystems, is sponsoring the development of **Unicode,** a uniform 16-bit encoding system. Unicode will enable computers and applications to talk to one another more easily and will accommodate most languages of the world. ASCII, with 128 (2^7) character codes, is sufficient for the English language but falls far short of the Japanese language requirements. The consortium is proposing that Unicode be adopted as a standard for information interchange throughout the computer community and the world. Unicode's 16-bit code takes up 2 bytes, allowing for 65,536 characters (2^{16}). Unicode will have codes for the alphabets of most of the world's languages (including Hebrew ש, Japanese ネ, and upper- and lower-case Greek Ψ). Universal acceptance of the Unicode standard will help facilitate international communication in all areas, from monetary transfers between banks to e-mail. With Unicode as a standard, software can be created more easily to work with a wider base of languages.

Unicode, like any advancement in computer technology, presents conversion problems. The 16-bit Unicode demands more memory than do traditional 8-bit codes. An *A* in Unicode takes twice the RAM and disk space of an ASCII *A*. Currently, 8-bit encoding systems provide the foundation for most software packages and existing databases. Should Unicode be adopted officially or unofficially (de facto) as a standard, programs must be revised to work with Unicode and existing data will need to be converted to Unicode. Information processing needs have simply outgrown the 8-bit standard, so conversion to Unicode or some other standard is inevitable. This conversion, however, will be time-consuming and expensive.

2–3   ANALYZING A COMPUTER SYSTEM, BIT BY BIT

We have learned that all computers have similar capabilities and perform essentially the same functions, although some might be faster than others. We have also learned that a computer system has input, output, storage, and processing components; that the *processor* is the "intelligence" of a computer system; and that a single computer system may have several processors. We have discussed how data are represented inside a computer system in electronic states called *bits*. We are now ready to expose the inner workings of the nucleus of the computer system—the processor.

Literally hundreds of different types of computers are marketed by scores of manufacturers. The complexity of each type may vary considerably, but in the end each processor, sometimes called the **central processing unit** or **CPU,** has only two fundamental sections: the *control unit* and the *arithmetic and logic unit*. Random-access memory (RAM) also plays an integral part in the internal operation of a processor. These three—random-access memory (same as primary storage), the control unit, and the arithmetic and logic unit—work together. Let's look at their functions and the relationships among them.

RAM: Random-Access Storage

RAM Technology: DRAM and SRAM   Unlike magnetic secondary storage devices, such as tape and disk, RAM (primary storage) has no moving parts. RAM, a *read-and-write memory*, enables data to be both read and written to memory. With no

In the first generation of computers (1951–1959), each bit was represented by a vacuum tube, about the size of a small light bulb. Today computers use chips, like this one, that can store millions of bits.   Courtesy of International Business Machines Corporation

mechanical movement, data can be accessed from RAM at electronic speeds, or close to the speed of light. Most of today's computers use CMOS (*C*omplementary *M*etal-*O*xide *S*emiconductor) technology for RAM. A state-of-the-art CMOS memory chip about one-eighth the size of a postage stamp can store about 4,000,000 bits, or more than 400,000 characters of data! Physically, memory chips are installed on **single in-line memory modules** or **SIMMs.** SIMMs are circuit boards with links directly to the processor.

The most common RAM technologies are **dynamic RAM (DRAM)** and **static RAM (SRAM).** DRAM is used in more computers than is SRAM. However, SRAM is faster than DRAM because it does not have to be refreshed hundreds of times a second like DRAM. It is also much more expensive and requires more space and power than does DRAM.

Nonvolatile memory is frequently the memory of choice for computer-controlled machine tools that must operate in harsh environments. Courtesy Deere and Company

There is one major problem with semiconductor storage: It is **volatile memory.** That is, when the electrical current is turned off or interrupted, the data are lost. Researchers are working to perfect a RAM technology that will retain its contents after an electrical interruption. Several **nonvolatile memory** technologies, such as **bubble memory,** have emerged, but none has exhibited the qualities necessary for widespread use as primary storage (RAM). Although much slower than RAM, bubble memory is superior to CMOS for use in certain computers because it is highly reliable, it is not susceptible to environmental fluctuations, and it can operate on battery power for a considerable length of time. Its durability makes bubble memory well suited for use with industrial robots and control devices and with hand-held computers.

Readin', 'Ritin', and RAM Cram   RAM provides the processor with *temporary* storage for programs and data. *All programs and data must be transferred to RAM from an input device (such as a keyboard) or from secondary storage (such as a disk) before programs can be executed and data can be processed.* RAM space is always at a premium; therefore, after program execution is terminated, the storage space it occupied is assigned to another program awaiting execution. PC users attempting to run too many programs at the same time face *RAM cram,* a situation in which there is not enough memory to run the programs.

Figure 2–5 illustrates how all input/output (I/O) is "read to" or "written from" RAM. Programs and data must be "loaded," or moved, to RAM from secondary storage for processing. This is a **nondestructive read** process; that is, the program and data that are read reside in both RAM (temporarily) and secondary storage (permanently).

The data in RAM are manipulated by the processor according to program instructions. A program instruction or a piece of datum is stored in a specific RAM location called an **address.** RAM is analogous to the rows of boxes you see in post offices. Each byte in RAM has an address just as each P.O. box has a number. Addresses permit program instructions and data to be located, accessed, and processed. The content of each address is constantly changing as different programs are executed and new data are processed.

ROM, PROM, and Flash Memory   A special type of internal memory, called *read-only memory (ROM),* cannot be altered by the user (see Figure 2–5). The contents of ROM (rhymes with *"mom"*), a nonvolatile technology, are "hard-wired" (designed into the logic of the memory chip) by the manufacturer and can be "read only." When you turn on a microcomputer system, a program in ROM automatically readies the computer system for use and produces the initial display-screen prompt.

MEMORY BITS
Internal Storage

- Volatile memory
  - Dynamic RAM (DRAM)
  - Static RAM (SRAM)
- Nonvolatile memory
  - Bubble memory
  - Flash memory
- ROM and PROM
  - Cache
  - Registers

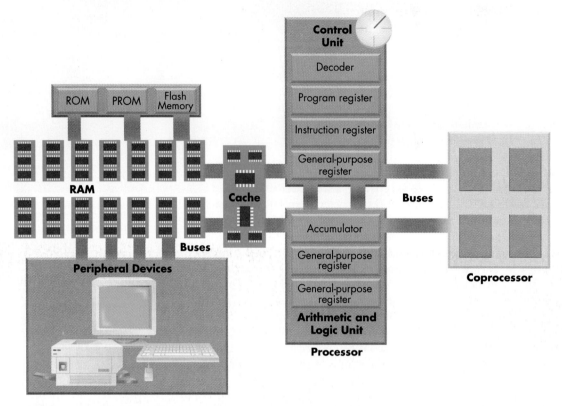

FIGURE 2–5 Interaction between Computer System Components
During processing, instructions and data are passed between the various types of internal memories, the processor's control unit and arithmetic and logic unit, the coprocessor, and the peripheral devices over the common electrical bus. A system clock paces the speed of operation within the processor and ensures that everything takes place in timed intervals.

Inside the Computer Explorer

A variation of ROM is **programmable read-only memory (PROM).** PROM is ROM into which you, the user, can load read-only programs and data. Some microcomputer software packages, such as electronic spreadsheets, are available as PROM units as well as on interchangeable disks. Generally, once a program is loaded to PROM, it is seldom, if ever, changed. ROM and PROM are used in a variety of capacities within a computer system.

Flash memory is a type of nonvolatile memory that can be altered easily by the user. Flash memory is a feature of many I/O and storage devices. The intelligence of these devices can be upgraded by simply downloading new software from a vendor-supplied disk to flash memory. Upgrades to early input/output and storage devices required the user to replace the old circuit board or chip with a new one. The emergence of flash memory has eliminated this time-consuming and costly method of upgrade. Look for nonvolatile flash memory to play an increasing role in computer technology as its improvements continue to close the gap between the speed and flexibility of CMOS RAM.

Cache Memory Programs and data are loaded to RAM from secondary storage because the time required to access a program instruction or piece of datum from RAM is significantly less than from secondary storage. Thousands of instructions or pieces of data can be accessed from RAM in the time it would take to access a single piece of datum from disk storage. RAM is essentially a high-speed holding area for data and programs. In fact, *nothing really happens in a computer system until the program instructions and data are moved from RAM to the processor.* This transfer of instructions and data to the processor can be time-consuming, even at microsecond speeds. To facilitate an

Issues in Computing

Should PC Ownership Be an Entrance Requirement for Colleges?

As the job market tightens, colleges are looking to give their students a competitive edge. With computer knowledge becoming a job prerequisite for many positions, hundreds of colleges have made the purchase of a personal computer a prerequisite for admission. Personal computers are versatile in that they can be used as stand-alone computers or they can be linked to the college's network, the Internet, or other personal computers. At these colleges, PCs are everywhere—in lounges, libraries, and other common areas.

Wouldn't it be great to run a bibliographic search from your dorm room or home? Make changes to a report without retyping it? Run a case search for a law class? Use the computer for math homework calculations?

Instead of making hard copies of class assignments, some instructors key in their assignments, which are then "delivered" to each student's electronic mailbox. Students can correspond with their instructors through their computer to get help with assignments. They can even "talk" to other students at connected colleges.

Extended Classroom At some colleges, owning a computer has been made a prerequisite for admission. Courtesy of International Business Machines Corporation

Discussion: If your college does not require PC ownership for admission, should it? If it does, should the policy be continued?

even faster transfer of instructions and data to the processor, computers are designed with **cache memory** (see Figure 2–5). Cache memory is used by computer designers to increase computer system throughput. **Throughput** refers to the rate at which work can be performed by a computer system.

Like RAM, cache is a high-speed holding area for program instructions and data. However, cache memory uses a technology that is about 10 times faster than RAM and about 100 times more expensive. With only a fraction of the capacity of RAM, cache memory holds only those instructions and data that are *likely* to be needed next by the processor.

Chips

The Processor: Nerve Center

The Control Unit Just as the processor is the nucleus of a computer system, the **control unit** is the nucleus of the processor. Recall from earlier in this section, the *control unit* and the *arithmetic and logic unit* are the two fundamental sections of a processor (see Figure 2–5). The control unit has three primary functions:

1. To read and interpret program instructions
2. To direct the operation of internal processor components
3. To control the flow of programs and data in and out of RAM

A program must first be loaded to RAM before it can be executed. During execution, the first in a sequence of program instructions is moved from RAM to the control unit, where it is decoded and interpreted by the **decoder.** The control unit then directs other processor components to carry out the operations necessary to execute the instruction.

The control unit contains high-speed working storage areas called **registers** that can store no more than a few bytes (see Figure 2–5). Registers handle instructions and data at a speed about 10 times faster than that of cache memory and are used for a variety of processing functions. One register, called the **instruction register,** contains the instruction being executed. Other general-purpose registers store data needed for immediate processing. Registers also store status information. For example, the **program register** contains the RAM address of the next instruction to be executed. Registers facilitate the movement of data and instructions between RAM, the control unit, and the arithmetic and logic unit.

The Arithmetic and Logic Unit   The **arithmetic and logic unit** performs all computations (addition, subtraction, multiplication, and division) and all logic operations (comparisons). The results are placed in a register called the **accumulator.** Examples of *computations* include the payroll deduction for social security, the day-end inventory, and the balance on a bank statement. A *logic* operation compares two pieces of datum. Then, based on the result of the comparison, the program "branches" to one of several alternative sets of program instructions. Let's use an inventory system to illustrate the logic operation. At the end of each day the inventory level of each item in stock is compared to a reorder point. For each comparison indicating an inventory level that falls below (<) the reorder point, a sequence of program instructions is executed that produces a purchase order. For each comparison indicating an inventory level at or above (= or >) the reorder point, another sequence of instructions is executed.

Buses: The Processor's Mass Transit System

Just as the mass transit systems in big cities must move large numbers of people, the computer has a similar system that moves millions of bits a second. Both transit systems use buses, although the one in the computer doesn't have wheels. All electrical signals travel on a common electrical bus. The term **bus** was derived from its wheeled cousin because passengers on both buses (people and bits) can get off at any stop. In a computer the bus stops are the control unit, the arithmetic and logic unit, internal memory (RAM, ROM, flash, and other types of internal memory), and the **device controllers** (small computers) that control the operation of the peripheral devices (see Figure 2–5). Even within a PC computer system, you have computers interacting with one another.

The bus is the common pathway through which the processor sends/receives data and commands to/from primary and secondary storage and all I/O peripheral devices. Instead of boarding the downtown bus or uptown bus, bits traveling between RAM, cache memory, and the processor hop on the **address bus** and the **data bus.** Source and destination addresses are sent over the address bus to identify a particular location in memory, then the data and instructions are transferred over the data bus to or from that location.

Making the Processor Work

We communicate with computers by telling them what to do in their native tongue— the machine language.

The Machine Language   You may have heard of computer programming languages such as Visual BASIC and C++. There are dozens of programming languages in common usage. However, in the end, Visual BASIC, C++, and the other languages are translated into the only language that a computer understands—its own **machine language.** Can you guess how machine-language instructions are represented inside the computer? You are correct if you answered as strings of binary digits.

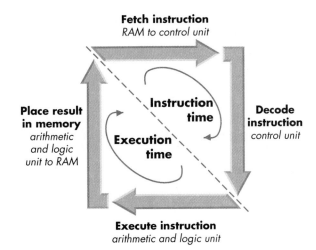

Fetch instruction
RAM to control unit

Instruction time

Decode instruction
control unit

Place result in memory
arithmetic and logic unit to RAM

Execution time

Execute instruction
arithmetic and logic unit

FIGURE 2–6   The Machine Cycle

The Machine Cycle: Making the Rounds   Every computer has a **machine cycle.** The speed of a processor is sometimes measured by how long it takes to complete a machine cycle. The timed interval that comprises the machine cycle is the total of the **instruction time,** or **I-time,** and the **execution time,** or **E-time** (see Figure 2–6). The I-time is made up of the first two activities of the machine cycle—fetch and decode the instruction. The E-time comprises the last two activities of the machine cycle—execute the instruction and store the results. The following actions take place during the machine cycle (see Figure 2–6):

Instruction time

● *Fetch instruction.* The next machine-language instruction to be executed is retrieved, or "fetched," from RAM or cache memory and loaded to the instruction register in the control unit.
● *Decode instruction.* The instruction is decoded and interpreted.

Execution time

● *Execute instruction.* Using whatever processor resources are needed (primarily the arithmetic and logic unit), the instruction is executed.
● *Place result in memory.* The results are placed in the appropriate memory position or the accumulator.

Processor Design: There Is a Choice

CISC and RISC: More Is Not Always Better   Most processors in mainframe computers and personal computers have a **CISC** (*c*omplex *i*nstruction *s*et *c*omputer) design. A CISC computer's machine language offers programmers a wide variety of instructions from which to choose (add, multiply, compare, move data, and so on). CISC computers reflect the evolution of increasingly sophisticated machine languages. Computer designers, however, are rediscovering the beauty of simplicity. Computers designed around much smaller instruction sets can realize significantly increased throughput for certain applications, especially those that involve graphics (for example, computer-aided design). These computers have **RISC** (*r*educed *i*nstruction *s*et *c*omputer) design. The RISC chip shifts much of the computational burden from the hardware to the software.

This high-power RISC-based Sun Microsystems Netra Internet Server helps companies establish a secure business presence on the Internet.   *Courtesy Sun Microsystems*

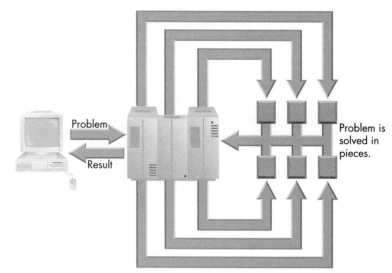

FIGURE 2–7   Parallel Processing
In parallel processing, auxiliary processors solve pieces of a problem to enhance system throughput.

Proponents of RISC design feel that the limitations of a reduced instruction set are easily offset by increased processing speed and the lower cost of RISC microprocessors.

Parallel Processing: Computers Working Together   In a single processor environment, the processor addresses the programming problem sequentially, from beginning to end. Today, designers are doing research on and building computers that break a programming problem into pieces. Work on each of these pieces is then executed simultaneously in separate processors, all of which are part of the same computer. The concept of using multiple processors in the same computer is known as **parallel processing.** In parallel processing, one main processor examines the programming problem and determines what portions, if any, of the problem can be solved in pieces (see Figure 2–7). Those pieces that can be addressed separately are routed to other processors and solved. The individual pieces are then reassembled in the main processor for further computation, output, or storage. The net result of parallel processing is better throughput.

Computer designers are creating mainframes and supercomputers with thousands of integrated microprocessors. Parallel processing on such a large scale is referred to as **massively parallel processing (MPP).** These super-fast supercomputers will have sufficient computing capacity to attack applications that have been beyond that of computers with traditional computer designs. For example, researchers hope to simulate global warming with these computers.

2–4   DESCRIBING THE PROCESSOR: DISTINGUISHING CHARACTERISTICS

People are people, and computers are computers, but how do we distinguish one from the other? When describing someone we generally note gender, height, weight, and age. When describing computers or processors we talk about *word size, speed,* and the *capacity* of their associated RAM (see Figure 2–8). For example, a computer might be described as a 64-bit, 100-MHz, 32-MB micro. Let's see what this means.

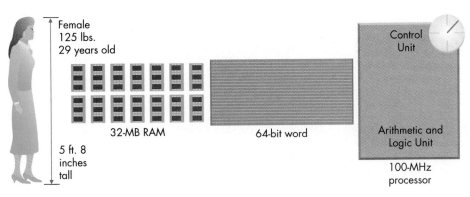

Female
125 lbs.
29 years old

5 ft. 8
inches
tall

32-MB RAM

64-bit word

Control
Unit

Arithmetic and
Logic Unit

100-MHz
processor

FIGURE 2–8 Describing a Computer
We describe computers much like we would a person, but we use different characteristics
(word size, speed, and RAM capacity).

Word Size: 16-, 32-, and 64-Lane Bitways

Just as the brain sends and receives signals through the central nervous system, the
processor sends and receives electrical signals through its common electrical bus—a
word at a time. A **word** describes the number of bits that are handled as a unit within
a particular computer system's bus or during internal processing.

Twenty years ago, a computer's word size applied both to transmissions through
the electrical *bus* and to *all internal processing*. This is no longer the case. In some of
today's computers, one word size defines pathways in the bus and another word size
defines internal processing capacity. Internal processing involves the movement of
data and commands between registers, the control unit, and the arithmetic and logic
unit (see Figure 2–5). Many popular micros have 32-bit internal processing but only
a 16-bit path through the bus. For certain input/output-oriented applications, a 32-
bit computer with a 16-bit bus may not realize the throughput of a full 32-bit computer.

The word size of modern microcomputers is normally 32 bits (four 8-bit bytes) or
64 bits (eight 8-bit bytes). Early micros had word sizes of 8 bits (one byte) and 16 bits
(two bytes). Workstations and mainframes have anywhere from 32-bit to 64-bit word
sizes. Supercomputers have 64-bit words.

Processor Speed: Warp Speed

A tractor can go 12 miles per hour (mph), a minivan can go 90 mph, and a slingshot
drag racer can go 240 mph. These speeds, however, provide little insight into the relative capabilities of these vehicles. What good is a 240-mph tractor or a 12-mph minivan? The same is true of computers. You have to place speed within the context of
design and application. Generally, micros are measured in *MHz;* workstations and
mainframes are measured in *MIPS;* and supercomputers are measured in *FLOPS.*

Megahertz: MHz The PC's heart is its *crystal oscillator* and its heartbeat is the *clock
cycle*. The crystal oscillator paces the execution of instructions within the processor. A

micro's processor speed is rated by its frequency of oscil-
lation, or the number of clock cycles per second. Most
personal computers are rated between 16 and 150 **megahertz, or MHz** (millions of clock cycles). The elapsed time
for one clock cycle is 1/frequency (1 divided by the frequency). For example, the time it takes to complete one
cycle on a 100-MHz processor is 1/100,000,000, or
0.00000001 seconds, or 10 nanoseconds (10 billionths of

Many field sales representatives carry notebook PCs
when they call on customers.
This Compaq notebook has a
32-bit processor with a speed
of 66 MHz and a RAM capacity of 12 MB.   Reprinted with
permission of Compaq Computer
Corporation. All Rights Reserved.

Emerging Technology

Computers: The Enabling Technology for the Disabled

Computer technology is having a profound effect on physically challenged people. With the aid of computers they now are better prepared to take control of their environments.

On the Move

Paraplegic Walks A little over a decade ago, Nan Davis stunned the world. A paraplegic since an automobile accident on the night of her high school graduation, she walked to the podium to receive her college diploma—with the help of a rehabilitative tool that uses FES, or functional electrical stimulation.

FES uses low-level electrical stimulation to restore or supplement the minute electrical currents the nervous system generates to control different parts of the body. This electrical stimulation is controlled by a microprocessor—a computer—that uses feedback from the body to adjust the electrical stimulation's length and intensity.

In Nan's case, FES took the form of electrodes to stimulate her leg muscles; a sensory feedback system; and a small, portable computer. The sensory feedback system tells the computer the position and movement of the legs so that it knows which muscles it must electrically stimulate next to produce a coordinated gait.

FES Comes of Age Although the use of FES to restore one's ability to stand, walk, and use the arms and hands is still in the experimental stage, many other FES applications are accepted

medical practice. The best-known application is the cardiac pacemaker that is attached directly to a faulty heart with electrodes. FES can also be used to control chronic pain, correct spinal deformities, improve auditory defects, and pace the rise and fall of the diaphragm during breathing.

Grasping the Technology This person, whose hands are paralyzed due to a spinal cord injury, uses an implanted FES system that causes her finger muscles to contract and allows her to grasp the telephone. Courtesy of MetroHealth Medical Center, Cleveland, Ohio

FES can also be used as a therapeutic tool to strengthen muscles idled by paralysis. Without exercise, muscles atrophy, circulation becomes sluggish, cardiovascular fitness declines, and pressure sores develop. These FES devices, which look like high-tech exercise bicycles, use a microprocessor to coordinate a system of electrodes and feedback sensors, allowing the user to push the pedals and turn a hand crank. Like anyone who engages in a regular exercise program, users of the FES devices report noticeable improvements in muscle tone, mass, and cardiovascular fitness. These devices cannot restore function, of course, but they can help the paralyzed to maintain their bodies while researchers continue to seek ways to help them walk again. In the meantime, many are thrilled just to see their bodies move again.

Scaling the Barriers at Work For most disabled workers—especially those with physical impairments—the barriers to gainful employment have been as steep as the stairs flanking many public buildings. This is changing thanks to federal legislation and revolutionary advances in computer hardware and software.

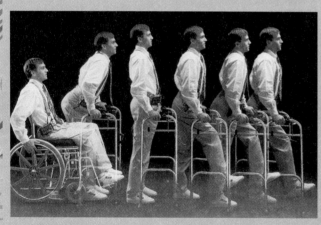

Paraplegic Walks The Parastep® System is a microcomputer controlled functional neuromuscular stimulation (FNS) device enabling standing and walking by people paralyzed with spinal cord injuries. This system comes from the medical engineering sciences known as neuroprosthetics.

The Parastep stimulator generates sequences of electrical pulses passed to target peripheral nerves through electrodes placed over muscles and nerves of the lower extremities. The user controls stimulation through a keypad on the stimulator unit or with control switches on the walker. Courtesy of Sigmedics, Inc.

The Americans with Disabilities Act of 1990 This legislation prohibits discrimination that might limit employment or access to public buildings and facilities. In fact, many call the law a bill of rights for people with physical limitations, mental impairments, and chronic illnesses. The legislation promises to benefit the nation, too. Of the approximately 43 million disabled workers, only about 28% hold full- or part-time jobs at a time when experts are projecting labor shortages and a shrinking pool of *skilled* workers.

Enabling Technology Under the law, employers cannot discriminate against any employee who can perform a job's "essential" responsibilities with "reasonable accommodations." Increasingly, these "accommodations" take the form of a personal computer with special peripherals and software. All told, almost 20,000 technology-based products are available for the disabled.

For example, getting a complete impression of the contents of a computer screen is a problem for the visually impaired, as is the ability to maneuver around such features as pull-down windows and click-on icons. The partially sighted can benefit from adaptive software packages that create large-type screen displays, while voice synthesizers can let the blind "read" memos, books, and computer screens.

Personal Reader This personal reader allows visually impaired people to "hear" books and typewritten material. An optical scanner reads the words into the computer system, where they are converted into English speech using a speech synthesizer (a device that produces electronic speech). Users can request any of nine different voices (including male, female, and child). Xerox Imaging Systems/Kurzweil, a Xerox Company

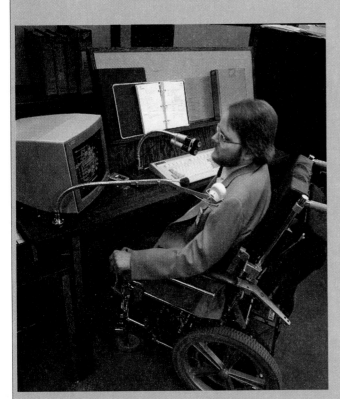

At Work The nature of the work and the availability of specially designed workstations have made computer careers particularly inviting to the physically disabled. The man in the photo works as a database administrator at a computer services company. Boeing Computer Services

For the hearing impaired, voice mail and a computer's beeps can be translated into visual cues, such as a screen display of text or flashing icons. Advancing communications and video technologies have made it possible for users to sit in front of their respective computer screens and have sign language conversations.

Virtually any type of physical movement can be used to input commands and data to a computer. This is good news for people with limited use of their arms and hands. Alternative input devices can range from a standard trackball (instead of a mouse) to the relatively slow sip-and-puff devices to faster voice-recognition systems. There are even software programs which allow keystroke combinations to be entered one key at a time.

Several studies, including ones by the U.S. Department of Labor and private firms, concluded that 80% of all accommodations would cost less than $500 per employee. Text-to-speech software, for example, can be purchased for as little as $150. More sophisticated PC-based accommodations are more costly, of course. The leading speech-recognition system, for example, costs about $9000, while a PC modified for a blind word processor can cost about $8000 (versus $2000 for a standard PC). Still, the prices of these technologies, like the prices of PCs themselves, continue to drop. The cost of a "reading" device, for example, fell from $40,000 to $2000 in about a decade. Furthermore, employers who provide "assistive technologies" to their employees are eligible for tax incentives. Employers benefit, too, by gaining highly motivated and productive workers. A study at a major chemical company found that workers with and without disabilities were equal or closely matched on safety and performance.

The Garland Division of E-Systems, Inc. has linked six Cray C-90 supercomputers, each containing 16 processors. The system is capable of crunching data at a peak rate of 64 GFLOPS (gigaflops). One GFLOP equals one billion floating point logic operations per second.   *Courtesy of E-Systems, Inc.*

a second). Normally several clock cycles are required to fetch, decode, and execute a single program instruction. The shorter the clock cycle, the faster the processor.

To properly evaluate the processing capability of a micro, you must consider both the processor speed and the word size. A 32-bit micro with a 66-MHz processor has more processing capability than does a 16-bit micro with a 66-MHz processor.

MIPS   The processing speed may be measured in **MIPS,** or *millions of instructions per second.* Although frequently associated with workstations and mainframes, MIPS is also applied to high-end PCs. Computers operate in the 20 to 1000 MIPS range. A 100-MIPS computer can execute 100 million instructions per second. Now that computers are performing at 1000 MIPS, look for *BIPS* (*billions of instructions per second*) to emerge as a measure of speed on high-end mainframe computers.

FLOPS   Supercomputer speed is measured in **FLOPS**—*floating point operations per second.* Supercomputer applications, which are often scientific, frequently involve floating point operations. Floating point operations accommodate very small or very large numbers. State-of-the-art supercomputers operate in the 30 to 100 **GFLOPS** range. One GFLOP (gigaflop) refers to one billion FLOPS.

Compare the number of characters in the Gettysburg Address to 1 KB (Kilobyte)

Compare the number of characters in this book to 1 MB (Megabyte)

Compare the number of people in China to 1 GB (Gigabyte)

Compare the number of gallons of water consumed each day in North America to 1 TB (Terabyte)

FIGURE 2–9   How Much Is a KB, an MB, a GB, and a TB?

RAM Capacity: Megachips

The capacity of RAM is stated in terms of the number of bytes it can store. As we learned in this chapter, a byte, or eight bits, is roughly equivalent to a character (such as *A, 1, &*).

Memory capacity for most computers is stated in terms of **megabytes (MB),** a convenient designation for 1,048,576 (2^{20}) bytes. Memory capacities of modern micros range from 4 MB to 32 MB. Memory capacities of early micros were measured in **kilobytes (KB),** which is 1024 (2^{10}) bytes of storage.

Some high-end mainframes and supercomputers have more than 1000 MB of RAM. Their RAM capacities are stated as **gigabytes (GB),** about one billion bytes. It's only a matter of time before we state RAM in terms of **terabytes (TB),** about one trillion bytes. GB and TB are frequently used in reference to high-capacity secondary storage. Occasionally you will see memory capacities of individual chips stated in terms of **kilobits (Kb)** and **megabits (Mb).** Figure 2–9 should give you a feel for KBs, MBs, GBs, and TBs.

Differences in Processor Personality

Word size, speed, and *RAM capacity* are the primary descriptors of processors. However, computers, like people, have their own "personalities." That is, two similarly described computers might possess attributes that give one more capability than the other. For example, one 64-bit, 100-MHz, 32-MB PC might permit the connection of four peripheral devices and another eight peripheral devices. Or, one might be configured with a coprocessor to speed up processing of numeric data. Just remember when you buy a PC that the basic descriptors tell most but not all of the story.

Now that you have had an opportunity to see what happens inside computers in general, let's take a closer look inside a personal computer.

The Microprocessor: Computer on a Chip

What is smaller than a postage stamp and found in wristwatches, sewing machines, and CD players? The answer—a **microprocessor.** The microprocessor is a small processor that embodies all elements of its cousins in larger mainframe computers: registers, control unit, arithmetic and logic unit, cache memory, and so on (see Section 2–3). Microprocessors play a very important role in our lives. You probably have a dozen or more of them at home and may not know it. They are used in telephones, ovens, televisions, thermostats, greeting cards, automobiles, and, of course, personal computers.

The microprocessor is a product of the microminiaturization of electronic circuitry; it is literally a "computer on a chip." We use the term *chip* to refer to any self-contained integrated circuit. The size of chips, which are about 30 thousandths of an inch thick, vary in area from fingernail size (about ¼-inch square) to postage-stamp size (about 1-inch square). These relatively inexpensive microprocessors have been integrated into thousands of mechanical and electronic devices—even elevators, band saws, and ski-boot bindings. In a few years virtually everything mechanical or electronic will incorporate microprocessor technology into its design.

The System Board: The Mother of All Boards

The **system board,** or **motherboard,** is the physical foundation of the PC. In a personal computer, the following are attached to the system board, a single circuit board:

- ▶ Microprocessor (main processor)
- ▶ Support electronic circuitry (for example, one chip handles input/output signals from the peripheral devices)
- ▶ Memory chips (RAM, DRAM, ROM, flash memory, cache memory, and so on)
- ▶ Bus (the path through which the processor communicates with memory components and peripheral devices)
- ▶ Expansion slots for linking other circuit boards and peripheral devices to the processor

Before being attached to the system board, the microprocessor and other chips are mounted onto a **carrier.** Carriers have standard-sized pin connectors that allow the chips to be attached to the system board.

The system board, the "guts" of a microcomputer, is what distinguishes one microcomputer from another. The central component of the system board, the microprocessor, is generally not made by the manufacturers of micros. It is made by companies, such as Motorola and Intel, that specialize in the development and manufacture of microprocessors.

Motorola Microprocessors Motorola manufactures two prominent families of microprocessors: the 68000, or 68K, family and the **PowerPC** family. The 68K family (68000, 68020, 68030, 68040, and 68060) has been the processor for the Apple line of computers and for hundreds of electronic devices from microwaves to automobiles. However, Apple and others are adopting the newer PowerPC technology.

Some industry observers are predicting that Motorola's PowerPC line of microprocessors may emerge as a new industry standard—but time will tell. They say this

In any PC, the system board is installed first, then everything else inside the system unit (power supply, disk drives, and so on) is connected to it. External peripheral devices are linked via cables which plug into standard connectors on the back side of the unit. Courtesy of International Business Machines Corporation

The Motorola's PowerPC family of microprocessors (top) can run all major industry standard platforms. Intel Corporation's Pentium™ is the microprocessor found in most PC-compatible computers. *Courtesy of International Business Machines Corporation*

is because the PowerPC is a product of an alliance between three of the computer industry's most powerful players: Motorola, Apple, and IBM. The PowerPC family includes the PowerPC 601, the PowerPC 603, the PowerPC 604, and the PowerPC 620. The first three are designed for use in PCs, including those manufactured by Apple and IBM. The PowerPC 620 is designed for use with everything from high-end workstations to supercomputers. The PowerPC provides users with tremendous flexibility in that it can run all major industry-standard **platforms.** A platform is defined by a combination of hardware and software for which software is developed. The two most popular platforms in state-of-the-art PCs are the *PowerPC with Apple's System 7* control software and the *Intel microprocessors with Microsoft Windows* software.

Intel Microprocessors The system board for the original IBM PC, the IBM PC/XT, and most of the *IBM-PC–compatible* micros manufactured through 1984, used the Intel 8088 microprocessor chip. The Intel 8088 chip is a slower version of the Intel 8086, which was developed in 1979. At the time of the introduction of the IBM PC (1981), the Intel 8086 was thought to be too advanced for the emerging PC market. Ironically, the more powerful Intel 8086 chip was not used in micros until the introduction of the low-end models of the IBM PS/2 series in 1987. The 8086 is considered the base technology for all microprocessors used in IBM-PC–compatible and the IBM PS/2 series computers.

The IBM PC/AT (Advanced Technology), which was introduced in 1984, employed an Intel 80286 microprocessor. As much as six times faster than the 8088, the 80286 provided a substantial increase in PC performance. The more advanced Intel 80386 and 80486 chips offered even greater performance for IBM-PC–compatible micros, which usually are called simply *PC compatibles.* When someone talks about a "286," "386," or "486" machine, he or she is referring to a micro that uses Intel 80286, 80386, or 80486 chip technology. Successor Intel microprocessors to the 486 fall in the **Pentium™** family of microprocessors. The Pentium chips are designed to better accommodate multimedia applications that involve sound and motion video. Figure 2–10 illustrates relative performance (speed in MIPS) of past, present, and future Intel microprocessors. Intel's successor to the Pentium, called the **P6,** is being installed in high-end workstations and may someday be the standard for PCs.

FIGURE 2–10 The Intel Family of Processors
Intel processors have been installed in 9 of every 10 of the over 160 million PCs in use today. This chart is an approximation of the relative speeds of popular Intel processors. It also compares these to one that reflects anticipated technology at the turn of the century. This processor will have about 10,000 times the speed of the Intel 8088 (2000 MIPs to .2 MIPs), the processor that ushered in the age of personal computing.

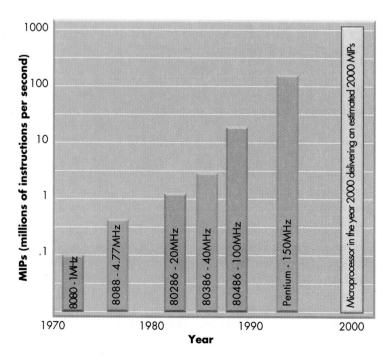

PowerPC versus Pentium™ The Pentium chip has two big advantages over the PowerPC chip: momentum and a proven record. Ninety percent of the PCs in use have an Intel or Intel-compatible microprocessor, consequently most of the software has been designed to run on Intel platforms. The PowerPC has its advantages as well. The RISC-based PowerPC is less expensive to produce and, therefore, costs less to buy. The PowerPC can run software for all popular platforms, including software that runs on the Pentium and other Intel chips. Proponents of the PowerPC argue that its simplicity in design makes it better for multimedia applications that combine motion video, audio, and animation.

Even with three influential companies sponsoring it, the PowerPC is fighting an uphill battle against Intel. It's a chicken-and-egg situation. Consumers want access to a wide variety of software applications before committing to PowerPC-based PCs, while software developers bide their time waiting for a show of market momentum before embracing the new PowerPC technology.

Although the Motorola and Intel chips get most of the press, a number of companies hope to challenge Motorola and Intel for a piece of the PC microprocessor market.

Connecting Peripheral Devices: Putting It Together

The system board, with its processor and memory, is ready for work; but alone, a system board is like a car without gas. The system board must be linked to I/O, storage, and communication devices to receive data and return results of processing.

Ports of Call In a PC, external peripheral devices (such as a printer and a mouse) come with a cable and a multipin connector. To link a device to the PC, you plug its connector into a receptacle in much the same way you plug a lamp cord into an electrical outlet. The receptacle, called a **port,** provides a direct link to the micro's common electrical bus.

External peripheral devices (outside the processor unit) can be linked to the processor via cables through either a **serial port** or a **parallel port.** The system board is normally designed with at least one of each plus a dedicated keyboard port. Some have a dedicated port for the mouse.

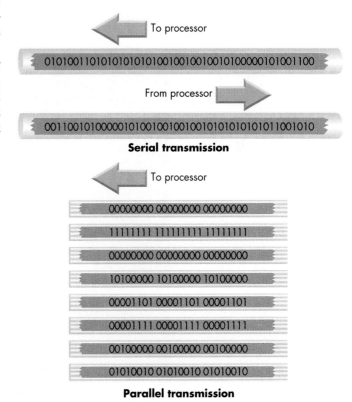

Serial transmission

Parallel transmission

FIGURE 2–11 Serial and Parallel Data Transmission In serial transmission, outgoing and incoming bits flow one-at-a-time through a single line. In parallel transmission, bytes flow together over eight separate lines.

▶ *Serial ports.* Serial ports facilitate the *serial transmission* of data, *one bit at a time* (see Figure 2–11). The mouse is usually connected to a serial port. The standard for micro serial ports is the 9-pin or 25-pin (male or female) **RS-232C connector.** One of the 9 or 25 lines carries the serial signal to the peripheral device and another line carries the signal from the device. The other lines carry control signals.

▶ *Parallel ports.* Parallel ports facilitate the *parallel transmission* of data; that is, several bits are transmitted simultaneously. Figure 2–11 illustrates how 8-bit bytes travel in parallel over 8 separate lines. Extra lines carry control signals. Parallel ports use the same 25-pin RS-232C connector or the 36-pin **Centronics connector.** These ports provide the interface for such devices as high-speed printers, magnetic tape backup units, and other computers.

▶ *Dedicated keyboard port.* The keyboard's dedicated serial port has a unique 5-pin or 7-pin round connector.

▶ *Dedicated mouse port.* Some system boards have a built-in serial port for the mouse.

Inside the Computer Explorer

A Fleet of Buses   The system board includes several empty **expansion slots** (see Figure 2–12) into which you can plug optional capabilities in the form of **expansion boards.** The expansion slots provide direct connections to the common electrical bus that services the processor and RAM. These slots enable a micro owner to enhance the functionality of a basic PC configuration with a wide variety of special-function *expansion boards,* also called **expansion cards.** These add-on circuit boards contain the electronic circuitry for many supplemental capabilities, such as extra ports or video capture capability. Expansion boards are made to fit a particular type of bus. The more popular types of buses for PC compatibles are introduced here.

ISA buses.   The most common PC expansion boards plug into an ISA (Industry Standard Architecture) **expansion bus.** The expansion bus, an extension of the common electrical bus, accepts the expansion boards that control the video display, disks, and other peripherals. For almost a decade, expansion bus technology stood still while processor and peripheral performance skyrocketed. As a result, we have bumper-to-bumper traffic on the interstate (high-speed data streams) exiting onto a single-lane covered bridge (the antiquated ISA bus). The ISA bus is slow, moving data in 16-bit words (compared to 32 bits within the processor) and at a much slower rate (8 MHz versus up to 100 MHz). A slow expansion bus forces the processor into a wait state, thereby causing a decrease in throughput.

MCA and EISA buses.   During the past few years, several improved expansion buses have been introduced to help boost throughput, but none has evolved as a standard.

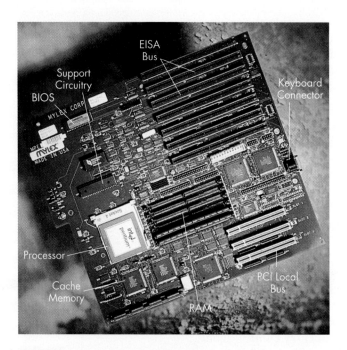

FIGURE 2–12   A System Board
This system board contains a 90-MHz Intel Pentium processor and ten expansion slots (seven EISA bus slots and three PCI local bus slots) for adding additional capabilities, such as a fax modem. The BIOS chip facilitates I/O between peripheral devices and the processor.   Courtesy of Mylex Corporation

IBM introduced the MCA (Micro Channel Architecture) bus and a consortium of high-profile PC manufacturers created and adopted the Extended Industry Standard Architecture, or EISA bus (rhymes with *"visa"*). Capable of processing 32 bits of data at a higher speed, MCA and EISA appeared to be the only solutions to higher performance in the PC-compatible environment. However, the added cost to the consumer was too much (as much as $1000) for either to emerge as a standard. MCA and EISA may be relegated to high-end PCs used in power applications, such as CAD.

Ironically, market pressure has forced the resurrection of ISA from the ashes of MCA and EISA. ISA can exist alongside innovative new ways to attach peripheral devices and special-function expansion boards.

Local Buses: PCI local bus and VL-bus. Recent innovations have resulted in linking expansion boards directly to the system's common bus, sometimes referred to as the **local bus.** The local bus offers channels that transfer data at the processor speeds (for example, 32 bits at 100 MHz). Two local bus solutions address the data stream bottleneck in PCs: Intel Corporation's **PCI local bus** and the Video Electronics Standards Association's (VESA) **VL-bus.** Both enable improved performance for today's high-speed peripherals, especially for graphics applications using high-resolution monitors. As a result, most new system boards are designed to accommodate a mix of expansion boards. Modern system boards normally include the popular ISA bus and either one or both of the PCI (Peripheral Component Interconnect) local bus and the VL-bus. The PCI local bus appears the choice of high-end users and the less expensive VL-bus the choice of entry-level users.

SCSI buses. The **SCSI bus,** or "scuzzy" bus, provides an alternative to the expansion bus. Up to seven SCSI (Small Computer System Interface) peripheral devices can be daisy-chained to a SCSI adapter (an expansion card), which means that the devices are connected along a single cable with multiple SCSI connectors. Components within the processor unit (perhaps a CD-ROM drive and tape backup unit) are daisy-chained on an internal cable while others (perhaps a printer and a scanner) are linked to the external cable (see Figure 2–13). Users who are running out of serial and parallel ports are looking to the SCSI bus for expansion. It's not unusual to find a CD-ROM drive, a tape backup unit, a printer, and perhaps an image scanner daisy-chained on a SCSI bus.

MEMORY BITS

Buses

- ISA buses
- MCA and EISA
- Local buses
—PCI local bus
—VL-bus
- SCSI bus

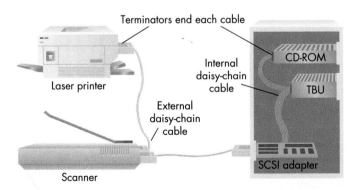

FIGURE 2–13 SCSI Bus
Two external devices, a printer and a scanner, are daisy-chained on the SCSI's external cable. Two internal devices, the CD-ROM and the tape backup unit, are daisy-chained on the SCSI's internal cable. Terminators are attached at the end of each cable to denote the end of the chain.

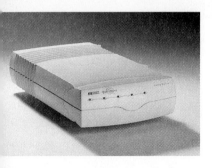

PC Growth: Adding Capabilities

Expansion: Slots for Boards   The *expansion slots* associated with the expansion buses (ISA, EISA, MCA) and local buses (PCI and VL-bus), and the *SCSI adapter* let you enhance processor functionality by adding *expansion boards*. The number of available expansion slots varies from computer to computer (see Figure 2–12). Keep in mind that an expansion board and/or peripheral device is designed for use with a particular type of expansion bus (ISA, VL-bus, SCSI, and so on). There are literally hundreds of expansion boards from which to choose. You will find these on most entry-level PCs.

Online users are often frustrated as they wait for applications to build or files to be downloaded. Cable modems (shown here) may put an end to this frustration, offering online services at speeds hundreds of times faster than traditional telephone-based modems. For example, a 45-minute file download over a traditional modem would take only 3 seconds over a cable modem. The cable modem is here now, but you may have to wait a year or so for your cable TV provider to upgrade its facilities. The cable modem hooks directly to your TV cable.   Photo courtesy of Hewlett-Packard Company

▶ *Graphics adapter.* These adapters permit interfacing with video monitors. The VGA (video graphics array) board enables the interfacing of high-resolution monitors with the processor.

▶ *Sound.* The sound card is becoming very popular and is included on most new PCs. The sound card makes two basic functions possible. First, it enables sounds to be captured and stored on disk. Second, it enables sounds to be played through external speakers, including music and spoken words. The sound card adds realism to computer games with stereo music and sound effects. It allows us to insert spoken notes within our word processing documents. The typical sound card will have receptacles for a microphone, a headset, an audio output, and a joystick.

▶ *Fax modem.* A **modem** permits communication with remote computers via a telephone-line link. The **fax modem** performs the same function as a regular modem plus it has an added capability—it enables a PC to emulate a **facsimile** or **fax** machine. Fax machines transfer images of documents via telephone lines to another location.

Expansion Boards

Depending on applications needs, you might wish to augment your system with some of these expansion boards.

GOING ONLINE

2.3
The Internet Tourbus

The Internet Tourbus ⟨http://csbh.mhv.net/~bobrankin/tourbus/⟩ is a popular point of embarkation for many newbies (someone new to the Internet). The Tourbus can take you to many interesting and exciting places. Take a ride on the Tourbus.

Hand in: The names and URL addresses of three of your favorite Tourbus stops.

▶ *Peripheral device interface.* The previously mentioned graphics adapter is the device interface for the monitor. Other peripheral devices, such as scanners (devices that capture images on hard-copy documents), very high-resolution printers, plotters (devices that provide precision plots of graphs), and external magnetic disk drives are sold with an interface card, as well as a cable. To install one of these devices you will need to insert its interface card into an empty expansion slot (see Figure 2–12), then connect the device's cable to the card. Devices with interface cards do not require the use of one of the PC's serial or parallel ports.

▶ *Serial and parallel ports.* Installation of this board provides access to the bus via auxiliary serial and parallel ports.

▶ *Network interface.* The network interface card (NIC) facilitates and controls the exchange of data between the micros in a PC *network* (several micros linked together). Each PC in a network must be equipped with an NIC. The cables that link the PCs are physically connected to the NICs.

▶ *SCSI interface card.* The SCSI bus can be built into the system board or installed as an expansion board.

▶ *Video capture.* This card enables full-motion color video with audio to be captured and stored on disk. Once on disk storage, video information can be integrated with text, graphics, and other forms of presentation.

Most expansion boards are *multifunction,* which means that they include two or more of these capabilities. For example, one popular **multifunction expansion board** comes with a serial port and a fax modem.

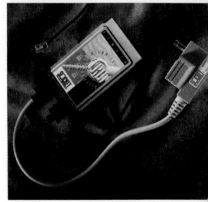

PC Cards: PCMCIA Technology   The **PCMCIA card,** sometimes called **PC card,** is a credit-card–sized removable expansion module that is plugged into a external PCMCIA expansion slot. Functionally, the PC card is like an expansion board. The Personal Computer Memory Card International Association (PCMCIA) was established in 1989 to create standards for the manufacture of PC cards. PC cards are like expansion boards in that they offer a wide variety of capabilities. PC cards can be expanded RAM, programmable nonvolatile flash memory, network interface cards, SCSI adapters, fax modems, sound cards, hard disk cards, and much more. For example, one PC card comes in the form of a Mobile GPS (global positioning system). The Mobile GPS card can be used to pinpoint the latitude and longitude of the user within 80 feet, anywhere on or near earth. Business travelers use GPS cards in conjunction with computer-based road maps to help them get around in unfamiliar cities.

Virtually all new portable computers are equipped with a PCMCIA-compliant interface. PDAs (personal digital assistants) and notebook PCs do not have enough space to accommodate the same permanent variety of expansion capabilities as do their desktop cousins. Interchangeable PC cards let laptop users insert capabilities as they are needed. For example, a user can insert a fax modem PC card to send e-mail, then do a *hot swap* (PC remains running) with a sound PC card to give a presentation.

Notebook PCs, because of their compact size, have fewer expansion slots than desktop PCs. For this reason, notebook PCs are designed with PCMCIA expansion slots. These PCMCIA removable expansion cards are plugged into PCMCIA expansion slots to give the system added capability. The top PCMCIA card contains a 340-MB hard disk. The bottom PCMCIA card contains a fax modem and LAN adapter (also called NIC).   Courtesy of Integral Peripherals/Courtesy of Socket Communications, Inc.

Why It's Important to Know What's Inside Your PC

Someday we won't have to worry about what's inside a PC. That day, however, will not be any time soon. If you want to take advantage of ever-advancing PC technology; if you want to get the most for your PC dollar; and if you want your PC to grow with your capabilities, you need to know what's inside your PC. You need to know the Pentium/PowerPC trade-offs. You need to know about the SCSI bus option. You need to know what to do with that PCMCIA slot on your notebook. You need to know that a mix of expansion buses may improve system throughput. You need to know because personal computing is very personal. You are the decision maker. A little knowledge about what's inside can save you big bucks and make you a more effective user.

IMPORTANT TERMS AND SUMMARY OUTLINE

2–1 DATA STORAGE: A BIT ABOUT THE BIT The two kinds of electronic signals are **analog** and **digital.** To make the most effective use of computers and automation, the electronics world is going digital. The music industry **digitizes** the natural analog signals that result from recording sessions, then stores the digital version on CDs. Computers are digital and, therefore, work better with digital data.

The two electronic states of the computer—on and off—are represented by a **bit,** short for *binary* dig*it*. These electronic states are compatible with the **binary** numbering system. Letters and decimal numbers are translated into bits for storage and processing on computer systems.

Data are stored temporarily during processing in **primary storage** (RAM) and permanently on **secondary storage** devices such as magnetic tape and disk drives.

2–2 ENCODING SYSTEMS: BITS AND BYTES Alphanumeric (**alpha** and **numeric**) characters are represented in computer storage by combining strings of bits to form unique bit configurations for each character. Characters are translated into these bit configurations, also called **bytes,** according to a particular coding scheme, called an **encoding system.**

The seven-bit **ASCII** encoding system is the most popular encoding system for PCs and data communication. The various versions of **extended ASCII,** an 8-bit encoding system, offer 128 more codes. Microsoft Windows uses the 8-bit **ANSI** encoding system.

Unicode, a uniform 16-bit encoding system, will enable computers and applications to talk to one another more easily and will accommodate most of the world's languages.

2–3 ANALYZING A COMPUTER SYSTEM, BIT BY BIT The processor is the "intelligence" of a computer system. A processor, which is also called the **central processing unit** or **CPU,** has only two fundamental sections, the **control unit** and the **arithmetic and logic unit,** which work together with RAM to execute programs. The control unit reads and interprets instructions and directs the arithmetic and logic unit to perform computation and logic operations.

RAM, or random-access memory, provides the processor with temporary storage for programs and data. Physically, memory chips are installed on **single in-line memory modules,** or **SIMMs.** The most common RAM technologies are **dynamic RAM (DRAM)** and **static RAM (SRAM).**

In RAM, datum is stored at a specific **address.** Most of today's computers use CMOS technology for RAM. CMOS is **volatile memory;** that is, the data are lost when the electrical current is turned off or interrupted. In contrast, **bubble memory** provides **nonvolatile memory.** All input/output, including programs, must enter and exit RAM. Programs are loaded to RAM from secondary storage in a **nondestructive read** process. Other variations of internal storage are ROM, **programmable read-only memory (PROM),** and **flash memory,** a nonvolatile memory.

Some computers employ **cache memory** to increase **throughput** (the rate at which work can be performed by a computer system). Like RAM, cache is a high-speed holding area for program instructions and data. However, cache memory holds only those instructions and data likely to be needed next by the processor. During execution, instructions and data are passed between very high-speed **registers** (for example, the **instruction register,** the **program register,** and the **accumulator**) in the control unit and the arithmetic and logic unit.

The **bus** is the common pathway through which the processor sends/receives data and commands to/from primary and secondary storage and all I/O peripheral devices. Like the wheeled bus, the bus provides data transportation to all processor components, memory, and **device controllers.** Source and destination addresses are sent over the **address bus,** then the data and instructions are transferred over the **data bus.**

Every **machine language** has a predefined format for each type of instruction. During one **machine cycle,** an instruction is "fetched" from RAM, decoded by the **decoder** in the control unit, executed, and the results are placed in memory. The machine cycle time is the total of the **instruction time (I-time)** and the **execution time (E-time)**.

Most mainframes and PCs use **CISC** (*complex instruction set computer*) architecture. Those using **RISC** (*reduced instruction set computer*) architecture realize increased throughput for certain applications.

In **parallel processing,** one main processor examines the programming problem and determines what portions, if any, of the problem can be solved in pieces. Those pieces that can be addressed separately are routed to other processors, solved, then recombined in the main processor to produce the result. Parallel processing on a large scale is referred to as **massively parallel processing (MPP).**

2–4 DESCRIBING THE PROCESSOR: DISTINGUISHING CHARACTERISTICS A processor is described in terms of its word size, speed, and RAM capacity.

A **word** is the number of bits handled as a unit within a particular computer system's common electrical bus or during internal processing.

Microcomputer speed is measured in **megahertz (MHz).** High-end PC, workstation, and mainframe speed is measured in **MIPS.** Supercomputer speed is measured in **FLOPS** and **GFLOPS.**

Memory capacity is measured in **kilobytes (KB), megabytes (MB), gigabytes (GB),** and **terabytes (TB).** Chip capacity is sometimes stated in **kilobits (Kb)** and **megabits (Mb).**

2–5 INSIDE THE PC The **microprocessor,** a product of the microminiaturization of electronic circuitry, is literally a "computer on a chip." In a microcomputer, the microprocessor, the electronic circuitry for handling input/output signals from the peripheral devices, and the memory chips are mounted on a single circuit board called a **system board,** or **motherboard.** Before being attached to the system board, the microprocessor and other chips are mounted onto a **carrier.**

Motorola manufactures two prominent families of microprocessors—the 68000, or 68K, family and the new **PowerPC** family. The PowerPC lets users run all major industry-standard **platforms.** Most PCs in use today have an Intel 80286, 80386, 80486, or **Pentium** microprocessor. Intel's **P6** is the successor to the Pentium.

In a PC, external peripheral devices come with a cable and a multipin connector. A **port** provides a direct link to the micro's bus. External peripheral devices can be linked to the processor via cables through either a **serial port** or a **parallel port.** The standard for micro serial ports is the **RS-232C connector.** The RS-232C and **Centronics connectors** are used with parallel ports.

The system board includes several empty **expansion slots** so you can purchase and plug in optional capabilities in the form of **expansion boards,** or **expansion cards.**

The most common PC expansion boards plug into a 16-bit ISA **expansion bus.** The expansion bus accepts the expansion boards that control the video display, disks, and other peripherals. MCA and EISA buses outperform the ISA bus by processing 32 bits of data at a higher speed; however, they may be too expensive for widespread acceptance. Recent innovations have resulted in linking expansion boards directly to the system's **local bus.** The **PCI local bus** and **VL-bus** offer two local bus solutions to the data stream bottleneck in PCs. The **SCSI bus,** or "scuzzy" bus, allows up to seven SCSI peripheral devices to be daisy-chained to a SCSI adapter.

Popular expansion boards include graphics adapter, sound, **fax modem** (enables emulation of a **facsimile** or **fax** machine), peripheral device interface, serial and parallel ports, network interface, SCSI interface card, and video capture. A **modem** permits communication with remote computers via a telephone-line link. Most are **multifunction expansion boards.**

The **PCMCIA card,** sometimes called **PC card,** provides a variety of interchangeable add-on capabilities in the form of credit-card–sized modules. The PC card is especially handy for the portable environment.

REVIEW EXERCISES

Concepts

1. Distinguish between RAM, ROM, PROM, and flash memory.
2. How many ANSI bytes can be stored in a 32-bit word?
3. Which two functions are performed by the arithmetic and logic unit?
4. List examples of alpha, numeric, and alphanumeric characters.
5. Write your first name as an ASCII bit configuration.
6. What are the functions of the control unit?
7. We describe computers in terms of what three characteristics?
8. What is the basic difference between CMOS technology and nonvolatile technology such as bubble memory?

9. For a given computer, which type of memory would have the greatest capacity to store data and programs: cache or RAM? RAM or registers? registers or cache?

10. Name two types of registers.

11. What do the *I* in *I-time* and the *E* in *E-time* stand for?

12. What is the relationship between a microprocessor, a motherboard, and a microcomputer?

13. List five functional enhancements that can be added to a microcomputer by inserting one or more optional expansion boards into expansion slots.

14. Why are some microcomputers sold with empty expansion slots?

15. Describe a hot swap as it relates to a PCMCIA-compliant interface.

16. Name two local buses for PC-compatible computers.

17. Order the following Intel microprocessors by performance: 80486, 8088, 80386, and Pentium.

18. Source and destination addresses sent to identify a particular location in a computer's memory are sent to which bus?

Discussion and Problem Solving

19. Create a 5-bit encoding system to be used for storing upper-case alpha characters, punctuation symbols, and the apostrophe. Discuss the advantages and disadvantages of your encoding system in relation to the ASCII encoding system.

20. Compute the time it takes to complete one cycle on a 66-MHz processor in both seconds and nanoseconds.

21. List at least 10 products that are smaller than a toaster oven and use microprocessors. Select one and describe the function of its microprocessor.

22. Explain how internal and external devices are linked to a PC via a SCSI adapter.

23. Convert 5 MB to KB, Mb, and Kb. Assume a byte contains eight bits.

SELF-TEST (BY SECTION)

2–1 **a.** What are the two kinds of electronic signals: (a) analog and digital, (b) binary and octal, or (c) alpha and numeric?

b. *Bit* is the singular of *byte*. (T/F)

c. The base of the binary number system is: (a) 2, (b) 8, or (c) 16?

d. Data are stored permanently on secondary storage devices, such as magnetic tape. (T/F)

2–2 **a.** The combination of bits used to represent a character is called a _____.

b. The proposed 16-bit encoding system is called _____.

2–3 **a.** Data are loaded from secondary storage to RAM in a nondestructive read process. (T/F)

b. The _____ is that part of the processor that reads and interprets program instructions.

c. The arithmetic and logic unit controls the flow of programs and data in and out of main memory. (T/F)

d. Put the following memories in order based on speed: cache, registers, and RAM.

e. The timed interval that comprises the machine cycle is the total of the _____ time and the _____ time.

f. The rate at which work can be performed by a computer system is called _____ .

2–4 **a.** The word size of most microcomputers is 64 bits. (T/F)

b. *MIPS* is an acronym for "millions of instructions per second." (T/F)

c. _____ is a common measure of supercomputer processor speed.

d. Which has the most bytes: (a) kilobyte, (b) gigabyte, or (c) megabyte?

2–5 **a.** The processing component of a motherboard is a _____.

b. The Intel _____ and the Motorola _____ are prominent microprocessors used in PCs.

c. The RS-232C connector provides the interface to a port. (T/F)

d. Peripheral devices are _____ along a cable to an SCSI adapter.

e. All PC components are linked via a common electrical _____.

f. Which two local bus solutions address the data stream bottleneck in PCs: (a) MCA and EISA, (b) PCI local bus and SCSI bus, or (c) PCI local bus and VL-bus?

Self-test Answers. **2–1 (a)** a; **(b)** F; **(c)** a; **(d)** T. **2–2 (a)** byte; **(b)** Unicode. **2–3 (a)** T; **(b)** control unit; **(c)** F; **(d)** from the slowest to the fastest memory: RAM, cache, registers; **(e)** instruction, execution; **(f)** throughput. **2–4 (a)** F; **(b)** T; **(c)** FLOPS or GFLOPS; **(d)** b. **2–5 (a)** microprocessor; **(b)** Pentium, PowerPC; **(c)** T; **(d)** daisy-chained; **(e)** bus **(f)** c.

IMAGE BANK

The Computer on a Chip

The invention of the light bulb in 1879 symbolized the beginning of electronics. Electronics then evolved into the use of vacuum tubes, then transistors, and now integrated circuits. Today's microminiaturization of electronic circuitry is continuing to have a profound effect on the way we live and work.

Current technology permits the placement of hundreds of thousands of transistors and electronic switches on a single chip. Chips already fit into wristwatches and credit cards, but electrical and computer engineers want them even smaller. In electronics, smaller is better. The ENIAC, the first full-scale digital electronic computer, weighed 50 tons and occupied an entire room. Today, a computer far more powerful than the ENIAC can be fabricated within a single piece of silicon the size of a child's fingernail.

Chip designers think in terms of nanoseconds (one billionth of a second) and microns (one millionth of a meter). They want to pack as many circuit elements as they can into the structure of a chip. High-density packing reduces the time required for an electrical signal to travel from one circuit element to the next—resulting in faster computers. Circuit lines on the initial Intel processors (early 1980s) were 6.5 microns wide. Today's are less than .5 microns. The latter holds 35 million transistors and is 550 times as powerful as the initial one. By the turn of the century, researchers expect to break the .2 micro barrier.

Chips are designed and manufactured to perform a particular function. One chip might be a microprocessor for a personal computer. Another might be for primary storage or the logic for a talking vending machine. Cellular telephones use semiconductor memory chips.

The development of integrated circuits starts with a project review team made up of representatives from design, manufacturing, and marketing. This group works together to design a product the customer needs. Next, team members go through prototype wafer manufacturing to resolve potential manufacturing problems. Once a working prototype is produced, chips are manufactured in quantity and sent to computer, peripheral, telecommunications, and other customers.

The manufacturing of integrated circuits involves a multistep process using various photochemical etching and metallurgical techniques. This complex and interesting process is illustrated here with photos, from silicon to the finished product. The process is presented in five steps: design, fabrication, packaging, testing, and installation.

DESIGN

1. Using CAD for Chip Design   Chip designers use computer-aided design (CAD) systems to create the logic for individual circuits. Although a chip can contain up to 30 layers, typically there are 10 to 20 patterned layers of varying material, with each layer performing a different purpose. In this multilayer circuit design, each layer is color-coded so the designer can distinguish between the various layers.   Photo courtesy of Micron Semiconductor, Inc.

INTERNET BRIDGE

Chips

2. Creating a Mask The product designer's computerized drawing of each circuit layer is transformed into a *mask*, or *reticle*, a glass or quartz plate with an opaque material (such as chrome) formed to create the pattern. The number of layers depends on the complexity of the chip's logic. The Pentium™ processor, for example, contains 20 layers. When all these unique layers are combined, they create the millions of transistors and circuits that make up the architecture of the processor. Photo courtesy of Micron Semiconductor, Inc.

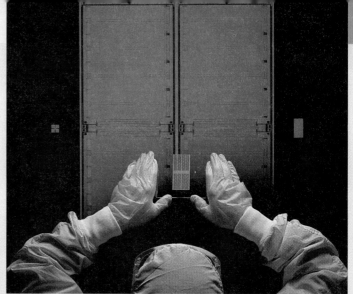

FABRICATION

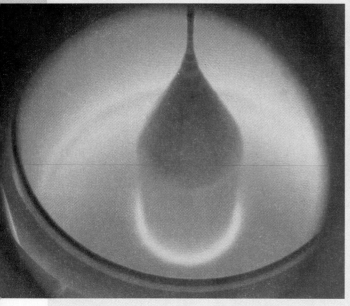

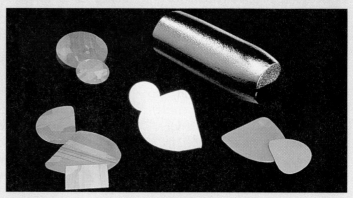

3. Creating Silicon Ingots Molten silicon is spun into cylindrical ingots. Because silicon, the second most abundant substance, is used in the fabrication of integrated circuits, chips are sometimes referred to as "intelligent grains of sand." © M/A-COM, Inc.

4. Cutting the Silicon Wafers The ingot is shaped and prepared prior to being cut into silicon wafers. Once the wafers are cut, they are polished to a perfect finish. © M/A-COM, Inc.

6. Keeping a Clean House Clean air continuously flows from every pore of the ceiling and through the holes in the floor into a filtering system at the manufacturing plant. A normal room contains some 15 million dust particles per cubic foot, but a clean room contains less than 1 dust particle per cubic foot. All of the air in a "clean room" is replaced seven times every minute.

Portions of the micro chip manufacturing process are performed in yellow light because the wafers are coated with a light-sensitive material called "photoresist" before the next chip pattern is imprinted onto the surface of the silicon wafer. Courtesy of Intel Corporation

5. Wearing Bunny Suits To help keep a clean environment, workers wear semi-custom-fitted Gor-tex® suits. They follow a hundred-step procedure when putting the suits on. Courtesy of Intel Corporation

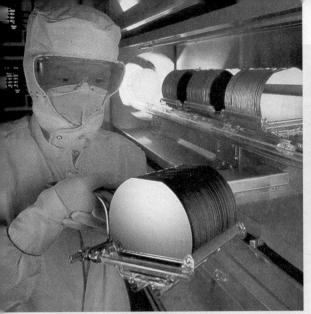

7. Coating the Wafers Silicon wafers that eventually will contain several hundred chips are placed in an oxygen furnace at 1200 degrees Celsius. In the furnace each wafer is coated with other minerals to create the physical properties needed to produce transistors and electronic switches on the surface of the wafer. Gould Inc.

8. Etching the Wafer A photoresist is deposited onto the wafer surface creating a film-like substance to accept the patterned image. The mask is placed over the wafer and both are exposed to ultraviolet light. In this way the circuit pattern is transferred onto the wafer. The photoresist is developed, washing away the unwanted resist and leaving the exact image of the transferred pattern. Plasma (superhot gases) technology is used to etch the circuit pattern permanently into the wafer. This is one of several techniques used in the etching process. The wafer is returned to the furnace and given another coating on which to etch another circuit layer. The procedure is repeated for each circuit layer until the wafer is complete. AT&T Technologies

9. Tracking the Wafers Fabrication production control tracks wafers through the fabricating process and measures layers at certain manufacturing stages to determine layer depth and chemical structure. These measurements assess process accuracy and facilitate real-time modifications. Courtesy of Micron Technology, Inc.

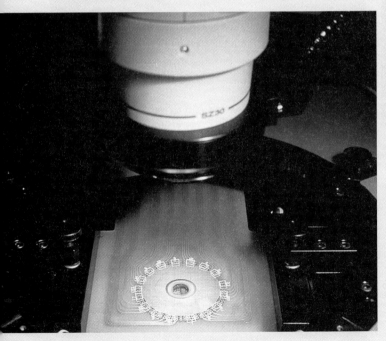

10. Drilling the Wafers It takes only a second for this instrument to drill 1440 tiny holes in a wafer. The holes enable the interconnection of the layers of circuits. Each layer must be perfectly aligned (within a millionth of a meter) with the others. Courtesy of International Business Machines Corporation

PACKAGING

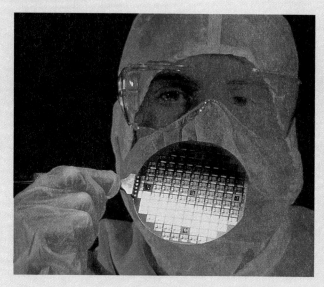

11. Removing the Etched Wafers The result of the coating/etching process is a silicon wafer that contains from 100 to 400 integrated circuits, each of which includes millions of transistors. National Semiconductor Corporation

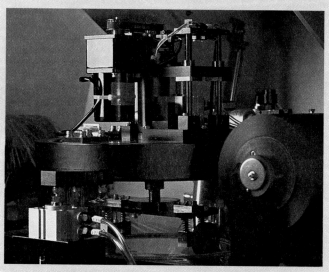

12. Mounting the Wafers Each wafer is vacuum mounted onto a metal-framed sticky film tape. The wafer and metal frame are placed near the tape; then all three pieces are loaded into a vacuum chamber. A vacuum forces the tape smoothly onto the back of the wafer and metal frame. Courtesy of Micron Technology, Inc.

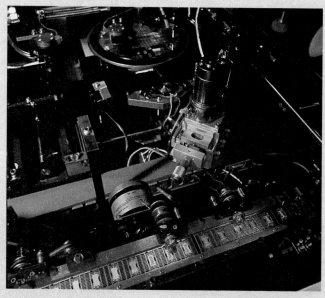

14. Attaching the Die Individual die are attached to silver epoxy on the center area of a lead frame. Each die is removed from the tape with needles plunging up from underneath to push the die while a vacuum tip lifts the die from the tape. Lead frames are then heated in an oven to cure the epoxy. The wafer map created in probe tells the die attach equipment which die to place on the lead frame. Courtesy of Micron Technology, Inc.

13. Dicing the Wafers A diamond-edged saw, with a thickness of a human hair, separates the wafer into individual processors, known as die, in a process called *dicing*. Water spray keeps the surface temperature low. After cutting, high pressure water rinses the wafer clean. In some situations, special lasers are used to cut the wafers. Courtesy of Micron Technology, Inc.

15. Packaging the Chips The chips are packaged in protective ceramic or metal carriers. The carriers have standard-sized electrical pin connectors that allow the chip to be plugged conveniently into circuit boards. Because the pins tend to corrode, the pin connectors are the most vulnerable part of a computer system. To avoid corrosion and a bad connection, the pins on some carriers are made of gold. Courtesy of International Business Machines Corporation

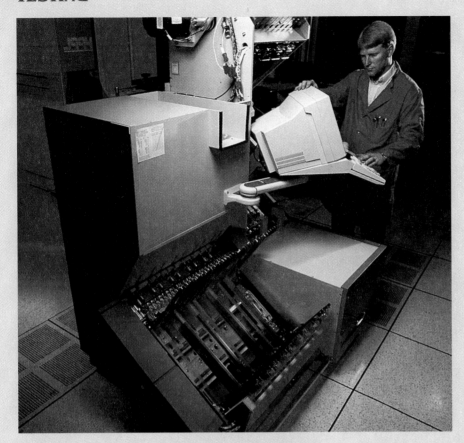

16. Testing the Chips Each chip is tested to assess functionality and to see how fast it can store or retrieve information. Chip speed (or access time) is measured in nanoseconds (a billionth, 1/1,000,000,000th of a second). The precision demands are so great that as many as half the chips are found to be defective. A drop of ink is deposited on defective chips. Courtesy of Micron Technology, Inc.

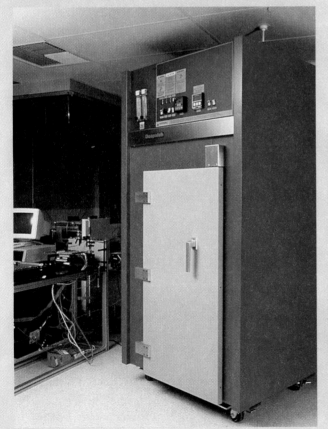

17. Burning In This burn-in oven runs performance tests on every chip simulating actual usage conditions. Each chip is tested by feeding information to the chip and querying for the information to ensure the chip is receiving, storing, and sending the correct data. Courtesy of Micron Technology, Inc.

18. Scanning All chips are scanned, using optics or lasers, to discover any bent, missing, or incorrectly formed leads. Courtesy of Micron Technology, Inc.

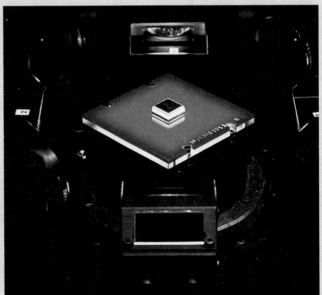

19. Creating Circuit Boards Pick and place equipment precisely positions various chips on the solder and contacts. Completed boards are then heated in the reflow ovens, allowing the lead coating and solder to melt together, affixing the chip to the printed circuit board. Courtesy of Micron Technology, Inc.

20. Installing the Finished Chips The completed circuit boards are installed in computers and thousands of other computer-controlled devices. Courtesy of E-Systems

INTERNET BRIDGE

Serendipitous Surfing

Software: Telling Computers What to Do

Let's Talk

The following conversation introduces many of the terms in this chapter. Read it now, then again after you have read the chapter.

The Scene:
The boss (Celeste), a certified cyberphobic, is seeking advice and compassion from her secretary (Jo Ellen).

Celeste: I'm beginning to feel out of sync now that we've linked the PCs in a local area network and standardized on the **Windows 95 platform.** Other managers are passing information and making decisions with the help of **applications software** for **workgroup computing** . . .

Jo Ellen: And you want in the loop?

Celeste: You bet I do.

Jo Ellen: Two months ago I didn't know the difference between the **foreground** and the **background.** I suffered a mild case of cyberphobia but overcame it by learning a little something new each day. Now it's a snap to **click** and **drag icons** around the **GUI.** Today, I'm even learning to write **macros** in the Lotus 1-2-3 **macro language.**

Celeste: You're so at ease with the computer. What's really your secret?

Jo Ellen: No secret—I just used my manuals, the online **help commands,** and Rick, the guy at the help desk.

Celeste: I think I'm ready to enter cyberland. Will you help me, Jo Ellen?

Jo Ellen: Sure, let's go in your office and **boot** your system.

(a couple of minutes later)

Jo Ellen: Let's begin with the **main menu** and call up a few **dialog boxes** to fine-tune your **default options.** Tomorrow we'll go over the basics: the **menu bar, scrolling, cursor** movement, and so on. How about I block out 30 minutes each morning for the next month on your electronic calendar?

Celeste: Maybe a month from now I'll be keeping my own calendar!

STUDENT LEARNING OBJECTIVES

▶ *To demonstrate an understanding of common system software concepts.*

▶ *To detail the purpose and objectives of an operating system.*

▶ *To understand the relationship between computers and programming languages.*

▶ *To distinguish between several different types of programming languages.*

▶ *To describe the capabilities of visual programming languages and natural languages.*

▶ *To describe what constitutes a platform.*

▶ *To distinguish between common platforms available to microcomputer users.*

▶ *To understand the scope of knowledge needed to interact effectively with a personal computer.*

▶ *To grasp concepts related to the effective use of computers and software.*

▶ *To describe various keyboard, mouse, and data entry conventions.*

At the Olympic Games in Lillehammer, Norway, a vast network of computers and terminals kept officials and the media up-to-the-minute on every competition at every venue. Officials and media personnel had immediate access to profiles of all the athletes as well as graphic illustrations that describe all aspects of the various sports and their venues. Shown here are the speed skating and ski jumping venues. Communications software (a type of system software) facilitates the transfer of information within the Olympics network. Applications software enables people to get the information they need to do their jobs.   Photos courtesy of International Business Machines Corporation

3–1 SOFTWARE IN PERSPECTIVE

Software, which refers to *programs,* tells the computer what to do. Let's put software into perspective. Suppose you are sick in bed and you ask a friend to get you a glass of ice water. In response to your request, your friend instinctively goes to the kitchen, opens the cabinet door and selects a glass, opens the refrigerator and gets some ice, turns the tap and fills the glass with water, returns to your bedside, and hands you the water. Now imagine making the same request to a computer. You would have to tell the computer not only where to get the water but also how to get there. You would have to tell the computer how many ice cubes, which end of the glass to fill, when to shut off the water, when to release the glass upon handing it to you, and much, much, more.

Any computer, whether it supports video games or an enterprise-wide information system, does nothing until directed to do so by a human. A computer does not make decisions, perform calculations, or manipulate data without exact, step-by-step instructions. These instructions, which take the form of a computer *program,* are how we tell a computer to perform certain operations. Let's put these instructions into perspective. The program in a wristwatch has about 1000 instructions. The programs that control the space shuttle during flight have about the same number of instructions as those for a cash register—about 400,000. Word processing and spreadsheet programs have over a million instructions.

We interact with software to direct the overall activities within a computer system. For example, if you wish to print a spreadsheet, you choose *Print* from your spreadsheet software's menu of options. The print-routine program is executed, performing the internal operations needed to print your spreadsheet.

At this point on your journey toward computer competency, you probably are feeling more comfortable with general computer hardware concepts. *Hardware,* however, is useless without *software,* and software is useless without hardware. This chapter should raise your comfort level with software.

The instructions in programs are logically sequenced and assembled through the act of **programming. Programmers,** people who write programs, use a variety of **programming languages,** such as C++ , Visual BASIC, and dBASE IV Language, to communicate instructions to the computer. Twenty years ago, virtually all programmers were computer specialists. Today, office managers, management consultants, engineers, politicians, and people in all walks of life write programs to meet business and domestic needs. And, some people do it for fun. Unless you plan on becoming a computer professional, it is unlikely that you will write programs in support of an enterprise-wide information system. You may, however, write programs to perform many personal tasks, such as preparing graphs from spreadsheet data and sequencing displays for multimedia presentations. As you develop expertise and confidence you may tackle more challenging programming tasks.

3–2 SYSTEM SOFTWARE: MAINTAINING CONTROL

We use the term *software* to refer to programs that tell the computer system what to do. There are, however, different types of software. The more you understand about the scope and variety of available software, the more effective you will be as a user. It's a lot like being in a big house—once you know its layout, you're able to move about the house much easier.

The House of Software

Once but a cottage, the house of software is now a roomy eight-room house (by the turn of the century, it will be a mansion). The blueprint for today's house of software is shown in Figure 3–1. We'll visit every room in the house by the time you finish this book. In the house, software is arranged in rooms by function. In Chapter 1, "The World of Computers," we peeked in all of the rooms except one—system software. In this chapter, we'll relax in the system software room awhile. An understanding of the scope and function of system software will make your visits to the other rooms more enjoyable and fruitful.

System Software in Perspective: Behind the Scenes

System software fills the entryway in the house of software (see Figure 3–1). The same is true when you turn on the computer. The first actions you see are directed by system software. **System software** takes control of the PC on start up, then plays a central role in all interactions with the computer. The *operating system* and the *graphical user interface (GUI),* both system software, are literally at the center of the software action (see Figure 3–2). Both are discussed in Section 3–3.

All of the software in the other rooms of the house depend on and interact with the operating system and its GUI. The GUI provides a user-friendly interface to the operating system. These programs, called **applications software,** are designed and created to perform specific personal, business, or scientific processing tasks, such as word processing, tax planning, or computer games. Figure 3–2 illustrates examples of and the relationship between system and applications software.

When we go out to a movie, we see only a few of those responsible for making the film—the actors. We don't see the director, the producers, the writers, the editors, and many others. Perhaps it's because of this visual link that we, the audience, tend to become adoring fans of glamorous actors. We tend to forget the others involved

Applications Explorer

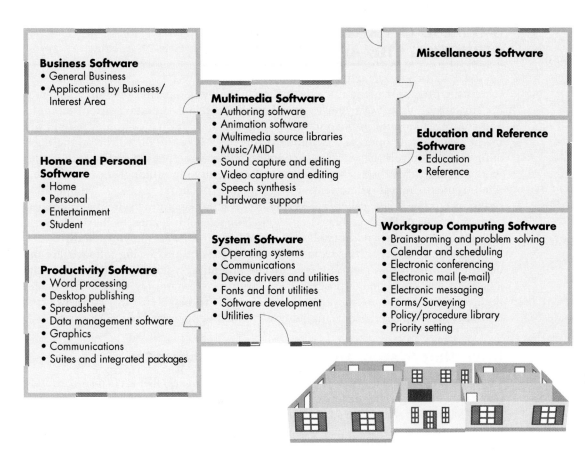

Business Software
• General Business
• Applications by Business/
  Interest Area

Home and Personal Software
• Home
• Personal
• Entertainment
• Student

Productivity Software
• Word processing
• Desktop publishing
• Spreadsheet
• Data management software
• Graphics
• Communications
• Suites and integrated packages

Multimedia Software
• Authoring software
• Animation software
• Multimedia source libraries
• Music/MIDI
• Sound capture and editing
• Video capture and editing
• Speech synthesis
• Hardware support

System Software
• Operating systems
• Communications
• Device drivers and utilities
• Fonts and font utilities
• Software development
• Utilities

Miscellaneous Software

Education and Reference Software
• Education
• Reference

Workgroup Computing Software
• Brainstorming and problem solving
• Calendar and scheduling
• Electronic conferencing
• Electronic mail (e-mail)
• Electronic messaging
• Forms/Surveying
• Policy/procedure library
• Priority setting

FIGURE 3–1 The House of Software
This blueprint shows the layout of the house of software. The rooms are laid out to feature software in eight major areas.

in the film, even the director, the person who ties it all together and literally makes it happen. It's much the same with software. As software users, we tend to shower our praise on that which we see most often—the *applications software.* On the other hand, *system software,* like the film director, stays in the background and ties it all together. We'll discuss the most prominent of these behind-the-scenes players, the operating system.

FIGURE 3–2 Relationship between the Operating System, the GUI, and Applications Software
The operating system coordinates all software activity within a computer system. Our interaction with the operating system is through the graphical user interface, the GUI. With applications software packages, such as spreadsheet and expert systems, we can address a variety of problems. For example, a manager can use spreadsheet software to create *templates* (models) for summarizing sales and maintaining the office's fixed inventory. A knowledge engineer can use expert system software to create a loan evaluation system to assist a bank's loan officers in making better, more consistent decisions.

3–3 THE OPERATING SYSTEM: DIRECTING THE ACTION

Just as the processor is the nucleus of the computer system, the **operating system** is the nucleus of all software activity (see Figure 3–2). The operating system monitors and controls all input/output and processing activities within a computer system. You might even call the operating system "the director." Like the film director, the operating system controls the set from "action" to "cut, print." The operating system is actually a family of *system software* programs that are usually, although not always, supplied by the computer system vendor when you buy a computer. One of the operating system programs, often called the **kernel,** loads other operating system and applications programs to RAM as they are needed. The kernel is loaded to RAM on system start up and remains *resident,* available in RAM, until the system is turned off.

All hardware and software, from the keyboard to word processing software, are under the control of the operating system. The operating system determines how valuable RAM is apportioned to programs, sets priorities for handling tasks, and manages the flow of information to and from the processor. To be an effective PC or workstation user, you will need a working knowledge of your system's operating system.

Operating System Objectives and Orientation

The operating system is what gives a *general-purpose computer,* like a PC or a corporate mainframe, its flexibility to tackle a variety of jobs. (Most *dedicated computers,* such as those that control appliances and arcade games, are controlled by a single-function program and do not need a separate operating system.) Windows 95, Macintosh System, OS/2, and UNIX are popular operating systems for PCs and workstations. These and other operating systems are discussed in Section 3–5. The use and functionality of the Windows 95 operating system is discussed in more detail in the Appendix, "The Windows Environment." One of the best ways to understand an operating system is to understand its objectives. All operating systems are designed with the same basic objectives in mind. These objectives are listed and explained in Figure 3–3.

The operating system objectives in Figure 3–3 apply to all computer systems; however, mainframe and micro operating systems differ markedly in complexity and orientation. On the mainframe, *multiuser operating systems* coordinate a number of special-function processors and monitor interaction with hundreds, even thousands, of terminals in a network. Most micro operating systems are designed primarily to support a *single user on a single micro.*

Living on a Budget: Allocating Computer Resources

We all must live within our means, including computers. A conscientious shopper can stretch the value of a dollar and a good operating system can get the most from its limited resources. Any computer system's most precious resource is its processor. Operating systems get the most from their processors through multitasking. **Multitasking** is the *concurrent* execution of more than one program at a time. Actually, a single computer can execute only one program at a time, but its internal processing speed is so fast that several programs can be allocated "slices" of computer time in rotation. This makes it appear that several programs are being executed at once.

The great difference in processor speed and the speeds of the peripheral devices makes multitasking possible. A 22-page-per-minute printer cannot even challenge the speed of a low-end PC. The processor is continually waiting for peripheral devices to complete such tasks as retrieving a record from disk storage or printing a report. During these waiting periods, the processor just continues processing other programs.

INTERNET BRIDGE

Operating Systems

1. To facilitate communication between the computer system and the people who run it.	The interface through which users issue system-related commands is part of the operating system.
2. To facilitate communication among computer system components.	The operating system facilitates the movement of internal instructions and data between peripheral devices, the processor, programs, and the computer's storage.
3. To maximize throughput.	The operating system coordinates system resources to maximize throughput, the amount of processing per unit of time.
4. To minimize the time needed to execute a user command.	In today's interactive systems, even small decreases in user wait time pay big dividends in user efficiency.
5. To optimize the use of computer system resources.	The operating system is continually looking at what tasks need to be done and what resources (processor, RAM, and peripheral devices) are available to accomplish these tasks. The incredible speed of a computer system dictates that resource-allocation decisions be made at computer speeds. Each millisecond the operating system makes decisions about what resources to assign to which tasks.
6. To keep track of all files in disk storage.	The operating system and its file and disk management utility programs enable users to perform such tasks as making backup copies of work disks, erasing disk files that are no longer needed, making inquiries about the number and type of files on a particular disk, and preparing new disks for use. The operating system also handles many file- and disk-oriented tasks that are transparent (invisible) to the end user. For example, operating systems keep track of the physical location of disk files so that we, as users, need only refer to them by name (for example, myfile or year-end-summary) when loading them from disk to RAM.
7. To provide an envelope of security for the computer system.	The operating system can allow or deny user access to the system as a whole or to individual files. Specific security measures, such as passwords, are discussed later in the book.
8. To monitor all systems capabilities and alert the user of system failure or potential problems.	The operating system can allow or deny user access to the system as a whole or to individual files. Specific security measures, such as passwords, are discussed later in the book.

FIGURE 3–3 Objectives of an Operating System

The operating system ensures that resources are allocated to competing tasks in the most efficient manner.

In a multitasking environment, programs running concurrently are controlled and assigned priorities by the operating system based on user criteria. For example, you can prepare a graphics presentation on CorelDRAW, while sending a Lotus 1-2-3 spreadsheet over the fax modem and backing up the hard disk to a tape. The **foreground** is that part of RAM that contains the active or current program. Other lower-priority programs, such as the fax transmittal and the backup in the example, are run in the **background** part of RAM. The operating system rotates allocation of the processor resource between foreground and background programs, with the foreground programs receiving the lion's share of the processor's time.

The Graphical User Interface: Goodie "Gooie"

To appreciate the impact and significance of graphical user interfaces, you need to understand what preceded them.

Text-based Software Through the 1980s, the most popular microcomputer operating system, **MS-DOS,** was strictly *text-based, command-driven* software. That is, we issued commands directly to DOS (the MS-DOS nickname) by entering them on the keyboard, one character at a time. For example, if you had wished to issue a command to copy a word processing document from one disk to another for your friend, you might have entered "copy c:\myfile a:\yourfile" via the keyboard at the DOS prompt, "C:\)".

C:\) copy c:\myfile a:\yourfile

When using command-driven, text-based software you must be explicit, whether entering a DOS command or an application program command. In the above example, you cannot just enter "copy" or even "copy MYFILE". You must enter the command that tells the micro where to find MYFILE and where to make the copy. If you omit necessary information in a command or the format of the command is incorrect, an error message is displayed and/or an on-screen prompt will request that you reenter the command. Command-driven DOS, in particular, demands strict adherence to command **syntax,** the rules for entering commands, such as word spacing, punctuation, and so on.

Graphics-based Software   Today, relatively few computers run with purely text-based operating systems. For the past decade, the trend has been toward a user-friendly, graphics-oriented environment called a **graphical user interface,** or **GUI** (pronounced *"G-U-I"* or *"gooie"*). Graphical user interfaces rely on graphics-based software, which permits the integration of text with high-resolution graphic images (see Figure 3–4).

All modern operating systems, including the **Windows 95** operating system, provide GUIs. GUI users interact with the operating system and other software packages by using a pointing device and a keyboard to issue commands. Rather than enter a command directly, as in a command-driven interface, the user chooses from options displayed on the screen. The equivalent of a syntax-sensitive operating system command is entered by pointing to and choosing one or more options from menus or by pointing to and choosing a graphics image, called an **icon.** An icon is a graphic rendering that represents a processing activity. For example, the file folder icon or the file cabinet icon generally represents processing activities associated with file management. Users might choose the "trash can" icon to delete a file from disk storage. Figure 3–4 shows a screen with a variety of symbolic icons. The Windows 95 operating system and its GUI are discussed in more detail in the Appendix.

GUIs have effectively eliminated the need for users to memorize and enter cumbersome commands. For example, GUIs permit a file to be copied from one disk to another disk by repositioning the file's icon from one area on the screen to another.

FIGURE 3–4   Icons
Each of the icons in this Microsoft Windows 95 display represents an available program. To run a program, simply use the mouse to point to and click on the desired icon.

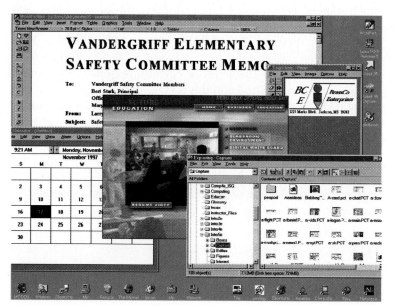

INTERNET BRIDGE

Programming

Many languages have emerged over thousands of years of spoken communication. Spanish is spoken throughout Central and South America. English has emerged as the international language of business. There are as many programming languages as there are spoken languages. In this section, we will sort out these languages and explain what they mean to you.

Computer Programs: The Power of Logic

We create software with programming languages. An applications software package, such as word processing, is made up of many programs. A single program addresses a particular problem—to compute and assign grades, to permit an update of a database, to monitor a patient's heart rate, to analyze marketing data, and so on. In effect, when you write a program, you are solving a *problem*. To solve a problem you must use your powers of *logic* and develop a procedure for solving the problem.

Creating a program is like constructing a building. Much of the brainwork involved in the construction goes into the blueprint. The location, appearance, and function of a building are determined long before the first brick is laid. With programming, the design of a program, or its *programming logic* (the blueprint), is completed before the program is written (the building is constructed). The traditional computer program consists of a sequence of instructions that are executed one after another. These instructions are executed in sequence unless their order is altered by a "test-on-condition" instruction or a "branch" instruction.

Each programming language has an instruction set with several instructions in each of the following *instruction classifications.*

  ▶ *Input/output instructions* direct the computer to "read from" or "write to" a peripheral device (for example, a printer or disk drive).

Programming has come a long way in 50 years. Early programmers had to set hundreds of switches manually to enter a program. To run another program, they had to reset the switches. Today, the technology assists us in the programming effort while providing us with a user-friendly interface. Photo courtesy of Hewlett-Packard Company/Courtesy of International Business Machines Corporation

▶ *Computation instructions* direct the computer to perform arithmetic operations (add, subtract, multiply, divide, and raise a number to a power). For example, PAY = HOURS * RATE computes gross earnings for hourly employees.

▶ *Control instructions* can alter the sequence of the program's execution or terminate execution. For example, a different sequence of instructions is executed when a customer's payment is posted after the due date.

▶ *Assignment instructions* transfer data internally from one RAM location to another.

▶ *Format instructions* are used in conjunction with input and output instructions (for example, where data are placed on a page).

With these few instruction sets, you can create software to model almost any business or scientific procedure, whether it be sales forecasting or guiding rockets to the moon.

Types of Programming Languages

We "talk" to computers within the framework of a particular programming language. There are many different programming languages, most of which have highly structured sets of rules. The selection of a programming language depends on who is involved and the nature of the "conversation." For example, we use one language to create enterprise-wide information systems and another to prepare a dynamic sales presentation. There are many different types of programming languages in use today.

Machine Language: Native Tongue   In Chapter 2, "Inside the Computer," we learned that all programs are ultimately executed in *machine language,* the computer's native language. Creating programs in machine language is a cumbersome process, so we write programs in more programmer-friendly programming languages. However, our resulting programs must be translated into machine language before they can be executed.

Procedure-oriented Languages   The introduction of more user-friendly programming languages (in 1955) resulted in a quantum leap in programmer convenience. Programmers could write a single instruction in lieu of several cumbersome machine language instructions. These early languages were **procedure-oriented languages.** Procedure-oriented languages require programmers to solve programming problems using traditional programming logic; that is, programmers code, or write, the instructions in the sequence in which they must be executed to solve the problem. Examples include *COBOL* (see Figure 3–5) and *FORTRAN,* both introduced in late 1950s.

Object-oriented Languages and OOP   In procedure-oriented languages, the emphasis is on *what* is done (the action). In **object-oriented languages,** the emphasis is on the *object* of the action—thus the object orientation. The top-down hierarchical structure of **object-oriented programming (OOP)** makes programs easier to design and understand. Also the trend in programming is toward greater use of images, videos, and sound. OOP (rhymes with *"hoop"*) handles these elements better than procedure-oriented languages. Examples include *Smalltalk* and *C++*.

The Fourth Generation: 4GLs   Most of the programming in procedure- and object-oriented languages is done by computer specialists. Programming in user-friendly **fourth-generation languages (4GLs)** is also done by computer specialists and a growing legion of end users. Users write 4GL programs to query (extract information from) a database and to create personal or departmental information systems.

Fourth-generation languages use high-level English-like instructions to retrieve and format data for inquiries and reporting. Most of the procedure portion of a 4GL program is generated automatically by the computer and the language software. That is, for the most part the programmer specifies what to do, *not* how to do it.

```
0100   IDENTIFICATION DIVISION.
0200   PROGRAM-ID.              PAYPROG.
0300   REMARKS.                 PROGRAM TO COMPUTE GROSS PAY.
0400   ENVIRONMENT DIVISION.
0500   DATA DIVISION.
0600   WORKING-STORAGE SECTION.
0700   01 PAY DATA.
0800        05 HOURS       PIC 99V99.
0900        05 RATE        PIC 99V99.
1000        05 PAY         PIC 9999V99.
1100   01 LINE-1.
1200        03 FILLER      PIC X(5).       VALUE SPACES.
1300        03 FILLER      PIC X(12).      VALUE "GROSS PAY IS."
1400        03 GROSS-PAY   PIC $$$$9.99.
1500   01 PRINT-LINE.      PIC X(27).
1600   PROCEDURE DIVISION.
1700   MAINLINE-PROCEDURE.
1800        PERFORM ENTER-PAY.
1900   PERFORM COMPUTE-PAY.
2000   PERFORM PRINT-PAY.
2100   STOP RUN.
2200   ENTER-PAY.
2300        DISPLAY "ENTER HOURS AND RATE OF PAY."
2400        ACCEPT HOURS, RATE.
2500   COMPUTE-PAY.
2600        MULTIPLY HOURS BY RATE GIVING PAY ROUNDED.
2700   PRINT PAY.
2800        MOVE PAY TO GROSS-PAY.
2900        MOVE LINE-1 TO PRINT-LINE.
3000        DISPLAY PRINT-LINE.
```

> Enter hours and rate of pay
> 43, 8.25
> Gross pay is $354.75

FIGURE 3–5 A COBOL Program
This COBOL program accepts the number of hours worked and the pay rate for an hourly wage earner, then computes and displays the gross pay amount. The interactive session below the program listing shows the input prompt, the values entered by the user, and the result.

Fourth-generation languages are effective tools for generating responses to a variety of requests for information. A few simple 4GL instructions are all that are needed to respond to the following typical management requests:

▶ Which employees have accumulated more than 20 sick days since May 1?

▶ Which deluxe single hospital rooms, if any, will be vacated by the end of the day?

▶ List departments that have exceeded their budgets alphabetically by the department head's name.

Visual Languages: Icons for Words   Programming for today's applications with their GUIs is far more complex than programming for the text-based applications of the 1970s and 1980s. Switching to the efficiency of object-oriented programming (OOP) helped programmers keep pace for a while, but the sheer volume of instructions needed to create GUI-based software can be overwhelming. Enter visual programming. As they say, a picture is worth a thousand words and so it is in programming. **Visual programming** takes object-oriented programming to the next level, replacing text-based instructions with symbolic icons, each of which represents an object or a common programming function (see Figure 3–6). Microsoft's **Visual BASIC** is one of the most popular visual languages for both the casual user and the professional software developer (see Figure 3–7).

FIGURE 3–6 Visual Programming
This visual program shows how icons are used to depict the programming activities (decision icon, main menu icon, sound icon, and so on) needed to create a program for an interactive information kiosk. The main flow of the program is represented at level 1. Each icon at level 1 may represent another group of icons at level 2 (see the Safety segment in the figure).

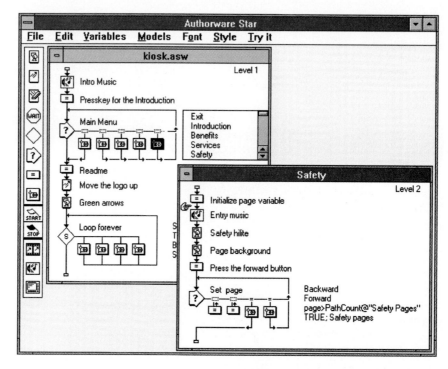

Natural Languages: The Ultimate Programming Language

Natural languages refer to software that enables computer systems to accept, interpret, and execute instructions in the native, or "natural," language of the end user—typically, English. The premise behind a natural language is that the programmer or user needs little or no training. The programmer simply writes, or perhaps speaks, processing specifications without regard for instruction syntax (the rules by which instructions are formulated). In theory, people using natural languages are not constrained by the instruction syntax inherent in traditional programming languages. In practice, however, there are limitations.

The state of the art of natural languages is still somewhat primitive. Researchers are currently working to develop pure natural languages that permit an unrestricted dialogue between us and a computer. Although the creation of such a language is difficult to comprehend, it is probably inevitable.

FIGURE 3–7 Visual BASIC
Microsoft Visual Basic, shown here, offers an easy-to-learn visual development environment. A Visual Basic programmer used visual programming capabilities to create the interface for an ATM (automatic teller machine). This screen asks the user to select a language to be used during the ATM interaction. The screen was created by moving appropriate objects to the form. Separate windows show programming code and properties for the highlighted "English" button.

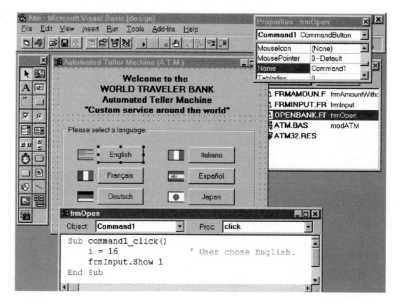

Programming and You

As you continue to gain experience with PCs and PC software, you, like so many before you, will probably begin to seek greater speed, power, and efficiency from your PC and its software. To gain speed and power, you will need to upgrade your hardware with the latest technology. To improve efficiency, you might wish to consider learning to write programs—yes, programs. You do not have to be a professional programmer. Most people who program are not. They are users who write programs to accomplish personal processing objectives. Many users who write programs get hooked on the benefits of programming by using time-saving macros.

Macros: Past and Present   As end users, we issue commands and initiate operations by selecting activities to be performed from a *hierarchy of menus.* A **menu** is simply a list of options for the user. When we choose an item on a menu, that operation is performed and the applications software causes the system to wait for further commands. We select operations (menu items) one at a time until we have accomplished what we wish to do. This one-at-a-time approach to system interaction is fine for one-time jobs, such as preparing and printing a sales summary bar chart. However, what if you prepare the same charts from an updated spreadsheet at the end of each week? Then, you might wish to consider creating a macro to do the job automatically. A **macro** is a sequence of frequently used operations or keystrokes that can be recalled as needed. A macro is actually a *short program,* containing a sequence of instructions to be performed.

The original macro concept grew from a need to automate repetitive interactions with applications software. The first macros (for spreadsheet and word processing software) simply recorded command interactions for replay at a later time. *Record-and-play macros* are handy for performing interactions that are done over and over. Straightforward macros can be created easily by recording operations as they are entered, then storing their sequence on disk for later recall. To **invoke,** or execute, the macro, you simply refer to it by name.

Today's users want more than record-and-play macros. For example, they want to be able to play macros that include user-defined conditions. In response to this need, software vendors began distributing their software with **macro languages.** Most of today's office software (word processing, spreadsheet, database, and so on) have their own powerful macro language. These languages are like procedure-oriented languages, except each is designed to support a particular piece of software. Users can write programs to do simple tasks or to create comprehensive office information systems (see Figure 3–8).

The Trend Is Set: Program Your Own   Professional programmers and system developers focus their energies on enterprise-wide information systems. Perhaps

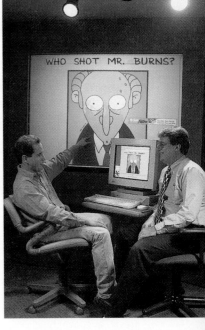

The Java language, created by Sun Microsystems, is a revolutionary new programming environment for the Internet. Java is designed for programmers who wish to develop new publishing and interactive multimedia applications for the Internet. Java enables both the professional and the casual programmer to create dynamic multimedia-based online applications.   Courtesy Sun Microsystems

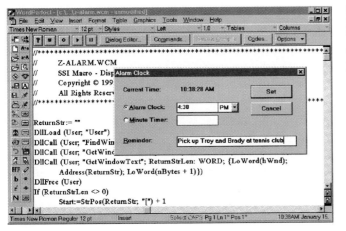

FIGURE 3–8 WordPerfect for Windows Macro Programming Language
This WordPerfect for Windows macro language program enables users to set an alarm clock. Once set, a window appears and a tone sounds at the designated time.

Issues in Computing

Modern-Day Bounty Hunters

The Business Software Alliance has offered the equivalent of $3900 to anyone in Britain who identifies a company that uses unlicensed software. Whistle-blowers can call a toll-free Software Crimeline to report the software abuse. Software vendors feel such measures are needed to curb software piracy.

Users groups are outraged, calling the scheme a return to the old East Bloc process of informing.

Discussion: Is placing a bounty on companies that abuse software copyrights justified?

more companies should make programmers available to end users to assist users with personal processing objectives, but, in reality, few do. In general, if you want to create a macro or write a macro program, you will need to do it yourself. There are literally millions of PC users who routinely play macros and run their own programs, most of whom never dreamed they would write a program. It's not unusual to talk with users who attribute savings of two to fifteen hours a week to the programs they wrote.

3–5 PLATFORMS: HOMES FOR SOFTWARE

A **platform** defines a standard for which software packages are developed. Software is created to run under a specific platform. Specifically, a platform is defined by two key elements:

▶ The processor (for example, Intel Pentium or PowerPC)

▶ The operating system (for example, Macintosh or Windows 95)

Generally, software created to run on one platform is not compatible with any other platform, and, therefore, cannot run under any other platforms.

The typical computer system, large or small, runs under a single platform. However, some can be configured to run several platforms. A multiplatform computer runs its native platform and *emulates* other platforms. Although emulation adds flexibility, programs running in emulation mode run more slowly than if run on the real thing.

The selection of a platform is important because it establishes boundaries for what you can and cannot do with your computer system. Before choosing a platform consider the following.

▶ Availability of appropriate commercial applications software for the platform

▶ Compatibility of platform with existing hardware, software, and expertise (A heavy investment in one platform often deters people from switching to another.)

PC Platforms

In the mainframe environment, platforms are the responsibility of computer specialists. Typically, in the PC environment, you—the individual user—are responsible for selecting the platform. The following discussion will provide some insight into that decision process. You must first decide whether to go with a *single-user* or *multiuser platform*.

Single-User Platforms   The most popular single-user platforms combine any PC-compatible micro with the *MS-DOS* or the *Windows 95* operating system, and the Macintosh with its *System* operating system.

PC compatibles with MS-DOS.   Through 1990 the platform of choice for the vast majority of PC users was defined by micros that are functionally compatible with the 1984 IBM PC-AT architecture (the Intel family of microprocessors) and run under MS-DOS. This platform dominated for these reasons.

1. Most users operated in the single-user environment, one application at a time.
2. Thousands of software packages have been created for this platform.
3. Millions of people are familiar with this platform and are reluctant to change.
4. Users have a tremendous financial investment in software and hardware that run under this platform.

Each and every year since 1990, DOS has been proclaimed dead by industry gurus and leading magazines. Recognizing the continued demand for MS-DOS, Microsoft's latest version of MS-DOS permits multitasking (the ability to run several applications simultaneously), one of the basic failings of the first six versions. Someday Windows aficionados may dance on the MS-DOS grave, but for now, the party will have to wait.

PC compatibles with MS-DOS and Windows.   Microsoft's **Windows** running within MS-DOS defines a PC platform (see Figure 3–9). MS-DOS remains a popular platform, but it is about 15 years old and is not designed to take advantage of modern PC technology. Microsoft's Windows offers some inviting solutions to the limitations of MS-DOS.

1. *Windows is user-friendly.* Windows employs a user-friendly GUI. MS-DOS users must memorize and enter cryptic text commands on the keyboard.
2. *Windows enables multiple programs to be run simultaneously.* This multitasking feature permits a user to print out a WordPerfect report while engaged in a Lotus 1-2-3 session.
3. *Windows enables users to work with large files.* Databases, spreadsheet files, and word processing documents can be as big as available memory will permit. Some micros have as much as 32 MB of RAM. With Windows, the text in this book (over 1 MB of memory) and many other books could be loaded to RAM—simultaneously! Without Windows, a file containing one or two chapters of this book might not fit into available RAM.

MEMORY BITS
PC Platforms

Single-user
• MS-DOS
• MS-DOS with Windows
• Windows 95
• System, the Macintosh platform

Multiuser
• UNIX
• Workgroup
  –Windows 95
  –Windows for Workgroups

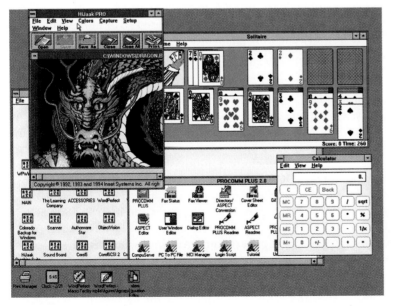

FIGURE 3–9 The MS-DOS with Windows Platform
The popular Microsoft Windows platform has a user-friendly graphical user interface (GUI).

4. *Windows permits information to be passed between applications.* With Windows, text in a word processing document can be transferred in seconds to a database record. A pie chart from a graphics program can be inserted into a word processing document just as easily. These types of information transfers, though not impossible, are cumbersome and time-consuming with MS-DOS.

Windows runs under MS-DOS, but programs written to take full advantage of its potential must conform to the *Windows CUA* (Common User Access). Think of Windows as a subplatform running under the MS-DOS platform. Windows, which offers a user-friendly graphical user interface, defines a new platform.

Most popular micro programs that gained their popularity as MS-DOS programs have been converted or they are being converted to run under the Windows platform. For example, WordPerfect for Windows is a by-product of the most popular MS-DOS program, WordPerfect. Windows provides an easy transition for MS-DOS users in that MS-DOS programs that do not conform to Windows standards can be run within Windows. These programs, called *non-Windows* programs, are no less effective when run within Windows, but they cannot take full advantage of the Windows capabilities.

PC compatibles with Windows 95: Chicago or bust. Code-named "Chicago" during development, Windows 95 is set to replace both MS-DOS and the original Windows. Windows 95, a truly user-friendly operating system, defines a new platform for the PC compatibles. This relatively new operating system (1995) opened to rave reviews when it demonstrated an interface that strikes a balance between usability for the novice and power for the expert.

Unlike its predecessor, Windows 95 does not require the antiquated MS-DOS operating system. Removing this limitation eliminates the original Windows' two most annoying problems—lack of speed and unexpected system crashes. The original Windows is inherently slow because it is unable to take full advantage of the hardware. Windows 95 can and does. The original Windows is famous for causing GPF (general protection faults) that lock up the PC, forcing the user to restart the system. With Windows 95, you can work with greater confidence and speed on Windows 95, Windows, or MS-DOS programs.

Windows 95 offers the **plug-and-play** capability. Plug-and-play refers to making a peripheral device or an expansion board immediately operational by simply plugging it into a port or an expansion slot. Users no longer have to juggle limited system resources, such as I/O ports, to eliminate system-level conflicts.

Some industry observers dubbed Windows 95 an "instant classic" before its official release. That may be, but only half of the PC world used Windows seven years after its introduction. If history repeats itself, Windows 95 may take a while to earn the platform-of-choice label. Windows 95 features and functionality are discussed in the Appendix.

The Macintosh platform. The Apple Macintosh family of microcomputers and **System,** its operating system, define another major platform. About one in every 10 PCs runs under this platform. Macintosh PCs, which are based on the Motorola family of microprocessors, use the NuBus 32-bit architecture. The Macintosh platform includes many sophisticated capabilities including multitasking, a GUI, virtual memory, and the ability to emulate the MS-DOS and MS-DOS/Windows platforms. Macintosh PCs also have the built-in ability to communicate with and share files with other Macintosh computers on a network. Figure 3–10 illustrates the interface for System 7.5, the Macintosh operating system.

Code-named Copland, Apple's next-generation operating system, is scheduled for release soon. Copland's user interface can be adjusted to fit the user's level of expertise.

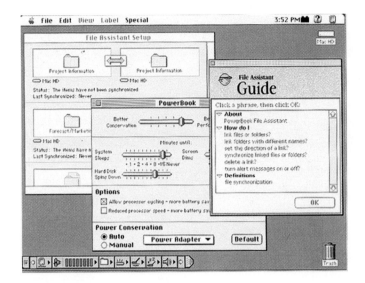

FIGURE 3-10 The System 7.5 GUI

Apple Computer Company introduced the GUI concept over a decade ago. The Macintosh System operating system continues the GUI tradition. Macintosh System provides enhanced features to simplify the mobile computing experience. Shown here are the control strip for easy access to controls, a control panel that consolidates power-management features, and file synchronization to ensure that users are always working on the most recent document.   Courtesy of Apple Computer, Inc.

PC platform options: Which to choose? A growing number of platform options await new and existing PC users, but which one is right for you? Your choice depends on your circumstances (knowledge, compatibility with office PCs, existing configuration, budget, and so on) and personal preferences. While you wait to make a decision, expect a marketing barrage from all players. Microsoft is committed to making Earth a Windows world. IBM sings to the tune of **OS/2** Warp (a competitor to Windows 95). Apple and IBM tell us the chip of the future is the PowerPC. The dominant platform of the PC era has been MS-DOS and more recently MS-DOS with Windows. That will change. You and millions of other users will determine the platform victor when you cast your vote (choose a platform for your PC).

Multiuser Platforms PC-level multiuser platforms fall into two groups: UNIX-based and those designed to support workgroup computing.

The UNIX-based platforms. The most popular multiuser platform is defined by UNIX and the type of PC on which it is run. UNIX is available with PC-compatible, Macintosh, and PowerPC-based PCs. Many of the popular PC software packages have been retrofitted to run under UNIX. For example, WordPerfect, a word processing package, has a product that runs under the UNIX platform. Much of the software written for this platform addresses office or department information systems. For example, a doctor's clinic might have three terminals for administration and three for user inquiry (for example, delinquent invoices).

Workgroup platforms. The new wave of multiuser platforms involves operating systems that support LAN-based **workgroup computing.** Workgroup computing allows people on network to use the network to foster cooperation and the sharing of ideas and resources. The most visible workgroup platforms are two Microsoft products—Windows 95 and **Windows NT,** another Microsoft operating system. **Groupware,** such as electronic messaging, calendar, brainstorming, and scheduling, is developed to run under workgroup platforms.

Platform Problems: Interoperability and Cross-Platform Technologies

Many companies purchase and maintain a fleet of automobiles for use by employees. Companies routinely exchange entire fleets of Chevys for Fords (and vice versa) without any loss of functionality. Employees simply come to work in a Chevy and drive

Emerging Technology

Tailoring PCs to the Needs of Mobile Workers

Electronic Fashion Statement

Thousands of mobile workers could benefit from using a computer—if only the computer were lighter, freed their hands, and didn't tether them to a desk or a power outlet. Now a new generation of wearable computers promises to extend the trend begun by laptop, notebook, and pen-based computers.

Prototypes of wearable computers, long a staple of science fiction, are already being promoted by Japan's NEC Corporation. In an effort to create truly personal computers that meld a computer and its user, NEC designers have divided the PC's components into cable-connected modules that fit into headsets, drape across shoulders, hang around the neck, and fasten around the waist, forearm, or wrist. Lightweight (about two pounds or less), the components would be covered in soft plastic and strapped on with Velcro.

Many of these prototypes combine existing or emerging technologies to create customized PCs for specific types of workers. The TLC (Tender Loving Care) PC for paramedics is a good example. At an accident scene, speech-recognition software would let the paramedic dictate symptoms and vital signs into a slender microphone hanging from a headset. The computer, draped across the medic's shoulders like a shawl, would compare this data to a CD-ROM medical directory in the shoulder unit. The computer would then project possible diagnoses and suggested treatments onto the headset's goggle-type display. The TLC unit would also improve upon the two-way radio medics now use to communicate with emergency-room doctors. Instead of describing symp-

toms over a two-way radio, medics could use a trackball-operated video camera and body sensor strapped to their palm to *show* doctors the patients' condition. The video and additional data would be beamed to the doctors by a satellite link on the medics' back. Headphones would let the medics get feedback and additional advice from the waiting doctors.

Wearable Computers and Body Nets

Given the industry's ongoing success in miniaturizing electronics and developing more powerful but lightweight batteries, we should expect a range of commercially viable wearable PCs to appear by the late 1990s. However, GRiD Systems Corporation, pioneer of the pen-based computer, isn't waiting. It has already introduced the Palmpad, a rugged 2.8-pound computer designed to be worn on a belt, slung over a shoulder, or strapped to a wrist. MIT's Media Lab has produced another wearable computer. This one is worn as a pair of eyeglasses. In it are a tiny computer and screen that you wear over one eye to read news feeds automatically downloaded throughout the day.

Perhaps the most intriguing concept in wearable computers is the Body Net. The Body Net will be a network of wearable computers strategically located over the body. For example, the shoe-based computer might detect your location, then transmit appropriate location-specific information for viewing on your eyeglasses computer. Perhaps by the twenty-first century, the PC will become as much an essential part of one's wardrobe as an indispensable business tool.

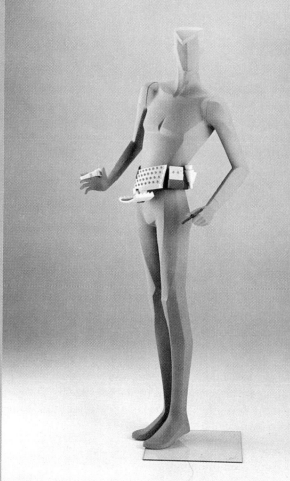

The Future of PCs? At NEC a handful of engineers and designers are creating what they believe to be the future of PCs—wearable PCs. Their objective is to blend the machine with the body.   Courtesy NEC Corporation, Tokyo, Japan

away in a Ford. It's not unusual for companies to rotate between major manufacturers every couple of years. The decision to go with Chrysler or Toyota doesn't commit a company over the long term. The choice of a computer platform, however, involves substantial commitment.

When you decide on a particular platform, you begin to purchase and create resources for that platform. When you or a company selects a particular platform, an ever-increasing investment in the platform demands a long-term commitment, at least five years. This type of commitment makes choosing a platform at the individual or company level a very important decision.

All companies have platform problems, some to a lesser extent than others. Those that standardized on platforms can enjoy the benefits of easily shared resources (from data to printers). Those that did not must do some work to achieve interoperability. **Interoperability** refers to the ability to run software and exchange information in a **multiplatform environment** (a computing environment of more than one platform). Enabling technologies that allow communication and the sharing of resources between different platforms are called **cross-platform technologies.** Multiplatform organizations use cross-platform technologies, both hardware and software, to link PCs, workstations, LANS, mainframes, and so on. Multiplatform environments are more the rule than the exception. Whenever possible, companies try to minimize the number of platforms represented in the company. The fewer the number of platforms, the less the hassle and expense associated with installing and maintaining cross-platform technologies.

3-6 INTERACTING WITH THE PC AND ITS SOFTWARE

The thesaurus lists these synonyms for the word *interact: blend, associate, hobnob, mingle, combine, mix, stir,* and *socialize.* To some extent we do all of these, even socialize, when we *interact* with PCs and their software. Most of us will interact directly with a personal computer or a workstation that may or may not be linked to a network. Or we will interact with a video display terminal (VDT) linked to a mainframe or a supercomputer in a remote location. The look and feel of a modern VDT is very much like that of the PC, except that the actual processing is done on a remote computer.

To interact effectively with a computer and its software, you need to be knowledgeable in four areas.

1. General software concepts (for example, windows, menus, uploading, and so on)
2. The operation and use of the hardware over which you have control (such as the PC, magnetic disk, and printer)
3. The function and use of the computer's operating system and/or its graphical user interface (GUI), both of which provide a link between you, the computer

User-friendly interfaces make it easier for us to interact with the computer. At the Blitz-Weinhard Brewing Co. in Portland, Oregon, operators can now supervise and interact with all production operations from the man-machine interface (MMI) without venturing to the plant floor (left). The PC-based system, created with InTouch software, is connected to the brewery's control system. The touch-sensitive screens give operators an accurate view of machine and process operations on the plant floor (center). Operator status checks show the equipment being monitored (right). Wonderware Corporation

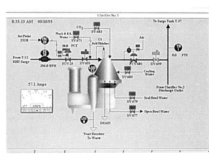

system, and the various applications programs (for example, a Lotus 1-2-3 spreadsheet program, an inventory management system)

4. The specific applications programs you are using

The first three areas are *prerequisites* to the fourth; that is, you will need a working knowledge of software concepts, hardware, and the operating system and/or a GUI before you can make effective use of Quicken (accounting), PowerPoint (presentation graphics), Paradox (database), or any of the thousands of software packages on the market today. In this book we lay the groundwork that will allow you to literally jump up the learning curve to effective use of computers. The hardware, software, operating system, and GUI concepts presented in this book can be readily applied to your computing environment. We also discuss the function and use of PC software that you will likely use at home and at work (word processing, spreadsheet, database, communications, and so on). Tutorials and exercises in supplemental materials to this book teach you how to use specific operating systems, GUIs, and general-purpose programs.

The remainder of this chapter is intended to give you some insight into the fundamental concepts that you will need to know to interact effectively with computers, especially PCs.

Computer Operation: Getting Started

Who operates computers? Probably you do. End users routinely do everything from unpacking boxes of hardware to installing and using the software. This is especially true for users of PCs and workstations.

Installing Hardware and Software   When you purchase a computer system, typically you will receive several boxes containing the various components of the system. Unless it is a portable computer, your system will come in several pieces: a keyboard, a mouse, a monitor, a printer, and a processor unit that houses the magnetic disk drives. Normally you can complete the installation of the hardware simply by linking the pieces of the system with the various types of cables. A computer, however, does nothing without software.

Many new PCs are sold with the operating system and, perhaps, a few user programs already installed (stored on the hard disk and ready to run). If not, you must install the software—first the operating system, then any applications software you intend to run. Even if your new system includes some software, you will likely install other software as well. **Software installation** involves copying the program and data files from the vendor-supplied master disks to the permanently installed hard disk. Software installation is a two-step process for the operating system and all applications software packages.

Software installation step 1: Install or set up software.   Commercial software is distributed on *3½-inch diskettes* or on *CD-ROM*. Generally the software is distributed on one to three diskettes, but the more sophisticated software can have 15 or more diskettes. Very complex software and multimedia software is distributed only on CD-ROM. This normally straightforward installation process can take up to an hour depending on the complexity of the software, the distribution media, and the speed of the PC.

Software installation from 3½-inch diskettes.   Installing programs from diskettes is a relatively standard and straightforward procedure.

▶ Insert Disk 1 in disk drive labeled A (or B). Hard disk drives are labeled consecutively beginning with C, D, and so on). Many PCs have only one hard disk labeled Drive C.

INTERNET BRIDGE

**Serendipitous
Surfing: Travel**

▶ If installing within Windows, enter *a:setup* or *a:install* as indicated by the program's documentation at the Windows 95 Start *Run* . . . Open the box or the Windows *File Run*. . . Command Line.

a:setup

If installing within MS-DOS, enter the command at the C:\\ prompt.

```
C:\>a:setup
```

The software is installed on hard disk Drive C unless you indicate otherwise.

▶ Remove Disk 1 and replace it with Disk 2, then Disk 3, and so on as directed until installation is complete. Depending on the software, you may be asked to respond to several questions. For example, you may be presented with a list of printers and asked to select yours.

Software installation from CD-ROM   Most CD-ROM–based software is designed to be run entirely, or at least in part, from the CD-ROM. This is true of most CD-ROM–based games and graphics programs. CD-ROM provides very high volume storage—over 600 MB. The average hard disk provides less storage than a single CD-ROM disc. Because CD-ROM is relatively slow, critical programs are loaded to the hard disk during installation to speed up the running of the overall software package.

The software installation procedure for CD-ROM–based programs is similar to that for diskettes. Simply preface the *setup* or *install* commands with the drive designator for the CD-ROM drive (often D, if only one hard disk). The installation procedure copies appropriate files to the hard disk. To run the CD-ROM–based software, the CD-ROM disc must be in the CD-ROM drive.

A single CD-ROM is far less expensive than 15 or 20 diskettes, so look for CD-ROM to gain popularity as media for software distribution.

Software installation step 2: Set system information.   Applications software is installed to accommodate the "typical" PC. You may need to revise some of the standard settings, such as type of printer, to better fit your PC's configuration. Some of these changes may be made during software installation. Also, applications software is installed for the "typical" user. If you wish to customize the application to better meet your processing needs, you may wish to revise certain **default options** (standard settings), such as location of data files, display colors, and so on.

HELP!   If you run into a problem after installation, help is never farther away than your keyboard. A handy feature available on nearly all modern software packages is the **help command.** When you find yourself in need of a more detailed explanation or instructions on how to proceed, tap the *Help* key, often assigned to Function Key 1 (F1), or choose *Help* from the main menu. Help is usually context-sensitive; that is, the resulting explanation relates to what you were doing when you entered the command. When you are finished reading the help information, the system returns you to your work at the same point you left it.

Power Up/Shut Down   Computers are similar to copy machines, toasters, and other electrical devices—you must turn them on by applying electrical power. The power-on procedure on almost any computer is straightforward—flip the on/off switch on the processor unit to *on*. Some input/output devices, such as the monitor and the printer, may have separate on/off switches. It is good practice to turn on needed input/output devices before turning on the processor.

When you **power up,** or add electrical power to a computer system, you also **boot** the system. The booting procedure is so named because the computer "pulls itself up

GOING ONLINE

3.3
Anyone for a Game?

Millions of people routinely play games over the Internet. Scan descriptions of some of the available games, then learn about one of them. Try keywords "games" and "Internet." Play the game.
Hand in: Information about the game, including its rules.

by its own bootstraps" (without the assistance of humans). When you boot the system, a ROM (read-only memory) program performs a **system check,** readies the computer for processing, and loads the operating system to RAM (see Figure 3–11).

Although the boot procedure officially ends with the display of the **system prompt** (for example, C:\) for MS-DOS) or the Windows 95 desktop, the operating system may execute predefined user instructions. Frequently, these instructions load an applications program, such as Excel, so your first interaction with the system may be with an application, not at the system prompt.

Unlike electrical appliances, you do not simply flip the computer switch to *off.* You must **shut down** in an orderly manner. This involves a normal exit from all active applications programs before shutting off the power. All applications programs have an **exit routine** that, when activated, returns you to a GUI, an operating system prompt, or a higher-level applications program. *Exit routines perform some administrative processing that, if bypassed, can result in loss of user data and problems during subsequent sessions.*

Entering Commands and Data: Computers Can Be Very Picky

Computers do *exactly* what you tell them to do—no more, no less. If you tell a computer to compute an employee's pay by adding hours worked to rate of pay (PAY = HOURS-WORKED + RATE), then that is what it does. The computer knows only what you tell it, not that you have given it an erroneous command to add (+) rather than multiply (*). All computers can do is interpret and do what you tell them to do.

Generally, the worst that can happen is that you get an error message or inaccurate results. Fortunately, most software packages have built-in safeguards that ask for confirmation before executing a command that might significantly alter or erase your work.

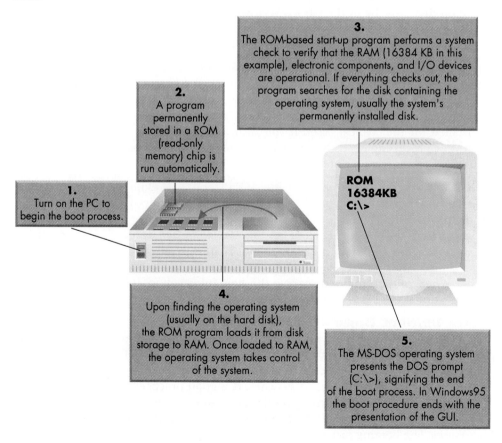

3.
The ROM-based start-up program performs a system check to verify that the RAM (16384 KB in this example), electronic components, and I/O devices are operational. If everything checks out, the program searches for the disk containing the operating system, usually the system's permanently installed disk.

2.
A program permanently stored in a ROM (read-only memory) chip is run automatically.

1.
Turn on the PC to begin the boot process.

**ROM
16384KB
C:\>**

4.
Upon finding the operating system (usually on the hard disk), the ROM program loads it from disk storage to RAM. Once loaded to RAM, the operating system takes control of the system.

5.
The MS-DOS operating system presents the DOS prompt (C:\>), signifying the end of the boot process. In Windows95 the boot procedure ends with the presentation of the GUI.

FIGURE 3–11 The Boot Procedure

Our interaction with computers is not always with a keyboard and mouse. Helicopter pilots at this Camp Pendleton, California, training facility might think they are flying a helicopter when they enter these domed flight simulators. They are actually flying a computer. The flight simulators combine a joystick, an actual instrument panel, a high-resolution visual system, and a motion system to give pilots the feeling of actual flight.   Courtesy of Evans & Sutherland Computer Corporation

Input and Control: Keyboards and Point-and-Draw Devices

The primary input devices found on all PCs, workstations, and many VDTs are the *keyboard* and a *point-and-draw device*. The function and use of these critical input devices are discussed in this chapter while other optional input devices are discussed in Chapter 5, "Input/Output: Computers in Action."

The Keyboard   The *keyboard* is your primary input and control device. You can enter data and issue commands via the keyboard. Figure 3–12 shows the keyboard commonly used by PC-compatible micros. Besides the standard QWERTY keyboard layout, most keyboards have **function keys.** When tapped, these function keys trigger the execution of software. For example, tapping one function key might call up a displayed list of user options commonly referred to as a *menu*. Function keys are numbered and assigned different functions in different software packages. For example, tapping the Function Key 7, F7, while working with word processing software might cause a document to be printed. HELP (context-sensitive user assistance) is often assigned to F1 (Function Key 1). Some software packages are distributed with **keyboard templates** that designate which commands are assigned to which function keys. The plastic templates are designed to fit adjacent to the function keys.

Most keyboards are equipped with a *numeric key pad* and *cursor-control keys* (see Figure 3–12). The key pad permits rapid numeric data entry. It is normally positioned to the right of the standard alphanumeric keyboard. Space limitations preclude keyboards on portable PCs from having a separate numeric key pad. The cursor-control keys, or "arrow" keys can be used to select options from a menu. The arrow keys also allow you to move the **text cursor** *up* (↑) and down (↓), usually a line at a time, and *left*

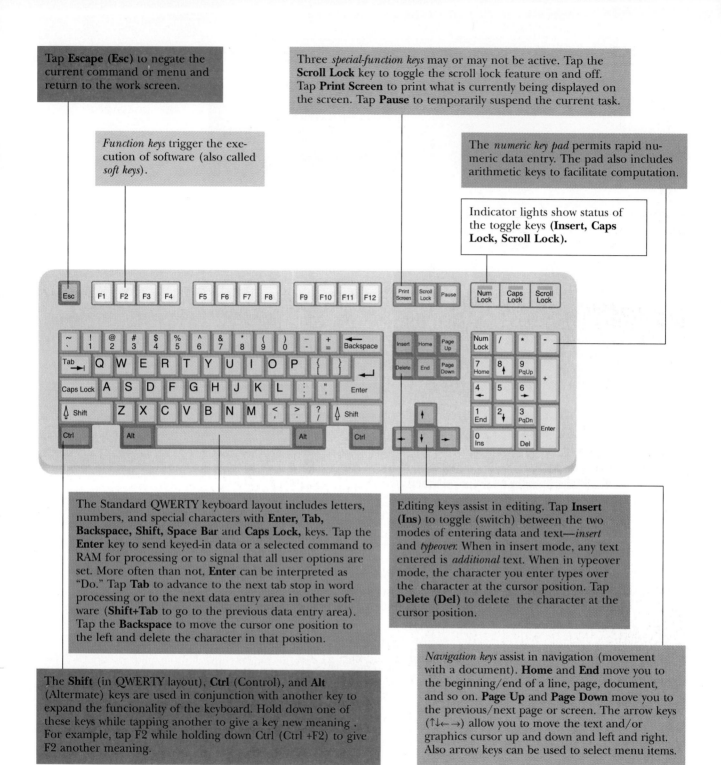

Tap **Escape (Esc)** to negate the current command or menu and return to the work screen.

Function keys trigger the execution of software (also called *soft keys*).

Three *special-function keys* may or may not be active. Tap the **Scroll Lock** key to toggle the scroll lock feature on and off. Tap **Print Screen** to print what is currently being displayed on the screen. Tap **Pause** to temporarily suspend the current task.

The *numeric key pad* permits rapid numeric data entry. The pad also includes arithmetic keys to facilitate computation.

Indicator lights show status of the toggle keys **(Insert, Caps Lock, Scroll Lock).**

The Standard QWERTY keyboard layout includes letters, numbers, and special characters with **Enter, Tab, Backspace, Shift, Space Bar** and **Caps Lock,** keys. Tap the **Enter** key to send keyed-in data or a selected command to RAM for processing or to signal that all user options are set. More often than not, **Enter** can be interpreted as "Do." Tap **Tab** to advance to the next tab stop in word processing or to the next data entry area in other software (**Shift+Tab** to go to the previous data entry area). Tap the **Backspace** to move the cursor one position to the left and delete the character in that position.

Editing keys assist in editing. Tap **Insert (Ins)** to toggle (switch) between the two modes of entering data and text—*insert* and *typeover.* When in insert mode, any text entered is *additional* text. When in typeover mode, the character you enter types over the character at the cursor position. Tap **Delete (Del)** to delete the character at the cursor position.

Navigation keys assist in navigation (movement with a document). **Home** and **End** move you to the beginning/end of a line, page, document, and so on. **Page Up** and **Page Down** move you to the previous/next page or screen. The arrow keys (↑↓←→) allow you to move the text and/or graphics cursor up and down and left and right. Also arrow keys can be used to select menu items.

The **Shift** (in QWERTY layout), **Ctrl** (Control), and **Alt** (Alternate) keys are used in conjunction with another key to expand the funcionality of the keyboard. Hold down one of these keys while tapping another to give a key new meaning . For example, tap F2 while holding down Ctrl (Ctrl +F2) to give F2 another meaning.

FIGURE 3–12 A Representative PC Keyboard

(←) and *right* (→), usually a character at a time. The text cursor always shows the location of the next keyed-in character on the screen. The text cursor can appear as several shapes depending on the application, but frequently you will encounter a blinking vertical line (|). To move the text cursor rapidly about the screen, simply hold down the appropriate arrow key.

For many software packages, you can use the arrow keys to view parts of a document or worksheet that extend past the bottom, top, or sides of the screen. This is known as **scrolling**. Use the up and down arrow keys (↑ ↓) to scroll vertically and the left and right keys (← →) to scroll horizontally. For example, if you wish to scroll vertically through a word processing document, move the up or down arrow key to the edge of the current screen and continue to press the key to view more of the document, one line at a time. Figure 3–13 illustrates vertical and horizontal scrolling in a spreadsheet.

In summary, the keyboard provides three basic ways to enter commands:

▶ *Key in* the command using the alphanumeric portion of the keyboard.

▶ Tap a *function key*.

▶ Use the *arrow keys* to select a *menu option* from the displayed menu. (Menus are discussed in detail in the next section.)

Other important keys common to most keyboards are illustrated and described in Figure 3–12.

Point-and-Draw Devices The hand-held mouse, or something like it, is a must-have item on PCs, workstations, and GUI-based VDTs. The mouse is either attached to the computer by a cable (the mouse's "tail") or linked via a wireless remote connection. The mouse is a small device that, when moved across a desktop, moves the **graphics cursor** accordingly. The graphics cursor, which can be positioned anywhere on the screen, is displayed as a bracket ([), an arrow (⇄), a crosshair (┼),or a variety of other symbols (for example, ☞). Depending on the application, the text and graphics cursors may be displayed on the screen at the same time. The graphics cursor is used to *point* and *draw*.

All movements of the mouse are reproduced by the graphics cursor on the screen. For example, when a mouse positioned to the right of the keyboard is moved up and away from its user, the graphics cursor moves toward the top right-hand corner of the screen. Use the mouse for quick positioning of the graphics cursor over the desired menu item or an icon. When positioned at a menu item or an icon, the graphics cursor is said to *point* to that item or icon.

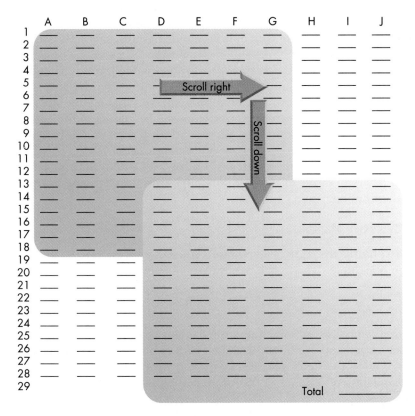

FIGURE 3–13 Scrolling
When a spreadsheet does not fit on a single screen, you can scroll horizontally (to the right as shown in the figure) and vertically (down in the figure) to view other portions of the spreadsheet.

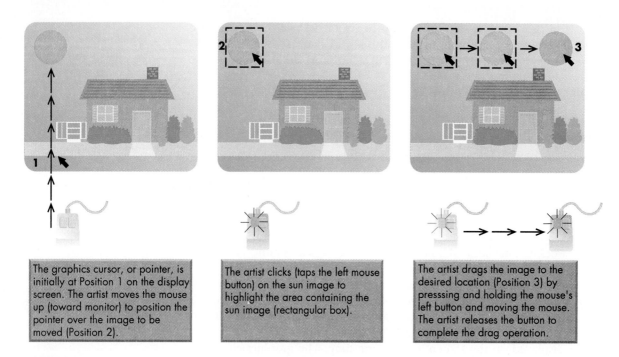

| The graphics cursor, or pointer, is initially at Position 1 on the display screen. The artist moves the mouse up (toward monitor) to position the pointer over the image to be moved (Position 2). | The artist clicks (taps the left mouse button) on the sun image to highlight the area containing the sun image (rectangular box). | The artist drags the image to the desired location (Position 3) by presssing and holding the mouse's left button and moving the mouse. The artist releases the button to complete the drag operation. |

FIGURE 3–14 The Mouse and the Graphics Cursor
In the example, a computer artist moves the sun image from the left to the right side of the screen.

Mice and other point-and-draw devices (discussed in Chapter 5) have one or more buttons. The Macintosh mouse has one button. The PC-compatible mouse normally has a left and right button (see Figure 3–14). You tap, or **click,** the left button to select a menu item or a program represented by an icon. The function of the right button varies between software packages, but often it is used to call up a menu of options germane to the current activity. A **double-click,** which is tapping a button twice in rapid succession, gives each button a different meaning. Some software packages permit a **simultaneous click,** or tapping both buttons simultaneously, to give the mouse added functionality.

Press and hold a button to **drag** the graphics cursor across the screen. When using a graphics software program, you drag the graphics cursor across the screen to create the image. When using a word processing program, you highlight a block of text to be deleted by dragging the graphics cursor from the beginning to the end of a block. In a GUI, you can point to an object, perhaps an icon, then drag it to a new position.

Click and drag operations are demonstrated in Figure 3–14 within the context of a graphics software package. In the example, a computer artist uses a mouse to reposition the sun in the drawing.

Menus and Button Bars

Software designers continue to create new and more efficient ways for us to issue commands and initiate operations. These include a variety of menus and button bars.

Menus   Traditionally, we tell computers what we wish to do by selecting activities to be performed from a *hierarchy of menus.*

Menu trees.   Menu hierarchies are sometimes called **menu trees.** When you select an item from the **main menu,** you are often presented with another menu of activities, and so on. Depending on the items you select, you may progress through as few as one and as many as eight levels of menus before processing is started for the desired activity.

Let's use presentation graphics software to illustrate how you might use a hierarchy of menus. Consider the following main menu.

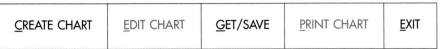

CREATE CHART	EDIT CHART	GET/SAVE	PRINT CHART	EXIT

Notice that two of the options in the main menu are dimmed. **Dimmed** options, which are usually gray, are disabled or unavailable. The current circumstance dictates whether an option is dimmed. In this example, there is no active chart to be edited or printed, so these options are dimmed.

One option on the main menu of the example graphics software package is *Create Chart.*

CREATE CHART	EDIT CHART	GET/SAVE	PRINT CHART	EXIT

If you select the *create chart* option, you are presented with another menu and an opportunity to choose one of five types of charts.

BAR	PIE	LINE	TEXT	ORGANIZATION

If you select the *text* option, another menu asks you to choose from three available types of text charts.

TITLE CHART	SIMPLE LIST	BULLET LIST

If you select the *bullet list* option, you are presented with the bullet list work screen on which you would enter the text for your bullet points.

Menu formats.   Menus are presented in four basic formats.

▶ *Menu bar.* The main menu is frequently presented as a **menu bar** in the **user interface** portion of the display. The user interface is that portion of the display dedicated to the presentation of user options. It is normally found around the perimeter of the work area. The menu bar provides a *horizontal list* of menu options, usually at the top of the screen (see Figure 3–15).

▶ *Pull-down menu.* The result of a menu selection from a menu bar at the top of the screen may be a subordinate menu bar or a **pull-down menu** (see Figure

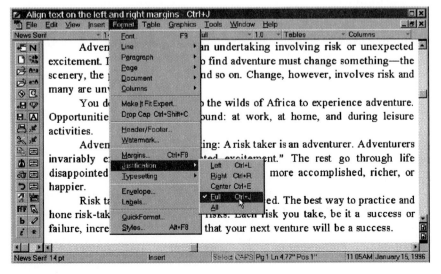

FIGURE 3–15 Menus
The WordPerfect for Windows main menu is presented in a menu bar above the user work area. In the example, the *Format* option in the bar menu is selected and the pull-down menu is presented. Selecting the *Justification* option results in a pop-out menu of justification options.

3–15). The subordinate pull-down menu is "pulled down" from the selected menu bar option and displayed as a *vertical list* of menu options. The entire pull-down menu is shown in a box directly under the selected menu bar option and over whatever is currently on the screen (see Figure 3–15).

▶ *Pop-up menu.* Like the pull-down menu, the **pop-up menu** is superimposed on the current screen in a window. Context-sensitive pop-up menus are often available by clicking the right mouse button.

▶ *Pop-out menu.* The **pop-out menu** is displayed next to the menu option selected in a higher-level pull-down or pop-up menu. The pop-out menu becomes the active menu, but the higher-level menu continues to be displayed (see Figure 3–15).

▶ *Floating menu.* You can activate a special-function menu such that it *floats* over the work area until you no longer need it. A menu that "floats" can be dragged with a mouse to any position on the work area. Floating menus streamline interaction with the software because you do not have to work through the main menu to get to a frequently used subordinate menu.

Most software packages provide users with three ways to select an item from a menu.

1. Use the left/right ($\leftarrow \rightarrow$) or up/down ($\uparrow \downarrow$) arrow keys to highlight the desired menu option and tap *Enter.*
2. Enter the **mnemonic** (pronounced *"neh MON ik"*) of the desired item. A letter or number within the text of the menu item is noted as its mnemonic, which means memory aid. The mnemonic is usually the first letter in the first word unless there is another option with the same first letter. Examine the underlined mnemonics in the menu bar in Figure 3–15 (File, Edit, View, Insert, Format, Table, and so on).
3. Use the mouse (or other point-and-draw device) to point to the desired option and click the left button.

Parameters and dialog boxes.   As you progress through a series of menus, eventually you are asked to enter the specifications, perhaps the location of the data to be graphed (graphics software) or the orientation of output on the printer paper (word processing software). These specifications are presented as parameters. **Parameters** are variables whose values must be defined by the user before the current command can be executed. Parameters are normally entered and revised in a dialog box. The text in a pop-up **dialog box** gives the user an opportunity to change default options or enter further information. Dialog boxes are discussed further in the Appendix, "The Windows Environment."

Menu summary.   All software, whether applications or system, is designed such that at any given point in a work session, the processing options are either displayed somewhere on the screen or can be displayed by tapping a key or clicking a mouse. So, if you are ever confused about what to do next or what can be done, the options usually are literally in front of your nose.

Button Bars   A software package's main menu is but the tip of a hierarchy of menus that may contain as many as 200 menu item options. You might go for years and not choose some of these options. Others, you will use frequently during interaction. Button bars have been created to give you ready access to these frequently used menu items. **Button bars** contain a group of rectangular graphics that represent a menu option or a command (see Figure 3–16). To execute a particular command, simply click on the button. The graphics on the buttons are designed to represent actions of the command. For example, a person running represents the *run* command and a printer represents the *print* command. You can customize your button bars to meet your processing needs.

FIGURE 3–16 Button Bar
This PROCOMM PLUS for Windows (a communications program) button bar contains buttons for frequently used menu options.

IMPORTANT TERMS AND SUMMARY OUTLINE

3–1 SOFTWARE IN PERSPECTIVE We interact with software, which refers to programs, to direct the overall activities within a computer system. The instructions in programs are logically sequenced and assembled through the act of **programming. Programmers,** people who write programs, use a variety of **programming languages** to communicate instructions to the computer. People in all walks of life write programs to meet business and domestic needs.

3–2 SYSTEM SOFTWARE: MAINTAINING CONTROL Software falls into two major categories: **system software** and **applications software.** System software takes control of the PC on start up, then plays a central role in all interactions with the computer. Applications software is designed and created to perform specific personal, business, or scientific processing tasks.

3–3 THE OPERATING SYSTEM: DIRECTING THE ACTION The **operating system** is the nucleus of all software activity. One of the operating system programs, called the **kernel,** loads other operating system and applications programs to RAM as they are needed.

All operating systems are designed with the same basic objectives in mind. Perhaps the most important objectives are to facilitate communication between the computer system and the people who run it and to optimize the use of computer system resources.

Operating systems get the most from their processors through **multitasking**, the current execution of more than one program at a time. High-priority programs run in the **foreground** part of RAM and the rest run in the **background.**

Through the 1980s, the most popular microcomputer operating system, **MS-DOS,** was strictly *text-based, command-driven* software that required strict adherence to command **syntax.** The trend now is **graphical user interfaces,** or **GUIs,** that use graphical **icons.** All modern operating systems, including the **Windows 95** operating system, have adopted the GUI concept.

3–4 PROGRAMMING LANGUAGES: COMPUTERTALK

We create software with programming languages. The design of a program, or its *programming logic* is completed before the program is written. Each language uses several types of instructions, including *input/output instructions, computation instructions, control instructions, assignment instructions,* and *format instructions.*

All programming languages are ultimately translated into *machine language* in order to be executed. In **procedure-oriented languages,** programmers code the instructions in the sequence in which they must be executed to solve the problem. COBOL and FORTRAN are examples.

Object-oriented languages, such as Smalltalk and C++, emphasize the *object* of the action. The hierarchical structure of **object-oriented programming (OOP)** makes programs easier to design and understand.

In **fourth-generation languages (4GLs),** the programmer need only specify *what* to do, not *how* to do it. One feature of 4GLs is the use of English-like instructions.

In **visual programming,** text-based instructions are replaced with symbolic icons, each of which represents a common programming function. **Visual BASIC** is an example.

Natural languages are programs that permit a computer to accept instructions without regard to format or syntax in the native language of the end user.

As end users, we can issue commands and initiate operations by selecting activities to be performed from a hierarchy of **menus.** A **macro** can also be used. To **invoke** the macro, you simply refer to it by name. Most of today's office software have their own **macro language.**

3–5 PLATFORMS: HOMES FOR SOFTWARE

A **platform** defines a standard for which software packages are developed. In the mainframe environment, platforms are the responsibility of computer specialists. Popular single-user platforms combine any PC-compatible micro with the MS-DOS, MS-DOS with **Windows** or the **OS/2** Warp operating system, as well as the Macintosh with its **System** operating system. PC-level multiuser platforms fall into two groups: UNIX-based and those designed to support **workgroup computing.** The most visible workgroup platforms, which run **groupware,** are two Microsoft products—Windows 95 and **Windows NT.** Windows 95 offers **plug-and-play** capability.

Those companies that do not standardize on a platform must work to achieve **interoperability,** which refers to the ability to run software and exchange information in a **multiplatform environment.** Enabling technologies that allow communication and the sharing of resources between different platforms are called **cross-platform technologies.**

3–6 INTERACTING WITH THE PC AND ITS SOFTWARE

The effective user will understand general computer software concepts, how to operate and use the hardware, the operating system and/or a graphical user interface (GUI), and one or more applications programs.

When you purchase a computer system, you receive several components. Hardware installation involves linking the pieces of the system with the various types of cables. **Software installation** involves copying the program and data files from the vendor-supplied master disks to the permanently installed hard disk. Software installation is a two-step process for the operating system and all applications software packages: Copy files to the permanently installed hard disk; and set system information, revising **default options** (standard settings) as needed. Use the **help command,** which is usually context-sensitive, when you need assistance.

When you **power up** a computer, you **boot** the system. First, a program in read-only memory (ROM) initializes the system and runs a **system check.** Next, the operating system is loaded to random-access memory (RAM), takes control of the system, and present the user with a **system prompt** or a GUI screen full of options. RAM provides temporary storage of data and programs during processing.

To **shut down** in an orderly manner, perform the **exit routine** from all active applications programs prior to shutting off the power.

When entering a command the user must be explicit. The primary input devices found on all PCs, workstations, and many VDTs are the *keyboard* and a *point-and-draw device.* In addition to the standard typewriter keyboard, most keyboards have **function keys.** Tapping a function key might present the user with a menu. Some software packages are distributed with **keyboard templates** that designate which commands are assigned to which function keys. Most keyboards are equipped with a numeric key pad and cursor-control keys. Use the cursor-control keys to position the **text cursor** and for **scrolling.**

The hand-held *mouse,* when moved across a desktop, moves the **graphics cursor** accordingly. The graphics cursor is used to *point* and *draw.* Use point-and-draw devices for quick positioning of the graphics cursor. Typically, you would **click** the mouse's left button to select a menu item. The **double-click** and **simultaneous click** give the mouse added functionality. You would press and hold a button to **drag** the graphics cursor across the screen.

Menu hierarchies are sometimes called **menu trees.** When you select an item from the **main menu,** you are often presented with another menu of activities. A menu can appear as a **menu bar** in the **user interface** portion of the display, a **pull-down menu,** a **pop-up menu,** or a **pop-out menu.** Menu options that are unavailable or disabled are **dimmed.**

Software packages provide users with three ways to select an item from a menu: Use the left/right or up/down arrow keys; enter the **mnemonic;** or use the mouse to position the graphics cursor at the desired option. Most menus present users with default options in a pop-up **dialog box.** User specifications needed for processing are presented in the form of **parameters.**

Button bars, which can be customized, contain a group of rectangular graphics that represent a menu option or command.

REVIEW EXERCISES

Concepts

1. Give two examples each of applications and system software.
2. What defines a platform?
3. Does the current program run in RAM's foreground or background?
4. Briefly describe two multiuser platforms for microcomputers.
5. Give an original example of a computation instruction.
6. Name two object-oriented programming languages.
7. What is the trademark of 4GLs?
8. What is the name given the software entities that provide the foundation for OOP?
9. What kind of programming languages use symbolic icons to represent common programming functions?
10. What is the purpose of function keys? Of cursor-control keys?
11. Contrast a menu bar with a pull-down menu.
12. Briefly describe two ways you can use a keyboard to enter commands to a software package.
13. During a software session, which key would you commonly press to move to the beginning of the work area? To negate the current command?
14. How is a pop-out menu displayed?
15. What does "booting the system" mean?

16. What must be accomplished to shut down in an orderly manner?
17. Which key is tapped to toggle between insert and typeover modes?
18. The help command is often assigned to which function key?

Discussion and Problem Solving

19. If each new generation of programming languages enhances interaction between programmers and the computer, why not write programs using the most recent generation of languages?
20. What is a macro and how can using macros save time? Give an example.
21. Explain in general terms what a natural language would do with the following command: "List all fixed inventory items in the purchasing department purchased prior to 1985." Give an example of what a response to the request might look like. Fixed inventory items would include items such as desks, chairs, lamps, and so on.
22. People have been saying that DOS is dead since 1990, but it continues to live. Will Windows 95 be the last nail in the MS-DOS coffin?
23. Multitasking allows PC users to run several programs at a time. Describe a PC session in which you would have at least two applications running at the same time.

SELF-TEST (BY SECTION)

3–1 Programmers use a variety of _____ _____ to communicate instructions to the computer.

3–2 **a.** _____ software takes control of the PC on start up.
b. Which type of software is designed to perform specific personal, business, or scientific processing tasks: (a) system, (b) applications, or (c) GUI?

3–3 **a.** The concurrent execution of more than one program at a time is called _____ .
b. GUIs are: (a) text-based, (b) graphics-based, or (c) label-based?
c. MS-DOS is a mainframe-based operating system. (T/F)

3–4 **a.** When programming in a procedure-oriented language, you tell the computer what to do and how to do it. (T/F)
b. C + + is: (a) a procedure-oriented language, (b) a problem-oriented language, or (c) an object-oriented language?
c. To _____, or execute, a macro, you refer to it by name.

3–5 **a.** A commonly used multiuser PC platform involves which of the following operating systems: (a) XIX, (b) UNIX, or (c) XINU?
b. The Macintosh family of PCs is unique in that they do not need an operating system. (T/F)

c. OS/2 Warp is a subset of Windows NT, a more sophisticated operating system. (T/F)

d. A computing environment that runs more than one platform is called a _____ environment.

3–6 a. Both the operating system and/or a _____ provide a link between the user, the computer system, and the applications programs.

b. A computer user must "kick the system" to load the operating system to RAM prior to processing. (T/F)

c. The MS-DOS operating system displays a system _____ to signal the user that it is ready to accept a user command.

d. Help commands are rarely context-sensitive. (T/F)

e. Use the _____ for rapid numeric data entry.

f. Menu hierarchies are sometimes called menu charts. (T/F)

g. Press and hold a mouse button to _____ the graphics cursor across the screen.

h. Which is not considered a common menu format: (a) floating; (b) pop-over; or (c) pop-up?

Self-test Answers. **3–1** programming languages. **3–2 (a)** System; **(b)** b. **3–3 (a)** multitasking; **(b)** b; **(c)** F. **3–4 (a)** T; **(b)** c; **(c)** invoke. **3–5 (a)** b; **(b)** F; **(c)** F; **(d)** multiplatform. **3–6 (a)** graphical user interface (GUI); **(b)** F; **(c)** prompt; **(d)** F; **(e)** numeric key pad; **(f)** F; **(g)** drag; **(h)** b.

CHAPTER 4

Storing and Retrieving Information: Disks and Tape Backup Units

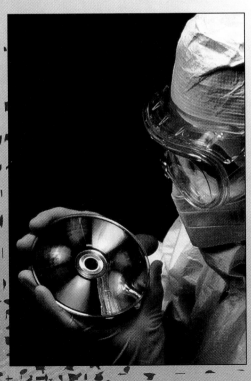

Courtesy of International Business Machine Corp.

Let's Talk

The following conversation introduces many of the terms in this chapter. Read it now, then again after you have read the chapter.

The Scene:
The executive director of the State University Alumni Association (Max) is meeting in his office with an analyst from the University Computer Center (Leah) and the president of the Alumni Association (Scottie).

Scottie: Our membership is disappointed with the Annual Alumni Directory. They don't like the $50 price tag, and they're complaining that it's out of date.

Max: And they're right! I say we go electronic with it. Can we do it, Leah?

Leah: Well, all the university administrators already have **direct access** to the entire **database,** which now has over 140,000 **records** on **magnetic disk.** Technically, providing greater access to it is not a problem, but you guys will have to address the security and privacy issues.

Max: Let's assume we can overcome these concerns. Is our current database complete?

Scottie: In this era of multimedia, our members may want more than name-and-address **ASCII files.** I suggest we give them the flexibility to attach their own **graphics files, audio files,** and even **video files** to their record.

Max: Great idea! I'd love to listen to my old friends and see some family photos.

Leah: If we do that, we'll need to go to **optical laser disk** storage to make this economically feasible. It sounds neat. Think about it—alums could change messages and their photos with the seasons.

Scottie: People want their databases on a computer, not in a book. Let's do the annual directory on **CD-ROM.**

Leah: You know, with **CD-R** coming down in price, we could do our own **CD-ROM publishing** right here in the Alumni Office. With a little **file compression** and a **CD production station,** we could provide a great service for the alumni.

Scottie: And, our members would love to be able to **import** selected portions of the alumni database on **the Internet** to their **spreadsheet files.**

Max: I'm excited! Forget the printed directory. What do you say we explore these options further?

STUDENT LEARNING OBJECTIVES

▶ *To distinguish between primary and secondary storage.*

▶ *To describe how data are stored and retrieved in computer systems.*

▶ *To demonstrate an understanding of the fundamental principles of sequential and random access.*

▶ *To distinguish between secondary storage devices and secondary storage media.*

▶ *To describe the principles of operation, methods of data storage, and use of magnetic disk and magnetic tape drives.*

▶ *To know types and sources of computer virus.*

▶ *To describe procedures for backing up disk files to data cartridge or diskette.*

▶ *To discuss the applications and use of optical laser disk storage.*

4–1 SECONDARY STORAGE AND FILES: DATA KEEPERS

Did you ever stop to think what happens behind the scenes when you

▶ Request a telephone number through directory assistance?

▶ Draw money from your checking account at an ATM?

▶ Check out at a supermarket?

▶ Download a file on the Internet?

Needed information, such as telephone numbers, account balances, item prices, or a stock summary file on the Internet, are retrieved from rapidly rotating disk-storage media and loaded to random-access memory (RAM) for processing. Untold terabytes (trillions of characters) of information representing millions of applications are stored *permanently* for periodic retrieval in **secondary storage,** such as magnetic disk. Interaction with secondary storage takes place in milliseconds. As soon as the directory assistance operator keys in the desired name, the full name and number are retrieved from disk storage and displayed. Moments later, a digitized version of voice recordings of numbers is accessed from disk storage and played in response to the caller's request: "The number is five, zero, one, two, two, four, nine."

Storage Technologies: Disk and Tape

Within a computer system, programs and information in all forms (text, image, audio, video) are stored in both *primary storage* and *secondary storage* (see Figure 4–1). Programs and information are retrieved from secondary storage and stored *temporarily* in high-speed primary storage (RAM) for processing.

Over the years, manufacturers have developed a variety of devices and media for the permanent storage of programs and information. Today the various types of **magnetic disk drives** and their respective storage media are the state of the art for permanent storage. **Magnetic tape drives** complement magnetic disk storage by providing inexpensive *backup* capability and *archival* storage. We will discuss these as well as the potential and applications of **optical laser disk** technology, a rapidly emerging alternative to magnetic disk and magnetic tape storage.

The Many Faces of Files

We have talked in general about the *file* in previous chapters. Now it's time for specifics. The **file** is the foundation of permanent storage on a computer system. To a computer, a file is simply a string of 0s and 1s (digitized data) that are stored and retrieved as an entity, a single unit.

Types of Files: ASCII to Video   There are many types of files, most of which are defined by the software that created them (for example, a word processing document or spreadsheet). Popular files are listed here.

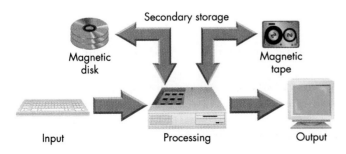

Secondary storage

Magnetic disk

Magnetic tape

Input   Processing   Output

FIGURE 4–1 Primary and Secondary Storage Programs and data are stored permanently in secondary storage and temporarily in primary storage (RAM).

There could be no better example of a graphics file than this grand prize winner in Corel Corporation's annual international art poster competition. A digitized version of this image, by Gerry Wilson, is maintained on magnetic disk storage.
Courtesy of Corel Corporation

▶ *ASCII file.* An **ASCII file** is a text-only file that can be read or created by any word processing program or text editor.

▶ *Data file.* A **data file** contains data organized into records.

▶ *Document file.* A word processing or desktop publishing **document file** contains integrated text and images.

▶ *Spreadsheet file.* A **spreadsheet file** contains rows and columns of data.

▶ *Source program file.* A **source program file** contains high-level instructions to the computer. These instructions must be translated to machine language prior to program execution.

▶ *Executable program file.* An **executable program file** contains executable machine language code.

▶ *Graphics file.* A **graphics file** contains digitized images.

▶ *Audio file.* An **audio file** contains digitized sound.

▶ *Video file.* A **video file** contains digitized video frames that when played rapidly (for example, 30 frames per second) produce motion video.

Files and Parking Lots   A *file* is to *secondary storage* as a *vehicle* is to a *parking lot.* A variety of vehicles, cars, buses, trucks, motorcycles, and so on are put in parking places to be picked up later. Just as single vehicles enter and exit, files are stored and retrieved as a unit. To help you find your vehicle, large parking lots are organized with numbered parking places in lettered zones. The same is true with files and secondary storage. Files are stored in numbered "parking places" on disk for retrieval. Fortunately, we do not have to remember the exact location of the file. The operating system does that for us. All we have to know is the name of the file. We assign user names to files then recall or store them by name. In the MS-DOS/Windows environment, filenames can be up to eight characters with an optional three-character extension (LETTER.DOC, PLAYGAME.EXE). Windows 95 and several other operating systems allow descriptive filenames of up to 255 characters. MAN_CP_3 could become Operations_Manual_Chicago_Plant_ver_3.

What to Do with a File   Everything we do on a computer has to do with a file and, therefore, secondary storage. What do we do with files?

▶ *We create, name, and save files.* We create files when we name and save a letter, a drawing, a program, or some digital entity to secondary storage.

▶ *We copy files, move files, and delete files.* We copy files from diskettes to a hard disk to install software. We move files during routine file management activities. When we no longer need a file, we delete it.

▶ *We retrieve and update files.* We continuously retrieve and update our files (update the entries in a spreadsheet or edit a memo).

▶ *We display, print, or play files.* Most user files that involve text and graphics can be displayed and printed. Audio and video files are played.

▶ *We execute files.* We execute program files to run our software. In the MS-DOS/Windows environment, executable files have one of these extensions: EXE, COM, BAT, and PIF (Windows only).

▶ *We download and upload files.* We download useful files from the Internet to our PCs. We sometimes work on, then upload updated files to our company's mainframe computer.

▶ *We export/import files.* The *file format,* or the manner in which a file is stored, is unique for each type of software package. For example, Word and WordPerfect are both word processing programs, but the format of their files is different. For a Word user to read a WordPerfect file, the WordPerfect file

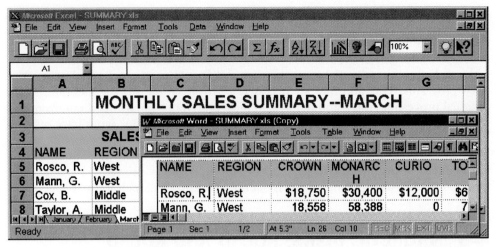

FIGURE 4–2
Importing Files
An Excel for Windows 95 spreadsheet is imported into a Word for Windows 95 document.

must be converted to the Word file format. To do this the user must **import** the WordPerfect document to a Word file format. When we import a file, we convert it from its foreign format to a format that is compatible with the current program. Figure 4–2 illustrates how a Quattro Pro for Windows spreadsheet can be imported into a WordPerfect for Windows document. When we **export** a file, we convert a file in the current program to a format needed by another program.

▶ *We compress files.* File formats for most software packages are inefficient, resulting in wasted space on secondary storage when you save files. When the air is squeezed out of a sponge, it becomes much smaller. When you release it, the sponge returns to its original shape—nothing changes. This is the way **file compression** works. A repeated pattern, such as the word *and* in text documents, might be replaced by a one-byte descriptor in a compressed file, saving two bytes for each occurrence of *and*. One technique used when compressing graphics files replaces those portions of an image that are the same color with a brief descriptor. Depending on the type and content of the file, file compression can create a compressed file that takes 10% to 90% less secondary storage (average is about 50%). Compressed files are decompressed when loaded to RAM for processing.

▶ *We protect files.* We can protect sensitive files by limiting access to authorized persons.

4–2 SEQUENTIAL AND DIRECT ACCESS: NEW TERMS FOR OLD CONCEPTS

An important consideration in both the design of an information system and the purchase of a computer system is the way that data and files are accessed. Magnetic tape can be used for *sequential access* only. Magnetic disks have *random-* or *direct-access* capabilities as well as sequential-access capabilities. You are quite familiar with these concepts, but you may not realize it. Operationally, the magnetic tape is the same as the one in home and automobile audiotape decks. The magnetic disk can be compared to a compact disk (CD).

Suppose you have Paul Simon's album, *The Rhythm of the Saints,* on CD. The first four songs on this CD are: (1) "The Obvious Child," (2) "Can't Run But," (3) "The Coast," and (4) "Proof." Now suppose you also have this album on a tape cassette. To play the third song on the cassette, "The Coast," you would have to wind the tape forward and search for it sequentially. To play "The Coast" on the CD, all you would have to do is select track number 3. This simple analogy demonstrates the two fundamental methods of storing and accessing data—*sequential* and *random.*

Magnetic disk drives are secondary storage devices that provide a computer system with **random-** *and* **sequential-processing** capabilities. In random processing, the desired programs, data, and files are accessed *directly* from the storage medium. In sequential processing, the computer system must search the storage medium, from the beginning, to find the desired programs, data, or files. Magnetic tapes have only sequential-processing capabilities. Today's online information systems demand immediate and direct access to information; therefore, virtually all active files and databases are maintained on media that permit random processing—primarily magnetic disk and optical laser disk. Magnetic tape is mainly a backup and archival storage medium.

4–3 MAGNETIC DISKS: ROUND AND ROUND

Because of its random- and sequential-processing capabilities, magnetic disk storage is the overwhelming choice of computer users, whether on micros, workstations, or supercomputers. A variety of magnetic disk drives (the hardware device) and magnetic disks (the media) are manufactured for different business requirements.

Hardware and Storage Media

There are two fundamental types of magnetic disks: interchangeable and fixed.

▶ **Interchangeable magnetic disks** can be stored offline and loaded to the magnetic disk drives as they are needed.

▶ **Fixed magnetic disks,** also called *hard disks,* are permanently installed, or fixed. All fixed disks are rigid and are usually made of aluminum with a surface coating of easily magnetized elements, such as iron, cobalt, chromium, and nickel.

In the past, interchangeable disks containing certain files and programs were taken from the shelf and loaded to the disk drives as needed. This is still true today but to a much lesser extent. Today's integrated software and databases require all data and programs to be online at all times. This is especially true for enterprise-wide information systems and in workgroup computing.

The different types of interchangeable magnetic disks and fixed disks are shown in Figure 4–3. As you can see, magnetic disk drives and their storage media are available in a wide variety of shapes and storage capacities. The type used would depend on the volume of data you have and the frequency with which those data are accessed.

Magnetic Disks: The Microcomputer Environment

PC Magnetic Disk Media   Virtually all PCs sold today are configured with at least one hard disk drive and one interchangeable disk drive. Having two disks increases system flexibility and throughput. The interchangeable disk drive provides a means for the distribution of data and software and for backup and archival storage. The high-capacity hard-disk storage has made it possible for today's PC user to enjoy the convenience of having all data and software readily accessible at all times.

The diskette.   Two types of disk drives are in widespread use on PCs. These disk drives accommodate interchangeable magnetic disks called **diskettes.**

▶ *5¼-inch diskette.* The 5¼-inch diskette is a thin, flexible disk that is permanently enclosed in a soft, 5¼-inch-square jacket. Because the magnetic-coated mylar diskette and its jacket are flexible like a page in this book, the diskette is also called a **floppy disk.**

**Peripherals
Explorer**

Early 5¼-inch diskettes recorded data on only one side of the disk. These were *single-sided* (SS) diskettes. Today all common-usage diskettes are *double-sided* and are labeled "DS" or simply "2." Similarly, diskettes are classified as *double-density* (DD), as opposed to the *single-density* of earlier diskettes. **Disk density** refers to the number of bits that can be stored per unit of area on the disk-face surface.

The *360-KB DS/DD* (double-sided, double-density) 5¼-inch diskette dominated during the 1980s and is still the only diskette that can be used on some PCs. However, the new 5¼-inch disk drives support both the popular 360-KB diskette and the *1.2-MB DS/HD* (double-sided, high-density) diskette. A 1.2-MB diskette has about three times the storage capacity of a 360-KB diskette.

▶ *3½-inch diskette.* The 3½-inch diskette is enclosed in a rigid plastic jacket. Like its 5¼-inch cousin, the 3½-inch diskette comes in two capacities, the 720-KB DS/DD and the 1.44-MB DS/HD diskettes. The 3½-inch diskette is preferred over the 5¼-inch diskette because of its durability, convenient size, and higher capacity.

Diskette technology continues to evolve. Some PC disk drives are able to store 2.88 MB on 3½-inch diskettes. The **floptical disk drive,** also called a **zip disk drive,** uses optical technology together with magnetic technology to read and write to 3½-inch 120-MB diskettes as well as the standard 3½-inch diskettes. These, however, are not in widespread use.

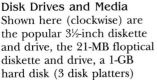

Courtesy of IBM Corp.

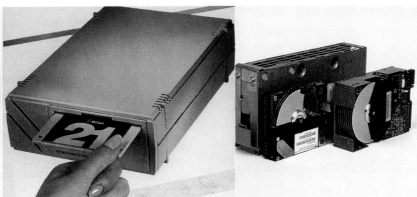

Courtesy of Iomega Corporation   Courtesy of IBM Corp.

FIGURE 4–3 Magnetic Disk Drives and Media Shown here (clockwise) are the popular 3½-inch diskette and drive, the 21-MB floptical diskette and drive, a 1-GB hard disk (3 disk platters) and a 1-GB hard disk (8 disk platters), and a 420-MB hard drive on a PCMCIA card that can be inserted in a PCMCIA slot on a PC.

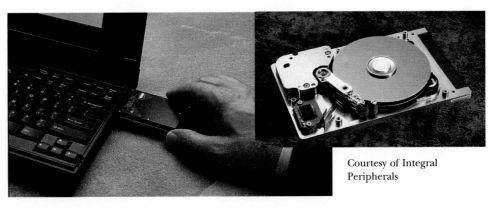

Courtesy of Integral Peripherals

Courtesy of Integral Peripherals

The hard disk.   The 1- to 5¼-inch hard disks have storage capacities from about 40 MB (megabytes) to 6 GB (gigabytes). A 6-GB hard disk can store as much data as four thousand 3½-inch high-density diskettes. That's a stack of floppies 44 feet high!

A hard disk contains several disk platters stacked on a single rotating spindle. Data are stored on all *recording surfaces*. For a disk with four platters, there are eight *recording surfaces* on which data can be stored (see Figure 4–4). The disks spin continuously at a high speed (from 3600 to 6000 revolutions per minute) within a sealed enclosure. The enclosure keeps the disk-face surfaces free from contaminants, such as dust and cigarette smoke. This contaminant-free environment allows hard disks to have greater density of data storage than the interchangeable diskettes. In contrast to a hard disk, a diskette is set in motion only when a command is issued to read from or write to the disk. An indicator light near the disk drive is illuminated only when the diskette is spinning.

The rotational movement of a magnetic disk passes all data under or over a **read/write head,** thereby making all data available for access on each revolution of the disk (see Figure 4–4). A fixed disk will have at least one read/write head for each recording surface. The heads are mounted on **access arms** that move together and literally float on a cushion of air over (or under) the spinning recording surfaces. The tolerance is so close that a particle of smoke from a cigarette will not fit between these "flying" heads and the recording surface!

Hard disks normally are permanently installed in the same physical unit as the processor and diskette drives. There are, however, *interchangeable hard disks* on the market. These interchangeable hard disk modules can be inserted and removed in a manner that is similar to the way you insert and remove tapes on a VCR. Only a small percentage of PCs are configured to accept interchangeable hard disks.

PC Magnetic Disk Organization   The way in which data and programs are stored and accessed is similar for both hard and interchangeable disks. The disk-storage medium has a thin film coating of one of the easily magnetized elements (cobalt, for example). The thin film coating on the disk can be magnetized electronically by the read/write head to represent the absence or presence of a bit (0 or 1).

Tracks and sectors: A disk floor plan.   Data are stored in concentric **tracks** by magnetizing the surface to represent bit configurations (see Figure 4–5). Bits are recorded using *serial representation;* that is, bits are aligned in a row in the track. The number of tracks varies greatly between disks, from as few as 40 on some diskettes to several thousand on high-capacity hard disks. The spacing of tracks is measured in **tracks per**

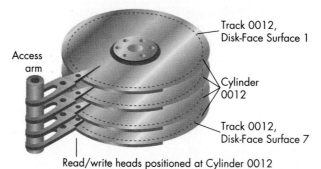

Access
arm

Track 0012,
Disk-Face Surface 1

Cylinder
0012

Track 0012,
Disk-Face Surface 7

Read/write heads positioned at Cylinder 0012

FIGURE 4–4 Fixed Hard Disk with Four Platters
and Eight Recording Surfaces
A cylinder refers to similarly numbered concentric tracks on the disk-face surfaces. In the illustration, the read/write heads are positioned over Cylinder 0012. At this position, the data on any one of the eight tracks numbered 0012 are accessible to the computer on each revolution of the disk. The read/write heads must be moved to access data on other cylinders.

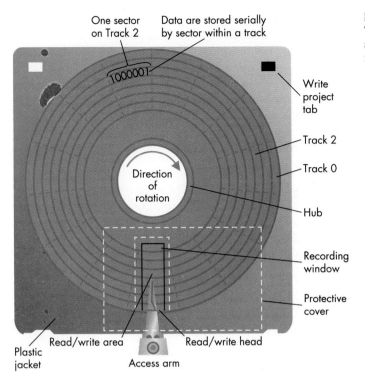

One sector on Track 2

Data are stored serially by sector within a track

`1000001`

Write project tab

Track 2

Track 0

Direction of rotation

Hub

Recording window

Protective cover

Read/write area

Read/write head

Plastic jacket

Access arm

FIGURE 4–5 Cutaway of a 3½-Inch Diskette
The access arm on this 3½-inch disk drive is positioned at a particular track (Track 2 in the example). Data are read or written serially in tracks within a given sector.

inch, or **TPI.** The 3½-inch diskettes are rated at 135 TPI. The TPI for hard disks can be in the thousands.

The *track density* (TPI) tells only part of the story. The *recording density* tells the rest. Recording density, which is measured in *bits per inch,* refers to the number of bits (1s and 0s) that can be stored per inch of track. Both the 720-KB and 1.44-MB diskettes have a track density of 135 TPI, but the recording density of the high-density disk is twice that of the double-density disk.

Microcomputer disks use **sector organization** to store and retrieve data. In sector organization, the recording surface is divided into pie-shaped **sectors.** The number of sectors depends on the density of the disk. The surface of the diskette in Figure 4–5 is logically divided into 15 sectors. Typically, the storage capacity of each sector on a particular track is 512 bytes or a multiple of 512 (for example, 1024), regardless of the number of sectors per track. Each sector is assigned a unique number; therefore, the *sector number* and *track number* are all that are needed for a **disk address** on a particular disk-face surface. The disk address represents the physical location of a particular file or set of data. To read from or write to a disk, an access arm containing the read/write head is moved, under program control, to the appropriate *track* (see Figures 4–4 and 4–5). When the sector containing the desired data passes under or over the read/write head, the data are read or written.

Cylinders: Tracks on tracks. Each of the high-density disk-face surfaces of a hard disk may have several thousand tracks, numbered consecutively from outside to inside. A particular **cylinder** refers to every track with the same number on all recording surfaces (see Figure 4–4). When reading from or writing to a hard disk, all access arms are moved to the appropriate *cylinder.* For example, each recording surface has a track numbered 0012, so the disk has a cylinder numbered 0012. If the data to be accessed are on Recording Surface 01, Track 0012, then the access arms and the read/write heads for all eight recording surfaces are moved to Cylinder 0012.

In Figure 4–4 the access arm is positioned over Cylinder 0012. In this position, data on any of the sectors on the tracks in Cylinder 0012 can be accessed without further movement of the access arm. If data on Surface 5, Track 0145 are to be read, the access arm must be positioned over Cylinder 0145 until the desired data pass under the read/write head.

Fortunately, software automatically monitors the location, or address, of our files and programs. We need only enter the name of the file to retrieve it for processing. In the case of a personnel master file with individual records, we simply enter the employee's name to retrieve his or her personnel record. The computer system searches the disk address associated with that person's record, locates it, and loads it to RAM for processing. Although the addressing schemes vary considerably between disks, the address normally will include the *cylinder (or track)*, the *recording surface*, and the *sector number.*

Formatting: Preparing a Disk for Use   Every PC user is eventually confronted with preparing a new diskette or hard disk for use. A new disk is coated with a surface that can be magnetized easily to represent data. However, before the disk can be used, it must be **formatted.** The formatting procedure causes the disk to be initialized with a recording format for your operating system. Specifically, it:

- Creates *sectors* and *tracks* into which data are stored.
- Sets up an area for the file allocation table. The **file allocation table (FAT)** tells the system where to find the files and file folders (groups of files) you eventually store on the disk, that is, what sector and track.

If you purchased a PC today, the hard disk probably would be formatted and ready for use. However, if you added a hard disk or upgraded your existing hard disk, the new disk would need to be formatted. Diskettes can be purchased as formatted or unformatted. Unformatted diskettes cost less, but they must be formatted prior to use.

Disk Access Time: Seek and Transmit   **Access time** is the interval between the instant a computer makes a request for transfer of data from a disk-storage device to RAM and the instant this operation is completed. The access of data from RAM is performed at electronic speeds—approximately the speed of light. But the access of data from disk storage depends on the movement of mechanical apparatus (read/write heads and spinning disks) and can take from 6 to 15 milliseconds—still very slow when compared with the microsecond-to-nanosecond internal processing speeds of computers.

Disk Caching: Speed Boost   The **data transfer rate** is the rate at which data are read from (written to) secondary storage to (from) RAM. Even though the data transfer rate from magnetic disk to RAM may be millions of bytes per second, the rate of transfer between one part of RAM to another is much faster. **Disk caching** (pronounced *"cashing"*) is a technique that enhances system performance by placing programs and data that are *likely* to be called into RAM for processing from a disk into an area of RAM. When an application program issues a call for the data or programs in the disk cache area the request is serviced directly from RAM rather than magnetic disk. Updated data or programs in the disk cache area eventually must be transferred to a disk for permanent storage. All state-of-the-art PCs come with software that takes full advantage of the potential of disk caching.

Diskette Care: Do's and Don'ts   A blank interchangeable disk, costing about a dollar, has a very modest value. But once you begin to use the disk, its value, at least to you, increases greatly. Its value includes the many hours you have spent entering data, preparing spreadsheets, or writing programs. Such a valuable piece of property should be handled with great care. Following are a few guidelines for handling interchangeable disks.

Do's

- *Do* store disks at temperatures between 50 and 125 degrees Fahrenheit.
- *Do* keep a backup of disks containing important data and programs.

- ▸ *Do* remove disks from disk drives before you turn off the computer.
- ▸ *Do* clean diskette drive read/write heads periodically with a diskette cleaning kit (available at most computer retailer locations).
- ▸ *Do* slide the *write-protect tab* to its open position on all important 3½-inch disks intended for read-only use (see Figure 4–5).

Don'ts

- ▸ *Don't* force a disk into the disk drive. It should slip in with little or no resistance.
- ▸ *Don't* touch the disk surface.
- ▸ *Don't* place disks near a magnetic field, such as magnetic paper-clip holders, tape demagnetizers, telephones, or electric motors.
- ▸ *Don't* expose disks to direct sunlight for a prolonged period.
- ▸ *Don't* insert or remove a disk from a disk drive if the "drive active" light is on.

Magnetic Disks: The Mainframe Environment

Direct-access storage devices (DASDs), such as magnetic disks, are the prerequisite for all information systems where the data must be online and accessed directly. An airline reservation system provides a good mainframe-oriented example of this need. Direct-access capability is required to retrieve the record for any flight at any time from any reservations office. The data must be current, or flights may be overbooked or underbooked.

Mainframes and supercomputers use a wide variety of fixed-disk media. The differences are primarily the size of the platter (up to 14 inches in diameter), the number of platters per disk drive, and the density at which data are recorded. The current technology enables a single disk drive to store more than 20 gigabytes of data. The way data and files are organized on mainframe disk systems is similar to that on microcomputer disk systems.

Computer Viruses: The Plague of Magnetic Disks

Computers can get sick just like people. A variety of highly contagious "diseases" can spread from computer to computer, much the way biological viruses do among human beings. A **computer virus** is a program that literally "infects" other programs and databases upon contact. It can also hide duplicates of itself within legitimate programs, such as an operating system or a word processing program. These viruses reside on and are passed between magnetic disks.

Types of Computer Viruses: Bad and Worse   There are many types of viruses. Some act quickly by erasing user programs and files on disk. Others grow like a cancer, destroying small parts of a file each day. Some act like a time bomb. They lay dormant for days or months but eventually are activated and wreak havoc on any software on the system. Many companies warn their PC users to back up all software prior to every Friday the thirteenth, a favorite date of those who write virus programs. Some viruses attack the hardware and have been known to throw the mechanical components of a computer system, such as disk-access arms, into costly spasms.

Sources of Computer Viruses: BBSs, Disks, and Computers   In the microcomputer environment, there are three primary sources of computer viruses (see Figure 4–6).

- ▸ *Electronic bulletin-board systems.* The most common source of viral infection is the public electronic bulletin board on which users exchange software. Typically, a user logs on to the bulletin board and downloads what he or she thinks is a game, a utility program, or some other enticing piece of freeware, but gets a virus instead.

GOING ONLINE

4.2
Getting the Picture

The Internet has millions of extraordinary images, including Saturn's rings, movie stars, Picassos, St. Martin beaches (shown here), and much more. Cruise the Net and select an image that strikes your fancy. Download it.

Hand in: The source (URL) and printed copy of an image of your choice.

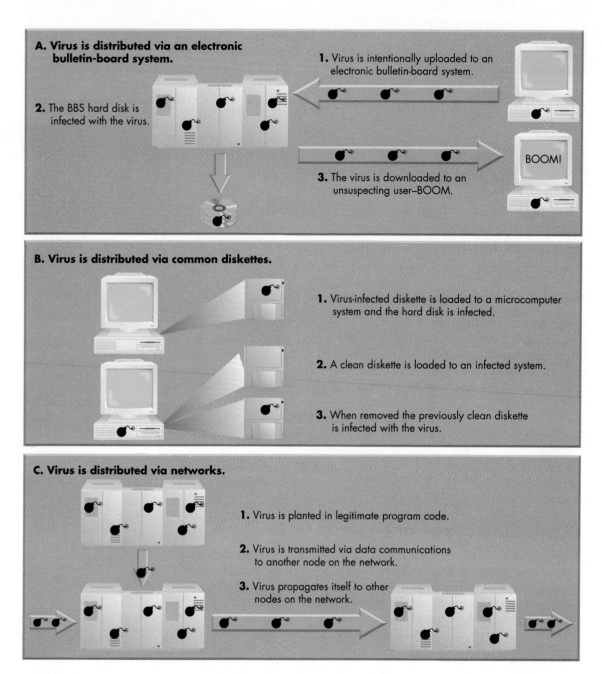

A. Virus is distributed via an electronic bulletin-board system.

1. Virus is intentionally uploaded to an electronic bulletin-board system.

2. The BBS hard disk is infected with the virus.

3. The virus is downloaded to an unsuspecting user–BOOM.

BOOM!

B. Virus is distributed via common diskettes.

1. Virus-infected diskette is loaded to a microcomputer system and the hard disk is infected.

2. A clean diskette is loaded to an infected system.

3. When removed the previously clean diskette is infected with the virus.

C. Virus is distributed via networks.

1. Virus is planted in legitimate program code.

2. Virus is transmitted via data communications to another node on the network.

3. Virus propagates itself to other nodes on the network.

FIGURE 4–6 How Viruses Are Spread

▶ *Diskettes.* Viruses are also spread from one system to another via common diskettes. For example, a student with an infected application disk might unknowingly infect several other laboratory computers with a virus which, in turn, infects the applications software of other students. Software companies have unknowingly distributed viruses with their proprietary software products.

▶ *Computer networks.* Viruses can spread from one computer network to another.

How serious a problem are viruses? They have the potential of affecting an individual's career and even destroying companies. (A company that loses its accounts receivables records could be a candidate for bankruptcy.) Antiviral programs, also called *vaccines,* exist, but they can be circumvented by a persistent (and malicious) programmer. The best way to cope with viruses is to recognize their existence and to take precautionary measures. Your chances of living virus free are greatly improved if you periodically check for viruses and are careful about what you load to your system's hard disk.

Magnetic Tape

4–4   MAGNETIC TAPE: RIBBONS OF DATA

Magnetic Tape and PCs

During the 1950s and 1960s, the foundation of many information systems was *sequential processing* using *magnetic tape* master files. Today, magnetic tape storage is no longer used for routine processing; however, it has three other important functions.

▶ *Protection against loss of valuable files.* Magnetic tape is used primarily as a backup medium for magnetic disk storage.

▶ *Archiving files.* Important files no longer needed for active processing can be archived to magnetic tape. For example, banks archive old transactions (checks and deposits) for a number of years.

▶ *File portability between computers.* Large amounts of information can be transferred between computers by writing to magnetic tape at the source site and reading from tape at the destination site.

A magnetic tape medium, such as the **magnetic tape cartridge,** can be loaded conveniently to a tape drive (the hardware device) for processing. Once loaded to a tape drive, the magnetic tape is online; that is, the data and programs on the tape are accessible to the computer system. When processing is complete, the tape is removed for offline storage until it is needed again for processing.

The magnetic tape cartridge, which is also called a **data cartridge,** is self-contained and is inserted into and removed from the tape drive in much the same way you would load or remove a videotape from a VCR. Like the videotape, the supply and the take-up reels are encased in a plastic shell.

Principles of Operation

Magnetic Tape Media   The mechanical operation of a magnetic tape drive is similar to that of an audiocassette tape deck. The tape, a thin polyester ribbon coated with a magnetic material on one side, passes under a *read/write head,* and the data are either

1. Read and transferred to RAM, or
2. Transmitted from RAM and written to the tape.

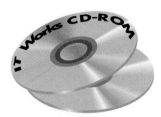

Peripherals Explorer

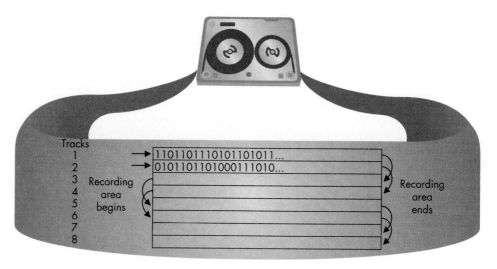

FIGURE 4–7 Cross-Section of a Magnetic Tape Data are recorded serially on this eight-track tape in a serpentine manner, two tracks at a time.

Tracks
1 — 1101101110101101011...
2 — 0101101101000111010...
3 Recording area begins
4
5
6
7
8

Recording area ends

Magnetic tape media come in several widths up to ½ inch and many different lengths, some over 2000 feet. Because the majority of us, as PC users, will use magnetic tape cartridges designed for use with PCs, our discussion of tape devices and media will focus on magnetic tape in the PC environment.

The tape format describes the characteristics of the tape. One of the most popular PC tape cartridge formats is the *QIC minicartridge*. The minicartridge tape drive normally is housed in the same physical unit as the processor and disk drives. The QIC (*QIC* stands for *quarter-inch cartridge*) minicartridge can hold from 250 MB to 1 GB of data. The actual amount of data a given tape cartridge can store depends on the precision of the magnetic tape drive.

The TBU: Tape Backup Unit The ¼-inch tape cartridges used with PCs record data in a continuous stream. Drives for ¼-inch tape cartridges, often called **tape backup units (TBUs),** store data in a **serpentine** manner. Data are recorded using **serial representation**; that is, the bits are aligned in a row, one after another, in tracks. The tracks run the length of the tape (see Figure 4–7). A tape cartridge can be formatted to have from 4 to 60 tracks, depending on the precision of the tape drive. The read/write head reads or writes data to one, two, or four tracks at a time. Figure 4–7 illustrates how data are written two tracks at a time. In the figure, data are written serially on the top two tracks for the entire length of the tape or until the data are exhausted. The tape is reversed, the read/write head is positioned over the next two tracks, and writing continues in a similar manner. If more backup capacity is needed, the computer operator is informed. A clean tape is inserted and writing continues.

A tape drive is rated by its *storage capacity* and its *data transfer rate*. You might recall that the data transfer rate is the rate at which data are read from (written to) secondary storage to (from) RAM. For example, a tape backup unit might have an 800-MB capacity with a data transfer rate of about 1 MB per second.

This robotic tape storage and retrieval unit holds up to 258 high-density tape cartridges, each with a capacity of 25 GB (gigabytes). The tape cartridges are automatically loaded and unloaded to a tape drive as they are needed for processing. Corporations, such as E-Systems, use tape storage and retrieval systems to back up massive master files on magnetic disk storage.   Courtesy of E-Systems, Inc.

4–5 BACKUP: BETTER SAFE THAN SORRY

At the Skalny Basket Company, in Springfield, Ohio, Cheryl Hart insisted on daily backups of the small family-owned company's accounts receivables files. The backups were inconvenient and took 30 minutes each day. Cheryl took the backup home each day in her briefcase, just in case. On December 23, she packed her briefcase and left for the Christmas holidays. Five days later at 3:00, Skalny Basket Company burned to the ground, wiping out all inventory and its computer system. The company was up in smoke, all except for a tape cassette which contained records of its $600,000 accounts receivables. Cheryl said, "We thought we were out of business. Without the tape, we couldn't have rebuilt."

Safeguarding the content of your disks may be more important than safeguarding hardware. The first commandment in computing, at any level, is

$$\mathfrak{BACK\ UP\ YOUR\ FILES.}$$

If data and programs on your disk files are destroyed, it may be impossible for them to be re-created within a reasonable period of time. If, on the other hand, the hardware is destroyed, it can be replaced fairly quickly. The impact of losing critical software or files makes *backup* a major concern.

When you create a document, a spreadsheet, or a graph and you wish to recall it at a later time, you *store* the file on disk. You can, of course, store many files on a single disk. If the disk is in some way destroyed (scratched, demagnetized, burned, and so on) or lost, you have lost your files unless you have a backup.

If your system is configured with a tape backup unit, then you easily can back up all files on a system. However, if you do not have a TBU, you still can back up critical files to diskettes. Backup techniques for tape and diskettes are discussed in the remainder of this section.

Backup to Magnetic Tape

If your backup requirements exceed 10 MB per day, you are a candidate for a tape backup unit. Anything under 10 MB can be handled with diskettes. The relatively inexpensive TBU is a good investment for the active PC user and for all administrators of local area networks (LANs).

Backup Methods   You can choose from three common backup methods.

Full backup	A full backup copies all files on a hard disk to magnetic tape.
Selective backup	Only user-selected files are backed up to magnetic tape.
Modified files only backup	Only those files that have been modified since the last backup are backed up to magnetic tape.

The frequency with which files are backed up depends on their *volatility*, or how often you update the files on the disk. If you spend time every day working with files, you should back them up each day. Others are backed up no more often than they are used. A six-tape backup rotation is illustrated in Figure 4–8.

At one time or another, just about everyone who routinely works with computers has experienced the trauma of losing work for which there was no backup. It is no fun seeing several days (or weeks) of work disappear, but it does emphasize the point that it is well worth the effort to make backup copies of your work.

Restoring Files   When loss of data or programs occurs, you will need to restore the backed-up file to disk. Because some updating will occur between backup runs, the re-creation of lost files means that subsequent updates and changes must be redone from the point of the last complete backup. For example, assume you experienced a disk crash on Thursday while doing routine backups as illustrated in Figure 4–8. To restore the backup files, you would restore the full backup tape from

MEMORY BITS

Characteristics of Magnetic Tape Backup Units

Media	Interchangeable cartridges
Type access	Sequential
Data representation	Serial
Storage scheme	Serpentine on tracks

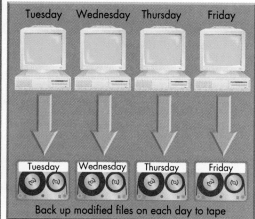

FIGURE 4–8 Tape Backup Rotation: Six Tapes

This six-tape backup rotation is common in small businesses and with individuals whose files have high volatility. Two total backups are done every Monday, one of which is taken to an off-site location. Only files that are modified on a given day are backed up for each of the other weekdays. If all files are lost on Friday, the total backup from Monday is restored to the hard disk, then modified backups are restored for Tuesday through Thursday.

Monday, then the modified backup from Tuesday, and finally the modified backup tape from Wednesday. Then you would need to redo any processing on Thursday prior to the disk crash.

Backup to Diskette

What if you don't have a tape backup unit? If you do not have a TBU (and most people do not), then you will need to back up your files to diskettes. Backing up a complete hard disk to diskette is not practical. To do so would require hundreds, perhaps thousands of diskettes. However, you should back up critical files to diskette.

Figure 4–9 illustrates and explains a backup procedure for critical files that are used daily. The procedure is the same whether your critical files are maintained on a hard disk or on one or more diskettes. In the figure, two generations of backup are maintained on Backup Sets A and B. Critical files disk are copied alternately to Backup Sets A and B each day. This technique is popular with individual users, especially those in an office setting.

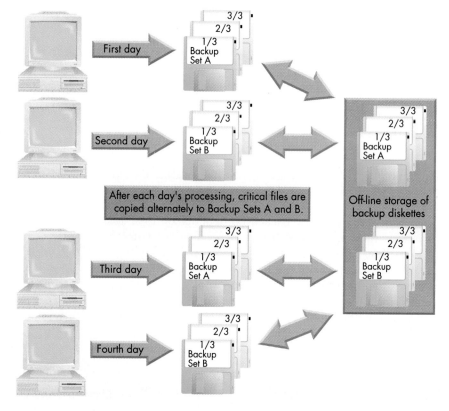

FIGURE 4–9 Diskette Backup Rotation: Two Backup Sets

After each day's processing, critical disk files are copied alternately to Backup Sets A and B. In this manner, one backup set (possibly several diskettes) is always current within a day's processing. If the critical work files and the most recent backup are accidentally destroyed, a third backup is current within two days' processing. Backup Sets A and B are alternated as the most current backup.

Peripherals Explorer

Some industry analysts have predicted that *optical laser disk* technology eventually may make magnetic disk and tape storage obsolete. With this technology, the read/write head used in magnetic storage is replaced by two lasers. One laser beam writes to the recording surface by scoring microscopic pits in the disk, and another laser reads the data from the light-sensitive recording surface. A light beam is easily deflected to the desired place on the optical disk, so a mechanical access arm is not needed.

Optical technology opens the door to new and exciting applications. Already, this technology is leading the way to the library of the future. Because the world's output of knowledge is doubling every four years, the typical library already is busting at the seams. It may be impractical to continue to build structures to warehouse printed materials. With declining budgets, perhaps the only long-term solutions for libraries is to move away from printed materials and toward knowledge in electronic format—possibly some form of optical disk. Perhaps in the not-too-distant future we will check out electronic books by downloading them from optical disk to our personal optical disk. In the library of the future, knowledge will be more readily available and complete. In theory, the library of the future will have every book and periodical ever written. And, a "book" will never be out on loan.

Optical laser disks are becoming a very inviting option for users. They are less sensitive to environmental fluctuations. And, they provide more direct-access storage at a cost that is much less per megabyte of storage than the magnetic disk alternative. Optical laser disk technology is still emerging and has yet to stabilize. At present there are three main categories of optical laser disks: *CD-ROM, WORM disks,* and *rewritable optical disks.*

The CD-ROM is the foundation technology for an explosion of multimedia applications. Multimedia kiosk information centers are popping up everywhere (left). The information provided by the interactive kiosks is frequently stored on CD-ROM. CD-ROMs have made it possible for us to enjoy motion video, audio, and sophisticated animation on our home PC (right).   Courtesy of International Business Machines Corporation/Courtesy of International Business Machines Corporation

Emerging Technology

CD-ROM Publishing: A New Approach to Publishing

A single CD-ROM can hold a massive amount of information, all of which is readily available to the user. A CD-ROM costs less to produce than a single newspaper, yet it can hold the information in a year's worth of newspapers. A CD-ROM can provide information in an interactive microcomputer format. This inexpensive mass-storage medium that offers interactivity with pizazz has not been overlooked by publishers.

CD-ROM Publishing Saves Money

Shearson Lehman Brothers, Inc. discovered it was paying more than $1 million using its PCs to access online financial information services that charge $20 to $400 an hour. Clearly, the company needed the data. An investment banker's recommendations are only as good as the data backing up those recommendations. But wasn't there a cheaper way to gather it? For Shearson Lehman and an increasing number of companies, research centers, universities, and libraries, CD-ROM publishing was the answer.

CD-ROM *publishing* refers to the collection and distribution of large financial, scientific, technical, legal, medical, and bibliographic databases, as well as reference works, catalogs, and manuals, on CD-ROM disks. Shearson Lehman's solution was to order a $30,000 subscription to One Source, a CD-ROM–based financial, business, and reference database from Lotus Development Corporation, which is updated weekly.

Information Service Offerings

One Source is just one of the more than 4000 databases offered on CD-ROM disks, often by the same information services that operate the online databases. Dialog Information Services, Inc., for example, offers many of its 400 databases both online and on CD-ROM. Other offerings include regularly updated databases on engineering developments, cancer research, and environmental issues surrounding pollution and hazardous wastes. Some of the databases contain bibliographic citations only; others contain the full text of articles, sometimes including all illustrations.

At many public libraries, the dogeared *Reader's Guide to Periodical Literature* has been replaced by workstations that sport a CD-ROM drive, an ink-jet printer, and InfoTrac, a service from Information Access Company. InfoTrac is a collection of CD-ROM–based indexes for more than 1100 popular magazines and journals; about 800 business, management, and trade journals; and such leading newspapers as *The New York Times* and *The Wall Street Journal*. Other InfoTrac CD-ROM disks let users retrieve financial and investment data.

CD-ROM–based databases are also available for specific industries. One example is Sabrevision, a national database for travel agencies that is updated quarterly.

Government Data on CD-ROM

CD-ROM publishing is proving invaluable to the U.S. government, which collects, maintains, and distributes the world's largest storehouse of information. Consider just one example from the U.S. Geological Survey's Geological Division, which maintains vast databases of satellite images of the earth for use by its scientists and by the public. The division once stored the database on 125-MB tapes; the price to the public was $2000 for each tape. The CD equivalent offers 680 MB of data for only $32 per disk.

Other government data available on CD-ROM disks include complete demographic data (from the U.S. Bureau of the Census); high-resolution displays of sonar-scanned oceanographic data (the product of a cooperative project between the U.S. Geological Survey, NOAA, and NASA); as well as CD-ROM disks on aquaculture, the Agent Orange defoliant, and acid rain (from the National Agricultural Library). And, over at the Library of Congress, the American Memory project is developing CD-ROM disks of sound recordings, book excerpts, manuscripts, photographs, and other primary source material that is organized around specific themes.

Magazines, Manuals, Catalogs, and Software

Magazines take on a new look when reformatted for multimedia. With a built-in audience, computer magazines such as *PC Magazine* and *Computerworld*, are leading the way into this new medium. Look for other mainline magazines to follow suit.

CD-ROM: *Moby Dick*, *Mozart*, and the *Daily Oklahoman*

History: Audio to Video   Introduced in 1980 for stereo buffs, the extraordinarily successful CD, or compact disk, is an optical laser disk designed to enhance the reproduction of recorded music. To make a CD recording, the analog sounds of music are translated into their digital equivalents and stored on a 4.72-inch optical laser disk. Seventy-four minutes of music can be recorded on each disk in digital format in 2 billion bits. (A bit is represented by the presence or absence of a pit on the optical disk.) With its tremendous storage capacity per square inch, computer industry entrepreneurs immediately recognized the potential of optical laser disk technology. In

Consulting and accounting firms have made the same discovery. Instead of sending auditors and consultants out with 20 pounds of printed, hard-to-search manuals, the firms now issue their staff CD-ROMs that can be used with multimedia-equipped laptop computers. The new systems cut printing costs as well as reduce the risk of mistakes that could lead to lawsuits.

Shop manuals and parts catalogs also lend themselves to CD-ROM publishing. The catalog from Intel Corporation, the major semiconductor manufacturer, delivers some 25,000 pages of technical data, wiring diagrams, schematics, and photographs to 300,000 design engineers worldwide. The massive amount of data can be stored on just two CD-ROM disks. Automobile and truck manufacturers also are providing parts catalogs to dealers on CD-ROM; the dealers find it faster and easier than going online to access a central mainframe. Retailers like CD-ROM–based catalogs because they can employ multimedia presentations to present thei products.

Many new commercial programs are also being shipped on CD-ROM disks to reduce the sheer number of magnetic disks required to deliver sophisticated programs. For example, Corel-Draw, Windows 95 Office, and Hijaak Pro are distributed on CD-ROM drive.

Reference Works

A representative title here is the *New Grolier Electronic Encyclopedia*, which packs all 21 volumes of *Grolier's Academic American Encyclopedia* onto a single CD-ROM disk. Like other CD-ROM titles, the encyclopedia includes audio excerpts, such as excerpts from famous speeches, musical passages, and the sounds of animals and birds. CD-ROMs that contain reference material are being created and updated every day. Reference CD-ROMs are available on a wide range of topics, including case law, pharmaceuticals, and the cinema. Whatever your special interest or occupation, there is a good chance that someone is planning on providing you with a reference CD-ROM to support your interest or occupation.

The Next Dimension in Publishing Traditional publishing (books) is sequential—one page after another. Publishing via CD-ROM lets the reader choose what comes next. The *PC Magazine CD,* shown here, is distributed each quarter. It contains the complete text of all issues of PC Magazine published during the past year. The CD-ROM also contains motion video, animation, and much more. Bill Gates' long awaited book, *The Road Ahead,* is published traditionally and on CD-ROM. The CD-ROM version includes the complete text with hundreds of hypertext links to further details (shown here) or multimedia presentations, a multimedia view of the future, an "Ask Bill" section, and much more.

effect, anything that can be digitized can be stored on optical laser disk: data, text, voice, still pictures, music, graphics, and motion video.

CD-ROM: The Technology   *CD-ROM,* a spinoff of audio CD technology, stands for *compact disk–read-only memory.* The name implies its application. Once inserted into the *CD-ROM drive,* the text, video images, and so on can be read into RAM for processing or display. However, the data on the disk are fixed—*they cannot be altered.* This is in contrast, of course, to the read/write capability of magnetic disks.

What makes CD-ROM so inviting is its vast capacity to store data and programs. The capacity of a single CD-ROM is up to 680 MB—about that of 477 DS/HD 3½-inch diskettes. To put the density of CD-ROM into perspective, the words in every book ever written could be stored on a hypothetical CD-ROM that is eight feet in diameter.

Optical Storage

Multimedia brings music to your PC. The Microsoft Multimedia Mozart CD-ROM lets you learn about the life of Wolfgang A. Mozart while enjoying his music.   Courtesy Microsoft

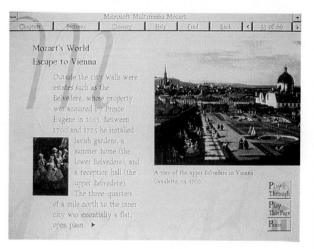

Magnetic disks store data in concentric tracks, each of which is divided into sectors (see Figure 4–5). The sectors on the inside tracks hold the same amount of information as those on the outside tracks. Although this wastes magnetic disk space, it optimizes the speed at which data can be written and retrieved because a magnetic disk spins at a constant speed. In contrast, CD-ROMs store data in a single track that spirals from the center to the outside edge (see Figure 4–10). The ultrathin track spirals around the disk thousands of times.

Data are recorded on the CD-ROM's reflective surface in the form of *pits* and *lands.* The pits are tiny reflective bumps that have been burned in with a laser. The lands are flat areas separating the pits. Together they record read-only binary (1s and 0s) information that can be interpreted by the computer as text, audio, images, and so on. Once the data have been recorded, a protective coating is applied to the reflective surface (the non-label side of a CD-ROM).

Popular CD-ROM drives are classified as double-spin, triple-spin, and quad-spin. These spin at two, three, and four times the speed of the original CD standard. The speed at which a given CD-ROM spins depends on the physical location of the data being read. The data passes over the movable laser detector at the same rate, no matter where the data are read. Therefore, the CD-ROM must spin more quickly when accessing data near the center.

The laser detector is analogous to the magnetic disk's read/write head. The relatively slow spin rates make the CD-ROM access time much slower than that of its magnetic cousins. A CD-ROM drive may take 10 to 50 times longer to ready itself to read the information. Once ready to read, the transfer rate also is much slower.

The introduction of *multidisk player/changers* enables ready access to vast amounts of online data. Like a compact disk audio player/changer, a desired CD-ROM disk is loaded to the CD-ROM disk drive under program control. These player/changers, sometimes called **jukeboxes,** can hold from 6 to more than 100 disks.

CD-ROM Applications   The tremendous amount of low-cost direct-access storage made possible by optical laser disks has opened the door to many new applications. Currently, most of the estimated 20,000 commercially produced CD-ROM disks contain reference material. This number is growing rapidly every year. The following is a sampling of available CD-ROM disks.

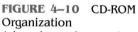

MEMORY BITS

Optical Laser Disk Technology

- CD-ROM (read only)
- CD-R (recordable)
- WORM disks (write once, read many)
- Rewritable optical disks

FIGURE 4–10   CD-ROM Organization
A laser beam detector interprets pits and lands, which represent bits (1s and 0s), located within the sectors in the spiraling track on the CD-ROM reflective surface.
Courtesy of Inernational Business Machines

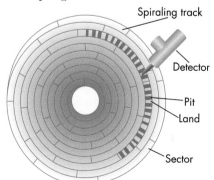

- *The New Groliers Multimedia Encyclopedia* (including text, thousands of stills, motion video sequences, and sounds)
- *The Oxford English Dictionary*
- *Microsoft Bookshelf* (dictionary, thesaurus, almanac, atlas, book of facts, and more)
- The 1990 U.S. Census (county level)
- The text of 450 titles (including *Moby Dick,* the *King James version of the Bible, Beowulf, The Odyssey,* and many more)

- Multilingual dictionaries (one disk contains translation dictionaries for 12 languages)
- Scientific writings for the Apple Macintosh
- *The Daily Oklahoman* newspaper (1981–1986)
- *Cinemania* (19,000 movie reviews from 1914 to 1991, actor biographies, movie stills, and more)
- *Great Cities of the World* (narratives, facts, photos, hotel and transportation information)
- *Space Quest IV* (space adventure game)
- Sound effects (thousands of sound clips)
- The Animals (multimedia zoo with 225 animals)
- World Atlas (thousands of maps and graphs, flags, audio of anthems, and more)
- *Desert Storm: The War in the Persian Gulf* (chronological multimedia presentation)

A few years ago, the price of recordable CD systems was about that of a luxury automobile. Today, this Pinnacle recordable CD system is priced for volume sales to both the consumer and commercial markets. The system gives users the capability to master their own CD-ROMs. Courtesy Pinnacle Micro

The cost of commercially produced CD-ROMs varies considerably from as little as $10 to several thousand dollars. Sales of commercial CD-ROM titles are doubling each year.

CD-ROM is the backbone of multimedia applications. Multimedia applications involve the integration of text, sound, graphics, motion video, and animation. Multimedia is discussed in detail in Chapter 9, "Graphics and Multimedia: Tickling Our Senses."

Creating CD-ROMs for Mass Distribution   During recording sessions, recording artists produce digital tapes of their work. The digital tape recordings are sent to a mastering facility that duplicates CDs for mass distribution. CD-ROMs are created in a similar manner. Most CD-ROMs are created by commercial enterprises and sold to the public for reference and multimedia applications. Application developers gather and create source material, then write the programs needed to integrate the material into a meaningful application. The resulting files are then sent to a mastering facility, often via magnetic tape. The master copy is duplicated, or "pressed," at the factory and the copies are distributed with their prerecorded contents (for example, the complete works of Shakespeare or the first 30 minutes of *Gone with the Wind*). Depending on the run quantity, the cost of producing and packaging a CD-ROM for sale can be less than a dollar apiece! CD-ROM is a very inexpensive way to distribute applications and information.

CD-R: Creating CD-ROMs Locally   Already more than half the world's PCs have CD-ROM drives. This rapid and universal acceptance of CD-ROM has given rise to an exciting new technology—**CD-R, compact disk-recordable.** A CD-R disk is functionally equivalent to a pre-recorded CD-ROM. A locally developed CD-R will play in any CD-ROM drive.

Locally produced CD-R disks are created on CD writers. **CD writers** are peripheral devices that can write once to a CD-R disk to create an audio CD or a CD-ROM. CD writers offer a low-cost alternative to the mastering of CD-ROMs. For under $2000, commercial enterprises can expand the capabilities of a PC to create one-of-a-kind CDs or CD-ROMs at a fraction of the cost of low-volume pressed disk manufacturing. A growing number of organizations are using CD-R and CD writers to create their own CD-ROMs, primarily for internal reference applications and for archiving. Many companies now produce CD-ROM sales manuals and update them quarterly. Sales manuals, which can span thousands of pages, are compressed to a single CD-ROM. Relatively inexpensive low-volume **CD production stations** are used to duplicate locally produced CD-ROMs.

Serendipitous Surfing: Sports

Comdisco, the world's largest independent computer-leasing company, uses an image processing system to store documents on optical disks for rapid, online retrieval. Documents on the system can be copied, viewed, printed, or faxed.   Courtesy of Harris Corporation

WORM Disks

Write once, read many optical laser disks, or **WORM disks,** are used by end user companies to store their own proprietary information. Like CD-ROMs, once the data have been written to the medium, they can only be read, not updated or changed. **WORM disk cartridges** can store greater volumes of information than CD-ROM. Typically, WORM applications involve image processing or archival storage. A single mainframe-based 200-gigabyte (GB) WORM disk can store more than 3 million digitized images the size of this page. A good example of an image processing application is an "electronic catalog." The retailer digitizes images of items for sale and stores these images for ready access on WORM disks. A customer can peruse a retailer's electronic catalog on a VDT, or perhaps a PC, and see the item while reading about it. And, with a few keystrokes the customer can order the item as well. The Library of Congress is using WORM technology to help alleviate a serious shelf-space problem. The pages of many books can be digitized and stored on a single WORM disk.

The WORM disk cartridge, which has a data storage life in excess of 30 years, provides an alternative to magnetic tape for archival storage. For example, one real estate company maintains a permanent record (digitized image) of all completed hardcopy transactions (contracts, deeds, and so on) on a PC-based WORM disk. A few WORM disk cartridges take up a lot less space than a row of file cabinets. The PC version of a WORM disk cartridge has a capacity of 600 MB.

Rewritable Optical Disks

Rewritable optical disks use several technologies, including **magneto-optical technology** (MO technology), to integrate optical and magnetic disk technology to enable read-*and*-write storage. The 5¼-inch rewritable disk cartridges can store up to 1 GB. However, the technology must be improved before the optical disks can be consid-

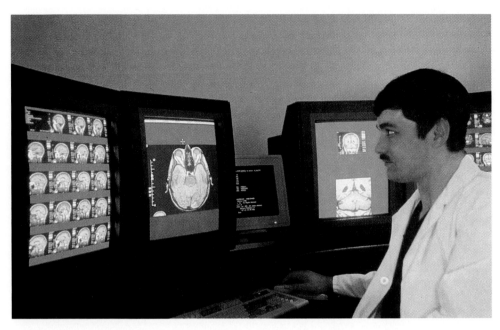

This image processing system is currently in use in a major hospital in Houston. Images resulting from radiological diagnostic procedures are stored online in an optical disk jukebox. Images are available for online retrieval on display stations located in radiology, intensive care, orthopedics, surgery, and many physician's offices. Placing the images online makes them more readily accessible and eliminates the need to generate expensive film.   Courtesy of E-Systems, Inc.

ered as a direct alternative to magnetic media. At present, rewritable optical disk drives are more expensive and less reliable than magnetic media. In addition, the disk-access times for rewritable optical disks are slow relative to magnetic media. For these reasons, most traditional information systems continue to rely on magnetic disks.

Rewritable optical disks are beginning to find their niche. Applications that call for large volumes of storage with relatively little update activity are made to order for rewritable optical disks. Also, applications that require hardware to operate in harsh environments may be candidates for rewritable optical disks. MO technology is very durable, able to withstand shock, magnetic fields, and a wide range of temperatures, from below freezing to 100 degrees Fahrenheit. Magnetic storage media may malfunction under less than ideal conditions. As optical laser disk technology matures to offer reliable, cost-effective read/write operation, it eventually may dominate secondary storage in the future as magnetic disks and tape do today.

4–7   STORAGE FORECAST: IS THERE A DISK IN YOUR FUTURE?

Storage is like money: No matter how much you have, you always want more. Each year, improvements are made in existing secondary storage devices as the storage industry strives to meet our craving for more storage.

Some scientists believe that holographic technology may give users everything they want in a storage device. Holographic memory systems enable the stacking of data on the recording surface. The different layers are read by changing the angle of the laser beam used for reading the data. Holographic memory systems will enable the entire Encyclopedia Britannica to be stored in a space the size and thickness of a penny.

Rotating storage may go the way of the steam engine when low-cost solid-state memory can store as much in less space. If nonvolatile chip technology continues to improve at the current pace, the entire Encyclopedia Britannica will fit into 8 tiny memory chips in the near future. Already, flash memory chips are being developed that will have 16 times more storage capacity than the largest flash chips currently available. The 30-MB flash memory chips could be used in place of hard drives in portable PCs. Perhaps someday the only moving parts on PCs will be the keyboard, the mouse, and the cooling fan. It's not unreasonable to expect 1 GB of flash memory in a PC by the end of the decade. If this happens, rotating storage may be relegated to archival storage.

What does being able to store more information in less space mean to you? It means videophones that can be worn like wristwatches. It means that you can carry a diskette-sized reader and all your college "textbooks" in your front pocket. We can expect at least one big leap in storage technology by the end of the century. That leap will forever change much of what we do and how we do it.

IMPORTANT TERMS AND SUMMARY OUTLINE

4–1 SECONDARY STORAGE AND FILES: DATA KEEPERS Data and programs are stored in **secondary storage** for permanent storage. **Magnetic disk drives** and **magnetic tape drives** are the primary devices for secondary storage. **Optical laser disk** technology is emerging as an alternative to magnetic disks and magnetic tapes.

The **file** is the foundation of permanent storage on a computer system. Popular file types include the **ASCII file, data file, document file, spreadsheet file, source program file, executable program file, graphics file, audio file,** and **video file.**

In the MS-DOS/Windows environment, *filenames* can be up to eight characters with an optional three-character *extension* (for example, *myphoto.bmp*).

Everything we do on a computer has to do with a file and, therefore, secondary storage. We can create, copy, move, retrieve, print, execute, download, **export, import,** compress, and protect files. **File compression** is used to economize on storage space.

4–2 SEQUENTIAL AND DIRECT ACCESS: NEW TERMS FOR OLD CONCEPTS Data are retrieved and manipulated either sequentially or randomly. Magnetic disk drives enable **random-** and **sequential-processing** capabilities. Magnetic tapes have only sequential-processing capabilities.

4–3 MAGNETIC DISKS: ROUND AND ROUND The two most popular types of **interchangeable magnetic disks** are the 5¼-inch and 3½-inch **diskettes** (or **floppy disks**). The microcomputer **fixed magnetic disk** is also called a hard disk. The multifunction **floptical disk drive (zip disk drive)** provides high-volume storage capacity on interchangeable diskettes.

In **sector organization,** the recording surface is divided into pie-shaped **sectors,** and each sector is assigned a number. Data are stored via serial representation in **tracks** on each recording surface. The spacing of tracks is measured in **tracks per inch,** or **TPI.** A particular **cylinder** refers to every track with the same number on all recording surfaces. **Disk density** refers to the number of bits that can be stored per unit of area on the disk-face surface. A particular set of data stored on a disk is assigned a **disk address** that designates its physical location (disk-face surface, track, sector). An **access arm** with one or more **read/write heads** is moved to the appropriate track to retrieve the data.

Before a disk can be used, it must be **formatted.** Formatting creates *sectors* and *tracks* into which data are stored and establishes an area for the **file allocation table (FAT).**

The **access time** for a magnetic disk is the interval between the instant a computer makes a request for transfer of data from a disk-storage device to RAM and the instant this operation is completed.

The **data transfer rate** is the rate at which data are read from (written to) secondary storage to (from) RAM. **Disk caching** enhances system performance.

Apply the dictates of common sense to the care of diskettes: Avoid excessive dust, avoid extremes in temperature and humidity, and don't fold, spindle, or mutilate the disks.

In the mainframe environment, **direct-access storage devices (DASDs)** are the prerequisite for virtually all information systems that demand direct-access processing.

A **computer virus** is a program that literally "infects" other programs and databases upon contact. Three primary sources of computer viruses are electronic bulletin-board systems, diskettes, and computer networks. Antiviral programs, also called *vaccines,* exist to help fight viruses.

4–4 MAGNETIC TAPE: RIBBONS OF DATA Today, magnetic tape storage is no longer used for routine processing; however, it has three other important functions. It is used as a backup medium, for archiving files, and for file portability between computers.

A **magnetic tape cartridge** (also called **data cartridge**) is loaded to a tape drive, where data can be read or written. The physical nature of the magnetic tape results in data being stored and accessed sequentially.

One of the most popular PC tape cartridge formats is the QIC minicartridge. A tape drive is rated by its *storage capacity* and its *data transfer rate.*

Drives for ¼-inch tape cartridges, often called **tape backup units (TBUs),** store data in a **serpentine** manner. Data are recorded in tracks using **serial representation.**

4–5 BACKUP: BETTER SAFE THAN SORRY The frequency with which a work disk is backed up depends on its volatility. It is common practice to maintain two generations of backup. Three common backup methods are full backup, selective backup of files, or backup of modified files only.

4–6 OPTICAL LASER DISKS: HIGH-DENSITY STORAGE Optical laser disk storage is capable of storing vast amounts of data. The three main categories of optical laser disks are **CD-ROM, WORM disk,** and **rewritable optical disk.**

A CD-ROM is inserted into the CD-ROM drive for processing. Most of the commercially produced read-only CD-ROM disks contain reference material or support multimedia applications. Multidisk player/changers are called **jukeboxes.**

A **compact disk-recordable (CD-R)** disk is functionally equivalent to a pre-recorded CD-ROM. Locally produced CD-R disks are created on **CD writers.** Relatively inexpensive low-volume **CD production stations** are used to duplicate locally produced CD-ROMs.

WORM disks are used by end user companies to store their own proprietary information. **WORM disk cartridges** can store greater volumes of information than CD-ROM. WORM applications involve image processing or archival storage.

Rewritable optical disks use **magneto-optical technology** to integrate optical and magnetic disk technology to enable read-*and*-write storage.

The choice of which technologies to choose for a system or an application is often a trade-off between storage capacity and cost (dollars per megabyte).

4–7 STORAGE FORECAST: IS THERE A DISK IN YOUR FUTURE? Each year, improvements are made in existing secondary storage devices as the storage industry strives to meet our craving for more storage.

REVIEW EXERCISES

Concepts

1. What are other names for diskette and direct processing?
2. Name and briefly describe four types of files.
3. What advantages will the Windows 95 operating system have over MS-DOS with respect to naming files?

4. Describe file compression and why it might be used.

5. CD-ROM is a spinoff of what technology?

6. A program issues a "read" command for data to be retrieved from a magnetic tape. Describe the resulting movement of the data.

7. Why must hard disks and diskettes be formatted?

8. What are the three main categories of optical laser disks?

9. What is the width of the magnetic tape in the QIC minicartridge?

10. List three topic areas available on CD-ROM.

11. What name is given to programs intended to damage the computer system of an unsuspecting victim? Name three sources of these.

12. Although magnetic tape storage is no longer used for routine processing, list two other functions it may serve.

Discussion and Problem Solving

13. A floppy disk does not move until a read or write command is issued. Once it is issued, the floppy begins to spin. It stops spinning after the command is executed. Why is a hard disk pack not set in motion in the same manner? Why is a floppy not made to spin continuously?

14. Every Friday night a company makes backup copies of all master files and programs. Why is this necessary? The company has both tape and disk drives. Which storage medium would you suggest for the backup? Why?

15. Describe the potential impact of optical laser disk technology on public and university libraries. On home libraries.

16. How many 250-MB QIC minicartridges would be needed to back up the contents of a 4-GB hard disk?

17. Describe at least two applications where rewritable optical laser disk would be preferred over hard disk for storage.

SELF-TEST (BY SECTION)

4–1 **a.** Data are retrieved from temporary secondary storage and stored permanently in RAM. (T/F)

b. An _____ file is a text-only file that can be read or created by any word processing program or text editor.

c. A *file* is to *secondary storage* as a *vehicle* is to a *parking lot*. (T/F)

d. WINTER.SALES and .ADD are valid filenames in the MS-DOS/Windows environment. (T/F)

e. When we _____ a file, we convert a file in the current program to a format needed by another program.

4–2 Magnetic disks have both _____- and _____-access capabilities.

4–3 **a.** The _____ disk drive uses optical technology together with magnetic technology to read and write to 120-MB diskettes as well as the standard 3½-inch diskettes.

b. In a disk drive, the read/write heads are mounted on an access arm. (T/F)

c. Interchangeable disks cannot be stored offline. (T/F)

d. The standard sizes for magnetic diskettes are _____ inch and _____ inch.

e. What percentage of the data on a magnetic disk is available to the system with each complete revolution of the disk: (a) 10%, (b) 50%, or (c) 100%?

f. The _____ _____ denotes the physical location of a particular file or set of data on a magnetic disk.

4–4 **a.** When activated, which tape backup unit feature results in increased capacity on the data cartridge: (a) data compression, (b) data reduction, or (c) tape stretching?

b. Tape backup units store data on tape cartridges in a _____ manner.

4–5 The frequency with which a work disk is backed up depends on its volatility. (T/F)

4–6 **a.** _____ _____ _____ storage technology uses laser beams to write to the recording surface.

b. CD-ROM is read-only. (T/F)

c. Disks that use magneto-optical technology are: (a) rewritable, (b) read-only, or (c) write-only?

d. CD writers are peripheral devices that can write once to a WORM disk. (T/F)

Self-test Answers. **4–1 (a)** *F;* **(b)** ASCII; **(c)** T; **(d)** F; **(e)** export. **4–2** random, sequential. **4–3 (a)** floptical (zip); **(b)** T; **(c)** F; **(d)** 5¼, 3½; **(e)** c; **(f)** disk address **4–4. (a)** a; **(b)** serpentine. **4–5** T. **4–6 (a)** Optical laser disk; **(b)** T; **(c)** a; **(d)** F.

CHAPTER 5

Input/Output: Computers in Action

Courtesy of Canon Computer Systems, Inc.

Let's Talk

The following conversation introduces many of the terms in this chapter. Read it now, then again after you have read the chapter.

The Scene:
A sales representative (Zeta) specializing in the sale of grocery store technology is calling on the vice president for operations (Paul) for an East Coast grocery chain.

Paul: Hello, Zeta. We don't want any more **speech synthesis** devices!

Zeta: I know, Paul. The **voice recognition** feedback at the cash registers didn't take off here or anywhere else. But what I have today is already in demand.

Paul: Let's see it.

Zeta: Let's see *them,* Paul. I've got two new products. First is a hand-held **scanner** with a **badge reader** for use by customers in a hurry and by those who have trouble walking through the store. Customers insert their **smart card** for ID purposes. Then, rather than picking items from the shelves, they simply **scan** the **bar code** of the desired item and continue shopping. On their way out, customers drop off their scanners and their contents are entered into the system. How about that for **source data automation?**

Paul: But what about the groceries?

Zeta: Well, the customer's account is charged, and an aisle-by-aisle list is printed for one of your professional shoppers. The order is gathered and boxed for pickup or delivery.

Paul: Sounds interesting. What's the other product?

Zeta: A **multimedia** kiosk that helps customers find what they need. An easy-to-use **trackball** lets customers move the cursor around a **Super VGA monitor,** which has a 1280 by 1024 **resolution** and a .28 **dot pitch.** A quiet **ink-jet printer** provides hard-copy output, mainly shopping lists and coupons.

Paul: So what's the value of the kiosk?

Zeta: For starters, the kiosk eliminates a thousand "Where is this?" questions each day, but it has many other benefits.

Paul: You've got my attention; tell me more.

STUDENT LEARNING OBJECTIVES

▶ *To explain alternative approaches to and devices for providing input to a system.*

▶ *To describe the operation and application of common output devices.*

▶ *To describe the use and characteristics of the different types of terminals.*

5–1 I/O DEVICES: LET'S INTERFACE

Data are created in many places and in many ways. Before data can be processed and stored, they must be translated into a form the computer can interpret. For this, we need *input* devices. Once the data have been processed, they must be translated back into a form we can understand. For this, we need *output* devices. These input/output (I/O) peripheral devices enable communication between us and the computer.

Just about everyone routinely communicates directly or indirectly with a computer, even people who have never sat in front of a personal computer or video display terminal. Perhaps you have had one of these experiences.

▶ Have you ever been hungry and short of cash? It's lunch time and you have only 47 cents in your pocket. No problem. Just stop at an automatic teller machine (ATM) and ask for some "lunch money." The ATM's keyboard (input) and monitor (output) enable you to hold an interactive conversation with the bank's computer. The ATM's printer (output) provides you with a hard copy of your transactions when you leave. Some ATMs talk to you as well (output).

▶ Have you ever called a mail-order merchandiser and been greeted by a message like this: "Thank you for calling BrassCo Enterprises Customer Service. If you wish to place an order, press one. If you wish to inquire about the status of an order, press two. To speak to a particular person, enter that person's four-digit extension or hold and an operator will process your call momentarily." The message is produced by a voice-response system—an output device. Your telephone and its key pad serve as an input device.

As you can see, input/output devices are quietly playing an increasingly significant role in our lives.

In this chapter we discuss *common* I/O devices and terminals with I/O capabilities. The number and variety of I/O devices is expanding as you read this, some of which are not so common. For example, AromaScan markets an electronic nose that can measure and digitally record smells. Perhaps the AromaScan smelling device will revolutionize aroma analysis in the food, drink, and perfume industries. Its cost, which is about the same as a BMW, may force us to do our sniffing the old-fashioned way.

5–2 TRADITIONAL INPUT DEVICES: KEY, POINT, AND DRAW

The Keyboard

There are two basic types of keyboards: the traditional alphanumeric keyboard and special-function keyboards.

Alphanumeric Keyboards: 12345 and QWERTY All PCs, workstations, and VDTs have a keyboard, the mainstay device for user input to the computer system. One of the most widely used keyboard layouts is the 101-key keyboard with the traditional *QWERTY* key layout, 12 function keys, a key pad, a variety of special-function keys, and dedicated cursor-control keys. PC, workstation, and VDT keyboards vary con-

There are many ways to interact with a computer system. While preparing a presentation, this medical consultant will use many of the input/output (I/O) devices discussed in this chapter.
Courtesy of Eastman Kodak Company

siderably in appearance. Portable computers have a simple QWERTY keyboard with a minimum number of function keys. Desktop computers are frequently configured with a 124-key PC keyboard that includes an extended set of function keys and extra unlabeled keys that can be programmed to perform user-defined keystroke sequences (macros) when tapped. Chapter 3, "Software: Telling Computers What to Do," contains detailed information on working with keyboards.

Special-Function Keyboards: Tap the French Fry Key Some keyboards are designed for specific applications. For example, the cash-register-like terminals at most fast-food restaurants have special-purpose keyboards. Rather than key in the name and price of an order of French fries, attendants need only press the key marked "French fries" to record the sale. These keyboards help shop supervisors, airline ticket agents, retail sales clerks, and many others interact more quickly with their computer systems.

Point-and-Draw Devices

The mouse and its cousins enable us to point to objects on the screen and to draw.

Mighty Mouse The keyboard is too cumbersome for some applications, especially those that rely on a graphical user interface (GUI) or require the user to point or draw. The effectiveness of GUIs depends on the user's ability to make a rapid selection from a screen full of graphic icons or menus. In these instances the mouse can position the pointer (graphics cursor) over an icon quickly and efficiently. The mouse and its operation are discussed in Chapter 3. Computer artists use mice to create images. Engineers use them to "draw" lines that connect points on a graph.

Mouse Cousins: Other Point-and-Draw Devices For the moment, the mouse remains the most popular point-and-draw device. However, a variety of devices are available that move the graphics cursor to point and draw, each with its advantages and disadvantages. Some desktop and tower PC users prefer the *joystick, trackball, mouse pen,* or the *digitizer tablet and pen.*

▶ *Joystick.* Video arcade wizards are no doubt familiar with the joystick and trackball. The **joystick** is a vertical stick that moves the graphics cursor in the direction the stick is pushed.

▶ *Trackball.* The **trackball** is a ball inset in a small external box or adjacent to and in the same unit as the keyboard. Trackballs are often configured with portable computers and workstations. The ball is "rolled" with the fingers to

Point-of-sale (POS) terminals at retail establishments, such as the one at this sound and video store, are usually equipped with special-function keyboards that enable rapid processing of sales transactions as well as alphanumeric input. Courtesy of International Business Machines Corporation

move the graphics cursor. Some people find it helpful to think of a trackball as an upside-down mouse with a bigger ball on the bottom.

▶ *Mouse pen.* The **mouse pen** is rolled across the desktop like a mouse and held like a pen.

▶ *Digitizer tablet and pen.* The **digitizer tablet and pen** are a pen and a pressure-sensitive tablet with the same *X–Y* coordinates as the screen. Some digitizing tablets also use a crosshair device instead of a pen. The movement of the pen or crosshair is reproduced simultaneously on the display screen. When configured with a PC, the digitizer tablet and pen enables the user to perform pen-based computing applications, such as drawing and entering handwritten data to the system.

To maintain maximum portability, laptop PCs are configured with trackballs and other devices that can be built into the unit, such as *trackpoints* and *trackpads*.

▶ *Trackpoints.* **Trackpoints** are usually positioned in or near a laptop's keyboard. They function like miniature joysticks but are operated with the tip of the finger.

▶ *Trackpads.* The **trackpad** has no moving parts. Simply move your finger about a touch-sensitive pad to move the graphics cursor.

Figure 5–1 provides a visual overview of point-and-draw devices.

Peripheral Explorer

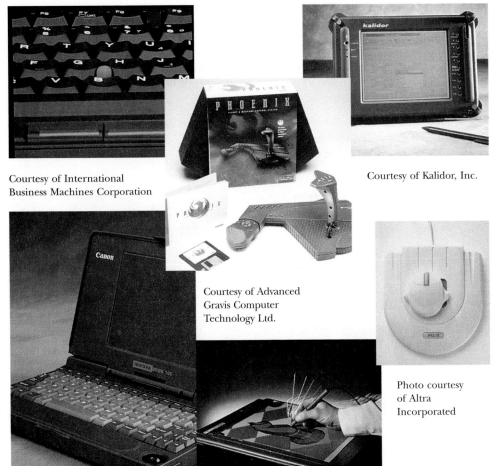

Courtesy of International Business Machines Corporation

Courtesy of Kalidor, Inc.

Courtesy of Advanced Gravis Computer Technology Ltd.

Photo courtesy of Altra Incorporated

Courtesy of Canon Computer Systems, Inc.

Photo courtesy of Altra Incorporated

FIGURE 5–1 Point-and-Draw Devices
This photo collage demonstrates the variety of ways we can point, draw, and click. The trackpoint is conveniently located within the keyboard (*top, left*). The digitizer tablet and pen is used by artists (*bottom, right*). The Phoenix Flight & Weapons Control System (joystick, *center*) is designed specifically for PC action games and flight simulation programs. Altra's Felix lets you move anywhere on the screen while moving its handle no more than an inch in any direction (*center, right*). The pen is used with this rugged Kalidor pen-based computer to enter information (*top, right*). This Canon notebook PC comes with a trackball (*bottom, left*).

5-3 SOURCE-DATA AUTOMATION: GETTING CLOSER TO THE ACTION

Data Entry Trend: Going Direct

The trend in data entry has been toward decreasing the number of transcription steps. This is accomplished by entering the data as close to the source as possible. For example, in most sales departments, salespeople key in orders directly to the system. In many accounting departments, bookkeepers and accountants record and enter financial transactions into the system from their PC or VDT keyboards. However, in many data entry situations, key entry transcription can be eliminated altogether. This is known as **source-data automation.**

Until recently, data entry has been synonymous with *keystrokes*. The keystroke will continue to be the basic mode of data entry for the foreseeable future, but the need for key-driven data entry has been eliminated in many applications. For example, you have probably noticed the preprinted **bar codes** on consumer products. At checkout counters these bar codes have eliminated the need for most key entry. Checkers need only pass the product over the *laser scanner*. The price is entered and the shelf inventory is updated as well.

Data entry is an area in which enormous potential exists for increases in productivity. The technology of data entry devices is constantly changing. New and improved methods of transcribing raw data are being invented and put on the market each month. These data entry methods and associated devices are discussed next.

Scanners: Making Hard Copy Soft

A variety of **scanners** read and interpret information on printed matter and convert it to a format that can be interpreted by a computer, primarily encoded alphanumeric characters and digitized images.

OCR and Bar Codes: Seeing Is Believing OCR (**optical character recognition**) is the ability to read printed information into a computer system. Bar codes represent alphanumeric data by varying the size of adjacent vertical lines. The United

Courtesy of Norand Corporation

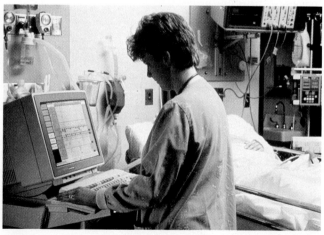

Photo courtesy of Hewlett-Packard Company

The trend in data entry is to enter data as close to the source as possible. This store clerk enters inventory data directly to a hand-held computer. The hand-held computer is networked to the store's main computer via a wireless link. Bedside terminals enable doctors and nurses to enter patient data at the source. Doctors order blood tests, schedule operating rooms, and review medical records while interacting with the hospital's computer system.

States Postal Service relies on OCR and bar code scanning to sort most mail. At the Postal Service, light-sensitive scanners read and interpret the ZIP code and POSTNET bar code on billions of envelopes each day. The ZIP information is then sent to computer-based sorting machines that route the envelopes to appropriate bins for distribution.

Scanners, such as those in supermarkets, use lasers to interpret the bar codes printed on products. Just as there are a variety of internal bit encoding systems, there are a variety of bar-coding systems. Compare the POSTNET bar codes on metered mail with those on packing labels with those on consumer products. One of the most visible bar-coding systems is the Universal Product Code (UPC). The UPC, originally used for supermarket items, is now being printed on other consumer goods. The advantage of bar codes over OCR is that the position or orientation of the code being read is not as critical to the scanner. In a supermarket, for example, the UPC can be recorded even when a bottle of ketchup is rolled over the laser scanner.

OCR and Bar Code Scanners and Applications

Two types of OCR and bar code scanners—*contact* and *laser*—read information on labels and various types of documents. Both bounce a beam of light off an image, then measure the reflected light to interpret the image. Hand-held contact scanners make contact as they are brushed over the printed matter to be read. Laser-based scanners are more versatile and can read data passed near the scanning area. Scanners of both technologies can recognize printed characters and various types of bar codes. Scanners used for OCR and bar code applications can be classified into three basic categories.

▶ *Hand-held label scanners.* These devices read data on price tags, shipping labels, inventory part numbers, book ISBNs, and the like. Hand-held label scanners, sometimes called **wand scanners,** utilize either contact or laser technology. You have probably seen both types used in various retail stores. Wand scanners also are used to read package labels in shipping and receiving and in inventory management.

▶ *Stationary label scanners.* These devices, which rely exclusively on laser technology, are used in the same types of applications as wand scanners. Stationary scanners are common in grocery stores and discount stores.

▶ *Document scanners.* Document scanners are capable of scanning documents of varying sizes. Document scanners read envelopes at the U.S. Postal Office. They read turnaround documents for utility companies. A **turnaround document** is *computer-produced output* that we can read and is ultimately returned as *computer-readable input* to a computer system. For example, when you pay your utility bills, you return a check and a stub for the invoice (the turnaround document). The stub is scanned and payment information is entered automatically to the utility company's system.

Federal Express couriers and handlers use the Super-Tracker, a hand-held OCR data collection device, to track the progress of packages from source to destination. Package status information, such as pickup or delivery times, is transmitted directly to the company's centralized database through the DADS (Digitally Assisted Dispatch System) units in the courier vans and sorting facilities. *Courtesy of Federal Express Corporation.*

Warehouse employees use wand scanners to assist them in materials handling and inventory management jobs. *Courtesy Intermec*

MEMORY BITS

Input Devices

- Keyboard
- Point-and-draw devices
- Scanners
- Image scanners (*page* and *hand*)
- Badge reader (for magnetic stripes and smart cards)
- Speeech-recognition systems
- Vision-input systems
- Digital cameras
- Hand-held data entry devices

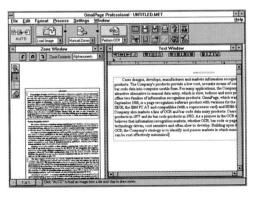

The key to successful character recognition is the software. The hard work begins once the scanner scans the image into the PC for processing. OCR software, such as OmniPage Professional shown here, interprets the image (left) and displays the recognized text (right). OmniPage Professional and other OCR packages have enabled businesses to convert an avalanche of paper into usable electronic text. *Courtesy of Caere Corporation*

Photo courtesy of Hewlett-Packard Company

Photo courtesy of Hewlett-Packard Company

Courtesy of Caere Corporation

Relatively inexpensive image scanners have given rise to a variety of image processing applications. Here (top), a graphic artist scans an image into the system on a page scanner. The inexpensive paper-driven scanner in the middle scans full pages as well. In the bottom photo, a manager uses a hand scanner to convert text in a magazine into electronic text that can be inserted into a word processing document.

Scanner technology has spawned an explosion of source-data automation applications. One of the more innovative uses of stationary scanners is along toll roads. Drivers who frequently use a particular toll road pay tolls in advance and receive labels for their cars. Stationary scanners along the toll road read the labels as cars pass at highway speeds. The electronic toll booths transmit the data directly to a central computer system. At the central site, the drivers' accounts are debited the amount of the toll.

Some professors rely on wand scanners in the classroom during multimedia-based presentations. Bar codes strategically placed throughout their lecture notes identify specific multimedia presentations. Within seconds after a professor scans a bar code, an image, an animation, a motion video, a text chart, or a pop quiz is displayed. Imagine seeing a "pop quiz" before the professor finishes the announcement!

Most retail stores and distribution warehouses, and all overnight couriers, are seasoned users of scanner technology. Salespeople, inventory management personnel, and couriers would much prefer to wave their "magic" wands than enter data one character at a time.

Image Scanners and Processing   Source-data automation allows direct entry of graphic information, as well as text-based information, via scanners. An **image scanner** uses laser technology to scan and **digitize** an image. The hard-copy image is scanned and translated into an electronic format that can be interpreted by and stored on computers. The image to be scanned can be a photograph, a drawing, an insurance form, a medical record—anything that can be digitized. Once an image has been digitized and entered to the computer system, it can be retrieved, displayed, altered, merged with text, stored, sent via data communications to one or several remote computers, and even faxed. This application, known as **image processing,** is experiencing rapid growth. As a result, image scanners may become a must-have peripheral in most offices.

Page and Hand Image Scanners.   Image scanners are of two types: *page* and *hand.* Either can be gray scale (the image is presented in shades of gray) or color. (Gray scale is discussed later in this chapter.) The *page image scanner* works like a desktop duplicating machine. That is, the image to be scanned is placed face down on the scanning surface, covered, then scanned. The result is a high-resolution digitized image. The *hand image scanner* is rolled manually over the image to be scanned. Because it must be guided across the image by the human hand, the resolution of a hand image scanner is not as high. Hand image scanners, about five inches in width, are appropriate for capturing small images or portions of large images.

Image scanners also scan and interpret the alphanumeric characters on regular printed pages. People use page scanners to translate printed hard copy to computer-readable format. For applications that demand this type of translation, page scanners can minimize or eliminate the need for key entry. Today's image scanners and the accompanying OCR software are very sophisticated. Together they can read and interpret the characters from most printed material, such as a printed letter or a page from this book.

Image Processing: Eliminating the Paper Pile.   Companies and even individuals are becoming buried in paper, literally. In some organizations, paper files take up most of the floor space. Moreover, finding what you want may take several minutes to hours. Or, you may never find what you want. Image processing applications scan and index thousands, even millions, of documents. Once these scanned documents are on the computer system they can be easily retrieved and manipulated. For example, banks use image processing to archive canceled checks and to archive documents associated with mortgage loan servicing. Insurance companies use image processing in claims processing applications.

Images are scanned into a digital format that can be stored on disk, often optical laser disk because of its huge capacity. For example, decades worth of hospital medical records can be reduced to optical laser disks that fit easily on a single shelf. The images are organized so they can be retrieved in seconds rather than minutes or hours. Medical personnel who wish a hard copy can simply print the image (a couple of seconds).

The State of Louisiana Department of Public Safety routinely supplies driver information to other state agencies and to outside organizations, such as insurance companies. The Department of Public Safety has the dual problem of keeping up with thousands of documents received each week and with servicing thousands of requests for driver information, mostly for problem drivers. Because this department has gone to image processing for driver information, other state agencies have direct access to the image bank over communication lines and the department has no trouble handling outside requests for information. So far, over 2000 terminals have been installed to fight the paper battle. The department's long-range plan calls for using image processing to minimize or eliminate paper and microfilm in as many applications as possible.

At this hospital, medical records are being converted to electronic images that are more easily stored, maintained, and retrieved than manual paper documents. Image processing is a natural application for medical records keeping. Courtesy of International Business Machines Corporation

The real beauty of image processing is that the material on digitized images can be easily manipulated. For example, any image can be easily faxed (without being printed) to another location. A fax is sent and received as an image. The content on the fax or any image can be manipulated. OCR software can be used to translate any printed text on the image to an electronic format. For example, a doctor might wish to pull selected printed text from various patient images into a word processing document to compile a summary of a patient's condition. The doctor can even select specific graphic images (X-rays, photos, or drawings) from the patient's record for inclusion in the summary report.

Magnetic Stripes and Smart Cards: Just Say Charge It

The magnetic stripes on the back of charge cards and badges offer another means of data entry at the source. The magnetic stripes are encoded with data appropriate for the application. For example, your account number and privacy code are encoded on a card for automatic teller machines.

Magnetic stripes contain much more data per unit of space than do printed characters or bar codes. Moreover, because they cannot be read visually, they are perfect for storing confidential data, such as a privacy code. Employee cards and security badges often contain authorization data for access to physically secured areas, such as the computer center. To gain access, an employee inserts a card or badge into a **badge reader.** This device reads and checks the authorization code before permitting the individual to enter a secured area. When badge readers are linked to a central computer, a chronological log of people entering or leaving secured areas can be maintained.

The enhanced version of cards with a magnetic stripe is called the **smart card.** The smart card, similar in appearance to other cards, contains a microprocessor that retains certain security and personal data in its memory at all times. Because the smart card can hold more information, has some processing capability, and is almost impossible to duplicate, smart cards may soon replace cards with magnetic stripes. Already, smart cards are being widely used in Europe and in parts of the United States.

Speech Processing: Getting on Speaking Terms with Computers

Speech-recognition systems can be used to enter certain kinds and quantities of data. Successful speech-recognition systems are limited to accepting words and tasks within

Serendipitous Surfing:
Reference

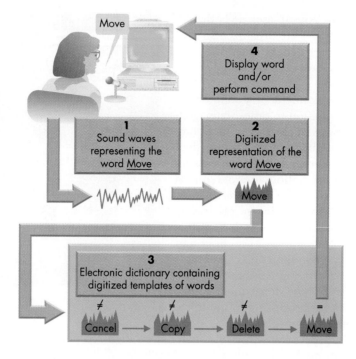

FIGURE 5–2 Speech Recognition
The sound waves created by the spoken word *Move* are digitized by the computer. The digitized template is matched against templates of other words in the electronic dictionary. When the computer finds a match, it displays a written version of the word.

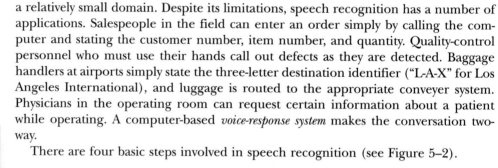

a relatively small domain. Despite its limitations, speech recognition has a number of applications. Salespeople in the field can enter an order simply by calling the computer and stating the customer number, item number, and quantity. Quality-control personnel who must use their hands call out defects as they are detected. Baggage handlers at airports simply state the three-letter destination identifier ("L-A-X" for Los Angeles International), and luggage is routed to the appropriate conveyer system. Physicians in the operating room can request certain information about a patient while operating. A computer-based *voice-response system* makes the conversation two-way.

There are four basic steps involved in speech recognition (see Figure 5–2).

1. *Say the word.* When you speak into a microphone, each sound is broken down into its various frequencies.
2. *Digitize the word.* The sounds in each frequency are digitized so they can be manipulated by the computer. Speech-recognition systems actually recognize *phonemes,* unique sounds that are the basic building blocks of speech. Speech-recognition software identifies the phonemes and groups them into words.
3. *Match the word.* The digitized version of the word is matched against similarly formed *templates* in the system's electronic dictionary. The digitized template is a form that can be stored and interpreted by computers (in 1s and 0s).
4. *Display the word or perform the command.* When a match is found, the word is displayed on a VDT or the appropriate command is performed (for example, "move" the marked text). In some cases, the word is displayed or repeated by a speech synthesizer for confirmation. If no match is found, the speaker is asked to repeat the word.

If you were to purchase a speech-recognition system for your PC, you would receive software, a generic vocabulary database, and a high-quality microphone with noise-canceling capabilities. The vocabulary may be only a few hundred words to enable navigation around Windows (exit, copy, drag mouse, and so on) and spreadsheets, or it may be 100,000 words for legal or medical dictation. Once you have installed the hardware and software, you would need to train the system to recognize your unique

The magnetic stripe on the back of your credit card opens the door to many applications. Not only can you obtain instant cash from automatic teller machines all over the world, but you can purchase a growing number of products and services by simply inserting your card in a badge reader. For example, thousands of gasoline service stations are now totally self-service, including self pay.
Phillips Petroleum Company

speech patterns. We all sound different, even to a computer. To train the system, we simply talk to it for at least 20 minutes—the longer the better. Even if we say a word twice in succession, it will probably have a different inflection or nasal quality. The system uses artificial intelligence techniques to learn our speech patterns and update the vocabulary database accordingly. The typical speech-recognition system never stops learning, for it is always fine-tuning the vocabulary so it can recognize words with greater speed and accuracy. Each user on a given PC would need to customize his or her own vocabulary database. Some speech-recognition systems are smart enough to recognize the speaker and switch to that person's customized vocabulary database for speech interpretation. To further customize our personal vocabulary database, we can add words that are unique to our working environment.

Most of the successes in speech recognition will be with *speaker-dependent systems.* For example, four doctors in a urology clinic might use speech recognition to dictate patient information. Each doctor would need to create a custom vocabulary database. *Speaker-independent speech-recognition systems* are much more limited. The size of the vocabulary database shrinks with the addition of each potential user. A speaker-independent system with about a 1000-word vocabulary can be effective as long as potential speakers know which 1000 words to use.

It is only a matter of time before we all will be communicating with our PCs in spoken English rather than through time-consuming keystrokes. Already thousands of attorneys, doctors, journalists, and others who routinely do dictation and write are enjoying the benefits of speech recognition. Speech recognition is also a tremendous enabling technology for the physically challenged.

Vision-Input Systems: Computer Eyes

The simulation of human senses, especially vision, is extremely complex. A computer does not actually see and interpret an image the way a human being does. A camera is needed to give computers "eyesight." To create the database, a vision system, via a camera, digitizes the images of all objects to be identified, then stores the digitized form of each image in the database. When the system is placed in operation, the camera enters the image into a digitizer. The system then compares the digitized image to

GOING ONLINE

5.2
The Stock Market

The Wall Street ticker tape runs through the Internet. Determine the value of the Dow Jones Industrial Index and the stock price for International Business Machines (IBM). DBC Online ⟨http://www3.dbc.com/⟩ offers free quotes and you do not have to register. *Note: Some sites charge for this information! Find a source that does not charge.*

Hand in: The value of the Dow Jones Industrial Index and the value of a share of IBM stock. Include date and time of day of the quotes. Also, include the name and address (URL) of your source.

DragonDictate for Windows is a flexible speech-recognition system that allows users to input text and control applications by speaking instead of typing. When this banker says a word, DragonDictate displays a word list that contains its "best guesses" as to what he said. Over time, the program adapts to the his voice; that is, its guesses get better as he uses it.
Courtesy of Dragon Systems, Inc.

be interpreted to the prerecorded digitized images in the computer's database, much like a speech-recognition system does with speech input. The computer identifies the image by matching the structure of the input image with those images in the database. This process is illustrated by the digital vision-inspection system in Figure 5–3.

As you can imagine, **vision-input systems** are best suited to very specialized tasks in which only a few images will be encountered. These tasks are usually simple, monotonous ones, such as inspection. For example, in Figure 5–3 a digital vision-inspection system on an assembly line rejects those parts that do not meet certain quality-control specifications. The vision system performs rudimentary gauging inspections, and then signals the computer to take appropriate action.

Vision input offers great promise for the future. Can you imagine traveling by car from your home town to Charleston, South Carolina, without the burden of driving? Sound far-fetched? Not really. Mercedes-Benz, the German automaker, is actively developing a system that will allow you to do just that. The copilot system is a step up from cruise control, freeing the driver from both the accelerator pedal and the steering wheel. Like cruise control, the driver would remain behind the wheel, even when the system is operational. The foundation technology is vision input. When traveling down the German autobahn, the system "sees" the lines on either side of the lane and makes minor adjustments in direction to keep the automobile centered in the lane. This part of the system works well; however, Mercedes-Benz engineers have many hurdles to overcome (exit ramps, pedestrians, and so on) before you see this feature in showroom automobiles. Someday the safest drivers on the road won't be driving at all.

FIGURE 5–3 Digital Vision-Inspection System In this digital vision-inspection system, the system examines parts for defects. If the digitized image of the part does not match a standard digital image, the defective part is placed in a reject bin.

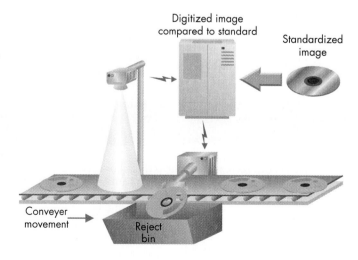

Digitized image compared to standard

Standardized image

Conveyer movement

Reject bin

Digital Cameras: Look, No Film

Most of us take photographs in the traditional manner with a traditional camera. We drop off our rolls of film for developing, then enjoy the results in the form of prints and slides. Some people use image scanners to digitize photos for use in newspapers, magazines, and so on. This process may change forever as the price of **digital cameras** continues to plummet (currently priced from $750 to $10,000). When you take a picture with a digital camera, a digitized image goes straight to 3½-inch diskette or CD-R. Once on disk it can be loaded to a computer and manipulated as you would other graphic images.

There are many applications for digital cameras, not the least of which is expanding the family photo album. As mentioned in Chapter 1, dermatologists use digital cameras to take close-up shots of lesions and skin disorders. Each time a patient comes in for an appointment, the doctor takes a file photo so that progress can be compared from visit to visit.

Hand-held Data Entry Devices

The typical *hand-held data entry device,* which is actually a small computer, has the following:

▶ A limited keyboard

▶ A calculator-like display

▶ Some kind of storage capability for the data, usually solid-state nonvolatile random-access memory

▶ A scanning device, capable of optical character recognition

After the data have been entered, the portable data entry device is linked with a central computer and data are *uploaded* (transmitted from the data entry device to a central computer) for processing.

Stock clerks in department stores routinely use hand-held devices to collect and enter reorder data. As clerks visually check the inventory level, they identify the items that need to be restocked. They first scan the price tag (which identifies the item), then enter the number to be ordered on the keyboard.

Hand-held pen-based PCs and PDAs (personal digital assistants) frequently are used as data entry devices. Pen-based computing and PDAs are introduced in Chapter 1, "The World of Computers." Pen-based PCs have pressure-sensitive writing pads that recognize hand-printed alphanumeric characters. Also, they permit the entering of graphic information. For example, police officers use pen-based PCs to document accidents, including recording the handwritten signatures of the participants.

5-4 OUTPUT DEVICES: COMPUTERS COMMUNICATE WITH US

Output devices translate bits and bytes into a form we can understand. The most common "output only" devices are discussed in this section. These include monitors, printers, plotters, screen image projectors, and voice-response systems.

Monitors and Graphics Adapters

Alphanumeric and graphic output are displayed on the televisionlike monitor. We define monitors in terms of the following:

▶ *Graphics adapter* (the electronic link between the motherboard and the monitor)

▶ *Size* (diagonal dimension of the display screen)

We may be entering an era of filmless photography. With this Canon digital camera, you can capture, view, print, store, and transmit almost any image. Up to 50 images can be recorded on a 2-inch floppy that is inserted in the camera. Once captured, images can be uploaded to a PC and used in countless applications, from the family photo album to training software. Courtesy of Canon U.S.A., Inc.

This hand-held data entry device is actually a small PC that is worn on the hand and the arm. Workers at McKesson Corporation wear their 13-ounce PCs. The wearable PCs contain a small screen, a key pad, and a bar code scanner. This receiving clerk can read bar codes and enter data while keeping both hands free to lift and move shipping containers. Photo courtesy of McKesson Corporation

Output

Resolution (detail of the display)

Color (monochrome or color)

Display quality

Graphics Adapters   The **graphics adapter** is the device controller for the monitor. Most graphics adapters are inserted into an expansion slot on the motherboard. Some, however, are built into the motherboard. The monitor cable is plugged into the graphics adapter board to link the monitor with the processor. All display signals en route to the monitor pass through the graphics adapter where the digital signals are converted to analog signals compatible with the monitor's display capabilities.

Graphics adapters have their own RAM, called **video RAM,** where they prepare monitor-bound images for display. The size of the video RAM is important in that it determines the number of possible colors, the resolution, and the speed at which signals can be sent to the monitor. A minimum of one megabyte (1 MB) of video RAM **(VRAM)** is recommended to accommodate the complexities of modern graphics-based software.

Monitor Size   Display screens vary in size from 5 to 30 inches (diagonal dimension). The monitor size for newly purchased desktop PCs has inched up from 9 inches to 15 inches over the past 10 years and is moving toward 17 inches. Output on a monitor is *soft copy.* This means it is temporary and available to the end user only until another display is requested (as opposed to the permanent *hard-copy* output of printers).

Monitor Resolution: Pixels and Dot Pitch   Monitors vary in their quality of output, or **resolution.** Resolution refers to the number of addressable points on the screen—the number of points to which light can be directed under program control. These points are sometimes called **pixels,** short for *picture elements.* Each pixel can be assigned a shade of gray or a color. The typical monitor is set to operate with 307,200 (640 by 480) addressable points. Monitors used primarily for computer graphics and computer-aided design may have more than 16 million addressable points. The high-resolution monitors project extremely clear images that look almost like photographs.

PC displays are in either **text mode** or **graphics mode.** MS-DOS–based programs operate in text mode, generally with 25 rows of up to 80 characters in length. Some monitors permit characters to be displayed with greater density (for example, 43 rows of up to 132 characters). All software applications developed to run under Microsoft's Windows, graphical user interfaces (GUIs), draw programs, and design programs operate in graphics mode. The trend in software development is toward the exclusive use of the graphics mode, even in word processing and spreadsheet software.

A monitor's resolution may be described in terms of its **dot pitch,** or the distance between the centers of adjacent pixels. Any dot pitch less than .31mm (millimeters) provides a sharp image. The crispness of the image improves as the dot pitch gets smaller. When you have an opportunity, use a magnifying glass to examine the pixels and observe the dot pitch.

Monochrome and Color Monitors   Monitors are either monochrome or color. Monochrome monitors display images in a single color, usually white, green, blue, red, or amber. A monochrome monitor can, however, display shades of one color. The industry uses the term **gray scales** to refer to the number of shades of a color that can be shown on a monochrome monitor's screen. Monochrome monitors are popular on low-end portable PCs. Relatively few new desktop PCs are configured with monochrome displays.

Most color monitors mix red, green, and blue to achieve a spectrum of colors, and are called **RGB monitors.** Several color video display standards have evolved since the introduction of the IBM PC in 1981. The four most popular monitors are listed here.

Output Devices

- Monitors
Described by graphics adapter, size, resolution (pixels and dot pitch), color (gray scales, RGB), and display quality
Types of monitors
—Televisionlike
—Flat-panel
—Touch screen
- Printers
—Dot-matrix printers
—Page printers (color option)
—Ink-jet printers (color option)
—Multifunction hydra
- Plotters
- Screen image projector
- Voice-response systems
—Recorded voice
—Speech synthesis

Courtesy of E-Systems

Courtesy of International Business Machines
Corporation

Courtesy of Sega of America Inc.

Courtesy General Parametrics Corporation

Monitors are an integral component of virtually all computer-based applications. (Clockwise from top left) An engineer at E-Systems needs a large high-resolution monitor for computer-aided design (CAD) applications. His laptop PC has a LCD flat-panel monitor. A growing number of public information kiosks use touch screen monitors. In video arcades, the action in Sega's Sonic and Knuckles (shown here) takes place on large, durable monitors. This Advanced Remote Control for Videoshow system enables the presentation of spectacular multimedia shows. The remote control includes a full-color LCD screen so that presenters can face their audience and still see what is on the big screen.

▶ *CGA.* The initial *c*olor *g*raphics *a*dapter standard offers four colors at 320 by 200 pixel resolution.

▶ *EGA.* The *e*nhanced *g*raphics *a*dapter offers 16 colors at 640 by 350 resolution.

▶ *VGA.* The *v*ideo *g*raphics *a*rray adapter offers 256 colors at 640 by 480 resolution.

▶ *Super VGA.* The Super VGA offers up to 16 million colors with resolutions from 800 by 600 to 1280 by 1024.

All four—CGA, EGA, VGA, and Super VGA—are in widespread use today.

A VGA-level monitor capable of displaying 256 colors is fine for most business and home applications. A super VGA with at least 65,536 colors is recommended for those who do desktop publishing and other graphics-intensive applications professionally.

**Peripherals
Explorer**

Emerging Technology

The I-Book Reader: Textbook of the Future

Books haven't changed much since Johann Gutenberg invented the printing press in the fifteenth century. The methods for producing books are, of course, far more sophisticated, but in the end, a book remains a sequential, static medium. This type of organization is made-to-order for novels, in which a story is read from page one to the end. The printed page, however, has its limits for just about any book or document that contains an index. This includes all varieties of reference books, encyclopedias, "how to" books, corporate manuals, and, of course, textbooks.

Over the next few years, the printed pages of college textbooks will begin their transformation to a technology-based presentation. Nobody knows for sure what the textbook of the future will look like. Most educators and publishers agree, however, that change is just over the horizon. Perhaps it's time to speculate on what that technology will look like and what it will bring to the classroom—or possibly the home, the office, the student union, the car . . .

The *interactive book*, or *i-book*, will offer many advantages over traditional books.

▶ Static figures will come alive with animation.
▶ Motion video will be available to demonstrate, elaborate, or clarify.
▶ More detailed information will be just a click or touch away.
▶ The i-book will help readers identify and overcome gaps in understanding.
▶ Readers will be able to click on or touch "active words" to display/play related material (for example, a definition, an exercise, or a demonstration).
▶ When linked to the Internet, readers of i-books will be given an opportunity to visit applicable Internet sites for further information.
▶ Margin notes can be written or spoken.
▶ Readers will be able to share information and thoughts via online communication with other readers.

The I-Book Reader

Any modern multimedia PC is ready for the i-book onslaught, but it doesn't offer the flexibility of books. We can open books and begin reading immediately in any lighted location. To some extent, multimedia notebook PCs give us this flexibility, but they cost several thousand dollars. Further miniaturization of hardware components and inevitable price reductions will eventually lead us to the *i-book reader*. The adjacent figure shows the authors' concept of the i-book reader, essentially a small special-function computer. Here are some of the i-book's proposed features.

▶ *Lightweight.* The first i-book readers will weigh about the same as a college textbook.
▶ *Solid-state memory.* System software and user data are recalled from nonvolatile solid-state memory. The i-book reader will not need a hard disk.
▶ *Digital versatile disk (DVD) drive.* The multimedia-based i-books will require huge amounts of storage for programs, text, images, video, audio, animated figures, virtual reality presentations, and so on. I-books probably will be distributed on DVDs, the next generation of CD-ROMs. DVDs have a read-only capacity of almost 20 gigabytes, about the capacity of 14 CD-ROMs.
▶ *Detachable touch screen viewer.* The i-book reader is in two parts, the *base unit,* which contains the processor and storage, and the *viewer.* The detachable viewer, which is tethered to the base unit, will provide the student with the flexibility to study the i-book in class, under a tree, or in bed. The touch screen capability lets the student communicate with the i-book. With improved technology, the viewer's self-retracting tether may be eliminated and replaced with a wireless connection.
▶ *Speaker and microphone.* Both the speaker and the microphone are embedded in the detachable viewer. The student will have the option of playing sound through a *headset.*
▶ *Network interface cards.* The NICs in the base unit will accept twisted-pair telephone wire or coaxial cable so that the i-book reader can be linked to LANs and the Internet.
▶ *A serial/parallel port.* The port will enable a direct connection to the student's PC and its resources (printer, disk drives, and so on).
▶ *Touchpad.* The more sophisticated i-book readers will have extras, such as a touchpad to expedite interaction with the i-book.

Display Quality: Be Flicker Free As a potential buyer of monitors, you should be aware of two more considerations that affect the quality of the display—the *refresh rate* and whether the monitor is *interlaced.* The phosphor coating on a monitor's CRT (cathode-ray tube) must be repainted or refreshed 50 to 80 times each second (Hz) to maintain clarity of the image. Generally, monitors with faster refresh rates have less flicker and are easier on the eyes. The less expensive monitors are interlaced; that is, they paint every other horizontal line on the screen, then fill in on a second pass (TVs

► *Eyeglasses viewer.* Students who want hands-free viewing may purchase an optional eyeglasses viewer. This viewer, which has two tiny monitors, is worn like eyeglasses. Students use the touchpad to interact with the i-book.

I-Book Summary

A handful of CD-ROM–based i-books are beginning to dot the educational landscape. However, you must have access to and be at a multimedia PC to use them. This first generation of i-books have only a few of the features we'll find in the second and third generation i-books described earlier. The next generation of i-books will emerge when i-book readers move from the laboratory to the bookstore and authors have had an opportunity to gain experience in *3-D writing*.

Traditional books are written and presented in one dimension, along a straight line (page 1 to the end). In contrast, the cyberauthor must learn to write in three dimensions. The author must allow the reader to *jump forward or backward* (along the traditional book line), to *jump to either side for supplemental information* (for example, animated figures, supportive images and video, virtual reality presentations, and self-administered quizzes), and *to go into greater depth*, the third dimension (for example, greater conceptual detail, definitions, in-depth analysis, and links to applicable Internet sites).

Now for the big question. When will this all happen? Probably a lot sooner than you would think!

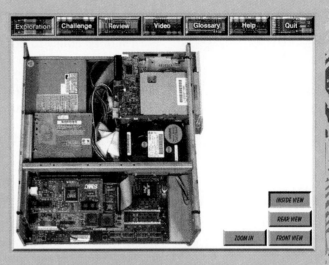

The IT Works CD-ROM that accompanies this book uses interactive methods to demonstrate computer concepts.

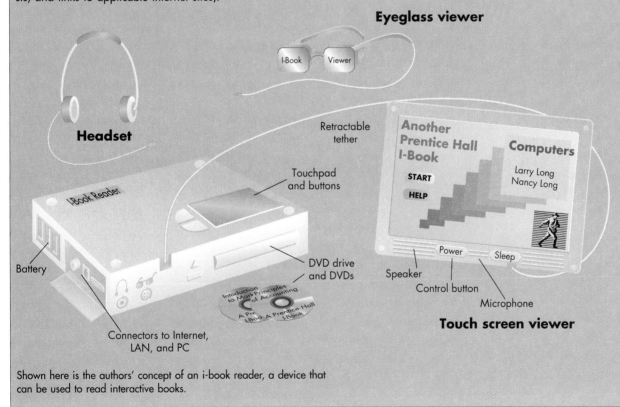

Shown here is the authors' concept of an i-book reader, a device that can be used to read interactive books.

are interlaced). This may result in some flicker. In contrast, *non-interlaced monitors* minimize flicker by painting the whole screen in one pass.

Flat-Panel Monitors: Thin Is In Some space-saving monitors are flat. Most **flat-panel monitors** are used in conjunction with laptop PCs. Flat-panel monitors use three basic types of technology: *LCD* (*l*iquid *c*rystal *d*isplay), the technology commonly used in digital wristwatches; *gas plasma*; and *EL* (*e*lectro*l*uminescent). Each has its advantages. For example, LCD displays use relatively little power and EL displays provide a wider

INTERNET BRIDGE

Printers

viewing angle. Up until the late 1980s, all flat-panel monitors were monochrome. With the recent introduction of color LCD monitors, laptop PC buyers now have a choice.

Touch Screen Monitors: Natural Monitors   **Touch screen monitors** permit input as well as output. Touch-sensitive screens enable users to choose from available options simply by touching the desired icon or menu item with their finger. We are born with an ability to point and touch. Educators realize this and are beginning to use touch screen technology in the classroom to teach everything from reading to geography. Interactive touch screen systems are installed in shopping centers, zoos, airports, grocery stores, post offices, and many other public locations. Within a few years the information you need will be at your fingertips wherever you go.

Printers: Lots of Choices

Printers produce hard-copy output, such as management reports, cash register receipts, memos, payroll checks, and program listings. Hundreds of printers are produced by dozens of manufacturers. There is a printer manufactured to meet the hard-copy output requirements of any individual or company, and almost any combination of features can be obtained. You can specify its size (some weigh less than a pound), speed, quality of output, color requirements, flexibility requirements, and even noise level. PC printers sell for as little as a good pair of shoes or for as much as a minivan. Mainframe printers can cost as much as an upscale house.

To make an informed choice when buying a printer, you need to ask yourself these questions:

▶ What's the budget?
▶ Is color needed or will black and white do?
▶ What will be the volume of output (pages per hour, day, or week)?
▶ How important is quality of the output?
▶ What special features are needed (ability to print envelopes, on legal size paper, on multi-part forms, and so on)?
▶ If the printer is to be shared on a network, what do the other users want?

Think about these questions as you read about various printer options. Keep in mind that you pay more for color, additional features, and each increment in speed and quality of output.

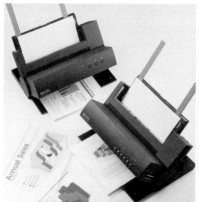

By the mid-1990s, the price of color printers plummeted to the point that they were economically feasible for virtually all computing environments, including the home. Now users can add color to their everyday business (memos, reports, spreadsheets, graphs) and home (banners, invitations) printing needs. These Hewlett-Packard color notebook (left), color ink-jet (middle), and color laser (right) printers provide high-quality color output. The notebook printer allows wireless printing from up to three feet away from a PC.   Photos courtesy of Hewlett-Packard Company

	Dot-Matrix Printers	Page Printers	Ink-Jet Printers
Pros	• Inexpensive • Can print multi-part forms • Can print on narrow and wide fanfold paper • Low per page cost (less than a penny per page) • Energy efficient	• High-resolution output (up to 1200 dpi) • Fast (4 to 32 ppm–text only) • Quiet • Many choices from which to choose (from under $400 for low-speed home/office models up to $20,000 for sophisticated shared printers) • Low cost per page (1 to 4 cents)	• High-resolution output (but less than that of page) • Quiet • Small (footprint can be smaller than a sheet of paper) • Energy efficient • Many choices from which to choose (black and white from $150 to full 4-color for about $400
Cons	• Noisy • Low-resolution output that gets worse as the ribbon ages • Slow (40 to 200 cps) • Poor quality graphics output • Requires add-on to handle cut sheets and envelopes • Limited font flexibility	• Cost • Limited to cut sheet media • Slow for graphics output	• Higher cost per page than page (2 to 8 cents) • Slower than page (1 to 3 ppm) • Special paper required for highest resolution output • Limited to cut sheet media
Color	Color ribbons can be used for highlighting.	Color page models produce high-resolution color output. At $.50 to $4.00 per color page, they can be expensive to operate.	Color ink-jet models may take over the low-end color market. Models under $400 are available that produce 720 dpi color output. Color output costs from $.10 to $1.20 per page.
Outlook	Dot-matrix technology is fading except for situations that require printing on multi-part forms.	High-speed, high-quality page printers will remain the mainstay of office printing for the foreseeable future. This is especially true for shared printers.	Ink-jet offers low-cost high-quality output. Home PC buyers with low volume output requirements may opt for color models in large numbers.

FIGURE 5–4
Printer Summary

Printer technology is ever changing. Three basic technologies dominate the PC printer arena: dot-matrix, ink jet, and page. The advantages and disadvantages of these technologies is summarized in Figure 5–4. All PC printers have the capability of printing graphs and charts and offer considerable flexibility in the size and style of print. All printers also can print in portrait or landscape format. **Portrait** and **landscape** refer to the orientation of the print on the page. Portrait format is like the page of this book—the lines run parallel to the shorter sides of the page. In contrast, landscape output runs parallel to the longer sides of the page. Landscape is frequently the orientation of choice for spreadsheet outputs with many columns.

Dot-Matrix Printers: Walking into the Sunset The **dot-matrix printer** forms images *one character at a time* as the print head moves across the paper. The dot-matrix printer is an *impact printer*, that is, it uses tiny *pins* to hit the ribbon and the paper, much as a typewriter does. The dot-matrix printer arranges printed dots to form characters and all kinds of images in much the same way as lights display time and temperature on bank signs. Several vertical column pins are contained in a rectangular print head. Print heads may have from 9 to 24 pins. The pins are activated independently to form a dotted character image as the print head moves horizontally across the paper. The quality of the printed output increases with the number of dots in the letter matrix (a rectangular arrangement of dots). Figure 5–5 illustrates how the dots can form characters as a print head moves across the paper to create a letter. The better dot-matrix printers form characters that appear solid, and they can be used for business letters as well as for draft output. Dot-matrix printers print up to 200 cps (characters per second).

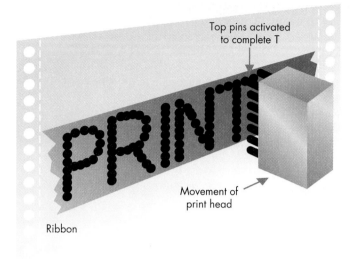

Top pins activated
to complete T

Movement of
print head

Ribbon

Most dot-matrix printers can accommodate both *cut-sheet paper* and *fanfold paper.* If your output is mostly single sheet (for example, letters and envelopes), you may need to purchase an *automatic sheet feeder.* The *tractor-feed* that handles fanfold paper is standard with most dot-matrix printers.

As long as people have a need to print on multi-part forms, there will be a need for impact dot-matrix printers. Impact printers, as opposed to nonimpact printers, touch the paper and can produce carbon copies along with the original. Another advantage of dot-matrix printers over the other types of printers is cost. However, this advantage is fading as the cost of high-speed, high-resolution page printers approaches that of dot-matrix printers. Those who do not print multi-part forms may opt for other types of printers in the future. The pros and cons of dot-matrix printers are summarized in Figure 5–4.

FIGURE 5–5
Dot-Matrix–Printer
Character Formation
Each character is formed in a matrix as the print head moves across the paper. The bottom pins are used for lowercase letters that extend below the line (for example, *g* and *p*). Notice how dots are overlapped to increase the density and, therefore, the quality of the image.

Page Printers: A Page at a Time   Nonimpact **page printers** use laser, LED (*light-emitting diode*), LCS (*liquid crystal shutter*), and other laser-like technologies to achieve high-speed hard-copy output by printing *a page at a time.* Page printers are also referenced simply as **laser printers.** The operation of a laser-based page printer is illustrated in Figure 5–6. The majority of laser printers print shades of gray; however, color laser printers are becoming increasingly popular as their price continues to drop.

Until the mid-1980s, virtually all printers configured with microcomputers were impact printers printing a character at a time. Now economically priced desktop page printers are becoming the standard for office microcomputer systems. These printers, capable of print speeds up to 32 pages per minute (ppm) for text-only printing, have redefined the hard-copy output potential of micros. Automatic sheet feeders, which hold from 100 to 400 blank pages, are standard equipment on desktop page printers. Most page printers print on a standard 8½-by 11-inch paper; however, some models can print on paper up to 17 by 22 inches.

All desktop page printers are capable of producing high-quality text and graphics output. Some can produce *near-typeset-quality (NTQ)* text and graphics as well. The resolution (quality of output) of the low-end desktop page printer is *300 dpi* (dots per inch). High-end desktop page printers, which are sometimes called *desktop typesetters,* are capable of at least 1200 dpi. The dpi qualifier refers to the number of dots that can be printed per linear inch, horizontally or vertically. That is, a 600-dpi printer is capable of printing 360,000 (600 times 600) dots per square inch. Commercial type-

FIGURE 5–6   Desktop Page Printer Operation
The enclosure of a desktop page printer is removed to expose its inner workings. (a) Prior to printing, an electrostatic charge is applied to a drum. Then laser beam paths to the drum are altered by a spinning multisided mirror. The reflected beams selectively remove the electrostatic charge from the drum. (b) Toner is deposited on those portions of the drum that were affected by the laser beams. The drum is rotated and the toner is fused to the paper to create the image.

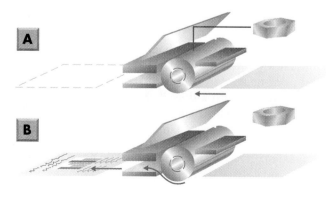

A

B

setting quality is a minimum of 1200 dpi and is usually in excess of 2000 dpi. Desktop page printers are also quiet (an important consideration in an office setting). The emergence of desktop page printers has fueled the explosion of *desktop publishing* (discussed in detail in Chapter 8, "Productivity Software: From Notes to Databases"). The pros and cons of page printers are summarized in Figure 5–4.

Ink-jet Printers: Popular in SOHO   To the naked eye, there is little difference between the print quality of nonimpact **ink-jet printers** and page printers. Although the output quality of ink-jet printers is more in line with page printers, their mechanical operation is more like that of the dot-matrix printer. The print head moves back and forth across the paper to write text and create the image. Just as the dot-matrix pins hit the ribbon and paper, several independently controlled injection chambers squirt ink droplets on the paper. The droplets, which dry instantly as dots, form the letters and images. Because the ink droplets are much smaller than the area resulting from pin thrusts, the resolution is much better for ink-jet than for dot-matrix printers. Resolutions for the typical ink-jet printer approach that of a 300-dpi page printer. Some newer models boast resolutions in excess of 700 dpi.

With a price tag about equal to a dot-matrix printer and a print quality close to that of a page printer, the ink-jet printer is emerging as the choice for budget-minded consumers. Look for SOHO (small office/home office) buyers to buy ink-jet printers by the millions. The high cost per page is not a deterrent for the low-volume output needs of the typical PC user. The pros and cons of ink-jet printers are summarized in Figure 5–4.

Color Printers: Over the Rainbow   A couple of years ago, color printers started at $7000. Today you can get a 720-dpi color ink-jet printer that produces near-photographic-quality output for under $500. The growing trend among printer consumers is to think (and possibly buy) color. You can purchase a color page printer or a color ink-jet printer. Generally, the more you pay the better the output. Page printers, which can cost up to $20,000, use one of three technologies. Color laser printers electrostatically adhere toner to the drum, then fuse toner to paper or transparencies. Thermal wax page printers melt wax-based inks that adhere to the paper or transparencies. Dye sublimation page printers press ink sheets against special paper, heating the color so they sink in. Ink-jet color printers use similar technologies for both black-and-white and color printers. Ink droplets are mixed to form the various colors. Color printers frequently are used to make colorful transparencies for presentations.

Hydra Printer: All in One   Traditionally, businesses have purchased separate machines to handle these paper-related tasks: computer-based printing, facsimile (fax), scanning, and copying. The considerable overlap in the technologies used in these machines has enabled manufacturers to create all-in-one multifunction printers called **hydra printers.** Hydra printers are relatively new, but they may well be the wave of the future. Watch for them.

Perhaps this Lanier hydra printer provides us with a glimpse into the office of the future. This multifunction printer acts as a copier, a fax machine, and a printer, providing PC users with a range of office capabilities. This printer services a LAN with four users.   Courtesy of Harris Corporation

Mainframe-based Page Printers Operating at peak capacity during an 8-hour shift, the fastest mainframe page printer can produce almost a quarter of a million pages—that's 50 miles of output. This enormous output capability is normally directed to people outside an organization. For example, large banks use page printers to produce statements for checking and savings accounts; insurance companies print policies on page printers; and electric utility companies use them to bill their customers.

Plotters: Precision Instruments

Dot-matrix, page, and ink-jet printers are capable of producing page-size graphic output, but are limited in their ability to generate high-quality, perfectly proportioned graphic output. For example, on a blueprint the sides of a 12-foot-square room must be exactly the same length. Architects, engineers, city planners, and others who routinely generate high-precision, hard-copy graphic output of widely varying sizes use another hard-copy alternative—**plotters.**

The two basic types of plotters are the *drum plotter* and the *flatbed plotter.* Both have one or more pens that move over the paper under computer control to produce an image. Several

Not all plotters use pens. This monochrome plotter uses ink-jet technology that permits output at five times the speed of pen-based plotters. This plotter is capable of a mechanical resolution of 0.0005 inches; that is, the output is accurate to within 5 ten-thousandths of an inch.   Photo courtesy of Hewlett-Packard Company

pens are required to vary the width and color of the line, and the computer selects and manipulates them. On the drum plotter, the pens and the drum move concurrently in different axes to produce the image. Drum plotters are used to produce continuous output, such as plotting earthquake activity, or for long graphic output, such as the structural view of a skyscraper. On some flatbed plotters, the pen moves in both axes while the paper remains stationary. However, on most desktop plotters, both paper and pen move concurrently in much the same way as on drum plotters.

Presentation Graphics: Be Persuasive

Business people have found that sophisticated and colorful graphics add an aura of professionalism to any report or presentation. This demand for *presentation graphics* has created a need for corresponding output devices. Computer-generated graphic images can be re-created on paper and transparency acetates with printers. Graphic

Screen image projectors can fill a room with information. Reprinted with permission of Compaq Computer Corporation. All Rights Reserved.

images also can be captured on 35-mm slides, displayed on a monitor, or projected onto a large screen.

The need for overhead transparencies and 35-mm slides is beginning to fade now that everything you need to give multimedia presentations, a **screen image projector** and a notebook PC, can fit into an attache case. Screen image projectors are used in conjunction with an ordinary overhead projector to project the output from the PC onto a large screen. The light from the overhead projector is directed through an LCD panel and the image is shown on a large screen for all to see.

Voice-Response Systems: Say It with Bits

Anyone who has used a telephone has heard "If you're dialing from a touch-tone phone, press 1." You may have driven a car that advised you to "fasten your seat belt." These are examples of talking machines that use output from a voice-response system. There are two types of **voice-response systems**: One uses a *reproduction* of a human voice and other sounds, and the other uses **speech synthesis.** Like monitors, voice-response systems provide temporary, soft-copy output.

The first type of voice-response system selects output from user-recorded words, phrases, music, alarms, or anything you might record on audiotape, just as a printer would select characters. In these recorded voice-response systems, the actual analog recordings of sounds are converted into digital data, then permanently stored on disk or in a memory chip. When output occurs, a particular sound is converted back into analog before being routed to a speaker. Chips are mass-produced for specific applications, such as output for automatic teller machines, microwave ovens, smoke detectors, elevators, alarm clocks, automobile warning systems, video games, and vending machines, to mention only a few. When sounds are stored on disk, the user has the flexibility to update them to meet changing application needs.

Speech synthesis systems, which convert raw data into electronically produced speech, are more popular in the microcomputer environment. All you need to produce speech on a PC are a sound expansion board, speakers (or headset), and appropriate software. Such software often is packaged with the sound board. To produce speech, sounds resembling the phonemes (from 50 to 60 basic sound units) are combined to make up speech. The existing technology produces synthesized speech with only limited vocal inflections and phrasing, however. Even with its limitations, the number of speech synthesizer applications is growing. For example, a visually impaired person can use the speech synthesizer to translate printed words into spoken words. Translation systems offer one of the most interesting applications for speech synthesizers and speech-recognition devices. Researchers are making progress toward enabling conversations among people who are speaking different languages. A prototype system has already demonstrated that three people, each speaking a different language (English, German, and Japanese), can carry on a computer-aided conversation. Each person speaks and listens to his or her native language.

5–5 TERMINALS: INPUT AND OUTPUT

Terminals enable interaction with a remote computer system in a wide variety of applications.

The Tube and the Telephone

The two most popular general-purpose terminals are the *video display terminal (VDT)* and the *telephone.* The VDT is affectionately known as "the tube," short for **cathode-ray tube.** A VDT's primary input mechanism is usually a *keyboard,* and the output is usually displayed on a *monitor.* Terminals come in all shapes and sizes and have a variety of input/output capabilities.

Terminals

Dumb Terminals Most terminals are dumb; that is, they have little or no intelligence (processing capability). The terminals you see in most hospitals or airports are dumb terminals. These terminals only display text and must be linked to a multiuser processor, such as a mainframe computer.

Smart X Terminals **X terminals** have processing capabilities and RAM comparable to some micros and workstations; however, they are not designed for standalone operation. The X terminal's processing capability enables the user to interact via a graphical user interface (GUI). All X terminals are configured with some type of point-and-draw device, such as a mouse, to permit efficient interaction with the GUI.

Dumb terminals support only text I/O within a single application. In contrast, the X terminal user can work with several applications at a time, any of which can display high-resolution graphics. Each application is displayed in its own window. Some X terminals can even run applications on different computers at the same time.

Terminals and PCs are taking on a new dimension as users interact not only with the computer but also with one another. The camera and microphone enable an audio-visual link that permits colleagues in different locations to literally talk with and see one another while viewing the same text or graphic information. Courtesy of International Business Machines Corporation

Telephone Terminals and Telephony The telephone's widespread availability is causing greater use of it as a terminal. You can enter alphanumeric data on the touch-tone key pad of a telephone or by speaking into the receiver (voice input). You would then receive computer-generated voice output. Salespeople use telephones as terminals for entering orders and inquiries about the availability of certain products into their company's mainframe computer. Brokerage firms allow clients to tap into their computers via telephone. After entering a password, clients can request a wide variety of services and information by working through a hierarchy of spoken menus. For example, they can request account balances and stock quotes. They can even request that a specific company's earnings report be sent to their fax machines.

The telephone by itself has little built-in intelligence; however, when linked to a computer, potential applications abound. **Telephony** is the integration of computers and telephones, the two most essential instruments of business. This integration is gaining momentum and should be complete by the turn of the century. Already, companies are beginning to implement innovative applications. In telephony the computer, perhaps a PC, acts as a front end to the telephone. The front-end PC can analyze incoming calls and take appropriate action (take a message, route call to appropriate extension, and so on). Generally we enter information on the telephone's 12-button key pad. In effect, telephony augments the 12 buttons to include a PC-based GUI.

This Human Designed Systems (HDS) X terminal includes a RISC-based processor. X terminal users have many of the advantages of PCs, including windows and user-friendly interfaces. Human Designed Systems, Inc.

▶ A mail-order house keeps customer records by customer telephone number. When a customer calls to phone in an order, the system detects the customer's telephone number (caller ID), routes the call to an available salesperson (or the one with the shortest wait time), and, finally, displays the customer's record on the salesperson's monitor before anyone says hello. If the salesperson is busy, the customer is given an opportunity to enter the order directly from a telephone.

▶ A school district uses telephony to reschedule district events. For example, a last-minute change of time for a school board meeting is automatically announced to the participants and the media community. The telephony system even negotiates scheduling conflicts with participants to arrive at an acceptable time for all concerned—all automatically.

▶ A major PC manufacturer asks customers calling in for sales or technical support to enter customer identification information via their telephone key pad. ID information is routed to the customer database. The telephony system then routes the caller to the appropriate person and displays customer background information for the support person.

Telephony promotes efficient interactions and as it matures, look for many routine communications to be handled entirely by computers (for example, scheduling of meetings). Much of what has to be done in a typical business phone call can be accomplished between cooperating computers. If and when we are needed, we will be asked to join the conversation.

Special-Function Terminals: ATMs and POSs

The number and variety of special-function terminals are growing rapidly. Special-function terminals are designed for a specific application, such as convenience banking. You probably are familiar with the *automatic teller machine (ATM)* and its input/output capabilities (see Figure 5–7). A badge reader (magnetic stripe) and a key pad enable input to the system. A monitor and a printer (for printing transaction receipts) provide output. Some ATMs use voice response as a monitor backup to alert people when to perform certain actions (for example, "Take your receipt").

The ATM idea has caught on for other applications. A consortium of companies is installing thousands of ATM-like terminals that will let you order and receive a wide variety of documents on the spot. For example, you can obtain an airline ticket, your college transcript, an IRS form, and much more.

Another widely used special-function terminal is the *point-of-sale (POS)* terminal. At a minimum, POS terminals in retail establishments have a key pad for input and at least one small monitor. Some have other input devices, such as a badge reader for credit cards and a wand scanner to read price and inventory data.

During the late 1980s, a number of grocery stores had POS terminals with voice-response systems that verbally confirmed the price on each item. The unnecessary noise added confusion to the checkout process without any increase in value to the store or the customer. These systems are now a part of computing history. That's the way it is with technology, especially input/output. Sometimes you have to try it to see if it works. Over the next few years we'll be confronted with many I/O experiments.

MEMORY BITS

Terminals

- General-purpose
  —Video display terminal (VDT)
  —X terminal
  —Telephone
- Special-function
  —Automatic teller machine (ATM)
  —Point-of-sale (POS) terminal

Terminals are being created to meet a variety of needs. This doctor at the Florida Hospital in Orlando is dictating into a dictation terminal. The terminal makes it easy for radiologists and other physicians to dictate findings into a central system.
Courtesy of Harris Corporation

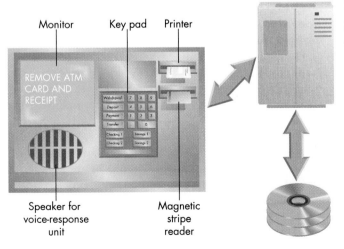

Monitor   Key pad   Printer

REMOVE ATM
CARD AND
RECEIPT

Speaker for
voice-response
unit

Magnetic
stripe
reader

FIGURE 5–7 Terminals for Banking Customers: Automatic Teller Machines
The widely used automatic teller machine (ATM) supports a variety of input/output methods. The magnetic stripe on the ATM card contains identification and security information that, when read, is sent to the bank's computer system. The ATM responds with instructions via its monitor. The customer enters an identification number and data via a key pad. In the figure, the computer processes the customer's request, then provides instructions for the customer via the monitor and verbally with a voice-response unit.

5–1 I/O DEVICES: LET'S INTERFACE   A variety of input/output (I/O) peripheral devices provide the interface between us and the computer.

5–2 TRADITIONAL INPUT DEVICES: KEY, POINT, AND DRAW   There are two basic types of keyboards: the traditional alphanumeric keyboard and special-function keyboards. A widely used keyboard layout is the 101-key keyboard with the traditional *QWERTY* key layout, 12 function keys, a key pad, a variety of special-function keys, and dedicated cursor-control keys. Some special-function keyboards are designed for specific applications. The mouse and its cousins enable us to point to objects on the screen and to draw. These include the **joystick, track-ball, mouse pen, digitizer tablet and pen, trackpoint,** and **trackpad.**

5–3 SOURCE-DATA AUTOMATION: GETTING CLO-SER TO THE ACTION   The trend in data entry has been toward **source-data automation.**

A variety of **scanners** read and interpret information on printed matter and convert it to a format that can be interpreted by a computer. **OCR (optical character recognition)** is the ability to read printed information into a computer system. **Bar codes** represent alphanumeric data by varying the size of adjacent vertical lines. Two types of OCR and bar code scanners—*contact* and *laser*—read information on labels and various types of documents. Scanners used for OCR and bar code applications can be classified into three basic categories—hand-held label scanners (called **wand scanners**), stationary label scanners, and document scanners (which are often used with **turnaround documents**).

An **image scanner** uses laser technology to scan and **digitize** an image. Image scanners provide input for **image processing.** Image scanners are of two types: *page* and *hand.*

Magnetic stripes, **smart cards,** and badges provide input to **badge readers.**

Speech-recognition systems can be used to enter limited kinds and quantities of data. They do this by comparing digitized representations of words to similarly formed templates in the computer system's electronic dictionary.

Vision-input systems are best suited to very specialized tasks in which only a few images will be encountered.

Digital cameras are used to take photos that are represented digitally (already digitized).

Hand-held data entry devices have a limited keyboard, a calculator-like display, storage, and often a scanning device.

5–4 OUTPUT DEVICES: COMPUTERS COMMUN-ICATE WITH US   Output devices translate bits and bytes into a form we can understand. The most common "output only" devices include monitors, printers, plotters, screen image projectors, and voice-response systems.

Monitors are defined in terms of (1) their **graphics adapter** (which has **video RAM** or **VRAM**); (2) size; (3) **resolution** (number of **pixels**); (4) color or monochrome; and (5) display quality.

PC displays are in either **text mode** or **graphics mode.** A monitor's resolution may be described in terms of its **dot pitch. Gray scales** are used to refer to the number of shades of a color that can be shown on a monochrome monitor's screen. **RGB monitors** mix red, green, and blue to achieve a spectrum of colors. The four most popular PC monitors are CGA, EGA, VGA, and Super VGA. The quality of the display is affected by the *refresh rate* and whether the monitor is *interlaced.*

Flat-panel monitors are used with laptop PCs. Three types of technology are common: *LCD, gas plasma,* and *EL.* **Touch screen monitors** permit input as well as output.

Three basic PC printer technologies include dot-matrix, ink jet, and page. Printers can print in **portrait** or **landscape** format. The **dot-matrix printer,** which is an impact printer, forms images *one character at a time* as the print head moves across the paper. Nonimpact **page printers (laser printers)** use laser, LED (light-emitting diode), LCS (liquid crystal shutter), and other laser-like technologies to achieve high-speed hard-copy output by printing *a page at a time.*

Nonimpact **ink-jet printers** have print heads that move back and forth across the paper squirting ink droplets to write text and create images. The ink-jet printer is emerging as the choice for budget-minded consumers.

The color option is available with most types of printers. Color ribbons are used for dot-matrix printers, ink droplets are mixed to form the various colors for ink-jet printers, and page printers use several technologies.

Hydra printers handle several paper-related tasks: computer-based printing, facsimile (fax), scanning, and copying. Mainframe-based page printers can have an enormous output capability.

Plotters, drum and flatbed, convert stored data into high-precision hard-copy graphs, charts, and line drawings.

The demand for *presentation graphics* has created a need for corresponding output devices, such as a **screen image projector.**

Voice-response systems provide recorded or synthesized audio output (via **speech synthesis**).

5–5 TERMINALS: INPUT AND OUTPUT Terminals enable interaction with a remote computer system. The general-purpose terminals are the *video display terminal (VDT)* and the *telephone.* The VDT is known as "the tube," short for **cathode-ray tube.** Terminals come in all shapes and sizes and have a variety of input/output capabilities.

Terminals that have little or no intelligence are called dumb terminals. **X terminals** with processing capabilities enable the user to interact via a graphical user interface. **Telephony** is the integration of computers and telephones.

A variety of special-function terminals, such as automatic teller machines and point-of-sale terminals, are designed for a specific application.

REVIEW EXERCISES

Concepts

1. Which output device, a plotter or a dot-matrix printer, generates graphs with the greatest precision?
2. What is meant when someone says that speech-recognition devices are "speaker-dependent"?
3. List devices, other than key-driven, that are used to input data into a computer system.
4. What is the device called that has fax, printer, scanner, and duplication capabilities?
5. What is the relationship between a joystick and a graphics cursor?
6. Name a device other than a monitor that produces soft-copy output.
7. Which kind of printer can produce near-typeset-quality output?
8. Which type of OCR scanner is designed to read documents of varying sizes?
9. What are two modes of a PC display?
10. List the following in order of improved resolution: VGA, CGA, and EGA.
11. What is a turnaround document? Give an example.
12. Identify all input and output methods used by an automatic teller machine.
13. What is a smart card?
14. Describe two applications for bar codes.

Discussion and Problem Solving

15. Describe the input/output characteristics of a workstation/PC that would be used by engineers for computer-aided design.
16. Some department stores use hand-held label scanners and others use stationary label scanners to interpret the bar codes printed on the price tags of merchandise. What advantages does one scanner have over the other?
17. What input/output capabilities are available at your college or place of work?
18. Compare today's vision-input systems with those portrayed in such films as *2001* and *2010.* Do you believe we will have a comparable vision technology by the year 2001?
19. Four PCs at a police precinct are networked and currently share a 100-cps impact dot-matrix printer. The captain has budgeted enough money to purchase one page printer (8 ppm) or two more 100-cps dot-matrix printers. Which option would you suggest the precinct choose and why?
20. In the next generation of credit cards, the familiar magnetic stripe probably will be replaced by embedded microprocessors in smart cards. Each will have limited processing capability. Suggest applications for this capability.

5–1 a. Input devices translate data into a form that can be interpreted by a computer. (T/F)
b. The primary function of I/O peripherals is to facilitate computer-to-computer data transmission. (T/F)

5–2 a. Only those keyboards configured with VDTs have function keys. (T/F)
b. Which of the following is not a point-and-draw device: (a) joystick, (b) document scanner, or (c) trackpoint?

5–3 a. Optical character recognition is a means of source-data automation. (T/F)
b. In speech recognition, words are _____ and matched against similarly formed _____ in the computer's electronic dictionary.
c. Vision-input systems are best suited to generalized tasks in which a wide variety of images will be encountered. (T/F)
d. The Universal Product Code (UPC) was originally used by which industry: (a) supermarket, (b) hardware, or (c) mail-order merchandising?
e. Image scanners are either page or _____ .
f. The enhanced version of cards with a magnetic stripe is called a badge card. (T/F)

5–4 a. The number of addressable points on the screen, called pixels, affects its _____ .

b. Most flat-panel monitors are used in conjunction with desktop PCs. (T/F)
c. Ink-jet printers are nonimpact printers. (T/F)
d. The tractor feed on dot-matrix printers enables printing on what kind of paper: (a) cut-sheet paper, (b) fanfold paper, (c) both cut-sheet and fanfold paper?
e. What type of printers are becoming the standard for office microcomputer systems: (a) laser printers, (b) dot-matrix printers, or (c) hydra printers?
f. _____ _____ systems convert raw data into electronically produced speech.
g. Another name for video RAM is DRAM chip. (T/F)

5–5 a. Which terminal permits system interaction via a GUI: (a) dumb terminal, (b) X terminal, or (c) text-based terminal?
b. _____ is the integration of computers and telephones.

Self-test Answers. **5–1 (a)** T; **(b)** F. **5–2 (a)** F; **(b)** b. **5–3 (a)** T; **(b)** digitized, templates; **(c)** F; **(d)** a; **(e)** hand; **(f)** F. **5–4 (a)** resolution; **(b)** F; **(c)** T; **(d)** b; **(e)** a; **(f)** Speech synthesis; **(g)** F. **5–5 (a)** b; **(b)** Telephony.

Networks and Networking: Linking the World

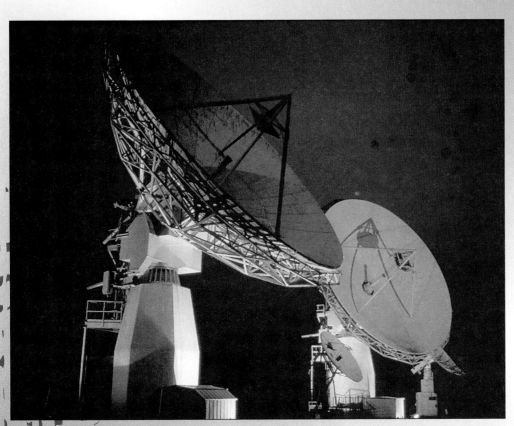

Western Union Corporation

Let's Talk

The following conversation introduces many of the terms in this chapter. Read it now, then again after you have read the chapter.

The Scene:
Three techies (Herb, his wife Carol, and Art) and one nontechy (Art's fiancé, Jana) are talking during a candle-lit dinner at Chez O'bere's.

Jana: This atmosphere is perfectly romantic!
Art: I'll say. The waiters are taking orders on **pocket computers** with a **wireless transceiver.**
Herb: It looks like their **radio signals** are transmitted to that **desktop PC** in the corner. It's probably linked to the **LAN server** by way of a **coaxial cable network bus.**
Carol: You know that **digital convergence** is imminent when your food orders are sent as messages from hand-held PCs to a **local net node** in the kitchen.
Jana: Enough of this tech talk. Are we dining out or talking shop?
Carol: You're right, Jana. It's difficult for people like us who work with **telecommunications** to overlook such a great application.
Art: I'm sorry, Jana. It's weird, but sometimes we find beauty in **network topologies,** especially those that enable **cooperative processing.**
Jana: Well, I hope the next time we come to Chez O'bere's, its technology won't overshadow the wonderful food and atmosphere.
Herb: Uh-oh, look at this note behind the pepper grinder. It says, "Coming Next Spring, Interactive Electronic Menus."

STUDENT LEARNING OBJECTIVES

▶ *To describe the concept of connectivity.*

▶ *To demonstrate an understanding of data communications terminology and applications.*

▶ *To detail the function and operation of data communications hardware.*

▶ *To describe alternatives and sources of data transmission services.*

▶ *To illustrate the various kinds of network topologies.*

▶ *To describe a local area network and its associated hardware and software.*

6-1 OUR WEIRD, WILD, WIRED WORLD

Millions of people are knowledge workers by day and surfers by night. As knowledge workers we need ready access to information. In the present competitive environment, we cannot rely solely on verbal communication for information transfer. Corporate presidents cannot wait until the Monday morning staff meeting to find out whether production is meeting demand. Field sales representatives can no longer afford to play telephone tag with headquarters personnel to get answers for impatient cus-

Courtesy NASA   AT&T Technologies

People have always yearned for better and faster ways to communicate with one another. In the nineteenth century, people were astounded that the Pony Express could carry a letter across the country in 10 days. Today, we pass information across the country or to the other side of the world at the speed of light. Communications satellites, such as this one being deployed from the space shuttle, enable digital and video signals to be relayed from and to points around the globe.

tomers. The president, the field rep, and the rest of us now rely on *computer networks* to retrieve and share information quickly. Of course, we will continue to interact with our co-workers, but computer networks simply enhance the efficiency and effectiveness of that interaction.

As surfers, we surf the Internet, America Online, CompuServe, Prodigy, or any of scores of commercial information services. Once logged on to one of these networks, cybersurfers chat with friends, strangers, and even celebrities. They go shopping, peruse electronic magazines, download interesting photos and songs, plan a vacation, play games, buy and sell stock, send e-mail, and generally hang out. It's official: We now live in a weird, wild, wired world where computer networks are literally networked to computer networks. This chapter is devoted to concepts relating to computer networks and communications technology. Chapter 7, "Going Online: Information Services, the Net, and More," talks about uses of this technology.

Digital Convergence: Coming Together as Bits and Bytes

Data communications, or **telecommunications,** is the collection and distribution of the electronic representation of information between two points. Information can appear in a variety of formats—data, text, voice, still pictures, graphics, and video. Raw information must be *digitized* before transmission between computers. (For example, numerical data and text might be translated into their corresponding ASCII codes.) Ultimately, all forms of digitized information are sent over the transmission media (for example, fiber optic cable) as a series of binary bits (1s and 0s). The technical aspects of data communications are discussed later in this chapter.

Serendipitous Surfing: Online Books

We are going through a period of **digital convergence.** TVs, PCs, telephones, movies, infomercials, college textbooks, newspapers, and much, much more are converging toward digital compatibility. The next edition of this textbook will come in two versions—one printed and the other digital. The digital version will be distributed on CD-ROM and parts of it will be made available through online information services. Movies that are now frames of cellulose are in the process of digital convergence. The 200,000 frames required for a full-length movie will converge to 16 billion bits (or 2 GB, the capacity of 3 CD-ROMs). Already the TV, PC, video game, stereo system, answering device, and telephone are on a collision course that will meld them into communications/information centers by the end of the century. Compaq Computer Corporation started the integration trend with a heavy-duty system for children called Mr. PC Head. The system combines the power of a PC with a stereo, telephone, and TV.

Digital convergence, combined with increased connectivity, will enable us all to take one giant leap into the future. We'll have video-on-demand such that we can view all or any part of any movie ever produced at any time, even in a window on our office PC. Instead of carrying a billfold, we might carry a credit-card-sized device. This device would contain all the typical billfold items from credit cards, to money, to pictures. These items, however, will be digital. When we buy a pizza, we simply enter a code into our electronic billfold to let the restaurant's POS system transfer funds from our bank account to theirs. The possibilities are endless.

Digital convergence is more than a convergence of technologies, it's also a convergence of industries. In a recent survey, 95 percent of the CEOs in the entertainment, telecommunications, cable, and computer industries agreed that their industries are converging.

With half the industrial world (and many governments) racing toward digital convergence, there is no question that we are going totally digital in the next few years. Our photo album will be digital. Our money will be digital. Already, Pacific Bell is transmitting digital movies to about a dozen theaters in Los Angeles where they are shown on high-definition projection units.

Connectivity: Getting to the Information

All of this convergence is happening so information will be more accessible to more people. To realize the potential of a digital universe of information, the business and computer communities are continually seeking ways to interface, or connect, a diverse set of hardware, software, and databases. In so doing, they are continually raising the level of **connectivity,** whether it be throughout a department, a company, or the world. Thirty years ago computers numbered in the tens of thousands. Today computers number in the tens of millions! Computers and information are everywhere. Our challenge is to connect them.

▶ Connectivity means that a marketing manager can use a PC to access information in a database on the finance department's local area network.

▶ Connectivity means that a network of PCs can route output to a common page printer.

▶ Connectivity means that a manufacturer's mainframe computer can communicate with a supplier's mainframe.

▶ Connectivity means that you can send your holiday newsletter via e-mail.

Connectivity is implemented in degrees. We can expect to become increasingly connected to computers and information both at work and at home during the coming years.

This office is one of four regional customer support centers, each of which is part of a computer network. The terminals and PCs at this office are linked to a local mainframe computer that is connected via a high-speed communications line to the company's headquarters in Salt Lake City, Utah. The regional mainframes also are used for local processing. NCR Corporation

The Beginning of an Era: Cooperative Processing

We are living in an era of **cooperative processing.** Information is the password to success in today's business environment. To get meaningful, accurate, and timely information, businesses must cooperate internally and externally to take full advantage of what is available. To promote internal cooperation, businesses are setting up *intracompany networking* (see Figure 6–1). For example, information maintained in the per-

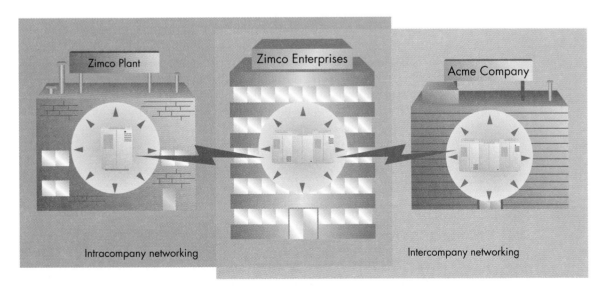

FIGURE 6–1 Intracompany and Intercompany Networking

FIGURE 6–2 Interactions between Customer and Supplier
In the figure, the traditional interaction between a customer company and a supplier company are contrasted with similar interactions via electronic data interchange (EDI).

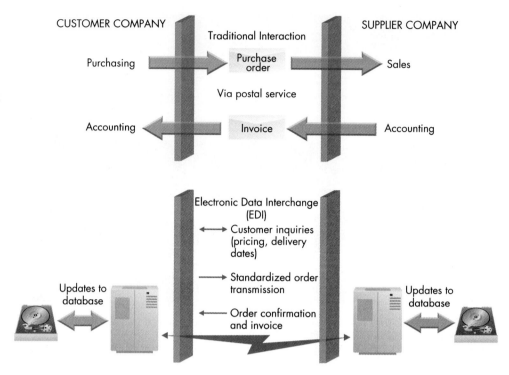

sonnel department is readily accessible to people throughout the company on a *need-to-know* basis.

Companies have recognized that they must cooperate with one another to compete effectively in a world market. They cooperate via *intercompany networking* (Figure 6–1) or, more specifically, via **electronic data interchange (EDI).** EDI uses computers and data communications to transmit data electronically between companies. Invoices, orders, and many other intercompany transactions can be transmitted from the computer of one company to the computer of another. For example, at major retail chains, such as Wal-Mart, over 90% of all orders are processed directly between computers via EDI. Figure 6–2 contrasts the traditional interactions between a customer and supplier company with interactions via EDI.

The phenomenal growth of the use of micros in the home is causing companies to expand their information system capabilities to allow linkages with home and portable PCs. This form of cooperative processing increases system efficiency while lowering costs. For example, in more than 100 banks, services have been extended to home PC owners in the form of home banking systems. Subscribers to a home banking service use their personal computers as terminals linked to the bank's mainframe computer system to pay bills, transfer funds, and ask about account status.

6–2 DATA COMMUNICATIONS HARDWARE: MAKING IT HAPPEN

Data communications hardware is used to transmit digital information between terminals and computers and between all kinds of computers. These primary hardware components include the modem, the front-end processor, the multiplexer, and the router. The integration of these devices with terminals and computer systems is illustrated in Figure 6–3 and discussed in the paragraphs that follow.

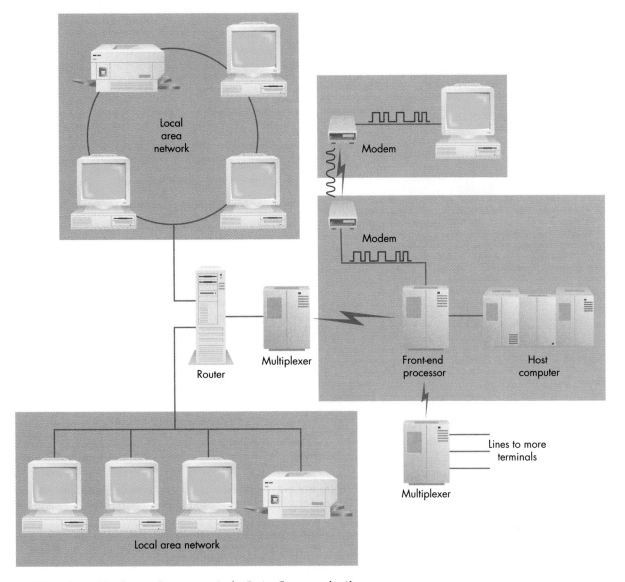

FIGURE 6–3 Hardware Components in Data Communications
Devices that handle the movement of data in a computer network are the modem, the multi-plexer, the front-end processor, router, and the host computer. Also in the figure, electrical digital signals are modulated (via a modem) into analog signals for transmission over telephone lines and then demodulated for processing at the destination. The lightening bolts indicate transmission between remote locations.

The Modem: Digital to Analog to Digital

If you have a micro, you can establish a communications link between it and any remote computer system in the world, assuming you have authorization to do so. However, to do this you must have ready access to a telephone line and your micro must be equipped with a *modem*. Most new PCs and many existing PCs are configured with modems.

Telephone lines were designed to carry *analog signals* for voice communication, not the binary *digital signals* (1s and 0s) needed for computer-based data communication. The modem (*mo*dulator-*dem*odulator) converts *digital* signals into *analog* signals so data

**Peripherals
Explorer**

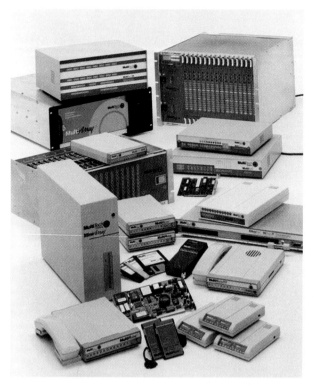

The applications of communications hardware are far more exciting than their appearance. Shown here are a wide variety of modems (internal, external, rack-mounted, PCMCIA card) and other communications hardware made by Multi-Tech Systems. Courtesy of Multi-Tech Systems, Inc.

can be transmitted over telephone lines (see Figure 6–3). The digital electrical signals are modulated to make sounds similar to those you hear on a touch-tone telephone. Upon reaching their destination, these analog signals are demodulated into computer-compatible signals for processing. The procedure is reversed for computer-to-terminal or computer-to-micro communication. A modem is always required when you dial up the computer on a telephone line. The modulation-demodulation process is not needed when a micro or a terminal is linked directly to a network by a transmission medium such as a coaxial cable.

Modems: Some Are In and Some Are Out   There are two types of modems for micros and terminals: *internal* and *external.* Most micros and terminals have internal modems; that is, the modem is on an optional add-on circuit board that is simply plugged into an empty expansion slot in the micro's processor unit or the terminal's housing. Laptops with PCMCIA-compliant interfaces use modems on interchangeable PC cards. The external modem is a separate component, as illustrated in Figure 6–3, and is connected via a serial interface port. To make the connection with a telephone line and either type of modem, you simply plug the telephone line into the modem just as you would when connecting the line to a telephone.

Fax Modems: Two for One   The *fax modem* performs the same function as a regular modem, with an added capability—it enables a PC to simulate a *facsimile* or *fax* machine. Fax machines transfer images of hard-copy documents via telephone lines to another location. The process is similar to using a copying machine except that the original is inserted in a fax machine at one location and a hard copy is produced on a fax machine at another location. PCs configured with a fax modem (an add-on circuit board or a PC card) can fax text and images directly from an electronic file to a remote facsimile machine or to another similarly equipped computer. They can also receive faxes (a printable file) sent from a fax machine or another PC. The fax modem is considered a must-have item on new PCs.

Special-Function Processors: Help along the Line

In Figure 6–3, the *host computer,* or central computer, is responsible for overall control of the computer system and for the execution of applications, such as a hotel reservation system. To improve the efficiency of a computer system, the *processing load* is sometimes *distributed* among several other special-function processors. The two communications-related processors in the computer system of Figure 6–3, the front-end processor and the multiplexer, are under the control of and subordinate to the host. In Figure 6–3, the host computer is a mainframe; however, the host could just as well be a micro, a workstation, or a supercomputer, depending on the size and complexity of the network.

The Front-End Processor   The terminal or computer sending a **message** is the *source.* The terminal or computer receiving the message is the *destination.* The **front-end processor** establishes the link between the source and destination in a process called **handshaking.** The front-end processor relieves the host computer of communications-related processing duties. These duties include the transmission of data to and from remote terminals and other computers. In this way, the host can concentrate on overall system control and the execution of applications software.

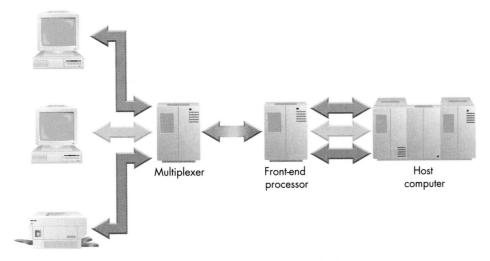

FIGURE 6–4 Concentrating Data for Remote Transmission
The multiplexer concentrates the data from several low-speed devices for transmission over a single high-speed line. At the host site, the front-end processor separates the data for processing. Data received from a front-end processor are interpreted by the multiplexer processor and routed to the appropriate device.

If you think of messages as mail to be delivered to various points in a computer network, the front-end processor is the post office. Each computer system and terminal/PC in a computer network is assigned a **network address.** The front-end processor uses these addresses to route messages to their destinations. The content of a message could be a prompt to the user, a user inquiry, a program instruction, an "electronic memo," or any type of information that can be transmitted electronically— even the image of a handwritten report.

The Multiplexer The **multiplexer** is an extension of the front-end processor. It is located down-line—at or near a remote site. The multiplexer collects data from several low-speed devices, such as terminals and printers. It then "concentrates" the data and sends the data over a single communications channel (see Figure 6–4) to the front-end processor. The multiplexer also receives and distributes host output to the appropriate remote terminals.

The multiplexer is an economic necessity when several low-speed terminals are at one remote site. One high-speed line connecting the multiplexer to the host is considerably less expensive than several low-speed lines connecting each terminal to the host. An airline reservation counter might have 10 terminals. Each terminal is connected to a common multiplexer, which in turn is connected to a central host computer. An airline might have one or several multiplexers at a given airport, depending on the volume of passenger traffic.

A microcomputer can be made to emulate the function of a multiplexer. This often occurs when a network of micros is linked to a mainframe computer.

Routers: Bridging the Gap

Computer networks are everywhere—in banks, in law offices, and in the classroom. In keeping with the trend toward greater connectivity, computer networks are being interconnected to give users access to a greater variety of applications and to more information. For example, one company linked several PC-based networks to the company's enterprise-wide mainframe network. This enabled end users on all networks to share information and resources.

**Serendipitous Surfing:
Government**

Communications protocols are rules established to govern the way data are transmitted in a computer network. Because networks use a variety of communications protocols and operating systems, incompatible networks cannot "talk" directly to one another. The primary hardware/software technology used to help alleviate the problems of linking incompatible computer networks is the **router.** Routers help to bridge the gap between incompatible networks. Upon receiving a message, the router performs the necessary protocol conversion and routes the message to its destination.

Organizations that are set up to interconnect computer networks do so over a **backbone.** The backbone is a collective term that refers to a system of routers and the associated transmission media (for example, fiber optic cable) that link the computers in an organization.

No Two Networks Alike

Networks are like snowflakes—no two are alike. Unlike snowflakes, however, networks never melt. Once created, networks seem to have a life of their own, growing with the changing needs of the organization. (Networks always grow. They never shrink.) Some networks have only PCs, with PCs performing the tasks of special-function processors and routers. Others have all these basic devices and more. There is a vast array of communications hardware and it's growing, especially with the trend to digital convergence. The more specialized devices are beyond the scope of this book.

6–3 THE DATA COMMUNICATIONS CHANNEL: DATA HIGHWAYS

A **communications channel** is the facility through which digital information is transmitted between locations in a computer network. During conversation, most people refer to a communications channel simply as the *line.*

Transmission Media: Wires and Wireless

Data, text, digitized images, and digitized sounds are transmitted as combinations of bits (0s and 1s) over a communications channel. A *channel's capacity* is rated by the number of bits it can transmit per second. The telephone lines that connect most homes to the telephone system can transmit about 28,800 **bits per second (bps),** or 28.8 K bps (thousands of bits per second). In practice, the word **baud** is often used interchangeably with *bits per second.* Technically speaking, however, it is quite different. But if someone says *baud* when talking about computer-based communications, that person probably means bits per second.

Data rates of 1540 K bps are available through **common carriers** such as American Telephone & Telegraph (AT&T). Common carriers provide channels for data transmission.

Twisted-Pair Wire: Old Faithful   **Twisted-pair wire** is the transmission media used to link your home or office telephone with the telephone system. A twisted-pair wire is actually two insulated copper wires twisted around each other. A single twisted-pair wire can handle a phone conversation or a data communications link. Over 20% of the traffic over long-distance telephone lines is data (fax or computer). Over 50% of the international transmissions are data.

Coaxial Cable   **Coaxial cable** contains electrical wire (usually copper wire) and is constructed to permit high-speed data transmission with a minimum of signal distortion. If you have ever hooked up a television, you probably are familiar with coaxial cable. Coaxial cable is laid along the ocean floor for intercontinental voice and

INTERNET BRIDGE

Transmission Media

data transmission. It is also used to connect terminals and computers in a "local" area (from a few feet to a few miles).

Fiber Optic Cable: Light Pulses   Very thin transparent fibers have been developed that will eventually replace the twisted-pair lines traditionally used in the telephone system. These hairlike fibers are bundled in a **fiber optic cable.** These cables carry data faster and are lighter and less expensive than their copper-wire counterparts. Twisted-pair wire and coaxial cable carry data as electrical signals. Fiber optic cable carries data as laser-generated pulses of light.

The differences between the data transmission rates of copper wire and fiber optic cable are tremendous. In the time it takes to transmit a single page of *Webster's Unabridged Dictionary* over twisted-pair copper wire (about 6 seconds), the entire dictionary could be transmitted over a single fiber!

Each time a communications company lays a new fiber optic cable, the world is made a little smaller. In 1956, the first transatlantic cable carried 50 voice circuits. Talking to Europe was expensive and a rare experience for most of us. Today, a single fiber can carry over 32,000 voice and data transmissions, the equivalent of 2.5 billion bits per second. Nowadays, people call colleagues in other countries or link up with international computers as readily as they call home.

Communications companies have gone into the construction business, repaving the information superhighway with fiber optic cable, at least between cities. Over the next decade, common carriers will need to extend fiber optic service to homes and businesses as well. We may not need to call 32,000 people at once, but bringing fiber optic cable to our homes will open the door to a myriad of exciting applications, like video on demand, videophones, and much more.

Another of the many advantages of fiber optic cable is its contribution to data security. It is much more difficult for a computer criminal to intercept a signal sent over fiber optic cable (via a beam of light) than it is over copper wire (an electrical signal).

MEMORY BITS

Transmission Media

- Twisted-pair wire
- Coaxial cable
- Fiber optic cable
- Wireless (microwave and radio signals)

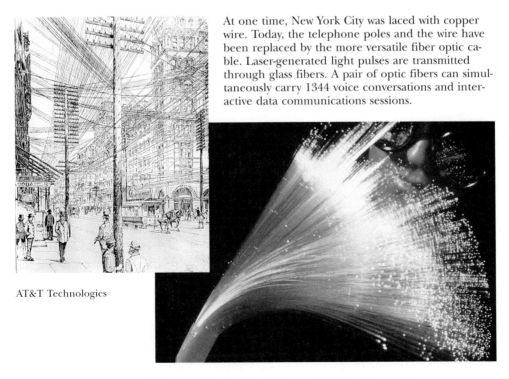

At one time, New York City was laced with copper wire. Today, the telephone poles and the wire have been replaced by the more versatile fiber optic cable. Laser-generated light pulses are transmitted through glass fibers. A pair of optic fibers can simultaneously carry 1344 voice conversations and interactive data communications sessions.

AT&T Technologies

Courtesy of International Business Machines Corporation

This lightweight, easily transportable, satellite communications system ensures that military troops can stay in touch anywhere in the world.
Courtesy of Harris Corporation

High-Speed Wireless Communication Communications channels do not have to be wires or fibers. Data can also be transmitted via **microwave signals** or **radio signals.** Transmission of these signals is *line-of-sight;* that is, the signal travels in a straight line from source to destination.

Microwave signals are transmitted between transceivers. Because microwave signals do not bend around the curvature of the earth, signals may need to be relayed several times by microwave repeater stations before reaching their destination. Repeater stations are placed on the tops of mountains, tall buildings, and towers, usually about 30 miles apart. Microwave transmission is used when running a cable is difficult or money can be saved. For example, a bank might opt to install its own microwave links between branch banks rather than to lease lines through a common carrier like AT&T.

Satellites have made it possible to reduce the line-of-sight limitation. Satellites are routinely launched into orbit for the sole purpose of relaying data communications signals to and from earth stations. Satellite data communication uses microwave signals. A satellite, which is essentially a repeater station, is launched and set in a **geosynchronous orbit** 22,300 miles above the earth. A geosynchronous orbit permits the communications satellite to maintain a fixed position relative to the earth's surface. Each satellite can receive and retransmit signals to slightly less than half of the earth's surface; therefore, three satellites are required to cover the earth effectively (see Figure 6–5). The main advantage of satellites is that data can be transmitted from one location to any number of other locations anywhere on (or near) our planet.

PCs Communicating without Wires One of the greatest challenges and the biggest expenses in a computer network is the installation of the physical links between its components. The **wireless transceiver** provides an alternative to running a permanent physical line (twisted-pair wire, coaxial cable, and fiber optic cable). Two PC-based wireless transceivers, each about the size of a thick credit card, replace a physical line between any source and destination. For example, wireless communication is routinely used to link these devices:

FIGURE 6–5 Satellite Data Transmission
Three satellites in geosynchronous orbit provide worldwide data transmission service.

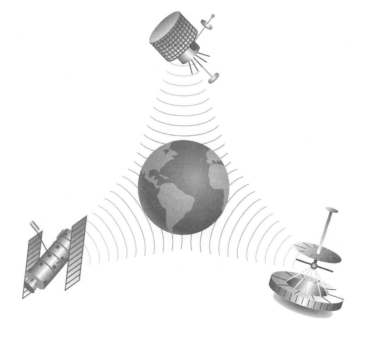

This notebook PC is linked to a LAN via a wireless transceiver (foreground). Wireless communication lets users take the PC and the LAN link with them to the conference room, the boss's office, or wherever they want to go within the range of the wireless link.   Courtesy of Harris Corporation

▶ Desktop PC and laptop PC

▶ Any PC and a LAN

▶ Any PC and a mainframe computer

▶ Terminal and multiplexer

▶ Laptop PC and page printer

The wireless transceiver hooks into the serial ports or the PCMCIA slots on the two computers. The transceivers, which have a limited range (about 50 feet), link computers via omnidirectional (360 degrees) radio waves. This means you can connect computers in adjacent rooms or even on different floors.

The source transmits digital signals via a physical link to a nearby transceiver, which, in turn, retransmits the signals over radio waves to another transceiver. Transceivers provide users with tremendous flexibility in the location of PCs and terminals in a network; however, the flexibility advantage is offset by the transceivers' limited channel capacity (about 115 K bps). Also, the number of terminals/PCs that can be linked via transceivers is limited by the frequencies allotted for this purpose.

The 1996 Olympics in Atlanta was the perfect venue for widespread use of wireless networks. Many sites at the games were made-to-order situations for wireless networks, temporary or difficult to wire. Wireless networks will allow judges, statisticians, and journalists to move with the action within and between venues.

Common Carriers: Anything but Common

It is impractical for companies to string their own fiber optic cable between distant locations, such as Philadelphia and New York City. It is also impractical for them to set their own satellites in orbit, although some have. Therefore, companies turn to *common carriers* for data communications, such as AT&T, MCI, Western Union, and

GOING ONLINE

6.3
What's New, Bill?

Software vendors have created informative Web sites to help us keep up with their latest software releases. Visit and peruse the Microsoft Web site ⟨http://www.microsoft.com⟩. Check out what Bill Gates, Microsoft's co-founder, said in one of his recent speeches.

Hand in: The text of the first couple of sentences from one of Bill Gates' speeches along with the location and date of the speech.

One of the services offered by common carriers is the facilitation of conferencing via telecommunications, called teleconferencing. Here, corporate colleagues in the United States and Japan are able to communicate effectively with one another without having to fly halfway around the world to do so. Photo courtesy of Hewlett-Packard Company

GTE, to provide communications channels for data transmission. Organizations pay communications common carriers for *private* or *switched* data communications service. Common carriers are regulated by the Federal Communications Commission (FCC).

A **private line** (or **leased line**) provides a dedicated data communications channel between any two points in a computer network. The charge for a private line is based on channel capacity (bps) and distance.

A **switched line** (or **dial-up line**) is available strictly on a time-and-distance charge, similar to a long-distance telephone call. You (or your computer) make a connection by "dialing up" a computer, then a modem sends and receives data. Switched lines offer greater flexibility than private lines in that a link can be made with any communications-ready computer near a telephone.

Low-speed modem-assisted transmission over conventional telephone lines will suffice for many applications, but some applications demand a higher channel capacity. Some common carriers offer a source-to-destination digital alternative using the **Integrated Services Digital Network (ISDN)** telecommunications standard. There is no need for modems in ISDN communication. ISDN services include several channel options, including a 144 K-bps channel and a 1540 K-bps channel.

ISDN may become obsolete when a new technology is implemented that permits high-speed communication over ordinary twisted-pair phone lines. With this new technology, anyone with standard telephone service will have access to a vast array of multimedia services. Telephone lines are connected to either a TV or a PC to enable interactive multimedia applications. The new technology is planned for implementation in most parts of the country by 1997.

When you apply for telephone service, you are asked if you want call waiting, caller ID, voice mail, and other additional services. All common carriers offer a variety of services over and above the basic data transmission service—for a fee, of course. These services may include electronic mail, data encryption/decryption, access to commercial databases, and code conversion for communication between incompatible computers. Some common carriers serve as an intermediary that helps facilitate EDI (electronic data interchange) between trading partners with incompatible hardware and software.

Data Transmission in Practice

A communications channel from Computer A in Seattle, Washington, to Computer B in Orlando, Florida (see Figure 6–6), usually would consist of several different transmission media. The connection between Computer A and a terminal in the same building is probably coaxial cable. The Seattle company might use a common carrier company such as AT&T to transmit the data. AT&T would then send the data through a combination of transmission facilities that might include copper wire, fiber optic cable, microwave signals, and radio signals.

6–4   NETWORKS: LINKING COMPUTERS AND PEOPLE

Each time you use the telephone, you use the world's largest computer network—the telephone system. A telephone is an endpoint, or a **node,** connected to a network of computers that routes your voice signals to any one of the 500 million telephones (other nodes) in the world. In a computer network the node can be a terminal, a

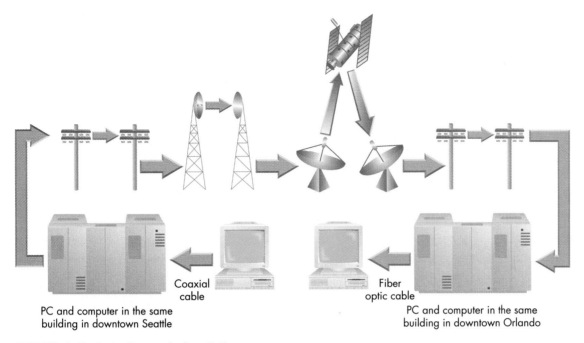

Coaxial
cable

Fiber
optic cable

PC and computer in the same
building in downtown Seattle

PC and computer in the same
building in downtown Orlando

FIGURE 6–6 Data Transmission Path
It's more the rule than the exception that data are carried over several transmission media
between source and destination.

computer, or any destination/source device (for example, a printer, an automatic
teller machine, or even a telephone). Computer networks are configured to meet the
specific requirements of an organization. Some have five nodes; others have 10,000
nodes. This section addresses the various approaches used to link nodes within an organization into a computer network.

Network Topologies: Star, Ring, and Bus

The basic computer **network topologies**—star, ring, and bus—are illustrated in Figure
6–7. A network topology is a description of the possible physical connections within
a network. The topology is the configuration of the hardware and shows which pairs
of nodes can communicate.

Star Topology   The **star topology** involves a centralized host computer connected
to several other computer systems that are usually smaller than the host. The smaller
computer systems communicate with one another through the host and usually share
the host computer's database. The host could be anything from a PC to a supercomputer. Any computer can communicate with any other computer in the network. Banks
often have a large home-office computer system with a star network of smaller mainframe systems in the branch banks.

Ring Topology   The **ring topology** involves computer systems approximately the
same size, with no one computer system as the focal point of the network. When one
system routes a message to another system, it is passed around the ring until it reaches
its destination address.

Bus Topology   The **bus topology** permits the connection of terminals, peripheral
devices, and microcomputers along a common cable called a **network bus.** The term
bus is used because people on a bus can get off at any stop along the route. In a bus
topology a signal is broadcast to all nodes, but only the destination node responds to
the signal. It is easy to add devices or delete them from the network as devices are

Networks

FIGURE 6–7 Network
Topologies
Network topologies include
(a) star, (b) ring, and (c) bus.

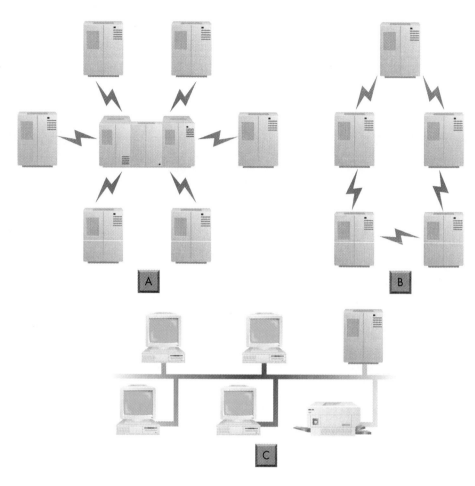

simply daisy-chained along the network bus. Bus topologies are most appropriate when the linked devices are physically close to one another. (See the discussion of local area networks that follows.)

Hybrid Topology   A pure form of any of these three basic topologies is seldom found in practice. Most computer networks are *hybrids*—combinations of these topologies.

Computer Systems Working Together: Client/Server Computing

Most computers, even PCs, exist as part of a network of computers. In this section we discuss the processing relationship between them.

Centralized Computing: A Bygone Era   Through the 1980s, processing activity within a computer network was accomplished, for the most part, by a centralized mainframe computer. The economies of scale were applicable. In this environment shared use of a centralized mainframe offered the greatest return for the hardware/software dollar. This is no longer true. PCs and workstations offer more computing capacity per dollar than mainframe computers. This reversal of hardware economics has caused information technology professionals to rethink the way they design and use computer networks.

During the era of centralized computers, users communicated with a centralized host computer that had dumb terminals with little or no processing capability. The mainframe performed the processing for all users, sometimes numbering in the thousands. With PCs and workstations exhibiting extraordinary price/performance, the trend in the design of computer networks is toward *client/server computing*.

This is the nerve center of EDSNET, Electronic Data Systems Corporation's global communications system. EDSNET facilitates data, voice, and video communication between a quarter of a million sites on five continents. Here in Plano, Texas (near Dallas), more than 100 operators manage the system. Operators view 12- by 16-foot screens to keep abreast of system activity. Fourteen smaller screens provide detailed information for trouble-shooting situations, and 13 clocks display times from around the world.   EDS photo by Steve McAlister

Decentralizing and Downsizing: A Growing Trend   In **client/server computing,** processing capabilities are distributed throughout the network, closer to the people who need and use them. A *server computer* supports many *client computers.*

▶ A **server computer,** which can be anything from a PC to a supercomputer, performs a variety of functions for its client computers, including the storage of data and applications software.

▶ The **client computer,** which is typically a PC or a workstation, requests processing support or another type of service (perhaps printing or remote communication) from one or more server computers.

In the client/server environment, both client and server computers perform processing. For example, the client computer system might run a database application *locally* (on the client computer) and access data on a *remote* (not local) server computer system. Client and server share processing duties to optimize application efficiency. In client/server computing, applications software has two parts—*the front end* and *the back end.*

▶ The client computer runs **front-end applications software** that performs processing associated with the user interface and applications processing that can be done locally (for example, database and word processing).

This company is moving toward a client/server computing environment. The users at client PCs in this office access a common database on this Compaq ProLiant PC server computer (foreground).   Reprinted with permission of Compaq Computer Corporation. All Rights Reserved.

▶ The server computer's **back-end applications software** performs processing tasks in support of its client computers. For example, the server might accomplish those tasks associated with storage and maintenance of a centralized corporate database.

In a client/server database application (see Figure 6–8), users at client PCs run front-end software to *download* (server-to-client) parts of the database from the server to their client PCs for processing. Upon receiving the requested data, perhaps data on customers in the mid-Atlantic region, the client user runs front-end software to work with the data. After local processing, the client computer may *upload* (client-to-server) updated data to the server's back-end software for processing. The server then updates the customer database. The database application is popular in client/server computing, but the scope and variety of applications are growing daily.

There is a mass migration *toward client/server computing* and *away from host-based networks.* Already more than 70% of all PCs are clients linked to at least one server computer and most workstations are either clients or servers. Because client computers have their own software and processing capability, they request only needed data. This results in reduced traffic over communications channels and increased speed and efficiency throughout the network. The trend toward client/server computing has resulted in companies downsizing their computers. **Downsizing** was coined to describe a policy that promotes increased reliance on smaller computers for *personal* and *enterprise-wide* processing tasks.

Network Line Control: Rules for Data Transmission

Communications Protocols: Transmitting by the Rules   *Communications protocols* describe how data are transmitted in a computer network. Communications protocols are defined in *layers,* the first of which is the physical layer. The physical

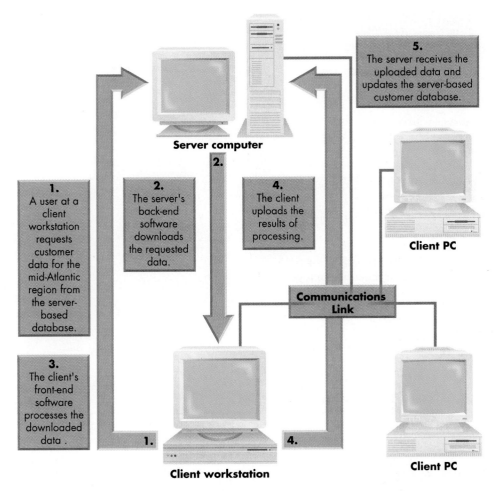

FIGURE 6–8 A Walkthrough of a Client/Server Database Application

layer defines the manner in which nodes in a network are connected to one another. Subsequent layers, the number of which vary between protocols, describe how messages are packaged for transmission, how messages are routed through the network, security procedures, and the manner in which messages are displayed. A number of different protocols are in common use.

Asynchronous and Synchronous Transmission Protocols fall into two general classifications: *asynchronous* and *synchronous* (see Figure 6–9). In **asynchronous transmission,** data are transmitted at irregular intervals on an as-needed basis. A modem is usually involved in asynchronous transmission. *Start/stop bits* are appended to the beginning and end of each message. The start/stop bits signal the receiving terminal/computer at the beginning and end of the message. In microcomputer data communications, the message is a single byte or character. Asynchronous transmission, sometimes called *start/stop transmission,* is best suited for data communications involving low-speed I/O devices, such as serial printers and micros functioning as remote terminals.

In **synchronous transmission,** the source and destination operate in timed synchronization to enable high-speed data transfer. Start/stop bits are not required in synchronous transmission. Data transmission between computers, routers, multiplexers, and front-end processors is normally synchronous.

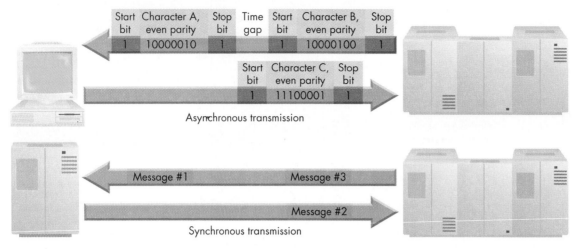

FIGURE 6–9 Asynchronous and Synchronous Transmission of Data
Asynchronous data transmission takes place at irregular intervals. In asynchronous transmission, the message is typically a single character. Synchronous data transmission requires timed synchronization between sending and receiving devices. The message is typically a block of characters.

A wide area network links air traffic controllers in this Federal Aviation Administration's regional facility in Seattle, Washington, to all other FAA locations.   Courtesy of Harris Corporation

6–5   LOCAL AREA NETWORKS: LOCAL NETS

With most PCs in industry, government, and education already linked to a LAN, a local area network, it is likely that you and your PC will be a part of one of these LANs. In this section we introduce you to those concepts that help you use your LAN effectively.

WANs, LANs, and TANs

A **WAN,** or **wide area network,** connects nodes in widely dispersed geographic areas, such as cities, states, and even countries. The WAN will normally depend on the transmission services of a common carrier to transmit signals between nodes in the network. In contrast, the *local area network* (*LAN*), or **local net,** connects nodes in close proximity, such as in a suite of offices or a building. The local net, including all data communications channels, is owned by the organization using it. Because of the proximity of nodes in local nets, a company can install its own communications channels (such as coaxial cable, fiber optic cable, or wireless transceivers); therefore, LANs do not need common carriers. **TAN,** or **tiny area network,** is a term coined to refer to very small LANs, perhaps two, three, or four nodes. For example, TANs are popular in home computing. They enable households to share resources (printer, modem, files) among the kids' PC, the parents' PC, and perhaps a parent's laptop from the office. When we refer to WANs, LANs, and TANs, we refer to all hardware, software, and communications channels associated with them.

These systems are linked via a LAN that is designed to enhance weather and flight information functions at air flight service stations.   Courtesy of E-Systems, Inc.

The focus of this section is the LAN. Strictly speaking, any type of computer can be incorporated within a LAN, but, in practice, PCs and workstations provide the foundation for local area networks. Micros in a typical LAN are linked to each other and share resources such as printers and disk storage. The distance separating devices in the local net may vary from a few feet to a few miles. As few as two and as many as several hundred micros can be linked on a single local area network. LANs with only a few nodes are sometimes called TANs.

Companies are incorporating more PCs into local area networks to facilitate communication among knowledge workers and to enable the sharing of valuable computing resources. LANs make good business sense because these and other available resources can be shared.

▶ *Applications software*. The cost of a LAN-based word processing program (for example, Word for Windows) is far less than the cost of a word processing program for each PC in the LAN.

▶ *Links to mainframes*. The mainframe becomes an accessible resource. It is easier to link the mainframe to a single LAN than to many individual PCs.

▶ *Communications capabilities*. A dedicated outside telephone line or a fax modem can be shared by many users.

▶ *I/O devices*. With a little planning, a single page printer, plotter, or scanner can support many users on a LAN with little loss of office efficiency. In a normal office setting, a single page printer can service the printing needs of up to 10 LAN users.

Emerging Technology

Working@Home

Traditionally, people get up in the morning, get dressed, and fight through rush hour to go to the office because that's where their work is. All this, however, is changing. People who work at home have accounted for more than half of all new jobs since 1987. For many knowledge workers, work is really at a PC or over the telephone, whether at the office or at home. PCs and communications technology make it possible for these people to access needed information, communicate with their colleagues and clients, and even deliver their work (programs, stories, reports, or recommendations) in electronic or hard-copy format. More and more people are asking: "Why travel to the office when I can telecommute?" Telecommuting is "commuting" to work via data communications. The trend toward PCs and networks has also fueled the growth of *cottage industries* where people work exclusively from their homes.

The Trend to Telecommuting

Millions of people are working at home full time: stockbrokers, financial planners, writers, programmers, buyers, teachers (yes, some teachers work exclusively with online students), salespeople, and graphic artists, to mention a few. A larger group is working at home at least one day a week: engineers, lawyers, certified public accountants, company presidents, mayors, and plant managers, to mention a few. Anyone who needs a few hours, or perhaps a few days, of uninterrupted time to accomplish tasks that do not require direct personal interaction is a candidate for telecommuting.

Through the early 1990s, telecommuting was discouraged. Management was reluctant to relinquish direct control of work-

ers. Managers were concerned that workers would give priority to personal, not business, objectives. Now we know that telecommuters are not only more productive, but they tend to work more hours. A recent Gartner Group study reported increases in productivity between 10% and 16% per telecommuter (as measured by employers). According to the study, each telecommuter experienced a two-hour increase in work time per day and saved the company about $4000 in annual facilities costs. It is only a matter of time before all self-motivated knowledge workers at all levels and in a variety of disciplines are given the option of telecommuting at least part of the time. Look at what companies are already doing.

- AT&T is encouraging its employees to telecommute on Tuesdays. Among other reasons, AT&T management is trying to support the lifestyle people think is desirable.
- The Canadian government hopes to save taxpayers hundreds of millions of dollars by encouraging telecommuting for public servants. Those who participated in a government-sponsored telecommuting pilot project reported a 73% increase in productivity.
- Pacific Bell offered telecommuting to its workers following the 1994 earthquake in Los Angeles. Ninety percent of the workers who took advantage of the "telecommuting relief package" were still working at home nine months after the earthquake. Half of those who opted to telecommute had not considered it before. Now half of those work at home five days a week. More than half of those are managers.

- *Storage devices.* Databases on a LAN can be shared. For example, some offices make a CD-ROM–based national telephone directory available to all LAN users.
- *Add-on boards.* Add-on boards, such as a fax modem boards, can be shared by many PCs.

Like computers, automobiles, and just about everything else, local nets can be built at various levels of sophistication. At the most basic level, they permit the interconnection of PCs in a department so that users can send messages to one another and share files and printers. The more sophisticated local nets permit the interconnection of mainframes, PCs, and the spectrum of peripheral devices throughout a large but geographically constrained area, such as a cluster of buildings.

In the near future you will be able to plug a terminal or PC into a network just as you would plug a telephone line into a telephone jack. This type of data communications capability is being installed in the new "smart" office buildings.

LAN Hardware

As we mentioned before, most LANs link PCs and workstations in the local area. The three basic hardware components in a PC-based LAN are the network interface cards, or NICs; the transmission media that connect the nodes in the network; and the servers.

The familiar surroundings of home inspire some people to do their best work. Others, however, are more comfortable working in traditional office setting. Reprinted with permission of Compaq Computer Corporation, All Rights Reserved

The Pros and Cons of Working at Home

Why Work at Home? Everyone has a different reason for wanting to telecommute. A programmer with two school-age children says, "I want to say good-bye when the kids leave for school and greet them when they return." A writer goes into the office once a week, the day before the magazine goes to press. She says, "I write all of my stories from the comfort of my home. An office that puts out a weekly magazine is not conducive to creative thinking." A company president states emphatically, "I got sick and tired of spending nights up in my office. By telecommuting, I'm at least within earshot of my wife and kids."

These are the most frequently citing reasons for working at home.

- *Increased productivity.* Telecommuters get more done at home than at the office.
- *Greater flexibility.* Telecommuters can optimize the scheduling of life events. For example, they can work late on Monday and take off for a few hours to exercise on Tuesday.
- *Improved relations with family.* Telecommuters spend more time with or around their family.
- *No commute.* The average commuter in a major metropolitan area spends the equivalent of one working day a week traveling to and from work. The telecommuter eliminates transportation expenses associated with the commute.
- *More comfortable and cheaper clothes.* Men willingly trade ties for T-shirts and women prefer sneakers to heels.
- *Cleaner air.* Telecommuting results in significantly less pollution, especially in large cities.

Arguments against Working at Home Working at home is not the answer for all workers. Some people are easily distracted and need the ready access to management and the routine of the office to maintain a business focus. Telecommuting is not possible when job requirements demand daily face-to-face meetings (for example, bank tellers and elementary school teachers). Telecommuters routinely interact with clients and colleagues over the telephone and e-mail. They even participate in online group meetings via groupware. However, those arguing against telecommuting say that this type of interaction does not permit "pressing of the flesh" and the transmittal of the nonverbal cues that are essential to personal interaction. These arguments, though valid, have done little to hamper the emergence of telecommuting as a mainstream business strategy.

Network Interface Cards The **network interface card (NIC),** which we described briefly in Chapter 2, "Inside the Computer," is a PC add-on card or PCMCIA card that facilitates and controls the exchange of data between the PC in a LAN. Each PC in a LAN must be equipped with an NIC. The cables or wireless transceivers that link the PCs are physically connected to the NICs. Whether as an add-on card or PCMCIA card, the NIC is connected directly to the PC's internal bus.

Only one node on a LAN can send information at any given time. The other nodes must wait their turn. The transfer of data and programs between nodes is controlled by the access method embedded in the network interface card's ROM. The two most popular access methods are *token* and *CSMA/CD*.

Token access method. When a LAN with a *ring* topology uses the **token access method,** an electronic *token* travels around a ring of nodes in the form of a *header.* Figure 6–10 demonstrates the token-passing process for this type of LAN. The header contains control signals, including one specifying whether the token is "free" or carrying a message. A sender node captures a free token as it travels from node to node, changes it to "busy," and adds the message. The resulting *message frame* travels around the ring to the addressee's NIC, which copies the message and returns the message

These Photonics transceivers use infrared technology to provide laptop and desktop PCs with wireless networking capabilities. The transceivers are connected to PCMCIA network interface cards (left) or expansion board NICs (right). Courtesy of Photonics Corporation

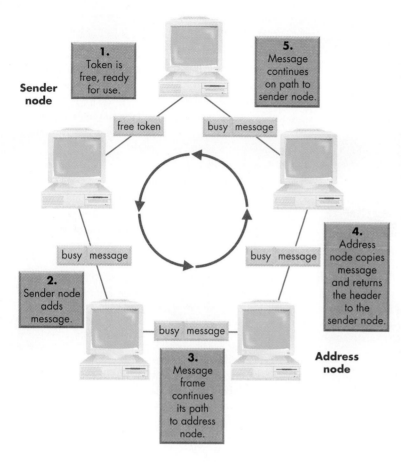

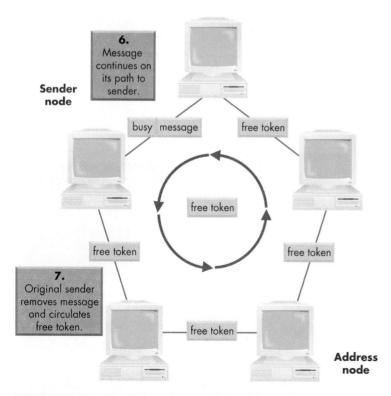

FIGURE 6–10 The Token Access Method in a LAN with a Ring Topology

frame to the sender. The sender's NIC removes the message frame from the ring and circulates a new free token. When a LAN with a *bus* topology uses the token access method, the token is broadcast to the nodes along the network bus. Think of the token as a benevolent dictator who, when captured, bestows the privilege of sending a transmission.

CSMA/CD access method. In the **CSMA/CD** (*C*arrier *S*ense *M*ultiple *A*ccess/*C*ollision *D*etection) **access method,** nodes on the LAN must contend for the right to send a message. To gain access to the network, a node with a message to be sent automatically requests network service from the network software. The request might result in a "line busy" signal. In this case the node waits a fraction of a second and tries again, and again, until the line is free. Upon assuming control of the line, the node sends the message and then relinquishes control of the line to another node. CSMA/CD LANs operate like a conversation between polite people. When two people begin talking at the same time, one must wait until the other is finished.

Moving the Data: LAN Transmission Media Three kinds of cables can be connected to the network interface cards: twisted-pair wire (the same wire cables used to connect telephones in a home), coaxial cable, and fiber optic cable. In wireless transmission, the cable runs from the transceiver to the NIC. Figure 6–11 illustrates how nodes in a LAN are connected along a network bus in a bus topology with a wiring hub at the end that allows several more nodes to be connected to the bus.

Servers: Serving the LAN In a LAN, a *server* is a component that can be shared by users on the LAN. The three most popular servers are the **file server,** the **print server,** and the **communications server.** These server functions may reside in a single PC or can be distributed among the micros that make up the LAN. When the server functions are consolidated, the server micro usually is *dedicated* to servicing the LAN. Some PCs are designed specifically to be dedicated **LAN servers.** The LAN server is high-end PC.

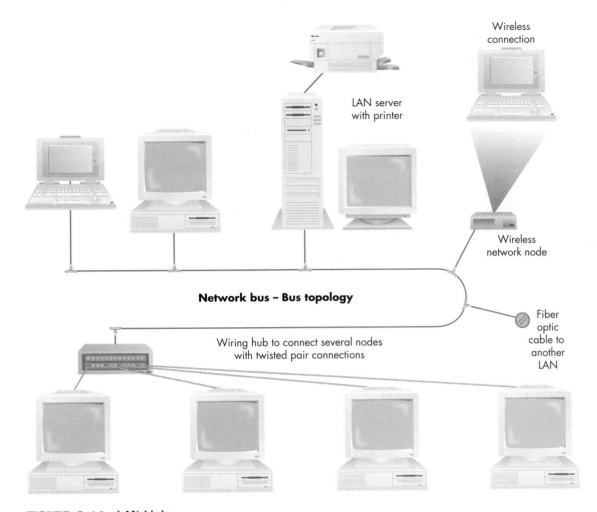

Network bus – Bus topology

LAN server
with printer

Wireless
connection

Wireless
network node

Fiber
optic
cable to
another
LAN

Wiring hub to connect several nodes
with twisted pair connections

FIGURE 6–11 LAN Links

In the figure, nodes in a LAN are linked via a bus topology. One of the nodes is linked to a
wiring hub that enables several PCs to be connected to the network bus. The wiring hub acts
like a multiplexer, concentrating transmissions from several nodes. The LAN is linked to
other LANs with fiber optic cable.

Until recently, you would purchase a traditional single-user micro and make it a
dedicated server. This continues to be an option with small- to medium-sized LANs,
but not in large LANs with 100 or more users. Now, micro vendors manufacture powerful micros designed specifically as LAN servers. LAN servers are configured with
enough RAM, storage capacity, and backup capability to handle hundreds of micros.

The *file server* normally is a dedicated micro with a high-capacity hard disk for storing the data and programs shared by the network users. For example, the master client
file, word processing software, spreadsheet software, and so on would be stored on
the server disk. When a user wants to begin a spreadsheet session, the spreadsheet
software is downloaded from the file server to the user's RAM.

The *print server* typically is housed in the same dedicated micro as the file server.
The print server handles user print jobs and controls at least one printer. If needed,
the server *spools* print jobs; that is, it saves print jobs to disk until the requested printer
is available, then routes the print file to the printer.

The *communications server* provides communication links external to the LAN—that
is, links to other networks. To accomplish this service, the communications server controls one or more modems.

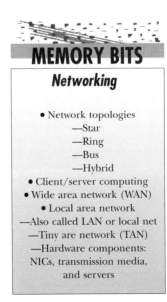

MEMORY BITS
Networking

- Network topologies
  —Star
  —Ring
  —Bus
  —Hybrid
- Client/server computing
- Wide area network (WAN)
- Local area network
—Also called LAN or local net
—Tiny are network (TAN)
—Hardware components:
NICs, transmission media,
and servers

Issues in Computing

Predicting Election Returns

Prior to 1951, people had to wait until the votes were counted to find out who won an election. That changed when a "giant brain," the Univac I computer, predicted Dwight Eisenhower the winner over Adlai Stevenson in the 1951 presidential election with only 5% of the votes counted. Today, computers are as much a part of Election Day as political rhetoric and flag waving. Critics, however, contend that these computer predictions keep many people away from the polls. Voters confess, "Why vote when the winner is already known?" The news media contend that it's the public's right to know.

Discussion: Should the media be allowed to report computer-based elections before the polls close?

LAN Software

In this section we explore LAN-based software, including LAN operating systems alternatives and a variety of applications software.

Network Operating Systems   **LAN operating systems,** the nucleus of a local net, come in two formats: *peer-to-peer* and *dedicated server.* In both cases, the LAN operating system is actually several pieces of software. Each processing component in the LAN has a piece of the LAN operating system resident in its RAM. The pieces interact with one another to enable the nodes to share resources and communication.

The individual user in a LAN might appear to be interacting with an operating system, such as MS-DOS or OS/2. However, the RAM-resident LAN software *redirects* certain requests to the appropriate LAN component. For example, a print request would be redirected to the print server.

Peer-to-peer LANs.   In a **peer-to-peer LAN,** all PCs are peers, or equals. Any PC can be a client to another peer PC or any PC can share its resources with its peers. Peer-to-peer LANs are less sophisticated than those that have one or more dedicated servers. Because they are relatively easy to install and maintain, peer-to-peer LANs are popular when small numbers of PCs are involved (for example, from 2 to 20). PCs running the Windows 95 operating system can be linked together in a peer-to-peer LAN.

LANs with dedicated servers.   In *LANs with dedicated servers,* the controlling software resides in the file server's RAM. LANs with dedicated servers can link hundreds of PCs in a LAN while providing a level of system security that is not possible in a peer-to-peer LAN. Two popular LAN operating systems are Novell's *NetWare* and Microsoft's *LAN Manager.*

Applications Software for LANs   LAN-based PCs can run all applications that stand-alone PCs can run plus those that involve electronic interaction with groups of people.

Shared applications software.   LANs enable the sharing of general-purpose software, such as WordPerfect (word processing) and Excel (spreadsheet). LAN-based applications software is licensed for sharing. The PCs on the LAN with a dedicated central server interact with a file server to load various applications programs. When a LAN-based PC is booted, software that enables the use of the network interface card, communication with the file server, and interaction with the operating system is loaded from the PC's hard disk to RAM. Depending on how the LAN system administrator

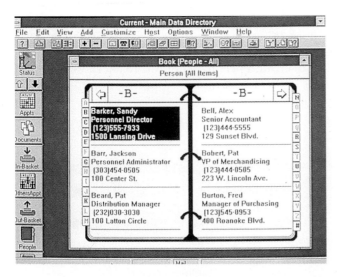
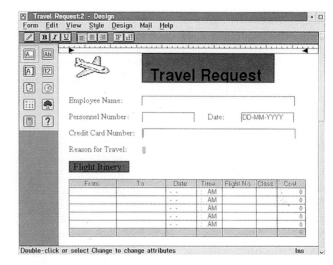

Users on a LAN can enjoy the benefits of workgroup computing. The online directory (left) helps expedite the routing of information to people on the workgroup. Electronic forms software (right) has made it possible to eliminate unnecessary paperwork.   Courtesy of International Business Machines Corporation/Courtesy of International Business Machines Corporation

configured the LAN, you may see a graphical user interface that lists software options or you may see a prompt from the operating system. When you select a software package, it is downloaded from the LAN's file server to your PC's RAM for processing. You can then work with shared files on the file server or with your own local files (those stored on your PC).

Groupware: Software for the group.   LANs have opened the door to applications that are not possible in the one-person, one-computer environment. For example, users linked together via a LAN can send electronic mail to one another. Scheduling meetings with other users on the LAN is a snap. This type of software is called groupware. *Groupware* is software whose application is designed to benefit a group of people. Local area networks and groupware provide the foundation for *workgroup computing*. The breadth of workgroup computing encompasses any application that involves groups of people linked by a computer network. The following is a sampling of workgroup computing applications.

- *Electronic mail (e-mail)*. E-mail enables people on a LAN to route messages to one another's electronic mailbox.
- *Calendar and scheduling*. People can keep online calendars and schedule meetings automatically. The scheduling software automatically checks appropriate users' electronic calendars for possible meeting times, schedules the meeting, and informs the participants via electronic mail.
- *Brainstorming and problem solving*. A LAN enables collaborative brainstorming and problem solving.
- *Setting priorities*. Groupware is available that enables LAN users to establish priorities for projects through collective reasoning.
- *Electronic conferencing*. Conferencing groupware lets LAN users meet electronically.
- *Electronic forms*. American businesses and government spend over $400 billion each year to distribute, store, and update paper forms. Electronic forms groupware lets LAN users create forms for gathering information from other LAN users.

Networks on the fly. The number and variety of workgroup computing applications can only increase. Already notebook PC users are creating networks on the fly. That is, they bring their computers to the meeting and attach them to a common cable or activate their wireless transceivers to create a peer-to-peer LAN. In effect, we have progressed from the *portable computer* to the *portable network.* Once part of a LAN, users can enjoy the advantages of groupware.

IMPORTANT TERMS AND SUMMARY OUTLINE

6–1 OUR WEIRD, WILD, WIRED WORLD Data communications (also called **telecommunications**) is the collection and distribution of the electronic representation of information from and to remote facilities. We rely on *computer networks* to retrieve and share information quickly; thus the current direction of **digital convergence. Connectivity** facilitates the electronic communication between companies and the free flow of information within an enterprise.

This is the era of **cooperative processing.** To obtain meaningful, accurate, and timely information, businesses have decided that they must cooperate internally and externally to take full advantage of available information. To promote internal cooperation, businesses are promoting intracompany networking. An application of intercompany networking is **electronic data interchange (EDI).**

6–2 DATA COMMUNICATIONS HARDWARE: MAKING IT HAPPEN Data communications hardware is used to transmit digital information between terminals and computers and between all kinds of computers. These primary hardware components include the modem, the front-end processor, the **multiplexer,** and the **router.**

Modems, both internal and external, modulate and demodulate signals so that data can be transmitted over telephone lines. The fax modem acts as a modem and enables a PC to simulate a facsimile machine.

The **front-end processor** establishes the link between the source and destination in a process called **handshaking,** then sends the **message** to a **network address.** The front-end processor relieves the host computer of communications-related tasks. The multiplexer concentrates data from several sources and sends it over a single communications channel.

Communications protocols are rules established to govern the way data are transmitted in a computer network. The primary hardware/software technology used to enable the interconnection of incompatible computer networks is the router. A **backbone** is composed of one or more routers and the associated transmission media.

6–3 THE DATA COMMUNICATIONS CHANNEL: DATA HIGHWAYS A **communications channel** is the facility through which digital information is transmitted between locations in a computer network. A channel's capacity is rated by the number of bits it can transmit per second (**bits per second** or **bps**). In practice, the word **baud** is often used interchangeably with *bits per second;* in reality, they are quite different.

A channel may be composed of one or more of the following transmission media: telephone lines of copper **twisted-pair wire, coaxial cable, fiber optic cable, microwave signals, radio signals,** and **wireless transceivers.** Satellites are essentially microwave repeater stations that maintain a **geosynchronous orbit** around the earth.

Common carriers provide communications channels to the public, and lines can be arranged to suit the application. A **private,** or **leased, line** provides a dedicated communications channel. A **switched,** or **dial-up, line** is available on a time-and-distance charge basis. Some common carriers offer a source-to-destination digital alternative using the **Integrated Services Digital Network (ISDN)** telecommunications standard.

6–4 NETWORKS: LINKING COMPUTERS AND PEOPLE Computer systems are linked together to form a computer network. In a computer network the **node** can be a terminal, a computer, or any other destination/source device. The basic patterns for configuring computer systems within a computer network are **star topology, ring topology,** and **bus topology.** The bus topology permits the connection of nodes along a **network bus.** In practice, most networks are actually hybrids of these **network topologies.**

In **client/server computing,** processing is distributed throughout the network. The **client computer** requests processing or some other type of service from the **server computer.** Both client and server computers perform processing. The client computer runs **front-end applica-**tions software and the server computer runs the **back-end applications software.** The trend toward client/server computing has resulted in companies **downsizing** their computers.

Asynchronous transmission begins and ends each message with start/stop bits and is used primarily for low-speed data transmission. **Synchronous transmission** permits the source and destination to communicate in timed synchronization for high-speed data transmission.

6–5 LOCAL AREA NETWORKS: LOCAL NETS A **WAN,** or **wide area network,** connects nodes in widely dispersed geographic areas. The *local area network (LAN),* or **local net,** connects nodes in close proximity and does not need a common carrier. A **TAN,** or **tiny area network,** is a very small LAN. The three basic hardware components in a PC-based LAN are the **network interface cards (NICs),** the transmission media, and the servers. The physical transfer of data and programs between LAN nodes is controlled by the access method embedded in the network interface card's ROM, usually the **token** or **CSMA/CD access method.** The three most popular servers are the **file server,** the **print server,** and the **communications server.** These server functions may reside in a dedicated **LAN server.**

The **LAN operating system** is actually several pieces of software, a part of which resides in each LAN component's RAM. In a **peer-to-peer LAN,** all PCs are equals. Any PC can share its resources with its peers. In LANs with dedicated servers, the controlling software resides in the file server's RAM.

LANs and *groupware* provide the foundation for *workgroup computing.* The breadth of workgroup computing encompasses any application that involves groups of people linked by a computer network. Workgroup computing applications include electronic mail, calendar and scheduling, brainstorming and problem solving, and others.

REVIEW EXERCISES

Concepts
1. Would EDI be more closely associated with intercompany networking or intracompany networking?
2. What is meant by *geosynchronous orbit,* and how does it relate to data transmission via satellite?
3. What is the unit of measure for the capacity of a data communications channel?
4. Expand the following acronyms: WAN, bps, and EDI.
5. What is the purpose of a multiplexer?
6. What is the relationship between a communications channel and a computer network?
7. What term describes the trend toward increased reliance on smaller computers?
8. List four workgroup applications.
9. What device converts digital signals into analog signals for transmission over telephone lines? Why is it necessary?
10. Why is it not advisable to increase the distance between microwave relay stations to 200 miles?

11. Name two subordinate processors that might be configured with a host computer to improve the overall efficiency of the computer system.
12. Name the three basic computer network topologies.
13. Name two popular LAN access methods. Which one passes a token from node to node?
14. Name three types of LAN servers.
15. Briefly describe the function of a router.

Discussion and Problem Solving

16. Describe circumstances in which a leased line would be preferred to a dial-up line.
17. What is the relationship between EDI and connectivity?
18. Describe how information can be made readily accessible to many people in a company, but only on a need-to-know basis.

19. The five PCs in the purchasing department of a large consumer-goods manufacturer are used primarily for word processing and database applications. What would be the benefits and costs associated with connecting the PCs in a local area network?
20. The mere fact that a system uses data communications poses a threat to security. Why?
21. Suppose you are a systems analyst for a municipal government. In the current incident-reporting system, transactions are batched for processing on the city's mainframe at the end of each day. You have been asked to justify to the city council the conversion from the current system to a LAN-based on-line incident-reporting system. What points would you make?

SELF-TEST (BY SECTION)

6–1 a. We are going through a period of digital convergence. (T/F)
b. The collection and distribution of the electronic representation of information between two points is referred to as _____ _____ .
c. Using computers and data communications to transmit data electronically between companies is called: (a) EDI, (b) DIE, or (c) DEI?
6–2 a. The modem converts _____ (digital or analog) signals to _____ (digital or analog) signals so that the data can be transmitted over telephone lines.
b. The terminal sending a message is the source and the computer receiving the message is the destination. (T/F)
c. Another name for a front-end processor is a multiplexer. (T/F)
d. _____ facilitate the interconnection of dissimilar networks.
6–3 a. It is more difficult for a computer criminal to tap into a fiber optic cable than a copper telephone line. (T/F)
b. A 9600-bits-per-second channel is the same as a: (a) 9.7-kps line, (b) 9.6 K-bps line, or (c) dual 4800X2 K-bps line.
c. The wireless transceiver replaces the physical link between the source and the destination in a network. (T/F)
d. The two basic types of service offered by common carriers are a private line and a switched line. (T/F)
e. The ISDN telecommunications standard is concerned with source-to-destination digital data transmission. (T/F)
6–4 a. An endpoint in a network of computers is called a _____.
b. The central cable called a network bus is most closely associated with which network topology: (a) ring, (b) star, or (c) bus?
c. The trend in the design of computer networks is toward: (a) distributed transmission, (b) client/server computing, or (c) CANs?
d. Synchronous transmission is best suited for data communications involving low-speed I/O devices. (T/F)
6–5 a. A LAN is designed for "long-haul" data communications. (T/F)
b. Which of the following is not a popular LAN access method: (a) token, (b) CSMA/CD, or (c) parity checking?
c. In a LAN with a dedicated server, the LAN operating system resides entirely in the server processor's RAM. (T/F)

Self-test Answers. 6–1 (a) T; **(b)** data communications; **(c)** a. **6–2 (a)** digital, analog; **(b)** T; **(c)** F; **(d)** Routers. **6–3 (a)** T; **(b)** b; **(c)** T; **(d)** T; **(e)** T. **6–4 (a)** node; **(b)** c; **(c)** b; **(d)** F. **6–5 (a)** F; **(b)** c; **(c)** F.

Going Online: Information Services, the Net, and More

Courtesy of Intel Corporation

Let's Talk

The following conversation introduces many of the terms in this chapter. Read it now, then again after you have read the chapter.

The Scene:
The place is a private chat room on a commercial information service where a widow, IdaB (Ida's online name), in Austin, Texas, and a retired railroad supervisor, RailroadRoy (Roy's online name), in Kingfisher, Oklahoma, are enjoying a cyber-romance.

RailroadRoy: Good evening, Ida. How are you tonight?

IdaB: I have a cold. :~) Worse, my 50-year-old son has left his good job in the city. :-(

RailroadRoy: Here's a dozen roses to pep you up. @->->- X12

IdaB: :-) Thanks. [*] Bill is taking a new job so he can **telecommute.** :-/ I'm a bit skeptical because I've never heard of Cyclometrics, his new company.

RailroadRoy: Me either, but I'll do some research. Let's **log off** now so I can get a **PPP** connection to the Cyclometrics **Web site.** Come back at 3:30 and I'll know more. **TTYL**

IdaB: Thanks, honey, bye now.***

(3:30)

RailroadRoy: Hi again, my little O :-). Check your **e-mail.** You'll find a file attached that contains more than you'll ever want to know about Cyclometrics.

IdaB: Hi, sweetie. [*] How'd you do it?

RailroadRoy: I visited its **World Wide Web site** on **the Internet at http://www.cyclometrics.com.** The company's got a sound financial statement, some innovative products, and a bright future.

IdaB: How do you know all that?

RailroadRoy: I clicked on a few **hypertext** links and even listened to an audio message from its president. You might want to visit the site yourself. It's really informative.

IdaB: Thanks, triple R. I'm going surfin'. See you tomorrow—same time. [[[[****]]]]

STUDENT LEARNING OBJECTIVES

▶ *To describe the purpose, use, and applications of general-purpose PC-based communications software.*

▶ *To demonstrate an awareness of the scope of services made available by online information services (America Online, CompuServe, Prodigy, and so on).*

▶ *To describe the Internet.*

▶ *To demonstrate an awareness of the scope of services made available over the Internet.*

▶ *To identify and describe common Internet capabilities.*

7–1 PC-BASED COMMUNICATIONS SOFTWARE

Your PC is a door to the world. To open the door, simply plug the phone line into your PC's modem and run your communications software. Once online, you can "chat" with friends in Europe, send Grandma a picture, schedule a meeting with your co-workers, pay the utility bill, play games with people you've never met, or conduct research for a report. Every day the number of things you can do online multiplies. Tens of millions are **telecommuting** to work each day over the digital highways. Telecommuters work from their homes via data communications links to their offices. This chapter explores your online options and shows how you, too, can enjoy and benefit from the wonders of PC-based communications software.

Telecommuting

Communications Software: The PC Takes On a New Role

Communications software is the key that unlocks the door to a new world of information and information-related services. With communications software, a micro becomes more than a small stand-alone computer: It becomes capable of interacting with a remote computer, whose location may be in the next room or in New Zealand.

There are a number of commercially available general-purpose communications packages, including PROCOMM PLUS, CommWorks, and QuickLink. Each of these packages has features that set it apart from the others. In this section we will emphasize the basic capabilities common to these and other full-function communications packages—terminal emulation, file transfer, host operation, and fax support.

▶ *Terminal emulation.* Communications software transforms a PC into an intelligent video display terminal (VDT) that can be linked to another computer (see Figure 7–1). The user at a terminal (or PC) logs on to a host computer to establish a communications link. A PC is not a terminal, but with the aid of communications software, information technology can emulate, or act like, one. When a micro is in **terminal emulation mode,** the keyboard, the monitor, and the data interface function like that of the terminal being emulated. Terminal emulation is necessary to enable a PC to gain access to certain computers (for example, those that support BBSs).

▶ *File transfer.* Communications software enables the transfer of files between a PC and another computer. Once the link between the PC and host has been established, any kind of digital file (data, program, text, image, sound, video) can be *downloaded* from disk storage on the host computer to disk storage on the PC. Files also can be *uploaded.* The file transfer capability supported by communications software can be invaluable when you need to transfer files between computers.

▶ *Host operation.* **Host mode** operation is the flip side of terminal emulation mode. Host mode operation allows you to set up your PC so remote users can call in and establish a communications link via terminal emulation. Once online, remote users can download or upload files.

Going Online

▶ *Fax support.* Communications software lets you send and receive faxes directly from your PC. (Your PC must be configured with an image scanner to fax hard-copy documents.) This feature eliminates the need to print a hard copy

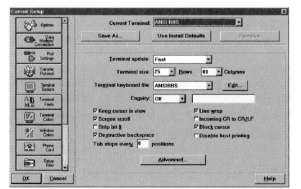

FIGURE 7–1 Terminal Emulation
PROCOMM PLUS communications software enables PC emulation of all commonly used terminals. Here, the terminal options setup screen specifies terminal emulation for the ANSI BBS terminal.

While waiting in an airport limo, this real estate executive uses his PC, communications software, and cellular phone to send a fax to the home office.   Reprinted with permission of Compaq Computer Corporation. All Rights Reserved/Courtesy of Harris Corporation

of a computer-based document and load it to a fax machine for transmission. To fax a word processing document, a spreadsheet document, or any other type of document, you would go through the same procedure. To send a fax, you print to a fax modem rather than a printer. Here is how it works.

1. Select the "Print" option in the pull-down "File" menu.
2. Select the "Fax" printer option in the print dialog box.
3. Enter the number of the destination fax machine and send the fax.

To receive a fax, simply activate the fax software and wait for the call. Each page of the fax transmission is placed in a separate file that can be displayed or printed as needed.

Preparing for an Interactive Session with a Remote Computer

When you use a PC, a modem, and data communications software to establish a link with another computer, the communications software will prompt you to specify the *telephone number* to be called and certain data communications *parameters*, or descriptors. These parameters may include the following:

▶ *Type of terminal emulation.* Specify the type of terminal to be emulated. Most host systems will hook up with several popular types of terminals. You will need to emulate a terminal that is accepted by the host. The options might include the generic ANSI BBS, TTY, VT-100, VT-52, IBM 3270, and others.

▶ *File transfer protocol.* Select the protocol used by the host to transfer files (for example, Zmodem, Xon/Xoff, Kermit, Xmodem). The protocol establishes the rules for transmitting and receiving data.

▶ *Port settings.* The PC's modem communicates through a serial port. You must tell the communications software which port is used and select options that specify how data are transmitted.

Serial port	Select the appropriate port. Serial ports are labeled COM1, COM2, COM3, and COM4 on PC-compatible computers.
bps or baud rate	Select the appropriate transmission rate. Common bps settings are 2400, 9600, 14,400, 19,200, and 28,800 bps (bits per second). Special high-speed lines may allow up to 115,200. *Bps* sometimes is labeled as *baud rate* even though, technically speaking, they are quite different.
Parity checking	In data communications, data in the form of coded characters are continuously transferred at high rates of speed. Both sending and receiving computers use a built-in checking procedure, called **parity checking,** to help ensure that the transmission is complete and accurate. Normally you would check either *none* (the most common setting) or *even* (CompuServe, the information service, uses even parity).
Data bits	Specify the number of bits in the character or byte (seven bits, for even parity, or eight bits).
Stop bits	"Stop" is actually a misnomer in that the stop bit is actually a timing unit. Usually you would select 1 for PC-based data communications.
Data flow (full or half duplex)	Select half or full duplex. Communications channels that transmit data in both directions, but not at the same time, are called **half duplex**. A channel that transmits data in both directions at the same time is called **full duplex**. Selecting half duplex causes each character you enter to be *echoed* (returned by the host). Most online services and BBSs expect full duplex.

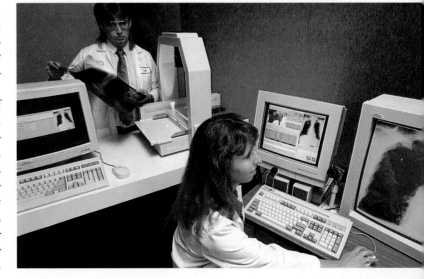

The medical communities in sparsely populated areas are going online to get the most out of their collective capabilities. Multimedia workstations enable teleconferencing and the sharing of medical information. Here, physicians are evaluating X-rays simultaneously with physicians in another city.   Courtesy of E-Systems, Inc.

Depending on the communications protocol, communications package, and hardware you are using, you may need to specify other parameters as well. For example, you might wish to display 43 lines of text rather than the default 25 as specified in the setup screen in Figure 7–1.

Communications software offers a variety of handy, time-saving features. For example, you can store the telephone number and the settings (parameters) for a particular bulletin-board system, information service, or mainframe computer in a *communications profile*. To establish a link with another computer, simply retrieve and activate the appropriate communications profile. From there, the communications software takes over and automatically dials and logs on to the remote computer. It will even redial if it gets a busy signal.

Logging On: Sign in Please

Now you are ready to log on. To interact with a remote computer, you must establish a link between your PC or terminal and the remote computer. All VDTs and most PCs are part of established computer networks. In these cases, the link to a LAN or a centralized computer is permanent, perhaps via a coaxial cable. However, if no link exists, the user must dial up the remote computer via the telephone system. In either case, the user must log on to the system once the link is made. The **log on** procedure, which may ask the user to enter a user ID and a user-defined **password,** helps protect a computer system against unauthorized access and use. Figure 7–2 walks you through the log on procedure.

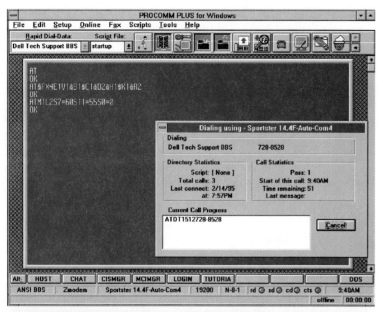

1. The communications software dials the telephone number specified for the "Dell [Computer Corporation] Tech Support BBS" profile (see inset of "Dialing" dialog box). Online users can prepare profiles of frequently called BBSs and information services to expedite the log on procedure.

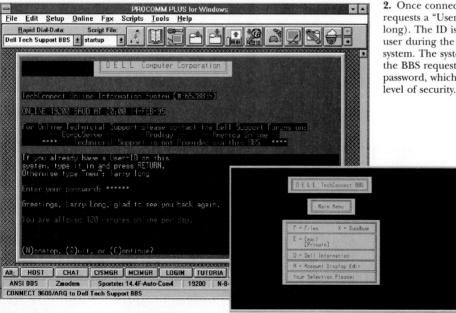

2. Once connected, the Dell BBS returns its banner and requests a "User-ID." The user enters a user ID (larry long). The ID is simply a character string chosen by the user during the initial interaction or assigned by the host system. The system uses the ID to identify the user. Then the BBS requests a password (entered as ******). The password, which is chosen by the user, provides another level of security.

3. Once the remote computer validates the user ID and password, the remote computer normally will present the user with a menu of options. Unauthorized users are disconnected. The Dell TechConnect BBS is more than a BBS. It allows users to download files, post messages for tech support people, and obtain information.

FIGURE 7–2 Log on Procedure
PROCOMM PLUS communications software, shown here, allows you to establish a communications link with a remote computer. The text transmission during the interactive session appears in the blue boxed area.

To terminate a session, the user must **log off** the system. This may be as simple as returning to the main menu and selecting the "log off" option or entering "bye" at the system prompt. Once log off is complete, the user must log on to begin another session.

Bulletin-Board Systems: Communications Software in Action

PCs that double as terminals can take advantage of a wide variety of communications-based applications. Later in this chapter we will discuss how to go online with a commercial information service, such as Prodigy, and how to surf the Internet. Another major area of online activity is the *bulletin-board system (BBS)*. The BBS is the electronic counterpart of a wall-mounted bulletin board. It enables users in a computer network to exchange ideas and information via a centralized message database. There are literally thousands of BBSs. Some are sponsored by the world's largest companies and some are run out of basements by teenagers. The person or group sponsoring the BBS is referred to as the **system operator,** or **sysop**.

Most cities with a population of 25,000 or more have at least one bulletin-board system, often sponsored by a local computer club. Members "post" messages, announcements, for-sale notices, and more "on" the computer bulletin board by transmitting them to a host computer—usually another PC. Members can also upload files to and download files from the BBS host.

Regional and national special-interest bulletin boards abound, focusing on anything from matchmaking to UFOs. The Clean Air BBS deals with health and smoking topics. The U.S. Census Bureau sponsors several BBSs. People looking for jobs might scan the listings on the Employ-Net BBS. Catch up on which fish are biting and which are not by tapping into the Fly-Fishers Forum BBS. The do-it-yourselfer might want to log on to the Popular Mechanics Online BBS. Enter your own movie review on the Take 3 BBS. Lawyers talk with one another on the Ye Olde Bailey BBS. A Denver BBS is devoted to parapsychology. Some senators and members of Congress sponsor BBSs to facilitate communication with their constituents. A number of BBSs are devoted to religious topics.

Leveraging PC Power

PCs have placed the power of computers at our finger tips. Communications software expands that capability by enabling micro users to become a part of any number of computer networks. Once part of the network, a user can take advantage of the awesome power of mainframe computers, the information in their databases, and the opportunity to communicate electronically with others on the network.

7–2 INFORMATION SERVICES: AMERICA ONLINE, COMPUSERVE, AND MANY MORE

More and more PC users are subscribing to commercial online information services, such as America Online, CompuServe, GEnie, Prodigy, Microsoft Network (MSN), The Source, Dow Jones News/Retrieval Service, DIALOG, and NewsNet. Information services have grown at a rate of 30% per year since 1990. Still, less than 25% of PC owners subscribe to an online information service, so there is plenty of room to grow. Look for information services to be one of the fastest growing industries during the 1990s. The largest information services, CompuServe, America Online, and Prodigy, already have several million subscribers each. Information services have several powerful mainframe computer systems that offer a variety of information services, from hotel reservations to daily horoscopes.

GOING ONLINE

7.2
Make Space for Space

Travel to the NASA Web site <http://www.nasa.gov> to learn about NASA's Goddard Space Flight Center.

Hand in: A brief historical description of the Goddard Space Flight Center, including the year it was created.

Going Online Explorer

To take advantage of these information services, you need a communications-equipped PC (modem and communications software) and a few dollars. You normally pay a *one-time fee* and a *monthly service charge.* For the initial fee, you get:

1. A communications software package designed specifically to interface with the information service.
2. A user ID and password.
3. A users' guide that includes telephone numbers that can be dialed to access the information service. (If you live in a medium-to-large city, the telephone number you dial is usually local.)

The monthly service charge varies from $5 to $20 for the most popular services. The charge can be much more for business-oriented services. Your monthly bill is based on how much you use the information service.

Figure 7–3 takes you on a visual tour of America Online, one of the most popular information services. This walkthrough figure shows you a few of the well-traveled roads on this stretch of the information highway, but it doesn't begin to show the true breadth and scope of America Online (AOL). If you were to spend every waking minute online for the next year, you would not be able to explore all of its features, bulletin boards, databases, download opportunities, and information services. In fact, you would probably fall behind. Existing services are updated and new services are added on AOL and all of the other information services every single day.

7–3 THE INTERNET: A WORLDWIDE WEB OF COMPUTERS AND INFORMATION

America Online (AOL), the information service, is one of the many beautiful stars in cyberspace. Now imagine being able to explore an entire universe with millions of beautiful stars, each offering databases, forums, e-mail, files of every conceivable type, information services, and more. That's *the Internet.*

What Is the Internet?

Once on the Internet, cybersurfers can tap into a vast array of information resources, have access to millions of retrievable files, "talk" on thousands of worldwide bulletin boards, send e-mail to any of millions of people, and take advantage of thousands of free and pay-for-use information services. Unlike AOL, CompuServe, Prodigy, and other information services, the Internet is coordinated by volunteers on an advisory committee. The Internet (*inter*connected *net*works), the world's largest network, is actually comprised of thousands of independent networks at academic institutions, military installations, government agencies, commercial enterprises, and other organizations.

Just how big is the Internet? The Net, the Internet's nickname, links more than 100,000 networks with over 4,000,000 hosts in almost every country in the world. Internet hosts are connected to the Internet 24 hours a day. Thousands more join this global network each month. The number of Internet users is expected to reach 180 million by the year 2000, up from an estimated 60 million in 1997.

The Internet is one of the federal government's success stories. Shortly after its creation in 1969, the first e-mail message was sent and the rest is history. The government is taking an active role in promoting cooperation between communications, software, and computer companies to create a *National Information Infrastructure (NII).* Most people would agree that the Internet is the basis for what may someday be the NII. The NII is also called the *information superhighway,* the *infobahn,* and many other names. The federal government wants to link schools, libraries, hospitals, corpora-

The Internet

(*text continues on page 203*)

FIGURE 7–3 Touring America Online

This multipage illustration takes you on a tour of 13 of the 14 America Online "departments." The "Internet Connection" department is featured in Figures 7–5 through 7–10.

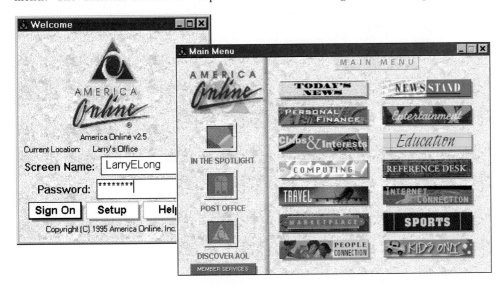

Sign On to America Online Prior to going online with America Online (AOL), you must install the AOL program disk to your PC's hard disk. The program contains communications software and a graphical user interface that allows you to navigate among the many AOL services. To go online, run the AOL program and go through the "sign on" procedure (see example). First you enter your AOL *screen name*— your online persona. Some people use their real name, but most use an alias, like SkyJockey, CaptBart, PrincesLea, and so on. Once you enter your password, which appears as asterisks, the software dials the AOL number, makes the connection, and displays the AOL main menu (see example). The main menu is divided into 14 departments, 13 of which are discussed and illustrated in this figure.

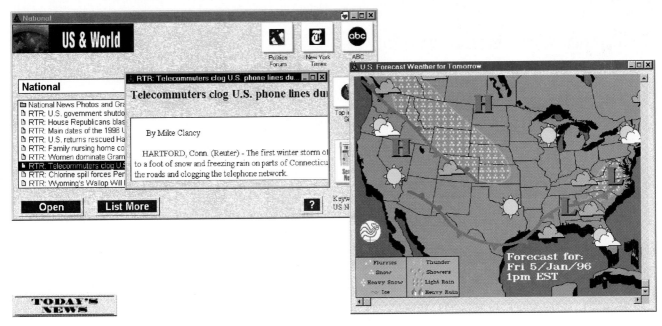

Today's News AOL's Today's News department offers up-to-the-minute news in five areas: United States and world, business, entertainment, sports, and weather. On-line news gives you the latest releases directly from the wire services. You can request general news or news about a specific topic. For example, you can request news about Australia, French politics, the plastics industry, or whatever interests you. In the example, the user chose to read an article on the space shuttle. The user could have elected to browse through an electronic version of *The New York Times* (click on New York Times icon). You can also request a short- or long-term weather forecast for any region in the world (see example).

Even television news is going online. PBS's *Nightly Business Report* now provides transcripts, market analysis, business news briefs, personal finance tips, and expert commentary over America Online. AOL members can be a part of the news by posting messages to *NBR* reporters and show guests.

(*Figure 7-3 cont. next page*)

FIGURE 7-3 (cont.)

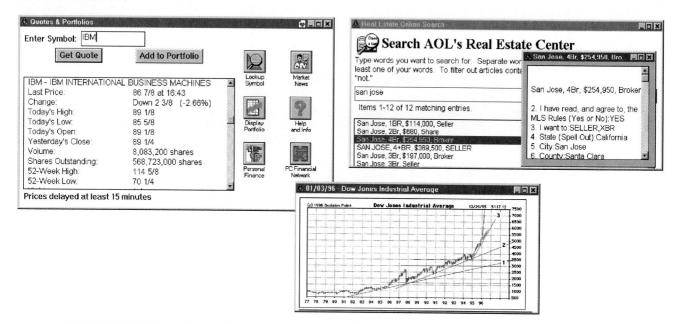

Personal Finance   Get up-to-the-minute quotes on stocks (see IBM quote), securities, bonds, options, and commodities. A wealth of financial information is available for the asking (see Dow Jones graph of averages over a twenty-three-year period). You also can use this service to help you manage a securities portfolio and to keep tax records. You can even purchase and sell securities from your PC.

Are you moving? If so, check out available real estate by scanning the listings for your destination city. In the example, the user searched through listings in San Jose, California.

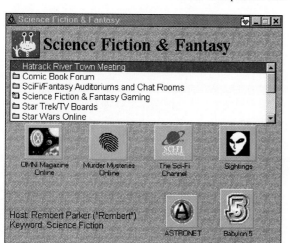

Clubs and Interests   Among the millions of people who go online each day, many belong to the same clubs and have interests similar to yours. You can share notes with fellow sci-fi fans (see example). Or, you can talk with fellow homeowners, environmentalists, bikers, aviators, and so on. Whatever your interest, there is probably an online *forum* that offers an opportunity to interact and share information (health tips, recipes, travel deals, art, and so on). The AOL forum, which may be called an *area* or *club* on other information services, is a theme-based electronic area in which people can share ideas, information, and files that relate to the theme (astrology, fiction writing, and so on).

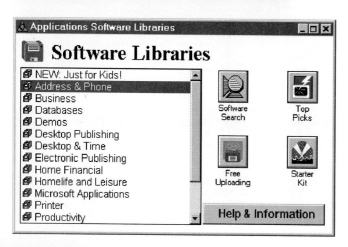

Computing   On any information service, the computing department is among the most active. PC enthusiasts can chat for hours about any subject relating to hardware or software. This AOL department lets you download any of thousands of programs (shareware, freeware, and those programs uploaded by AOL members), from games to CAD (computer-aided design) programs (see Software Libraries example). AOL maintains a list of the 500 most frequently downloaded software packages. You can catch up on the latest technology news and talk directly with hardware and software vendors through the "Industry Connection."

Travel You can plan your own vacation or business trip over AOL. All you have to do is check airline (see flight availability example), train, and cruise schedules, then make your reservations. You can even charter a yacht in the Caribbean, locate the nearest bed-and-breakfast inn, or rent a lodge in the Rockies.

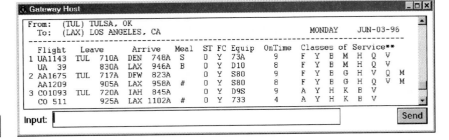

Marketplace The AOL Marketplace is the ultimate in one-stop shopping. You can get everything from pickup trucks to contact lenses, often at discount prices. You can even order personalized greeting cards to be delivered (see example). Electronic shopping adds a new dimension to shopping—information. For example, you can research financial services, telephone companies, car insurance agencies, or a particular product. Photo quality displays are available for many products.

Shop at your leisure. The online store is never closed and there is no clerk rushing you to a decision. Online shopping helps you get the most for your money. It's easy to comparison shop or check out the recommendation of *Consumer Reports*. If you are in the market for a new automobile, you can find out exactly what the dealer paid for a particular automobile.

Online shopping is changing the landscape of merchandising. Look what is happening to the recording industry. Traditionally, the recording industry has distributed music in the form of records, cassette tapes, and CDs. When CD-R (recordable CD) becomes as popular as CD-ROM, we may be buying our music online. The foundation has been laid. In 1994, Geffen Records began experimenting with information services as an alternate means of distribution. "Head First," a song left off an Aerosmith CD, was offered free to CompuServe subscribers. In this experiment, CompuServe did not charge for download connect time (about 60 minutes for the 4.3 MB song) and Aerosmith waved royalties.

People Connection An online information service is a community where people chat about the weather, gather after work to relax at a virtual pub, go shopping, ask advice, and share things. This electronic community, however, doesn't reflect society as a whole. Whether we will admit it or not, how we look, where we live, our economic status, and so on affects who we talk with and often the subject. This emerging electronic society allows people to set aside traditional social mores and interact freely regardless of race, creed, color, sex, age, appearance, ability, education, and so on. Cybersurfers have an opportunity to meet and converse with those who might be outside their social circle in real life. Members of the electronic society have talked openly with the President and Vice President of the United States. They have talked with the rich and famous. Even more importantly, they have talked with those who are younger or older, richer or poorer, or of different religions. In an electronic society, you are a player. For a few pennies, you can cross geographic, political, economic, and social boundaries and be heard by thousands, if not millions, of other players.

AOL offers a variety of ways for members to communicate, primarily *chat rooms, message boards*, and *e-mail*. The nomenclature for people-to-people online communications capabilities varies between commercial information services and the Internet. For example, an electronic bulletin board is called a *message board* (AOL), *newsgroup* (the Internet), *forum* (CompuServe), *table* (Delphi), and simply *bulletin board* (Genie).

Chat rooms. People "enter" AOL chat rooms and talk with real people in real time. In the example, 21 people in the "romanceconnection" chat room are talking trivia. It's like having a conference call, except the people involved key in their responses. You can "listen in" or be an active part of the electronic conversation. AOL sponsors three types of chat rooms: public (special-topic rooms defined by AOL), member (special-topic rooms defined by AOL members), and private (rooms created by members for private conversations). Chat rooms are found in all AOL departments, not just the People Connection.

AOL chat rooms have a couple of interesting features. You can send an instant message directly to a particular individual in the room. Your message appears on that individual's screen near the scrolling chat

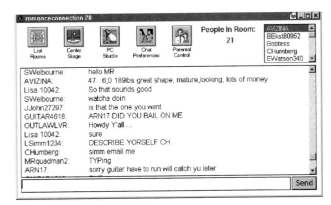

(Figure 7-3 cont. next page)

FIGURE 7-3 (cont.)

room conversation. Also, you can view the profile of a particular person in the room by clicking on that person's screen name (see the box in the upper-right corner in the "romanceconnection" example). Most AOL members maintain an online member profile that can be viewed on request. The profile contains basic information about the AOL member. If no profile is posted, you have no way of knowing whether you're talking with a middle-aged woman, an elementary schoolboy, or an intelligent parrot.

Often, special guests are invited to auditoriums (a large chat room with slightly different rules) to meet with AOL members. When Vice President Al Gore participated in an online conference held over CompuServe, 900 people "showed up" for the conference, of which, over 300 got responses. During the conference, Gore noted that two-way interactive communication was far superior to the one-way communication of broadcast TV.

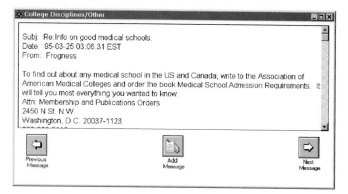

Message boards. The AOL message board is what is generically known as an electronic bulletin board. Electronic bulletin boards provide a great platform for the exchange of ideas and information. People post electronic messages, just as you might pin a note to a wall-mounted bulletin board. You can post a message or respond to an existing message on any of thousands of special-topic AOL message boards. In either case, your message is posted to the message board for all to see. In the example, Frogness posted a message to the "College Disciplines/Other" message board. AOL message boards are denoted in the GUI by the pushpin icon. Pushpin icons are prominent in most AOL forums.

Messages are culled periodically to remove old messages. The life of a message is anywhere from a few days to a few weeks, depending on the way the message board is set up. Normally, the life span of a message is determined by the volume of replies. The life is extended if the original message continues to get replies.

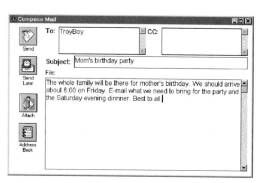

E-mail. Send e-mail to and receive it from other AOL members. Each AOL member has an electronic mailbox (identified by the screen name). E-mail sent to a particular member can be "opened" and read only by that member. To send an e-mail message, the user simply enters the screen name of the recipient (TroyBoy in the example), keys in a message, and clicks the send icon to place the message in the recipient's electronic mail box.

E-mail messages are limited to simple ASCII text to enable ease of transmission between dissimilar computers. Therefore, you can not embed graphics and do fancy formatting as you might in a word processing document. You can, however, attach a file to an e-mail message. For example, you might wish to send a program or a digitized image along with your message. The file is sent to AOL's central computers where it can be downloaded by the recipient.

AOL's e-mail has many features. For example, you can forward the mail easily to other interested persons. You can even send your e-mail to a fax machine. E-mail features and services continue to grow. One of the information services translates e-mail messages posted in French and German into English, and vice versa.

The combined volume of mail handled by United States Postal Service is about half a billion pieces each day, currently about twice that of all electronic communications (e-mail and fax). As we begin to send birthday invitations and greetings cards via e-mail, the volume of electronic mail will be double that of traditional mail in the near future.

News Stand AOL has a growing number of alliances with popular magazines and newspapers: *The New York Times,* (see example), *Chicago Tribune, San Jose Mercury, The Atlantic Monthly, Wired, Popular Photography,* and *Road & Track,* to mention a few. Online magazines and newspapers are now a reality. The electronic version is not just a digital version of the print media, it is much more. For starters, news can be delivered as it happens not with the morning newspaper or a weekly magazine. Stories that might be cut or condensed in print media are placed online in their entirety. Also, you can find topics of special interest whether in the current or past issues. In the *The New York Times* example, the user searched past issues for articles that included the words *Microsoft, Bill,* and *Gates.*

Online newspapers, in particular, include more in-depth information especially on local issues, such as a school-by-school summary of daily activities and the lunch menu, write-ups of social activities, and so on. Much of the material in online newspapers is supplied by interested persons, not by newspaper staff (for examples, school lunch menus). Both online magazines and newspapers offer cross-references to related stories and news sources. Both offer forums for online discussions.

Entertainment The Entertainment Department is just that—entertainment. You can read reviews of the most recently released movies, videos, CDs, plays, and books. The Hollywood Online forum offers pictures of movie and TV stars (see example), classic sound clips, a movie-talk message board, and more. You can play single-player games, such as digital football, and multiplayer games, such as MegaWars. Or, you might prefer to match wits with another trivia buff. You can visit the cartoon forum for some laughs.

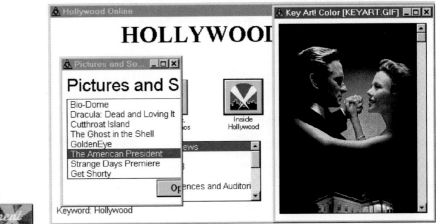

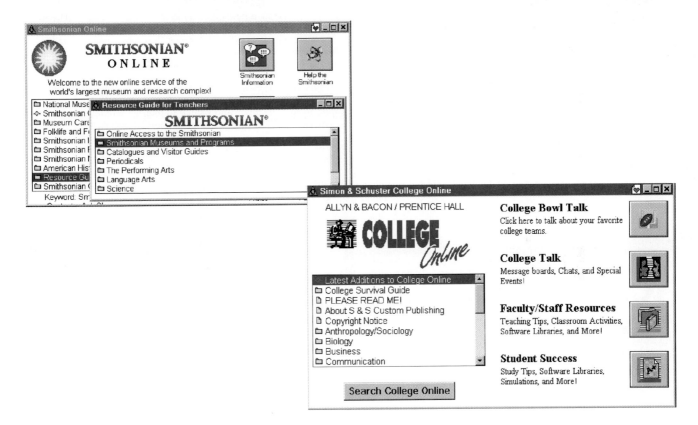

Education The Education Department is a potpourri of forums associated with learning and knowledge. Elementary teachers can tap into the Resource Guide for Teachers at the Smithsonian (see example). College professors and students can tap in to the Simon & Schuster College Online forum (see example) where they can talk with one another, obtain teaching hints and student study tips, scan through software libraries, and keep up with what's new with Simon & Schuster multimedia activities. (Prentice Hall, the publisher of this book, is the primary sponsor of this forum.)

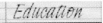

The education resources available to members include National Geographic Online, the Library of Congress Online, *Compton's Encyclopedia*, and much, much more. The Electronic University Network offers online students an opportunity to obtain baccalaureate degrees and postgraduate degrees in a wide range of subjects. You can choose from a variety of educational packages, from learning arithmetic to preparing for the Scholastic Aptitude Test (SAT). You can even determine your IQ!

(*Figure 7-3 cont. next page*)

FIGURE 7-3 (cont.)

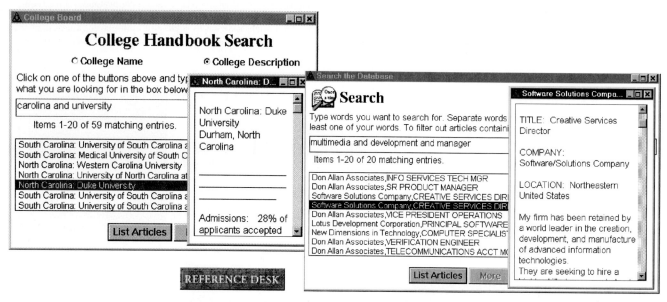

Reference Desk   The information society is adopting a new approach to seeking information. The traditional approach involved finding print sources, then thumbing through them one-by-one. This approach is a bit cumbersome for today's knowledge worker. The Reference Desk department allows users to search through dozens, even hundreds of books, documents, or databases in minutes. For example, students seeking a college might want to query the College Handbook service for information about colleges of interest. In the example, a college student who wanted to attend a university in North or South Carolina entered the search string "carolina and university." The resultant search lists all college profiles that mention both "carolina" and "university." The student then double-clicked on "Duke University" for more information. In the other example, an AOL member who wanted to manage multimedia development projects searched a Job Listings database with the search string "multimedia and development and manager."

There are literally hundreds of databases that offer information in as many areas. For example, politicians can scan through various government publications on key words. You can recall articles on any conceivable subject from dozens of newspapers, trade periodicals, and newsletters. Lawyers have access to a complete law library online. No matter what your question, you can probably find an answer in the Reference Desk department.

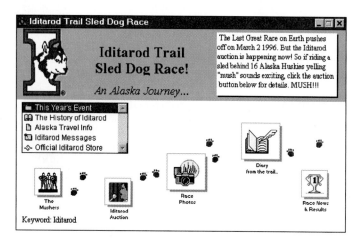

Sports   In the Sports department, you can get up-to-the-minute scores for college and professional sporting events. Sports enthusiasts who revel in statistics need look no further—it's easy to find out who did what, when, and to whom. Sports fans can go to chat rooms and talk to one another about their favorite sport, team, or sports figure. You can even follow the annual Iditarod Trail Sled Dog Race from the warmth of your home (see examples).

(Figure 7-3 cont. on next page)

Kids Only   Kids Only is KOOL (Kids Only OnLine) and kids love it. Kids Only is actually a hodgepodge of services from all AOL departments, but just for kids. The chat rooms in the "Tree House" are designed for kids, as are the reading materials, such as *Disney Adventure*. Of course, one of the most popular Kids Only forums is "Goosebumps."

tions, agencies at all levels of government, and much more by the twenty-first century. The role of government is unclear. Currently the administration appears to be more of a catalyst than an active participant.

From ARPANET to the Internet: Some Historical Perspective

A lot happened in 1969, including Woodstock and the first landing on the moon. Amidst all of this activity, the birth of what we now know as the Internet went virtually unnoticed. A small group of computer scientists on both coasts were busy creating a national network that would enable the scientific community to share ideas over communications links. At the time this was truly a giant leap because computers were viewed more as number crunchers than as aids to communication.

The Department of Defense's Advanced Research Project Agency (ARPA) sponsored the project, named ARPANET, to create a new community of geographically dispersed scientists who are united by technology. The first official demonstration linked UCLA with Stanford University, both in California. Ironically, this historic event had no reporters, no photographers, and no records. No one remembered the first message, only that it worked. By 1971, the ARPANET included more than 20 sites, including Harvard and MIT. By 1981, the ARPANET linked 200 sites. This grand idea of interconnected networks caught on like an uncontrolled forest fire, spreading from site to site throughout the United States. Other countries wanted in on it, too.

ARPANET broke new ground. The diversity of computers and the sites forced ARPA to develop a standard protocol (rules of data communications) that would enable communication between diverse computers and networks. ARPANET eventually lost its reason to exist, as other special-interest networks took its place. In 1990, ARPANET was eliminated, leaving behind a legacy of networks that evolved into the Internet. At that time, commercial accounts were permitted access to what had been a network of military and academic organizations.

Making the Internet Connection

How do you get on the Internet? There are three basic ways to connect your PC to the Internet. These ways are summarized in Figure 7–4 and explained below.

1. *Connect via an information service.* The easiest way to gain access to the Internet is to subscribe to a commercial information service, such as America Online or Prodigy (see Figure 7–4). This is a popular choice for people working from

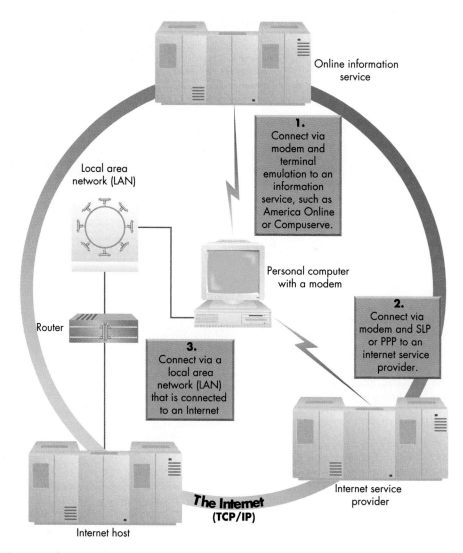

FIGURE 7–4 Ways to Connect to the Internet

their home or small businesses and for those who wish to link their home PC to the Internet. These information services provide an electronic *gateway* to the Net that allows access to many of the Net's most popular features. Figures 7–5 through 7–10 demonstrate interaction with the Internet through the America Online gateway, and Figure 7–11 shows the Prodigy gateway.

The gateway is necessary to link information service subscribers to the Net. Communications over the Net are built around the **Transmission Control Protocol/Internet Protocol (TCP/IP)**. All Internet hosts must have the ability to communicate via TCP/IP. TCP/IP is different from the protocol used within the AOL network, Prodigy network, and other information service networks. Their Internet gateways enable communication between the information services' native communications protocols and TCP/IP.

2. *Connect via an Internet service provider.* The only way to get full Internet service via a dial-up connection is through an Internet service provider (see Figure 7–4). Some information services double as Internet service providers. A number of Internet hosts offer Internet service for a fee. You dial into the provider, as you would an information service. However, once online, you are on the Internet, not a gateway, and have access to everything the Internet has to offer. To get this access, you must have an account with a service provider and software that enables a direct link via TCP/IP. Your dial-up connection is

made through a *SLIP* (Serial Line Internet Protocol) or *PPP* (Point-to-Point Protocol) server on the service provider's Internet host. A "Slip" connection is slow in that it is limited to phone line speeds (usually 9600 bps, 14.4 k bps, or 28.8 k bps).

3. *Direct via network connection.* A direct connection to the Internet is preferable to a dial-up link (alternatives 1 and 2 above) because interaction with the Internet is much faster. This means you do not have to wait so long between requests. It's not unusual to wait several minutes for an Internet response on a dial-up line. To have a direct connection, your PC must be configured with TCP/IP software and be connected to a LAN that is linked to an Internet host (see Figure 7–4).

Do you want to be a *newbie*? Newbies are what seasoned surfers call novice Internet users. If you do, there is a good chance that your college or company's computer network is linked to the Internet. Obtaining access may be as easy as asking the network administrator to assign you an Internet address and password.

The Internet Address: username@lan.host.com

People on the Internet send/receive e-mail/files and interact with other networks through an Internet address. Think of an Internet address as you would your mailing address. Each has several parts with the most encompassing part at the end. When you send mail outside the country, you note the country at the end of the address. The Internet address has two parts and is separated by an @ symbol. Consider this Internet address:

spenc_ba@cis.stateuniv.edu

▶ *User ID.* On the left side of the @ separator is the user ID (usually all or part of the user's name). Organizations often standardize the format of the user name so users don't have to memorize so many user names. One popular format is shown in the above example: the first five letters of the last name (*spenc*er), an underscore (_), and the first two letters of the first name (*ba*rbara).

▶ *Host/network identifier.* That portion to the right of the @ identifies the host or network. The host/network identifier adheres to rules for the domain hierarchy. At the top of the domain hierarchy is the country code for all countries except the United States. For example, the address for information about UUNET Canada, Inc. is *info@uunet.ca*. Other common country codes are *au* (Australia), *dk* (Denmark), *fr* (France), and *jp* (Japan). The country code is replaced with affiliation categories for addresses within the United States. The U.S. top-level domains denote affiliation.

Colleges are in the *edu* category. At the next level might be the name of a college or business (*stateuniv* or *prenhall*). Large organizations might have networks within a network and need subordinate identifiers. The example Internet address, *spenc_ba@cis.stateuniv.edu,* identifies the *cis* local area network at *stateuniv*. The Physics Department LAN at State University might be identified as *physics.stateuniv.edu.* Note that the top level is on the right and that the levels are separated by periods.

Internet Applications: E-Mail, Newsgroups, FTP, the Web, and More

There are at least as many applications in the Internet as there are houses in Moscow. To a newbie, navigating around the Internet is like driving around Moscow without a road map or a knowledge of the Russian language. You can see and enjoy the build-

U. S. Top-level Domain Affiliation ID	Affiliation
edu	Education
com	Commercial
gov	Government
int	International
mil	Military
net	Network resources
org	Usually nonprofit organizations

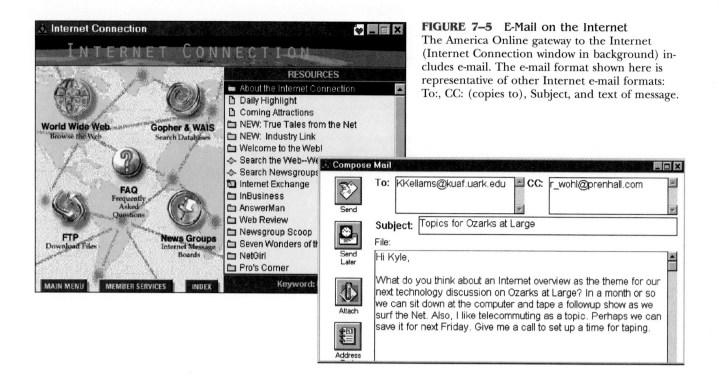

FIGURE 7–5 E-Mail on the Internet
The America Online gateway to the Internet (Internet Connection window in background) includes e-mail. The e-mail format shown here is representative of other Internet e-mail formats: To:, CC: (copies to), Subject, and text of message.

ings but you might not know how you got there or where you are going. To truly appreciate Moscow, you would need to learn a little of the Russian language and the layout of the city. The same is true of the Internet. This takes time and a lot of practice. In this brief space, we can only hope to expose you to the main thoroughfares. As you gain experience and confidence, you can veer off onto the Internet's side streets.

Surfers on the Net prefer to use GUI-based software whenever available. Each commercial information service offers its own GUI. There are many commercial software packages available that let you point-and-click your way around the Internet (for example, Internet in a Box). The GUIs shown in Figures 7–5 through 7–10 are from America Online. What you see in these examples may be different from what you see on your Internet connection, but what you enter and the resultant information are the same.

E-mail on the Net   Internet e-mail is like company e-mail or AOL e-mail, but with a great many more electronic mailboxes. You can send an e-mail message to anyone on the Net, even talk show host David Letterman *(lateshow@cbs.com)*. He may not reply because of the volume of mail, but you can request a subscription service that sends the Top-Ten list and show highlights to your e-mail address. Use Internet e-mail to give your congressperson a few political hints. Internet e-mail is illustrated in Figure 7–5.

Newsgroups and Mailing Lists   A *newsgroup* is the Internet version of an electronic bulletin board. *Newsgroups* is a misnomer in that you seldom find any real news. They are mostly electronic discussion groups. Almost 30,000 newsgroups entertain global discussions on thousands of topics. If you're unable to reach David Letterman via e-mail, you can talk about Dave on an Internet newsgroup *(alt.fan.letterman,* the name of the newsgroup). Sometimes Dave joins the fun. If Letterman is not your cup of tea, you can join another newsgroup and talk about Rush Limbaugh *(alt.fan.rush-limbaugh.tv-show),* Madonna *(alt.fan.madonna),* or Elvis *(alt.fan.elvis-presley).* Real Elvis fans can learn about recent Elvis sightings on the *alt.elvis.sighting* newsgroup. Internet newsgroups are illustrated in Figure 7–6.

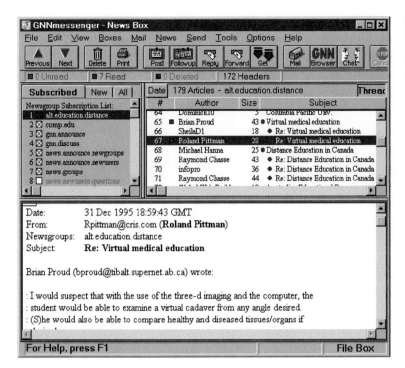

FIGURE 7–6 Newsgroups on the Internet
People frequenting this distance-learning-theme newsgroup (alt.education.distance) post messages related to distance-learning. In the example, a response to a "Virtual medical education" message is displayed.

The Internet *mailing list* is a cross between a newsgroup and e-mail (see Figure 7-7). Mailing lists are like newsgroups in that people discuss issues of common interest. There are mailing lists for most, if not all, of your personal interest areas. Here is the way a mailing list works. You scan or search available mailing lists, then *subscribe* to those that interest you. To subscribe, you simply send an e-mail message to the mailing list sponsor. Generally there is no subscription fee. The sponsor puts you on the list. Once on the list you receive every e-mail message sent to the mailing list by subscribers. To send e-mail to all subscribers to the list, simply send e-mail to the mailing list address. This is called "sending mail to the list." Subscribing to a mailing list can be stimulating and, possibly, overwhelming—remember, each message posted is

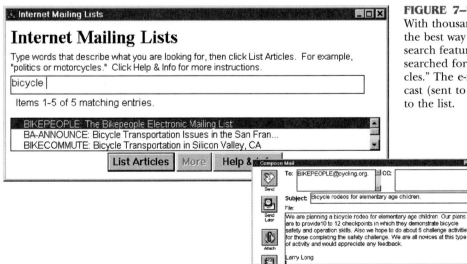

FIGURE 7–7 Mailing Lists on the Internet
With thousands of mailing lists on the Internet, the best way to find what you want is to use the search feature. In the example, the user searched for a mailing list that addresses "bicycles." The e-mail message shown here is broadcast (sent to more than one) to all subscribers to the list.

Issues in Computing

Prescreening of Online Communications

Millions of people have access to and participate in the bulletin boards and online forums. Some information services feel obligated to give their subscribers an environment that is free of offensive language. These information services use an electronic scanner to "read" each message before it is posted to a bulletin board or a forum. In a split second the scanner flags those words and phrases that do not comply with the information service's guidelines. The scanner even catches words or phrases that may be disguised with asterisks and so on. Generally the guidelines are compatible with accepted norms in a moral society. These include the use of grossly repugnant material, obscene material, solicitations, and threats. The scanner also scans for text that may be inappropriate for a public discussion, such as the use

of pseudonyms, attempts qat trading, presentation of illegal material, and even speaking in foreign languages. Messages that do not pass the prescreening process are returned automatically to the sender.

Some might cry that their rights to freedom of expression are violated. This, of course, is a matter that may ultimately be decided in a court of law. In the meantime, those who wish a more open discussion have plenty of opportunities. On some national bulletin boards and information services, anything goes.

Discussion: Is prescreening of electronic communications a violation of freedom of expression?

broadcast to all on the list. If you subscribe to a couple of active mailing lists, your Internet mailbox could be filled with dozens if not hundreds of messages—each day! So, if you can't get enough of David Letterman through a newsgroup, send "Subscribe TOP5" to *listserve@gitvm1.gatech.edu* to subscribe to the "TOP 5: Letterman-Style Comedy Discussion List."

FTP: Downloads for the Asking The **File Transfer Protocol (FTP)** allows you to download and upload files on the Internet. Tens of thousands of FTP sites offer millions of useful files—most are free for the asking. *FTPing* is a popular activity on the Net. You can download exciting games, colorful art, music from up-and-coming artists, statistics, published and unpublished books, maps, photos, utility and applications programs, anything that can be stored digitally. Many FTP sites invite users to contribute (upload) files of their own.

You must be an authorized user (know the password) to access many FTP sites. Many, however, are **anonymous FTP sites** that maintain public archives. Anonymous FTP allows anyone on the Net to transfer files without prior permission. The trick to successful FTPing is knowing where to look. Figure 7–8 walks you through a search for FTP files related to "music."

Telnet: Remote Login Telnet refers to a class of Internet application programs that let you log into a remote computer using the Telnet communication protocol. **Telnet** is a *terminal emulation* protocol that allows you to work from a PC as if it were a terminal linked directly to a host computer. Thousands of Internet sites around the world have Telnet interfaces. Once online to one of these sites, you can run a normal interactive session as if you were sitting at an on-site terminal. You can run programs, search databases, execute commands, and take advantages of many special services. For example, you can search through the county library's electronic card catalog, play chess with students from other campuses, scan the pages of *USA Today*, or run programs to analyze data from an experiment.

Information Servers: From Gopherspace to the Web No person or group of people monitors or tracks information on the Internet, consequently, there is no source or index that tells you what information is on the Net or how to find it. The

Internet has thousands of databases, such as the *Congressional Record*, NIH clinical information, a list of job openings for the entire United States, the lyrics to "Yesterday" by the Beatles—you name it and it's probably on the Net. These databases are located on information servers. An **information server** is an Internet host with a repository of information that is made available over the Internet. To get the information you

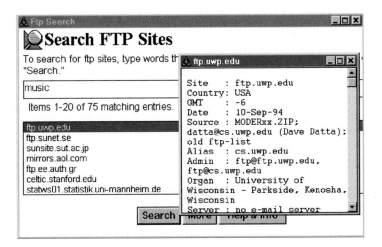

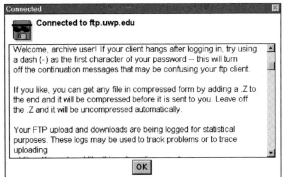

1. A search of anonymous FTP archives on "music" yields 75 sites, including *ftp.uwp.edu* (The University of Wisconsin—Parkside). A site description is superimposed over the search screen.

2. The user enters the desired Internet host address (*ftp.uwp.edu*) connect to the FTP site. FTP site information is displayed once the connection is made.

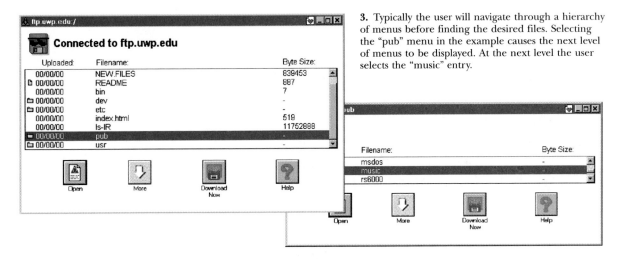

3. Typically the user will navigate through a hierarchy of menus before finding the desired files. Selecting the "pub" menu in the example causes the next level of menus to be displayed. At the next level the user selects the "music" entry.

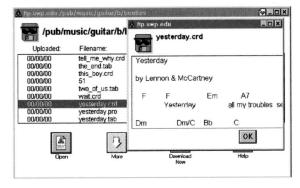

4. In the resulting menu the user selects "guitar" (not shown) to display a menu with yet another menu. The menu (also not shown) includes letters of the alphabet as entries. Desiring the lyrics and chords for "Yesterday," the user selects "b," then "Beatles" from successive menus. The next level displays retrievable files. All the user has to do from here to download the file is to highlight the desired file and click the "Download Now" button. The highlighted file is displayed in the foreground window.

FIGURE 7–8 FTPing on the Internet
The figure illustrates how one might search through anonymous FTP archives to find files related to "music."

want, you must look for it. There are three ways to search the Internet: *search, browse,* or *ask someone.*

▶ *Searching the Net.* The Net helps those who help themselves. It offers a variety of resource discovery tools to help you find the information or service you need. Several of the many Internet search tools are discussed in this section.

▶ *Browsing the Net.* Browsing is good if you are just looking for a good recipe or information on computer viruses. When you browse the Net you work through menu trees, selecting paths that meet your immediate information needs.

▶ *Asking someone.* People on the Net are a family, ready to help those in need. Don't hesitate to post an inquiry to a newsgroup or mailing list when you need help. Of course, the subject matter should relate to the theme of the newsgroup or mailing list. Many newsgroups maintain FAQ (frequently asked questions) files that you can view or download. Your question may have been asked and answered before.

1. At the top of the gopher menu tree is an alphabetic list of topic areas. Choosing "Census" displays another menu.

2. The user opted to view the "Detailed Occupation..." document from the "U.S. Census Summaries" menu.

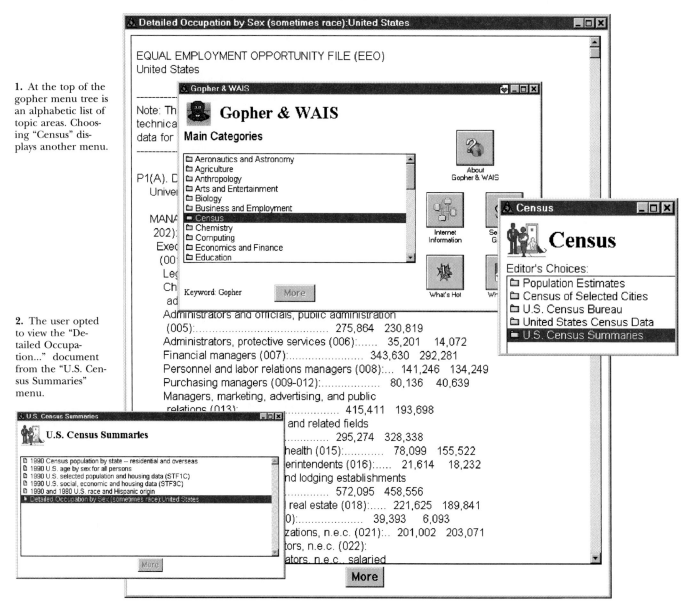

3. The user can scroll through the requested document, store it in a file, or print it.

FIGURE 7–9 Searching Gopherspace

Gopherspace: Go-for information. Gopherspace is the home of thousands of Gopher servers throughout the world. The **Gopher** system was developed at University of Minnesota, the home of the Golden Gophers. Think of the Gopher system as a huge menu tree that allows you to keep choosing menu items until you find the information you want. Figure 7–9 illustrates how to search gopherspace via the America Online Internet gateway.

WAIS: Wide Area Information Server. **WAIS** (pronounced "ways") offers another approach to information retrieval. WAIS servers allow you to search by content, rather than poking around a hierarchy of menus to find the information you need. Figure 7–10 illustrates how to conduct a WAIS search using America Online.

WWW: World Wide Web. The **World Wide Web,** which is a mouthful, is affectionately called **the Web, WWW,** and **W3.** Two attributes set WWW servers apart from other Internet servers.

▶ *Multimedia.* Information on WWW may be graphics, audio, video, and, of course, text. Gopher, WAIS, and other servers deal primarily with text-based documents and databases.

GOING ONLINE

7.3
Your Internet Hot List

By now you're a seasoned traveler on the Net and have, no doubt, created your own Internet Hot List.

Hand in: Names and addresses (URLs) on your personal hot list (at least five sites).

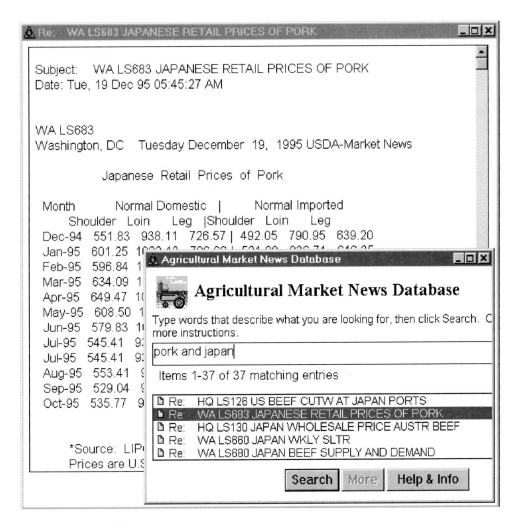

FIGURE 7–10 Searching WAIS
In this example, the user used an Internet search tool to request a list of documents relating to "pork" and "japan." The "Japan Retail Prices of Pork" (highlighted) is shown in the background.

Emerging Technology

Cybertalk: A New Way to Communicate

When online, we key in, rather than speak, our words and emotions. People who frequent bulletin boards and online forums have invented keyboard shortcuts to speed up the written interaction and convey emotions. These are among the most frequently used keyboard shortcuts.

AFJ	April fool's joke
<--AFK	Away from keyboard
BRB	Be right back
BTW	By the way...
F2F	Face-to-face
FAQ	Frequently asked questions
<GG>	Grin
IMHO	In my humble opinion...
IRL	In real life

LOL	Laughing out loud
ROFL	Rolling on the floor laughing
TPTB	The powers that be
TTYL	Talk to you later
<VBG>	Very big grin
WAG	A guess
Wizard	A gifted or experienced user
YKYBHTLW	You know you've been hacking too long when . . .

To shout online, key in words in all capital letters. Do this only when you really wish to make a point.

Because in cyberspace there is no eye contact or voice inflection, cybernauts use "emoticons" (emotion icons), called "smileys," to express emotions. They must be effective because many couples who meet on the information highway are eventually married. Their courtship may have involved some of these smileys.

*	Kiss
:-)	Smiling
:'-(	Crying (sad)
:'-)	Crying (happy)
:-(	Sad
<:(	Dunce
:-o	Amazed
:-l	Bored
:-I	Indifferent
8-)	Wearing sunglasses
::-)	Wearing glasses

:-`)	User with a cold
:-@	Screaming
:-&	Tongue tied
:-Q	Smoker
:-D	Laughing
:-/	Skeptical
O :-)	Angel
;-)	Wink
:c)	Pigheaded
@—>—>—	A rose
[[[***]]]	Hugs and kisses

Creating smileys has emerged as a pop art. These smileys were created by online users with a sense of humor. Turn the page sideways and see if you recognize any familiar faces.

:-)X	Sen. Paul Simon
+-(:-)	The Pope
==):-D	Don King
[8-]	Frankenstein
==):-)=	Abe Lincoln
@@@@@@@@:)	Marge Simpson
/:-)	Gumby
7:-)	Ronald Reagan
\	
8-]	FDR
*<(:')	Frosty the Snowman
(8-o	Mr. Bill
~8-)	Alfalfa
@;^[)	Elvis

▶ *Hypertext links.* Information on most information servers is accessed through menu hierarchies or by keyword searches through document descriptions, titles, or filenames. Multimedia resources on WWW are linked via **hypertext**. WWW documents are created using HTML (HyperText Markup Language). Words or phrases within hypertext documents can be marked and highlighted (see Figure 7–11) to create interactive links to related text or multimedia information. Hypertext links on WWW are displayed as blue and underlined text. When you click on the hypertext link (the highlighted words or phrases) you are whisked away to the URL (uniform resource locator) address specified in the hypertext link. The link could take you to another location in the same document or to another document on a WWW server on another continent. The transition between hypertext links appears seamless to the WWW user.

MEMORY BITS

On the Internet

- E-mail
- Newsgroups
- FTP
- Telnet
- Gopher
- WAIS
- World Wide Web

Growth of the WWW has been spectacular, due to the emergence of user-friendly Web browsers. The GUI-based Web browsers take the mystery out of surfing the Internet. With Web browsers, even newbies can navigate and browse (poke around and search) the Net with ease. Netscape Navigator, Mosaic, Cello, Spyglass Mosaic, Netcom Netcruiser, and other Web browsers are GUI-based client software packages (run on a PC) that replace the often cryptic lingo of the Internet.

There are, however, a growing number of commercial browsers that offer more comprehensive functionality across Internet capabilities. Also, the commercial information services have created their own GUI tools for interacting with the Internet.

Browsing the Net

Vast, enormous, huge, immense, massive—none of these words is adequate to describe the extent of applications, retrievable files, communication services, and information services available over the Internet. Perhaps *the Internet* may someday emerge as a euphemism for anything that is almost unlimited in size and potential. In this section we mention a few more of the many sights you can see on the Net.

The recent introduction of the Java language has opened the door for more exciting online applications. Instead of simply reading pages from an Internet site, the HotJava browser (shown here) enables users to execute computer applications locally. To do this, the HotJava browser downloads "applets," small applications that run on the user's PC. *Courtesy Sun Microsystems*

▶ *The Electronic Newsstand on the Internet.* The Electronic Newsstand opened for business in 1993 with eight magazines: *The Economist,* the *New Yorker, National Review, The Source, The New Republic, New Age Journal, Journal of NIH Research,* and *Outside Magazine.* Today the Newsstand has several hundred and is growing. The magazines are as diverse as those who surf the Net: *ComputerWorld, Yoga Journal,* and *Discover, Inc.* The Electronic Newsstand doesn't include everything in the current issue, but it does include a table of contents and one or two selected articles from the current issue. Past issues, however, are included in the archival file.

▶ *MUDers on the Internet.* One of the exits on the Internet highway leads to MUD (Multi-User Domain), online role-playing adventure games. MUDs are challenging games that provide text descriptions of circumstances and situations rather than the graphic images of video games. This scenario description is typical: "You have fallen down a secret passageway into a chamber that is lit only by the full moon shining through a small opening in the ceiling. On the east wall there is a Latin inscription and a wooden door that is bolted on the outside. Distant voices are barely audible through the door." A player explores his or her realm by entering simple commands such as "go," "east," "west," and so on. As you might expect, not-so-nice creatures occupy the same realm and are out to get you.

The monsters and denizens of cyberspace present special challenges but the real challenges are posed by MUDers. Players define their character and even their personality: You might be a Rambo-like character or the Wicked Witch of the East. Each day tens of thousands of players spend hours, even days, online slaying evil creatures and joining other adventurers on their quest.

FIGURE 7–11 Surfing the World Wide Web

The World Wide Web is emerging as the foundation service on the Internet. That is, the downloadable FTP files, the Gopher and WAIS databases, newsgroups, e-mail, and other Internet applications are being organized within and offered through World Wide Web sites. The highly graphic World Wide Web home pages give users the flexibility to point and click their way to desired services or information. For example, one of the WWW hypertext links might be "FTP files." This Internet session is typical of how people use client software (the Netscape Navigator browser in this example) to surf World Wide Web servers. This chapter closes with a sampling of World Wide Web sites and applications from around the world.

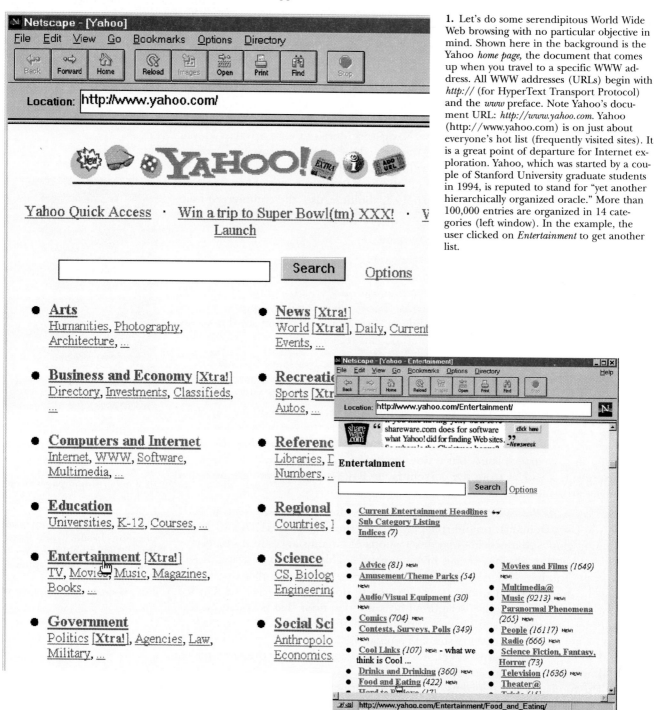

1. Let's do some serendipitous World Wide Web browsing with no particular objective in mind. Shown here in the background is the Yahoo *home page,* the document that comes up when you travel to a specific WWW address. All WWW addresses (URLs) begin with *http://* (for HyperText Transport Protocol) and the *www* preface. Note Yahoo's document URL: *http://www.yahoo.com.* Yahoo (http://www.yahoo.com) is on just about everyone's hot list (frequently visited sites). It is a great point of departure for Internet exploration. Yahoo, which was started by a couple of Stanford University graduate students in 1994, is reputed to stand for "yet another hierarchically organized oracle." More than 100,000 entries are organized in 14 categories (left window). In the example, the user clicked on *Entertainment* to get another list.

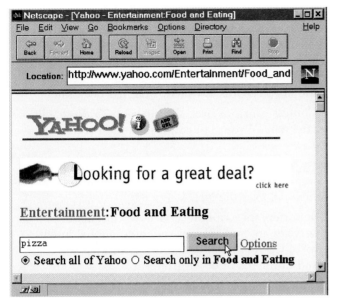

2. Clicking on *Food and Eating* presented another categorized list of sites, each with a brief description. Shown here is the search tool that heads each list. The thought of food and eating makes us hungry. Is it possible to order pizza over the Internet? Let's see. Yahoo lets you navigate through a hierarchy of categories or simply search all or selected sites by keyword. To begin a WWW search, we need to enter at least one keyword. Let's enter "pizza" and see what pops up.

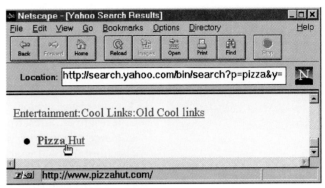

3. The search turns up a long list of pizza sites, including Pizza Hut (shown here). Simply click on the blue underlined word(s) to go to the site.

4. Pizza Hut delivers. Just enter name, address, and phone number at the Pizza Hut home page. Pizza Hut's World Wide Web server uses your address and phone number to determine your home town and the nearest Pizza Hut.

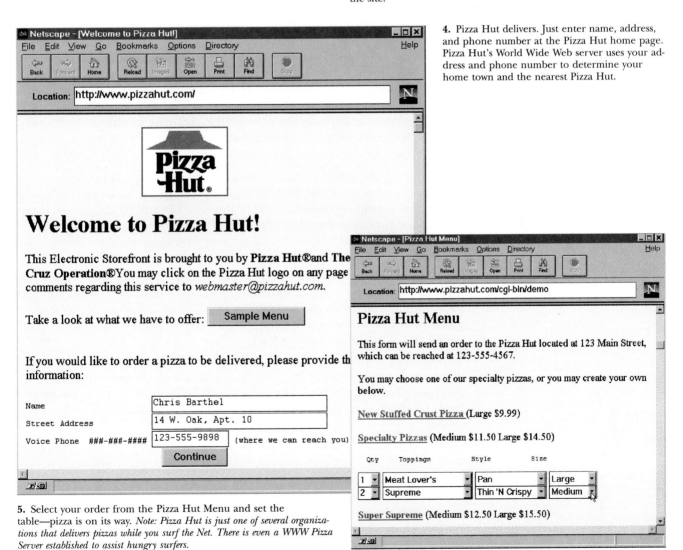

5. Select your order from the Pizza Hut Menu and set the table—pizza is on its way. *Note: Pizza Hut is just one of several organizations that delivers pizzas while you surf the Net. There is even a WWW Pizza Server established to assist hungry surfers.*

GOING ONLINE

7.4
Newsgroups

Thousands of special-interest newsgroups pepper cyberspace. Join a newsgroup of your choice. Post a message to the newsgroup. Wait several days.

Hand in: A printed copy of your message and any replies to your message. Include the address of the newsgroup.

▶ *Love and war.* The Internet is a romance connection. Many married couples met and courted over the Net. Talk show host Rush Limbaugh had an electronic courtship that led to matrimony. Where there is marriage there is divorce. Some couples prefer to negotiate their divorce settlement over Internet e-mail. This written approach to arbitration allows parties to choose their words more carefully and to keep records of exactly what has been said.

▶ *The electronic confessional.* Confess your sins over the Internet. To do so, choose a sin from a menu, enter the date of your last confession, then receive your penance.

▶ *Be an informed traveler.* Savvy travelers often shop around for the best deal on a hotel room, make their own reservations, and get information on local attractions and nearby restaurants—all over the Net.

▶ *Subscription services.* The Net offers subscription services for just about every interest area. Subscription services are available for the international intelligence community, podiatrists, CD-ROM manufacturers, tennis players, high school football coaches, and hundreds of other groups.

▶ *E-mail and geography.* A Wisconsin teacher encourages her fifth graders to correspond with e-mail pen pals in all 50 states. The teacher conceived the idea to help students learn geography and practice communication skills. Kids ask their "pen pals" about everything from pizza prices to politics.

Down the Road

Only one in three adult Americans have heard of the information superhighway, and most of those have little understanding of what it is, according to a nationwide Harris poll. In fact, most people are still waiting at the on ramp. Each day, however, more travelers drive up the on ramp and enter the information superhighway. Increasing traffice on the electronic highway has prompted an increase in online applications. Over the next few years, look for the information superhighway to have a dramatic impact on our lives. Let's gaze into the crystal ball.

▶ *The electronic family reunion.* The function of the telephone will be incorporated into a video phone or, perhaps, into our computers so we can both hear and see the person on the other end of the line. You will be able to use the information superhighway, your television or PC, and multiple video-phone hookups to hold an electronic family reunion. You can even share photos and view family videos.

▶ *Entertainment everywhere.* Many of the initial offerings traveling the information superhighway will be aimed at entertaining us. We'll have *video-on-demand;* that is, you will be able to choose what television program or movie you want to watch and when you want to watch it. Some programs will be interactive, allowing you to influence the plot line.

▶ *The home library.* The information superhighway will make it possible for you to browse through vritually any book from your PC or terminal. If you wish to purchase a hard-copy version of a book, it will be charged via **EFT (electronic funds transfer),** then printed and bound on your personal high-speed color printer.

▶ *Mail at the speed of light.* Most of what we now know as mail will travel electronically over the superhighway, even greetning cards and family photos.

▶ *The cashless society.* We are already well on our way toward a *cashless society.* Traditional gas pumps are being replaced with ones that accept credit cards—swipe the card and pump the gas. In Phoenix, bus fares can be paid with VISA or MasterCard. Cars on turnpikes zoom past tool stations as scanners identify the vehicle and debit the owner's account.

▶ *Shop at home.* More and more people are opting for the convenience and value of electronic shopping. It's no longer necessary to drive from store to store to seek a particular style of sneaker. Many people in Chicago and San Francisco do their grocery shopping through Peapod, an online grocery-shopping service. Groceries are delivered to their doorsteps within 90 minutes.

▶ *High-tech voting and polling.* In the not-too-distant fugure we will record our votes over the information superhighway. Such a system will reduce the costs of elections and encourage greater voter participation.

Internet Issues

The Internet is a digital Wild West, without law and order. Nevertheless, the lure of this new frontier has an endless stream of wagon trains "heading west." Like the Wild West, anyone can come along. The Internet is public land; therefore, accessibility is one of the inherent problems on the Internet. With unlimited accessibility come mischievous hackers, the plague of computer networks. (Most hackers are good, doing what they can to make things better for those who travel in cyberspace.) The bad hackers are continually doing what they can to disrupt the flow of information. These electronic assaults are on the routers and other communications devices that route data from node to node on the Net. Such actions are like changing the road signs along the interstate highway system. Hackers don't stop at changing the road signs; they also plant computer viruses on the Internet, disguised as enticing downloadable files. Once downloaded, the virus infects the PC and creates havoc, often destroying files. Hackers have stolen valuable software, traded secrets, and hijacked telephone credit-card numbers. Hackers have distributed copyrighted photos and songs over the Internet. Hackers run online securities scams.

People on the Internet reflect real life—most are good and a few are bad. The bad elements deal in garbage. Some Internet newsgroups are dominated by bigots and cranks who push everything from neo-Nazi propaganda to pornographic images. Women on the Internet are sometimes hounded by electronic lechers. The language spoken in the heat of a passionate electronic debate can range from rude to libelous. Fortunately, responsible people are fighting back. When somebody posts something outlandish, inappropriate, or out of phase with the societal norms to a newsgroup or mailing list, they get *flamed.* Flaming results in a barrage of scathing messages from irate Interneters.

The Internet rivals the towering majesty of Mount Everest, but there is a dark side of every mountain. At the foot of this great mountain of information is a rocky pasture. Watch your step as you cross this pasture, then enjoy the climb up Mount Internet.

7–4 CRUISING THE NET

Serendipitous Surfing: Magazines

With an estimated 5,000,000 host sites, the Internet offers a vast treasure trove of information and services to an estimated 50,000,000 users. The number of users continues to explode as more and more newbies (Net novices) begin to cruise the Net. By the turn of the century, about 150,000,000 people will pass through the newbie stage on their way to becoming seasoned travelers on the Internet.

Emotions of newbies run high when they enter the on ramp for the first time. They simultaneously are shocked, amazed, overwhelmed, appalled, and enlightened. The Internet is so vast that these same emotions are experienced by seasoned users as well. The remainder of the chapter includes examples of a few of the tens of thousands of stops along the Internet.

Serendipitous Surfing: Business

Prodigy The big three, Prodigy, America Online, and CompuServe (all three shown here on this and top of next page), as well as Genie, Microsoft Network, The source, Dow Jones News/Retrieval Service, AT&T Interactive, DIALOG, NewsNet, and other commercial information services, offer a wealth of enlightening and entertaining online services.

There is something for children of all ages on Prodigy and other information services. Shown here is *Sports Illustrated for Kids*. Prodigy's "Highlights" are in 16 categories. *SI for KIDS* is also available directly over the Internet from the Sports Illustrated Web site. Look for big changes in commercial information services as the Internet realizes its promise in terms of content and accessibility. To maintain their base of over 10 million customers, commercial information services will need to add value to their product to differentiate their services from what is available on the Net.

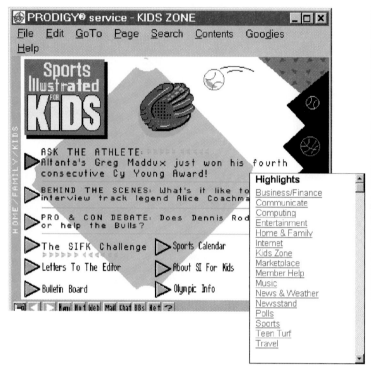

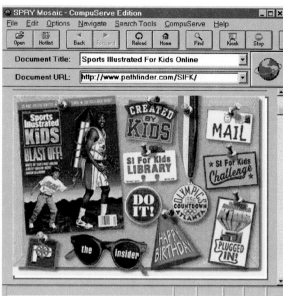

America Online (AOL) Suppose one of your friends, a member of Saucon Valley Country Club in Bethlehem, Pennsylvania, has invited you to the annual member/guest golf tournament. You can find out more about Saucon Valley by tapping the AOLGolf database on AOL. The database contains extensive information on Saucon Valley and on every golf course in America. AOL's main menu lists 14 categories.

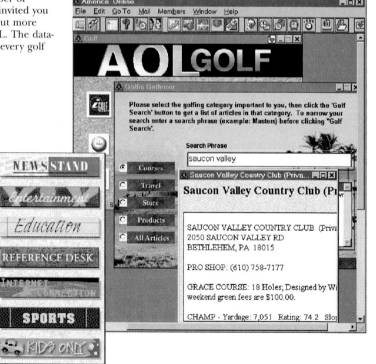

CompuServe People-oriented people can enjoy the interactive version of *People* magazine on CompuServe. You can track the stars, download photo images of the beautiful people, engage in online chats, and much more. CompuServe's main menu lists 17 categories.

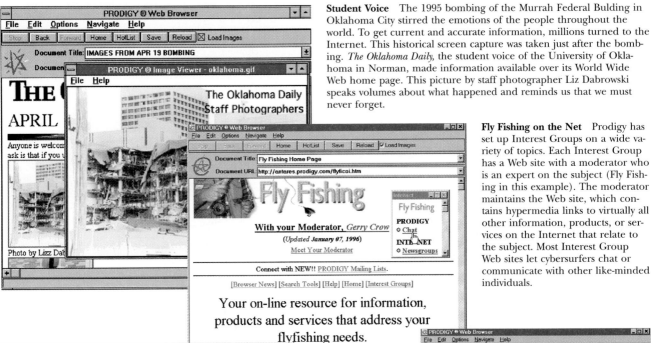

Student Voice The 1995 bombing of the Murrah Federal Building in Oklahoma City stirred the emotions of the people throughout the world. To get current and accurate information, millions turned to the Internet. This historical screen capture was taken just after the bombing. *The Oklahoma Daily,* the student voice of the University of Oklahoma in Norman, made information available over its World Wide Web home page. This picture by staff photographer Liz Dabrowski speaks volumes about what happened and reminds us that we must never forget.

Fly Fishing on the Net Prodigy has set up Interest Groups on a wide variety of topics. Each Interest Group has a Web site with a moderator who is an expert on the subject (Fly Fishing in this example). The moderator maintains the Web site, which contains hypermedia links to virtually all other information, products, or services on the Internet that relate to the subject. Most Interest Group Web sites let cybersurfers chat or communicate with other like-minded individuals.

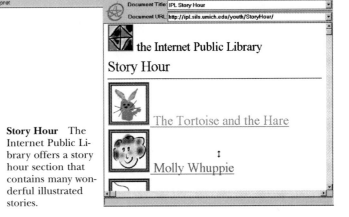

The Centennial Olympic Games To make the Centennial Olympics the best games ever, Atlanta built and refurbished many venues, one of which is its Web site on the Internet.

Story Hour The Internet Public Library offers a story hour section that contains many wonderful illustrated stories.

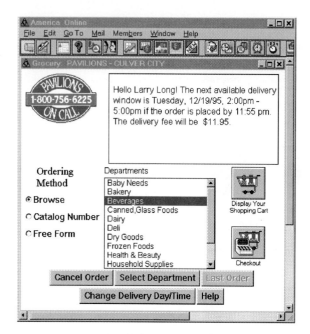

Virtual Grocery Store Shoppers Express is a rapidly expanding service on America Online which allows busy people to do their grocery shopping at their PCs. The service has agreements with grocery stores and chains throughout the United States. Shoppers click items into a virtual grocery cart. The real grocery cart is filled by a professional shopper at a partner grocery store and your order is delivered to your home.

Internet Greeting Cards E-mail messages now outnumber written messages eight to one. It's only a matter of time before online greeting cards overtake traditional greeting cards. Several Web sites, such as this one, give you the facilities to create and send your own "greeting cards"—for free. You choose the images and the words. You can even add audio and animation to your online cards. Online greeting cards arrive on time and you save the expense of a card, an envelope, and a stamp.

Toy Story Walt Disney Company's *Toy Story* has its own web page where fans can learn more about Woody, Buzz, and their friends. The site includes images, movie information, and other "important stuff." Movie studios usually create Web sites for their high-profile films prior to their release.

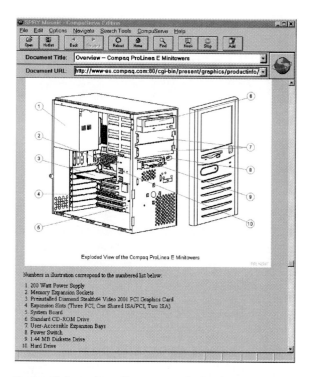

Product Information Customer service has become the byword of corporate America. Competition demands that companies provide customers with the best possible service, including a comprehensive Web site. Compaq's Web site (shown here), which is representative, provides product information, technical support, and much more.

White House Tour When you take your cybertour of the White House, be sure to sign the guest book. During the tour, you can listen to the comments of the President and the Vice President, meet the first family, and see the White House. The tour includes much more, including information on the executive branch and a long list of related publications. You can send e-mail to the President via the *Speak Out* feature on the "Welcome to the White House" home page. Each day, the White House receives over 150,000 e-mail messages, mostly from college-educated (75%) males (80%) under the age of 50 (85%).

The Worst of the Web Cybersurfers are ever vigilant in their search for the worst that the Net has to offer. Critics abound on the Internet. People and companies who create Web sites should be aware that cybercritics will eventually pass judgment on the quality of their site. A select few make one of the "best" or "worst" lists. This site won a Bobbie Award for being a runner-up in the most useless business page category.

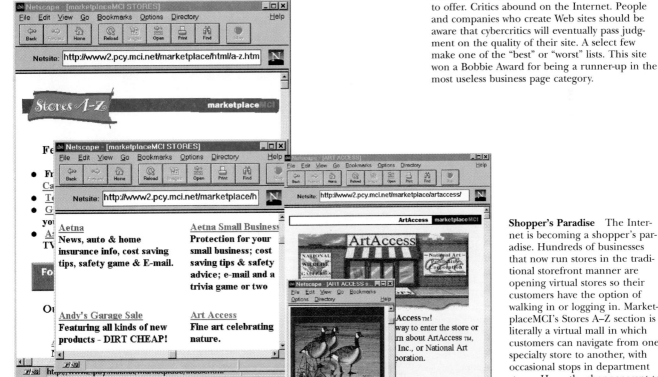

Shopper's Paradise The Internet is becoming a shopper's paradise. Hundreds of businesses that now run stores in the traditional storefront manner are opening virtual stores so their customers have the option of walking in or logging in. MarketplaceMCI's Stores A–Z section is literally a virtual mall in which customers can navigate from one specialty store to another, with occasional stops in department stores. Here, the shopper went to the Art Access store to look for a print for the living room.

The Ultimate Travel Brochure
The Internet has emerged as "the" source for travel information. It's easy to get information about any destination in the Caribbean or any other popular vacation haven. For example, this traveler requested a comparison of the hotels on Grand Cayman.

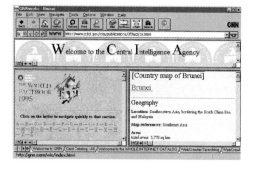

Peeping In on the CIA See your taxpayer dollars at work on the CIA Web server. The site contains some very interesting information on the CIA mission and these comprehensive online books: *A Fact Book on Intelligence* and *The World Fact Book 1994*. *The World Fact Book 1996* has comprehensive information on every country in the world, including Brunei (shown here).

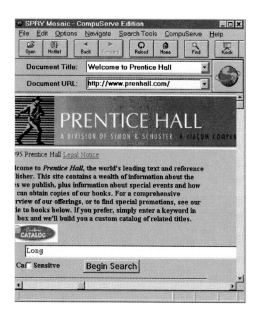

College Textbooks The publisher of this book, Prentice Hall, has a comprehensive Web site over which students and professors can communicate with one another and download important class materials. Users can thumb through the Prentice Hall College Division's catalog to obtain information about any book it offers. Or, they can use the Prentice Hall search tool to find more about books by a particular author or on a particular subject. Online users also can order books through the Prentice Hall Web site.

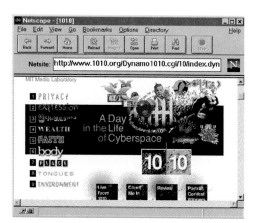

An Internet Time Capsule In celebration of the MIT Media Lab's 10th Anniversary, the lab took a snapshot of cyberspace. It did this by asking Net surfers to tune in on each of 10 consecutive days and make contributions relative to the theme of the day (for example, privacy). The contributions could be anything that could be digitized or thoughts provided in a survey or during online discussions. The results are published on the lab's Web site in a permanent archive that reflects the Internet during this 10-day period in time.

Taking a Virtual Tour of the Louvre Save the plane fare and enjoy the works of the masters over the Internet. The virtual tour lets you search the Louvre in Paris by artist or go to a particular period (Baroque, Impressionism, and so on). The Louvre is home to the Mona Lisa, the Venus de Milo, and many other masterpieces.

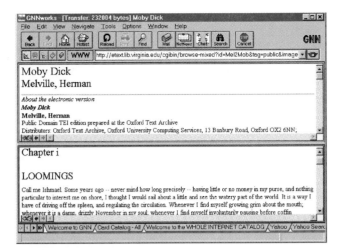

Online Books "Call me Ishmael." The opening line from Melville's *Moby Dick* as well as the rest of his book can be found at a number of Internet sites, including the electronic text library at the University of Virginia (shown here). Thousands of public domain works of literature from *Beowulf* to the complete works of Shakespeare can be found on the Net.

Nutritional Profile The WebCrawler (top left window), one of the most popular Internet search tools, enables the users to navigate to sites based on keyword searches. In the example, the user entered the keywords *nutrition* and *profile* to find a site that would provide him with a nutrition profile. The WebCrawler had 119 "hits," one of which was the Mirical Nutrition Corporation Web site (shown here). At this Internet stop, he obtained a comprehensive nutritional profile simply by entering pertinent personal information. The report shows the optimum amount of food and nutrients (29, in this case) for a person with the attributes shown.

Online Newspapers *USA Today* and many other newspapers, even weekly newspapers in small towns, sponsor Internet Web sites. The comprehensive *USA Today* site provides up-to-the-minute news in five categories (news, sports, money, life, and weather) as well as a variety of other information-based services.

NASA's Online Resources The National Aeronautics and Space Administration is more than willing to share its massive resources with the general public.

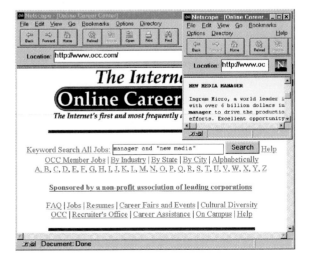

Looking for a Job? The Net has many places, both commercial and nonprofit, that specialize in matching job applicants with employers. Already, most professional positions are listed on the Net. A good place to start your job search is the Online Career Center, which offers a comprehensive list of online job services and resume banks. The Online Career Center can be searched for jobs by key word, location, salary, and so on. In the example, the user searches the database for positions that included "manager" and "new media" in the job description (see window). For a small fee, the service (shown here) will put your resume online. Frequently the screening process progresses via e-mail, with both parties passing information back and forth.

7–1 PC-BASED COMMUNICATIONS SOFTWARE
Millions of people who are **telecommuting** use these basic capabilities common to full-function communications packages: terminal emulation, file transfer, host operation, and fax support. When a PC is in **terminal emulation mode,** the keyboard, the monitor, and the data interface function like that of the terminal being emulated. When in **host mode** operation, the PC is set up to let remote users call in and establish a communications link.

When using communications software, you set these parameters: *type of terminal emulation, file transfer protocol,* and *port settings* (which include the serial port, bps or baud rate, **parity checking,** data bits, stop bits, and **half** or **full duplex** data flow options).

To **log on,** a user enters a user ID and a user-defined **password.** To terminate, the user must **log off.**

A variety of information services are available to PC owners with communications capabilities. Bulletin-board systems (BBSs) are popular throughout the country. The person or group sponsoring the BBS is referred to as the **system operator,** or **sysop.**

7–2 INFORMATION SERVICES: AMERICA ONLINE, COMPUSERVE, AND MANY MORE PC users with communications-equipped PCs can subscribe to commercial online services such as America Online, CompuServe, GEnie, Prodigy, and Microsoft Network (MSN).

America Online offers such choices as news, financial information, online forums, computing information, travel, shop at home, chat rooms, message boards, e-mail, online magazines and newspapers, entertainment highlights, a reference desk, sports, topics for kids only, and more. AOL offers a variety of ways for members to communicate, primarily *chat rooms, message boards,* and *e-mail.*

7–3 THE INTERNET: A WORLD WIDE WEB OF COMPUTERS AND INFORMATION The Internet is comprised of thousands of independent networks in virtually every type of organization. The Department of Defense's ARPANET project was the genesis of the Internet.

You can connect your PC to the Internet *via an information service,* which provides a gateway built around the **Transmission Control Protocol/Internet Protocol (TCP/IP);** *via an Internet service provider* in which your dial-up connection is made through a SLIP or PPP server; or *via a direct network connection.* Newbies are novice Internet users.

The Internet address has two parts, the user ID and the host/network identifier, which are separated by an @ symbol.

There are many applications in the Internet: e-mail, newsgroups, mailing lists, and more. **File Transfer Protocol (FTP)** allows you to download and upload files on the Internet. You must be an authorized user to access some FTP sites, but many are **anonymous FTP sites** that permit public access.

Telnet is a *terminal emulation* protocol that allows you to work from a PC as if it were a terminal linked directly to a host computer.

An **information server** is an Internet host with a repository of information that is made available over the Internet. To get information on the Internet, you *search, browse,* or *ask someone.* The **Gopher** system is a menu tree that allows you to look for information by choosing menu items until you find what you want. The Wide Area Information Server **(WAIS)** lets you search by content rather than with a hierarchy of menus.

The **World Wide Web,** also called **the Web, WWW,** and **W3,** is another Internet server. Two attributes set WWW servers apart from other Internet servers: multimedia and **hypertext** links. The document that comes up when you travel to a specific WWW address is called the home page. All WWW addresses (URLs) begin with *http.* Clicking the hypertext link in a WWW document will link you to another document.

The information superhighway is a network of high-speed data communications links that eventually will connect virtually every facet of our society. Traffic on the superhighway will be anything that can be digitized. A wide range of information and telecommunication services are now available and more are planned for the information superhighway. These applications include video phones, video-on-demand, interactive television, virtual libraries, soft-copy publishing (with a hard-copy option), multimedia catalogs, electronic mail (including a video option), total **electronic funds transfer (EFT),** electronic shopping, electronic voting and polling, and much more.

Accessibility is one of the inherent problems on the Internet, opening the door to electronic assaults on routers and other communications devices.

7–4 CRUISING THE NET The Internet's more than 5,000,000 host sites offer a vast treasure of information and services to an estimated 50,000,000 users.

REVIEW EXERCISES

Concepts

1. Name three data communications parameters that may need to be specified to establish a communications link between a PC and another computer.
2. If you were the sponsor of a bulletin-board system, what would you be called?
3. Which Internet server lets you search by content, WAIS or Gopher?
4. Which of these data transmission rates is not possible over a normal telephone line: 9600 bps, 14,400 bps, 19,200 bps, 28,800 bps, or 115,200 bps?
5. Name five commercial online information services.
6. Briefly describe four America Online departments.
7. What is a newbie?
8. What is the organizational affiliation of these Internet addresses: smith_jo@mkt.bigco.com; politics@washington.senate.gov; and hugh_roman@cis.stuniv.edu.
9. Describe what you do to send a fax from a PC.
10. In an Internet address, how are levels separated in the host/network identifier?
11. What is an information server on the Internet?
12. Expand the following acronyms: NII, TCP/IP, bps, and URL.
13. In what ways is the World Wide Web different from other servers on the Internet?
14. Which action would result in more Internet e-mail,

posting a message to a newsgroup or subscribing to a popular mailing list?

Discussion and Problem Solving

15. Describe five things you would like to do on the Internet.
16. Discuss the pros and cons of FTPing on the Internet.
17. What kind of work would you like to be doing in five years? Explain how you might telecommute to accomplish part or all of your work.
18. The Internet is a digital Wild West. Should access be more tightly controlled to help bring law and order to the Internet?
19. Discuss how you would justify spending of $10 to $20 a month to subscribe to an online information service.
20. Gambling could be one of the most profitable computer applications ever. Americans spent 70 times as much on gambling last year as they spent on movies. Gambling is being proposed as a possible application on the information superhighway. Argue for or against this proposal.
21. The federal government is calling for "universal service" such that everyone has access to the "information superhighway." Is this an achievable goal?

SELF-TEST (BY SECTION)

7–1 a. When a PC is in terminal emulation mode, the keyboard, the monitor, and the data interface function like that of the host being emulated. (T/F)
b. Which of the following is not an example of a file transfer protocol: (a) VT-100; (b) Kermit; or (c) Xmodem?
c. Bps is sometimes labeled as _____.

d. Communications links that transfer information in both directions, but not at the same time, are called half duplex. (T/F)
e. Parity checking helps to ensure that data transmission is complete and accurate. (T/F)
f. Most online information services and BBSs expect: (a) half duplex; (b) full duplex; or (c) all duplex?

7-2 a. Which of the following is not an online commercial information service: (a) Microsoft Network; (b) the Web; or (c) AOL?

b. The nomenclature for people-to-people online communications capabilities is standard between commercial information services. (T/F)

c. You would look for online magazines in which AOL department: (a) Marketplace; (b) Personal Finance; or (c) News Stand?

7-3 a. The Internet is not a commercial information service like Prodigy. (T/F)

b. ARPANET was the first commercially available communications software package. (T/F)

c. TCP/IP is the communications protocol for: (a) the Net; (b) AOL; or (c) all internal e-mail?

d. To eliminate the spread of viruses, only downloading of files is permitted on the Internet. (T/F)

e. Which server on the Internet offers hypertext links: (a) WAIS; (b) WWW; or (c) Gopher?

7-4 a. Yahoo is an Internet site. (T/F)

b. Which of the following labels is associated with an Internet address: (a) bps; (b) pbs; or (c) http?

Self-test Answers. **7-1 (a)** F; **(b)** a; **(c)** baud rate; **(d)** T; **(e)** T; **(f)** b. **7-2 (a)** b; **(b)** F; **(c)** c. **7-3 (a)** T; **(b)** F; **(c)** a; **(d)** F; **(e)** b. **7-4 (a)** T; **(b)** c.

The Windows Environment

What Is Windows?

Windows (running under MS-DOS), Windows for Workgroups (running under MS-DOS), and Windows 95 define the dominant platforms for the PC-compatible environment. Windows for Workgroups is Windows with additional networking and workgroup capabilities. Windows 95 is the successor to both Windows and Windows for Workgroups. Prior to 1996, virtually all new PCs were sold with MS-DOS and Windows installed on the hard disk. Now PCs come with Windows 95. The terms, concepts, and features discussed in this section generally apply to both; however, the examples show the most recent version—Windows 95. The name *Windows* describes basically how the software functions. The GUI-based Windows series run one or more applications in *windows*—rectangular areas displayed on the screen. The Windows series has introduced a number of new concepts and terms, all of which apply to the thousands of software packages that have been and are being developed to run under the Windows platforms. These are discussed in this section.

Understanding Windows and Windows 95: Help

Books and tutorial software are complementary learning tools. This is especially true when it comes to learning Windows, Windows 95, or any other software package. The explanations in the following sections will make more sense once you begin interacting with Windows and other GUIs. We recommend that you visit the PC lab and run Help to learn more about Windows or Windows 95, whichever is installed.

Non-Windows versus Windows Applications

Non-Windows Applications   Any software application that does not adhere to the Microsoft Windows standard is a **non-Windows application.** Non-Windows applications will run under Windows or Windows 95, but these software packages cannot take advantage of many helpful Windows features.

Windows Applications   Programs that adhere to Windows conventions are **Windows applications.** These conventions describe:

▶ Type and style of window

▶ Arrangement and style of menus

▶ Use of the keyboard and mouse

▶ Format for screen image display

The GUI for Windows versions of Word, CorelDRAW, Quicken, Pagemaker, and all other Windows applications have the same look and feel. *When you learn the GUI for Windows or Windows 95, you also learn the GUI for all Windows-based software packages.*

The Windows and Windows 95 graphical user interfaces use both the mouse and the keyboard as input devices. Interaction with Windows or a Windows application is most efficient when options are chosen with a mouse and characters are entered via the keyboard.

When working with the mouse:

▶ Point and *click* the left button to **select** an item (an application program, a menu option, a box, and so on). When you select an item, the item is highlighted in some way. *Generally, selection does not result in the initiation of a processing activity.*

▶ Point and *double-click* the left button to **choose** an item. *Choosing an item results in some kind of action.*

▶ Point and *drag* to move or resize a window on the display screen.

When working with the keyboard:

▶ Enter text as needed (for example, a path for a file: c:\wp\wp.exe).

▶ Activate the current menu bar by tapping the ALT key.

▶ Enter the underlined letter of the menu option in the active menu to choose that option.

▶ Use the arrow keys to highlight menu options in an active menu.

▶ Use the **shortcut key,** which can be a key or a key combination (for example, ALT + F4 may be *Exit* and CTRL + C may be *Copy*) to issue commands within a particular application without activating a menu.

▶ Use the **hotkey,** also a key or key combination, to cause some function to happen in the computer, no matter what the active application.

The Desktop

The screen upon which icons, windows, and so on are displayed is known as the **desktop.** The Windows and Windows 95 desktop may contain a *background, one active window, one or more inactive windows,* and *icons* (see Figure A–1). The background can be anything from a single-color screen, as shown in Figure A–1 to an elaborate artistic image. All windows and icons are superimposed over the background, be it plain or an artistic image.

The Window A typical rectangular Windows **application window** is illustrated in Figure A–1. An application window contains an **open application** (a running application), such as Paint or WordPerfect. Several applications can be open or running simultaneously, but there is only one **active window** at any given time. (You can tell that Paint is the active window in Figure A–1 because its title bar is highlighted.) Application commands issued via the keyboard or mouse apply to the active window,

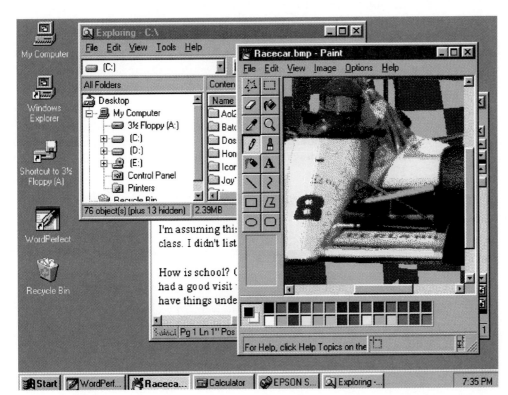

FIGURE A–1 The Windows 95 Desktop The appearance of the Windows 95 desktop depends on the user's application mix and visual needs at a particular time. This user has three open application windows (Windows Explorer, WordPerfect for Windows, and Paint, the active window) and two applications that have been shrunk to application icons (HiJaak PRO and Calculator) in the task bar at the bottom of the desktop. The task bar lists all open applications.

FIGURE A–2 Elements of an Application Window

Application icon   Menu bar   Title bar   Minimize   Minimize   Exit

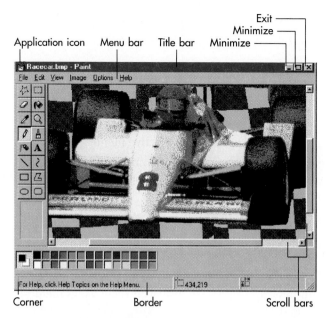

Corner   Border   Scroll bars

which is highlighted. The elements of an application window are: the title bar, the menu bar, the work space, the scroll bars, and the corners and borders. Each is described in the following sections and illustrated in Figure A–2.

Title bar. The horizontal **title bar** at the top of each window runs the width of the window from left to right (see Figure A–2). The elements of the title bar include the *application icon, window title and active filename, minimize button, maximize/restore button,* and *exit button.* Point and click the mouse on these elements to change the presentation of the window.

▶ *Application icon in title bar.* Point and click on the application icon in the title bar (the control menu box in Windows) to display the pull-down control menu (see Figure A–3), which is also called the *system menu.* Most of the options on the control menu are available without having to display the menu. For example, one of the options is *Move.* To move a window, the user simply uses the mouse to point to the window title area and drags the window to the desired location. The keyboard user would need to choose the *Move* option and use the cursor-control keys to move the window. Control menu options vary, depending on the type of application being displayed in the window, but most will have some or all of the following options.

Restore   When available, users can restore an enlarged window to its previous size (a window or an icon). The *Restore* option is dimmed and not available unless the window is enlarged. (*Restore* is dimmed in Figure A–3.)

FIGURE A–3 The Control Menu

Move   The *Move* option enables the user to use the cursor-control keys to reposition the active window on the desktop.

Size   The *Size* option enables the user to change the height or width of the active window with the cursor-control keys.

Minimize The *Minimize* option **shrinks** the active window to a button in the task bar (see Figure A–1) or, in Windows, an icon at the bottom of the desktop. That is, the application in the window is deactivated and the window disappears from the screen, but the application remains open in the form of a button or an icon.

Maximize The *Maximize* option enlarges the active window to fill the entire screen.

Close   Choosing *Close* deactivates and removes the active window (and its application) from the desktop.

Edit   Choosing *Edit* results in a **cascading menu** that permits users to transfer information between windows. A cascading menu is a pop-up menu that is displayed when a command from the active menu is chosen.

▶ *Window title and active filename.* The title of the application is contained in the title bar ("Paint" in Figure A–1). Next to the title is the name of the file displayed in the application work space ("RACECAR.BMP" in Figure A–2).

▶ *Maximize/minimize/restore buttons.* Mouse users can point and click on the maximize (□, ▲ in Windows) and minimize (– ,▼ in Windows) buttons (at the right end of the title bar in Figure A–2) to enlarge the window to fill the screen or to shrink it to an icon. The restore button replaces the maximize button when the window is enlarged.

Menu bar.   The menu bar for an application window runs the width of the window just below the title bar (see Figure A–2). The menu bar lists the menus available for that application. Choosing an option from the menu bar results in a pull-down menu. The *File, Edit,* and *Help* menus are available for most applications. Other menu options depend on the application.

Certain conventions apply to user interactions with any menu, whether a menu bar, a pull-down menu, or a cascading menu.

▶ *Only the boldface options can be chosen.* Dimmed options are not available for the current circumstances. For example, the *Copy* option would not be available in an Edit menu if nothing had been identified to be copied.

▶ *Choosing a menu option followed by an ellipsis (. . .) results in a dialog box.* The text in the pop-up dialog box asks the user to choose parameters or enter additional information.

▶ *Corresponding shortcut keys are presented adjacent to many options in Windows menus.* For example, the Close option on the Edit menu in Figure A–3 can be executed by the Alt + F4 shortcut key combination.

▶ *Choosing a menu option followed by an arrow (▶) results in a cascading menu.*

▶ *A user-recorded check mark (✓) to the left of the menu option indicates that the option is active and applies to any related commands.* For example, many programs have a tool bar and a status bar that can be hidden or displayed depending on whether or not there is a check mark next to the entry in the View pull-down menu.

▶ *There are three ways to choose a menu option.*

1. Point and click the mouse on the option.
2. Use the keyboard cursor-control keys to select (highlight) the option and tap the Enter key to choose it.
3. Use the keyboard to enter the underlined letter of the menu option. For example, in Figure A–3, enter M (Move), n (Minimize), and so on.

On most application windows, the last option on the menu bar is *Help*. Choose the online Help menu whenever you need context-sensitive information regarding basic skills, shortcut keys, procedures, features, or commands. Windows 95 and programs written for Windows 95 have **wizards** that lead you step by step through many common user procedures, such as installing new software or creating the format for a desktop publishing–produced newsletter.

Work space. The **work space** is the area in a window below the title bar or menu bar (see Figure A–2). Everything that relates to the application noted in the title bar is displayed in the work space. For example, in Figure A–2, an image of a race car is in the work space of the Paint program. The work space of a word processing program contains the word processing document.

Scroll bars. Depending on the size of a window, the entire application may not be visible. When this happens the window is outfitted with **vertical** and/or **horizontal scroll bars** (see Figure A–2). Each bar contains a **scroll box** and two **scroll arrows**. Use the mouse or keyboard to move a box up/down or left/right on a scroll bar to display other parts of the application. To move the scroll box with the mouse, simply drag it to another location on the scroll bar or click the scroll arrows.

Corners and borders. To resize a window, use the mouse and point to a window's border or corner. The graphics cursor changes to a double arrow when positioned over a border or corner. Drag the border or corner in the directions indicated by the double arrow to the desired shape.

Types of Windows: Application, Document, and Dialog Box The three types of windows in the Windows GUI are the *application window* (see Figure A–1), the *document window*, and the *dialog box*.

Document windows, which are windows within an application window, are displayed in the parent application window's work space. For example, the Word for Windows application in Figure A–4 has three open documents (resume.doc, baron.doc, and marketing.doc), each of which is shown in a document window.

Typically, you, the user, must okay or revise entries in the dialog box before a command can be executed. The dialog box may contain any of these nine elements.

1. *Tabs.* The tabs enable similar properties to be grouped within a dialog box (for example, "Appearance" in Figure A–5).
2. *Text box.* Enter text information in the text box or accept the default entry that is displayed (see Figure A–5).
3. *Command buttons.* Point and click on the *OK* rectangular command button to carry out the command with the information provided in the dialog box. Choose *Cancel* to retain the original information (see Figure A–5).
4. *Option buttons.* Circular option buttons preface each item in a list of mutually exclusive items (only one can be activated). Point and click a button to insert a black dot in the button and activate the option (see Figure A–5).
5. *List boxes.* A list box displays a list of available choices for a particular option (see Figure A–5). Long lists will have a vertical scroll bar.
6. *Drop-down list boxes.* The drop-down list box is an alternative to the list box (see Figure A–5) when the dialog box is too small for a list box to be displayed.

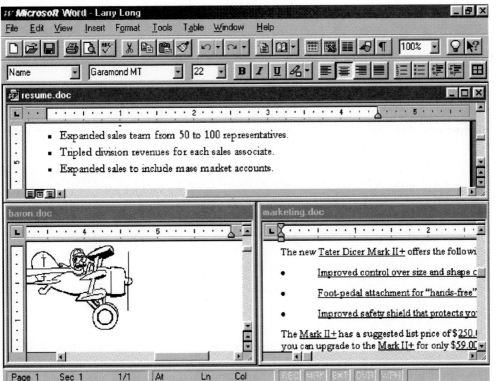

FIGURE A–4 Application and Document Windows
In this example display, the Word for Windows application has three open document windows. The highlighted window, resume.doc, is the active document window.

7. *Drop-down color palette.* The drop-down color palette displays a matrix of available font, line, and fill colors (see Figure A–5).

8. *Scroll bar adjustment.* The scroll bar adjustment enables users to change parameters, such as the speed at which the cursor blinks.

9. *Check boxes.* Check boxes preface options that can be switched on or off as needed. Point and click on a box to insert an *X* and activate the option.

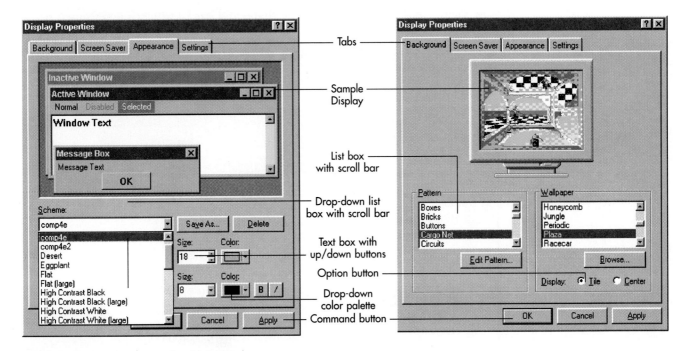

FIGURE A–5 Elements of a Dialog Box
Many common dialog box elements are shown in the Desktop properties dialog boxes. Not shown are the scroll bar adjustment and check box elements.

Icons: Pretty Pictures Icons, the graphical representation of a Windows element, play a major role in the Windows environment. Commonly used icons include *application icons, shortcut icons, document icons,* and *disk-drive icons.*

Application icons. An active application window can be minimized to a button on the task bar, thereby making it inactive. The **application icon,** usually a graphic rendering of the software package's logo, is positioned on the button or, in Windows, at the bottom of the desktop. Point and double-click on the button or icon to restore the window and the application to active status. Typically, you would minimize application windows that may not be needed for a while to make room on the desktop for other windows.

Shortcut icons. A **shortcut icon** to any application, document, or printer can be positioned on the desktop or in a folder. In Windows 95, documents and programs are stored in **folders.** In the original Windows, folders were known as **directories.** The shortcut icon has an arrow in its lower left corner (see Figure A–1). Shortcuts are double-clicked to begin an application. They have other uses as well. For example, you can drag a file to a printer shortcut to print the file.

Document icons. The active document window, which is a window within an application window, can be minimized to a **document icon.** Point and double-click on the document icon to restore the document window.

Disk-drive icons. The disk-drive icons graphically represent five disk-drive options: floppy, hard, network (hard), RAM, and CD-ROM. The floppy (A), hard-disk (C and D), and CD-ROM (E) icons shown in Figure A–6 resemble the faceplates of the disk drives. Typically, PCs have only one or two floppy drives, assigned to A and B.

Taking in the Scenery: Viewing Windows The Windows environment lets you view multiple applications in windows on the desktop display. An application window can be opened in several ways, usually by pointing and clicking on the application icon in the Program Manager window. Once open, a window can be resized, minimized (and restored), maximized (and restored), and, finally, closed.

Essentially, any applications software for the Windows environment can be:

▶ Viewed and run in a window, the shape and size of which is determined by the user.

▶ Run full-screen; that is, filling the entire screen, with no other application windows or icons showing.

FIGURE A–6 Explorer
The Windows 95 Explorer makes everything on the computer readily accessible to the user. Click on a disk icon to show the content of the disk. Click on an application icon to open an application.

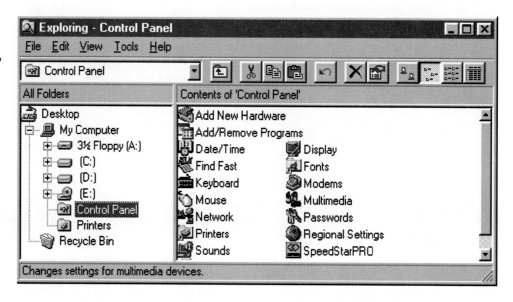

 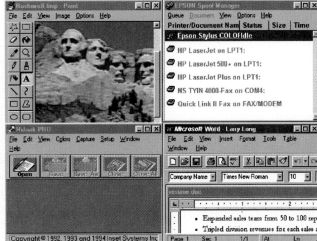

FIGURE A–7 Arrangement of Windows
Open application windows can be displayed as cascading windows (*left*) or tiled windows (*right*).

Some non-Windows applications run only as full-screen applications and cannot be run in a window. When multiple applications are running, the user can use the Move and Resize capabilities to arrange and size the windows to meet viewing needs. Of course, open windows can be minimized to free viewing space on the desktop.

Within a given application window, such as Word for Windows, multiple document windows can be sized, shrunk, and arranged by the user within the work space (see Figure A–4). As an alternative, the user can request that the document windows be automatically presented as **cascading windows** or **tiled windows** (see Figure A–7). Choose these options from the *Windows* menu option in the menu bar of any Windows application. The *Cascade* option overlaps open document windows so that all title bars are visible. The *Tile* option fills the work space in such a way that no document window overlaps another. Scroll bars are provided on those document windows for which the space is not adequate to display the window's content.

Switching Between Windows   In the Windows environment, users can open as many applications as available RAM will permit. The active window is always highlighted in the **foreground.** When located in the foreground all parts of the window are visible. Other open windows are in the **background,** or behind the foreground (see Figures A–1 and A–7). Do the following to switch between open applications:

▶ Point and click anywhere on the desired inactive window.

▶ Point and double-click the desired application button in the task bar or application icon.

Moving On: Terminating an Application and a Windows Session   Perform three operations before ending a Windows session:

1. *Save your work.* The *Save* option in the *File* menu updates the existing file to reflect the changes made during the session. The *Save as* option allows users to save the current file under another filename.
2. *Close all open windows.* After saving your work, exit each window by pointing and double-clicking the application icon in the title bar. You may also exit a Windows application through its menu bar (*File* then *Exit*).
3. *Shut down Windows.* In Windows 95, click *Start* in the task bar, then *Shut Down.* In Windows, click *File,* then *Exit Windows* in the Program Manager title bar.

One of the most inviting aspects of the Windows environment is the ability to copy and move information (text, graphics, sound clips, video clips, or a combination) from one application to another. Windows offers several methods for sharing information.

The Clipboard: The Information Way Station

The most common method of sharing information among applications is to use the Windows **clipboard** and the *Edit* option in the menu bar. Think of the clipboard as an intermediate holding area for information. The information in the clipboard can be en route to another application or it can be copied anywhere in the current document. *Edit* is an option in the menu bar of most Windows applications and an option in the control menu of most non-Windows applications. Choosing Edit results in a pull-down menu from the menu bar and a cascading menu from the control menu. Options common to most Edit menus are *Cut, Copy, Paste,* and *Delete.* The **source application** and **destination application** can be one and the same or they can be entirely different applications.

The procedure for transferring information via the clipboard is demonstrated in Figure A–8. This example illustrates the *Copy* procedure. Choosing the *Cut* option causes the specified information to be removed from the source application and placed on the Windows clipboard. Whether *Copy* or *Cut,* the clipboard contents remain unchanged and can be pasted as many times as needed.

Object Linking and Embedding: OLE

Another way to link applications is through **object linking and embedding** or **OLE.** Loosely, an **object** is the result of any Windows application. The object can be a block of text, all or part of a graphic image, or even a sound clip. OLE gives us the capability to create a **compound document** that contains one or more objects from other applications. A document can be a word processing newsletter, a Paint drawing, a spreadsheet, and so on. The object originates in a **server application** and is linked to a destination document of a **client application.** For example, when a Paint (server application) drawing (object) is linked to a WordPad (client) newsletter (destination document), the result is a compound document (see Figure A–9).

Object Linking: Dynamic Connection OLE lets you *link* or *embed* information. When you link information, the link between source and destination documents is dynamic; that is, any change you make in the source document is reflected in the destination document. Object linking is demonstrated in Figure A–9. Linking doesn't actually place the object into the destination document: It places a pointer to the source document (a disk-based file). In linking, the object is saved as a separate file from the source document. The source document must accompany the destination to maintain the integrity of the destination document (a compound document); that is, if you give a friend a copy of the destination document, you must also give the friend the source as well. Your friend's PC must have both the server and client application to display the compound document. Linking is helpful when the object is used in several destination documents because when you change the source, it is updated in all documents to which it is linked.

Object Embedding: Implant Operation When you embed information, you insert the actual object, not just a pointer. Where linking is dynamic, embedding is not. You can change the source within the destination document, but the original (if there is one) is unchanged. A source document is not required in object embedding.

1. *Mark the information.* Drag the select cursor (the Pick tool in Paint) from one corner of the information to be copied to the opposite corner of the area and release the mouse button. The information to be transferred is highlighted.

2. *Copy the marked information to the clipboard.* Choose Edit in the source application's (Paint) menu bar or control menu to display the options. Choose Copy to place the specified information in the Windows clipboard, leaving the sourec application unchanged.

3. *Switch to the destination application and place the graphics cursor at the desired insertion point.*

4. *Paste the marked information.* Choose Edit in the destination application's (WordPad) bar menu or control menu to display the application options. Choose the paste option to copy the contents of the clipboard to the cursor position in the destination application.

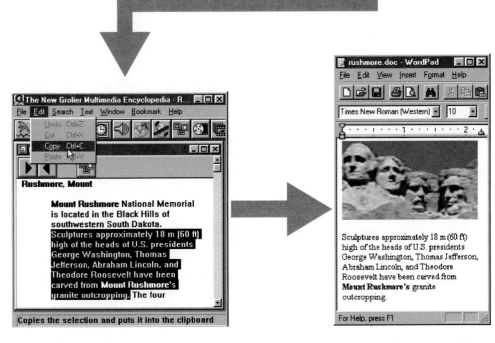

5. *Mark the information*

6. *Copy the marked information to the clipboard*

7. *Switch to the destination application and place the graphics cursor at the desired insertion point.*

8. *Paste the marked information*

FIGURE A–8 Copy and Paste via the Clipboard
This walkthrough demonstrates the procedure for transferring information among multiple Windows applications: Paint (a paint program), WordPad (a word processing program), and an online encyclopedia. In the example, the faces portion of the Mount Rushmore image in a Paint document is marked and copied (to the clipboard), then pasted to a WordPad document. Supporting text in the *New Grolier Multimedia Encyclopedia* is marked and copied to the same WordPad document via the clipboard.

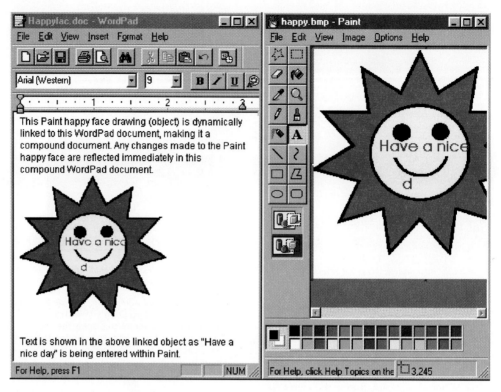

FIGURE A–9 Object Linking
Part of the Paint image is linked to a WordPad document to create a compound document. The WordPad text describes the procedure.

A Thousand Look-Alikes

The discussion in Sections A–1 and A–2 is intended to introduce you to fundamental concepts and terminology associated with the Windows environment. Thousands of software packages written specifically for the Windows environment have adopted these same concepts and terminology and are designed to take advantage of Windows capabilities. Once you understand the Windows environment, you will feel comfortable with the user interfaces of all software written for this environment.

A–3 MIGRATING TO WINDOWS 95

More than seven years transpired before Microsoft Windows passed the 50% installed plateau for the PC compatibles. After seven years on the market, 50% of the users still preferred the MS-DOS platform. If history repeats itself, acceptance of Windows 95 may be slow in coming for MS-DOS users and Windows users. Millions of PC users who feel comfortable with the MS-DOS and/or Windows platforms may be reluctant to migrate to Windows 95. Some users must upgrade their PC's processor (Intel 386-level processor or better), RAM (8 MB or better), and hard disk (requires about 40 MB of disk storage) before Windows 95 becomes an option.

Windows 95 has full backward compatibility with MS-DOS and Windows programs. Those who plan to upgrade to Windows 95 will find that most of the concepts and terminology they learned with Windows apply to Windows 95 as well. They will also find a number of very enticing features. The main Windows 95 features are illustrated and described briefly in the overview in Figure A–10. Windows and MS-DOS may linger a while, but the migration has begun.

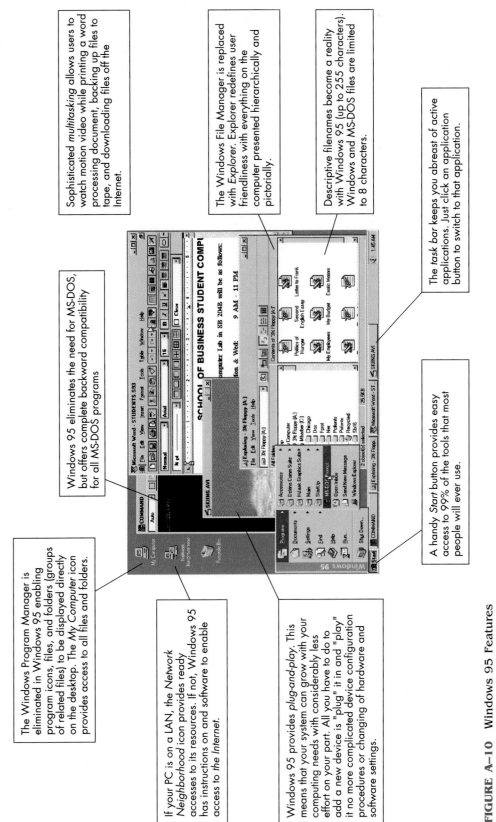

The Windows Program Manager is eliminated in Windows 95 enabling program icons, files, and folders (groups of related files) to be displayed directly on the desktop. The *My Computer* icon provides access to all files and folders.

If your PC is on a LAN, the *Network Neighborhood* icon provides ready accesses to its resources. If not, Windows 95 has instructions on and software to enable access to *the Internet*.

Windows 95 provides *plug-and-play*. This means that your system can grow with your computing needs with considerably less effort on your part. All you have to do to add a new device is "plug" it in and "play" it no more complicated device configuration procedures or changing of hardware and software settings.

Windows 95 eliminates the need for MS-DOS, but offers complete backward compatibility for all MS-DOS programs

Sophisticated *multitasking* allows users to watch motion video while printing a word processing document, backing up files to tape, and downloading files off the Internet.

The Windows File Manager is replaced with *Explorer*. Explorer redefines user friendliness with everything on the computer presented hierarchically and pictorially.

Descriptive filenames become a reality with Windows 95 (up to 255 characters). Windows and MS-DOS files are limited to 8 characters.

The *task bar* keeps you abreast of active applications. Just click an application button to switch to that application.

A handy *Start* button provides easy access to 99% of the tools that most people will ever use.

FIGURE A–10 Windows 95 Features
This figure illustrates important new features of Windows 95, Microsoft's platform for PC-compatible computers that replaces the Windows with MS-DOS and the Windows for Workgroups with MS-DOS platforms.

REVIEW EXERCISES

1. In the Windows environment, how is an item, such as an application program or a menu option, selected with a mouse? How is the item chosen?

2. In the Windows environment, what is the screen area called upon which icons, windows, and so on are displayed?

3. List four elements of the Windows application window.

4. What area is just below the Windows title bar or menu bar?

5. Name the three types of windows in the Windows graphical environment.

6. What results when a Windows menu option, which is followed by an ellipsis (. . .), is chosen?

7. In the Windows environment, is the active window highlighted in the foreground or the background?

8. What is the intermediate holding area called through which information is transferred between Windows applications?

9. In what type of presentation are open windows overlapped such that all title bars are visible?

10. What is displayed in a Windows 95 task bar?

11. What does OLE stand for?

CHAPTER 8

Productivity Software: From Notes to Databases

Courtesy of International Business Machines Corporation

Let's Talk

The following conversation introduces many of the terms in this chapter. Read it now, then again after you have read the chapter.

The Scene: *The executive board of the newly formed RPOA (Rosemont Property Owners' Association) is convening to plan the agenda for the coming year. In attendance are the president (Michelle), VP (Stan), treasurer (Neil) and secretary (Bernie).*

Michelle: Welcome, neighbors, to our very first meeting of the RPOA. We've got lots to do.

Bernie: Where do we begin: the bylaws, the Rosemont newsletter, the neighborhood **database,** or the dues?

Neil: As for the dues, we're 95% paid up. I've already set up a **spreadsheet template** to keep track of dues and expenses. Here's a **summary report** *(passing a printout to each person)* that shows a $1,252.71 balance at First National.

Michelle: Stan, you volunteered to take care of the newsletter, didn't you?

***Stan* (laughing):** No, but I guess my **desktop publishing** experience makes me the logical choice. If anyone has an item for the newsletter, could you give it to me as an **ASCII file** or **word processing document** on diskette? I've got a **scanner,** so we can include photos as well. I'll use my **clip art** library to add seasonal touches.

Michelle: Great, Stan. I'll take care of the neighborhood database. Here's what I've done so far *(showing a database printout)*. It's **sorted** by last name. The database is on a Microsoft Access **relational database,** so we can add and delete **fields** from the **record.** Look it over and tell me if any changes are needed. I've set it up so we can use **mail merge** for our address labels.

Bernie: And, I've got a copy of the bylaws from my old neighborhood association. Stan, if you could **scan** this *(handing the paper to Stan)* and give me a disk file, we can **edit** this **boilerplate** to create our bylaws.

Stan: This **typeface** is easily scanned. I'll get you a diskette by Tuesday.

Michelle: It looks like we're well on our way to a great year!

STUDENT LEARNING OBJECTIVES

▶ *To describe the function and applications of word processing software.*

▶ *To understand word processing concepts.*

▶ *To describe the function and applications of desktop publishing software.*

▶ *To understand desktop publishing concepts.*

▶ *To describe and illustrate the relationships between the levels of the hierarchy of data organization.*

▶ *To describe the function and applications of spreadsheet software.*

▶ *To understand common spreadsheet concepts.*

▶ *To describe the function and applications of database software.*

▶ *To understand common database software concepts.*

▶ *To describe the concepts associated with programming and programs.*

8–1 PERSONAL COMPUTING WITH POPULAR PRODUCTIVITY PACKAGES

Personal computing encompasses everything from 3-D games, to going online, to computer-based education, to music composition. Tens of thousands of software packages add variety to the potential of personal computing. The foundation of personal computing over the last decade, however, has been software in these four categories: word processing software, desktop publishing software, spreadsheet software, and database software. Over the years, these packages have won unanimous user acceptance because of their tremendous contribution to personal productivity. This chapter provides a conceptual and functional overview of each of these types of software.

8–2 WORD PROCESSING: THE MOST POPULAR PC APPLICATION

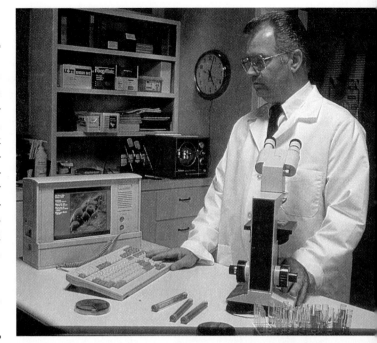

At work, at home, at school, and even during leisure activities, we spend much of our time writing. At work we send memos and write procedures manuals. At home we keep to-do lists and prepare party announcements. At school we write reports and essays. During leisure time, we keep diaries and write letters to our family and friends. These are just a few of the myriad of day-to-day writing activities that can be made easier and more professional through the use of word processing software and desktop publishing software. This section addresses word processing software. Today's sophisticated *word processing software* packages do much more than text-oriented word processing. For example, most packages let you integrate images with text and some let you integrate audio, such as voice annotations, within your on-screen word processing document.

Most jobs require a fair amount of writing and/or drawing. This is true for architects, teachers, lawyers, insurance agents, executives, and it is true for this medical researcher. Word processing skills will benefit him as he writes up his findings. Reprinted with permission of Compaq Computer Corporation, All Rights Reserved.

Concepts and Features

The material in this section provides you with a *conceptual overview* of word processing software, as opposed to a *hands-on tutorial*. You need *both* in order to be an effective user of word processing software. In the typical introductory hands-on laboratory, you learn how to perform basic word processing operations in Word, WordPerfect, or some other word processing package.

Over time, through experience and experimentation, you will learn how to take advantage of all that your word processing package has to offer. If you're in a hurry, your college probably offers advanced hands-on labs for word processing and other popular productivity software packages (spreadsheet, database, graphics, and so on). Microsoft Word is used in the examples for this text.

Creating a Document   The term *document* is a generic reference to whatever is currently in the word processing work area (text and/or images) or to a file containing stored text and/or images (perhaps a report or an outline). To create an original document, such as a report, you simply begin entering text from the keyboard and occasionally enter commands that enhance the appearance of the document when it is printed (spacing, italics, and so on). If you wish to work with the document later, you will need to save it to disk storage for later recall. When you recall a document from disk storage, you can *edit* (revise) it, then save the revised version of the document to disk storage. Once you are satisfied with the content and appearance of the document, you can print it.

Having word processing skills is like having money in the bank for this and millions of other college students. This student uses her skills to write reports, compose short stories, organize class notes, write letters home, and for many other applications. Courtesy of International Business Machines Corporation

INTERNET BRIDGE

Word Processing/DTP

Formatting a document. Before you begin keying in the text of a word processing document, you may need to *format* the document to meet your application needs. You do this by specifying what you wish the general appearance of the document to be when it is printed. However, if you are satisfied with the software's preset format specifications, you can begin keying in text right away. Typically, the preset format, or *default settings*, fit most word processing applications. For example, the size of the output document is set at letter size (8½ by 11 inches); the left, right, top, and bottom margins are set at 1 inch; tabs are set every ½ inch; and line spacing is set at 6 lines per inch.

Entering and editing text. Text is entered and subsequently edited in either **typeover mode** or **insert mode**. To *toggle,* or switch, between typeover and insert modes, you tap the insert (or INS) key. Word processing permits **full-screen editing,** which means that you can move the text cursor to any position in the document to insert or type over text. You can browse through a multiscreen document by *scrolling* a line at a time, a screen at a time, or a page (the text that corresponds to a printed page) at a time.

Most modern word processing packages are considered **WYSIWYG** (pronounced "*WIZ e wig*"), short for "What you see is what you get." What you see on the screen is essentially what the document will look like when it is printed—the type of font, font size, graphics, and all. The **font** refers to the style, appearance, and size of print. Fonts are described in more detail in the section on desktop publishing.

This process of preparing a word processing document is illustrated in Figure 8–1, which presents the draft copy and subsequent revisions to a memo written by B. J.

FIGURE 8–1 Creating a Memo: A Walkthrough
This multipage illustration walks you through the process of creating a simple memo, demonstrating basic word processing concepts along the way. The example is illustrated in Microsoft Word for Windows 95.

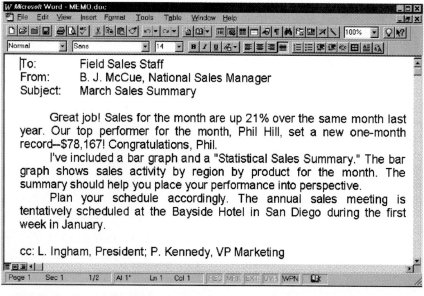

1. B. J. McCue, the national sales manager for BrassCo Enterprises, created this draft copy of a memo to the sales staff. As text is entered, it automatically *wraps* to the next line when it reaches the right margin. In word processing, *tap the ENTER key only when you wish to begin a new line of text.* In the memo, B. J. tapped ENTER after the opening three information lines, after each paragraph in the body of the memo, and after the "copy to" (cc) line. B. J. also tapped ENTER to insert each of the blank lines. The TAB key was tapped at the beginning of each paragraph to indent the first line of the paragraph.

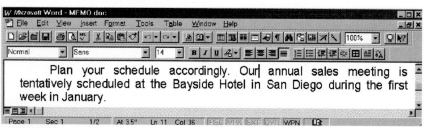

2. When in typeover mode, the character you enter *types over* the character at the cursor position. For example, in the last sentence of the memo, B. J. began with *The* and realized that *Our* is a better word. To make the correction in typeover mode, B. J. positioned the cursor at the *T* and typed *O-u-r,* thereby replacing *The* with *Our.* When in insert mode, any text entered is *additional* text.

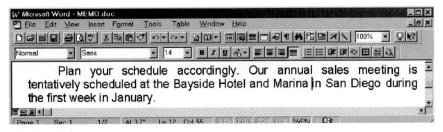

3. B. J. forgot to enter the full name of the hotel (Bayside Hotel and Marina) in the last line of the draft memo. To complete the name, B. J. selected the insert mode, placed the cursor at the *i* in the word *in* (after *Bayside Hotel*), and entered *and Marina* followed by a space. Notice how text at the end of the sentence is automatically wrapped to the next line. This type of text movement is called *word wrap.*

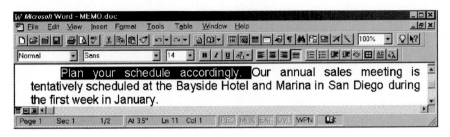

4. After reading over the memo, B. J. decided to edit the memo to make it more readable. B. J. moved the first sentence in the last paragraph to the end of the memo. To perform this operation, B. J. marked the block by dragging the cursor from the beginning of the block (*P* in *Plan*) to the end of the block (the position following the period at the end of that sentence). On most word processing systems, the portions of text marked for a block operation are usually displayed in *reverse video.*

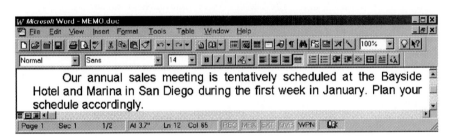

5. To complete the move operation begun in Step 4, B. J. selected the *cut* option in the Edit menu to remove the block from the memo and place it in the clipboard. Then B. J. used the mouse to position the cursor at the destination location (after a space following the end of the paragraph) and selected the *paste* option to complete the move operation.

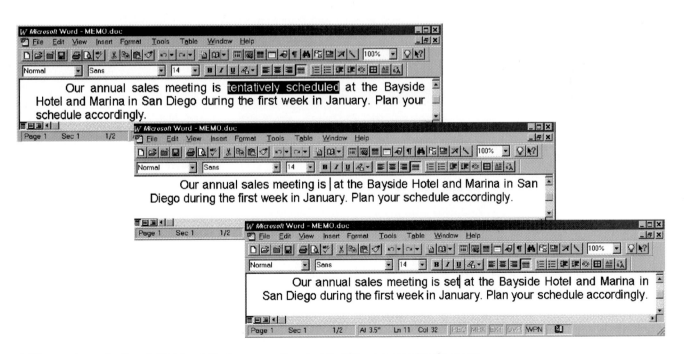

6. The meeting at the Bayside Hotel and Marina was confirmed while B. J. was composing the memo. To reflect the confirmation, B. J. used the block-delete command to drop the phrase *tentatively scheduled,* then inserted the word *set.*

(**Figure 8-1** continues on next page)

FIGURE 8-1 (continued)

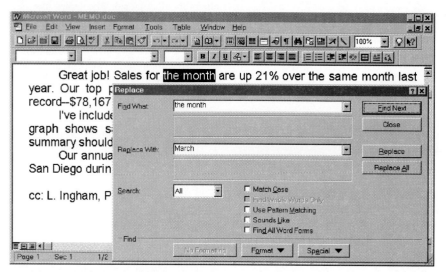

7. While looking over the memo, B. J. decided that it would read better if all generic references to *the month* were replaced by the name of the month, *March*. The necessary revisions in the memo can be made by using the *find and replace* feature. This feature allows B. J. to search the entire memo for all occurrences of *the month*. After entering the find string and clicking on the Find Next button, the cursor is positioned at the first occurrence of *the month*. B. J. can easily edit each occurrence to reflect *March*. However, rather than change each occurrence, B. J. entered a replace string in the *Find and Replace Text* dialog box—*March*.

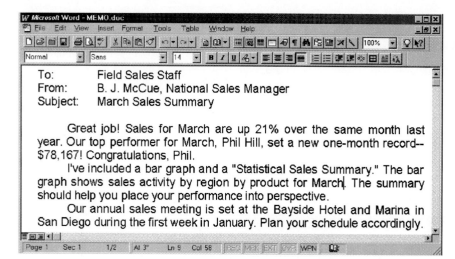

8. The *find and replace* feature lets B. J. replace occurrences of the find string (*the month*) with the replace string (*March*) either selectively (Replace button) or globally (Replace All button). When B. J. clicked on the Replace All button in the dialog box (Step 7), all occurrences of *the month* were replaced with *March*.

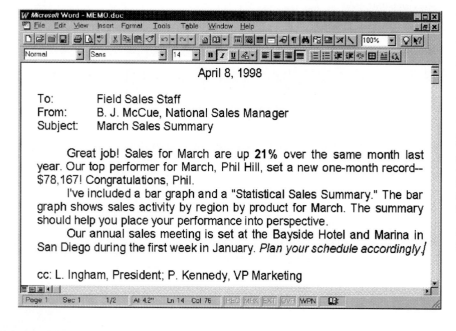

9. B. J. used several other valuable word processing features to enhance the appearance and readability of the memo before distributing it to the field sales staff. First, the manager decided to enter the current date at the top of the memo and use the automatic *centering* feature to position it at the center of the page.

In the memo, B. J. decided to highlight the remarkable 21% increase in sales by requesting that it be printed in boldface type. To do so, the manager marked *21%* and issued the boldface command. To make the point that sales representatives should plan now for the January meeting, B. J. followed a similar procedure to set the last sentence in italics.

Note also that B. J. has chosen full justification (alignment of both left and right margins) for a cleaner appearance.

McCue, the national sales manager for BrassCo Enterprises, a manufacturer of quality brass products. In Figure 8–1, Step 1, B. J. has created a draft copy of a memo to the sales staff. The initial revisions using typeover mode and insert mode are illustrated in Steps 2 and 3. Steps 4 through 9 in Figure 8–1 demonstrate features common to word processing software packages. The example in Figure 8–2 illustrates these and other word processing features.

INTERNET BRIDGE

Serendipitous Surfing: Money Management

FIGURE 8–2 Features Overview
Common capabilities of word processing software are illustrated in this printout.

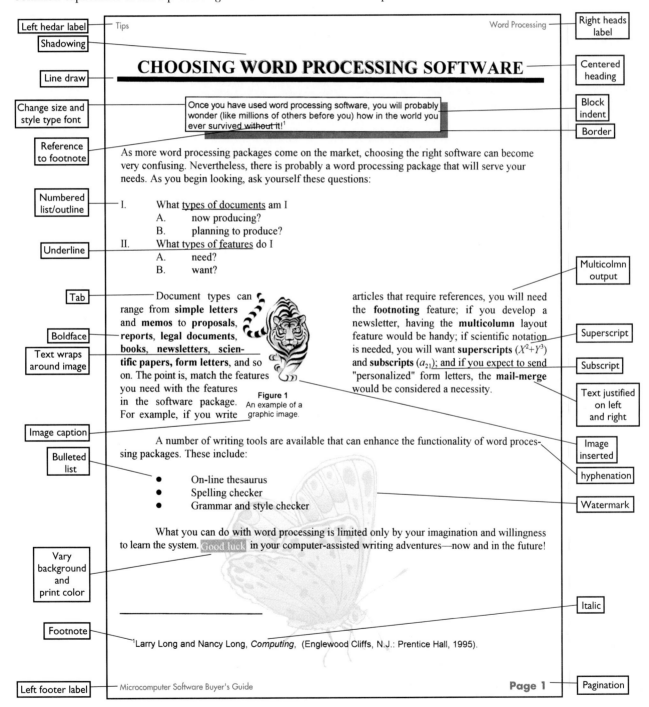

Left hedar label · Tips
Shadowing
Line draw

CHOOSING WORD PROCESSING SOFTWARE

Word Processing · Right heads label
Centered heading

Change size and style type font

Once you have used word processing software, you will probably wonder (like millions of others before you) how in the world you ever survived without it![1]

Block indent
Border

Reference to footnote

As more word processing packages come on the market, choosing the right software can become very confusing. Nevertheless, there is probably a word processing package that will serve your needs. As you begin looking, ask yourself these questions:

Numbered list/outline

I. What <u>types of documents</u> am I
    A. now producing?
    B. planning to produce?
II. What <u>types of features</u> do I
    A. need?
    B. want?

Underline

Multicolmn output

Tab

Document types can range from **simple letters** and **memos** to **proposals, reports, legal documents, books, newsletters, scientific papers, form letters**, and so on. The point is, match the features you need with the features in the software package. For example, if you write

Figure 1
An example of a graphic image.

articles that require references, you will need the **footnoting** feature; if you develop a newsletter, having the **multicolumn** layout feature would be handy; if scientific notation is needed, you will want **superscripts** (X^2+Y^3) and **subscripts** (a_{21}); and if you expect to send "personalized" form letters, the **mail-merge** would be considered a necessity.

Boldface

Text wraps around image

Superscript

Subscript

Text justified on left and right

Image caption

A number of writing tools are available that can enhance the functionality of word processing packages. These include:

Bulleted list

- On-line thesaurus
- Spelling checker
- Grammar and style checker

Image inserted
hyphenation

Watermark

What you can do with word processing is limited only by your imagination and willingness to learn the system. Good luck in your computer-assisted writing adventures—now and in the future!

Vary background and print color

Italic

Footnote

[1]Larry Long and Nancy Long, *Computing*, (Englewood Cliffs, N.J.: Prentice Hall, 1995).

Left footer label · Microcomputer Software Buyer's Guide

Page 1 · Pagination

Printing a document or sending a fax features. To print a document, ready the printer and select the *print* option on the main menu. If your PC is configured with a fax modem, you can fax your word processing document as easily as you would print it. To send a fax, simply select the fax modem driver as your "printer," and select the *print* option. The fax modem software asks you for a telephone number, then dials the number and faxes the current document.

Integrating Tables and Graphs

The *table* feature, found in most commercial word processing packages, facilitates the tabular presentation of data. The user sets up a table format by entering the number of rows and columns desired. The "Statistical Sales Summary" alluded to in the example memo of Figure 8–1 is presented in a table in Figure 8–3. Once data have been entered into the table, spreadsheet-type functions can be performed on the entries. For example, in Figure 8–3, user-defined formulas calculate, then display the sum for each row.

FIGURE 8–3 Integrating Text with Graphics The bar graph and the "Statistical Sales Summary" referred to in the memo of Figure 8–1 are combined in the same word processing document. To create the table shown in this figure, B. J. McCue told the software to generate a table with six rows and five columns. B. J. enhanced the appearance of the table by choosing a mix of line styles and by shading cells (first row). Finally, B. J. entered the text, data, and formulas (totals in last column) in the cells. The formulas in the *totals* column sum the amounts in their respective rows.

B. J. created the bar graph in a two-step process. First, B. J. marked the product headings (Crown, Monarch, Curio) and the data under headings. Next, B. J. told the software to create a bar graph based on the marked headings and data. B. J. positioned the resulting chart such that the text of the memo would contour around the chart.

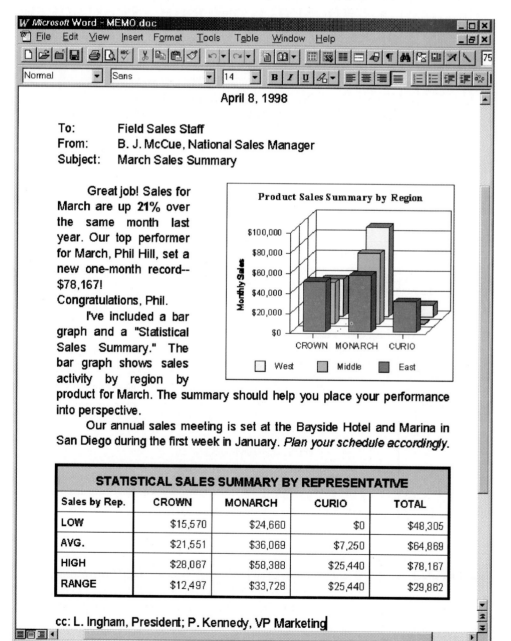

STATISTICAL SALES SUMMARY BY REPRESENTATIVE				
Sales by Rep.	CROWN	MONARCH	CURIO	TOTAL
LOW	$15,570	$24,660	$0	$48,305
AVG.	$21,551	$36,069	$7,250	$64,869
HIGH	$28,067	$58,388	$25,440	$78,167
RANGE	$12,497	$33,728	$25,440	$29,862

Today's sophisticated word processing programs can do much more than work with words. For example, WordPerfect for Windows has a feature that lets you create bar and pie charts. The bar graph in Figure 8–3 was created automatically from the data in the table.

Writing Tools: Dotting the *i*'s and Crossing the *t*'s

Modern word processing programs offer a variety of helpful writing tools. These writing tools are introduced in this section and illustrated in Figure 8–4.

▶ *Spelling checker.* The **spelling checker** checks every word in the text against an **electronic dictionary** and alerts you if a word is not in the dictionary (see Figure 8–4).

▶ *Online thesaurus.* Most commercial word processing packages have an **online thesaurus** to help you find the right word (see Figure 8–4).

▶ *Grammar and style checkers.* Grammar and style checkers are the electronic version of a copy editor. A **grammar and style checker** highlights grammatical concerns and deviations from conventions (see Figure 8–4).

Putting Word Processing to Work

You can create just about any type of text-based document with word processing—letters, reports, books, articles, forms, memos, tables, and so on. However, the features of commercial word processing packages go beyond the generation of text documents. This section summarizes these applications of word processing software.

Merging Documents with a Database   Word processing software provides the capability of merging data in a database with the text of a document. The most frequently used application of this capability is the *mail-merge* application. This application is illustrated in Figure 8–5. In the example, B. J. McCue decided to revise the memo of Figure 8–3 so that personalized letters could be sent to each BrassCo sales representative. To do this, B. J. created a *database file* with name and address data that could be merged with a *form file* (the letter with references to entries in the database).

Boilerplate: Electronic Recycling   The mail-merge example is a good illustration of the use of **boilerplate.** Boilerplate is existing text that can be customized for a variety of word processing applications. One beauty of word processing is that you can accumulate text on disk storage that eventually will help you meet other word processing needs. You can even *buy* boilerplate (for example, text for business letters).

The legal profession offers some of the best examples of the use of boilerplate. Simple wills, uncontested divorces, individual bankruptcies, real estate transfers, and other straightforward legal documents may be as much as 95% boilerplate. Even more-complex legal documents may be as much as 80% boilerplate. Once the appropriate boilerplate has been merged into a document, the lawyer edits the document to add transition sentences and the variables, such as the names of the litigants. Besides the obvious improvement in productivity, lawyers can be relatively confident that their documents are accurate and complete. The use of boilerplate is common in all areas of business, education, government, and personal endeavor.

Hypertext Links   Not all word processing documents are designed to be printed. For example, many companies are opting to put their reference materials in electronic, rather than printed, documents. Electronic versions of product catalogs, procedures manuals, personnel handbooks, and so on are now common in the business community. They are easier to create, maintain, and distribute. One of the main reasons for this trend to online documents is the ability to place *hypertext links* in documents.

GOING ONLINE

8.1
Be in Touch

In an e-mail message to one of your classmates and to your instructor, describe some of the exciting things that you've found while surfing the Net.
Hand in: A copy of your e-mail message.

**Applications
Explorer**

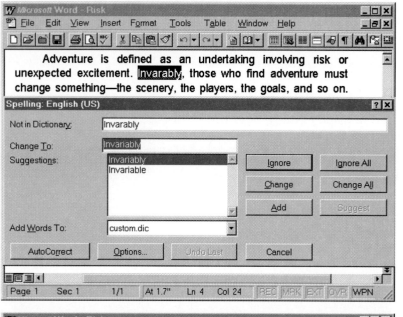

FIGURE 8–4 Writing Tools

Writing tools available with most commercial word processing packages include the spelling checker, the online thesaurus, and the grammar and style checker.

The spelling checker does as its name implies—checks the spelling. Upon finding an unidentified word, the spelling checker normally will give you several options:
▲ You can opt to replace the highlighted word with one of the suggested words. In the example, *Invarably* is flagged. The spelling checker suggested two possibilities: *Invariably* and *Invariable.*
▲ You can key in the correct spelling in your word processing document.
▲ You can ignore the highlighted word and continue scanning the text (the Ignore and Ignore All buttons) in the example). Normally, you do this when a word is spelled correctly but is not in the dictionary (for example, a company name such as BrassCo).
▲ You can add the word to the dictionary and continue scanning the text.

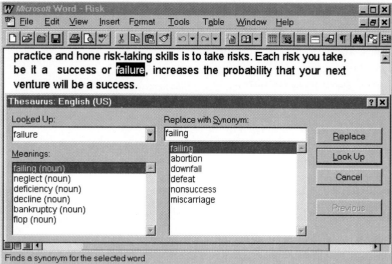

The Word for Windows 95 thesaurus feature helps you find the right word. In the example, the user requested synonyms for the word *failure.* The user extended the search by requesting synonyms for the word *flop.*

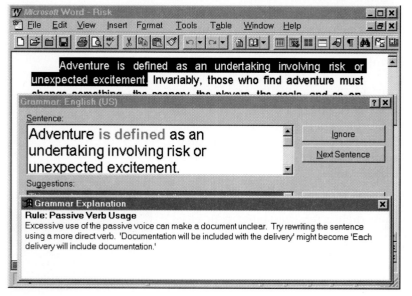

Grammar and style checkers scan word processing documents for grammar, style, usage, punctuation, and spelling errors. In the example, the program advises the user to consider using a more direct verb in the displayed sentence. The user has the option of taking no action and going on to the next problem, editing the problem, marking it for later examination, or ignoring similar problems for the rest of the scan.

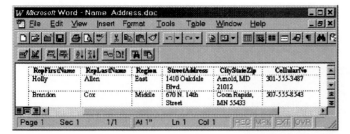

FIGURE 8–5 The Mail-Merge Application

B. J. McCue used the mail-merge capability to send personalized letters to all the field sales representatives. Two specially formatted document files must be created to merge data with a text document: the *database file* and the *form file*. The two are merged to create the personalized letters.

B. J. McCue created the *database file* by entering the name and address information for each field representative. The database file contains *records*, which are made up of related *fields*. There is a record for each rep. Each record has six fields, each of which is described at the top of the database display. This database file is merged with the form file (the letter) to generate the personalized letters.

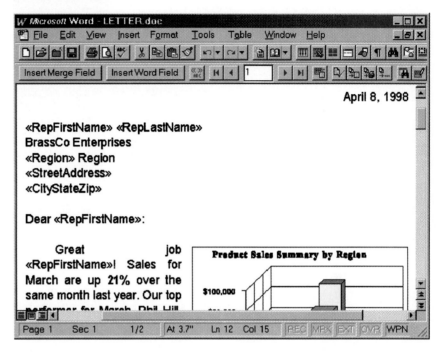

To prepare the *form file*, B. J. revised the memo of Figure 8–3. B. J. deleted the memo heading and inserted merge codes in the text of the letter to indicate where the data are to be merged. Name and address data from the database file are merged with the form file in the inside address, the salutation, and the body of the letter.

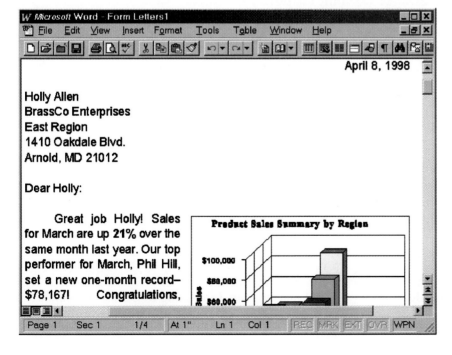

The database and form files are merged to create a third file containing the personalized letters. During the merge process a single letter document (form file) is merged with a single record (in database file). The example illustrates what happens when Holly Allen's record is merged with the form file letter. The merge process is repeated until all records are processed. The resulting document, which contains all personalized letters, is ready to print. The name and address database file can be merged with an envelope form file to print the envelopes.

FIGURE 8-6 Hypertext Links

Performing the *vacuum tube* hypertext link in the WordPerfect for Windows document titled "The Computer on a Chip" causes another document to be displayed in its place. After viewing the linked document, the user can opt to return to the original document.

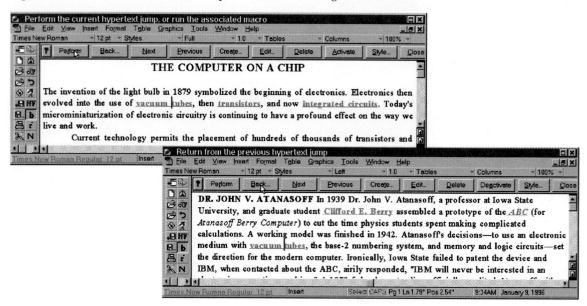

Hypertext links let you tie parts of a document or different documents together. Words or phrases within documents can be highlighted as hypertext (see Figure 8–6). When you encounter a hypertext entry, you can jump (link) to another place in the same document or to another document for more information. In Windows-based programs, hypertext links are displayed in green and underlined (see Figure 8–6). Hypertext links make it easy to skip around a document to find what you want. The uses of hypertext are endless.

Word Processing: Working Faster and Smarter Word processing is the perfect example of how automation can be used to increase productivity and foster creativity. It reduces the effort you must devote to the routine aspects of writing so you can focus your attention on its creative aspects. As a result, most word processing users will agree that their writing styles have improved. The finished product is less verbose, better organized, without spelling errors, and, of course, more visually appealing.

8-3 DESKTOP PUBLISHING: FREEDOM OF THE PRESS

Word Processing/DTP

Desktop publishing has given new meaning to the phrase *freedom of the press.* Instead of being tied to the typesetter and the print shop, millions of users now create newsletters, brochures, user manuals, pamphlets, flyers, restaurant menus, periodicals, greeting cards, graduation certificates, and thousands of other printed items. **Desktop publishing,** sometimes abbreviated as **DTP,** refers to the capability of producing *typeset-quality camera-ready copy* for publication from the confines of a desktop. Desktop publishing software can help you produce camera-ready copy for every conceivable type of printed matter, from business cards to catalogs. The resulting camera-ready copy is reproduced by a variety of means, from duplicating machines to commercial offset printing. This concept is changing the way organizations and individuals meet their printing needs.

Desktop Publishing and Word Processing: What's the Difference?

Like DTP software, word processing software also enables us to produce camera-ready copy for newsletters, brochures, user manuals, and so on. In fact, the end result may be similar, but getting there is quite different. In word processing, the emphasis is on *words*, the text that makes up the documents. In word processing, we fill the document with words, then add images, borders, shading, and so on around the running text. The text runs from the beginning to the end of the letter, handbook, or whatever document is being created. In desktop publishing, the emphasis is on overall document composition. Various types of *objects* are pulled together and laid out on a page. An object can be a block of text, an image, a line, an ellipse, and so on. DTP's page layout capabilities combined with its precision have made DTP software the choice of professional designers of publication materials.

The content for the text and image objects used in a DTP document is usually created within another program (for example, WordPerfect for Windows or Paintbrush, a graphics program). Once created, the text or image is transferred into a DTP object and placed on the page.

Although the business community still relies on professional publication designers to do the page makeup for long, complex documents, many jobs can be completed by the nonprofessional user. Consider these examples.

- Junior high school students use DTP to prepare their school newspapers.
- Marketing managers use DTP to prepare their own ad pieces.
- Restaurant owners use DTP to lay out menus.
- College department heads use DTP to prepare departmental brochures.
- Personnel directors use DTP to create employee handbooks.

GOING ONLINE

8.2
Going to the Movies
The Internet is a great place to determine whether or not you should invest time and money at the cinema. Go online and read what people have to say about a current movie. Enter "movies" and "reviews" in the Yahoo (http://www.yahoo.com) or WebCrawler (http://www.webcrawler.com) search box for plenty of commentary on the movies.

Hand in: A printed copy and identify the source of a movie review, a summary of the review, or someone's comments on a movie.

Concepts and Features

Traditionally, drafts of documents to be professionally printed are delivered to commercial typographers to be typeset. The typeset text is physically pasted together with photos, artwork, ruled lines, and so on to achieve the final layout. Desktop publishing eliminates the typesetting and cumbersome manual paste-up process. The output of the desktop publishing process is *camera-ready copy* that can be reproduced for distribution.

The quality of the DTP-produced camera-ready copy is dependent on the quality of available input and output devices. The typical office will have a standard image scanner and perhaps a 600 to 1000 dpi (dots per inch) laser printer. This is sufficient for most printing needs. The camera-ready copy produced in this type of environment is called *near-typeset-quality*. Professional graphics studios and printers will have very high-resolution scanners and printers capable of producing *typeset-quality* camera-ready copy in color, as well as black and white.

The Components of Desktop Publishing   The components required for desktop publishing include:

- Document-composition software
- Microcomputer
- Desktop page printer
- Image scanner
- Typefaces and fonts
- Clip art
- Illustration software

The image scanner is one of the components of the desktop publishing environment. Relatively inexpensive hand image scanners have opened the door for more people to get into desktop publishing.
Courtesy Logitech

Document-composition software. The document-composition software enables users to design and make up the page or pages of a document. When people talk of desktop publishing software, they are actually talking about document-composition software. Popular professional-level DTP packages include Quark Incorporated's *QuarkXPress,* Corel Corporation's *Corel Ventura,* and Aldus Corporation's *PageMaker.* Popular entry-level DTP packages include *Microsoft Publisher,* Timeworks International Corporation's *Publish It!,* and Softkey International Corporation's *PFS: Publisher. Microsoft Publisher* is used as the basis for the examples in this section.

To create a DTP document with a program like Microsoft Publisher, you go through the *document-composition process.* This process involves integrating graphics, photos, text, and other resources into a visually appealing *document layout.* Figure 8–7 illustrates the basic steps in the document-composition process. Follow these steps to produce finished, professional-looking documents.

Microcomputer. DTP is one of the most technologically demanding PC applications. A high-end microcomputer is a prerequisite for effective desktop publishing. The typical micro used for DTP will be fast and will be configured with a high-resolution *monitor,* a *mouse,* plenty of RAM, and a high-capacity *hard disk.* A large screen monitor (at least 17 inches) is recommended for PC users who are routinely involved in desktop publishing.

Desktop page printer. The quality of the resultant camera-ready copy is directly proportional to the quality of the printer. The casual DTP user will need a page printer with at least 600 dpi resolution. Professional DTP studios have high-end printers (2000 dpi or greater).

Image scanner. Image scanners are used to digitize images, such as photographs. Image scanners re-create an electronic version of text or an image (photograph or line drawing) that can be manipulated and reproduced under computer control. Like printers, image scanners come with a variety of capabilities. Hand image scanners produce an electronic image, but the result is not nearly as clear as the image produced by a high-resolution page scanner.

Typefaces and fonts. Most DTP-produced documents use a variety of **typefaces.** A typeface refers to a set of characters of the same type style (Helvetica, Courier, Swiss Light, *Park Avenue,* Dutch Roman, and so on). A *font* is described by its typeface, its height in points (8, 10, 14, 24, and so on; 72 points to the inch), and its presentation attribute (light, roman [or normal], medium, **bold,** *italic,* ***bold italic,*** **extra bold,** and so on).

FIGURE 8–7 The DTP Document-Composition Process
This walkthrough illustrates, generally, how DTP documents are created. The document being prepared within Microsoft Publisher is a two-page newsletter put out monthly by the PC User's Group (PCUG).

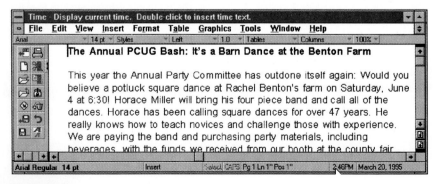

1. *Prepare text.* Generally, the text to be placed in DTP documents is prepared with a word processing program. Here the text for a PC User's Group newsletter is prepared in WordPerfect for Windows, a word processing program.

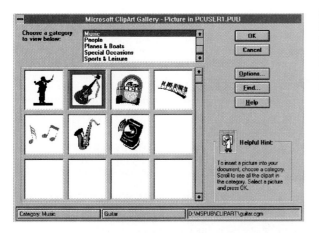

2. *Prepare or identify nontext-related resources.* The images in this example (see Step 6) come from two sources: clip art (see the heading art, the guitar, and the PC users) and screen captures (see the Windows 95 display). Microsoft Publisher comes with a variety of clip art. Clip art images can be selected from the clip art browser (shown here). Had the example required original art, the art would have had to have been prepared using a seperate illustration program.

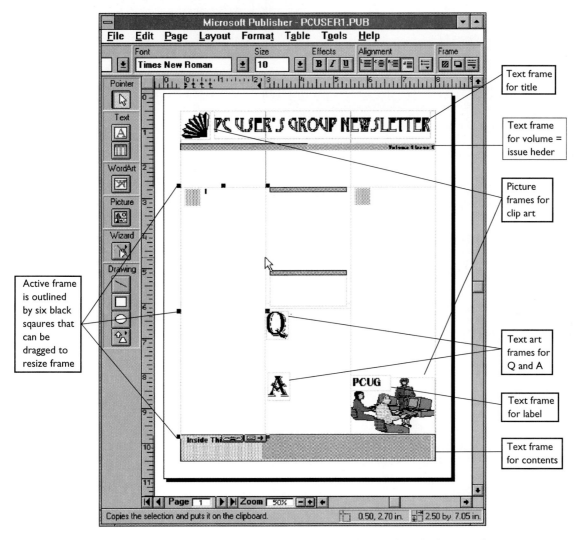

3. *Lay out the document page(s) and add frames.* Set up the page, indicating margins, number of columns, and so on. When you set up the page, nonprinting *layout guides* are displayed. Once the layout is complete, you can use these layout guides to help you position the text and picture frames to fit your needs.

There are two ways to lay out a publication. You can *start from scratch* and make all layout decisions yourself or you can *use a template.* Templates are predesigned publications that include the basic elements for a particular application (newsletter, business card, handbook, brochure, formal invitation, menu, résumé, and so on). Every DTP package comes with a variety of templates from which to choose. Professional publication designers frequently start from scratch. Most of the rest of us either use a template *as is* or *customize* it to meet our publication needs. The PC User's Group modified a Microsoft Publisher template to create the layout shown here.

(**Figure 8-7** continues on next page)

FIGURE 8-7 (continued)

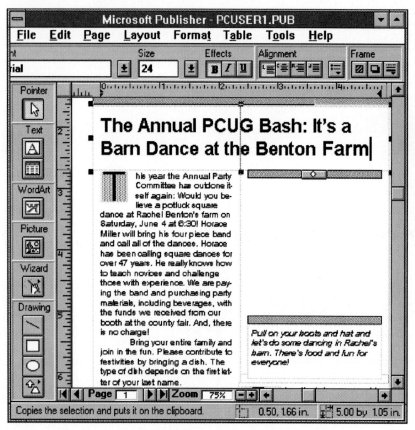

4. *Fill in the text frames.* For publications that require little text, enter the text directly into the text frame. For longer text-based publications, like newsletters, it is actually quicker to create and edit the text with a word processing program. Once you have the text the way you want it, transfer it to the text frame via the *Windows clipboard* or *import it* to the text frame. If the text has been *tagged* with certain attributes (boldface, italics, and so on) and you wish to retain these attributes in the DTP document, it is better to import the file.

The story about "The Annual PCUG Bash" and the other stories were created using WordPerfect for Windows in Step 1. The text from the word processing document is transferred into the DTP document one frame at a time. The "Bash" text is transferred to the first column text frame (highlighted in Step 3). The "Bash" heading is placed in a text frame over the story (shown here).

5. *Fill in the picture frames.* The picture frame in the middle of the first page is filled with the guitar clip art highlighted in the Clip Art Browser in Step 2. A screen capture showing the Windows 95 GUI was used to fill a picture on page 2 (see Step 6).

6. *Fine-tune the layout.* The DTP display is WYSIWYG—that is, "What you see is what you get" when the document is printed. If what you see is not what you want, then you can use the mouse to reposition frames containing text and pictures to the desired locations.

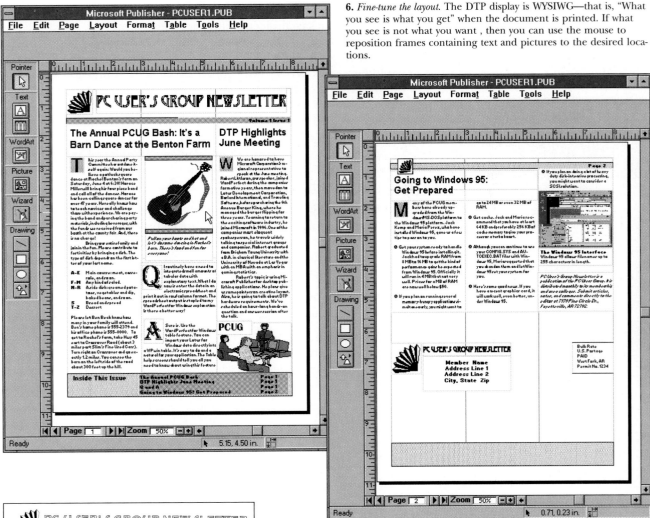

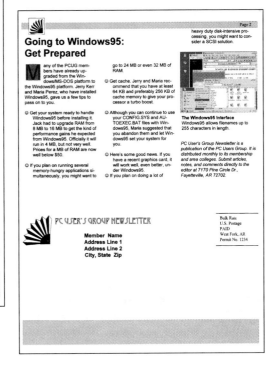

7. *Print the camera copy.* Once the WYSIWYG display shows what you want, use a desktop page printer to produce the finished camera-ready copy.

8. *Publish the document.* Reproduce the camera copy for distribution.

Clip art. No DTP environment would be complete without a healthy supply of **clip art.** Clip art refers to prepackaged electronic images stored on disk to be used as needed. The tiger and butterfly in Figure 8–2 are clip art. Several pieces of clip art are used in the DTP example in Figure 8–7 (the heading art, the guitar, the PC users). Clip art items could be a clock, a rose, two people talking, a hamburger, or just about anything you can imagine. It's not unusual for the active PC user to have hundreds, if not thousands, of pieces of clip art. Clip art ranges in sophistication from crude line drawings to very detailed and colorful artistic images, with the latter requiring far greater disk space.

One of the handiest features of desktop publishing software is the *clip art browser.* The clip art browser lets you preview postage-stamp size renderings of available clip art (see Step 2, in Figure 8–7).

Illustration software. An illustration program (paint or draw software) is nice to have if you intend to create original illustrations for inclusion in a DTP document. All Windows users have access to Paintbrush, a paint program. The casual DTP user may be able to get by without illustration software, using clip art in lieu of original illustrations.

Desktop Publishing Resources A number of resources are pulled together in a typical DTP-produced document, such as a newsletter. These resources might include the following.

▶ *Text files.* Text files generally are created within a word processing program. Although DTP software provides the facility to create and edit text, it is much easier to do these tasks with a word processing program.

▶ *Clip art.* Clip art resources needed to produce the DTP document must be identified.

▶ *Original artwork.* Original artwork is created with a paint or draw program and stored in files.

▶ *Photographs and hard-copy graphics.* Photos and graphics must be scanned into digital files.

▶ *Screen displays.* Applicable screen displays are captured into files.

All such resources should be prepared or identified prior to beginning work on the DTP document. A long report or a book may involve hundreds of resources, all of which are stored in separate files.

During the document-composition process, each resource is assigned to a rectangular **frame.** (see Step 3, Figure 8–7). A frame is created to hold a particular type of resource. Generally, frames are classified as either *text frames* or *picture frames.* Text is placed in text frames. All types of images, from clip art to scanned photographs, are placed in picture frames. To create a frame, a DTP user simply selects the desired type of frame from a tool bar, then drags the cursor between opposite corners of where the frame is to be placed. A frame can be positioned within a frame. For example, a frame containing text can be placed entirely within a frame containing an image.

8–4 DATA MANAGEMENT IN PRACTICE: BITS TO DATABASES

Our upbringing prepared us better for word processing software than it did for data management software. If you are like most people, you probably felt very comfortable about the prospects of using word processing. After all, you have been preparing to

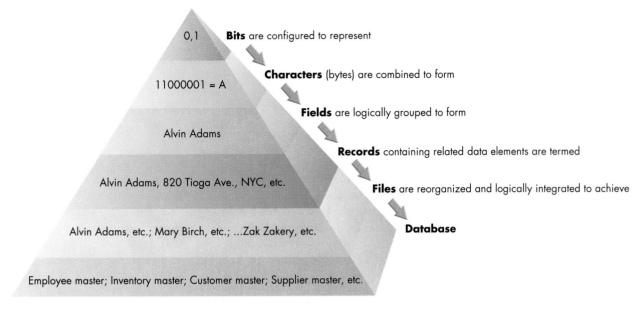

FIGURE 8–8 The Hierarchy of Data Organization

use word processing software since the day you said your first word. At home and at school you were taught spelling, grammar, sentence structure, and writing style. Through formal learning and experience you expanded your vocabulary and learned how documents, such as letters, should look. In short, when you call up word processing software, you are well prepared to use it.

Just as you need to learn sentence structure and grammar to be an effective user of word processing software, you need to learn fundamental data management principles to be an effective user of spreadsheet and database software. These principles, which are new to most people taking this course, include the terms and concepts associated with the *hierarchy of data organization*. This hierarchy is the basis for any information processing activity involving spreadsheet or database software.

The six levels of the hierarchy of data organization are illustrated in Figure 8–8. They are *bit, character, field, record, file,* and *database*. Each succeeding level in the hierarchy is the result of combining the elements of the preceding level. Data are logically combined in this fashion until a database is achieved. The following paragraphs explain each level of the hierarchy and how it relates to the succeeding level.

Bits and Characters

In a computer system, a *character* (A, B, C, 1, 2, and so on) is represented by a group of *bits* (1s and 0s) that are configured according to an encoding system, such as ASCII. In ASCII, a *C* is represented inside a computer as 1000011 and a 5 is represented as 0110101. Whereas the bit is the basic unit of primary and secondary storage, the character is the basic unit for human perception. When we enter a command on a PC or a terminal, each character is automatically encoded into a bit configuration. The bit configurations are decoded on output so we can read and understand the output. In terms of data storage, a character is usually the same as a *byte*.

Fields: First Name, ZIP Code, and Part Number

The **field** is the lowest level in the data hierarchy at which we can derive any meaning from the data. For example, a single character (such as *A*) has little meaning out of context. But when characters are combined to form a name (for example, *Alicia*

**Serendipitous Surfing:
Humor**

or *Alvin*), they form a logical unit. A field is best described by example: social security number, first name, street address, marital status. These are all fields, the basic subdivisions of a record.

An address is often represented as four fields: street address, city, state, and ZIP code. If we treated the entire address as one field, it would be cumbersome to print because the street address is normally placed on a separate line from the city, state, and ZIP code. Because name-and-address files are often sorted by ZIP code, it is also a good idea to store the ZIP code as a separate field.

Records: Describing Events or Items

A *record* is a description of an event (for example, a sale, a hotel reservation) or an item (for example, a customer, a part). Related fields describing an event or an item are logically grouped to form a record. For example, the following example shows some of the fields that might be found in a typical employee record. It also shows the values of the fields for a particular employee record (Alvin E. Adams): "Department" and "Marital status" are *coded* for ease of data entry and to save storage space.

FIELDS	Employee security number	Last name	First name	Middle initial	Dept. (coded)	Marital status (coded)	Salary
Values	445447279	Adams	Alvin	E	Acct	S	50000

Files: Related Records

A *file* is a collection of related records. The employee file contains a record for each employee. An inventory file contains a record for each inventory item. The accounts receivable file contains a record for each customer. Files are sorted, merged, and processed by a **key field.** For example, in an employee file the key might be "social security number," and in an inventory file the key might be "part number." A file is said to be a **flat file** when it does not point to or physically link with another file.

The Database: Integrated Data Resource

The **database** is the integrated data resource for a computer-based information system. In essence, a database is a collection of files that are in some way logically related to one another. That is, one file might contain logical links that identify one or more files containing related information. This concept is demonstrated in Section 8–6.

8–5 SPREADSHEET: THE MAGIC MATRIX

INTERNET BRIDGE

Spreadsheet/Database

The name *spreadsheet* aptly describes this software's fundamental application. The spreadsheet has been a common business tool for centuries. Before computers, the ledger (a book of spreadsheets) was the accountant's primary tool for keeping records of financial transactions. Instructors' grade books are also in spreadsheet format.

Spreadsheet software is simply an electronic alternative to thousands of traditionally manual tasks. We are no longer confined to using pencils, erasers, and hand calculators to deal with rows and columns of data. Think of anything that has rows and

Courtesy of International Business Machines Corporation

Data management is part of our daily lives at home and at work, whether we use computers or not. This policeman's PC has several databases, including one with information on all vehicles registered in the county. This woman is cataloging her audio CDs on a database while listening to one. (CD-ROM drives can play audio CDs.) Modern kitchens frequently include a cooking island and PC-based database containing all of the recipes that used to be stored on 3 by 5 cards.

columns of data and you have identified an application for spreadsheet software: income (profit-and-loss) statements, personnel profiles, demographic data, home inventories, and budget summaries, just to mention a few. Because spreadsheets parallel so many of our manual tasks, they are enjoying widespread acceptance.

The conceptual coverage that follows is generic; that is, it applies to all spreadsheets. The examples in the figures are from Lotus 1-2-3 for Windows (a Lotus Development Corporation product).

Concepts and Features

B. J. McCue, the national sales manager for BrassCo Enterprises, a manufacturer of an upscale line of brass coat hanger products (the Crown, the Monarch, and the Curio), uses spreadsheet software to compile a monthly sales summary. We will use B. J.'s March sales summary shown in Figure 8–9 to demonstrate spreadsheet concepts. B. J. uses a monthly sales *template* each month. The template, simply a spreadsheet model, contains the layout and formulas needed to produce the summary il-

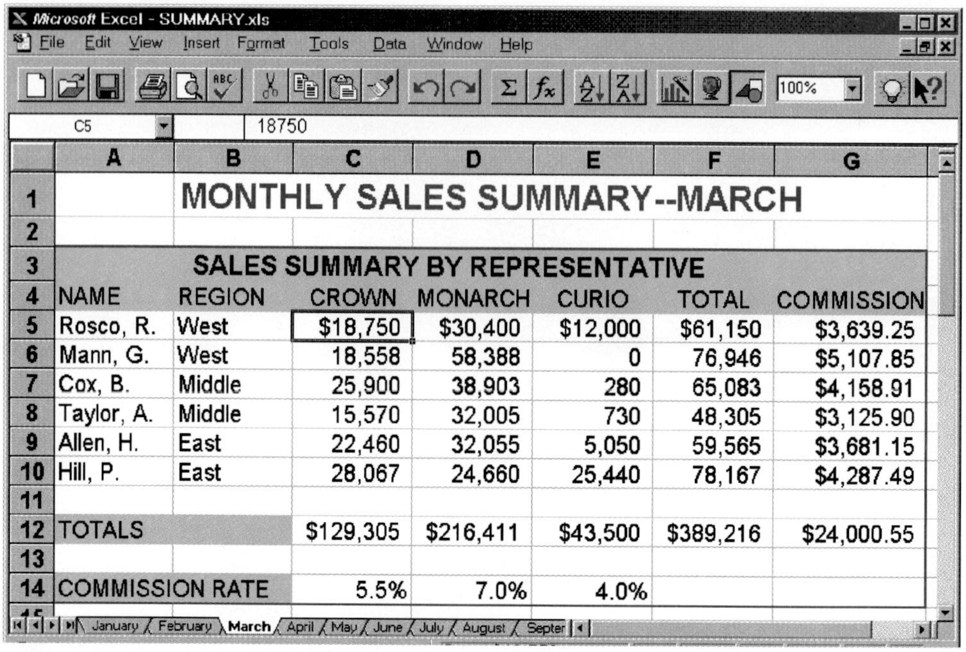

Microsoft Excel - SUMMARY.xls

File Edit View Insert Format Tools Data Window Help

C5 18750

	A	B	C	D	E	F	G
1		MONTHLY SALES SUMMARY--MARCH					
2							
3		SALES SUMMARY BY REPRESENTATIVE					
4	NAME	REGION	CROWN	MONARCH	CURIO	TOTAL	COMMISSION
5	Rosco, R.	West	$18,750	$30,400	$12,000	$61,150	$3,639.25
6	Mann, G.	West	18,558	58,388	0	76,946	$5,107.85
7	Cox, B.	Middle	25,900	38,903	280	65,083	$4,158.91
8	Taylor, A.	Middle	15,570	32,005	730	48,305	$3,125.90
9	Allen, H.	East	22,460	32,055	5,050	59,565	$3,681.15
10	Hill, P.	East	28,067	24,660	25,440	78,167	$4,287.49
11							
12	TOTALS		$129,305	$216,411	$43,500	$389,216	$24,000.55
13							
14	COMMISSION RATE		5.5%	7.0%	4.0%		

January / February / March / April / May / June / July / August / Septer

FIGURE 8–9 A Monthly Sales Summary Spreadsheet Template
This Microsoft Excel for Windows 95 spreadsheet template is the basis for the explanation and demonstration of spreadsheet concepts. Lines and shading are added to improve readability.

lustrated in Figure 8–9. B. J. entered only the data for the current month (March in the example) and the spreadsheet template did all of the needed calculations. For example, B. J. entered the *sales amounts* for each salesperson and the spreadsheet software calculated the *totals* and the *commissions.*

Organization: Rows and Columns Spreadsheets are organized in a *tabular structure* with *rows* and *columns.* The intersection of a particular row and column designates a **cell.** As you can see in Figure 8–9, the rows are *numbered* and the columns are *lettered.* Single letters identify the first 26 columns (A, B, . . . Z); double letters are used after that (AA, AB, . . . AZ; BA, BB, . . . BZ).

Data are entered and stored in a cell at the intersection of a column and a row. During operations, data are referred to by their **cell address.** A cell address identifies the location of a cell in the spreadsheet by its column and row, with the column designator first. For example, in the monthly sales summary of Figure 8–9, C4 is the address of the column heading for product Crown, and D5 is the address of the total amount of Monarch sales for R. Rosco ($30,400).

In the spreadsheet work area (the rows and columns), a movable highlighted area "points" to the *current cell.* The current cell is highlighted with either a dark border around the current cell or a different color. This highlighted area, called the **pointer,** can be moved around the spreadsheet with the arrow keys or the mouse. To add or edit (revise) an entry at a particular cell, the pointer must be positioned at that cell. The address and content of the current cell (the location of the pointer) are displayed in the user-interface portion of the spreadsheet, the area above and/or below the spreadsheet work area (above in Figure 8–9). Specifically, the information for a particular cell (Cell C5 in Figure 8–9) is displayed in a *cell status line.* The content, or resulting value (for example, from a formula), of each cell is shown in the spreadsheet work area. Notice in Figure 8–9 that when the pointer is positioned at C5, the actual

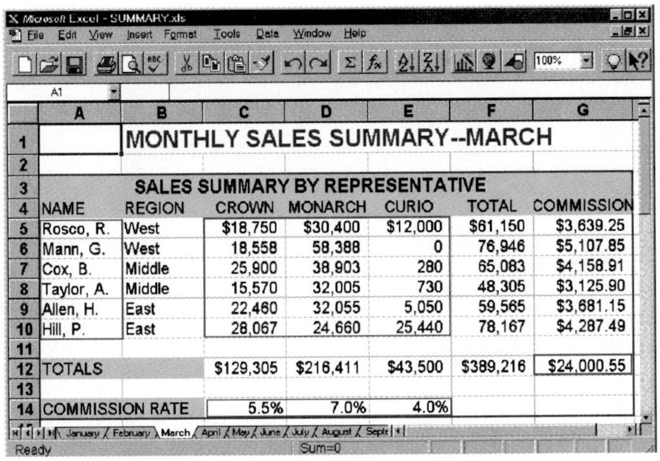

FIGURE 8-10 Spreadsheet Ranges
The highlighted cells in this spreadsheet display illustrate the four types of ranges: cell (G12), column (A5..A10), row (C14..E14), and block (C5..E10).

numeric value (18750) is displayed as the *cell contents box* in the user interface, and an optional *formatted* version ($18,750) is displayed in C5.

Ranges: Groups of Cells   Many spreadsheet operations ask you to designate one or more **ranges** of cells (also called blocks). The four types of ranges are highlighted in Figure 8–10.

▶ *Cell range.* A single cell (Example range is G12.)

▶ *Column range.* All or part of a column of adjacent cells (Example range is A5..A10.)

▶ *Row range.* All or part of a row of adjacent cells (Example range is C14..E14.)

▶ *Block range.* A rectangular group of cells (Example range is C5..E10.)

A particular range is indicated by the addresses of the endpoint cells separated by two periods. Any cell can comprise a single-cell range. The range for the commission percentages in Figure 8–10 is C14..E14, and the range for the row labels (salespeople's names) is A5..A10. The range of sales amounts for the three products is indicated by any two opposite-corner cell addresses (for example, C5..E10 or E5..C10).

When you want to copy, move, erase, or format (change font, display as currency, and so on) part of the spreadsheet, you must first define the range you wish to act on.

Cell Entries   To make an entry in the spreadsheet, simply move the pointer to the appropriate cell, and key in the data. To *edit* (revise) or replace an existing entry, you also move the pointer to the appropriate cell. Once you have completed work on a particular entry, press the ENTER key or an arrow key to insert the entry in the actual spreadsheet. Spreadsheet packages allow the user to vary the column width to improve readability.

Types of Cell Entries   To make an entry in the spreadsheet, simply move the pointer to the appropriate cell, and key in the data. The major types of entries are *label* entry, *numeric* entry, and *formula* entry. Labels and numeric data are entered in Figure 8–11.

Label entries.   A label entry is a word, a phrase, or any string of alphanumeric text (spaces included) that occupies a particular cell. Whenever you begin an entry with a letter, the spreadsheet software automatically assumes that you are entering a label. In Figure 8–11, "NAME" in Cell A4 is a label entry, as is "COMMISSION" in G4 and "MONTHLY SALES SUMMARY—MARCH" in B1.

FIGURE 8–11 Entering Headings and Data
Only label and numeric entries are included in this spreadsheet. All headings, the NAME data, and the REGION data are label entries. The ranges C5..E10 and C14..E14 contain numeric data.

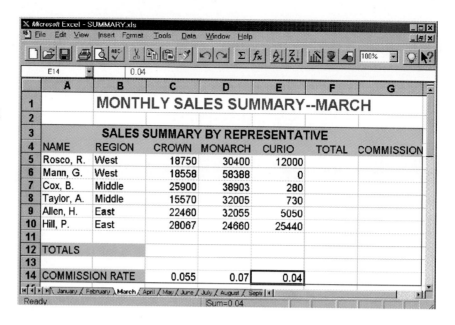

Microsoft Excel - SUMMARY.xls

	A	B	C	D	E	F	G
1		MONTHLY SALES SUMMARY--MARCH					
2							
3		SALES SUMMARY BY REPRESENTATIVE					
4	NAME	REGION	CROWN	MONARCH	CURIO	TOTAL	COMMISSION
5	Rosco, R.	West	18750	30400	12000		
6	Mann, G.	West	18558	58388	0		
7	Cox, B.	Middle	25900	38903	280		
8	Taylor, A.	Middle	15570	32005	730		
9	Allen, H.	East	22460	32055	5050		
10	Hill, P.	East	28067	24660	25440		
11							
12	TOTALS						
13							
14	COMMISSION RATE		0.055	0.07	0.04		

January / February / March / April / May / June / July / August / Sept

Ready — Sum=0.04

Numeric and formula entries. In Figure 8–12, the dollar sales values in the range C5..E10 are *numeric*. The dollar sales values in the ranges F5..G10 and C12..G12 are results of *formulas*. Cell F5 contains a formula, but it is the numeric result (for example, 61150 in Figure 8–12) that is displayed in the spreadsheet work area. With the pointer positioned at F5, the formula appears in the cell contents box in the user-interface panel. The formula value in F5 computes the total sales made by the salesperson in Row 5 for all three products (that is, total sales is + C5 + D5 + E5). The actual numeric value appears in the spreadsheet work area (see Figure 8–12).

Spreadsheet formulas use standard notation for **arithmetic operators:** + (add), − (subtract), * (multiply), / (divide), ^ (raise to a power, or exponentiation). The formula in F5 (cell contents box in Figure 8–12) computes the total sales for R. Rosco. The range F6..F10 contains similar formulas that apply to their respective rows (+ C6 + D6 + E6, + C7 + D7 + E7, and so on). For example, the formula in F6 computes the total sales for G. Mann. Figure 8–12 provides a summary of the actual cell contents for all cells.

Putting Spreadsheet Software to Work

The possibilities of what B. J. McCue, you, and others can do with spreadsheet software and PCs are endless. Find any set of numbers and you have identified a potential application for spreadsheet software.

Spreadsheet Templates: Models The spreadsheet in Figure 8–12 is a *template,* or a model, for B. J. McCue's monthly sales summary. All B. J. has to do is enter the sales data for the current month in the range C5..E10. All other data are calculated with formulas.

Most spreadsheet applications eventually take the form of a spreadsheet template. Once created, the template becomes the basis for handling a certain type of data (for example, monthly sales data). Spreadsheet templates are modified easily. For example, any of these modifications of Figure 8–12 would require only a few minutes:

▶ Add another column to accommodate a new product.

▶ Delete a row to accommodate one less salesperson.

▶ Compute the standard deviation for Crown sales data.

MEMORY BITS

Spreadsheet Organization

- Tabular structure
  —Numbered rows
  —Lettered columns
- Row/column intersect at cell
- Cell address locates cell
- Pointer highlights current cell
- Common cell entry types
  —Label
  —Numeric
  —Formula

FIGURE 8–12 Entering and Copying Spreadsheet Formulas

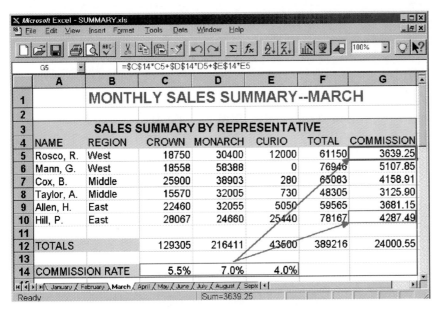

Copying Formulas The actual content of F5 is the formula in the cell contents box (= + C5 + D5 + E5). The result of the formula appears in the spreadsheet at F5 (61150). In creating the spreadsheet template for the monthly sales summary, B. J. McCue entered only three formulas (see cell contents summary below).

- The formula in F5 to sum the product sales for each salesperson was copied to the range F6..F10.
- The formula in G5 to compute the commission for each salesperson was copied to the range G6..G10.
- The formula in C12 to sum the sales for each product was copied to the range D12..G12.

Copying Formulas That Include Absolute Cell Addresses Each of the commission computation formulas in the range G5..G10 has the same multipliers—the commission rates in the range C14..E14. Because the relative positions between the commission formulas in G5..G10 and the commission rates in C14..E14 vary from row to row, the commission rates are entered as absolute cell addresses. If the contents of a cell containing a formula are copied to another cell, the relative cell addresses in the copied formula are revised to reflect the new position, but the absolute cell addresses are unchanged. Notice in the cell contents summary below how the absolute addresses ($C$14, $D$14, and $E$14) in the copied formulas (G6..G10) remained the same in each formula and the relative addresses were revised to reflect the applicable row.

	A	B	C	D	E	F	G
1				MONTHLY SALES SUMMARY—MARCH			
2							
3			SALES SUMMARY BY REPRESENTATIVE				
4	NAME	REGION	CROWN	MONARCH	CURIO	TOTAL	COMMISSION
5	Rosco,R.	West	18,750	30,400	12,000	+C5+D5+E5	+$C$14*C5+$D$14*D5+$E$14*E5
6	Mann,G.	West	18,558	58,388	0	+C6+D6+E6	+$C$14*C6+$D$14*D6+$E$14*E6
7	Cox,B.	Middle	25,900	38,903	280	+C7+D7+E7	+$C$14*C7+$D$14*D7+$E$14*E7
8	Taylor,A.	Middle	15,570	32,005	730	+C8+D8+E8	+$C$14*C8+$D$14*D8+$E$14*E8
9	Allen,H.	East	22,460	32,055	5,050	+C9+D9+E9	+$C$14*C9+$D$14*D9+$E$14*E9
10	Hill,P.	East	28,067	24,660	25,440	+C10+D10+E10	+$C$14*C10+$D$14*D10+E14$*E10
11							
12	TOTALS		@SUM(C5..C10)	@SUM(D5..D10)	@SUM(E5..E10)	@SUM(F5..F10)	@SUM(G5..G10)

Cell Contents Summary This cell contents summary illustrates the actual content of the cells in the above spreadsheet.

- Change the rate of commission for the Crown from 5.5% to 6.0%.
- Sort the sales summary portion (A5..G10) alphabetically by name.
- Sort the sales summary portion (A5..G10) in descending order by commission.

Spreadsheet Graphics   Most commercial spreadsheet packages are *integrated packages* that combine spreadsheet, presentation graphics, and database capabilities. The graphics component enables users to present spreadsheet data as business graphs. B. J. McCue's monthly sales summary template also includes a "Sales Summary by Region" in Rows 16 through 20 (see Figure 8–13). B. J. responded to a series of prompts to generate a graph. The first prompt asks B. J. to select the type of graph to be generated. B. J. then identifies the source of the data, enters labels and titles, and so on. In Figure 8–13 the sales figures for each region (Range C18..E20) are plotted in a *stacked-bar graph*. The resulting graph permits B. J. McCue to understand better the regional distribution of sales.

FIGURE 8–13
Spreadsheet Graphs
Regional sales for each of the three products (Range C18..E20) are represented in this stacked-bar graph. This graph can be displayed full screen or it can be printed.

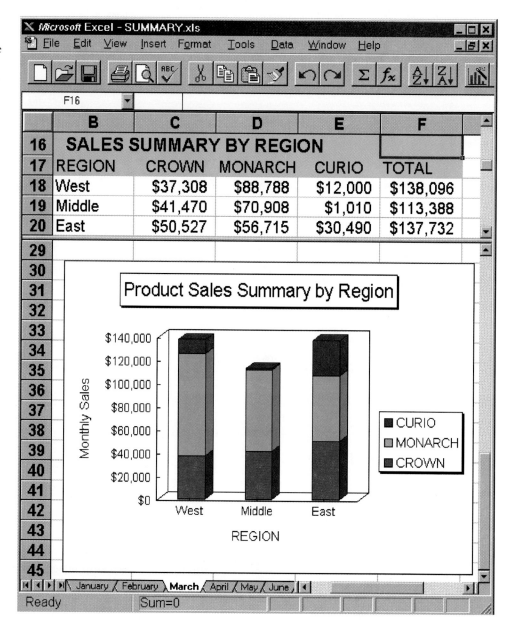

With database software you can create and maintain a database and extract information from it. To use database software, you first identify the format of the data, then design a display format that permits interactive entry and revision of the database. Once the database is created, its data can be deleted or revised and other data can be added.

All database software packages have these fundamental capabilities:

1. To create and maintain a database (add, delete, and revise records)
2. To extract and list information that meets certain conditions
3. To make an inquiry (for example, "What is the total amount owed by all customers?")
4. To sort records in ascending or descending sequence by primary, secondary, and tertiary fields
5. To generate formatted reports with subtotals and totals

The more sophisticated packages include a variety of other features, such as spreadsheet-type computations, presentation graphics, and programming.

Database Software and Spreadsheet Software: What's the Difference?

Both database and spreadsheet software packages enable us to work with data as rows and columns in a spreadsheet and as records in a database. Spreadsheet software offers greater flexibility in the manipulation of rows and columns of data. Everything relating to spreadsheet-based data is easier with spreadsheet software—creating formulas, generating charts, what if analysis, and so on. Database software offers greater flexibility in the manipulation of records within a database. Everything relating to a database is easier with database software—queries, data entry, linking databases, report generation, programming, and so on.

In short, spreadsheet packages are great number crunchers and are very helpful for small database applications. Database software packages may be too cumbersome for any serious number crunching, but they are terrific for creating any kind of personal or business information system.

Concepts and Features

Creating a Database with Database Software   The concepts and features of database software packages are very similar. The database example we give here is generic and can be applied to all database packages. The displays in the accompanying figures are taken from Paradox for Windows (a product of Borland International).

In a database, related *fields,* such as employee, ID, and department, are grouped to form *records* (for example, the employee record in the TRAINING table in Figure 8–14). Most PC-based database packages use the *relational* approach to database management, which organizes data into *tables* in which a *row* is equivalent to a *record.* The database *table* is conceptually the same as a *file.* One or more tables comprise a **relational database.** A relational database refers to all of the tables in the database and the relationships between them.

The best way to illustrate the concepts of database software is by example. Ed Rockford, BrassCo's education coordinator, uses a PC-based database software package to help him with his record-keeping tasks. To do this, Ed created an education database with two tables: COURSE and TRAINING. The COURSE table (see Figure 8–14) contains a record for each course that BrassCo offers its employees and for sev-

GOING ONLINE
8.4
Be My Guest!

Go to the White House Web site (http://www.whitehouse.gov/), sign the guest book, and take a virtual tour of the President's residence.

Hand in: The first sentence of the President's most recent State of the Union Address.

Spreadsheet/Database

FIGURE 8–14 Education Database: COURSE Table and TRAINING Table
The Microsoft Access COURSE table contains a record for each course that BrassCo Enterprises offers its employees. The TRAINING table contains a record for each BrassCo employee who is enrolled in or has taken a course. The fields for each table are described in the text.

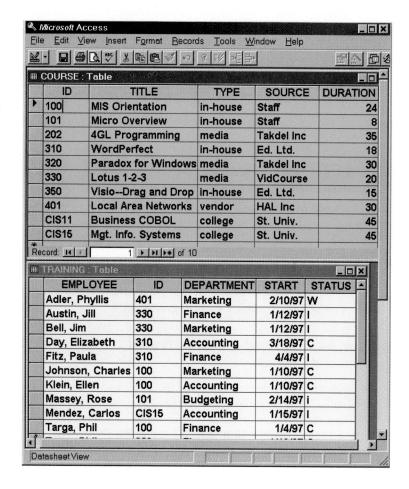

eral courses at State University. BrassCo provides tuition reimbursement for selected courses at the State University. Each record (row) in the COURSE table contains the following fields:

- ▶ IDentification number of course (supplied by BrassCo; provides a link to the TRAINING table)
- ▶ TITLE of course
- ▶ TYPE of course (in-house, multimedia, college, or vendor seminar)
- ▶ SOURCE of course (BrassCo staff or commercial supplier of course)
- ▶ DURATION of course (number of hours required for an employee to complete course)

The ID field uniquely identifies each record in the COURSE table.

The TRAINING table (see Figure 8–14) contains a record for each BrassCo employee who is enrolled in or has taken a course. Each record contains the following fields:

- ▶ EMPLOYEE (name of BrassCo employee; last name first)
- ▶ IDentification number of course taken by employee (provides a link to COURSE table)
- ▶ DEPARTMENT (department affiliation of employee)
- ▶ START (date course was begun)
- ▶ STATUS (employee's status code: *I* = incomplete, *W* = withdrawn from course, *C* = completed course)

No single field in the TRAINING table uniquely identifies each record. However, the combined EMPLOYEE and course ID do identify each record. To access a particular record in the TRAINING table, you must specify both the EMPLOYEE and ID (for example, Targa, Phil, 330). The two tables can be linked because they have the course ID field in common.

The structure of the database table. The first thing you do to set up a database table is to specify the structure of the database table. You do this by identifying the characteristics of each field in it. This is done interactively, with the system prompting you to enter the field name, the field type, and so on (see Figure 8–15). For example, in the first row of Figure 8–15, the *field name* is ID; the *field type* is A for "alphanumeric"; and the *field size,* or field length, is five positions. The field names for the COURSE and TRAINING tables are listed at the top of each table in Figure 8–14 (ID, TITLE, TYPE, and so on). An *alphanumeric* field type can be a single word or any alphanumeric (numbers, letters, and special characters) phrase up to several hundred characters in length. For *numeric* field types, you can specify the number of decimal positions that you wish to have displayed. Because the course durations all are defined in whole hours, the DURATION field is displayed in whole numbers in the table of Figure 8–14.

Entering and editing a database. Once you have defined the structure of the database table, you are ready to enter the data. The best way to enter data is to establish a *screen format* that allows convenient data entry. The data entry screen format is analogous to a hard-copy form that contains labels and blank lines (for example, a medical questionnaire or an employment application). Data are entered and edited (added, deleted, or revised) one record at a time with database software as they are on hard-copy forms. The data entry screen format for the COURSE database table is shown in Figure 8–16.

Query by Example Database software also permits you to retrieve, view, and print records based on **query by example.** In query by example, you set conditions for the selection of records by composing one or more example *relational expressions.* A relational expression normally compares one or more field names to numbers or character strings using the **relational operators** (= [equal to], > [greater than], < [less than], and combinations of these operators). Several conditions can be combined with **logical operators** (*AND, OR,* and *NOT*). Figure 8–17 demonstrates three query by example examples—one condition, two conditions, and calculation with one condition.

COURSE : Table		
Field Name	Data Type	Description
ID	Text	Size 5
TITLE	Text	Size 20
TYPE	Text	Size 8
SOURCE	Text	Size 10
DURATION	Number	
Field Properties		

TRAINING : Table		
Field Name	Data Type	Description
ID	Text	Size 5
EMPLOYEE	Text	Size 20
DEPARTMENT	Text	Size 10
START	Date/Time	
STATUS	Text	Size 1
Field Properties		

FIGURE 8–15 Structure of the COURSE and TRAINING Tables
This display shows the structure of the COURSE and TRAINING tables of Figure 8–12. The COURSE record (top) has four alphanumeric (A) fields and one numeric (N) field. The TRAINING record (bottom) has four alphanumeric (A) fields and one date field.

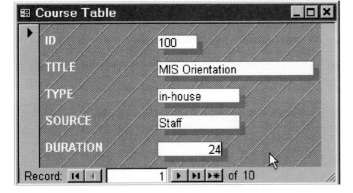

Course Table	
ID	100
TITLE	MIS Orientation
TYPE	in-house
SOURCE	Staff
DURATION	24
Record:	1 of 10

FIGURE 8–16 Data Entry Screen Format
The screen format for entering, editing, and adding records to the COURSE table is illustrated.

FIGURE 8–17 Query by Example

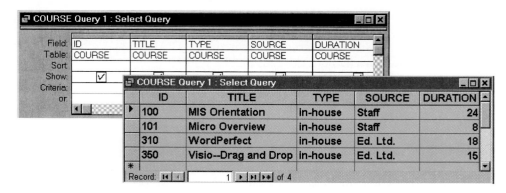

QBE: One Condition. Ed Rockford wanted a listing of all in-house seminars. He requested a list of all courses that meet the condition *TYPE − in-house* in the COURSE table (see Figure 8–14). All records that meet this condition (see criteria in query box) are displayed in the answer window (bottom).

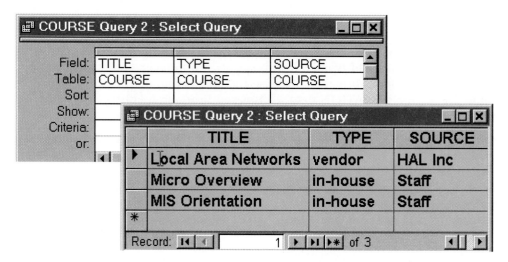

QBE: Two Conditions. To produce the results shown here, Ed Rockford set up his query by example to select only those courses that were taught by the BrassCo staff (SOURCE = staff) *OR* offered by a vendor (TYPE = vendor). In Microsoft Access for Windows 95, the software package used in the database examples, expressions linked by the OR operator are placed on separate lines in the query box. In addition, the education coordinator selected only three fields to be included in the results display. The OR operator can be applied between fields (see example) or within fields. For example, the query by example, *TYPE = college or in-house,* would display only the records of TYPE college or in-house.

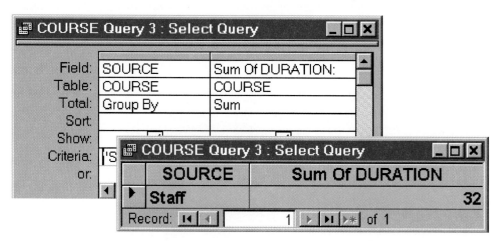

QBE: Calculation with One Condition. Besides query by example, you can also make inquiries to the database that result in a display of calculated information. For example, Ed Rockford wanted to know the total number of course hours taught by in-house staff. The query (SOURCE = Staff; DURATION: sum) and result (32 hours) are shown here.

Relational Operators		Logical Operators AND and OR	
COMPARISON	OPERATOR	OPERATION (for the condition to be true)	OPERATOR
Equal to	=	Both subconditions must be true	AND
Less than	<		
Greater than	>	At least one subcondition must be true	OR
Less than or equal to	<=		
Greater than or equal to	>=	The condition is not true	NOT
Not equal to	<>		

The following relational expressions establish conditions that will select or extract records(noted to the right of the expression) from the COURSE table in Figure 8–14.

QUERY BY EXAMPLE (COURSE table)	RECORDS DISPLAYED (ID)
TYPE=in-house AND DURATION<=10	101
SOURCE=VidCourse OR =Takdel Inc.	202, 320, 330
DURATION>=15 AND <=25	100, 310, 330, 350
ID=CIS11	CIS11

The following queries by example extract records from the TRAINING table in Figure 8–14.

QUERY BY EXAMPLE (TRAINING table)	RECORDS DISPLAYED (EMPLOYEE)
DEPARTMENT=Marketing	Adler, Bell, Johnson
START<=1/10/95	Johnson, Klein, Targa
STATUS=I AND DEPARTMENT=Finance	Austin, Fitz

Issues in Computing

Better Sales through Better Information

Two decades ago manufacturers called the shots in retailing with high-powered ad campaigns and product promotions. Today, the scanning of each individual product into an online computer system has reversed the situation—retailers are in command. In the past, high-volume retailers didn't know which products were selling or contributing to profit until months after the sale. Some never knew. Now managers can look at sales figures and profitability for individual products on a real-time basis. Chains can pool data to determine trends for local, regional, and national sales.

Information sells products. Some stores are searching for another level of information. Frequent shoppers are given their own bar codes so that product sales can be associated with in-dividual customers. You can see where this is leading. Retailers can obtain a profile of their customers' buying habits that will enable them to better target product marketing campaigns. In fact, promotions can be directed to specific customers for specific products. For example, if the store knows that the customer drinks lots of diet caffeine-free Coca Cola, it can notify the customer of a one-month discount on that beverage. This could be done automatically via e-mail, regular mail, fax, or at the time of purchase, perhaps on a cash register receipt.

Discussion: Should retail stores be allowed to gather and maintain personal information on their customers?

Software Applications

These queries of the COURSE table in Figure 8–14 involve calculations.

QUERY BY EXAMPLE (COURSE table)	RESULTS
TYPE: calc count (count unique values)	4 (college, in-house, media, vendor)
TYPE=in-house; DURATION: calc average	16.25 (average duration of in-house courses)

MEMORY BITS

Database Inquiries

- Query by example (create relational expressions with)
  —Relational operators (= , > , <)
  —Logical operators (AND, OR, NOT)
- Sorts (identify)
  —Primary key field
  —Secondary key field (if needed)

Sorting: Rearranging Records   The records in a database table also can be sorted for display in a variety of formats. For example, the COURSE table in Figure 8–14 has been sorted and is displayed in ascending order by course identification number (ID). To obtain this sequencing of the database records, Ed Rockford selected ID as the *key field*, thus causing an ascending sort of the COURSE table.

Ed also wants a presentation of the COURSE table that is sorted by ID within TYPE. This involves the selection of a *primary* and a *secondary key field*. Secondary key fields are helpful when duplicates exist in the primary key field (for example, there are three records for TYPE = media). Ed selects TYPE as the primary key field, but he wants the courses offered by each TYPE to be listed in ascending order by ID. To achieve this record sequence, he selects ID as the secondary key field. A version of the COURSE table that has been sorted by ID within TYPE is shown in Figure 8–18. Notice in Figure 8–18 that the TYPE field entries are in alphabetical order and that the three "media" records are in sequence by ID (202, 320, 330). If the need arises, Ed can perform sorts that require the identification of primary, secondary, and tertiary key fields.

Generating Reports   A database is a source of information, and database software provides the facility to get at this information. A *report* is the presentation of information derived from one or more databases. The simple listings of selected and ordered records in Figure 8–17 are "quick and dirty" reports. Such reports are the bread and butter of database capabilities.

FIGURE 8–18 COURSE Table Sorted by ID within TYPE
This display is the result of a sort operation on the COURSE table with the TYPE field as the primary key field and the ID field as the secondary key field.

COURSE : Table

TYPE	ID	TITLE	SOURCE	DURATION
college	CIS11	Business COBOL	St. Univ.	45
college	CIS15	Mgt. Info. Systems	St. Univ.	45
in-house	100	MIS Orientation	Staff	24
in-house	101	Micro Overview	Staff	8
in-house	310	WordPerfect	Ed. Ltd.	18
in-house	350	Visio--Drag and Drop	Ed. Ltd.	15
media	202	4GL Programming	Takdel Inc	35
media	320	Paradox for Windows	Takdel Inc	30
media	330	Lotus 1-2-3	VidCourse	20
vendor	401	Local Area Networks	HAL Inc	30

Record: 1 of 10

Database software allows you to design the *layout* for and to create customized, or formatted, reports. This means that you have some flexibility in spacing and can include titles, subtitles, column headings, separation lines, and other elements that make a report more readable. Managers often use this capability to generate periodic reports, such as the summary of employee enrollment in courses at BrassCo shown in Figure 8–19.

Database: The Next Step The database capabilities illustrated and discussed in this section merely "scratch the surface" of the potential of database software. For example, with relative ease, you can generate sophisticated reports that involve subtotals, calculations, and programming. In addition, data can be presented as a graph. You can even change the structure of a database (for example, add another field). Database software's programming capability has enabled users to create thousands of useful PC-based information systems.

Employee Enrollment in Courses

EMPLOYEE	ID	TITLE	STATUS
Adler, Phyllis	401	Local Area Networks	W
Austin, Jill	330	Lotus 1-2-3	I
Bell, Jim	330	Lotus 1-2-3	I
Day, Elizabeth	310	WordPerfect	C
Fitz, Paula	310	WordPerfect	I
Johnson, Charles	100	MIS Orientation	C
Klein, Ellen	100	MIS Orientation	C
Massey, Rose	101	Micro Overview	i
Mendez, Carlos	CIS15	Mgt. Info. Systems	I
Targa, Phil	330	Lotus 1-2-3	C
Targa, Phil	100	MIS Orientation	C

FIGURE 8–19 Customized Report
To obtain this report, the BrassCo education coordinator needed both the COURSE and TRAINING tables of Figure 8–14 from the education database. The two tables are linked via the common ID field.

IMPORTANT TERMS AND SUMMARY OUTLINE

8–1 PERSONAL COMPUTING WITH POPULAR PRODUCTIVITY PACKAGES Although there are many software packages that add variety to the potential of personal computing, the foundation of personal computing has been software in these four categories: word processing software, desktop publishing software, spreadsheet software, and database software.

8–2 WORD PROCESSING: THE MOST POPULAR PC APPLICATION Word processing lets you create text-based documents into which you can integrate images.

When you format a document, you are specifying the size of the page to be printed and how you want the document to look when it is printed. The preset format, or *default settings,* may fit your word processing application. To enter and edit text, you toggle between **typeover mode** and **insert mode.** Word processing permits **full-screen editing.** Most word processing packages are considered **WYSIWYG,** short for "What you see is what you get." The **font** refers to the style, appearance, and size of print.

Features common to word processing software packages include block operations (*copy, delete, cut,* and *paste*). The find feature permits the user to search the entire word processing document and identify all occurrences of a particular search string. The replace feature enables replacement either selectively or globally.

Word processing has variety of features that enable users to enhance the appearance and readability of their documents, including justification, boldface, underlining, indentation, header and footer labels, pagination, watermarks, multicolumn text, tables, and more.

You can print or fax a document by selecting the print option on the main menu.

Some word processing packages have a table feature that expedites the presentation of tabular data and let you create bar and pie charts.

Several helpful writing tools are designed to enhance the functionality of word processing programs. The **spelling checker,** an **online thesaurus** and a **grammar and style checker.**

Word processing software provides the capability of merging data in a database with the text of a document. The *mail-merge* application is an example. Here you merge a *database file* with a *form file.*

Boilerplate is existing text that can in some way be customized so it can be used in a variety of word processing applications. *Hypertext links* let you tie parts of a document or different documents together.

8–3 DESKTOP PUBLISHING: FREEDOM OF THE PRESS DTP (desktop publishing) refers to the capability of producing *typeset-quality camera-ready copy* for publication from the confines of a desktop. In word processing software, the emphasis is on *words,* and in desktop publishing, the emphasis is on overall document composition.

The components required for desktop publishing include document-composition software, a high-end microcomputer, a desktop page printer, an image scanner, **typefaces** and fonts, **clip art,** and illustration software.

The document-composition process involves integrating graphics, photos, text, and other elements into a visually appealing document layout. The steps are: (1) prepare text, (2) prepare or identify nontext-related resources, (3) lay out the document page(s) and add frames, (4) fill in the text frames, (5) fill in the picture frames; (6) fine-tune the layout, (7) print the camera-ready copy, and (8) publish the document.

Most DTP-produced documents use a variety of typefaces and fonts.

A number of resources are pulled together in a typical DTP-produced document: text files, clip art, original artwork, photographs and hard-copy graphics, and screen displays. During the document-composition process, each file is assigned to a rectangular **frame.** A frame holds the text or an image of a particular file.

8–4 DATA MANAGEMENT IN PRACTICE: BITS TO DATABASES Spreadsheet and database software principles include the terms and concepts associated with the six levels of the hierarchy of data organization. The six levels of the hierarchy of data organization are bit, character (or byte), **field,** record, file, and **database.** The first level is transparent to the programmer and end user, but the other five are integral to the design of any information processing activity. A string of bits is combined to form a character. Characters are combined to represent the content of fields. Related fields are combined to form records. Records combine to form files. Files are sorted, merged, and processed by a **key field.** A file is said to be a **flat file** when it does not point to or physically link with another file. A **database** is a collection of files that are in some way logically related to one another.

8–5 SPREADSHEET: THE MAGIC MATRIX Spreadsheet software provides an electronic alternative to thousands of manual tasks that involve rows and columns of data. Spreadsheets are organized in a tabular structure of rows and columns. The intersection of a particular row and column designates a **cell.** During operations, data are referred to by their **cell addresses.** The **pointer** can be moved around the spreadsheet to any cell address with the arrow keys.

To make an entry, to edit, or to replace an entry in a spreadsheet, move the pointer to the appropriate cell. Revise the entry in much the same way you would revise the text in a word processing document. The appearance of data in a spreadsheet can be modified to enhance readability.

The four types of **ranges** are a single cell, all or part of a column of adjacent cells, all or part of a row of adjacent cells, and a rectangular block of cells. A particular range is depicted by the addresses of the endpoint cells (for example, C5..E10).

Three major types of entries to a cell are label, numeric, and formula. A label entry is any string of alphanumeric text (spaces included) that occupies a particular cell. A numeric entry is any number. A cell may contain a formula, but it is the numeric results that are displayed in the spreadsheet. Spreadsheet formulas use standard programming notation for **arithmetic operators.**

A spreadsheet template can be used over and over for different purposes by different people. If you change the value of a cell in a spreadsheet, all other affected cells are revised accordingly.

Most commercial spreadsheet packages are *integrated packages* that combine spreadsheet, presentation graphics, and database capabilities.

8–6 DATABASE: A DYNAMIC DATA TOOL
Database software lets users create and maintain a database and extract information from it. Once the database is created, its data can be deleted or revised, and other data can be added to it.

Both database and spreadsheet software packages enable us to work with tabular data and records in a data-base. Spreadsheet software offers greater flexibility in the manipulation of tabular data. Database software offers greater flexibility in the manipulation of records within a database.

Database software uses the **relational database** approach to data management. Relational databases are organized in tables where a row is a record and a column is a field.

In database software, the user-defined structure of a database table identifies the characteristics of each field in it. Related fields are grouped to form records.

Database software also permits you to retrieve, view, and print records based on **query by example.** To do this, users set conditions for the selection of records by composing a relational expression containing **relational operators** that reflects the desired conditions. Several expressions can be combined into a single condition with **logical operators.**

Records in a database can be sorted for display in a variety of formats. To sort the records in a database, select a primary key field and, if needed, secondary key fields. Database software can create customized, or formatted, reports.

REVIEW EXERCISES

Concepts
1. Describe the function of word processing software.
2. Name three things that might be specified when formatting a word processing document.
3. What is meant when a document is formatted to be justified on the right and on the left?
4. Identify the two modes in which text is entered. Which mode would you select to change *the table* to *the long table?* Which mode would you select to change *pick the choose* to *pick and choose?*
5. Give an example of when you might issue a global find-and-replace command.
6. What productivity software package has the capability of producing typeset-quality camera-ready copy for printing jobs?
7. Name two software components and two hardware components of a desktop publishing system.
8. What is the shape and significance of a desktop publishing frame?
9. What term is used to refer to prepackaged electronic images?
10. Briefly describe the difference between word processing and desktop publishing software.
11. What are the six levels of the hierarchy of data organization?
12. Name two possible key fields for a personnel file. Name two for an inventory file.
13. Describe the layout of a spreadsheet.
14. Give an example of each of the four types of ranges.
15. Give examples of the three types of entries that can be made in a spreadsheet.
16. List three different ways to define the range A4..P12.
17. What is the relationship between a field, a record, and the structure of a database table?
18. Give examples and descriptions of at least two other fields that might be added to the record for the TRAINING table (Figure 8–14).
19. Which records would be displayed if the selection condition for the COURSE table (Figure 8–14) were DURATION > 20 AND TYPE = media?

Discussion and Problem Solving
20. Customer-service representatives at BrassCo Enterprises spend almost 70% of their day interact-

ing directly with customers. Approximately one hour each day is spent preparing courtesy follow-up letters, primarily to enhance good will between BrassCo and its customers. Do you think the "personalized" letters are a worthwhile effort? Why or why not?

21. With the advent of desktop publishing, the number of printed items bearing the company logo has increased dramatically. Many companies require that all such documents be approved by a central DTP review board prior to distribution. What concerns prompted these managers to establish the review board?

22. Give at least two examples (not mentioned in the text) of possible uses for online word processing documents with hypertext links.

23. Describe 10 specific publications that are candidates for desktop publishing.

24. All commercial spreadsheet packages manipulate rows and columns of data in a similar manner. What makes one spreadsheet package more desirable than another?

25. If you were asked to create a PC-based inventory management system for a privately owned retail shoe store, would you use spreadsheet software, database software, or both? Why?

26. Describe two types of inquiries to a database that involve calculations.

27. Under what circumstances is a graphic representation of data more effective than a tabular presentation of the same data?

SELF-TEST (BY SECTION)

8–1 The foundation of personal computing over the last decade has been 3-D computing games. (T/F)

8–2 **a.** Preset format specifications are referred to as _____ .

b. To add a word in the middle of an existing sentence in a word processing document, you would use the insert mode. (T/F)

c. An online thesaurus can be used to suggest synonyms for a word in a word processing document. (T/F)

d. _____ is existing text that can in some way be customized so it can be used in a variety of word processing applications.

e. In a word processing document, different documents can be tied together by: (a) cybertext links, (b) hydratext links, or (c) hypertext links?

8–3 **a.** The type of printer normally associated with desktop publishing is the dot-matrix printer. (T/F)

b. The purpose of desktop publishing is to produce _____ copy.

c. What device creates an electronic version of a hard-copy image: (a) image scanner, (b) image-reduction aid, or (c) vision-entry device?

d. During the document-composition process, each file is assigned to a rectangular _____ .

8–4 What do you call a data file that does not point to or physically link with another file: (a) flat file, (b) round file, or (c) domed file?

8–5 **a.** The term *spreadsheet* was coined at the beginning of the personal computer boom. (T/F)

b. Data in a spreadsheet are referred to by their cell _____ .

c. The spreadsheet pointer highlights the: (a) relative cell, (b) status cell, or (c) current cell?

d. D20..Z40 and Z20..D40 define the same spreadsheet range. (T/F)

e. A model of a spreadsheet designed for a particular application is sometimes called a _____ .

8–6 **a.** If the COURSE database table in Figure 8–14 is sorted in descending order by ID, the third course record would be Local Area Networks. (T/F)

b. The definition of the structure of a database table would not include which of the following: (a) field names, (b) selection conditions for fields, (c) field lengths?

c. The relational operator for greater than or equal to is _____ .

d. What record(s) would be selected from the COURSE table in Figure 8–14 for the condition SOURCE = VidCourse: (a) 310, (b) 330, or (c) no records are selected?

e. What record(s) would be selected from the TRAINING table in Figure 8–14 for the condition ID = 100 and DEPARTMENT = finance: (a) Targa, Phil/330, (b) Targa, Phil/100, or (c) Johnson, Charles/100?

Self-test Answers. **8–1** F. **8–2** (a) default settings; **(b)** T; **(c)** T; **(d)** Boilerplate; **(e)** c. **8–3** (a) F; **(b)** camera-ready; **(c)** a; **(d)** frame. **8–4** a. **8–5** (a) F; **(b)** addresses; **(c)** c; **(d)** T; **(e)** template. **8–6** (a) T; **(b)** b; **(c)** > = ; **(d)** b; **(e)** b.

Graphics and Multimedia: Tickling Our Senses

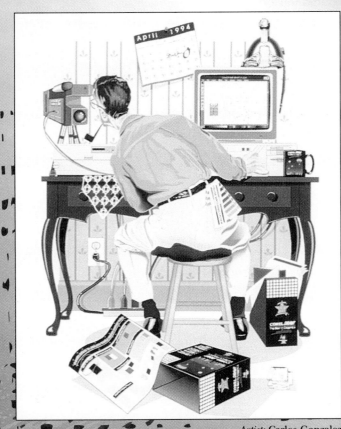

Artist: Carlos Gonzalez
Courtesy of Corel Corporation

Let's Talk

The following conversation introduces many of the terms in this chapter. Read it now, then again after you have read the chapter.

The Scene:
Three education students (Anne, Rich, and Carolyn) are putting the finishing touches on their group term project about the first university, the University of Paris. Now, they are planning their presentation to the class.

Anne: What about doing a computer-assisted presentation? We can use my new **multimedia** notebook PC.

Carolyn: That's a great idea, Anne. I'll create a couple of attention-getting **MIDI files** on my **synthesizer.**

Rich: And, I'll set up my 200-watt amp and a couple of 12-inch woofers for the sound output. It'll sound like we're in a theater.

Carolyn: Then, the only other hardware we'll need is a **screen image projector.** I'll reserve the department's for presentation day.

Anne: Microsoft **PowerPoint** came with my **software suite** and it sure makes it easy to prepare and integrate **text charts, maps,** and images. We can even do a little **animation.**

Carolyn: We could also **download** some **bit-mapped** images from the University of Paris's **Web site** to use in the **slide presentation.**

Rich: And if the site has both historic and modern images of the campus, we can use **morphing** techniques to blend the old with the new.

Anne: Well, if we want to get fancy, we might as well do the whole presentation on the PC. We could record audio **wave files** to introduce each slide.

Rich: Now we're talking! We can also shoot some video with my camcorder and use the media center's **video capture card** to convert the videotape to **video files.**

Carolyn: I'd love to direct the opening and closing video segments!

Anne: And for the *coup de grâce*, let's log on to the University of Paris's Web site and take the class on a multimedia tour of the campus.

Carolyn: I'm starting to feel an "A" coming on. Let's get to work!

STUDENT LEARNING OBJECTIVES

▶ *To understand graphics software concepts.*

▶ *To describe the functions of different types of graphics software.*

▶ *To understand multimedia concepts and applications.*

▶ *To identify hardware and software associated with multimedia.*

▶ *To describe the functions of different types of software associated with multimedia.*

Word processing software, desktop publishing software, spreadsheet software, and database software (discussed in Chapter 8) are wonderful tools. Indeed, you could become an effective PC user and never venture far from the capabilities of these four high-visibility products. However, if you wish to add pizazz to these and other software products, you will want to familiarize yourself with graphics and multimedia software. That pizazz could be anything from colorful illustrations to full multimedia presentations involving sound, animation, and motion video.

The next section introduces you to an array of graphics software options to help you create and work with images. Section 9–3 then introduces you to the exciting world of multimedia. Multimedia applications, which overlap with graphics applications, combine text, sound, graphics, motion video, and/or animation.

9–2 GRAPHICS: CREATING AND WORKING WITH IMAGES

A dollar may not buy what it used to, but a picture is still worth a thousand words. This time-honored maxim may be one of the many reasons for the explosion of graphics software. *Graphics software* facilitates the creation, manipulation, and management of computer-based images. With graphics software you can issue a command to plot a mathematical equation. Issue another command and voilà—the plot is bigger, smaller, rotated, squeezed, stretched, or even "painted" with different colors and textures. Graphics software helps you create pie graphs, line drawings, company logos, maps, clip art, blueprints, flowcharts, retouched photographs, or just about any image that you can conjure in your mind.

We will discuss these graphics software within the context of five common capabilities:

- Paint
- Draw
- Photo illustration
- Presentation graphics
- Animation

When you purchase graphics software, keep in mind that commercial software is often bundled to include two or more of these capabilities.

We describe the function, concepts, and use of each of these graphics capabilities in this section. However, before you can fully understand graphics software, first you need to know the fundamentals of how images are displayed.

Displaying and Printing Graphic Images

Graphic images can be maintained as **raster graphics, vector graphics,** or **metafiles.** In raster graphics, the image is composed of patterns of dots called *picture elements* or *pixels.* In vector graphics, the image is composed of patterns of lines, points, and other geometric shapes (vectors). The naked eye cannot distinguish one method of graphics display from another; however, the differences are quite apparent when you try to manipulate them. The metafile is a class of graphics that combines the components of raster and vector graphics formats.

Graphics

GOING ONLINE

9.1
Staying Healthy

The Internet has many sites devoted to health issues. Browse through a few of them.

Hand in: A printed copy of at least three health tips. Trace the path that led you to one of these tips (search tools used, keywords used, and the sequence of URLs).

Raster Graphics   Raster graphics, displayed as dot patterns, are created by digital cameras, scanners, graphics paint software, and screen-capture software. Faxes, for example, rely on raster graphics. Dots on the screen are arranged in rows and columns. The low-end PC monitor has about 300,000 pixels in 480 rows and 640 columns. Very high-resolution monitors will have thousands of rows and columns and millions of pixels. Each dot or pixel on a monitor is assigned a number that denotes its position on the screen grid (120th row and 323rd column) and its color. On a monochrome (one-color) monitor, the pixel denotes the position and a shade of one color.

As with all internal numbers in a computer system, the numbers that describe the pixel attributes (position and color) are binary bits (1s and 0s). The number of bits needed to describe a pixel increases with the monitor's resolution and the number of colors that can be presented. Because the image is projected, or "mapped," onto the screen based on binary bits, the image is said to be **bit-mapped.** In conversation, the term *bit-mapped* may be used more frequently than the term *raster graphics*.

A bit-mapped image and the display of a word processing document share many similarities. Just as you can replace one word with another in word processing, you can replace one color with another in a bit-mapped image. Carrying the analogy one step further, you also can do block operations—move, copy, and delete—on a user-defined area in a graphics display.

Vector Graphics   Vectors, which are lines, points, and other geometric shapes, are configured to create the vector graphics image. The vector graphics display, in contrast to the raster graphics display, permits the user to work with objects, such as a drawing of a computer. Draw software and computer-aided design software use vector graphics to meet the need to manipulate individual objects on the screen. Draw software is illustrated in Figure 9–1. Notice how the screen portion of the overall image is actually made up of four objects.

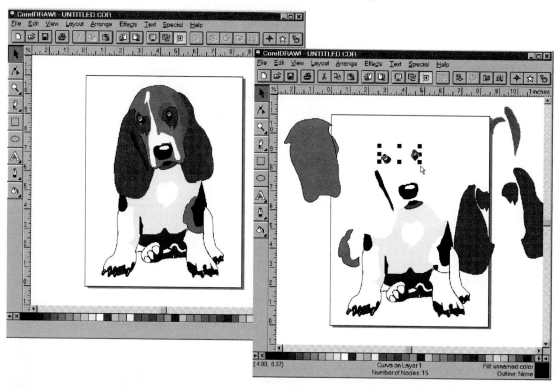

FIGURE 9–1   CorelDRAW: A Draw Program
CorelDRAW, shown here, is a vector graphics program. The user draws, then integrates objects to create the drawing. The front portion of the puppy is made up of several vector objects. The rectangle shows that the puppy's eyes are one of the objects that comprise the image. CorelDRAW's interface is similar to Paint's (see Figure 9–2); however, CorelDRAW's drawing features are much more sophisticated.

Vector graphics images take up less storage than bit-mapped images. Each pixel in the bit-mapped image must be fully described internally to the computer, including the background colors. Vector graphics are defined in geometric shapes, each of which can define the attributes of many pixels. For example, a vector graphics image of a blue square may encompass thousands of pixels when displayed, but the image is stored with a few simple descriptors: location of one of the corners, angle to horizontal, length of a side, and color.

Printing Graphics Images In general, printers provide higher-resolution output than do screen displays. The resolution of a 600 dpi page printer is far greater than that of a VGA monitor, and lines that may appear uneven on a monitor will be more uniform when printed.

Paint Software

Paint software provides the user with a sophisticated electronic canvas for the creation of bit-mapped (raster graphics) images. The Windows 95 Paintbrush program is introduced and illustrated in Figure 9–2. Paintbrush is a paint program distributed with Microsoft's Windows and Windows 95. The user interfaces of paint programs are similar. Once you are familiar with the common tools in the user interface on a typical paint screen, you are ready to use the program. The enlarged view shown in Figure 9–2 illustrates the pixel makeup of the original image.

Although you can perform amazing feats with paint software, one important similarity remains between it and the traditional canvas: Whatever you draw on either one becomes part of the whole drawing. Because the canvas is a *bit map*, you must erase or draw over any part with which you are dissatisfied. For example, suppose you draw a green circle. You would not be able simply to replace the circle with a blue square. The paint software does not remember the circle or any other representation of an object on the screen. To replace the circle with the square, you would have to draw over (or erase) the pixels that make up the green circle, then draw in the blue square.

Draw Software

Both paint and **draw software** enable users to create imaginative images. Perhaps the best way to explain draw software is to address the differences between it and paint

> **MEMORY BITS**
>
> **Graphic Images**
>
> - Raster graphics
>   —Image as pixels
>   —Bit-mapped image
> - Vector graphics
>   —Image as line patterns and geometric shapes
>   —Permits manipulation of objects within image

FIGURE 9–2 Paint: A Paint Program

User Interface The user interface for Paint, which is distributed with Windows 95, is representative of paint programs. The parts of the interface include:
- *Drawing area.* The image is created in this area.
- *Graphics cursor.* A point-and-draw device, such as a mouse, is used to move the graphics cursor to draw images and to select options. When positioned in the drawing area, the graphics cursor takes on a variety of shapes, depending on the tool selected. Outside the drawing area, it is an arrow.
- *Main menu.* Pull-down menus appear when any of the items in the main bar menu are selected. Go to the main menu to load and save drawings, zoom in on a particular area for detailed editing, change the attributes of the screen fonts, copy parts of the screen, and so on.
- *Tool box.* One of the tools in the tool box is active at any given time. Use the tools to draw; to move, copy, or delete parts of the screen; to create geometric shapes; to fill defined areas with colors; to add text; and to erase.
- *Linesize box.* This box contains the width options for the drawing line. Other boxes can appear in this space depending on which tool is selected.
- *Color palette.* This box contains colors and patterns used with the drawing tools.

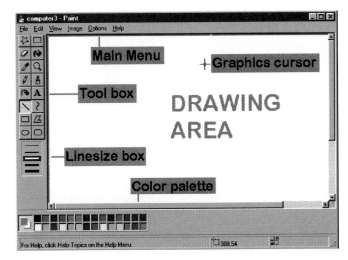

(**Figure 9-2** continues on next page)

FIGURE 9–2 (cont.)

Creating an Image This screen shows the steps in creating a PC image. Each step demonstrates a paint software feature.

- *Step A.* The *box* and *rounded box* tools are used to create the outlines for the monitor and the processor unit. Notice that the *text tool* (denoted by "A" in the tool box) is used to label the steps.
- *Step B.* The area containing the bit-mapped image created in Step A was *copied* to position B, then the *paint fill tool* was used to fill in *background colors*. The image in each of the following steps was created from a copy of the image of the preceding step.
- *Step C.* The *line tool* is used to draw the vents on the front of the processor unit. Drag the graphics cursor from one point to another and release the mouse button to draw the line. The two box areas for the disks were created with the box and line tools.
- *Step D.* When the *brush tool* is active, the *foreground color* is drawn at the graphics cursor position. Use the brush tool for freehand drawing, such as the addition of the pedestal for the monitor. The disk slots and the disk-active lights were drawn with the line tool. Notice that the line width and the foreground color were changed to draw the disk slots and the lights.
- *Step E.* A logo (upper-left corner of processor box) and a bar graph are added. The *PC* in the black logo box was drawn one pixel at a time. The *zoom* feature explodes a small segment of the draw area to enable the user to draw one pixel at a time (see the next screen). The bar graph was drawn with the line tool. Notice that each line was drawn with a different color from the color palette.
- *Step F.* In this final step, the beige color is *erased* to gray. Paint software permits the user to selectively switch one color for another within a user-defined area or in the entire drawing area. The keyboard was drawn with the box, line, and erase tools, then *tilted* for a three-dimensional look.

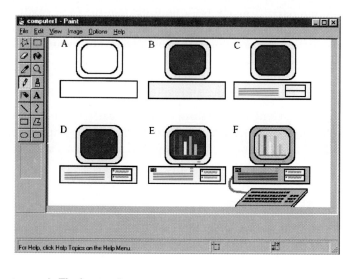

Zoom Feature In the illustration, the paint software user has zoomed in on the upper-left corner of the processor box in the completed PC image (Step F). Each square is a pixel. Any changes made in the enlarged version of the image are reflected in the window in the upper left corner of the work area. The window reflects the size of the image as it would normally appear on the screen.

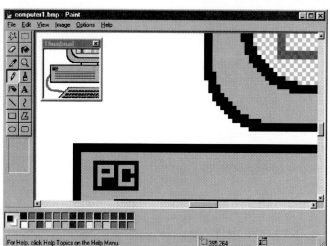
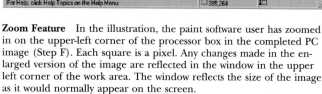

The Shrink–Grow Feature The PC image in the upper-left corner was copied from Step F above. The original image was selected with the pick tool, then copied to the clipboard. The clipboard contents were then loaded to a clean drawing area. The PC image in Step F is reduced and enlarged with the shrink–grow feature of paint software. Notice that image resolution suffers when the image is shrunk or enlarged (for example, the disk slots).

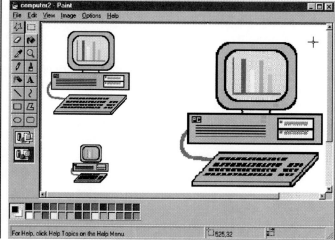

software. Consider the same example we used in the paint software discussion—a drawing of a green circle to be replaced with a blue square. As draw software permits you to isolate and manipulate representations of individual objects, you simply delete the entire green circle and copy a blue square to that position. This is not possible with paint software because it manipulates pixels, not objects.

Draw software relies on vector graphics, so a specific object can be moved, copied, deleted, rotated, tilted, flipped horizontally or vertically, stretched, and squeezed. Think of a screen image produced by draw software as a collage of one or more objects (see Figure 9–1 for a demonstration of how objects are combined to create an image).

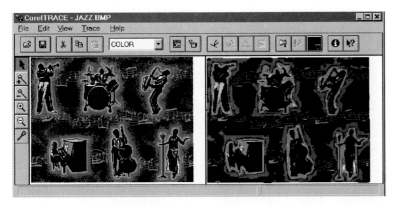

FIGURE 9–3 Converting Bit-Mapped Images to Vector Graphics Images
Programs, such as CorelTRACE shown here, are available that convert bit-mapped images into vector graphics images that can be manipulated with draw software. Here, the jazz image on the left is converted to a vector graphics image (right). The conversion process resulted in the creation of 968 separate images.

Software is available that converts any bit-mapped image (a scanned image or a paint software image) to a vector format. The conversion, however, is far from complete (see Figure 9–3). Artists will often use such programs to create templates that can be the basis for original vector artwork.

Photo Illustration Software

Photo illustration software enables us to create original images as well as to dress up existing digitized images, such as photographs and electronic paintings. Images can be retouched with special effects to dramatically alter the way the images appear (see Figure 9–4) on the next page. Photo illustration software is to an image as word processing software is to text. A word processing package allows you to edit, sort, copy, and generally do whatever can be done to electronic text. Photo illustration software allows you to do just about anything imaginable to digitize photos or drawings. The result of a photo illustrator's effort is a composite image with stunning special effects. For example, you can show the changes that take place as one image is modified to become an entirely different image (see Figure 9–4). This process is called **morphing,** a term derived from the word *metamorphosis.* You also can feather images to blend with their surroundings, enter artistic text over the image, change colors, include freehand draw-

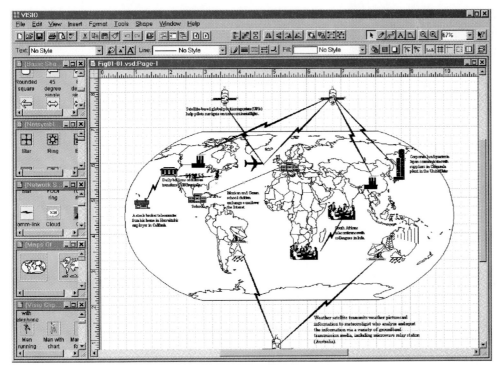

Visio, a product of Shapeware, Inc., lets you create professional-looking drawings. Five Visio templates are open to the left of the drawing area. Images are chosen, then dragged to the drawing area and dropped. Once positioned on the drawing area, images can be moved and resized to meet user needs. In this drawing, a world map image was dragged to the drawing area and enlarged to fill the screen. Other images were dragged from the adjacent templates and dropped on the map. Various connectors link the images. This Visio drawing was the authors' original drawing for Figure 1–1 in Chapter 1.

FIGURE 9–4 Photo Illustration Software

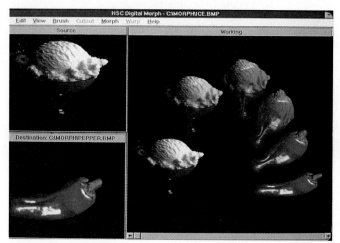

Morphing. A dish of ice cream is transformed into a red pepper with Digital Morph in a process called morphing. The illustrator identifies source and destination images, then applies the morph feature to create this amazing special effect. Image supplied by HSC Software Copyright 1994

Glass Block. The glass block effect is applied to an image in Corel Photo-Paint. Glass block is one of many available special effects.

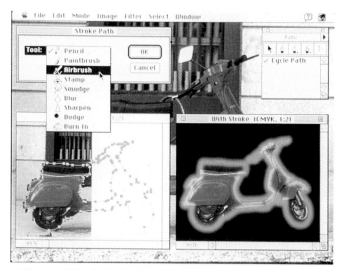

Air Brush. The air brush effect is one of the special effects options in Adobe Photoshop. Courtesy Adobe Systems

Photo Touchup. HiJaak TouchUp is used to modify this person's image. The retouched images are shown as thumbnail sketches in HiJaak Browser. Graphics browsers let you view many images so you can more easily select what you want. Inset Systems Inc. HiJaak® Graphics Suite™ TIF

Filtering. An artist's rendering of a European train station is shown at midday and at dusk. Photo illustration software enabled the artist to filter the original midday drawing to create what appears to be an evening drawing. Courtesy of Evans and Sutherland Computer Corporation

ings, isolate objects for special treatment, distort specific objects (for example, *glass blocking*), and much more.

An interesting application of what photo illustration software can do is the electronic aging of missing children. Artists combine a child's snapshot with a database of measurements showing how human facial dimensions change in a fairly predictable way over time. Such retouched snapshots have helped find hundreds of children since the mid-1980s.

Presentation Graphics Software

In the business world, the rules for the way you present yourself have changed. A typewritten letter with white-out corrections is no longer acceptable. The same is true of crude, manually produced business graphics. People now expect professional-looking graphics, even for simple communications.

Using Technology to Make the Point During the past decade, the use of *presentation graphics software* has become a business imperative. A progressive sales manager would never consider reporting a sales increase in tabular format. A successful year that otherwise would be obscured in rows and columns of sales figures will be vividly apparent in a colorful bar graph. Those in other areas of business also want to "put their best foot forward." To do so, they use computer-generated presentation graphics.

A number of studies confirm the power of presentation graphics. These studies uniformly support the following conclusions:

▶ People who use presentation graphics are perceived as being better prepared and more professional than those who do not.

▶ Presentation graphics can help persuade attendees or readers to adopt a particular point of view.

▶ Judicious use of presentation graphics tends to make meetings shorter.

Whether you're preparing a report, a presentation, a newsletter, or any other form of business communication, it pays—immediately and over the long term—to take advantage of the capabilities of presentation graphics.

Output Options With presentation graphics software you can create a variety of graphics from data in a spreadsheet or a database, or you can enter the data within the presentation graphics program. Among the most popular presentation graphics are **pie graphs** and **bar graphs** (see Figure 9–5). It is also possible to produce other types of graphs, range bar charts, and scatter diagrams, which are annotated with *titles, labels,* and *legends.*

Most spreadsheet, database, and some word processing packages come with presentation graphics software. However, dedicated presentation graphics packages have a wider range of features that enable you to prepare more dynamic and visually appealing graphics. Dedicated presentation graphics packages provide users with the tools they need to customize their graphs. For example, a company can add another dimension to a sales summary bar graph by topping the bars with clip art that represents the sales area (a bar of soap, an airplane, a refrigerator).

Besides traditional business graphs, presentation graphics software provides the ability to prepare *text charts* (see list of key points in Figure 9–6), *organization charts* (such as the block chart in Figure 9–6 showing the hierarchical structure of an organization), and *maps.*

Besides offering the ability to prepare graphs and charts from user-supplied data, some presentation graphics packages let you create and store original drawings. This capability is functionally similar to that of paint and draw packages, but without their sophisticated features. Companies frequently use this capability to draw and store the image of their company logo to insert on memos, reports, and graphs.

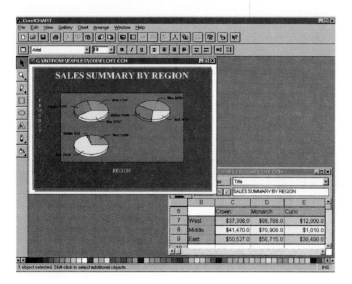
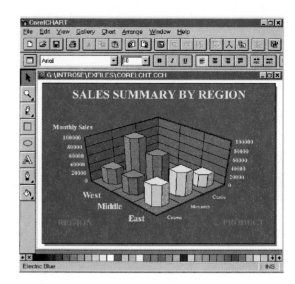

FIGURE 9–5 Pie and Bar Graphs

Shown here are a trilogy of pie graphs and a three-dimensional bar graph prepared with CorelCHART. Both graphs present the March sales data for BrassCo. These data were imported to CorelCHART from the Microsoft Excel example in Chapter 8 (Figure 8–13).

Preparing a Graph Usually the data needed to produce a graph already exist in a spreadsheet or a database. These data can be imported to the presentation graphics software. The graphics software leads you through a series of prompts, the first of which asks you what type of graph is to be produced—a bar graph, a pie graph, a line graph, and so on. You then select the data to be plotted or graphed. You can also enter names for the labels. Once you have identified the source of the data (perhaps a spreadsheet or a database), have entered the labels, and perhaps have added a title, you can display and print the graph.

FIGURE 9–6 Text and Organization Charts

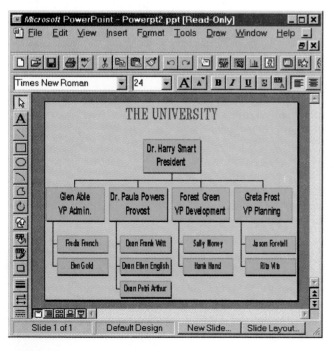
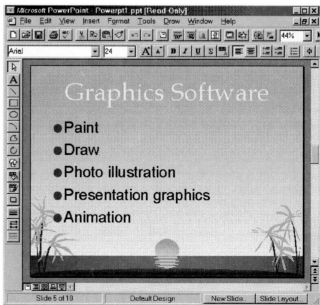

Presenting a Graph The use of sophisticated and colorful graphics adds an aura of professionalism to any report or presentation. The actual physical presentation of a graph depends on the available hardware (for example, a color page printer). Computer-generated graphic images can be re-created on paper and transparency acetates with a printer or on 35-mm slides with a desktop film recorder. Also, they can be displayed on a monitor or projected onto a large screen with a screen image projector. These output devices are discussed in Chapter 5, "Input/Output: Computers in Action."

Making a Presentation At the heart of any good presentation graphics software is the capability that allows you to put together an informative and exciting *slide presentation*. A presentation may involve slides, an outline, speaker notes, and even handouts. Normally you would begin building the slides by designing and creating the graphs, charts, and images that are to be shown. Figure 9–7 illustrates a slide presentation that was created with presentation graphics software.

Ultimately the slides you create can be made into 35-mm slides (for use with a 35-mm projector), transparency acetates (for use with an overhead projector), or they can be displayed dynamically using a PC. The latter capability lets you assemble presentation graphics in a synchronized PC-based presentation. The PC-based presentation can be made to an individual or small group on a single PC or it can be projected onto a large screen. You can integrate a visually interesting transition between the various slides during a PC-based presentation. For example, the current graph or image can be made to *fade out* (dissolve to a blank screen) while the next is fading in. Or the current image can be *wiped* away with the next.

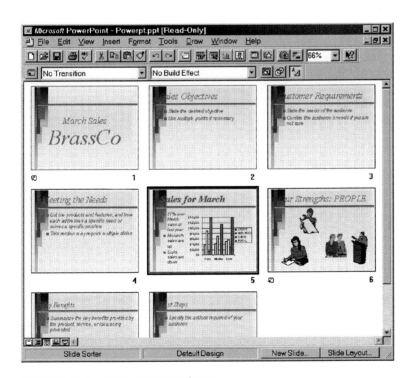
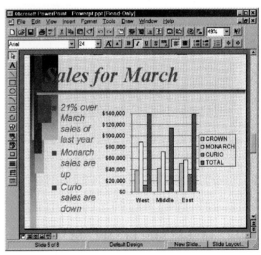

FIGURE 9–7 Slide Presentations
Microsoft PowerPoint, one of the most popular presentation graphics programs, helps you prepare and present slides for formal presentation. PowerPoint has a variety of slide templates from which you can choose. You can work with the entire presentation (left) or with a single chart (right). Slides are easily rearranged by simply dragging a slide to a new position.

Animation

The next step up from the static display is the dynamic display, that is, the movement within slides. **Animation,** or movement, is accomplished by the rapid repositioning (moving) of objects on the display screen. For example, animation techniques give life to video-game characters.

Animation software, which may be a component of presentation graphics software, lets you further enhance presentations with rudimentary animation. Animating presentation graphics involves the rapid movement of an object, perhaps the image of a dollar sign, from one part of the screen to another (see Figure 9–8). The animation is accomplished by moving the object in small increments of about ¼ inch in rapid succession, giving the illusion of movement. Most good presentation software packages have several built-in animation features that help you include animation in text and graphs. The *animated bullet build* feature can be applied to a simple text chart to integrate animation into the presentation of the bullet points on the chart. The *animated charting* feature can be applied to bar and pie graphs to animate the presentation of the important aspects of the graph.

The judicious use of animation can enliven any presentation. Some of the most important presentations take place in courtrooms. How can a lawyer best present evidence to help the judge and jury understand the case? This is a special challenge in

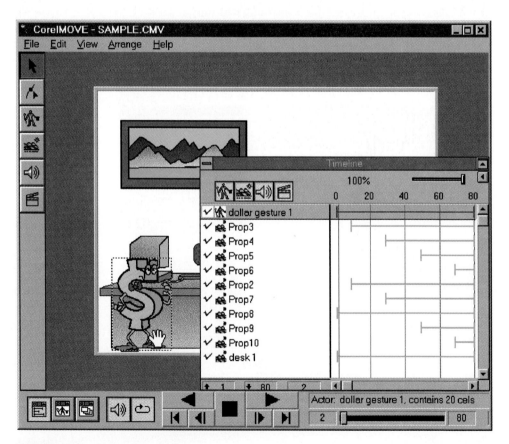

FIGURE 9–8 Animation Software

CorelMOVE, a type of animation software, enables users to add animation to their presentations. In this animation, the dollar sign "actor" jumps up on a desk and gestures to the bullet points as they appear on the screen in sequence. The actor moves along a user-defined line. The Timeline dialog box depicts the sequence in which the actor and props (bullet points) appear on the screen.

Issues in Computing

Collecting and Distributing Personal Information

Online information services not only provide information, they collect information—from you. Your online information service may be compiling data on you, including your social security number, credit-card number, demographic information, and interest areas. This information is then made available to online customers. For example, online users can request the last known address for any person in the United States. Users also can determine how long an individual has had a particular phone number or lived at a particular address. Some online services also provide information on how to get to more online information, such as driving records.

Discussion: Would you be for or against legislation that would require all telecommunications companies, including online information services, to tell people what information is being collected on them and how it's being used?

---

personal injury suits, where technical experts often present conflicting testimony. An increasing number of lawyers are illustrating expert testimony with animated computer graphics. In re-creating a plane crash, for example, data from the plane's data recorder can be used to prepare an animated graphic showing the exact flight path, while the cockpit voice recorder plays in the background. Several animations were used during the prosecution's case for the 1995 O. J. Simpson trial.

Applications of Computer Graphics

Until recently, PC-based applications were limited to numbers, letters, and crude graphics. The emergence of sophisticated high-resolution graphics has resulted in an avalanche of new applications in almost every area of endeavor. Figure 9–9 provides an overview of some of these exciting applications.

The emergence of computer graphics has not only changed what we see on the screen, but what we do as well. For example, computer graphics applications can now be found in almost every phase of medical training, diagnosis, and treatment. In fact, scholars of medical ethics predict that doctors who don't use these and other computer-based aids might eventually be sued for providing inadequate medical treatment. One especially valuable diagnostic technology is computed axial tomography, or the CAT scan, a rotating X-ray device that constructs a three-dimensional view of body structures. Medical schools are replacing traditional anatomy lessons and dissection labs with "electronic cadavers," databases of three-dimensional images created by combining measurements taken from human cadavers with CAT scans, magnetic resonance imaging, and still and video photographic images.

One of the computer world's basic maxims is, "The goal of computing is insight, not numbers." The same could be said of scientific research, where a wealth of data is both a blessing and a curse. Computer graphics are now helping scientists of every type gain new insights. Consider just these few examples.

▶ *Archeology.* A blend of database technology and three-dimensional computer mapping, modeling, and imaging have helped researchers reconstruct and preserve the ruins and artifacts of Pompeii. Like modern architects, archaeologists can now tour electronic models of ancient buildings and get a better idea of how the Pompeiians lived and died.

▶ *Astrophysics.* With the help of extremely powerful computers, researchers have been able to create three-dimensional simulations of the sun's surface that will help them understand the boiling turbulence of the convection zone,

FIGURE 9–9 Applications of Graphics Software

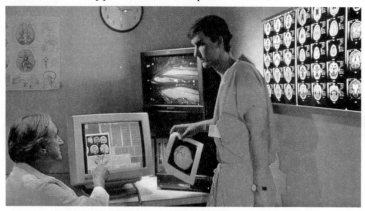

Preparing for Surgery Preparation and accuracy are especially important for any surgery. These University of Pittsburgh doctors are using computer graphics to help them make more informed decisions before and during surgery. Photo courtesy of Hewlett-Packard Company

Computer Graphics and Education Ms. Frizzle loads her students on the Magic School Bus and takes them on tours of everything from the brain to the solar system (shown here). Courtesy of Microsoft Corporation

Adding Color to Black-and-White Classics This movie is just one of many black-and-white films that have been *colorized* with the aid of computer graphics technology. The colorizing process uses an electronic scanner to break each frame into 525,000 dots the computer can store and manipulate. The art director reviews the frames at the beginning, middle, and end of the scene and selects a specific color for every object. A computer graphics artist then uses a digitizing tablet to "hand paint" these frames as per the art director's instructions. Computer software then colors the remaining frames. Mobile Image Canada Limited

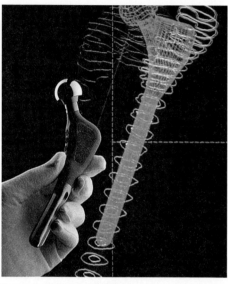

Creating Customized Surgical Implants The same computer-aided design and manufacturing techniques used in industry are being used to create artificial hips and other replacement bones and joints. Special software translates CAT scans and other medical images of a patient's body into a precise drawing, which doctors and medical engineers use to create a final design. The software then uses this design to control the manufacture of the finished implant. Similar techniques are being used to create other medical devices, such as replacement heart valves. Courtesy Techmedia

Computer Graphics in Industry Employees at Ponderay Newsprint find computer graphics displays easier to interpret than screens filled with numbers. Courtesy Wonderware Corporation

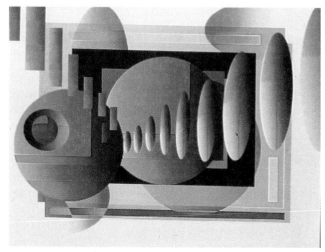

Computer Art Modern art has been taken to new levels of sophistication with the advent of computer graphics. Courtesy Truevision

where superheated material from the sun's core mixes with cooler material near the surface.

▶ *Oceanography.* Computer-enhanced graphics can be used to plot raw data collected by satellite, creating three-dimensional color-coded maps that help oceanographers envision the interplay of water temperature and movement with the terrain of the ocean floor.

These insights prove yet another truism of the computer world: "Computers really don't make difficult things easier; they make impossible things possible." This ability—to make the impossible possible—has made computer graphics one of the most exciting tools for computer users in all fields.

9–3 MULTIMEDIA: TEACHING THE COMPUTER TO SING AND DANCE

Probably no other computer "buzzword" is causing as much excitement today as *multimedia.* To understand the excitement, just consider the "show biz" appeal of these few examples.

▶ *Microsoft Bookshelf for Windows,* a single CD-ROM disk, contains seven reference works, including a "talking" dictionary that demonstrates correct pronunciations, a book of quotations that includes digitized recordings of such dignitaries as John F. Kennedy, an atlas that plays every country's national anthem, and a concise encyclopedia illustrated with high-resolution graphics and narrated animations showing how certain processes work. And, like any computer file, the CD-ROM can be searched by key word or phrase, taking a lot of the tedium out of research. *Bookshelf* is just one of a growing list of multimedia software titles that merge entertainment and education.

▶ A computerized information kiosk at the Montreux Jazz Festival allowed users to call up biographies, photos, and performance videos of all performers.

▶ Thousands of workers are now learning Word, Lotus 1-2-3, and other popular applications via interactive multimedia tutorials that are enlivened with music, graphics, and motion. A Department of Defense study concluded that such tutorials take about a third less time, cost about a third less, and are more effective than traditional training methods.

With multimedia, the PC is transformed into an exciting center for learning, work, or play.

Multimedia Applications: What's the Big Deal?

Multimedia is more sensual than traditional PC applications in that it tickles our senses while interacting with us and presenting us with information. Multimedia adds a new dimension of sound to the visual aspects of computing. You can now hear talking and singing voices, an entire orchestra, and many exciting sound effects that add to the functionality and enjoyment of an application (and you can even hear it in stereo). Figure 9–10 features a few of the endless applications for multimedia.

Multimedia

Multimedia applications let users access and interact with a PC that is capable of integrating text, high-resolution still graphics, motion video, animation, and sound. With multimedia, we are part of the action as the screen comes alive with motion and sound. The best way to understand multimedia is to experience it firsthand on a PC. No verbal description can do it justice.

For now, multimedia is a big deal. It's new, different, and very effective. In a few years, however, we probably won't say much about multimedia, for *all* applications will be multimedia.

FIGURE 9–10 Multimedia Applications

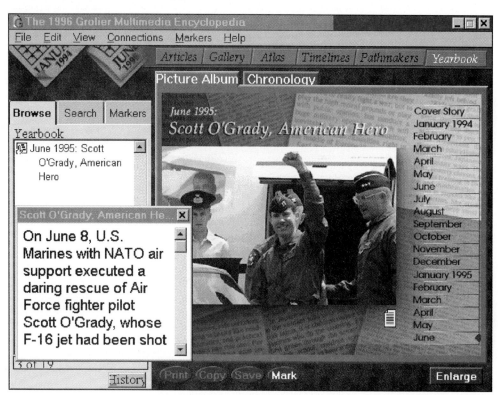

The Multimedia Encyclopedia The multimedia encyclopedia is a good place to start your multimedia adventure. The *Grolier Multimedia Encyclopedia* (shown here) contains over 10 million words about thousands of persons, places, and things. The CD-ROM encyclopedia uses the full capabilities of multimedia to enrich the presentation of information. For example, you can travel through time using maps that chart journeys filled with sights, sounds, and motion. How would you like to sail with Magellan or march with General Robert E. Lee? The encyclopedia offers narrated essays which use photos, music, and sound to explore such topics as the human body and space exploration. "Thumbing" through an encyclopedia will never be the same. In the example, the user tapped the Yearbook feature to view and read about some of the important events that took place in June 1995.

Multimedia in the Home Virtually all new PCs purchased for home use have full multimedia capability. At home, the multimedia PC is becoming the center for entertainment, reference, learning, home administration, writing and publishing, and more. Courtesy of International Business Machines Corporation

Informative Kiosks The multimedia kiosk is popping up everywhere. The manner in which we obtain information is changing rapidly. How often have you wandered through a department store looking for someone to help you? In the near future, the closest interactive kiosk, whether in a department store or a corporate office, should be able to answer most of your questions. Courtesy of International Business Machines Corporation

A Microcomputer Summary of the Twentieth Century The TIME Almanac of the Twentieth Century CD-ROM contains photographs, videos, maps, charts, and articles of events of the twentieth century. Shown here is a video clip of Elvis Presley's first day in the army.

Elvis Presley, the "King of Rock-and-Roll," was drafted by the army in 1957. Millions of fans mourned his enlistment.

Back

VIDEOS

COVERS

CHARTS

RESEARCHER | Before TIME | 1920s | 1930s | 1940s | 1950s | 1960s | 1970s | 1980s | 1990s | NEWSQUEST

Back | < | > | Search | Show | Copy | Print | Mark | Note | Help

Corporate Training To save network technicians critical time in off-site training, this telephone company uses multimedia training courses that can be accessed directly from the individual's PC or workstation.   Courtesy of Dynatech Corporation

Multimedia and Education People retain 10% of the information they see; 20% of what they hear; 50% of what they see and hear; and 80% of what they see, hear, and do. These statistics present a strong argument for interactive learning via multimedia. With the right software, this multimedia-capable Power Macintosh becomes an effective electronic teacher. This electronic teacher is more than a treasure chest of knowledge. It can answer students' questions and guide them through the learning process.   Courtesy of Apple Computer, Inc. (Jeff Haeger, photographer)

(**Figure 9-10** continues on next page)

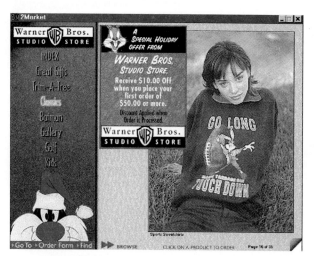

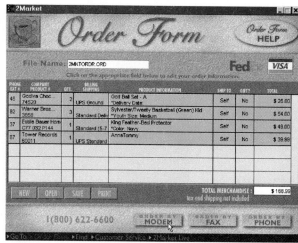

Shopping for Those Who Hate to Shop The 2Market CD-ROM contains dozens of multimedia catalogs (Eddie Bauer, Warner Brothers Studio Store, and many more). Shoppers can browse through thousands of products or find products by item or category. As you shop you simply click on the items you wish to add to your order form. When you are finished shopping, all you have to do is click on the "Modem" button to send your order.

Multimedia Titles Already there are thousands of multimedia titles covering topics from Mozart to movies. For example, movie buffs will love Microsoft's Cinemania. It is filled with movie reviews, video and audio clips, biographies, and cinema insights—all very accessible on CD-ROM.

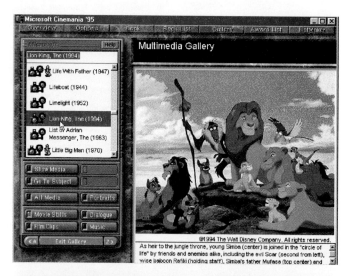

Learning Languages The multimedia PC is an excellent language instructor. Shown here is The Language Company's Vocabulary Builder (Spanish version). Whenever possible images are used as visual clues and memory aids. In this exercise an image is highlighted (la cueva, or cave, in this example), the word is spoken by the system, then the learner is given an opportunity to speak the word. The learner's spoken word is recorded for playback and evaluated by the program on a scale that goes from tourist to native.

Let the Games Begin The multimedia PC is rapidly becoming the delivery system for video games. The expanding popularity of PC-based games is evident in any software store, where the games section may be larger than all of the other software sections combined. Aspiring pinball wizards can play Sierra's 3-D Ultra Pinball alone or with their friends.

Emerging Technology

Myst Is More Than a Game—It's an Experience

The title of this box exemplifies how co-creator Rand Miller feels about his popular multimedia surrealistic adventure he and his brother, Robyn Miller, created. Let's take a closer look into this fantastic virtual exploration.

Your Challenge

Myst is a story of intrigue and adventure. You begin the game on Myst Island and you are not sure why you are there or what you are to do. All you know is what you see and observe and that you must explore and collect clues around the island. The island, as you come to learn, was created by Atrus, a man who perfected an amazing art of writing books that transport readers into fantastic worlds (called Ages). However, Atrus, his wife Catherine, and their sons are not to be found on the island. It seems that there is a plot against Atrus and his work. Your challenge is to uncover the story of Myst and find Atrus and his family.

Moving around in Myst is incredibly intuitive. You move by clicking the mouse where you would like to go. If you want to examine, use, or pick up an object, just click on it, or click and drag it. In fact, expect to click on everything you see. You are encouraged to keep track of all your clues (for example, the note found on the crumpled paper, the garbled video message from each son, the distinguishing features of each Age) in hopes of discovering the betrayer of ages past.

The Making of Myst

The company Cyan was formed in 1988 when brothers Rand and Robyn Miller began working together developing children's software for the Macintosh. Myst was their first goal-oriented game that was aimed primarily at an older audience (14 and up).

Myst was two years in the making. The Cyan team first developed the story line and worked through the logic puzzles by play-testing and role-playing. They wanted to maintain a feeling of exploration. There is no violence in Myst and you, the player, can't die. The Millers and their team at Cyan created everything, from the intriguing story line, to the graphics, to the soundtrack and sound effects.

The Cyan team used the computer to build their sets. The 2500 3-D rendered graphics are just a part of what makes you feel as though you are actually there, walking through concealed passageways, riding a secret

elevator, and seeing the incredible amount of detail and richness of the environment. According to Rand, "We create a wire frame model of a tree, scanned in a piece of bark and gave the computer various parameters which include lighting, fog, reflectivity, and texture. We come back many hours later, the 3-D program has rendered an entire forest!"

Dealing with the constraints of the speed of CD-ROM technology presented problems for the team. They wanted to get the graphics and the sound to the screen as quickly as possible. To accomplish this the team had to push the limits of existing technology.

The Myst CD-ROM contains 40 minutes of original music and lots of haunting sound effects. The gong you hear coming from the tower clock started by hitting a wrench with a piece of metal and digitizing its sound. Myst has 66 minutes of full-motion video and animation. If you're already a Myst fan, you will be interested to know that the Cyan team is hard at work on more Myst mysteries.

The Origin of Myst Island All of the 2500 pieces of art in Myst are original. Nothing is photo-based. Courtesy of Strata, Inc.

GOING ONLINE

9.3
What's the Latest News?

Use the Internet to check out today's news. *USAToday* (http://www.usatoday.com) is always informative.

Hand in: the headlines for at least three online articles and the name and source (URL) of the news.

Multimedia Hardware and Software: Making It Happen

What do you need to put the thrill of multimedia into your computing life? The answer depends, to a great extent, on what you want to do with multimedia. Most approach it in stages.

Getting Started with Multimedia   Do you want to experience multimedia? If so, you will need the following hardware components.

- ❱ *Personal computer.* You will need a PC with at least an Intel 386™ level processor.

- ❱ *High-resolution monitor.* A VGA or better monitor is needed to provide vivid displays of images. Many of the more recent multimedia programs require a graphics card and a monitor capable of displaying 256 colors.

- ❱ *CD-ROM drive.* The CD-ROM brings high-volume, low-cost storage to multimedia applications. You can take a ride around the block with diskette-based multimedia, but if you want to travel the world, you need a CD-ROM drive. It's impractical to load multimedia programs with sound and motion video to the hard disk because these resources take up too much space.

- ❱ *Sound card.* The sound card enables sounds to be captured and stored on disk and sounds to be played through external speakers or headphones.

- ❱ *External speakers or headphones.* The sound card has a small amplifier that can play sounds directly to small speakers or headphones. If you wish to fill the room with sound, you can feed the sound from the sound card directly into your stereo system's amplifier.

- ❱ *Microphone.* The microphone, which provides sound input directly to the sound card, lets you record sound in digitized format.

- ❱ *Multimedia support software.* Starter multimedia software would normally include that which is distributed with the sound card or operating system. This may include a variety of software (see Figure 9–11). One type of software enables you to assemble sounds to be played in a user-defined sequence. Text-to-speech synthesizer software enables text on the screen to be read aloud to the user. **Authoring software** lets you create multimedia applications that integrate sound, motion, text, animation, and images. Another software package lets you use your CD-ROM drive to play your audio CDs.

- ❱ *Multimedia applications software.* Users can choose from thousands of multimedia CD-ROM titles, from flight simulators to encyclopedias. CD-ROM titles cost from $10 to $10,000. The lower-priced CD-ROMs ($10 to $200) are for the mass market while the higher-priced ones contain reference material, primarily for the corporate environment.

If you own any of the current Macintosh models, you already have most of the hardware needed to run multimedia applications. Just attach a *CD-ROM drive* (if you don't have one) and you're ready to go. Most new PCs are configured for multimedia applications. The new low-end laptops may need an external CD-ROM to run multimedia applications.

The Multimedia Upgrade Kit   Over 80% of existing PCs will not run multimedia applications. If yours is one of them, you don't need to purchase a new system to take advantage of multimedia. If you own a reasonably powerful IBM-PC compatible (Intel 386 and up), you can buy a **multimedia upgrade kit.** These kits contain a CD-ROM drive, a sound card, multimedia software, external speakers, a microphone, and several CD-ROM titles. Of course, you can purchase the multimedia components individually as well. The bundled upgrade kit offers two major advantages. First, you can save money (about 20%). Second, you can be confident that the various multi-

INTERNET BRIDGE

Serendipitous Surfing:
Law and Justice

Audiostation. The Audiostation interface mimics the look of familiar home stereo components. Shown here are the CD player and the audio mixer. The CD player lets you play standard audio CDs on the CD-ROM drive. Audiostation lets you listen to Elvis Presley while working on a spreadsheet

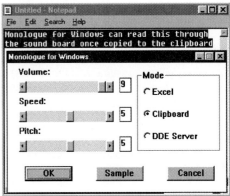

Monologue for Windows. Monologue for Windows will read aloud whatever text is is in the Windows clipboard. Text can be copied to the clipboard from any application.

Sound Recorder. Sound Recorder, which is distributed with Windows and Windows 95, enables you to record and edit sound files. With sound Recorder you can add special effects, such as echo, and even play a sound in reverse.

Audio Calendar. The Audio Calendar is an online calendar that lets you set alarms to alert you to important events (see bell icon at 9:00) and include audio notes to yourself (see speaker icon at 11:00).

FIGURE 9–11 Microcomputer Software That May Come with the Sound Card or Operating System

media components will work together. Compatibility can be a problem with microcomputer media components.

Growing with Multimedia The next stage of multimedia growth comes when you decide to *develop* sophisticated multimedia applications—either your own multimedia title, an interactive tutorial, or an information kiosk. At this point, you or your company may need to invest in some or all of the following hardware and software.

▶ *Video camera, videocassette recorder/player, audiocassette player, CD-audio player, and television.* These electronic devices are emerging as staples in many households and companies. The video camera lets you capture motion video source material that can be integrated with multimedia applications. The videocassette recorder/player and audiocassette player are needed when you edit prerecorded motion video and sounds for inclusion in an application. The CD-audio player is handy when combining CD-based audio material with CD-ROM source material. The television provides an alternative output device.

▶ *Synthesizer.* A good synthesizer can reproduce a variety of special effects and sounds, including those of almost any musical instrument. A synthesizer with a keyboard can be played to create source music for inclusion in a multimedia application.

▶ *Video capture card.* This expansion card lets you capture and digitize full-motion color video with audio. The digitized motion video can then be used as source material for a CD-ROM-based multimedia application.

▶ *Color scanner.* The color scanner is needed if you wish to capture color images from hard-copy source material.

▶ *Applications development software.* If you plan to develop sophisticated multimedia applications, you will need to upgrade to professional application develop-

FIGURE 9-12 Authoring Software
Authoring software, such as HSC InterActive, lets you integrate multimedia elements into a logical sequence of events. Most authoring packages enable visual programming in which users drag appropriate icons to an editing screen to attach content (sound effects, graphics, text, and so on) and perform programming functions (display menu, make decision, and so on). Properties are assigned to each icon depending on its function. For example, conditional expressions would be described for a decision icon. Other icons might identify images to display or sounds to play. Image supplied by HSC Software, copyright 1994

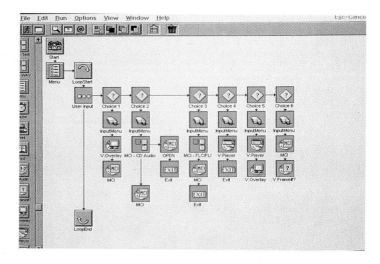

ment tools and high-level authoring software. Figure 9–12 demonstrates how an authoring language uses design icons, each of which has a special meaning, to integrate multimedia elements into a logical sequence of events.

▶ *Microcomputer source library.* The source library contains digitized versions of art, video, and audio that you can use as needed to complement a multimedia application.

Multimedia Resources

Multimedia applications draw content material from a number of sources. The resources that comprise multimedia applications are described in this section.

Text Files A little over a decade ago, computer-based applications were designed around text and numbers. We entered words, letters, and numbers to get output made up of words, letters, and numbers. A few programs included crude graphics. Text files remain an integral part of multimedia applications, but in many instances, text-based descriptions are being replaced with graphic descriptions. Applications are being designed to show and demonstrate rather than tell. An animation of the workings of the human heart is far more effective than a description with words of how it works. The text files used in multimedia applications are normally created with word processing software.

Database Files Many CD-ROM titles involve the use of databases. For example, one CD-ROM title contains information on every city in the United States (name, population, major industries, and so on). Another's database contains financial data by corporation for the past decade. The CD-ROM that accompanies this book has an interactive study guide that pulls questions from a Paradox for Windows database. Traditionally, database products have been designed to handle text; however, this is changing. Recent releases of popular database packages enable the storage of images and sound along with alphanumeric data.

Sound Files Sound files are of two types: *waveform* and *non-waveform.* The waveform files, or **wave files,** contain the digital information needed to reconstruct the analog waveform of the sound so it can be played through speakers. The Windows and Windows 95 waveform files are identified with the WAV extension (for example, SOUNDFIL.WAV).

The non-waveform file contains instructions as to how to create the sound, rather than a digitized version of the actual sound. For example, an instruction might tell the computer the pitch, duration, and sound quality of a particular musical note. The most common non-waveform file, which is primarily for recording and playing music, is known as the **MIDI file.** MIDI files are identified with the MID extension (for example, MUSICFIL.MID). MIDI stands for *Musical Instrument Digital Interface.* MIDI provides an interface between PCs and electronic musical instruments, like the synthesizer. MIDI offers the musician an opportunity to explore the full potential of synthesized music. To take maximum advantage of the MIDI capabilities, you will need a sound card that supports MIDI and a MIDI-compatible instrument. A typical MIDI application has the PC recording notes played by a musician on a synthesizer. The musician then adds additional instruments to the original track (layering) to create a full orchestral sound.

MEMORY BITS

Multimedia Resources

- Text files
- Database files
- Sound files
- Image files
- Animation files
- Motion video files

Image Files   Multimedia is visual. To be visual, you need lots of images. These are the primary sources of images.

▶ *You.* You can create your own images using the graphics software and techniques discussed earlier in this chapter.

▶ *Clip art.* Anyone serious about creating multimedia material will have a hefty clip art library. Word processing, desktop publishing, and other productivity software are distributed with a clip art library. A good commercial graphics package will include up to 30,000 pieces of clip art (usually on CD-ROM). Even larger clip art libraries are available commercially.

▶ *Scanned images.* If you have a scanner, you can scan and digitize any hard-copy image (photographs, drawings, and so on).

▶ *Photo images.* Photo image libraries are available commercially (on CD-ROM) and as downloadable files over the Internet and commercial information services (CompuServe, Prodigy, and so on).

Animation Files   You can create your own animation using animation software, such as CorelMOVE, or you can purchase a commercial animation library. The latter contains animation templates that can be applied to different presentation needs.

Motion Video Files   Obtaining relevant motion video for a particular multimedia application can be a challenge. You will need a video camera and a video capture board to produce original motion video for inclusion in a multimedia application. Depending on the presentation need, you may need actors, props, and a set, as well. For example, you will frequently see video clips of on-screen narrators in multimedia presentations and tutorials. Videos are produced as you would any video product (set, actor, and so on), then digitized for storage on a CD-ROM.

Unlike clip art, animation, and photo images, there are no commercially available libraries of motion video files. However, if you see something on TV you like, you can probably obtain the rights to use it (usually for a fee).

Creating a Multimedia Application: Putting the Resources Together

Developing any of these multimedia applications can be as much fun to create as using them.

▶ *Presentations.* These are slide shows for formal presentations.

▶ *Kiosks.* Interactive kiosks with touch-sensitive screens provide public users with detailed information about a city, a company, a product, and so on.

▶ *Tutorials.* Multimedia is rapidly becoming the foundation of computer-based training. For example, companies prepare interactive tutorials to introduce newcomers to company procedures.

▶ *Online reference.* CD-ROM-based multimedia documents are beginning to replace technical reference manuals, product information booklets, and the like. Electronic versions of reference materials are easier to use and much lighter.

▶ *Interactive publications.* Books, magazines, and newspapers are already being distributed as multimedia publications. The printed page will never be able to share sights and sounds. Look for this book and other printed material to come out as interactive products in the near future.

Refer to Figure 9–10 for a visual overview of different types of multimedia applications.

Once you have prepared and/or identified the sight and sound resource material, you're ready to put it together. A wide variety of software packages are available to help you accomplish this task.

▶ *Presentation graphics programs.* Presentation graphics programs like PowerPoint and CorelSHOW (see Figure 9–13) can help you prepare and create stimulating multimedia presentations. Such programs are easy to learn and use.

▶ *Authoring programs.* To create *interactive* multimedia tutorials and titles, you will need an authoring program, such as HSC InterActive (see Figure 9–12), Toolbook, or Macromedia Director. The HyperCard authoring system is bundled with Macintosh computers. Low-end authoring programs can be pur-

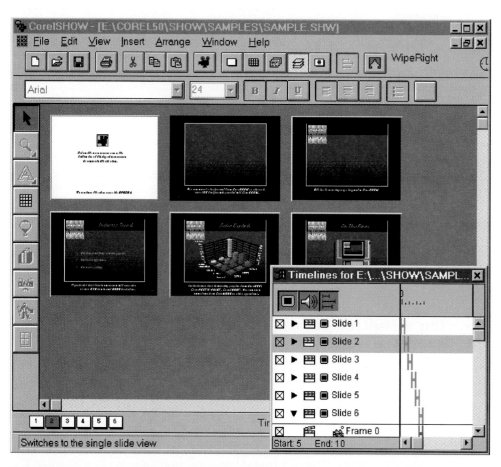

FIGURE 9–13 Presentation Graphics and Multimedia
Presentation graphics software, such as CorelSHOW pictured here, allows the integration of sight and sound during a multimedia presentation. The Timelines dialog box lets you determine how long a slide is displayed and when to play sounds (see speaker icon).

chased for under $100, but professional authoring software may cost several thousand dollars. The icon-driven interface of some consumer-market authoring packages makes multimedia very accessible and doable by people with little or no system design or programming experience. The user simply drags the icons (system building blocks) to a flowline to integrate the multimedia elements.

▶ *Multimedia programming.* The creation of sophisticated commercial multimedia titles, such as *The Grolier Multimedia Encyclopedia,* may require the use of several multimedia development tools, including high-end authoring programs and microcomputer programming languages. Visual Basic and C++, both program development tools, are part of any developer's multimedia tool kit.

Multimedia: The Possibilities

Multimedia possibilities stretch the human imagination to its limits. Already we see that multimedia will change the face of publishing. Many feel that *interactive books* based on multimedia technology have the potential to be more accessible and effective than traditional books, especially as learning tools. Early indications are that passive entertainment, such as TV and movies, may have to move aside to make way for interactive multimedia entertainment that involves the viewer in the action.

Multimedia applications touch our lives no matter which way we turn. They are in the malls to help us select the right product. Many magazines are delivered in multimedia format. The multimedia versions of board games look nothing like those of past generations. Multimedia products are beginning to invade classrooms from kindergarten to colleges. They help us learn Italian, appreciate music, and much more. We can explore the wonders of Tahiti, Kiev, or other exotic destinations simply by inserting a CD-ROM. It's amazing to think about what we can do now with multimedia. What we can do in the future boggles the mind.

9–4   SOFTWARE SUITES: ALL IN ONE PACKAGE

During the first 15 years of personal computing, software companies conceptualized, developed, and sold *stand-alone software.* Word processing packages were designed to do word processing tasks with little regard for their interaction with the other major software applications. The same was true of spreadsheet, database, and other types of software. PC users purchased software as needed from a variety of vendors, choosing the packages that best met their immediate needs. A representative software portfolio might have included Word Perfect for Windows (Corel), Lotus for Windows (Lotus Development Corporation), Paradox for Windows (Borland International), Microsoft Publisher (Microsoft), and PowerPoint (Microsoft).

During the last few years, major software vendors have been creating and pushing **software suites.** Software suites include, to varying degrees, most of the major business applications packages or capabilities introduced in Chapters 7 through 9; that is, those of communications (including Internet browsers), word processing, desktop publishing, spreadsheet, database, graphics, and multimedia. The various programs within a given software suite have a common interface and are integrated for easy transfer of information among programs.

Software suites offer great value. A suite may cost as little as 30% to 50% of the cost of the individually priced programs. That value, however, may have some drawbacks. The word processing package in the suite may not read your old word pro-

FIGURE 9–14 The Software Suite
Microsoft Word (word processing), Microsoft Excel (spreadsheet), Microsoft Access (database), Microsoft PowerPoint (presentation graphics), and a variety of other helpful programs are included with this Windows 95 version of Microsoft Office, a software suite. Office suites are constantly updating the mix of applications software to meet market demands. For example, some suites may include desktop publishing software (such as Microsoft Publisher, shown here) and an Internet browser.

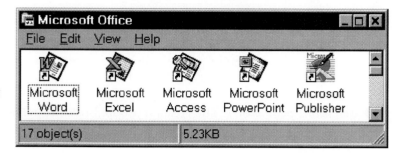

cessing files. The spreadsheet package may not be as good as the one in another suite. The suite may not include communications software. Each suite has its advantages and disadvantages. When you buy a suite, you get value and a little more integration; however, you give up the flexibility to get exactly what you may need. The dominant suite in the Windows arena is Microsoft Office Professional (see Figure 9–14).

IMPORTANT TERMS AND SUMMARY OUTLINE

animation 48
authoring software 56
bar graph 45
bit-mapped 40
draw software 41
metafile 39

MIDI file 59
morphing 43
multimedia upgrade kit 56
paint software 41
photo illustration software 43
pie graph 45

raster graphics 39
software suite 61
vector graphics 39
wave file 58

9–1 ADDING PIZAZZ In addition to word processing, desktop publishing, spreadsheet, and database software, you will want to familiarize yourself with graphics and multimedia software if you wish to add pizazz to these and other software products.

9–2 GRAPHICS: CREATING AND WORKING WITH IMAGES Graphics software facilitates the creation, manipulation, and management of computer-based images. Graphics software is discussed within the context of five capabilities: paint, draw, photo illustration, presentation graphics, and animation.

Graphic images are presented as **raster graphics, vector graphics,** and **metafiles.** In raster, or **bit-mapped,** graphics, the image is composed of patterns of dots (pixels). In vector graphics, the image is composed of patterns of lines, points, and other geometric shapes (vectors). The metafile is a class of graphics that combines the components of raster and vector graphics formats.

Paint software, which works with bit-mapped images, provides the user with a sophisticated electronic canvas. Whatever you draw on either the traditional or the electronic canvas becomes part of the whole drawing. Tools in a paint program's user interface include the drawing area, the graphics cursor, the main menu, the tool box, the linesize box, and the color palette.

Draw software lets you create a screen image, then isolate and manipulate representations of individual objects within the overall image. Draw software relies on vector graphics, so a specific object can be dealt with independently.

Photo illustration software enables us to create original images as well as to dress up existing digitized images, such as photographs and electronic paintings. Images can be retouched with special effects, such as **morphing,** where you can show the changes that take place as one image is modified to become an entirely different image.

Presentation graphics software enables users to create a wide variety of visually appealing and informative presentation graphics. Among the most popular are **pie graphs** and **bar graphs.** Presentation graphics software also permits the preparation of text charts, organization charts, maps, and original drawings that can be shown in a slide presentation.

Animation is accomplished by the rapid repositioning of objects on the display screen. Animation software lets you further enhance presentations with rudimentary animation with such tools as animated bullet build and animated charting features.

9–3 MULTIMEDIA: TEACHING THE COMPUTER TO SING AND DANCE Multimedia refers to a computer system that lets users access and interact with computer-based text, high-resolution still graphics, motion visuals, animation, and sound. Three elements in particular distinguish multimedia: sound, motion, and the opportunity for interaction.

A basic multimedia system includes a PC, a high-resolution monitor, a CD-ROM drive, a sound card, external speakers or headphones, a microphone, multimedia support software, and multimedia applications software. A **multimedia upgrade kit** may be used to update your existing PC so you can run multimedia applications.

The next stage of multimedia growth would include some or all of the following hardware and software: a video camera, a videocassette recorder/player, an audiocassette player, a CD-audio player, a television, a synthesizer, a video capture card, a color scanner, professional applications development software, and a source library.

Multimedia applications draw content material from a number of sources, including text files, database files, sound files, image files, animation files, and motion video files. Sound files are of two types: *waveform* (or **wave file**) and *non-waveform* (or **MIDI file**). Sources for image files include those the user creates, clip art, scanned images, and photo images.

There are a variety of software packages available to help you create multimedia applications. These include presentation graphics programs and multimedia development tools, including high-end **authoring software** and multimedia programming languages.

Multimedia possibilities stretch the human imagination to its limits and its applications are touching our lives no matter which way we turn.

9–4 SOFTWARE SUITES: ALL IN ONE PACKAGE **Software suites** include most of the major business applications packages of communications, word processing, desktop publishing, spreadsheet, database, graphics, and multimedia. The various programs within a given software suite have a common interface and are integrated for easy transfer of information among programs.

REVIEW EXERCISES

Concepts

1. What term is frequently used in place of *raster graphics?*
2. Which type of graphics software package provides a computer-based version of the painter's canvas?
3. Which type of graphics software package enables the generation and presentation of a wide variety of charts and graphs?
4. Which type of graphics software enables users to assemble presentation graphics in a synchronized demonstration?
5. Which paint software tool permits freehand drawing?
6. Name three special effects made possible with photo illustration software.
7. Name at least three hardware devices over and above those needed to run a word processing program that are needed to run multimedia applications.
8. Name three common household electronic devices that a developer of multimedia applications might use when developing multimedia applications.
9. Which type of expansion card lets you capture full-motion color video with audio on magnetic disk?
10. Briefly describe three multimedia applications discussed in this chapter.

11. What is the difference between a waveform file and a non-waveform file?
12. Name four programs that you might find in a software suite.
13. What class of graphics combines the components of raster and vector graphics formats?

Discussion and Problem Solving

14. Describe the advantages of a multimedia-based encyclopedia over a traditional printed encyclopedia. Describe the advantages of a traditional printed encyclopedia over a multimedia-based encyclopedia.
15. Use paint software, such as Paint (comes with Windows 95), to create an image of your choice.
16. Why might the term *multimedia* not be such a "buzzword" in the not-so-distant future?
17. What is one advantage and one disadvantage of multimedia upgrade kits?
18. Describe two scenarios for which information kiosks would be applicable.
19. Create a series of bulleted text charts (manually or with presentation graphics software) that you might use to make a presentation to the class on presentation graphics software.

9–1 As a rule of thumb, you cannot be an effective user of word processing software without knowing something about multimedia software. (T/F)

9–2 a. Presentation graphics software allows users to create charts and graphics. (T/F)
b. In raster graphics, the image is composed of patterns of: (a) vectors, (b) pictures, or (c) dots?
c. Which of the following would not be a tool in a paint program's tool box: (a) rectangle tool, (b) color palette, or (c) add text tool?
d. _____ charts show the hierarchical structure of an organization.
e. Draw software relies on vector graphics to permit manipulation of specific objects within an image. (T/F)
f. A photo illustration process called _____ shows the changes that take place as one image is modified to become an entirely different image.

9–3 a. Which of the following would not be considered one of the major elements of multimedia: (a) sound, (b) sequential access, or (c) the opportunity for interaction?
b. The _____ card has a small amplifier through which sound can be played.
c. HyperCard is an example of an _____ program that lets you create multimedia applications that integrate sound, motion, text, animation, and images.
d. The video synthesizer expansion card lets you capture and digitize full-motion color video with audio. (T/F)
e. MIDI files are (a) waveform files, (b) non-waveform files, or (c) minidigital files?
f. JAZZTOP.MID could be the filename for a sound file. (T/F)

9–4 Which of the following is not usually associated with a software suite: (a) stand-alone packages, (b) common interface, or (c) value?

Self-test Answers. **9–1** F. **9–2(a)** T; **(b)** c; **(c)** b; **(d)** Organization; **(e)** T; **(f)** morphing. **9–3 (a)** b; **(b)** sound; **(c)** authoring; **(d)** F; **(e)** b; **(f)** T. **9–4** a.

IMAGE BANK

PC Buyer's Guide

Each year millions of people go through the process of buying a PC, PC peripherals, and PC software. They also subscribe to commercial information services, print magazines, and CD-ROM magazines. During the last few years PC-related expenses have emerged as the third most significant expense—right behind homes and automobiles. The process is always an adventure, whether you're a first-time buyer or you're buying a replacement system. The information presented here will help you enjoy your adventure and spend your money wisely.

The emphasis in this PC Buyer's Guide is on the actual buying process. Hardware and software concepts are discussed in detail in other sections of the book.

STEPS IN BUYING A PC

Buying a PC can be a harrowing experience or a thrilling and fulfilling one. If you approach the purchase of a PC haphazardly, expect the former. If you go about the acquisition methodically and with purpose, expect the latter. Follow this 10-step procedure to get the biggest bang for your buck.

Step 1: Achieve Computer Competency

You do not buy an automobile before you learn how to drive, and you should not buy a PC without a good understanding of its capabilities and how you intend to use it. In effect, this book is a comprehensive buyer's guide: The informed buyer will know and understand its con-

tent. Every college and vocational college offers courses leading to computer competency.

Step 2: Decide How Much You Are Willing to Spend

Assess your circumstances and decide how much you are willing to commit to the purchase of a PC system. Generally, *purchase the best system you can afford*. If you don't and you are a typical user, you will end up replacing or upgrading it sooner than you think. You can pay now or pay later. If you must buy a smaller system, make sure it is easily upgradable to the next level.

Step 3: Determine Your Information and Computing Needs

The adage "If you don't know where you are going, any road will get you there" certainly applies to choosing a PC. Your goal is to figure out where you want to go by answering this question: "How can I use a PC to simplify my work, increase my pleasure, or both?"

For most people, this means deciding which types of software packages they want to use. The choices here truly are vast including word processing, spreadsheet, database, data communications, personal finance, graphics, edutainment, games, and much more. This

A computer-competent colleague can be a real help during the learning process.   Courtesy of Apple Computer, Inc. (photo by John Greenleigh)

Some people prefer the flexibility and portability of a notebook computer. Photo courtesy of Hewlett-Packard Company

is an important decision because software needs frequently determine hardware needs.

Step 4: Assess the Availability and Quality of Software and Information Services

Determine what software and commercial information services are available to meet your needs. Good sources of this type of information include general computer periodicals (*PC Magazine*, *Byte*, *Computer-Life*, and *MacWorld*, to name a few), salespeople at computer stores, your computer/software instructor, a local computer club, your colleagues at work, and acquaintances who have knowledge in the area. If you have access to the

Software in retail outlets is usually organized by platform and function (for example, Windows 95, spreadsheets). Courtesy of Egghead Software

Internet and/or an online information service, you can request information from vendors and tap into the thoughts of those who have used the software or information service.

Thousands of software packages are available commercially, and they vary greatly in capability and price. Considering the amount of time you might spend using PC software, any extra time you devote to evaluating the software will be time well spent.

Step 5: Choose a Platform

At this point in the PC decision process you will need to decide on a platform. Platforms are important because software is written to run under a particular platform. The various platforms are discussed in detail in Chapter 3, "Software: Telling Computers What to Do." Of course, you will need to select a platform that supports your software and information needs (Step 4).

When making the platform decision, consider compatibility with the other PCs in your life: your existing PC (if you have one), the one at work/home, and/or the one in your college lab.

Step 6: Identify the Desired Type of PC

PCs come in many flavors: pocket PCs, notebook PCs, desktop PCs, and tower PCs. Choose the PC that fits your lifestyle and application needs.

Step 7: Identify One or More PC Systems for Further Examination

If your software needs are typical, you will have a number of PC alternatives available to you within a given platform. Identify one or more that meet criteria established in the first six steps.

Virtually all new desktop and tower PCs will be configured to handle the system requirements for modern software packages, including multimedia and data communication applications. Nevertheless, you should check each alternative against these *minimum hardware requirements for PC compatibles.*

▶ 66 MHz 486-level processor (100 Pentium is desirable)

▶ 8 MB (12 MB is desirable with Windows 95)

▶ Hard disk drive (500 MB to 1.8 GB)

- CD-ROM drive (triple- or quad-speed is desirable)
- Super VGA monitor (640 X 480 with 256 colors)
- Sound card, speakers, and a microphone
- Fax modem (14.4 k bps with 28.8 k bps desirable)
- Mouse (or other point-and-draw device) and enhanced keyboard

Virtually all new PCs are sold with Windows 95 installed on the hard disk. Windows 95 runs both 16-bit and 32-bit software, where MS-DOS/Windows runs only 16-bit software. Note: Only high-end notebook PCs are configured for multimedia applications (CD-ROM, sound board, and speakers).

Step 8: Determine the Processor-Related Features You Want

Once you have narrowed your choice of PC systems to one, two, or perhaps three, you are ready to determine which processor-related features you want. Become familiar with the options of these systems. For example, assess the availability of expansion slots, parallel ports, and serial ports. You can go with a basic processor (see Step 7) or, if your budget allows, you can select a more powerful processor and add a few "bells and whistles." Expect to pay for each increase in convenience, quality, and speed.

Step 9: Determine the Peripheral Devices You Want

Peripheral devices come in a wide variety of speeds, capacities, and qualities. The peripherals you select depend on your specific needs, volume of usage, and the amount of money you are willing to spend. If you plan on doing a lot of graphics work, you might wish to consider getting a color image scanner. You might wish to pay a little more to get a 1.8 GB hard disk. A large monitor (17 inches or bigger) can

If you wish to scan images for inclusion in printed documents, you might wish to consider an image scanner. Courtesy Caere Corporation

relieve eye strain. You can pay as little as $150 or as much as $10,000 for a printer. This choice depends on the anticipated volume of hard-copy output, the quality of the output, and whether you need color output.

Step 10: "Test Drive" Several Alternatives

Once you have selected several software and hardware alternatives, spend enough time to gain some familiarity with them. Do you prefer one keyboard over another? Is the word processing system compatible with the one used at the office? Is one user's guide easier to understand than another?

Many software packages have demonstration and/or tutorial disks. When you load the demo or tutorial disk on the PC, an instructional program interactively "walks you through" a simulation (demonstration) of the features and use of the software. It is a good idea to work through the demo to get a feeling for the product's features and ease of use.

This model uses a tower configuration, which is designed to rest on the floor and to provide more expansion slots. Courtesy of International Business Machines Corporation

Frequently, software is bundled with a PC, thus confusing the issue. You might like the software bundled with your second choice PC. If this is the case, don't hesitate to ask the vendor about the possibility of bundling the software you want with the PC you want.

Salespeople at most retail stores are happy to give you a "test drive"—just ask. Use these sessions to answer any questions you might have about the hardware or software.

Step 11: Select and Buy Your System

Apply your criteria, select, and then buy your hardware and software. PCs with similar functionality may differ as much as 40% in price. Don't let a fancy name or a multi-million-dollar ad campaign distract you from what should be your primary considerations—functionality and price.

FACTORS TO CONSIDER WHEN BUYING A PC

▶ *Future computing needs.* What will your computer and information-processing needs be in the future? Make sure the system you select can grow with your needs. For example, the difference between a 700-MB and a 1.8 GB hard disk may be several hundred dollars. However, if you estimate your disk-storage needs to be in excess of 700 MB within a couple of years, you may be better off in the long run buying the 1-GB disk.

▶ *Who will use the system?* Plan not only for yourself but also for others in your home or office who will use the system. Get their input and consider their needs along with yours. For example, if you're purchasing for a home with teenagers, you might want to consider a joystick.

▶ *Service.* Computing hardware is very reliable. Even so, the possibility exists that one or several of the components eventually will malfunction and have to be repaired. Before purchasing a PC, identify a reliable source of hardware maintenance. Most retailers service what they sell. If a retailer says the hardware must be returned to the manufacturer for repair, consider another retailer or another system. If you plan on purchasing via mail order, identify a nearby computer-repair store or a computer retailer that does repair work on the system you intend to buy.

Most retailers or vendors will offer a variety of maintenance contracts. Maintenance-contract options range from same-day, on-site repairs that cover all

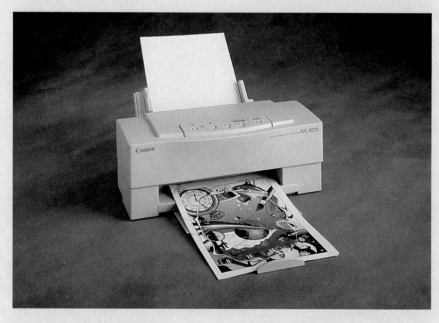

The color ink-jet printer has emerged as the standard for home computing.   Courtesy of Canon Computer Systems, Inc.

parts and service to a carry-in service that does not include parts. Most domestic users elect to treat their PCs like their televisions and cars: When the warranty runs out, they pay for repairs as they are needed. Under normal circumstances, this strategy will prove the least expensive. Business users are sometimes willing to pay extra for the convenience of an on-site maintenance contract.

Service extends beyond hardware maintenance. Service is also an organization's willingness to respond to your inquiries before *and* after the sale. Some retailers and vendors offer classes in the use of the hardware and software they sell.

Most hardware and software vendors offer a *technical support hot line*. The extent of the hot-line service varies considerably. Some

companies provide their licensed users with a toll-free 24-hour hot line—free of charge for as long as they own the product. At the other end of the spectrum, companies charge their users as much as $50 an hour for using their technical support hot lines. Typically, companies will provide hot-line service for a limited period of time (six months or a year), then charge after that. Some vendors offer other tech support options including a free BBS (with online tech support, answers to frequently asked questions, and solutions to common problems) and fax support (automated fax-back of documentation and solutions to common problems).

▶ *Hardware obsolescence.* In 1995 you could buy a PC that costs half as much and offers a

Make sure the program you want has good documentation before you buy it. Reprinted with permission of Compaq Computer Corporation. All Rights Reserved.

12000% improvement in performance over a 1985 PC. If you decide to wait until the price goes down a little more, you may never purchase a computer. If you wait another six months, you probably will be able to get a more powerful PC for less money, but what about the lost opportunity?

There is also a danger in purchasing a PC that is near the end of its life cycle. If you are planning on using a PC frequently at school, home, or work, focus your search on PCs with state-of-the-art technology. You may get a substantial discount on a PC with dated technology, but will it run next year's software?

▶ *Software obsolescence.* Software can become obsolete as well. Software vendors are continually improving their software packages. Make sure you are buying the most recent release of a particular software package.

▶ *Product documentation (internal and external).* PC products are consumer items and are distributed with user manuals, just like automobiles and VCRs. In most cases, the person who purchases the product installs it and uses it.

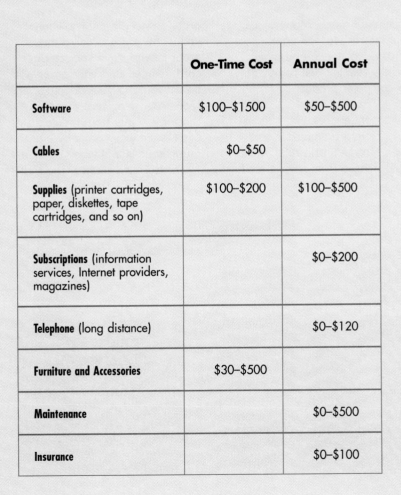

	One-Time Cost	**Annual Cost**
Software	$100–$1500	$50–$500
Cables	$0–$50	
Supplies (printer cartridges, paper, diskettes, tape cartridges, and so on)	$100–$200	$100–$500
Subscriptions (information services, Internet providers, magazines)		$0–$200
Telephone (long distance)		$0–$120
Furniture and Accessories	$30–$500	
Maintenance		$0–$500
Insurance		$0–$100

To install it and use it, you will need effective product documentation. Inevitably you will spend many hours with the product's documentation. Make sure that it is good.

▶ *Other costs.* The cost of the actual PC system is the major expense, but there are many incidental expenses that can mount up and influence your selection of a PC. If you have a spending limit, consider these costs when purchasing a PC (the cost ranges listed are for a first-time user).

WHERE TO BUY

PC Retailers

Ten years ago PCs were considered a highly technical specialty item and were sold almost exclusively through PC retail outlets. Today, PCs and PC software have emerged as popular consumer items. PCs and associated hardware and software can be purchased at thousands of convenient locations.

▶ *Computer retailers.* About a dozen national retail chains and many regional retail chains specialize in the sale of PC hardware and/or software. Most market and service a variety of small computer systems. There are also more than 1000 computer stores that are not affiliated with a national or regional chain.

▶ *Department stores.* PCs and PC software are sold in the computer/electronics departments of most department store chains.

▶ *Discount stores.* Discount stores sell a wide range of PC hardware and software.

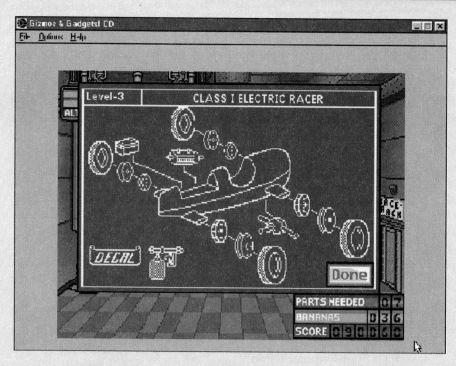

The fastest growing segment of the software market is education software. Gizmos and Gadgets, a product of The Learning Company, combines education and entertainment (edutainment) in this science adventure.

▶ *Other retail stores.* Many office supply stores, college bookstores, audio/video stores, and other specialty retailers sell computers and computer products.

▶ *Mail-order services.* The alternative to buying a computer and related products at a retail outlet is to purchase them from a mail-order service. If you know what you want, you can call a mail-order service, give your credit-card number, and your order will be delivered to your doorstep. Mail order is a great way to shop if you buy from reputable dealers. Be wary of fly-by-night organizations that won't be there when you need service. The best

Retail stores are one of the PC consumer's many sources for hardware and software. Egghead Discount Software specializes in software.   Courtesy of Egghead Software

mail-order services give you their street address (not a P. O. box) and offer a 30-day unconditional money-back guarantee on all merchandise. Accept nothing less.

▶ *Direct marketers.* Some manufacturers of PC hardware and/or software are direct marketers; that is, they sell directly to the customer. For the most part, the direct marketer's "store window" is an advertisement in a PC trade magazine. The customer telephones, faxes, or mails the order, and the direct marketer sends the requested product(s) by return mail.

▶ *Used-computer retailers.* The used-computer retailer was as inevitable as the used-car dealer. A computer that is no longer powerful enough for one user may have more than enough power for another.

▶ *Classified ads.* Frequently, people wishing to upgrade will opt to advertise their existing systems in the classified ad sections of their local newspapers.

The sale price of a PC, a peripheral device, or a software package may vary substantially from one source to another. It pays to shop around. A software suite may be offered at list price ($899) from the manufacturer, at $650 from one local computer retailer, at $599 from another, and at $389 from a mail-order service. Of course, the selling price does not tell the whole story. For example, the local retailers may promise to provide some technical support after the sale.

The "Perks" of Employment or Being a Student

You might be able to acquire a PC and/or software through your employer or college. Many companies offer their employees a "PC perk." In cooperation with vendors, companies and colleges make volume purchases of PCs and software at discount rates, then offer them to employees and students at substantial savings. The employee-purchase program is so popular in some organizations that they set up internal computer stores.

Shareware: Affordable Software

Thousands of software authors have created a wide variety of excellent programs, from business graphics to trivia games. However, most of these creative authors do not have the funds needed to launch their creations in the commercial software marketplace. The alternative is to make their software available as *shareware.* Shareware is software made readily available to PC users via electronic bulletin boards, online services (Prodigy, CompuServe, and so on), and other low-cost distribution channels. Shareware distribution companies sell diskettes and CD-ROMs containing shareware. You pay the same nominal amount per diskette (from $1.75 to $5.00) or you can purchase a CD-ROM containing hundreds of programs for as little as $20.

When you download or order shareware, it is implied that you will register the software with the developer if you like it and intend to use it. The registration fees vary from $10 for utility programs to $100 for full-featured word processing packages. Software developers use several methods to encourage registration of their software. At a minimum, developers provide technical support and update information to registered users. Some shareware is distributed with start-up documentation only, with complete documentation sent to registered users. Some shareware developers make shareware enhancements available only to registered users.

You can get programs that print signs and banners, help you with

The docking station gives the notebook PC added convenience and capability. Courtesy of International Business Machines Corporation

your taxes, teach you to speak Japanese, help you manage projects, provide access to many delicious recipes, and suggest lottery numbers. You can get complete systems for church accounting, stamp collection, billing and invoicing, and investment management. You can get full-featured packages for word processing, spreadsheet, database, and graphics. And, if you're intimidated by the thought of learning a spreadsheet, why not try "Templates of Doom," a shareware program that uses an adventure game to teach spreadsheet basics. Scores of games are available from golf to martial arts. These are just the tip of the shareware iceberg.

INSTALLATION TIPS

▶ *Location selection.* Select a location for your computer system. The location should be away from people traffic; have access to a telephone line (for communications applications); have plenty of non-glare lighting; and be within a controlled environment (temperature, dust, and humidity).

The few hours extra hours you spend designing your work place will pay big dividends during the countless hours you spend at the PC. Courtesy of International Business Machines Corporation

- *Create an ergonomically designed work place.* See Chapter 11, "Computers in Society," for more on work-place design considerations.
- *Plan for growth.* It's inevitable that your space requirements will grow (more CD-ROMs, other peripherals, manuals, and so on).
- *Complete and send registration cards for all hardware and software.* These cards are important for warranty protection and for access to technical support. Write down product serial numbers on the inside covers of the respective user's manuals.
- *Read and consolidate all manuals.* Read installation instructions before beginning any installation procedure. Keep all manuals together and readily accessible.
- *Keep shipping material for at least the period of the warranty.*
- *Clearly label all external connectors.* Some, but usually not all, connectors are labeled by the manufacturer. You may need to label extra serial ports, sound card connectors, and so on.

SYSTEM MAINTENANCE TIPS

- *Back up critical files.* The critical element in any computer system is the hard disk because that is where you keep your program and data files. Back up these files regularly to diskette or tape.
- *Keep your hard disk healthy.* Periodically use disk management software to reorganize fragmented files for faster operation and to check for and fix disk problems.
- *Clean the 3.5-inch disk drive.* Periodically use a disk cleaning kit to clean read/write heads.
- *Run a virus program.* Periodically run a virus program to maintain a virus-free operation.
- *Delete unused directories and files.* Over time, PC hard disks get cluttered with obsolete and unused programs and data. Periodically examine hard disk contents and delete directories/files as needed.
- *Clean the monitor.* Use the special cloth distributed with your monitor to maintain a dust-free screen for better viewing.
- *Replace the printer cartridge as needed.* Output quality usually dictates the need for a new cartridge.
- *Upgrade software.* It's a good idea to upgrade the operating system and frequently used programs as new releases become available.

UPGRADING EXISTING PCS

Once you purchase and begin to use a PC, the buying doesn't stop. It is inevitable that your PC will grow with the technology and your ever-expanding processing needs. This growth means that occasionally you may need to upgrade the PC. The upgrade might involve switching processors (for example, an Intel 486 to an Intel Pentium), adding a hard drive, adding an expansion board (for example, 28.8 k-bps fax modem), upgrading to a color printer, adding peripherals (for example, a joystick), installing a multimedia upgrade kit, and so on.

More than 80% of existing PCs will not run multimedia applications. But, that percentage is changing as millions of PC novices are upgrading their existing PCs. Here's how they do it.

Step 1: Remove the cover of the processor unit to expose the expansion slots.
Step 2: Insert the sound board in an empty expansion slot.
Step 3: Insert the CD-ROM in an empty half-height drive bay.
Step 4: Attach the appropriate cables to the CD-ROM drive and sound card (power connector, sound cable, and data ribbon cable).
Step 5: Replace the cover.
Step 6: Plug the speaker and microphone jacks into the external portion of the sound board. A joystick, which is purchased separately, can be attached to the sound board's game port.
Step 7: Install the software.

The multimedia upgrade takes about an hour and costs from $250 to $700, depending on the quality of the kit.

PC BUYER'S WORKSHEET

After you have looked at two or three systems, their features, options, and specifications tend to blur in your mind. It is difficult to remember whether the first system had a 100-MHz processor or a 100-day money-back warranty. The best way to make an informed purchase decision is to capture pertinent information in a way that will allow an easy comparison between alternatives. You can use the, PC Buyer's Worksheet, on the following page to *gather information on proposed systems* and/or to *document the ideal system for your needs.*

The entire family will enjoy the benefits of a multimedia upgrade kit.
Courtesy of International Business Machines Corporation

PC BUYER'S WORKSHEET

Vendor _____

Contact person _____ Telephone number (   )   ext.

PRODUCT	MAKE	MODEL	WARRANTY	COST
Processor unit				$
Processor speed in MHz:				
RAM in MB				
Cache in KB				
BUS # 1 type: slots:				
BUS # 2 type: slots:				
Serial ports: Parallel ports:				
Special feature # 1:				
Special feature # 2:				
Keyboard				$
Point-and-draw device				$
Monitor				$
Size: Resolution: Dot pitch:				
Hard disk drive				$
Capacity: Access time: Transfer rate:				
Diskette drive				$
CD-ROM drive				$
Access time: Transfer rate:				
Tape backup unit				$
Capacity: Transfer rate:				
Printer				$
Type: Speed: Resolution:				
Sound card				$
Speakers				$
Fax modem				$
K bps: Fax software:				
Other I/O Device # 1:				$
Specs:				
Other I/O Device # 2:				$
Specs:				
Total System Cost		$		

PROGRAM		VERSION	COST
Name: Description:			$
Name: Description:			$
Name: Description:			$
Name: Description:			$
Total Software Cost	$		

Information Systems: The MIS, DSS, and EIS

Courtesy of Harris Corporation

(cont. on p. 77)

Let's Talk

The following conversation introduces many of the terms in this chapter. Read it now, then again after you have read the chapter.

The Scene:
An information system consultant (Patricia) has been called into the Sixth National Bank of Palo Alto by its chief information officer (Sam) to discuss systems approaches to improve the bank's handling of loan applications.

Sam: Patricia, we have 38 loan officers in 12 different locations. We need an **information system** that will help us make more uniform decisions on loan applications. Our **MIS** is simply too structured.

Patricia: How about a **decision support system?**

Sam: We actually tried **DSS,** but the tools were too hard to use because our current system is very low tech. About 90% of the loan applications can be processed with **programmed decisions** based on our written guidelines. The really tough decisions are made by Henry Hughes, who's been with SNB for 38 years. Henry applies his own secret criteria to these loan applications. But, he's retiring in December!

Patricia: Sounds like you need a **knowledge-based system.**

Sam: We talked about purchasing an **assistant system** from a company out of L.A., but that system balked when confronted with a difficult decision.

Patricia: With Henry and his wisdom leaving, you may need the full boat—an **expert system.**

Sam: You think so?

Patricia: If I can spend a few days with Henry, I'll be able to translate his years of experience into **factual knowledge** and **rules.** We can integrate Henry's input with your existing written guidelines to create the **knowledge base.**

Sam: It just might work.

Patricia: Henry may be retiring, but his wealth of knowledge can live on.

STUDENT LEARNING OBJECTIVES

▶ *To describe how information needs vary at each level of organizational activity.*

▶ *To distinguish between programmed decisions and nonprogrammed decisions.*

▶ *To identify the elements, scope, and capabilities of an information system.*

▶ *To describe the circumstances appropriate for batch and transaction-oriented data entry.*

▶ *To define data processing system, management information system, decision support system, executive information system, expert system, and software agent.*

▶ *To identify characteristics associated with data processing systems, management information systems, decision support systems, executive information systems, expert systems, and software agents.*

10–1 AN END TO BUSINESS AS USUAL

A highly competitive world market is pressuring corporate managers into a desperate search for solutions—no more business as usual. Those with a genuine desire to survive and flourish are doing everything they can to improve profitability. Companies are adopting no smoking policies to lower the cost of insurance premiums. Unions are accepting wage concessions. Executives are flying coach rather than first class. The days are gone when good management and hard work would invariably result in success and profits. Now that these corporate qualities have become prerequisites for survival, managers are seeking strategies that can give their companies the competitive advantage. These strategies often involve computers and information technology. In this highly competitive era, the judicious use of available technology can make the difference between profitability and failure.

New and innovative uses of information technology are being implemented every day. Even so, the business community is still in the early stages of automation. Each company has a seemingly endless number of opportunities to use technology to achieve a competitive edge. Health care, entertainment, publishing, and all organizations that wish to remain competitive are integrating more and more information technology into all they do.

Money spent on information technology yields tremendous returns. Properly implemented, information technology can improve product and service quality, reduce costs, increase productivity, and even improve employee morale. Information technology facilitates communication between people spread across organizational and geographic boundaries. The return for the corporate investment in information technology is astonishing. A Massachusetts Institute of Technology survey of 400 large companies revealed that the return on the information technology dollar exceeded 50%. The best news is that these savings are ultimately passed on to us, the consumers.

Not only are computers and information technology changing the way we do things, they are changing the function and purpose of major companies. As we move toward the end of the century, the distinction between companies will begin to blur. We can expect companies to merge and provide vertical integration of information technology–based products and services. For example, look for banks, brokerage firms, insurance companies, and other financial services companies to begin offering similar products and services. It only makes sense for companies to leverage their capabilities, and companies in all industries are doing it.

10–2 INFORMATION AND DECISION MAKING

To be successful, managers must fully understand and use four major resources: money, materials, people, and information. Managers have become adept at taking full advantage of the resources of *money, materials,* and *people;* but only recently have they begun to make effective use of the fourth major resource—*information.*

Making Decisions to Produce Products and Services

The four levels of information activity within a company are *strategic, tactical, operational,* and *clerical.* Computer-based information systems process data at the clerical level and provide information for managerial decision making at the strategic, tactical, and operational levels.

▶ Strategic-level managers determine long-term strategies and set corporate objectives and policy consistent with these objectives.

▶ Tactical-level managers are charged with the responsibility of implementing the objectives and policies set forth at the strategic level of management. To do this, managers identify specific tasks that need to be accomplished.

No matter where you are, computers can help you process data and make better decisions. Here, a group of mountain climbers are using a solar-charged notebook PC during their ascent of Mount Everest. The 1.8-pound solar panel is needed to recharge the notebook's batteries. The climbers used the notebook PC to record their use of supplies and to help them plan routes for the next day's climb.   Reprinted with permission of Compaq Computer Corporation. All Rights Reserved.

▶ Operational-level managers complete specific tasks as directed by tactical-level managers.

The business system model shown in Figure 10–1 helps place the decision-making environment in its proper perspective. As you can see, it is necessary for managers to use all the resources at their disposal more effectively, meet corporate objectives, and perform the management functions of *planning, organizing, leading,* and *controlling.*

Figure 10–1 illustrates how the corporate resources of *money, materials* (including facilities and equipment), *people,* and *information* become "input" to the various functional units, such as operations, sales, and accounting. People use their talent and knowledge, together with these resources, to produce products and services.

The business system acts in concert with several *entities,* such as employees, customers, and suppliers (see Figure 10–1). An entity is the source or destination of information flow. An entity also can be the source or destination of materials or product flow. For example, suppliers are a source of both information and materials. They are also the destination of payments for materials. The customer entity is the destination of products and the source of orders.

FIGURE 10–1 A Business System Model

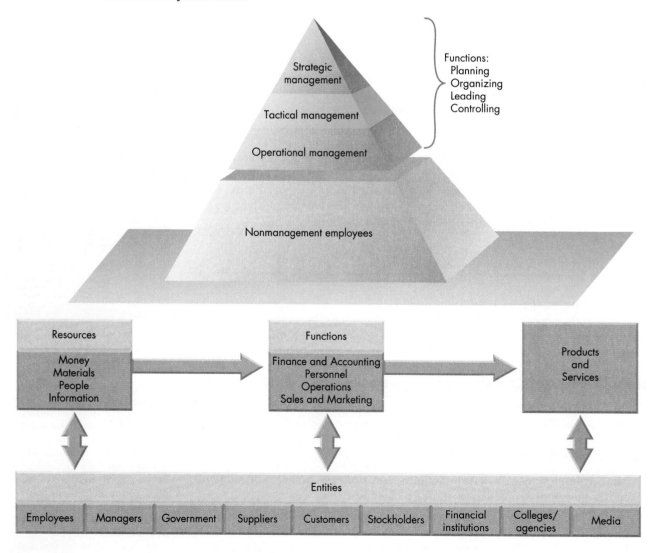

Companies are beginning to make their information resources available to customers. This retailer has installed an information kiosk that helps customers with their gift-buying decisions. Customers describe the person(s) for whom a gift is intended by entering sex, age, and lifestyle information. They also indicate how much they are willing to spend and they identify the occasion (birthday, wedding, anniversary, and so on). The system responds with gift ideas.
Courtesy of International Business Machines Corporation

Filtering Information: Getting the Right Information to the Right Person

The quality of an information system is judged by its output. A system that generates the same 20-page report for personnel at both the clerical and strategic levels defeats the purpose of an information system. The information needs at these two levels of activity are substantially different. For example, an administrative assistant might need names, dates of employment, and other data to enroll employees in a pension plan. The president of the company does not need that level of detail but does need information on overall employee pension contributions.

The key to developing quality information systems is to *filter* information so that people at the various levels of activity receive just the information they need to accomplish their job functions—no more, no less. **Filtering** information results in the *right information* reaching the *right decision maker* at the *right time* in the *right form*.

Clerical Level   Clerical-level personnel, those involved in repetitive tasks, are concerned primarily with *transaction handling*. You might say that these non-management clerical employees process data. For example, in a sales information system, order entry clerks key in customer orders on their terminals. In an airline reservation system, ticket agents confirm and make flight reservations.

Operational Level   Personnel at the operational level have well-defined short-term tasks that might span a day, a week, or as long as three months. Their information requirements often consist of *operational feedback*. In the sales information system, for example, the manager of the Eastern Regional Sales Department for Bravo International, a small high-tech firm, might want an end-of-quarter sales summary report (see Figure 10–2).

Managers at the operational, tactical, and strategic levels often request **exception reports** that highlight critical information. They can make such inquiries directly to the system using a query language (see the example in Figure 10–2).

The information available for an operational-level decision is often conclusive. That is, the most acceptable alternative can be clearly identified based on information available to the decision maker. At this level, personal judgment and intuition play a reduced role in the decision-making process.

FOUR-YEAR SALES TREND BY PRODUCT($1000)

PRODUCT	1994	1995	1996	1997	4-YEAR AVERAGE
ALPHAS	3,604	3,866	4,001	4,640	4,028
BETAS	1,106	2,240	2,855	3,590	2,448
GAMMAS	2,543	2,587	2,610	2,613	2,588
DELTAS	0	450	2,573	5,846	2,217
TOTALS	7,253	9,143	12,039	16,689	

FIGURE 10–2 Filtering of Information

A strategic-level sales-trend-by-product report shown in tabular and graphic formats. The sales-trend report and bar graph are prepared in response to inquiries from Bravo International's president, a strategic-level manager. Knowing that it is easier to detect trends in a graphic format than in a tabular one, the president requests that the trends be summarized in a bar graph. From the bar graph, the president easily can see that the sales of Alphas and Gammas are experiencing modest growth while the sales of Betas and Deltas are better.

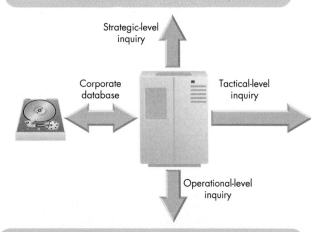

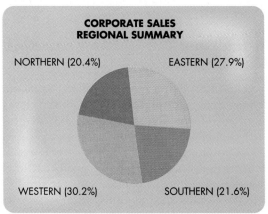

CORPORATE SALES
REGIONAL SUMMARY($1000)-1ST QUARTER

REGION	ALPHAS	BETAS	GAMMAS	DELTAS	TOTAL
EASTERN	321	233	224	367	1145
SOUTHERN	180	202	196	308	886
WESTERN	369	250	150	472	1241
NORTHERN	250	170	162	254	836
TOTALS	1120	855	732	1401	4108

A tactical-level sales summary report shown in tabular and graphic formats. The sales summary report and pie graph are prepared in response to inquiries from Bravo International's national sales manager, a tactical-level manager. The report presents dollar-volume sales by sales region for each of the company's four products. To get a better sense of the relative sales contribution of each of the four regional offices during the first quarter, the national sales manager requested that the total sales for each region be presented graphically in a pie graph.

SALES DEPARTMENT - EASTERN REGION
SALES SUMMARY ($1000) - 1ST QUARTER

SALESPERSON	ALPHAS	BETAS	GAMMAS	DELTAS	TOTAL
BAKER	70	10	14	65	159
COOK	60	40	37	77	214
JONES	55	28	40	57	180
LUCAS	20	50	48	68	186
MILLER	45	34	28	48	155
OTT	39	47	29	42	157
RITTER	32	24	28	10	94
TOTALS	321	233	224	367	1145

SALES DEPARTMENT - EASTERN REGION
SALES SUMMARY ($1000) - 1ST QUARTER
SALESPERSONS WITH SALES<$15,000 FOR ANY PRODUCT

SALESPERSON	ALPHAS	BETAS	GAMMAS	DELTAS	TOTAL
BAKER	70	10	14	65	159
RITTER	32	24	28	10	94

An operational-level sales summary and exception report. These sales reports are prepared in response to inquiries from an operational-level manager. The top report shows dollar-volume sales by salesperson for each of Bravo International's four products: Alphas, Betas, Gammas, and Deltas. In the report, the sales records of the top (Cook) and bottom (Ritter) performers are highlighted so that managers can use this range as a basis for comparing the performance of the other salespeople.

The eastern regional sales manager used a fourth-generation language to produce the exception report (bottom). The manager's request was: "Display a list of all eastern region salespeople who had sales of less than $15,000 for any product in this quarter." The report highlights the subpar performances of Baker and Ritter.

Tactical Level   At the tactical level, Bravo International managers concentrate on achieving a series of goals required to meet the objectives set at the strategic level. The information requirements are usually *periodic,* but on occasion managers require one-time and what if reports. *"What if" reports* are generated in response to inquiries that depict "what if" scenarios ("What if sales increase by 15% next quarter?"). Tactical managers are concerned primarily with operations and budgets from year to year. In the sales information system, the national sales manager, who is at the tactical level, might want the "Corporate Sales" report of Figure 10–2.

The information available for a tactical-level decision is seldom conclusive. That is, the most acceptable alternative cannot be identified from information alone. At this level, most decisions are made by using personal judgment and intuition in conjunction with available information.

Strategic Level   Bravo International's strategic-level managers are objective-oriented. Their information system requirements are often *one-time reports, "what if" reports,* and *trend analyses.* For example, the president of the company might ask for a report that shows the four-year sales trend for each of the company's four products and overall (Figure 10–2).

The information available for a strategic-level decision is almost never conclusive. To be sure, information is critical to strategic-level decision making, but virtually all decision makers at this level rely heavily on personal judgment and intuition.

Decisions: Easy Ones and Tough Ones

The two basic types of decisions are **programmed decisions** (easy ones) and **nonprogrammed decisions** (tough ones). Purely programmed decisions address well-defined problems. The decision maker has no judgmental flexibility because the actual decision is determined by existing policies or procedures. In fact, many such decisions can be made by a computer without human intervention! For example, the decision required to restock inventory levels of raw materials is often a programmed decision. This decision can be made by an individual or by a computer-based information system. When the inventory level of a particular item drops below the reorder point, perhaps a two months' supply, a decision is made to replenish the inventory by submitting an order to the supplier.

Nonprogrammed decisions involve unstructured problems (hard-to-define problems for which the rules are unclear). Such decisions are also called **information-based decisions** because the decision maker needs information in order to make a rational decision. The information requirement implies the need for managers to use

Here, flight controllers at the Johnson Space Center in Houston, Texas, witness the landing of the Space Shuttle *Discovery.* NASA's computer systems make routine programmed decisions, leaving the operators more time to make the more difficult information-based decisions. The trend toward relegating programmed decisions to computers is apparent in all industries.   NASA

judgment and intuition in the decision-making process. Corporate policies, procedures, standards, and guidelines provide substantial direction for nonprogrammed decisions made at the operational level, less direction at the tactical level, and little or no direction at the strategic level. The greater the programmability of a decision, the greater the confidence of the decision maker that the most acceptable alternative has been selected.

10–3 ALL ABOUT INFORMATION SYSTEMS

The Information System: What Is It?

Hardware, software, people, procedures, and *data* are combined to create an *information system* (see Figure 10–3). The term *information system* is a generic reference to a computer-based system that does two things:

▶ *Provides information processing capabilities for an individual or, perhaps, an entire company.* The processing capability refers to the system's ability to handle and process information (for example, order processing).

▶ *Provides information people need to make better, more informed decisions.* Information systems provide decision makers with *on-demand reports* and *inquiry capabilities* as well as *routine periodic reports.* Information systems can make programmed decisions without people being involved.

Six types of information systems are discussed in this chapter: *data processing systems, management information systems, decision support systems, executive information systems, expert systems,* and *software agents.* Each is described later in this chapter. The remainder of this section addresses important concepts that relate to information systems in general. These concepts apply to all types of information systems: PC-based systems, LAN-based systems, mainframe-based systems, and enterprise-wide client/server systems.

The Information System: What Can It Do?

Not surprisingly, an information system has the same four capabilities as a computer system: *input, processing, storage,* and *output* (see Figure 10–4).

Input The information system input capability can accept

▶ *Source data.* Source data result from the recording of a transaction or an event (for example, a bank deposit or the receipt of an order).

▶ *An inquiry.* An inquiry is any request for information.

▶ *A response to a prompt.* You might enter a *Y* or an *N.*

▶ *An instruction.* "Store file" or "Print invoice" could be instructions.

▶ *A message to another user on the system.*

▶ *A change.* When you edit a word processing document, you are entering change data.

Processing The information system processing capability encompasses

▶ *Sorting.* Use the sort capability to arrange data or records in some order (for example, alphabetizing a customer file by last name).

▶ *Retrieving, recording, and updating data in storage.* For example, a customer's record is retrieved from a database for processing, expense data are entered into an accounting system's database, and a customer's address is changed on a marketing database, respectively.

▶ *Summarizing.* Information may be presented in a condensed format to reflect totals and subtotals.

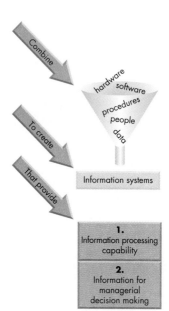

FIGURE 10–3 Creating an Information System

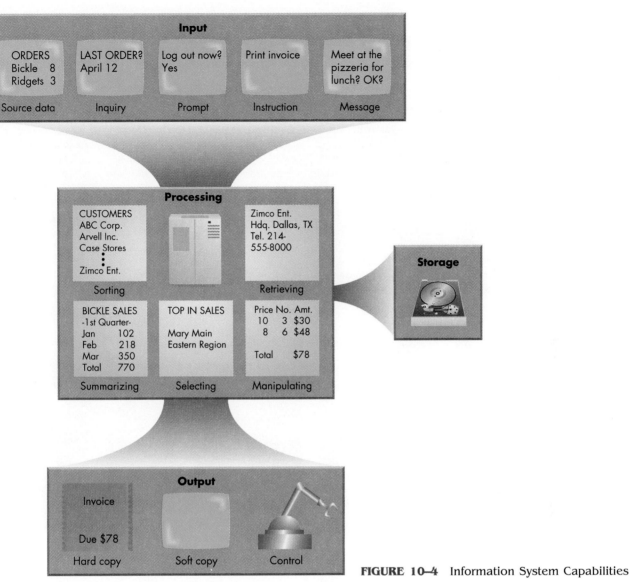

FIGURE 10–4 Information System Capabilities

▶ *Selecting.* Records can be selected by criteria (for example, "Select all employees with 25 or more years of service in the company").

▶ *Manipulating.* Arithmetic operations (addition, multiplication, and so on) and logic operations (comparing an employee's years of service to 25 to determine if they are greater than, equal to, or less than 25) can be performed.

Storage　The information system storage capability permits it to store *data, text, images* (graphs, pictures), and *other digital information* (voice messages) so that they can be recalled easily for further processing.

Output　The information system output capability allows it to produce output in a variety of formats:

▶ *Hard copy.* Printed reports, documents, and messages are hard copy.

▶ *Soft copy.* Temporary displays on terminal screens or voice mail messages are soft copy.

▶ *Control.* Instructions to industrial robots or automated processes are also output from an information system.

Emerging Technology

Robots and Robotics

Our vision of robots may still be in the days of Star Wars' R2D2 or Rosie Jetson's household robot, but things have changed in the last 10 years in the field of robotics. We often think of robotics, which is the integration of computers and robots, as associated with manufacturing and the use of industrial robots. Industrial robots are quite good at repetitive tasks and those that require precision movements, moving heavy loads, and working in hazardous areas. Nevertheless, robots are emerging as major players not only in manufacturing but in non-manufacturing industries, such as health care and other service industries. Already we can give robots crude human sensory capabilities and some degree of artificial intelligence. As these capabilities mature over the next decade, look for robots in other areas of the work place, in our homes, and even on stage and in museums.

Rudimentary Robotics The "steel-collar" work force throughout the world is made up of hundreds of thousands of industrial robots. The most common industrial robot is a single mechanical arm controlled by a computer. The arm, called a *manipulator*, has a shoulder, a forearm, and a wrist and is capable of performing the motions of a human arm. The manipulator is fitted with a hand designed to accomplish a specific task, such as painting, welding, picking and placing, and so on. The automotive industry is the largest user of such robots (for painting and welding) and the electronics industry (for circuit testing and connecting chips to circuit boards) is second.

Teaching Robots to Do Their Job A computer program is written to control the robot just as one is written to print payroll checks. It includes such commands as when to reach, in which direction to reach, how far to reach, when to grasp, and so on. Most robots are programmed to reach to a particular location, find a particular item, and then place it somewhere else. This simple application of robotics is called *pick and place*. Instead of a grasping mechanism, other robots are equipped with a

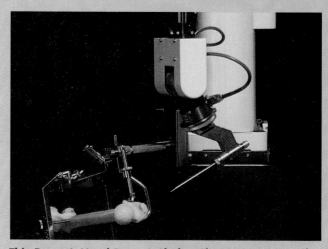

This Doctor's Hand Doesn't Shake The ROBODOC Surgical Assistant helps in the hip replacement. With a human surgeon present, ROBODOC machines a cavity in the patient's femur bone before the prosthetic implant is inserted. Courtesy of Integrated Surgical Systems Inc.

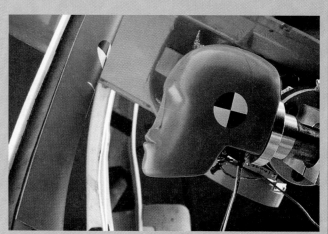

Mobile Robots Can Deliver What can work 24 hours a day, weighs 575 pounds, stands 4-feet-7-inches tall, always talks politely, blinks a lot, and is extremely dependable? It's HelpMate®, a trackless, robotic courier designed to perform material transport tasks for healthcare facilities. This robot can deliver mail, medication, supplies, and meal trays to the nursing units throughout the hospital. It can even use the elevator! Courtesy of Transactions Research Corporation

What a Headache At Ford's Auto Safety Center, a robot directs a crash dummy headform at targets in a vehicle interior. An impactor at the end of a robotic arm fires the headform at speeds up to 15 mph to gather data. The test results are used to improve occupant safety. Courtesy of Ford Motor Company

variety of industrial tools such as drills, paint guns, welding torches, and so on. Once programmed, robots do not need much attention. One plant manufactures vacuum cleaners 24 hours a day, 7 days a week!

Robots Come to Their Senses   Industrial robots are being equipped with rudimentary sensory capabilities, such as vision, that enable them to simulate human behavior. A robot with the added dimension of vision can be given some intelligence. (Robots without intelligence simply repeat preprogrammed motions.) Even though the technology for the vision systems is primitive, a robot can be "taught" to distinguish between dissimilar objects under controlled conditions. With this sensory subsystem, the robot has the capability of making crude but important decisions.

As vision system technology continues to improve, more and more robots will have *navigational capabilities* (the ability to move). Now most robots are stationary; those that are not can only detect the presence of an object in their path or are programmed to operate within a well-defined work area where the positions of all obstacles are known. Service industries using mobile-robot technology applications include hospitals, security and patrol, hazardous waste handling, bomb disposal, nuclear plant cleanup, rehabilitation programs, and the military.

Opportunities for Robots Are Growing

The number and variety of robotics applications are growing each day (see accompanying photographs). Even surgeons are using robots to help in brain surgery. In this application, robots can be set up to manipulate the surgical drill and biopsy needle with great accuracy, thereby making brain surgery faster, more accurate, and safer. Other surgical applications of robotics include help with hip replacements, knee replacements, and pelvic and spinal surgeries.

The future of robotics offers exciting opportunities. Companies are sure to take advantage of these opportunities to stay competitive. Who knows, we may someday have robots as workmates

The Robot Team   The precise, untiring movement of computer-controlled industrial robots helps assure quality in the assembly of everything from electrical components to automobiles. Here in this Chrysler Motors Corporation plant, 66 industrial robots apply spot welds. About 300 robots weld, seal, train, paint, clean, and handle material at this plant.   Chrysler Motors Corporation

Sweeping the Floors   This modular multifunction service robot can act as a kind of "surrogate body" for a human being. It can be equipped as an autonomous mobile robotic industrial sweeper vacuum cleaner. Or, when outfitted with the surveillance package, it can perform security surveillance and other monitoring tasks.   Courtesy of Cyberworks, Inc.

Robot Traffic   These computer-controlled automated guided vehicles (AGVs) are mobile robots. These AGVs are used in plants and warehouses for material and inventory handling. Photo courtesy of Litton Industries, Inc.

The Manual System: Opportunities for Automation

When we speak of an information system today, we imply an automated system. The elements of an information system are hardware, software, people, procedures, and data. The automated elements (the hardware and software) do not play a part in *manual systems*. Manual systems consist of people, procedures, and data. In terms of numbers, the overwhelming majority of systems in industry, government, and education are still manual. This is true of large organizations with hundreds of computers and of two-person companies. Tens of thousands of manual systems have been targeted to be upgraded to computer-based information systems. Ten times that many are awaiting tomorrow's creative users and computer professionals to identify their potential for computerization.

Both manual systems and computer-based information systems have an established pattern for work and information flow. In a manual payroll system, for example, a payroll clerk receives time sheets from supervisors; the clerk retrieves each employee's records from folders stored alphabetically in a file cabinet. The clerk uses a calculator to compute gross and net pay, then manually writes (or types) the payroll check and stub. Finally, the payroll clerk compiles the payroll register, which is a listing of the amount paid and the deductions for each employee, on a tally sheet with column totals. About the only way to find and extract information in a manual payroll system is to thumb through employee folders, a painstaking process.

Today most payroll systems have been automated. But look in any office in almost any company and you will find rooms full of filing cabinets, tabbed three-ring binders, circular address files, or drawers filled with 3×5 inventory cards. These manual systems are opportunities to improve a company's profitability and productivity through the application of computer and information technologies.

Function-Based and Integrated Information Systems

An information system can be either function-based or integrated. A **function-based information system** is designed for the exclusive support of a specific application area, such as inventory management or accounting. Its database and procedures are, for the most part, independent of any other system. The databases of function-based information systems invariably contain data that are maintained in other function-based systems within the same company. For example, much of the data needed for an accounting system would be duplicated in an inventory management system. It is not unusual for companies with a number of autonomous function-based systems to maintain customer data in 5 to 10 different databases. When a customer moves, the address must be updated in several databases (accounting, sales, distribution, and so on). This kind of data redundancy is an unnecessary financial burden to a company.

During the past decade, great strides have been made in the integration of function-based systems. The resulting **integrated information systems** share a common database. The common database helps minimize data redundancy and allows departments to coordinate their activities more efficiently.

Getting Data into the System: Data Entry Concepts

INTERNET BRIDGE

**Artificial
Intelligence**

Online versus Offline   As we discussed earlier, the four fundamental components of a computer system are input, processing, storage, and output. In a computer system, the input, output, and data storage components receive data from and transmit data to the processor over some type of transmission medium (coaxial cables, wireless transceivers, and so on). These hardware components are said to be *online* to the processor. Hardware devices that are not accessible to or under the control of a processor are said to be *offline*. A peripheral device that is connected to the processor, but not turned on, is considered offline. The concepts of online and offline also apply to data. Data are said to be *online* if they can be accessed and manipulated by the processor. All other machine-readable data are *offline*.

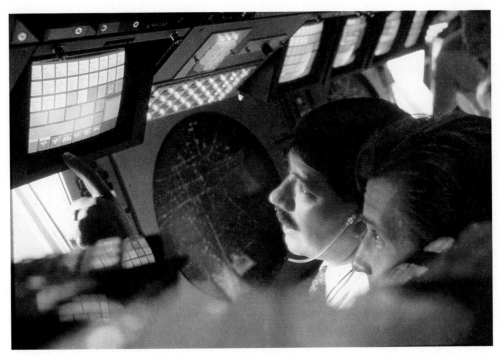

An integrated information system links people throughout the organization through a common database. When an air traffic controller routes an airplane, every controller has access to this routing information.   Courtesy of Harris Corporation

When you are logged in to a LAN from a PC, the data on a LAN file server are said to be online. When you log off you are offline. A CD-ROM in a cabinet is offline until it is inserted into the CD-ROM drive, at which time it is online.

Source Data   Most data do not exist in a form that can be "read" by the computer. For example, supervisors may record manually the hours worked by the staff on the time sheet. Before the payroll checks can be computed and printed, the data on these time sheets must be *transcribed* (converted) into a *machine-readable format* that can be interpreted by a computer. This is done in an *online* operation by someone at a PC or terminal. The time sheet is the **source document** and, as you might expect, the data on the time sheet are the **source data.**

Not all source data have to be transcribed. For example, the numbers printed at the bottom of your bank checks are your individual account number and bank number. They are already machine-readable, so they can be read directly by an input device. The UPC bar codes on consumer goods are machine-readable.

The paperless office is a goal that may be unreachable in the foreseeable future; however, many companies are encouraging greater use of source data automation to eliminate paperwork. This retailer enters order data directly to the system via a wireless data terminal, not to a hard-copy order form.
Courtesy of Norand Corporation

Approaches to Data Entry   The term *data entry* describes the process of entering data into an information system. Information systems are designed to provide users with display-screen prompts to make online data entry easier. The display on the operator's screen, for example, may be the image of the source document (such as a time sheet). A *prompt* is a brief message to the operator that describes what should be entered (for example, "Enter hours worked").

Data can be entered on a terminal or PC in the following ways:

▶ *Batch processing*. In **batch processing,** transactions are grouped, or batched, and entered consecutively, one after the other.

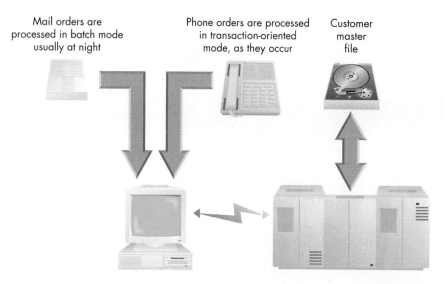

Mail orders are processed in batch mode usually at night

Phone orders are processed in transaction-oriented mode, as they occur

Customer master file

FIGURE 10–5 Batch and Transaction-Oriented Processing
The typical order entry system accepts orders by mail and by phone.

▶ *Transaction-oriented processing.* In **transaction-oriented processing,** transactions are entered to the system as they occur.

To illustrate the difference between batch and transaction-oriented processing, consider the order processing system for Bravo International (see Figure 10–5). The system accepts orders by both mail and phone. The orders received by mail are accumulated, or batched, for data entry—usually at night. There are no handwritten source documents for phone orders; people taking the phone orders interact with the computer via PCs or terminals and enter the order data online while talking with the customer.

Most data entered into mainframe-based enterprise-wide systems or into local area network–based systems is done online. This is true for both batch and transaction-oriented processing. In a mainframe environment, terminal and PC operators enter data *directly* into the host computer system for processing as shown in Figure 10–5. In a LAN, PC users interact directly with the file server. The primary advantage of transaction-oriented data entry is that records on the database are updated immediately, as the transaction occurs. With batch data entry, records are batched periodically. In a transaction-oriented environment, the database remains continuously up-to-date and can be queried at any time. In the example of Figure 10–5, a salesperson can check the availability of an item and tell the customer when to expect delivery.

10–4 DATA PROCESSING SYSTEMS

Data processing systems, or **DP systems,** are concerned with transaction handling and record-keeping, usually for a particular functional area. Data are entered and stored in a file format, and stored files are updated during routine processing. Periodic outputs include *action documents* (invoices) and *scheduled reports,* primarily for operational-level managers. The major drawback of data processing systems is that they are inflexible and cannot accommodate data processing or information needs that are not already built into the system. Most companies have moved beyond the scope of DP systems and now have systems with the flexibility of providing management with information in support of an ever-changing decision-making environment.

10–5 MANAGEMENT INFORMATION SYSTEMS

MIS/DSS/EIS

In the not-too-distant past, most payroll systems were data processing systems that did little more than process time sheets, print payroll checks, and keep running totals of annual wages and deductions. As managers began to demand more and better information about their personnel, payroll *data processing systems* evolved into human resource **management information systems.** A human resource management information system is capable of predicting the average number of worker sick days, monitoring salary equality between minority groups, making more effective use of available personnel skills, and providing other information needed at all three levels of management—operational, tactical, and strategic.

Here, engineers from San Diego Gas and Electric and Harris Corporation review final test information for a Harris XA/21 energy management system. The management information system controls and optimizes power flow while providing management with valuable information. *Courtesy of Harris Corporation*

The Management Information System: What Is It?

If you were to ask any five executives or computer professionals to define a management information system, or **MIS,** the only agreement you would find in their responses is that there is no agreement on its definition. An MIS has been called a method, a function, an approach, a process, an organization, a system, and a subsystem. The following working definition of *management information system* will be used in this book: *An MIS is a computer-based system that optimizes the collection, transfer, and presentation of information throughout an organization through an integrated structure of databases and information flow.*

The MIS versus the Data Processing System

The basic distinctions between an MIS and a DP system are summarized as follows:

- ▶ The integrated database of an MIS enables greater flexibility in meeting the information needs of management.
- ▶ An MIS integrates the information flow between functional areas (accounting, marketing, and so on) where DP systems tend to support a single functional area.
- ▶ An MIS caters to the information needs of all levels of management where DP systems focus on operational-level support.
- ▶ Management's information needs are supported on a more timely basis with an MIS (online inquiry capability) than with a DP system (usually scheduled reports).

Characteristics of Management Information Systems

The following are *desirable* characteristics of an MIS:

- ▶ An MIS supports the data processing functions of transaction handling and record-keeping.
- ▶ An MIS uses an integrated database and supports a variety of functional areas.
- ▶ An MIS provides operational-, tactical-, and strategic-level managers with easy access to timely but, for the most part, structured information.

GOING ONLINE

10.2
Some Advice Please

Go online to find comments on or reviews of any person, place, or thing (for example, a professional tennis player, Alaska, or a comic strip). You can find hundreds of newsgroups devoted to talking about celebrities and products (for example, cars).

Hand in: A printed comment or review along with the name and address (URL) of the source.

An MIS is somewhat flexible and can be adapted to meet changing information needs of the organization.

An MIS provides an envelope of system security that limits access to authorized personnel.

The MIS in Action

All major airlines rely on management information systems to facilitate day-to-day operations and provide valuable information for short- and long-term planning. At the core of such an MIS is the airline reservation subsystem. Airline reservation agents interact with the MIS's integrated database via remote terminals to update the database the moment a seat on any flight is filled or becomes available.

An airline MIS does much more than keep track of flight reservations. Departure and arrival times are closely monitored so that ground crew activities can be coordinated. The system offers many kinds of management information needs: the number of passenger miles flown, profit per passenger on a particular flight, percent of arrivals on time, average number of empty seats on each flight for each day of the week, and so on.

You may be interested to know that airlines routinely overbook flights; that is, they book seats they do not have. The number of extra seats sold is based on historical "no-show" statistics compiled by the MIS from data in the integrated database. Although these statistics provide good guidelines, occasionally everyone does show up!

The influence of management information systems is just as pervasive in hospitals (patient accounting, point-of-care processing, and so on), insurance (claims-processing systems, policy administration, actuarial statistics, and so on), colleges (student registration, placement, and so on), and other organizations that use computers for information processing and to gather information for decision making.

10–6   DECISION SUPPORT SYSTEMS

The Decision Support System: What Is It?

Managers spend much of their day gathering and analyzing information before making a decision. Decision support systems were created to assist managers in this task. **Decision support systems (DSS)** are interactive information systems that rely on an integrated set of user-friendly hardware and software tools to produce and present information targeted to support management in the decision-making process. On many occasions, decisions makers can rely on their experience to make a quality decision, or they need look no further than the information that is readily available from the integrated corporate MIS. However, decision makers, especially at the tactical and strategic levels, are often confronted with complex decisions whose factors are beyond their human abilities to synthesize properly. These types of decisions are "made to order" for decision support systems.

A decision support system can help close the information gap and allow managers to improve the quality of their decisions. To do this, DSS hardware and software employ the latest technological innovations, planning and forecasting models, user-oriented 4GLs, and even artificial intelligence.

In many cases, the DSS facilitates the decision-making process, helping a decision maker choose between alternatives. Some DSSs can automatically rank alternatives based on the decision maker's criteria. Decision support systems also help remove the tedium of gathering and analyzing data. For example, managers are no longer strapped with such laborious tasks as manually entering and totaling rows and columns of numbers. Graphics software helps managers generate illustrative bar and pie graphs in a matter of minutes. And, with the availability of a variety of user-oriented DSSs, managers can get the information they need without having to depend on direct technical assistance from a computer professional.

The DSS versus the MIS

As we have mentioned before, management information systems are best at supporting decisions that involve *structured* problems, such as when to replenish raw materials inventory and how much to order. This type of routine operational-level decision is based on production demands, the cost of holding the inventory, and other variables that depend on the use of the inventory item. The MIS integrates these variables into an inventory model and presents specific order information (for example, order quantity and order date) to the manager in charge of inventory management.

In contrast to the MIS, decision support systems are designed to support decision-making processes involving *semistructured* and *unstructured* problems. A semistructured problem might be the need to improve the delivery performance of suppliers. The problem is partially structured in that information comparing the on-time delivery performance of suppliers can be obtained directly from the integrated database supporting the MIS. The unstructured facets of the problem, such as extenuating circumstances, rush-order policy and pricing, and so on, make this problem a candidate for a DSS.

An example of an entirely unstructured problem would be the evaluation and selection of an alternative to the raw material currently used. A decision maker might enlist the aid of a DSS to provide information on whether it would be advisable to replace a steel component with a plastic or aluminum one. The information requirements for such a decision are diverse and typically beyond the scope of an MIS.

Another distinction we can make between an MIS and a DSS is that an MIS is designed and created to support a set of applications. A DSS is a set of decision support tools that can be adapted to any decision environment.

Characteristics of Decision Support Systems

The following are *desirable* characteristics of a DSS:

- A DSS helps the decision maker in the decision-making process.
- A DSS is designed to address semistructured and unstructured problems.
- A DSS supports decision makers at all levels, but it is most effective at the tactical and strategic levels.
- A DSS is an interactive, user-friendly system that can be used by the decision maker with little or no assistance from a computer professional.
- A DSS makes general-purpose models, simulation capabilities, and other analytical tools available to the decision maker.
- A DSS can be readily adapted to meet the information requirements of any decision environment.
- A DSS can interact with the corporate database.
- A DSS is not executed in accordance with a pre-established production schedule.

The DSS Tool Box

A decision support system is made up of a set of decision support tools that can be adapted to any decision environment (see Figure 10–6). The combination of these general-purpose tools helps managers address decision-making tasks in specific application areas (the evaluation and promotion of personnel, the acquisition of companies, and so on). DSS tools include the following:

GOING ONLINE

10.3
Hello, Mrs. Robinson

Musicians routinely cruise the Internet contributing everything from original music to arrangements of popular songs. Explore some of these music sites.

Hand in: A copy of the words to the first verse of Paul Simon's classic song "Mrs. Robinson" and to one of your favorite songs. Identify the source (URL) for each song. *Hint: Start with keywords "paul," "simon," and "robinson."*

Serendipitous Surfing:
Distance Learning

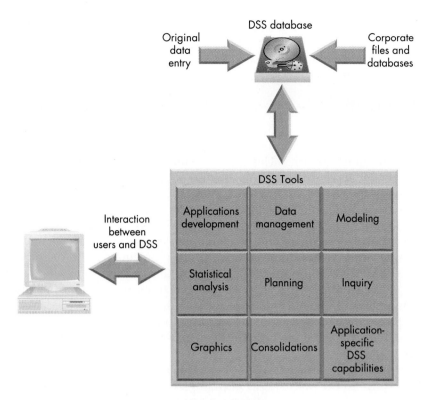

FIGURE 10–6 The Decision Support System
A decision support system is a set of software and hardware tools that can be adapted to any decision environment.

▶ *Applications development.* Some decision support systems provide users with the capability of developing computer-based systems to support the decision-making process. These applications typically involve the input, processing, and storing of data and the output of information. The ease with which DSS applications can be created has spawned a new term—**throwaway systems.** Often DSS applications are developed to support a one-time decision and are then discarded.

▶ *Data management.* Each DSS software package has its own unique approach to database management—that is, the software mechanisms for the storage, maintenance, and retrieval of data. This DSS tool is necessary to ensure compatibility of a DSS database and an integrated set of DSS tools. Typically, this DSS tool enables access to a wide variety of databases. For example, the DSS data management tool can *import* and use data from a mainframe-based database or a PC-based spreadsheet. The DSS data management tool also can do the reverse, that is, *export* DSS data for use by another program.

▶ *Modeling.* Decision support systems enable managers to use mathematical modeling techniques to re-create the functional aspects of a system within the confines of a computer. These simulation models are appropriate when decisions involve a number of factors. For example, models are often used when uncertainty and risk are introduced, when several decision makers are involved, and when multiple outcomes are anticipated. In these cases, each decision needs to be evaluated on its own merit.

In the business community, managers use modeling DSS software to simulate sales, production, demand, and much more. Simulation techniques are

System Development

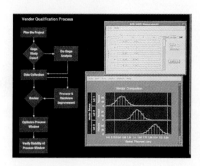 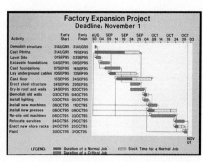 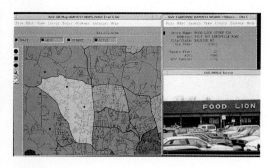

SAS Institute has long been a leader in the creation of DSS and EIS software. SAS/QC software (left) helps identify problems, design experiments to improve a product or process, use control charts, and analyze process capability. SAS/OR software (middle) provides a range of decision support tools for solving management problems. SAS/GIS software (right) enables maps to be combined with other types of information to create geographic information system. SAS/QC(R), SAS/OR(R), and SAS/GIS(R) software, courtesy of SAS Institute Inc. SAS, SAS/QC, SAS/OR, SAS/GIS are registered trademarks of SAS Institute Inc., Cary, NC, USA

being applied to other aspects of life as well. Simulations have proven effective in predicting social, environmental, and biological trends.

▶ *Statistical analysis.* The DSS statistical analysis capability includes everything from simple statistics such as *average, median,* and *standard deviation* to more analytical techniques such as *regression analysis* and *exponential smoothing* to complex procedures such as *multivariate analysis.* Risk analysis and trend analysis are common applications of DSS statistical tools.

▶ *Planning.* Managers are often faced with making decisions that will be implemented at some time in the future. To help them get a glimpse into the future, they rely on DSS software that permits *forecasting, "what if" analysis,* and *goal seeking.* In what if analysis, managers make inquiries such as, "What would be the impact on sales if we boost the advertising budget by 30%?" In goal seeking, managers make inquiries such as, "How much do we need to increase the advertising budget to achieve a goal of $120 million in sales for next year?"

▶ *Inquiry.* DSS software enables managers to make online inquiries to the DSS database using English-like commands (for example, a natural language interface with a fourth-generation language). Users who query corporate databases are able to communicate with computers in much the same language that they would use to communicate with their colleagues.

▶ *Graphics.* With the graphics DSS tool, managers can create a variety of presentation graphics based on data in the DSS database, including bar graphs, pie graphs, and line graphs. The graphics tool allows you to "drill down" into a graph to uncover additional information. For example, a user viewing a *monthly* sales bar graph can "drill down" and display a *weekly* sales bar graph for any given month.

▶ *Consolidations.* DSS tools are available that enable the consolidation of like data from different sources. An example use of this DSS tool is the consolidation of financial statements from subsidiary companies into a single corporate financial statement.

▶ *Application-specific DSS capabilities.* DSS tools that support a particular decision environment, such as financial analysis and quality control, are being introduced routinely into the marketplace.

The executive information system (EIS) can be as mobile as the executives who use it. This executive relies on the EIS during presentations.
Courtesy of International Business Machines Corporation

Executive Information Systems: The Executive's DSS

Just as user managers and the computer community are finally getting a handle on the scope and functionality of decision support systems, a new type of information system is conceived. Now we have the **executive information system.** Like its predecessors, the MIS and the DSS, the term *executive information system,* or **EIS,** has been introduced with fanfare and anticipation but without a common understanding of what it is. The EIS offers the same decision support tools as the DSS but each tool is designed specifically to support decision making at the executive levels of management, primarily the tactical and strategic levels. Like the MIS and the DSS, the EIS may eventually gain an identity of its own, but today's commercially available executive information systems look suspiciously like what most managers have come to know as decision support systems.

10–7 EXPERT SYSTEMS

Expert Systems/ Software Agents

The kinds of problems that can be addressed by computers extend well past those usually associated with computation. They can now address problems requiring the kind of intelligence associated with people. Research in *artificial intelligence (AI)* has added a new dimension to computing—the ability to reason and possess crude sensory perceptions. This enables computers to take on many new tasks. For example, it has proven to be an effective marriage counselor and a wise corporate colleague. The software that gives the computer these human-like capabilities is the expert system.

The Expert System: What Is It?

The **expert system** is a recent addition to the circle of information systems. Like the DSS, expert systems are computer-based systems that help managers resolve problems or make better decisions. However, expert systems, which are also referred to as *cased-based reasoning systems,* do this with a decidedly different twist. An expert system is an interactive computer-based system that responds to questions, asks for clarification, makes recommendations, and generally helps the user in the decision-making process. In effect, working with an expert system is much like working directly with a human expert to solve a problem because the system mirrors the human thought process. It even uses information supplied by a real expert in a particular field such as medicine, taxes, or geology. Expert systems are particular adept at making critical decisions that we aren't making because of lack of time, interest, resources, knowledge, and so on. In many ways, expert systems re-create the decision process better than humans do. We tend to miss important considerations or alternatives—computers don't.

This loan officer works with an expert system when advising loan applicants.   Courtesy of International Business Machines Corporation

An expert system applies preset IF-THEN rules to solve a particular problem, such as determining a patient's illness. Like management information systems and decision support systems, expert systems rely on factual knowledge, but expert systems also rely on *heuristic knowledge* such as intuition, judgment, and inferences. Both the factual knowledge and the heuristic rules of thumb are acquired from a *domain expert,* an expert in a particular field, such as jet engine repair, life insurance, or property assessment. The expert system uses this human-supplied knowledge to model the human thought process within a particular area of expertise. Once completed, an expert system can approximate the logic of a well-informed human decision maker.

Technically speaking, an *expert system* is the highest form of a **knowledge-based system.** In practice, the terms *expert system* and *knowledge-based system* are used interchangeably. The less sophisticated knowledge-based systems are called **assistant systems.** An assistant system helps users make relatively straightforward decisions. Assistant systems are usually implemented to reduce the possibility that the end user will make an error in judgment rather than to resolve a particular problem. For example, assistant systems are used to help people make online charge-card approvals and quote rates for life insurance.

In effect, expert systems simulate the human thought process. To varying degrees, they can *reason, draw inferences,* and *make judgments.* Here is how an expert system works. Let's use a medical diagnosis expert system as an example. Upon examining a patient, a physician might use an expert diagnosis system to get help in diagnosing the patient's illness or, perhaps, to get a second opinion. First the doctor would relate the symptoms to the expert system: male, age 10, temperature of 103°, and swollen glands about the neck. Needing more information, the expert system might ask the doctor to examine the parotid gland for swelling. Upon receiving an affirmative answer, the system might ask a few more questions and even ask for lab reports before giving a diagnosis. A final question for the physician might be whether the patient had been previously afflicted with or immunized for parotitis. Based on the information, the expert system would diagnose the illness as parotitis, otherwise known as the mumps.

In recent years expert systems have been developed to support decision makers in a broad range of disciplines, including medical diagnosis, oil exploration, financial planning, tax preparation, chemical analysis, surgery, locomotive repair, weather prediction, computer repair, trouble-shooting satellites, computer systems configuration, nuclear power plant operation, newspaper layout, interpreting government regulations, and many others.

MEMORY BITS

Information Systems

- Data processing (DP) system
  —Functional area support
  —Transaction handling and record-keeping
- Management information system (MIS)
  —Integrated database
  —DP functions plus management information
- Decision support system (DSS)
  —Interactive system
  —Various tools that support decision making
- Executive information system (EIS)
  —Subset of DSS
  —Decision support at tactical and strategic levels
- Expert system
  —Interactive knowledge-based system
  —Simulates human thought process
- Software agent
  —Has the authority to act on our behalf
  —Performs a variety of tasks

An Expert System Example: Technical Support

Anyone who has owned a printer for any length of time has had it act up or, worse, refuse to act at all. You don't have many alternatives when this happens. You can try to decipher an often-incomplete manual, call a knowledgeable friend, or bite the bullet and call an expensive professional. Now, Compaq printers offer a more palatable alternative—an expert system. These expert systems do what Compaq call-in technical service people used to do—work their customers through the problem to a solution. A knowledge base was extracted from the knowledge of technical service personnel who have handled thousands of such calls. The knowledge base contains:

1. The identification of problem(s) to be solved
2. Possible solutions to the problem(s)
3. How to progress from problem to solution (primarily through facts and rules of inference)

All of this knowledge is integrated in an interactive online expert system that can help users solve most problems in a matter of minutes.

This expert system is probably the beginning of a new trend in technical support. Hardware and software vendors can't afford very many calls from a customer before their profit from the sale of a product has eroded. Major vendors have hundreds (a few have thousands) of people doing nothing but handling calls for technical support. In some companies, 25% of their employees staff the tech support lines. In a very few years, look for vendors to integrate more and more expert systems in to their tech support strategies. The trend to this alternative form of customer service may not reach its full potential until most customers have CD-ROM–based PCs. Compaq estimates that the expert system for one line of printers will reduce customer services costs by $10 million to $20 million a year.

Are Expert Systems in Your Future?

One of the myths surrounding expert systems is that they will replace human experts. While expert systems augment the capabilities of humans and make them more productive, they will never replace them. Expert systems and humans complement one another in the decision-making process. The computer-based expert system can handle routine situations with great accuracy, thereby relieving someone of the burden of a detailed manual analysis. Humans can combine the insight of an expert system with their flexible intuitive abilities to resolve complex problems.

The number and variety of expert system applications have increased dramatically with the advent of powerful, cost-effective PCs. Expert systems advise financial analysts on the best mix of investments; help taxpayers interpret the tax laws; help computer repairpersons diagnose the problems of a malfunctioning computer; and help independent insurance agents select the best overall coverage for their business clients.

In the short period of their existence, expert systems have operated impressively and they continue to improve. Decision makers in every environment are developing or contemplating developing an expert system. Attorneys will hold mock trials with expert systems to "pre-try" their cases. Doctors routinely will ask a second opinion. Architects will "discuss" the structural design of a building with an expert system. Military officers will "talk" with the "expert" to plan battlefield strategy. City planners will "ask" an expert system to suggest optimal locations for recreational facilities.

Some computer industry observers believe that expert systems are the wave of the future and that each of us will have "expert" help and guidance at home and in our respective professions.

10–8 SOFTWARE AGENTS: WORKING FOR US

In days of yore, well-to-do people had butlers and maids to do their bidding, day and night (some still do). A recent innovation in information technology may enable a return to the days of yore—sort of. In cyberland, **software agents** will "live" in our computer systems and assist us with the chores of life, both at home and at work. Software agents, like expert systems, are a type of artificial intelligence.

A software agent has the authority to act on our behalf, just as a human agent does. We set the goals for our agents and the agents act to reach those goals. The agent reacts to meet the demands of a specified goal.

> ▶ The agent may remain in continuous motion working toward an ongoing goal.

> ▶ The agent performs an action when a specified event occurs.

> ▶ The agent performs actions needed to accomplish a one-time goal.

For example, you might ask an agent to alert you one week prior to birthdays of selected friends and relatives (an ongoing goal). A week before a birthday, the agent will alert you (an action triggered by an event).

> Ryan's 30th birthday is Monday, March 3.
> Last year you sent a humorous e-mail birthday greeting.

At this point the agent is poised to respond to your request. The agent is set up to send an e-mail or postal greeting, send flowers (you specify price range), or arrange a party and send out announcements. If you wish, you can instruct the agent to purchase and deliver a present to Ryan (a one-time goal). The agent's response is based on the information contained in Ryan's profile (mutual friends, preferences, and so on). If you give an agent the authority to handle all birthdays, you may never have to worry about birthdays again. Of course, if the agent plans a party, you should attend.

In a few years, our agents will be helping us do a wide variety of jobs.

> ▶ A sailor might instruct the agent to alert her to favorable wind conditions at the local lake. To do this the agent must tap weather information on a regular basis.

> ▶ The agent can sort through e-mail. The agent scans each message and routes junk e-mail to the electronic equivalent of file 13.

> ▶ We can ask our agents to scan online newspapers and magazines for articles in our interest areas (for example, college basketball, folk music, environmental issues).

> ▶ We can tell the software agent the type of vacation we want to book and it will comb through online databases, looking for the best combination of price and luxury. When the agent reports back, we can make our selection and the agent will make the reservations.

As you can see, the possibilities for agents are endless. Agents are already at work doing hundreds of tasks; however, we may have to wait a few years before the agents automatically send flowers on Mother's Day. The wait may be shorter than you think because companies are already developing software agents and a number of major companies, including America Online and AT&T, are developing products and services that will accommodate these agents.

Software agents scurry around the network helping this network administrator handle a wide range of network management tasks.
Courtesy of Dynatech Corporation

INTERNET BRIDGE

Computers at Work

It won't be long before our computers are online 24 hours a day to our office, home, college, and the information superhighway. As we evolve to an environment in which PCs are perpetually online, look for software agents to take on an ever increasing workload. Unlike butlers and maids who slept at night and rested on weekends, software agents never stop working for us.

IMPORTANT TERMS AND SUMMARY OUTLINE

assistant system 95
batch processing 87
data processing (DP) system 88
decision support system (DSS) 90
exception report 79
executive information system (EIS) 94
expert system 95

filtering 79
function-based information system 86
information-based decision 81
integrated information system 86
knowledge-based system 95
management information system (MIS) 88

nonprogrammed decision 81
programmed decision 81
software agent 97
source data 87
source document 87
throwaway system 92
transaction-oriented processing 88

10–1 AN END TO BUSINESS AS USUAL New and innovative uses of information technology are being implemented every day. Each company has a seemingly endless number of opportunities to use technology to achieve a competitive edge for money spent on information technology yields tremendous returns.

10–2 INFORMATION AND DECISION MAKING Traditionally managers have been very adept at taking full advantage of the resources of money, materials, and people, but only recently have they begun to make effective use of information, the other resource. By **filtering** information, the right information reaches the right decision maker at the right time in the right form.

Information systems help process data at the clerical level and provide information for managerial decision making at the operational, tactical, and strategic levels. Managers at the operational, tactical, and strategic levels often request **exception reports** that highlight critical information. For decisions made at the tactical and strategic levels, information is often inconclusive, and managers also must rely on their experience, intuition, and common sense to make the right decision.

The two basic types of decisions are **programmed decisions** and **nonprogrammed decisions.** Purely programmed decisions address well-defined problems. Nonprogrammed decisions, also called **information-based decisions,** involve ill-defined and unstructured problems.

10–3 ALL ABOUT INFORMATION SYSTEMS Hardware, software, people, procedures, and data are combined to create an information system. An information system provides companies with data processing capabilities and the company's people with information.

Types of information systems include *data processing systems, management information systems, decision support systems, executive information systems, expert systems,* and *software agents.* An information system has the same four capabilities as a computer system: input, processing, storage, and output. The processing capabilities include sorting; accessing, recording, and updating data in storage; summarizing; selecting; and manipulating.

An information system can be either function-based or integrated. A **function-based information system** is designed for the exclusive support of a specific application area. **Integrated information systems** share a common database.

In a computer system, the input, output, and data storage components that receive data from and transmit data to the processor are said to be *online.* Hardware devices that are not accessible to or under the control of a processor are said to be *offline.* **Source data** on **source documents** must be transcribed into a machine-readable format before they can be interpreted by a computer. Data entry describes the process of entering data into an information system.

When transactions are grouped together for processing, it is called **batch processing.** In **transaction-oriented processing,** transactions are entered as they occur.

10–4 DATA PROCESSING SYSTEMS **Data processing (DP) systems** are file-oriented, function-based systems that focus on transaction handling and record-keeping and provide periodic output aimed primarily at operational-level management.

10–5 MANAGEMENT INFORMATION SYSTEMS The authors offer the following definition of a **management information system,** or **MIS:** An MIS is a computer-based system that optimizes the collection, transfer, and presentation of information throughout an organization through an integrated structure of databases and information flow.

An MIS not only supports the traditional data processing functions but also relies on an integrated database to provide managers at all levels with easy access to timely but structured information. An MIS is flexible and can provide system security.

An MIS is oriented to supporting decisions that involve structured problems.

10–6 DECISION SUPPORT SYSTEMS **Decision support systems** are interactive information systems that rely on an integrated set of user-friendly hardware and software tools to produce and present information targeted to support management in the decision-making process.

A **DSS** supports decision making at all levels by making general-purpose models, simulation capabilities, and other analytical tools available to the decision maker. A DSS can be readily adapted to meet the information requirements of any decision environment.

In contrast to the MIS, decision support systems are designed to support decision-making processes involving semistructured and unstructured problems.

A decision support system is made up of a set of software tools and hardware tools. The categories of DSS software tools include applications development (frequently resulting in **throwaway systems**), data management (including the ability to import and export data), modeling, statistical analysis, planning, inquiry, graphics, consolidations, and application-specific DSS capabilities. We

use the term *import* to describe the process of converting data in one format to a format that is compatible with the calling program, in this case the data management tool. The DSS data management tool also can do the reverse, that is, *export* DSS data for use by another program, perhaps a DBMS or a PC-based database package.

The **executive information system's (EIS)** tool box is designed specifically to support decision making at the tactical and strategic levels of management.

10–7 EXPERT SYSTEMS **Expert systems,** which are associated with an area of research known as artificial intelligence, help managers resolve problems or make better decisions. They are interactive systems that respond to questions, ask for clarification, make recommendations, and generally help in the decision-making process. An expert system is the highest form of a **knowledge-based system,** but in practice the two terms are used interchangeably. The less sophisticated knowledge-based systems are called **assistant systems.**

The user interface component of an expert system enables the interaction between end user and expert system needed for heuristic processing. Some computer industry observers believe that expert systems are the wave of the future and that each of us will have "expert" help and guidance at home and in our respective professions.

10–8 SOFTWARE AGENTS: WORKING FOR US **Software agents,** a type of artificial intelligence, have the authority to act on our behalf, just as human agents do. We set the goals for our software agents and they act to reach those goals.

REVIEW EXERCISES

Concepts

1. MIS is an abbreviation for what term?
2. What is the purpose of an exception report?
3. What elements are combined to create an information system?
4. What are the levels of organizational activity, from specific to general?
5. Which type of information system would most closely approximate working directly with a human expert to solve a problem?
6. Which of the following information systems is designed specifically for decision support at the tactical and strategic levels of management: expert systems, management information systems, DP systems, or executive information systems?

7. In which type of processing are transactions grouped together for processing?
8. What are the two basic types of decisions?
9. What is meant by filtering information?
10. List seven items in the DSS software tool box.
11. Distinguish between online operation and offline operation.
12. What do expert systems and assistant systems have in common?

Discussion and Problem Solving

13. For each of the three levels of management illustrated in the business system model in Figure 10–1, what would the horizon (time span) be for planning decisions? Explain.

14. In general, top executives have always treated money, materials, and people as valuable resources, but only recently have they recognized that information is also a valuable resource. Why do you think they waited so long?

15. It is often said that "time is money." Would you say that "information is money"? Discuss.

16. Give examples of reports that might be requested by an operational-level manager in an insurance company. By a tactical-level manager. By a strategic-level manager.

17. Contrast a DP system with an MIS. Contrast an MIS with a DSS.

18. Describe a specific decision environment that would be appropriate for the implementation of an expert system.

19. Suppose the company you work for batches all sales data for data entry each night. You have been asked to present a convincing argument to top management about why funds should be allocated to convert the current system to transaction-oriented data entry. What would you say?

20. Describe one way that a software agent might be able to help you at home. Describe another application for software agents that would help you at work.

21. Reflect on your activities of the past week and identify those activities that generate source data for information systems.

SELF-TEST (BY SECTION)

10–1 Money spent on information technology yields tremendous returns. (T/F)

10–2 **a.** Tactical-level managers are charged with the responsibility of implementing the objectives and policies set forth at the _____ level of management.
b. It is easier for a manager to detect trends presented in a graphic format than in a tabular format. (T/F)
c. Nonprogrammed decisions are also called: (a) computer-oriented decisions, (b) information-based decisions, or (c) human decisions?

10–3 **a.** The summarizing activity would be associated with which capability of an information system: (a) input, (b) output, or (c) processing?
b. An integrated information system is designed for the exclusive support of a specific application area. (T/F)
c. A CD-ROM sitting on a shelf is said to be _____ (online or offline).

10–4 The focus of data processing systems is _____ and _____.

10–5 **a.** An MIS provides an envelope of system security that limits access to authorized personnel. (T/F)
b. Which type of information system integrates the information flow between functional areas: (a) DP system, (b) MIS, or (c) DSS?

10–6 **a.** Decision support systems are designed to support decision-making processes involving semistructured and unstructured problems. (T/F)
b. A DSS is most effective at which two levels of management: (a) clerical and operational, (b) operational and tactical, or (c) tactical and strategic?
c. DSS applications that are discarded after providing information support for a one-time decision are called _____.
d. An MIS is a subset of an EIS. (T/F)

10–7 **a.** An assistant system is the highest form of a knowledge-based system. (T/F)
b. Which type of information system has the greatest potential to reduce dependencies on critical personnel: (a) MIS, (b) expert system, or (c) DP system?

10–8 Software agents fall under which of these software umbrellas: (a) operating systems, (b) data management, or (c) artificial intelligence?

Self-test Answers. **10–1** T. **10–2 (a)** strategic; **(b)** T; **(c)** b. **10–3 (a)** c; **(b)** F; **(c)** offline. **10–4** transaction handling, record-keeping. **10–5 (a)** T; **(b)** b. **10–6 (a)** T; **(b)** c; **(c)** throwaway systems; **(d)** F. **10–7 (a)** F; **(b)** b. **10–8** c.

CHAPTER 11

Computers in Society

Courtesy of International Business Machines Corporation

Let's Talk

The following conversation introduces many of the terms in this chapter. Read it now, then again after you have read the chapter.

The Scene:
Company picnic conversations usually are about "the company." At the BestCo picnic, a claims adjustor (David), an assistant VP of operations (Julia), and a receptionist (Sandra) talk openly.

Sandra: Julia, I understand you've been put in charge of evaluating **system security.**

Julia: Yes, our **physical security** is in pretty good shape. Our network is **fault-tolerant** with a **UPS** for each server. But, our **logical security** needs improvement.

David: With our open work areas, we probably do need another level of security over and above **user IDs** and **passwords.**

Julia: I agree—we're doing two things to protect user access. As soon as all systems are upgraded with sound boards, users will need to enter their **voice print** to gain access to sensitive data.

Sandra: What a great idea. What else are we doing?

Julia: You should get a memo tomorrow announcing the complete redesign of all cubicles and offices.

David: Hallelujah! It's about time.

Julia: We hired a human factors consultant to ensure that all work places are **ergonomically** designed. We purchased over four hundred ergonomic keyboards to minimize **RSIs—repetitive-stress injuries.**

Sandra: Maybe these new workstations will help my **carpal tunnel syndrome.**

David: As long as we're talking about improving the work place, how about scrapping the **computer monitoring?** It makes me feel like someone's looking over my shoulder all day.

Sandra: I'm with you, David.

Julia: Management is looking at personal privacy issues one at a time. They've decided to stop monitoring interoffice e-mail. But, computer monitoring may remain in place for a while.

David: Well, I'm really looking forward to working in a modern office. Anyone for seconds on the baked beans?

STUDENT LEARNING OBJECTIVES

▶ *To become aware of the relationship between career mobility and computer knowledge.*

▶ *To identify ergonomic and environmental considerations in the design of the knowledge worker's work place.*

▶ *To explore ethical questions concerning the use of information technology.*

▶ *To identify points of security vulnerability for a computer center, an information system, and a PC.*

11-1 THE VIRTUAL FRONTIER

The *virtual frontier* may be the last great frontier. Much of what lies beyond the virtual horizon is uncharted and potentially dangerous territory. Even so, wagon trains filled with brave pioneers set out each day to blaze new electronic trails. The virtual frontier is sometimes likened to the Wild West because there are no rules. Responsible pioneers accept and live by society's acceptable rules of behavior, but the seedier elements of society are quick to observe that there is no virtual sheriff.

The virtual frontier encompasses the electronic highways that comprise the Internet, thousands of BBSs, scores of information services, and thousands of private networks. The *information superhighway* metaphor is frequently used as a collective reference to these electronic links that have wired our world. This metaphor, though some feel it is inappropriate, is used by many and will probably remain in common usage for some time. There is no official name for our wired world. The government is beginning talk about a *National Information Infrastructure* (*NII*), while the media continues to create more descriptors for the virtual frontier, such as *I-way, infobahn,* and *cyberspace.* Whatever it is or will be called, it eventually will connect virtually every facet of our society.

It's difficult to fathom the hardships endured by nineteenth-century pioneers who headed west for a better life. Imagine a hearty pioneer woman pushing a Conestoga wagon through the mud while her husband coaxes their oxen to pull harder. The hardships along the electronic trails are not as physical or life-threatening, but they exist. We're still sloshing through the virtual mud in the virtual frontier. When we find a road, it's more like a trail or a roadway under construction than a highway. The few highways that exist are narrow, filled with potholes, and have many detours.

The virtual frontier is growing much like the Wild West. In the western frontier, cities grew from nothing overnight. In the virtual frontier, major services or capabilities unheard of a few years ago are being introduced every day. In the Wild West, many years passed before the ranchers and the farmers could be friends. The same may be true of telecommunications industries in the virtual frontier. Outlaws roamed the Wild West creating havoc until law and order was established. Electronic outlaws may have their way in the virtual frontier, as well, until cybercops armed with strict cyberlaws drive them out of town.

The opportunity for a better life enticed pioneers to risk all and follow the setting sun. Eventually the Wild West was tamed and they realized their dreams. The modern-day version of the Wild West presents us with the same opportunity. The important thing to remember is that the information superhighway is truly a frontier that may not be tamed in the foreseeable future. The fact that it is a frontier, with its risks, makes it even more exciting. In this chapter we address some of the issues confronting the virtual frontier and computing in general.

11-2 THE JOB OUTLOOK IN THE INFORMATION SOCIETY

Jobs

Whether you are seeking employment or a promotion as a teacher, an accountant, a writer, a fashion designer, a lawyer (or in any of hundreds of other jobs), someone is sure to ask, "What do you know about computers?" Today, interacting with a computer is part of the daily routine for millions of knowledge workers and is increasingly common for blue-collar workers. No matter which career you choose, in all likelihood you will be a frequent user of computers.

Upon completion of this course, you will be part of the computer-competent minority, and you will be able to respond with confidence to any inquiry about your knowledge of computers. But what of that 90% of our society that must answer "nothing" or "very little"? These people will find themselves at a disadvantage.

The virtual frontier extends to the satellites that enable global positioning systems such as AccuTrans, shown here. AccuTrans provides vehicle location and status to managers of large transportation systems. AccuTrans will help eliminate the problem of lost buses and stranded passengers.   Courtesy of E-Systems, Inc.

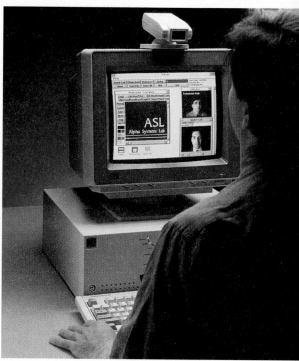

This user's system has video teleconferencing capability. The system transmits and receives over standard telephone lines to a similarly equipped system. Remote users interact with one another and pass information back and forth in a shared virtual workspace.   Courtesy of Alpha Systems Lab

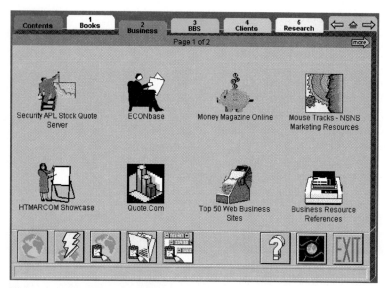

Vizion is an intelligent gateway to the Internet, BBSs, and other commercial and public online services. It's one of a number of user-friendly software packages that can help you get to where you're going on the information superhighway. Hundreds of destinations are a click away. Shown here are some of the destinations in the Business "folio." There are 18 other Vizion folios (BBS, Books, Research, Sports, Travel, Shopping, and so on).

These computer specialists develop and maintain a variety of administrative information systems. All of these people need a solid foundation of computer knowledge to accomplish their jobs effectively.   Courtesy of International Business Machines Corporation

Opportunities for Computer Specialists

If you are planning a career as a computer specialist, opportunities have never been better. Almost every company, no matter how small or large, employs computer specialists, and most of these companies are always looking for qualified people. For the last decade, people with computer and information systems education have been at or near the top of the "most wanted" list. With millions (yes, millions!) of new computers being purchased and installed each year, it is likely that this trend will continue. Of course, the number of people attracted to the booming computer field is also increasing. One of the many reasons for this migration to the computer fields is that computer careers are consistently ranked among the most desirable jobs. A recent *Money* magazine called computer systems analyst the best job in America. The magazine ranked 100 jobs in terms of earnings, long- and short-term job growth, job security, prestige rating, and "stress and strain" rating. Physician, physical therapist, electrical engineer, and civil engineer round out the top five. The systems analyst is but one of dozens of computer specialist careers. Others are programmers, network administrators, PC specialists, computer operators, Internet site specialists, educators specializing in computer education, and on and on.

The variety and types of computer specialist jobs are ever changing. For example, there's the information detective. Companies and individuals call on these high-tech detectives to help them answer such questions as: Has my child's sitter had any driving accidents? Has my materials supplier ever filed for bankruptcy? Did this applicant for the sales manager position really earn an MBA at Harvard? Another related job is the professional Internet researcher. Someone who really knows his or her way around the Internet can do in minutes what might take a Net newbie days to do. A good detective or researcher can make in excess of $100 an hour and never leave the comfort of home!

Career Opportunities for the Computer-Competent Minority

Opportunities abound for computer-competent people pursuing almost any career—from actuaries to zoologists. Every facet of automation is moving closer to the people who use it. In fact, most professions put you within arm's reach of a personal computer, workstation, or terminal.

- The terminal has become standard equipment at hospital nursing stations and is often found in operating rooms.
- Draftspeople have traded drawing tables for computer-aided design (CAD) workstations.
- Teachers are integrating the power of computer-based training (CBT) into their courses.
- Economists would be lost without the predictive capabilities of their decision support system (DSS).
- Truck dispatchers query their information systems before scheduling deliveries.
- Advertising executives use computers to help them plan ad campaigns.
- Construction contractors keep track of on-site inventory on portable laptop computers.
- The microcomputer is the secretary's constant companion for everything from word processing to conference scheduling.
- Stockbrokers often have terminals on both sides of their desks. (Some dedicated brokers have one by their bed at night as well to keep up with Asian markets.)

Computer competency is already a prerequisite of employment in many professions, such as business and engineering. Within a few years, computer competency may well be a requirement for success in most professions. Career mobility is becoming forever intertwined with an individual's current and future knowledge of computers.

Career advancement ultimately depends on your abilities, imagination, and performance, but understanding computers can only enhance your opportunities. All things being equal, the person who has the knowledge of and the will to work with computers will have a tremendous career advantage over those who do not.

Our Jobs Are Changing

As information technology continues to move to the forefront in our society, jobs in every discipline are being redefined. For example, 10 years ago sales representatives carried manuals and products to the customer site. Today, they still knock on doors, but to a much lesser extent because much of what used to be personal interaction is now electronic interaction (e-mail, fax, and EDI, or Electronic Data Interchange). The sales rep is no longer the sole source of product/service information. Customers can get up-to-date information off bulletin boards or vendor-distributed CD-ROMs. They also routinely place their orders electronically, without involvement from the sales representative. Radical changes in the way we do our jobs are not limited to the business community. Poets, the clergy, politicians, professors, and others are continually evaluating what they do and how they do it within the context of emerging technology.

Some jobs are being eliminated. Others, however, are being created. The revenue accounting department at a major U.S. airline was reduced from 650 to 350 with the implementation of a new computer-based system. Those remaining had to be retrained to work with the new system. Those displaced had to be retrained for other work opportunities in an increasingly automated society. For example, the Home Shopping Network jumped from 600 employees to 5000 in about 10 years, most of whom are knowledge workers. The explosion of information technology has resulted in thousands of new companies that provide a myriad of previously unknown products and services. America Online, an intensely information technology–related business employing thousands, didn't exist a decade ago.

Information technology continues to steamroll into our lives, affecting all that we do—even our jobs. Each of us has a choice. We can resist information technology and

Professionals in all areas of endeavor continue to include greater use of technology in their jobs. Today advanced precision farming techniques enable producers to optimize their resources. RDI Technologies' AgMAPP, shown here, is a comprehensive GIS (Geographic Information System) that blends the power of computers with the precision of global positioning system (GPS) technology. The combined technologies enable producers to map fields by simply driving the perimeter and to record location-specific information on soil and yields. With the resulting information they can increase output by adopting variable rate application (see example) and other ixx-based farming strategies.

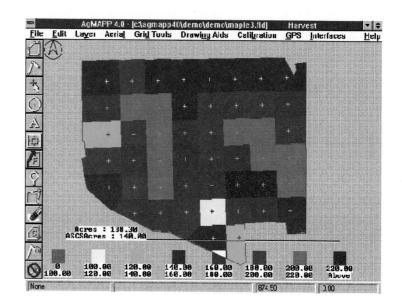

hope for the best, or we can embrace it and use it to improve our jobs and our job performance. The fact that you are reading this indicates that you have chosen the latter.

11–3 THE WORK PLACE: ERGONOMICS AND GREEN COMPUTING

Our work place is changing because we are more attuned to *ergonomic* considerations and the growing importance of *green computing*.

Ergonomics and Work-Place Design

For close to a hundred years, the design of automobiles was driven by two overwhelming considerations: marketing and functionality. Engineers were asked to design cars that had plenty of marketing features and could go from point A to point B. Surprisingly little attention was given to the human factor; that is, the connection between the driver and passengers and the automobile. About 20 years ago, executives discovered that they could boost sales and enhance functionality by improving this human connection; thus began the era of ergonomically designed automobiles. **Ergonomics** is the study of the relationships between people and their machines.

Today, human factors engineers apply the principles of ergonomic design to ensure that the interface between people and cars is *safe, comfortable, effective,* and *efficient.* The emergence of ergonomics is having a similar impact on the relationship between knowledge workers and their work places. Two decades ago, computers numbered in the thousands. Now they number in the millions and ergonomics has emerged as an important consideration in work-place design.

Reasons for Concern

One of the best ways to avoid health problems related to computing is through a program of exercise. The Computer Athlete fitness program transforms your fitness equipment into an interactive video arcade center. An infrared light beam detects your exercise motions and feeds the information to a virtual reality game. The thrill of competition will inspire you to race against and eliminate your competitors. Courtesy of Computer Athlete Inc.

During the 1980s the knowledge worker's work place gained attention when workers began to blame headaches, depression, anxiety, nausea, fatigue, and irritability on prolonged interaction with a terminal or PC. These and other problems often associated with extended use of a terminal or PC are collectively referred to as *video operator's distress syndrome,* or *VODS.* Although there was little evidence to link these problems directly with using terminals or PCs (the same problems occurred in other work environments), VODS caused people to take a closer look at the work place and the types of injuries being reported. As the number of *repetitive-stress injuries* (*RSIs*) increased for knowledge workers, workstation ergonomics became an increasingly important issue for corporate productivity.

A poorly designed work place has the potential to cause *cumulative trauma disorder* (*CTD*), a condition that can lead to a permanent disability of motor skills. CTD now accounts for more than half of work-related problems. CTD typically occurs when people ignore human factors considerations while spending considerable time at the keyboard. Other workstation-related injuries include mental stress, eyestrain, headaches, muscular injuries, and skeletal injuries. Hand and wrist problems have always been the main complaint, with the repetitive-stress injury called *carpal tunnel syndrome* (*CTS*) heading the list of complaints.

Ergonomics

The manufacturer bills this as the "first truly ergonomic industrial terminal to improve worker productivity." This wireless scanning terminal fits comfortably in the user's hand. Everything about this terminal was designed to give factory and warehouse workers maximum flexibility.
Courtesy of Norand Corporation

Much has been written about the health concerns associated with monitors. Talk about the radiation emitted by monitors has unduly frightened office workers. A controversial, and apparently flawed, study in the late 1980s concluded that women who are exposed to the radiation emitted from terminals and PCs may have a higher rate of miscarriage than those who are not. A comprehensive four-year federal government study completed in 1991 concluded that women who work with terminals and PCs and those who do not have the same rate of miscarriage.

Work-Place Design: An Evaluation

Proper work-place design, whether on the factory floor or in the office, is good business. Any good manager knows that a healthy, happy worker is a more productive worker. A good manager also knows that the leading causes of lost work time are back/shoulder/neck pain and CTD.

The key to designing a proper work place for the knowledge worker is *flexibility*. The knowledge worker's work place should be designed with enough flexibility to enable it to be custom-fitted to its worker. Figure 11–1 highlights important considerations in work-place design. Look for ANSI (American National Standards Institute) to provide added direction in standards for work-place design. Also, ergonomics problems in the work place are being addressed in legislation and in proposed regulations from the Occupational Safety and Health Administration (OSHA).

One of the most important factors in ergonomic programs is employee training. Workers should be shown how to analyze their workstations and make necessary adjustments (such as monitor contrast and brightness or chair lumbar support). Attention to the overall environment can reduce stress and increase worker performance. For example, equipping impact printers with acoustical enclosures can reduce the noise level. Indirect lighting can reduce glare. Proper ventilation eliminates health

The Hardware
Monitor location (A). The monitor should be located directly in front of you at arm's length with the top at forehand level. Outside windows should be to the side of the monitor. *Monitor features*. Monitor should be high-resolution with anti-glare screens. *Monitor maintenance*. The monitor should be free from smudges or dust buildup.
Keyboard location (B). The keyboard should be located such that the upper arm and forearms are at a 90-degree angle. *Keyboard features*. The keyboard should be ergonomically designed to accommodate better the movements of the fingers, hands, and arms.

The Chair
The chair should be fully adjustable to the size and contour of the body. *Pneumatic seat height adjustment (C); Seat and back angle adjustment (D); Back-rest height adjustment (E); Recessed armrests with height adjustment (F); Lumbar support adjustment (for lower back support) (G); Five-leg pedestal on casters (H)*.

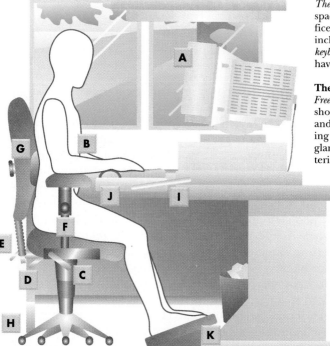

The Desk
The swing space. Use wraparound work space to keep the PC, important office materials, and files within 18 inches of the chair. *Adjustable tray for keyboard and mouse (I)*: The tray should have height and swivel adjustments.

The Room
Freedom of movement. The work area should permit freedom of movement and ample leg room. *Lighting*. Lighting should be positioned to minimize glare on the monitor and printed materials.

Other Equipment
Wrist rest (J). The wrist wrest is used in conjunction with adjustable armrests to keep arms in a neutral straight position at the keyboard. *Footrest (K)*. The adjustable footrest takes pressure off lower back while encouraging proper posture.

FIGURE 11–1 Ergonomic Considerations in Work-Place Design
Knowledge workers, most of whom spend four or more hours each day at a PC or terminal, are paying more attention to the ergonomics (efficiency of the person–machine interface) of the hardware, including chairs and desks.

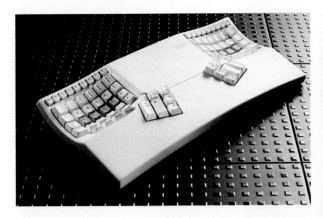

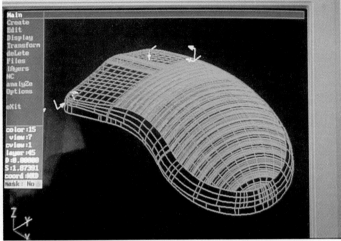

The Kinesis Ergonomic Keyboard is contoured to fit the shape and movements of the human body. The design puts less stress and strain on muscles, reducing the user's risk for fatigue in hands, wrists, and arms. The keyboard also reduces risk factors for developing painful injuries, such as carpal tunnel syndrome, tendinitis, and cumulative trauma disorders (CTDs).   Courtesy of Kinesis™ Corporation

During the development of the Microsoft ergonomic mouse, human factors engineers were asked to optimize both functionality and the interface with the user.   Courtesy of Microsoft Corporation

concerns caused by the ozone emitted by laser printers. (Excessive exposure to ozone can cause headaches and nausea.) Cubicles can be installed that foster teamwork and improve morale.

Each knowledge worker can contribute to the quality of his or her work place by following a couple of simple rules. First, make the adjustments necessary to custom fit your work place. Second, take periodic mini-breaks; that is, look away from the monitor and/or generally alter your body orientation for a few seconds (make a fist, turn your head from side to side, roll your shoulders, walk around your desk, wiggle your toes, and so on).

Green Computing

The dawning of the age of green computing is upon us. As a society we are adopting a more environmentally sound position with respect to the use and manufacture of computing hardware. Computers drain critical resources such as electricity and paper. The electrical, chemical, and bulk-waste side effects of computing have emerged as important issues in computing.

The United States government now requires its agencies to purchase PCs, monitors, and printers that comply with the Environmental Protection Agency's *Energy Star* guidelines. To comply with Energy Star requirements, monitors and processors in standby mode (not in use) can consume no more than 30 watts of power. Printers are permitted a range of 30 to 45 watts. Computer manufacturers have been moving toward more energy-efficient products in hopes of reducing manufacturing costs and increasing product competitiveness.

It costs about $250 a year to keep a PC and laser page printer running 24 hours a day. We could save a lot of money and fossil fuel if every user were conscientious about turning off PCs and peripheral devices when not in use. Judicious computing can even save trees—why print a letter when e-mail is faster and better for the environment? Green computing means printing only what needs to be printed, saving the cellulose pulp for more meaningful applications.

Other recommendations by green computing proponents include buying equipment from vendors who are manufacturing environmentally safe products; purchasing recycled paper; recycling paper and toner printer cartridges (which would probably end up in landfills); buying reconditioned components rather than new ones; recycling old PCs and printers; shopping electronically to save gas; and telecommuting once or twice a week.

The repetitive-stress injuries (RSIs) associated with the keyboard may be eliminated at some time in the future as more people move to speech-recognition technology to interact with their PCs. This executive dictates directly to a computer system. This technology, however, has it problems. Some people who currently engage in day-long chats with computers complain of hoarseness and sore throats. Fortunately, this voice strain is usually associated with new users who tend to bark the commands rather than speaking normally. *Courtesy of International Business Machines Corporation*

11–4 THE QUESTION OF ETHICS

The computer revolution has generated intense controversy. This controversy has raised questions about what is and is not ethical with regard to activities involving information technology. These ethics issues are so important to our society that many prominent educators have recommended that information technology ethics be integrated into all college curricula. They believe that if people are made aware of the consequences of their actions that fewer people will be motivated to plant dangerous computer viruses, contaminate information systems with false information, or post pornographic material to the Internet. Ethics-conscientious people will be more likely to protect personal privacy, honor the copyright laws, and report unethical activity. Educators warn us of dire consequences should we fail to instill a sense of ethics in future generations. If ethical abuses are left unabated, all roads on the information superhighway will be toll roads for encrypted data. If this were to happen, we would become a more secretive society, far less willing to share accumulated knowledge.

Standards of Conduct: A Code of Ethics

About 25 years ago, one of the largest computer professional societies adopted a code of ethics. The code warns the members, who are mostly professionals in the information technology fields, that they can be expelled or censured if they violate it. Other professional societies publish a code of ethics as well. Rarely, however, has any action been taken against delinquent members. Does this mean there are no violations? Of course not. A carefully drafted code of ethics provides some guidelines for conduct, but professional societies cannot be expected to police the misdoings of their membership. In many instances, a code violation is also a violation of the law.

A code of ethics provides direction for computer professionals and users so that they act responsibly in their application of information technology. The following code of ethics is in keeping with the spirit of those encouraged by professional societies.

INTERNET BRIDGE

Ethics in Computing

1. Maintain the highest standard of personal and professional behavior.
2. Avoid situations that create a conflict of interest.
3. Do not violate the confidentiality of your employer or those you serve.
4. Continue to learn so your knowledge keeps pace with the technology.
5. Never misrepresent or withhold information that is germane to a problem or situation of public concern.

6. Use information judiciously and maintain system integrity at all times.
7. Do not violate the rights or privacy of others.
8. Take appropriate action when exposed to unethical or illegal practices.
9. Do not exploit the shortcomings of an employer's computer system for personal gain.
10. Accomplish each task to the best of your ability.

If you follow this 10-point code, it is unlikely that anyone will question your ethics. Nevertheless, well-meaning people routinely violate this simple code because they are unaware of the tremendous detrimental impact of their actions. With the speed and power of computers, a minor code infraction easily can be magnified to a costly catastrophe. For this reason, the use of computers in this electronic age is raising new ethical questions, the most visible of which are discussed in the following sections.

The Misuse of Personal Information

Depending on which poll you accept, about 40% of all white-collar workers are cyberphobic, resisting new technology. Half of these refuse to use voice mail or e-mail. The most common reason cited for their anti-technology attitude is the fear of loss of privacy.

Sources of Personal Data The issue with the greatest ethical overtones is the privacy of personal information. Some people fear that computer-based record-keeping offers too much of an opportunity for the invasion of an individual's privacy. There is indeed reason for concern. For example, credit-card users unknowingly leave a "trail" of activities and interests that, when examined and evaluated, can provide a surprisingly comprehensive personal profile.

The date and location of all credit-card transactions are recorded. In effect, when you charge lunch, gasoline, or clothing, you are creating a chronological record of where you have been and your spending habits. From this information, a good analyst could compile a very accurate profile of your lifestyle. For example, the analyst could predict how you dress by knowing the type of clothing stores you patronize. On a more personal level, records are kept that detail the duration, time, and numbers of all your telephone calls. With computers, these numbers easily can be matched to people, businesses, institutions, and telephone services. So each time you make a phone call, you also leave a record of whom or where you call. Enormous amounts of personal data are maintained on everyone by the IRS, your college, your employer, your creditors, your hospital, your insurance company, your broker, and on and on. The profile can be fine-tuned by examining your Internet activity on such activities as messages posted to bulletin boards, newsgroups frequented, and the kinds of software downloaded.

We all have an obligation to adopt a code of ethics when working with computers. This worker deals with sensitive international communications. The system she is using is a multilanguage optical character recognition system. The system applies language processing and image pattern recognition techniques to automatically retrieve, sort, recognize, and categorize documents written in different languages.   Courtesy of E-Systems, Inc.

Here on the floor of the Chicago Mercantile Exchange, brokers complete buy and sell orders that result in name, address, and other personal information being added to one or more databases. On average, each American is listed in about 60 government and 80 private-sector databases. On a typical day, each person's name is passed between computers 10 times. People who are socially, economically, and politically active may be listed in hundreds of databases.   Cromemco, Inc.

Issues in Computing

Telecommuting Policies

A few years ago working at home via data communications, or telecommuting, was a carrot offered only to trusted employees. Today telecommuting is a mainstream business strategy. Over 40,000,000 people work out of their homes, an increase of over 8% in the last year. The argument for promoting telecommuting becomes more compelling as the studies roll in. One study found that 75% of telecommuters polled reported greater productivity and 83% said their home lives had improved. The results of a comprehensive survey of Fortune 1000 executives showed that 92% of them felt telecommuting produced advantages for their companies, such as reduced absenteeism, improved employee retention, reduced employee stress, lower real estate costs, and improved employee morale. Even the federal government is promoting telecommuting, with hopes of having 60,000 telecommuting employees by 1998. Big cities are encouraging telecommuting to reduce traffic problems and pollution.

All of the statistics point to a trend among businesses to policies which permit telecommuting. Even so, telecommuting remains a volatile issue in many organizations.

Discussion: Telecommuting is not an employee option in many organizations. What would you say to the management of these companies to encourage them to adopt a policy supporting telecommuting?

We hope that information about us is up-to-date and accurate. Unfortunately, much of it is not. Laws permit us to examine our records, but first we must find them. You cannot just write to the federal government and request to see your files. To be completely sure that you examine all your federal records for completeness and accuracy, you would have to write and probably visit more than 5000 agencies that each maintain computer-based files on individuals. The same is true of computer-based personal data maintained in the private sector.

Violating the Privacy of Personal Information   Most will agree that the potential exists for abuse, but are these data being misused? Some say yes. Consider the states that sell lists of the addresses and data on their licensed drivers. At the request of a manager of several petite women's clothing stores, a state provided the manager with a list of all licensed drivers in the state who were women between the ages of 21 and 40, less than 5 feet 3 inches tall, and under 120 pounds. You be the judge. Is the sale of such a list an abuse of personal information? Does the state cross the line of what is considered ethical practice?

Personal information has become the product of a growing industry. Companies have been formed that do nothing but sell information about people. Not only are the people involved not asked for permission to use their data, they are seldom even told that their personal information is being sold! A great deal of personal data can be extracted from public records. For example, one company sends people to county courthouses all over the United States to gather publicly accessible data about people who have recently filed papers to purchase a home. Computer-based databases are then sold to insurance companies, landscape companies, members of Congress seeking new votes, lawyers seeking new clients, and so on. Such information even is sold and distributed over the Net. Those placed on these electronic databases eventually become targets of commerce and special-interest groups.

The use of personal information for profit and other purposes is growing so rapidly that the government has not been able to keep up with abuses. Antiquated laws, combined with judicial unfamiliarity with computers, make policing and prosecuting abuses of the privacy of personal information difficult and, in many cases, impossible.

Issues in Computing

Computer Matching   In **computer matching,** separate databases are examined and individuals common to both are identified. The focus of most computer-matching applications is to identify people engaged in wrongdoing. For example, federal employees are being matched with those having delinquent student loans. Wages are then garnisheed to repay the loans. In another computer-matching case, a $30-million fraud was uncovered when questionable financial transactions were traced to common participants.

The Internal Revenue Service also uses computer matching to identify tax cheaters. The IRS gathers descriptive data, such as neighborhood and automobile type, then uses sophisticated models to create lifestyle profiles. These profiles are matched against reported income on tax returns to predict whether people seem to be underpaying taxes. When the income and projected lifestyle do not match, the return is audited.

Proponents of computer matching cite the potential to reduce criminal activity. Opponents of computer matching consider it an unethical invasion of privacy.

Law enforcement officials, from FBI agents to local police, routinely use computer matching techniques to fight crime.   Courtesy of Harris Corporation

Securing the Integrity of Personal Information   Computer experts feel that the integrity of personal data can be more secure in computer databases than in file cabinets. They contend that we can continue to be masters and not victims if we implement proper safeguards for the maintenance and release of this information and enact effective legislation to cope with the abuse of it.

The Privacy Question: No Easy Answers   The ethical questions surrounding the privacy of personal information are extremely complex and difficult to resolve. For example, consider the position of the American Civil Liberties Union. On one hand, the ACLU is fighting to curb abuses of personal information and on the other, it is lobbying the government for greater access to government information, which may include personal information. Are these goals in conflict?

As automation continues to enrich our lives, it also opens the door for abuses of personal information. Research is currently being done which may show that people with certain genetic and/or personality makeups have a statistical predisposition to a physical problem or a mental disorder, such as early heart failure or depression. Will employers use such information to screen potential employees?

By now it should be apparent to you that we may never resolve all of the ethical questions associated with the privacy of personal information. Just as the answer to one question becomes more clear, another is raised by an ever-growing number of applications that deal with personal information.

Anyone who records transactions on a computer system is a candidate for computer monitoring. Overnight couriers, who simultaneously communicate with customers and computers, are candidates. Courtesy of Federal Express Corporation. All rights reserved.

Computer Monitoring

One of the most controversial applications of information technology is **computer monitoring.** In computer monitoring, computers continuously gather and assimilate data on job activities to measure worker performance. Today computers monitor the job performance of more than 7 million American workers and millions more worldwide. Most of these workers interact with a mainframe computer system via terminals or work on a LAN-based PC. Others work with electronic or mechanical equipment that is linked to a computer system.

Many clerical workers who use terminals are evaluated by the number of documents they process per unit of time. At insurance companies, computer monitoring systems provide supervisors with information on the rate at which clerks process claims.

Supervisors can request other information, such as time spent at the terminal and keying-error rate.

Computers also monitor the activities of many jobs that demand frequent use of the telephone. The number of inquiries handled by directory-assistance operators is logged by a computer. Some companies employ computers to monitor the use of telephones by all employees.

Although most computer monitoring is done at the clerical level, it is also being applied to higher-level positions, such as commodities brokers, programmers, loan officers, and plant managers. For example, CIM (computer-integrated manufacturing) enables corporate executives to monitor the effectiveness of a plant manager on a real-time basis. At any given time executives can tap the system for productivity information, such as the rate of production for a particular assembly.

Not all computer monitoring is aimed at assessing ongoing job performance. For example, some organizations encourage management scrutiny of employee electronic mail. In this form of monitoring, management opens and reads employee e-mail to ensure that internal communications are work-related and of a certain level of quality. Many organized worker groups have complained that this form of monitoring is an unnecessary invasion of privacy and can actually be counterproductive.

Workers complain that being constantly observed and analyzed by a computer adds unnecessary stress to their jobs. However, management is reluctant to give up computer monitoring because it has proved itself a tool for increasing worker productivity. In general, affected workers are opposing any further intrusion into their professional privacy. On the other hand, management is equally vigilant in its quest for better information on worker performance.

Computer Crime

The ethical spectrum for computer issues runs from that which is ethical, to that which is unethical, to that which is against the law—a computer crime. There are many types of computer crimes, ranging from the use of an unauthorized password by a student to a billion-dollar insurance fraud. The first case of computer crime was reported in 1958. Since then, all types of computer-related crimes have been reported: fraud, theft, larceny, embezzlement, burglary, sabotage, espionage, and forgery. We know computer crime is a serious problem, but we don't know how serious. It is estimated that each year the total money lost from computer crime is greater than the sum total of that taken in all robberies. In fact, no one really knows the extent of computer crime because much of it is either undetected or unreported. In those cases involving banks, officers may elect to write off the loss rather than announce the crime and risk losing the good will of their customers. Computer crimes involving the greatest amount of money have to do with banking, insurance, product inventories, and securities.

The good news is that only a small percentage of the people with an inclination toward crime are computer-competent and capable of committing computer crimes. The bad news is that the criminal element in our society, like everyone else, is moving toward computer competency. There is, however, more good news. Business-related crime, in general, is decreasing because of the improved controls made possible through automation. Computers have made it more difficult for people to commit business crimes. For the most part, computer crimes are committed by trusted computer users with authorized access to sensitive information.

Computers and the Law Companies try to employ information technology within the boundaries of any applicable law. Unfortunately, the laws are not always clear because many legal questions involving the use of information technology are being debated for the first time. For example, is e-mail like a letter or a memo, subject to freedom-of-information laws? Or, is it private, like telephone calls? This question is yet to be resolved. To no one's surprise, computer law is the fastest growing type of law practice.

INTERNET BRIDGE
Computer Crime

Laws governing information technology are beginning to take shape. Prior to 1994, federal laws that addressed computer crime were limited because they applied only to those computer systems that in some way reflected a "federal interest." The Computer Abuse Amendments Act of 1994 expanded the scope of computer crimes to computers "used in interstate commerce." Effectively this means any computer, including PCs, with a link to the Internet. These laws make it a felony to gain unauthorized access to a computer system with the intent to obtain anything of value, to defraud the system, or to cause more than $1000 in damage. Although most states have adopted computer crime laws, they are only the skeleton of what is needed to direct an orderly and controlled growth of information technology applications.

Existing federal and state laws concerning the privacy of personal information are being updated every year. At the same time, new laws are written. Current federal laws outline the handling of credit information, restrict what information the IRS can obtain, restrict government access to financial information, permit individuals to view records maintained by federal agencies, restrict the use of education-related data, and regulate the matching of computer files. States have or are considering laws to deal with the handling of social security numbers, criminal records, telephone numbers, financial information, medical records, and other sensitive personal information.

Computer crime is a relatively recent phenomenon. As a result, legislation, the criminal justice system, and industry are not yet adequately prepared to cope with it. Only a handful of police and FBI agents in the entire country have been trained to handle cases involving computer crime. And when a case comes to court, few judges and even fewer jurors have the background necessary to understand the testimony.

Defrauding the System   Most computer crimes fall under the umbrella of computer fraud. These crimes involve a premeditated or conscious effort to defraud a computer-based system. Here are some examples.

▶ A U.S. Customs official modified a program to print $160,000 worth of unauthorized federal payroll checks payable to himself and his co-conspirators.

▶ A 17-year-old high school student tapped into an AT&T computer and stole more than $1 million worth of software.

▶ One person illegally transferred $10,200,000 from a U.S. bank to a Swiss bank. He probably would have gotten away with this electronic heist if he hadn't felt compelled to brag about it.

▶ Three data entry clerks in a large metropolitan city conspired with welfare recipients to write over $2 million of fraudulent checks. Apparently the computer-based system had few controls to thwart this type of fraud.

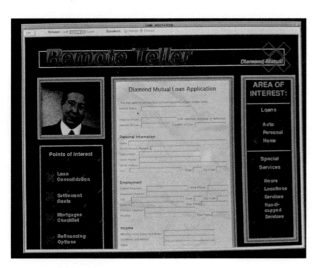

This Remote Teller can save time and money for both the financial industry and the loan applicant. Borrowers complete loan applications while interacting with an automated system. The multimedia teller is capable of answering the questions of a typical loan applicant. The Remote Teller system is designed to minimize the potential for fraud.   Courtesy of International Business Machines

Emerging Technology

The Promise of Virtual Reality

Imagine that your job is to monitor the operation of a vast telecommunications network. Cables snake underground and underwater. Data flows between communications satellites and earth and across wiring inside building walls. Now imagine that a graphic image of this vast grid and its data flows could be laid out below you, as you float above, an "infonaut" looking for the kink that is blocking service to millions of customers. Far below you see a pulsing light. There's the problem. With a gestured command, you fix it—without leaving your office. That's the promise of virtual reality, and it's moving from computer fantasy to computer fact. In fact, US West and a number of other telecommunications firms are already experimenting with such systems.

Virtual reality (VR), a term coined in 1970 by Myron Krueger, combines computer graphics with special hardware to immerse users in *cyberspace*, an artificial three-dimensional world. Instead of passively viewing data or graphics on a screen, users can move about, handle "virtual" representations of data and objects, and get visual, aural, and tactile feedback. In the world of computers, the term *virtual* refers to an environment that is *simulated by hardware and software* (for example, virtual memory, virtual department store).

And what about marriage in cyberspace? A bride, a groom, and their minister entered cyberspace by entering pods at the CyberMind Virtual Reality Center in San Francisco. They said their vows amid a virtual recreation of the lost city of Atlantis. The scene included palaces, chariots, carousels, and even doves.

Dressing for Cyberspace

To enter cyberspace, users don special hardware for the feeling of total immersion in a three-dimensional world.

▶ *Headpiece.* The goggles-like head-mounted display (HMD) blocks out visual sensations from the real world and substitutes images presented on *two small video screens*—one for each eye, creating a

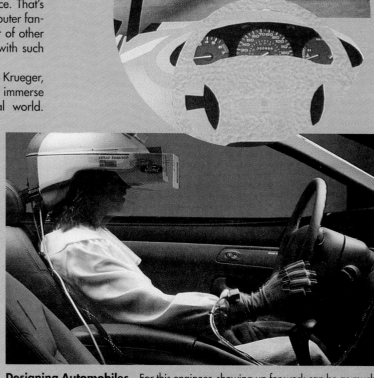

Designing Automobiles   For this engineer, showing up for work can be as much fun as going to the video arcade. But she's not playing games. She's experimenting with the use of virtual reality to help design cars for the future. This operator wears a helmet and goggles equipped with two small screens (see inset of the 3-D image). A special glove fitted with sensors covers her right hand and allows her to manipulate objects during the design process.   Courtesy of Ford Motor Company/Courtesy of Ford Motor Company

These are all examples of fraud. Any illegal entry into a computer system, direct or indirect, for the purpose of personal gain is considered fraud.

Computers can be both an invitation to fraud and a tool to thwart fraud. For example, the automated system in place in the pits at the Chicago Board of Trade and the Chicago Mercantile Exchange has made it possible for traders to fill personal orders either simultaneously or ahead of their customers to get better prices. A system, involving hand-held computer trading devices, could be implemented that would electronically record every trade in sequence, preventing such abuses. However, the

Thrills without Spills Virtual reality takes this hang glider to the twenty-first century so he can fly among the skyscrapers of Los Angeles. Virtual hang gliders ride in an actual hang glider harness positioned in front of a box that contains an image generator displaying pictures of a futuristic Los Angeles. Courtesy of Evans and Sutherland Computer Corporation

three-dimensional effect. The headpiece also contains *motion,* or *balance, sensors;* move your head and the computer will shift the view presented on the video screens. Just flip up the visor on your headpiece to see what is going on in the real world. Or, flip it down to enter the virtual world.

▶ *Headphones.* Headphones block out room noise and substitute three-dimensional *holophononic* sounds. Generally the headphones are built into the helmet.

▶ *Data glove.* The ensemble is completed by a data glove outlined with *fiber-optic sensors* and cables. The glove can be used, like a floating mouse, to "gesture" a command or to grasp and move virtual objects about.

Each piece of hardware is tethered to a power pack and to one or more powerful computers via two-way data transfer cables that record the user's movements and provide real-time feedback.

Will the Promise Be Kept?

Virtual reality is still in its infancy, but the breadth and success of existing VR applications have shown us that VR will play an important role in the future. Already, architects can "walkthrough" proposed buildings. Researchers are exploring life forms on a VR version of an Antarctic lake bottom. A Japanese department store uses a "virtual kitchen" for planning custom-designed remodeling projects. Exercise bikes can cycle through a virtual town. Virtual reality arcades (VRcades) let players be a part of the game. Acrophobics don VR headsets to overcome their fear of heights.

Although some VR applications can be run on powerful PCs, the most realistic experiences are created with sophisticated systems that cost as much as a new Mercedes. Moreover, the equipment is cumbersome and the graphics are often fairly crude. Still, many experts predict that hardware costs will continue to drop and software will become more refined. If so, virtual reality will emerge as the user interface of the future.

Chicago Board of Trade and the Chicago Mercantile Exchange are reluctant to implement it.

Attempts to defraud a computer system require the cooperation of an experienced computer specialist. A common street thug does not have the knowledge or the opportunity to be successful at this type of computer crime. Over 50% of all computer frauds are internal; that is, they are committed by employees of the organization being defrauded. About 30% of those defrauding employees are computer specialists.

Virtual Reality

Negligence and Incompetence   Not all computer crime is premeditated. Negligence or incompetence can have a negative impact on people outside the organization. Such crimes are usually a result of poor input/output control. For example, after she paid in full, a woman was sent dunning notices continually and was visited by collection agencies for not making payments on her automobile. Although the records and procedures were in error, the company forcibly repossessed the automobile without thoroughly checking its procedures and the legal implications. The woman had to sue the company for the return of her automobile. The court ordered the automobile returned and the company to pay her a substantial sum as a penalty.

The Cracker Problem   Another problem is the criminal activities of overzealous *hackers*, sometimes called *crackers* for the way they "crack" through network security. These "electronic vandals" have tapped into everything from local credit agencies to top-secret defense systems. The evidence of unlawful entry, perhaps a revised record or access during nonoperating hours, is called a **footprint.** Some malicious crackers leave much more than a footprint—they infect the computer system with a *computer virus.* Viruses, which infect programs and databases, can be found at all levels of computing. Viruses are written by outlaw hackers and programmers to cause harm to the computer systems of unsuspecting victims.

The Computer Abuse Amendments Act of 1994 changed the standard for criminal prosecution from "intent" to "reckless disregard," thus increasing the chances of successful prosecution of crackers. Recently, two computer crackers were sentenced to federal prison for their roles in defrauding long-distance carriers of more than $28 million. The crackers stole credit-card numbers from MCI. One who worked at MCI was sentenced to three years and two months and the other to a one-year prison term.

Some people are concerned that criminally oriented hackers are glorified by the media, creating heroes for a new generation of computer criminals. This glorification may begin to fade as we read about more and more crackers serving hard time.

Highway Robbery: Crime on the Internet   Security on the Internet, the foundation of the information superhighway, is an ongoing problem. Internet-related intrusions are increasing, averaging over 200 a month. The Internet is so vulnerable that computer science professors have been known to ask their students to break into files at a particular site on the Internet. Successful students bring back proof of system penetration to show they understand the protocols involved.

The Internet's cybercops on the Computer Emergency Response Team at Carnegie Mellon University often work around the clock to thwart electronic vandalism and crime on the Internet. CERT concentrates its efforts on battling major threats to the global Internet. Lesser problems are left to the Internet service providers to police. A few years ago, the cybercops tracked hackers who were out to prove their ingenuity. Now cyberthiefs are after more than self-esteem: They want to steal something. They do this by intercepting credit-card numbers, rerouting valuable inventory, downloading copyright software, or making illegal monetary transactions. Unfortunately, as soon as CERT people plug a hole in the Internet, another is found. The problem won't go away and will become more difficult to cope with as perpetrators gain sophistication.

Security experts say that the best way to deal effectively with crime on the Internet is the universal adoption and use of an international encryption standard. At present, most people and companies are reluctant to do this because it would effectively end open worldwide communication. However if abuse continues, encryption may be the only solution.

Software Piracy and the Theft of Intellectual Property   Software is automatically protected by federal copyright law from the moment of its creation. This is the same law that protects other intellectual property (books, audio recordings, films, and so on). The Copyright Law of 1974 gives the owner of the copyright "the exclu-

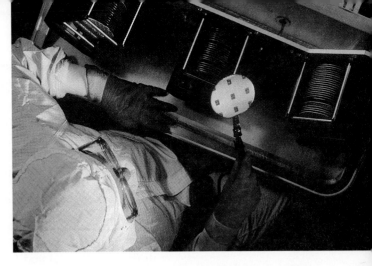

sive rights" to "reproduce the copyrighted word." Those who purchase copyright software have the right to copy to an original computer and to make an archival copy. Unless specifically stated in the license agreement, the purchasers can load the software to only one computer. The general rule is: one software package per computer. Any other duplication, whether for sale or for the owner's personal use, is an infringement of copyright law.

It is copyright infringement to allow simultaneous use of a single-user version on a LAN by more than one person. LAN versions of software packages are sold with a *site license* that permits a specific number of users. Also, the Software Rental Amendments Act of 1990 prohibits the rental, leasing, or lending of copyright software.

Copyright laws protect literature, music, the design of a silicon chip, and software. A sophisticated circuit design may be the result of a multi-million-dollar research effort. Courtesy of Harris Corporation

The unlawful duplication of proprietary software, called **software piracy,** is making companies vulnerable to legal action by the affected vendors. The term **pilferage** is used to describe the situation where a company purchases a software product without a site-usage license agreement, then copies and distributes it throughout the company. If piracy is done "willfully and for the purpose of commercial advantage or private financial gain," perpetrators are subject to fines up to $250,000 and 5 years in jail. Software piracy doesn't pay. Two pirates in Canada were forced to walk the plank with a $22,500 fine. This and similar rulings have sent the message loud and clear: Software piracy is no longer tolerated.

Vendors of software for personal computers estimate that for every software product sold, two more are illegally copied. Software piracy is a serious problem, and software vendors are acting vigorously to prosecute people and companies who violate their copyrights. Worldwide, the software industry loses an estimated 7 to 10 billion dollars a year to software piracy.

The information superhighway poses big problems for software vendors. How do you keep people from distributing copies of software over the Internet or through a BBS? In all likelihood, software will eventually be encrypted such that the purchaser receives a cryptographic key to decode the program and data files. The key would exist in the program, identifying the owner and the buyer. If the buyer illegally distributes the program over an electronic highway, cybercops will be able to trace the action back to the source of the crime.

Some managers confront the issue head on and state bluntly that software piracy is a crime and offenders will be dismissed. This method has proven effective. Some, who are in reality accomplices, look the other way as subordinates copy software for office and personal use.

Other intellectual property, such as a chip design or a new concept in productivity software, is equally vulnerable to theft. Numerous cases involving intellectual property are currently being contested in the courts.

11–5 COMPUTER AND SYSTEM SECURITY

To minimize unethical abuses of information technology and computer crime, individuals and organizations must build an envelope of security around hardware and embed safeguards into the information systems. There are too many points of vulnerability and too much is at stake to overlook the threats to the security of any computer system. These threats take many forms—white-collar crime, natural disasters (earthquakes, floods), vandalism, and carelessness.

In this section we discuss commonly applied measures that can help to neutralize security threats to a computer center, an information system, and a PC.

Sendipitous Surfing: Music

Computer-Center Security

Enterprise-wide information systems provide information and processing capabilities to workers throughout a given organization. Generally, such systems are handled by mainframe computers and/or network server computers located in centralized computer centers. The center can be anything from a secure room for the LAN server to an entire building for the organization's mainframe computers and the information services staff. Whether a room or a building, the computer center has a number of points of vulnerability; these are *hardware, software, files/databases, data communications,* and *personnel.* Each is discussed separately in this section and illustrated in Figure 11–2.

Hardware If the hardware fails, the information system fails. The threat of failure can be minimized by implementing security precautions that prevent access by unauthorized personnel and by taking steps to keep all hardware operational.

Common approaches to securing the premises from unauthorized entry include closed-circuit TV monitors, alarm systems, and computer-controlled devices that check employee badges, fingerprints, or voice prints before unlocking doors at access points. Computer centers also should be isolated from pedestrian traffic. Machine-room fires should be extinguished by a special chemical that douses the fire but does not destroy the files or equipment.

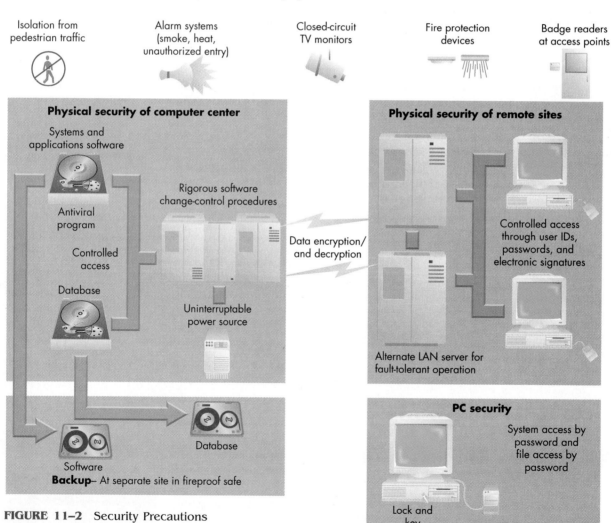

FIGURE 11–2 Security Precautions
Some or all of the security measures noted in the figure are in force in most organizations. Each precaution helps minimize the risk of a computer center's, a PC's, or an information system's vulnerability to crime, disasters, and failure.   Courtesy of International Business Machines Corporation

Any complex system is subject to failure. However, for many organizations, network failure is simply unacceptable. For example, if the network supporting the Hilton Hotel reservation system went down for a couple of hours, thousands of reservations and, perhaps, millions of dollars would be lost. When network downtime is unacceptable, the network must be made **fault-tolerant;** that is, the network must be designed to permit continuous operation, even if important components of the network fail. To accomplish this, parts of the system must be duplicated. For example, the system might have a parallel host processor or an alternate LAN server. Fault-tolerant networks are designed to enable alternate routing of messages. Of course, no network can be made totally fault-tolerant. The degree to which a network is made fault-tolerant depends on the amount of money an organization is willing to spend on its system.

Computers must have a "clean," continuous source of power. To minimize the effects of "dirty" power or power outages, each critical computer should draw its power from an **uninterruptible power source** (**UPS**). Dirty power, with sags and surges in power output or brownouts (low power), causes data transmission errors and program execution errors. A UPS system serves as a buffer between the external power source and the computer system. In a UPS system, the computer is powered by batteries that deliver clean power, which in turn are regenerated by an external power source. If the external power source fails, the UPS system permits operation to continue for a period of time after an outage. This allows operators to either "power down" normally or switch to a backup power source, usually a diesel-powered generator. Until recently, UPS systems were associated only with mainframe computer systems and LAN servers. Now they are economically feasible for microcomputer systems.

Software Unless properly controlled, the software for an information system can be modified for personal gain, or vandalized and rendered useless. Close control of software development and the documentation of an information system is needed to minimize the opportunity for computer crime and vandalism.

Unlawful modification of software. Bank programmers certainly have opportunities to modify software for personal gain. In one case, a couple of programmers modified a savings system to make small deposits from other accounts to their own accounts. Here's how it worked: The interest for each savings account was compounded and credited daily; the calculated interest was rounded to the nearest penny before being credited to the savings account; programs were modified to round down all interest calculations and put the "extra" penny in one of the programmer's savings accounts. It may not seem like much, but a penny a day from thousands of accounts adds up to a lot of money. The "beauty" of the system was that the books balanced and depositors did not miss the 15 cents (an average of ½ cent per day for 30 days) that judiciously was taken from each account each month. Even auditors had difficulty detecting this crime because the total interest paid on all accounts was correct. However, the culprits got greedy and were apprehended when someone noticed that they repeatedly withdrew inordinately large sums of money from their own accounts. Unfortunately, other enterprising programmers in other industries have been equally imaginative.

Operational control procedures built into the design of an information system will constantly monitor processing accuracy. Unfortunately, cagey programmers have been known to get around some of them. Perhaps the best way to safeguard programs from unlawful tampering is to use rigorous change-control procedures. Such procedures require programmers to obtain authorization before modifying an operational program. Change-control procedures make it difficult to modify a program for purposes of personal gain.

Viruses. Michelangelo, Friday the 13th, Stoned, and Jerusalem are words that strike fear in PC users. They're names of computer viruses. The infamous Michelangelo virus hits on March 6, the artist's birthday, destroying stored data. Friday the 13th

GOING ONLINE

11.3
Shop 'Til You Drop

Do some shopping at any electronic mall, such as market placeMCI 〈http://www2. pcy. mci.net/marketplace〉. Identify two items you would like to buy, then shop around for a good deal.

Hand in: The names of at least two products, where you could purchase them (names and URL addresses), and their cost.

causes its damage on that day. Even though computer viruses have no metabolism of their own, some people are convinced that they fit the definition of a living system because they use the metabolism of a host computer for their parasitic existence.

The growing threat of viruses has resulted in tightening software controls. *Virus software,* which has been found at all levels of computing, "infects" other programs and databases. The virus is so named because it can spread from one system to another like a biological virus. Viruses are written by outlaw programmers to cause harm to the computer systems of unsuspecting victims. Left undetected a virus can result in loss of data and/or programs and even physical damage to the hardware.

Individuals and companies routinely run antiviral programs, called *vaccines,* to search for and destroy viruses before they can do their dirty work. Many organizations encourage employees to run antiviral programs prior to March 6th and Friday the 13th. IBM researchers are working on an electronic *immune system* that would automatically detect viruses and neutralize them with digital antibodies. The immune system inoculates other computers on the network, stopping the spread of the virus.

Files/Databases   The database contains the raw material for information. Often the files/databases are the lifeblood of a company. For example, how many companies can afford to lose their accounts receivable file, which documents who owes what? Having several *generations of backups* (backups to backups) to all files is not sufficient insurance against loss of files/databases. The backup and master files should be stored in fireproof safes in separate rooms, preferably in separate buildings.

Data Communications   The mere existence of data communications capabilities poses a threat to security. A knowledgeable criminal can tap into the system from a remote location and use it for personal gain. In a well-designed system, this is not an easy task. But it can be and has been done! When one criminal broke a company's security code and tapped into the network of computers, he was able to order certain products without being billed. He filled a warehouse before he eventually was caught. Another tapped into an international banking exchange system to reroute funds to an account of his own in a Swiss bank. In another case, an oil company consistently was able to outbid a competitor by "listening in" on the latter's data transmissions. On several occasions, overzealous hackers have tapped into sensitive defense computer systems; fortunately, no harm was done.

How do companies protect themselves from these criminal activities? Some companies use **cryptography** to scramble messages sent over data communications channels. Someone who unlawfully intercepts such a message would find meaningless strings of characters. Cryptography is analogous to the code book used by intelligence people during the "cloak-and-dagger" days. Instead of a code book, however, a key is used in conjunction with **encryption/decryption** hardware to unscramble the message. Both sender and receiver must have the key, which is actually an algorithm that rearranges the bit structure of a message.

Personnel   The biggest threat to a company's security system is the dishonesty and/or negligence of its own employees. Managers should pay close attention to who gets hired for positions with access to computer-based information systems and sensitive data. Many companies flash a message on each terminal display such as: "All information on this system is confidential and proprietary." It's not very user-friendly, but it gets the message across to employees that they may be fired if they abuse the system. Someone who is grossly negligent can cause just as much harm as someone who is inherently dishonest.

Information Systems Security

Information systems security is classified as physical or logical. **Physical security** refers to hardware, facilities, magnetic disks, and other items that could be illegally accessed, stolen, or destroyed. For example, restricted access to the mainframe machine room is a form of physical security.

Logical security is built into the software by permitting only authorized persons to access and use the system. Logical security for online systems is achieved primarily by using *user IDs* and *passwords*. Only those people with a need to know are given user IDs and told the password. On occasion, however, these security codes fall into the wrong hands. When this happens, an unauthorized person can gain access to programs and sensitive files simply by dialing up the computer and entering the codes.

Keeping user IDs and passwords from the computer criminal is not easy. One approach is to educate employees about techniques used to obtain user IDs and passwords, such as tailgating. The tailgater simply continues a session begun by an authorized user when the user leaves the room.

Some companies have added another layer of security with the *electronic signature*. The electronic signature, which is built into hardware or software, can be a number or even a digitized signature of an individual. The host or server computer checks the electronic signature against an approved list before permitting access to the system. This thwarts the tailgater who attempts to use illegally obtained passwords on unauthorized PCs or software.

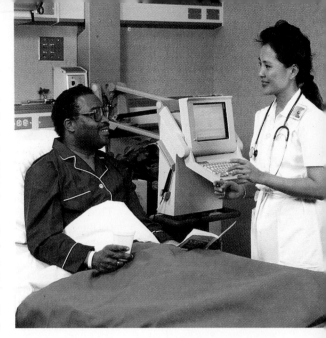

Progressive hospitals restrict staff access to patient medical histories on a need-to-know basis. An employee's user ID and password determine what portions of the database can be accessed.   Courtesy of International Business Machines Corporation

PC Security

Twenty-five years ago, the security problem was solved by wrapping the mainframe-based computer center in an envelope of physical security. Today the security issue is far more complex. PCs more powerful than the mainframes of 25 years ago pepper the corporate landscape. We even carry them with us. It's impractical to apply mainframe standards of security to PCs. If we did, we would all be working in concrete buildings under heavy security and mobile computing would end.

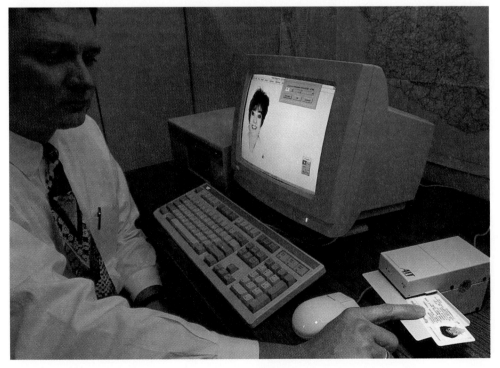

This Secure ID Document System provides instant access to sensitive real-time information for such applications as border monitoring, health care, and voter registration. A virtually tamper proof identification card includes information on the bearer which can easily be verified using scanner technology.   Courtesy of E-Systems, Inc

Mainframe security is carefully planned and controlled by security professionals. In contrast, PC security frequently is the responsibility of the individual users who may or may not have security training. As PC users we have an ongoing obligation to be ever aware of security concerns. Generally, our PCs are readily accessible to other people in the area.

The conscientious PC user has several physical and logical security measures that can be used to safeguard valuable and/or sensitive information. The most frequently used physical tools include the *lock and key* and the *badge reader*. The lock and key, which come standard on most modern PCs, work like an automobile ignition switch. That is, the PC functions only when the lock is turned to the enable position. The badge reader is an optional peripheral device that reads magnetic stripes on badges, such as credit cards. The PC is disabled until an authorized card is inserted in and read by the badge reader. Multimedia systems equipped with the proper software can use *voice prints* to add an extra layer of security.

Often the content of your PC's screen bares your soul or perhaps sensitive corporate data. Some people place a special filter over the screen that permits only straight-on viewing. People use it in the office, airplane, or wherever they need to feel secure about their display.

User IDs and *passwords* remain the foundation of logical security. Users of LAN-based PCs must enter IDs and passwords before being allowed access to LAN resources. Stand-alone PCs also can be set up in a similar manner. Individual files can be secured by assigning them unique passwords. For example, if you were using a word processing package to prepare personnel performance evaluations, you could secure these files by assigning each a password. To recall a file at a later session, you or anyone else would have to enter the name of the file and the associated password to gain access to it.

The user ID is your electronic identifier and may be known by your friends and colleagues. The password, however, is yours alone to protect and use.

▶ Never tell anyone your password.

▶ Never write your password down.

▶ Change your password frequently.

Level of Risk

No combination of security measures will completely remove the vulnerability of a computer center, an information system, a PC, or a file. Security systems are implemented in degrees. That is, an information system can be made marginally secure or very secure, but never totally secure. Each company must determine the level of risk that it is willing to accept. Unfortunately, some corporations are willing to accept an enormous risk and hope that those rare instances of crime and disaster do not occur. Some of them have found out too late that *rarely* is not the same as *never!*

11-6 YOUR CHALLENGE

Your newly acquired base of knowledge has positioned you to mainstream into the information society. However, the computer learning process is ongoing. The dynamics of rapidly advancing computer technology demands a constant updating of skills and expertise. By their very nature, computers bring about change. With the total amount of computing capacity in the world doubling every two years, we can expect even more dramatic change in the future. The cumulative effects of these changes are altering the basic constructs of society and the way we live, work, and play. Terminals and PCs have replaced calculators and ledger books; electronic mail speeds

What's next? The world is changing so quickly that it is difficult to speculate on what it will be like in five years. We know, however, that innovative people are continuously working to apply technology solutions to problems in every facet of life. For example, this is no ordinary minivan; it's a self-driving vehicle created by scientists at Carnegie Mellon University. The vehicle uses a video camera in conjunction with a notebook PC to control steering, speed, and braking. The minivan has logged over 6000 autonomous miles. Perhaps the cruise control of the future may relieve us from steering duties! Courtesy Carnegie Mellon University

communication; word processing has eliminated typewriters; computer-aided design has rendered the drawing table obsolete; computer-based training has become a part of the teaching process; EFT may eventually eliminate the need for money; online shopping is affecting consumer buying habits . . . and the list goes on.

We as a society are, in effect, trading a certain level of computer dependence for an improvement in the quality of life. This improvement in the way we live is not a foregone conclusion. Just as our highways play host to objectionable billboards, carjackings, and automobile accidents, the information superhighway is sure to have back roads lined with sleaze, scams, and cyberthiefs. It is our challenge to harness the power of the computer and direct it toward the benefit of society.

Never before has such opportunity presented itself so vividly. This generation, *your generation,* has the technological foundation and capability of changing dreams into reality.

IMPORTANT TERMS AND SUMMARY OUTLINE

computer matching 112
computer monitoring 113
cryptography 122
encryption/decryption 122
ergonomics 107

fault-tolerant 121
footprint 118
logical security 123
physical security 122

pilferage 119
software piracy 119
uninterruptible power source (UPS) 121

11–1 THE VIRTUAL FRONTIER The virtual frontier encompasses the electronic highways that comprise the Internet, thousands of BBSs, scores of information services, and thousands of private networks. It is sometimes likened to the Wild West because there are no rules. The opportunity for a better life is enticing pioneers to explore the virtual frontier.

11–2 THE JOB OUTLOOK IN THE INFORMATION SOCIETY People who can include computer knowledge on their résumés will have an advantage over those who cannot. Computer competency is a prerequisite of employment in many professions, and in a few more years it may well be a requirement in most professions.

Virtually every organization employs or is considering

employing computer specialists. More and more of these computer specialist positions are being filled in user groups. The systems analyst is but one of dozens of computer specialist careers. Others are programmers, network administrators, PC specialists, computer operators, Internet site specialists, educators specializing in computer education, and on and on.

As information technology continues to move to the forefront in our society, jobs in every discipline are being redefined. Some jobs are being eliminated while others are being created.

11–3 THE WORK PLACE: ERGONOMICS AND GREEN COMPUTING Human factors engineers are applying the principles of **ergonomic** design to ensure that the interface between knowledge worker and work place is safe, comfortable, effective, and efficient. The knowledge worker's work place should be designed with enough flexibility to enable it to be custom-fitted to its worker. Attention to the overall environment (lighting, noise, ventilation) can reduce stress and increase worker performance.

Problems associated with extended use of a terminal or PC are collectively referred to as *video operator's distress syndrome,* or *VODS.* As the number of *repetitive-stress injuries* (*RSIs*) increased for knowledge workers, workstation ergonomics became an increasingly important issue for corporate productivity. A poorly designed work place has the potential to cause *cumulative trauma disorder* (*CTD*), a condition that can lead to a permanent disability of motor skills.

Green computing adopts a more environmentally sound position with respect to the use and manufacture of computing hardware. The EPA's Energy Star guidelines are being used to standardize energy usage for monitors and processors. Good green computing includes sending e-mail (rather than paper); purchasing recycled paper; buying reconditioned components; and telecommuting once or twice a week.

11–4 THE QUESTION OF ETHICS A code of ethics provides direction for computer professionals and users so they can apply computer technology responsibly.

The dominant ethical issue is the privacy of personal information. As automation continues to enrich our lives, it also opens the door for abuses of personal information. Personal information has become the product of a growing industry. Not only are the people involved not asked for permission to use their data, they are seldom even told that their personal information is being sold. **Computer matching** involves the examination of separate databases to identify individuals common to both. **Computer monitoring** is used to measure worker performance.

Computer crime is a relatively recent phenomenon; therefore, laws governing information technology are

few, and those that do exist are subject to a variety of interpretations. Computer crimes are frequently a result of computer fraud, negligence, or incompetence. Crackers tap into computer systems and sometimes leave evidence of unlawful entry, called a **footprint,** or infect the computer system with a virus, which is intended to cause harm to the computer systems of unsuspecting victims. **Software piracy** and **pilferage** are computer crimes.

Security on the Internet is an ongoing problem as Internet-related intrusions are increasing. The Internet's cybercops on the Computer Emergency Response Team at Carnegie Mellon University are ever vigilant in the fight against Internet crimes. The only effective answer to Internet crime is the universal adoption and use of an international encryption standard.

11–5 COMPUTER AND SYSTEM SECURITY The threats to the security of computer centers and information systems call for precautionary measures. A computer center can be vulnerable in its hardware, software, files/databases, data communications, and personnel.

Any complex system is subject to failure, but when network downtime is unacceptable, the network must be made **fault-tolerant;** that is, the network must be designed to permit continuous operation, even if important components of the network fail.

Organizations use a variety of approaches to secure the computer center, including the installation of an **uninterruptible power source** (**UPS**) and the use of **cryptography** to scramble messages sent over data communications channels. A key is used in conjunction with **encryption/decryption** hardware to unscramble the message.

The growing threat of viruses has resulted in the tightening of software controls. Virus software "infects" other programs and databases. Antiviral programs, called *vaccines,* search for and destroy viruses.

Maintain several generations of backups, storing them in fireproof safes in separate rooms or buildings.

Information systems security is classified as **logical security** or **physical security.** Logical security for online systems is achieved primarily by using user IDs and passwords. Another security measure is the electronic signature.

In the PC environment, people use several methods to control accessibility, including the *lock and key* and the *badge reader.* Properly equipped PCs can use *voice prints* to add an extra layer of security.

Security systems are implemented in degrees, and no computer center, LAN server, PC, or system can be made totally secure.

11–6 YOUR CHALLENGE The computer offers us the opportunity to improve the quality of our lives. It is our challenge to harness the power of the computer and direct it to the benefit of society.

REVIEW EXERCISES

Concepts

1. List at least three terms that are commonly used to refer to our wired world.
2. What name is given to programs intended to damage the computer system of an unsuspecting victim?
3. Most computer monitoring takes place at which level of activity: clerical, operational, tactical, or strategic?
4. What is the objective of computer matching?
5. What term is used to describe the situation where a company copies and distributes software without a site-usage license agreement?
6. What is green computing? Give two examples of green computing.
7. What is a fault-tolerant system?
8. Expand the following abbreviations: VODS, RSI, and CTD.
9. What precautions can be taken to minimize the effects of hardware failure?
10. Describe the optimal position for a monitor relative to its user.

Discussion and Problem Solving

11. Information technology is touching all aspects of your life. Are you prepared for it? Explain.
12. Evaluate your work place at home, school, or work. Use the guidelines presented in Figure 11–1.
13. What can you do, that you are not doing now, that would be a move toward green computing?
14. In the past, bank officers have been reluctant to report computer crimes. If you were a customer of a bank that made such a decision, how would you react?
15. Why would a judge sentence one person to 10 years in jail for an unarmed robbery of $25 from a convenience store and another to 18 months for computer fraud involving millions of dollars?
16. Describe what yesterday would have been like if you had not used the capabilities of computers. Keep in mind that businesses with which you deal rely on computers and that many of your appliances are computer-based.
17. Discuss the kinds of personal information that can be obtained by analyzing a person's credit-card transactions during the past year.
18. Internet cybercops at CERT are no longer concerned with minor intrusions to Net security. What are their interests?
19. Currently, the Internet is open and all types of information flow freely, including pornographic text and images. A law enforcement official in Florida calls the Internet a "pedophile's playground." One of the most important issues facing the information superhighway is censorship. Argue for or against censorship.
20. Two lawyers used the Internet to broadcast thousands of e-mail messages advertising their services. They were subsequently flamed (sent angry e-mail messages) and vilified by Internet users for what they believed to be an inappropriate use of the Net. The attorneys broke no laws. Was the reaction of Internet users justified? Explain.

SELF-TEST (BY SECTION)

11–1 The _____ is a metaphor frequently used as a collective reference to the electronic links that have wired our world.

11–2 Contrary to popular belief, the emergence of information technology does not eliminate jobs. (T/F)

11–3 **a.** The study of the relationships between people and their machines is called: (a) humanology, (b) human economics, or (c) ergonomics?
b. A monitor emits radiation. (T/F)
c. What is the approximate cost of running a PC and a laser printer 24 hours a day for a year: (a) $10, (b) $50, or (c) $250?

11–4 **a.** The number of federal government agencies that maintain computer-based files on individuals is between: (a) 50 and 100, (b) 500 and 1000, or (c) 5000 and 10,000?
b. In _____ , computers continuously gather and assimilate data on worker activities for the purpose of measuring worker performance.
c. Gaining unauthorized access to any computer system with the intent of defrauding the system is

a: (a) violation of public ethics, (b) misdemeanor, or (c) felony?

d. Many legal questions involving computers and information processing are yet to be incorporated into the federal laws. (T/F)

e. The evidence of unlawful entry to a computer system is called a _____ .

f. What law is violated when an organization duplicates proprietary software without permission: (a) civil rights, (b) antitrust, or (c) copyright?

11–5 a. Logical security for online systems is achieved primarily by user IDs and _____ .

b. Virusology is the study of the assignment of security codes. (T/F)

c. Although expensive, some companies implement the security measure needed to be totally secure. (T/F)

11–6 The total computing capacity in the world is increasing at slightly less than 5% per year. (T/F)

Self-test Answers. **11–1** information superhighway. **11–2** F. **11–3 (a)** c; **(b)** T; **(c)** c. **11–4 (a)** c; **(b)** computer monitoring; **(c)** c; **(d)** T; **(e)** footprint; **(f)** c. **11–5 (a)** passwords; **(b)** F; **(c)** F. **11–6** F.

GLOSSARY

Absolute cell address A cell address in a spreadsheet that always refers to the same cell.

Access arm The disk drive mechanism used to position the read/write heads over the appropriate track.

Access time The time interval between the instant a computer makes a request for a transfer of data from a secondary storage device and the instant this operation is completed.

Accumulator The computer register in which the result of an arithmetic or logic operation is formed. (Related to *arithmetic and logic unit*.)

Active window The window in Microsoft Windows or Windows 95 with which the user may interact.

Address (1) A name, numeral, or label that designates a particular location in primary or secondary storage. (2) A location identifier for nodes in a computer network.

Address bus Pathway through which source and destination addresses are transmitted between RAM, cache memory, and the processor. (See also *data bus*.)

Alpha (1) A reference to the letters of the alphabet. (Compare with *numeric* and *alphanumeric*.) (2) A RISC-based microprocessor from Digital Equipment Corporation.

Alphanumeric Pertaining to a character set that contains letters, digits, punctuation, and special symbols. (Related to *alpha* and *numeric*.)

Analog signal A continuous wave form signal that can be used to represent such things as sound, temperature, and velocity. (See also *digital signal*.)

Animation The rapid repositioning of objects on a display to create movement.

Anonymous FTP site An Internet site that permits FTP (file transfer protocol) file transfers without prior permission.

ANSI The American National Standards Institute is a non-government standards-setting organization which develops and publishes standards for "voluntary" use in the United States.

Application icon A pictograph in the Microsoft Windows desktop that represents a minimized application window.

Application window A rectangular window containing an open, or running, application in Microsoft Windows.

Applications programmer A programmer who translates analyst-prepared system and input/output specifications into programs. Programmers design the logic, then code, debug, test, and document the programs.

Applications software Software designed and written to address a specific personal, business, or processing task.

Argument That portion of a function which identifies the data to be operated on.

Arithmetic and logic unit That portion of the computer that performs arithmetic and logic operations. (Related to *accumulator*.)

Arithmetic operators Mathematical operators (add [+], subtract [-], multiply [*], divide [/], and exponentiation [^]) used in programming and in spreadsheet and database software for computations.

Artificial intelligence (AI) The ability of a computer to reason, to learn, to strive for self-improvement, and to simulate human sensory capabilities.

ASCII [*American Standard Code for Information Interchange*] An encoding system.

ASCII file A generic text file that is stripped of program-specific control characters.

Assembler language A second generation programming language that uses easily recognized symbols, called mnemonics, to represent instructions.

Assistant system This knowledge-based system that helps users make relatively straightforward decisions. (See also *expert system*.)

Asynchronous transmission A protocol in which data are transmitted at irregular intervals on an as-needed basis. (See also *synchronous transmission*.)

Audio file A file that contains digitized sound.

Authoring software Software that lets you create multimedia applications that integrate sound, motion, text, animation, and images.

Automatic teller machine (ATM) An automated deposit/withdrawal device used in banking.

Back-end applications software This software on the server computer performs processing tasks in support of its clients, such as tasks associated with storage and maintenance of a centralized corporate database. (See also *front-end applications software*.)

Backbone A system of routers and the associated transmission media that facilitates the interconnection of computer networks.

Background (1) That part of RAM that contains the lowest priority programs. (2) In Windows, the area of the display over which the foreground is superimposed. (Contrast with *foreground*.)

Backup file Duplicate of an existing file.

Backup Pertaining to equipment, procedures, or databases that can be used to restart the system in the event of system failure.

Badge reader An input device that reads data on badges and cards.

Bar code A graphic encoding technique in which printed vertical bars of varying widths are used to represent data.

Bar graph A graph that contains bars that represent specified numeric values.

Batch processing A technique in which transactions and/or jobs are collected into groups (batched) and processed together.

Baud (1) A measure of the maximum number of electronic signals that can be transmitted via a communications channel. (2) Bits per second (common-use definition).

Binary A base-2 numbering system.

Bit A *bi*nary digi*t* (0 or 1).

Bit-mapped Referring to an image that has been projected, or mapped, to a screen based on binary bits. (See also *raster graphics*.)

Bits per second (bps) The number of bits that can be transmitted per second over a communications channel.

Boilerplate Existing text in a word processing file that can in some way be customized to be used in a variety of word processing applications.

Boot The procedure for loading the operating system to primary storage and readying a computer system for use.

Bubble memory Nonvolatile solid-state memory.

Bug A logic or syntax error in a program, a logic error in the design of a computer system, or a hardware fault. (See also *debug*.)

Bulletin-board system (BBS) The electronic counterpart of a wall-mounted bulletin board that enables users in a computer network to exchange ideas and information via a centralized message database.

Bus An electrical pathway through which the processor sends data and commands to RAM and all peripheral devices.

Bus topology A computer network that permits the connection of terminals, peripheral devices, and microcomputers along an open-ended central cable.

Button bar A software option that contains a group of pictographs that represent a menu option or a command.

Byte A group of adjacent bits configured to represent a character or symbol.

C A transportable programming language that can be used to develop software.

C++ An object-oriented version of the C programming language.

Cache memory High-speed solid-state memory for program instructions and data.

CAD See *computer-aided design*.

Carrier Standard-sized pin connectors that permit chips to be attached to a circuit board.

Cascading menu A pop-up menu that is displayed when a command from the active menu is chosen.

Cascading windows Two or more windows that are displayed on a computer screen in an overlapping manner.

Cathode-ray tube See *CRT*.

CBT See *computer-based training*.

CD production station A device used to duplicate locally produced CD-ROMs.

CD writer A peripheral device that can write once to a CD-R disk to create an audio CD or a CD-ROM.

CD-R [*C*ompact *D*isk-*R*ecordable] The medium on which CD writers create CDs and CD-ROMs.

CD-ROM disk [*C*ompact-*D*isk–*R*ead-*O*nly *M*emory disk] A type of optical laser storage media.

CD-ROM drive A storage device into which an interchangeable CD-ROM is inserted for processing.

Cell address The location—column and row—of a cell in a spreadsheet.

Cell The intersection of a particular row and column in a spreadsheet.

Central processing unit (CPU) See *processor*.

Centronics connector A 36-pin connector that is used for the electronic interconnection of computers, modems, and other peripheral devices.

Channel capacity The number of bits that can be transmitted over a communications channel per second.

Channel The facility by which data are transmitted between locations in a computer network (e.g., terminal to host, host to printer).

Chief information officer (CIO) The individual responsible for all the information services activity in a company.

Chip See *integrated circuit*.

Choose To pick a menu item or icon in such a manner as to initiate processing activity.

CISC [*C*omplex *I*nstruction *S*et *C*omputer] A computer design architecture that offers machine language programmers a wide variety of instructions. (Contrast with *RISC*.)

Click A single tap on a mouse's button.

Client application (1) An application running on a networked workstation or PC that works in tandem with a server application. (See also *server application*.) (2) In object linking an embedding, the application containing the destination document.

Client computer Typically a PC or a workstation which requests processing support or another type of service from one or more server computers. (See also *server computer*.)

Client/server computing A computing environment in which processing capabilities are distributed throughout a network such that a client computer requests processing or some other type of service from a server computer.

Clip art Prepackaged electronic images that are stored on disk to be used as needed in computer-based documents.

Clipboard An intermediate holding area in internal storage for information en route to another application.

Clone A hardware device or a software package that emulates a product with an established reputation and market acceptance.

Coaxial cable   A shielded wire used as a medium to transmit data between computers and between computers and peripheral devices.

COBOL   [*Common Business Oriented Language*] A third-generation programming language designed to handle business problems.

Code   (1) The rules used to translate a bit configuration into alphanumeric characters and symbols. (2) The process of compiling computer instructions into the form of a computer program. (3) The actual computer program.

Command   An instruction to a computer that invokes the execution of a preprogrammed sequence of instructions.

Common carrier   A company that provides channels for data transmission.

Common User Access (CUA)   The standard by which all software applications designed to be run under Microsoft's Windows must adhere.

Communications channel   The facility by which data are transmitted between locations in a computer network.

Communications protocols   Rules established to govern the way data in a computer network are transmitted.

Communications server   The LAN component that provides external communications links.

Communications software   (1) Software that enables a microcomputer to emulate a terminal and to transfer files between a micro and another computer. (2) Software that enables communication between remote devices in a computer network.

Compatibility   Pertaining to the ability of computers and computer components (hardware and software) to work together.

Compile   To translate a high-level programming language into machine language in preparation for execution.

Compiler   A program that translates the instructions of a high-level language to machine-language instructions that the computer can interpret and execute.

Compound document   A document, such as a word processing document, that contains one or more linked objects from other applications.

Computer   An electronic device capable of interpreting and executing programmed commands for input, output, computation, and logic operations.

Computer competency   A fundamental understanding of the technology, operation, applications, and issues surrounding computers.

Computer matching   The procedure whereby separate databases are examined and individuals common to both are identified.

Computer monitoring   Observing and regulating employee activities and job performance through the use of computers.

Computer network   An integration of computer systems, terminals, and communications links.

Computer operator   One who performs those hardware-based activities needed to keep production information systems operational in the mainframe environment.

Computer system   A collective reference to all interconnected computing hardware, including processors, storage devices, input/output devices, and communications equipment.

Computer virus   See *virus*.

Computer-aided design (CAD)   Use of computer graphics in design, drafting, and documentation in product and manufacturing engineering.

Computer-aided software engineering (CASE)   An approach to software development that combines automation and the rigors of the engineering discipline.

Computer-based training (CBT)   Using computer technologies for training and education.

Computerese   A colloquial reference to the language of computers and information technology.

Configuration   The computer and its peripheral devices.

Connectivity   Pertains to the degree to which hardware devices, software, and databases can be functionally linked to one another.

Context-sensitive   Referring to an on-screen explanation that relates to a user's current software activity.

Control clerk   A person who accounts for all input to and output from a computer center.

Control unit   The portion of the processor that interprets program instructions, directs internal operations, and directs the flow of input/output to or from RAM.

Cooperative processing   An environment in which organizations cooperate internally and externally to take full advantage of available information and to obtain meaningful, accurate, and timely information. (See also *intra-company networking*.)

Coprocessor   An auxiliary processor that handles a narrow range of tasks, usually those associated with arithmetic operations.

CPU   See *processor*.

Cracker   An overzealous hacker who "cracks" through network security to gain unauthorized access to the network. (Contrast with *hacker*.)

Cross-platform technologies   Enabling technologies that allow communication and the sharing of resources between different platforms.

CRT   [*Cathode-Ray Tube*] The video monitor component of a terminal.

Cryptography   A communications crime-prevention technology that uses methods of data encryption and decryption to scramble codes sent over communications channels.

CSMA/CD access method   [*Carrier Sense Multiple Access/Collision Detection*] A network access method in which nodes on the LAN must contend for the right to send a message.

Current window   The window in a GUI in which the user can manipulate text, data, or graphics.

Cursor, graphics   Typically an arrow or a cross hair which can be moved about a monitor's screen by a point-and-draw device to create a graphic image or select an item from a menu. (See also *cursor, text*.)

Cursor, text A blinking character that indicates the location of the next keyed-in character on the display screen. (See also *cursor, graphics.*)

Cursor-control keys The arrow keys on the keyboard that move the cursor vertically and horizontally.

Custom programming Program development to create software for situations unique to a particular processing environment.

Cyberphobia The irrational fear of, and aversion to, computers.

Cylinder A disk storage concept. A cylinder is that portion of the disk that can be read in any given position of the access arm. (Contrast with *sector.*)

Data Representations of facts. Raw material for information. (Plural of *datum.*)

Data bits A data communications parameter that refers to a timing unit.

Data bus A common pathway between RAM, cache memory, and the processor through which data and instructions are transferred. (See also *address bus.*)

Data cartridge Magnetic tape storage in cassette format.

Data communications The collection and distribution of the electronic representation of information between two locations.

Data communications specialist A person who designs and implements computer networks.

Data compression A method of reducing secondary storage requirements for computer files.

Data entry The transcription of source data into a machine-readable format.

Data entry operator A person who uses key entry devices to transcribe data into machine-readable format.

Data file This file contains data organized into records.

Data flow diagram A design technique that permits documentation of a system or program at several levels of generality.

Data item The value of a field. (Compare with *field.*)

Data path The electronic channel through which data flows within a computer system.

Data processing (DP) Using the computer to perform operations on data.

Data processing (DP) system Systems concerned with transaction handling and record-keeping, usually for a particular functional area.

Data transfer rate The rate at which data are read/written from/to secondary storage to RAM.

Database The integrated data resource for a computer-based information system.

Database administrator (DBA) The individual responsible for the physical and logical maintenance of the database.

Database record Related data that are read from, or written to, the database as a unit.

Database software Software that permits users to create and maintain a database and to extract information from the database.

Debug To eliminate bugs in a program or system. (See also *bug.*)

Decision support system (DSS) An interactive information system that relies on an integrated set of user-friendly hardware and software tools to produce and present information targeted to support management in the decision-making process. (Contrast with *MIS* and *EIS.*)

Decode To reverse the encoding process. (Contrast with *encode.*)

Decoder That portion of a processor's control unit that interprets instructions.

Default options Preset software options that are assumed valid unless specified otherwise by the user.

Density The number of bytes per linear length or unit area of a recording medium.

Desktop The screen in Windows upon which icons, windows, a background, and so on are displayed.

Desktop film recorders An output device that permits the reproduction of high-resolution computer-generated graphic images on 35-mm film.

Desktop PC A non-portable personal computer that is designed to rest on the top of a desk. (Contrast with *laptop PC* and *tower PC.*)

Desktop publishing (DTP) Refers to the capability of producing typeset-quality camera-ready copy for publication from the confines of a desktop.

Desktop publishing software Software that allows users to produce near-typeset-quality copy for newsletters, advertisements, and many other printing needs, all from the confines of a desktop.

Destination application, clipboard The software application into which the clipboard contents are to be pasted. (Contrast with *source application.*)

Detailed system design That portion of the systems development process in which the target system is defined in detail.

Device controller Microprocessors that control the operation of peripheral devices.

Device driver software Software that contains instructions needed by the operating system to communicate with the peripheral device.

Dial-up line See *switched line.*

Dialog box A window that is displayed when the user must choose parameters or enter further information before the chosen menu option can be executed.

Digital signal Electronic signals that are transmitted as in strings of 1s and 0s. (See also *analog signal.*)

Digital camera A camera that records images digitally rather than on film.

Digital convergence The integration of computers, communications, and consumer electronics, with all having digital compatibility.

Digitize To translate data or an image into a discrete format that can be interpreted by computers.

Dimmed A menu option, which is usually gray, that is disabled or unavailable.

Digitizer tablet and pen A pressure-sensitive tablet with the same *x–y* coordinates as a computer-generated screen. The outline of an image drawn on a tablet with a stylus (pen) or puck is reproduced on the display.

Direct conversion An approach to system conversion whereby operational support by the new system is begun when the existing system is terminated.

Direct access See *random access.*

Direct-access file See *random file.*

Direct-access processing See *random processing.*

Direct-access storage device (DASD) A random-access secondary storage.

Disk, magnetic A secondary storage medium for random-access data storage available in permanently installed or interchangeable formats.

Disk address The physical location of a particular set of data or a program on a magnetic disk.

Disk caching A hardware/software technique in which frequently referenced disk-based data are placed in an area of RAM that simulates disk storage. (See also *RAM disk.*)

Disk cartridge An environmentally sealed interchangeable disk module that contains one or more hard disk platters.

Disk density The number of bits that can be stored per unit of area on the disk-face surface.

Disk drive, magnetic A magnetic storage device that records data on flat rotating disks. (Compare with *tape drive, magnetic.*)

Disk optimizer A program that reorganizes files on a hard disk to eliminate file fragmentation.

Diskette A thin interchangeable disk for secondary random-access data storage (same as *floppy disk*).

Docking station A device into which a notebook PC is inserted to give the notebook PC expanded capabilities, such as a high-capacity disk, interchangeable disk options, a tape backup unit, a large monitor, and so on.

Document file The result when work with an applications program, such as word processing, is saved to secondary storage.

Document icon A pictograph used by Windows within an application to represent a minimized document window.

Document window Window within an application window that is used to display a separate document created or used by that application.

Document-conversion program Software that converts files generated on one software package into a format consistent with another.

Domain expert An expert in a particular field who provides the factual knowledge and the heuristic rules for input to a knowledge base.

DOS [*D*isk *O*perating *S*ystem] See *MS-DOS.*

Dot pitch The distance between the centers of adjacent pixels on a display.

Dot-matrix printer A printer that arranges printed dots to form characters and images.

Double click Tapping a button on a point-and-draw device twice in rapid succession.

Download The transmission of data from a remote computer to a local computer.

Downsizing Used to describe the trend toward increased reliance on smaller computers for personal as well as enterprise-wide processing tasks.

Downtime The time during which a computer system is not operational.

DP See *data processing.*

Drag A point-and-draw device procedure by which an object is moved or a contiguous area on the display is marked for processing.

Drag-and-drop software Software that lets users drag ready-made shapes from application-specific stencils to the desired position on the drawing area to do drawings for flowcharting, landscaping, business graphics, and other applications.

Draw software Software that enables users to create electronic images. Resultant images are stored as vector graphics images.

Driver module The program module that calls other subordinate program modules to be executed as they are needed (also called a *main program*).

DTP See *desktop publishing.*

Dynamic RAM (DRAM) A type of RAM technology that requires stored data to be refreshed hundreds of times per second.

E-mail See *electronic mail.*

E-time See *execution time.*

EBCDIC [*E*xtended *B*inary *C*oded *D*ecimal *I*nterchange *C*ode] An 8-bit encoding system.

Echo A host computer's retransmission of characters back to the sending device.

Education coordinator The person within an organization who coordinates all computer-related educational activities.

Edutainment software Software that combines *edu*cation and enter*tainment.*

EFT [*E*lectronic *F*unds *T*ransfer] A computer-based system allowing electronic transfer of money from one account to another.

EGA [*E*nhanced *G*raphics *A*dapter] A circuit board that enables the interfacing of high-resolution monitors to microcomputers.

EISA [*E*xtended *I*ndustry *S*tandard *A*rchitecture] A bus architecture for PC-compatible processors.

Electronic data interchange (EDI) The use of computers and data communications to transmit data electronically between.

Electronic dictionary A disk-based dictionary used in conjunction with a spelling-checker program to verify the spelling of words in a word processing document.

Electronic funds transfer See *EFT.*

Electronic mail A computer application whereby messages are transmitted via data communications to "electronic mailboxes" (also called *E-mail*). (Contrast with *voice message switching.*)

Electronic messaging A workgroup computing application that enables electronic mail to be associated with other workgroup applications.

Encode To apply the rules of a code. (Contrast with *decode*.)

Encoding system A system that permits alphanumeric characters and symbols to be coded in terms of bits.

Encryption/decryption The encoding of data for security purposes. Encoded data must be decoded or deciphered to be used.

Enterprise-wide information system Information systems which provide information and processing capabilities to workers throughout a given organization.

Ergonomics The study of the relationships between people and machines.

Exception report A report that has been filtered to highlight critical information.

Executable program file A file that contains programs that can be executed run.

Execution time The elapsed time it takes to execute a computer instruction and store the results (also called *E-time*).

Executive information system (EIS) A system designed specifically to support decision making at the executive levels of management, primarily the tactical and strategic levels.

Exit routine A software procedure that returns you to a GUI, an operating system prompt, or a higher-level applications program.

Expansion board These add-on circuit boards contain the electronic circuitry for many supplemental capabilities, such as a fax modem, and are made to fit a particular type of bus. (Also called *expansion cards*.)

Expansion bus An extension of the common electrical bus which accepts the expansion boards that control the video display, disks, and other peripherals. (See also *bus*.)

Expansion card See *expansion board*.

Expansion slots Slots within the processing component of a microcomputer into which optional add-on circuit boards may be inserted.

Expert system An interactive knowledge-based system that responds to questions, asks for clarification, makes recommendations, and generally helps users make complex decisions. (See also *assistant system*.)

Expert system shell The software that enables the development of expert systems.

Export The process of converting a file in the format of the current program to a format that can be used by another program. (Contrast with *import*.)

Extended ASCII An 8-bit extension of the ASCII encoding system that includes 128 non-standard ASCII symbols.

Facsimile (fax) The transferring of images, usually of hard-copy documents, via telephone lines to another device that can receive and interpret the images.

Fault tolerant Referring to a computer system or network that is resistant to software errors and hardware problems.

Fax modem A modem that enables a PC to emulate a facsimile machine. (See also *modem*.)

Fax See *facsimile*.

Feedback loop A closed loop in which a computer-controlled process generates data that become input to the computer.

Fetch instruction That part of the instruction cycle in which the control unit retrieves a program instruction from RAM and loads it to the processor.

Fiber optic cable A data transmission medium that carries data in the form of light in very thin transparent fibers.

Field The smallest logical unit of data. Examples are employee number, first name, and price. (Compare with *data item*.)

File (1) A collection of related records. (2) A named area on a secondary storage device that contains a program or digitized information (text, image, sound, and so on).

File allocation table (FAT) MS-DOS's method of storing and keeping track of files on a disk.

File compression A technique by which file size can be reduced. Compressed files are decompressed for use.

File server A dedicated computer system with high-capacity disk for storing the data and programs shared by the users on a local area network.

File Transfer Protocol (FTP) A communications protocol that is used to transmit files over the Internet.

Filtering The process of selecting and presenting only that information appropriate to support a particular decision.

Fixed disk See *hard disk*.

Flash memory A type nonvolatile memory that can be altered easily by the user.

Flat files A file that does not point to or physically link with another file.

Flat-panel monitor A monitor, thin from front to back, that uses liquid crystal and gas plasma technology.

Floating menu A special-function menu that can be positioned anywhere on the work area until you no longer need it.

Floppy disk See *diskette*.

Floppy disk drive A disk drive that accepts either the 3.5-inch or 5.25-inch diskette.

FLOPS [*Fl*oating *P*oint *O*perations *P*er *S*econd] A measure of speed for supercomputers.

Floptical disk drive A disk drive that uses optical technology to read and write to 20-MB diskettes as well as the standard 3 1/2-inch diskettes.

Flowchart A diagram that illustrates data, information, and work flow via specialized symbols which, when connected by flow lines, portray the logic of a system or program.

Flowcharting The act of creating a flowchart.

Font A typeface that is described by its letter style, its height in points, and its presentation attribute.

Footprint (1) The evidence of unlawful entry or use of a computer system. (2) The floor or desktop space require for a hardware component.

Foreground (1) That part of RAM that contains the highest priority program. (2) In Windows, the area of the display containing the active window. (Contrast with *background*.)

Formatted disk A disk that has been initialized with the recording format for a specific operating system.

FORTRAN [*FOR* mula *TRAN* slator] A high-level programming language designed primarily for scientific applications.

Fourth-generation language (FOURTH GENERATION LANGUAGE) A programming language that uses high-level English-like instructions to retrieve and format data for inquiries and reporting.

Frame A rectangular area in a desktop publishing–produced document into which ele-ments, such as text and images, are placed.

Front-end applications software Client software that performs processing associated with the user interface and applications processing that can be done locally.

Front-end processor A processor used to off-load certain data communications tasks from the host processor.

Full-duplex line A communications channel that transmits data in both directions at the same time. (Contrast with *half-duplex line*.)

Full-screen editing This word processing feature permits the user to move the cursor to any position in the document to insert or replace text.

Function A predefined operation that performs mathematical, logical, statistical, financial, and character-string operations on data in a spreadsheet or a database.

Function key A special-function key on the keyboard that can be used to instruct the computer to perform a specific operation.

Function-based information system An information system designed for the exclusive support of a specific application area, such as inventory management or accounting.

Functional specifications Specifications that describe the logic of an information system from the user's perspective.

Gb See *gigabit*.

GB See *gigabyte*.

General system design That portion of the systems development process in which the target system is defined in general.

General-purpose computer Computer systems that are designed with the flexibility to do a variety of tasks, such as CAI, payroll processing, climate control, and so on.

Geosynchronous orbit An orbit that permits a communications satellite to maintain a fixed position relative to the surface of the earth.

GFLOPS A billion FLOPS. (See *FLOPS*).

Gigabit (Gb) One billion bits.

Gigabyte (GB) One billion bytes.

Gopher A type of menu tree to "go for" items on the Internet, thus bypassing complicated addresses and commands.

Graceful exit Quitting a program according to normal procedures and returning to a higher-level program.

Grammar and style checker An add-on program to word processing software that highlights grammatical concerns and deviations from effective writing style in a word processing document.

Graphical user interface (GUI) A user-friendly interface that lets users interact with the system by pointing to processing options with a point-and-draw device.

Graphics adapter A device controller which provides the electronic link between the motherboard and the monitor.

Graphics-conversion program Software that enables files containing graphic images to be passed between programs.

Graphics file A file that contains digitized images.

Graphics mode One of two modes of operation for PC monitors. (Contrast with *text mode*.)

Graphics software Software that enables you to create line drawings, art, and presentation graphics.

Gray scales The number of shades of a color that can be presented on a monochrome monitor's screen or on a monochrome printer's output.

Group windows A window within the Windows Program Manager that contains groups of program-item icons.

Groupware Software whose application is designed to benefit a group of people. (Related to *workgroup computing*.)

Hacker A computer enthusiast who uses the computer as a source of recreation. (Contrast with *cracker*.)

Half-duplex line A communications channel that transmits data in one direction at the same time. (Contrast with *full-duplex line*.)

Half-size expansion board An expansion board that fits in half an expansion slot.

Handshaking The process by which both sending and receiving devices in a computer network maintain and coordinate data communications.

Hard copy A readable printed copy of computer output. (Contrast with *soft copy*.)

Hard disk A permanently installed, continuously spinning magnetic storage medium made up of one or more rigid disk platters. (Same as *fixed disk*; contrast with *interchangeable disk*.).

Hard disk drive See *hard disk*.

Hardware The physical devices that comprise a computer system. (Contrast with *software*.)

Help command A software feature that provides an on-line explanation of or instruction on how to proceed.

Help desk A centralized location (either within an organization or outside of it) where computer-related questions about product usage, installation, problems, or services are answered.

High-level language A language with instructions that combine several machine-level instructions into one instruction. (Compare with *machine language* or *low-level language*.)

Horizontal scroll bar A narrow screen object located along the bottom edge of a window that is used to navigate side to side through a document.

Host computer The processor responsible for the overall control of a computer system.

Host mode A mode of PC operation in which remote users can call in and establish a communications link via terminal emulation. (Contrast with *terminal emulation.*)

Hotkey A seldom used key combination that, when activated, causes the computer to perform the function associated with the key combination.

Hydra printer Multifunction machines that can handle several paper-related tasks such as computer-based printing, facsimile, scanning, and copying.

Hypermedia Software that enables the integration of data, text, graphics, sounds of all kinds, and full-motion video. (See also *hypertext.*)

Hypertext Data management software that provides links between key words in the unstructured text-based documents. (See also *hypermedia.*)

I/O [*Input/Output*] Input or output or both.

I-time See *instruction time.*

IBM Personal Computer (IBM PC) IBM's first personal computer (1981). This PC was the basis for PC-compatible computers.

Icons Pictographs used in place of words or phrases on screen displays.

Idea processor A program or word processing feature that allows the user to organize and document thoughts and ideas in outline form.

Image processing A reference to computer applications in which digitized images are retrieved, displayed, altered, merged with text, stored, and sent via data communications to one or several remote locations.

Image scanner A device which can scan and digitize an image so that it can be stored on a disk and manipulated by a computer.

Impact printer A printer that uses pins or hammers which hit a ribbon to transfer images to the paper.

Import The process of converting data in one format to a format that is compatible with the calling program. (Contrast with *export.*)

Inference engine The logic embodied in the software of an expert system.

Information Data that have been collected and processed into a meaningful form.

Information resource management (IRM) A concept advocating that information be treated as a corporate resource.

Information service A commercial network that provides remote users with access to a variety of information services.

Information society A society in which the generation and dissemination of information becomes the central focus of commerce.

Information superhighway A metaphor for a network of high-speed data communication links that will eventually connect virtually every facet of our society.

Information system A computer-based system that provides both data processing capability and information for managerial decision making.

Information technology A collective reference to the integration of computing technology and information processing.

Information-based decision See *nonprogrammed decision.*

Ink-jet printer A nonimpact printer in which the print head contains independently controlled injection chambers that squirt ink droplets on the paper to form letters and images.

Input Data entered to a computer system for processing.

Input/output A generic reference to input and/or output to a computer.

Input/output-bound operation The amount of work that can be performed by the computer system is limited primarily by the speeds of the I/O devices.

Insert mode A data entry mode in which the character entered is inserted at the cursor position.

Instruction A programming language statement that specifies a particular computer operation to be performed.

Instruction register The register that contains the instruction being executed.

Instruction time The clapsed time it takes to fetch and decode a computer instruction (also called *I-time*).

Integrated circuit (IC) Thousands of electronic components that are etched into a tiny silicon chip in the form of a special-function electronic circuit.

Integrated information system An information system that services two or more functional areas, all of which share a common database.

Integrated Services Digital Network (ISDN) A digital telecommunications standard.

Interactive Pertaining to online and immediate communication between the user and the computer.

Interchangeable disk A magnetic disk that can be stored offline and loaded to the computer system as needed. (Contrast with *hard disk*, or *fixed disk.*)

Internet, the (the Net) A global network that connects more than tens of thousands of networks, millions of large multiuser computers, and tens of millions of users in more than 100 countries.

Interoperability The ability to run software and exchange information in a multiplatform environment.

Invoke Execute a command or a macro.

Joystick A vertical stick that moves the cursor on a screen in the direction in which the stick is pushed.

Jukebox A storage device for multiple sets of CD-ROMs, tape cartridges, or disk modules enabling ready access to vast amounts of online data.

Kb See *kilobit.*

KB See *kilobyte.*

Kernel An operating system program that loads other operating system programs and applications programs to RAM as they are needed.

Key field The field in a record that is used as an identifier for accessing, sorting, and collating records.

Key pad That portion of a keyboard that permits rapid numeric data entry.

Keyboard A device used for key data entry.

Keyboard templates Typically, a plastic keyboard overlay that indicates which commands are assigned to particular function keys.

Kilobit (Kb) 1024, or about 1000, bits.

Kilobyte (KB) 1024, or about 1000, bytes.

Knowledge base The foundation of a knowledge-based system that contains facts, rules, inferences, and procedures.

Knowledge engineer Someone trained in the use of expert system shells and in the interview techniques needed to extract information from a domain expert.

Knowledge worker Someone whose job function revolves around the use, manipulation, and dissemination of information.

Knowledge-acquisition facility That component of the expert system shell that permits the construction of the knowledge base.

Knowledge-based system A computer-based system, often associated with artificial intelligence, that helps users make decisions by enabling them to interact with a knowledge base.

LAN operating system The operating system for a local area network.

LAN server A high-end PC on a local area network whose resources are shared by other users on the LAN.

Landscape Referring to the orientation of the print on the page. Printed lines run parallel to the longer side of the page. (Contrast with *portrait.*)

Laptop PC Portable PC that can operate without an external power source. (Contrast with *desktop PC* and *tower PC.*)

Laser printer A page printer that uses laser technology to produce the image.

Layout A reference to the positioning of the visual elements on a display or page.

Leased line See *private line.*

Librarian The person in a computer center who keeps track of interchangeable disks and tapes, and maintains a reference library of printed and computer-based material.

Line printer A printer that prints a line at a time.

Load To transfer programs or data from secondary to primary storage.

Local area network (LAN or local net) A system of hardware, software, and communications channels that connects devices on the local premises. (Contrast with *wide area network.*)

Local bus A bus that links expansion boards directly to the computer system's common bus.

Local net See *local area network.*

Log off The procedure by which a user terminates a communications link with a remote computer. (Contrast with *log on.*)

Log on The procedure by which a user establishes a communications link with a remote computer. (Contrast with *log off.*)

Logic error A programming error that causes an erroneous result when the program is executed.

Logical operators AND, OR, and NOT operators can be used to combine relational expressions logically in spreadsheet, database, and other programs. (See also *relational operators.*)

Logical security That aspect of computer-center security that deals with user access to systems and data.

Loop A sequence of program instructions executed repeatedly until a particular condition is met.

Low-level language A language comprising the fundamental instruction set of a particular computer. (Compare with *high-level programming language.*)

Machine cycle The cycle of operations performed by the processor to process a single program instruction: fetch, decode, execute, and place result in memory.

Machine language The programming language that is interpreted and executed directly by the computer.

Macintosh Apple Computer's mainline personal computer.

Macintosh System The operating system for the Apple Macintosh line of personal computers.

Macro A sequence of frequently used operations or keystrokes that can be invoked to help speed user interaction with microcomputer productivity software.

Macro language Programming languages whose instructions relate specifically to the functionality of the parent software.

Magnetic stripe A magnetic storage medium for low-volume storage of data on badges and cards. (Related to *badge reader.*)

Magnetic tape cartridge Cartridge-based magnetic tape storage media.

Magnetic tape drive See *tape drive, magnetic.*

Magnetic tape See *tape, magnetic.*

Magnetic-ink character recognition (MICR) A data entry technique used primarily in banking. Magnetic characters are imprinted on checks and deposits, then scanned to retrieve the data.

Magneto-optical disk An optical laser disk with read and write capabilities.

Magneto-optical technology An erasable recording technology that incorporates attributes of both magnetic and optical storage technologies.

Mail merge A computer application in which text generated by word processing is merged with data from a database (e.g., a form letter with an address).

Main menu The highest-level menu in a menu tree.

Main program Same as *driver module.*

Mainframe computer A large computer that can service many users simultaneously in support of enterprise-wide applications.

Management information system (MIS) A computer-based system that optimizes the collection, transfer, and presentation of information throughout an organization, through an integrated structure of databases and information flow. (Contrast with *decision support system* and *executive support system.*)

Massively parallel processing (MPP) An approach to the design of computer systems that involves the integration of thousands of microprocessors within a single computer.

Master file The permanent source of data for a particular computer application area.

Mb See *megabit.*

MB See *megabyte.*

MCA [*Micro Channel Architecture*] The architecture of the high-end IBM PS/2 line of microcomputers.

Megabit (Mb) 1,048,576, or about one million, bits.

Megabyte (MB) 1,048,576, or about one million, bytes.

Megahertz (MHZ) One million hertz (cycles per second).

Memory See *RAM.*

Menu A display with a list of processing choices from which a user may select.

Menu bar A menu in which the options are displayed across the screen.

Menu tree A hierarchy of menus.

Message A series of bits sent from a terminal to a computer, or vice versa.

MHZ See *megahertz.*

MICR See *magnetic-ink character recognition.*

MICR inscriber An output device that enables the printing of characters for magnetic ink character recognition on bank checks and deposit slips.

MICR reader-sorter An input device that reads the magnetic ink character recognition data on bank documents and sorts them.

Microcomputer (or micro) A small computer (See also *personal computer, PC*).

Microprocessor A computer on a single chip. The processing component of a microcomputer.

Microsecond One millionth of a second.

Microwave signal A high-frequency line-of-sight electromagnetic wave used in wireless communications.

MIDI [*Musical Instrument Digital Interface*] An interface between PCs and electronic musical instruments, like the synthesizer.

MIDI file A non-waveform file result for MIDI applications.

Millisecond One thousandth of a second.

Minicomputer (or mini) A midsized computer.

Minimize Reducing a window on the display screen to an icon.

MIPS Millions of instructions per second.

MIS planner The person in a company who has the responsibility for coordinating and preparing the MIS plans.

Mnemonics A memory aid often made up from the initials of the words in a term or process.

Modem [*MOdulator-DEModulator*] A device used to convert computer-compatible signals to signals that can be transmitted over the telephone lines, then back again to computer signals at the other end of the line.

Monitor A televisionlike display for soft-copy output in a computer system.

Morphing Using graphics software to transform one image into an entirely different image. The term is derived from the word *metamorphosis.*

Motherboard See *system board.*

Mouse A point-and-draw device that, when moved across a desktop a particular distance and direction, causes the same movement of the cursor on a screen.

Mouse pen A point-and-draw device that is rolled across the desktop like a mouse and held like a pen.

MS-DOS [*MicroSoft–Disk Operating System*] A microcomputer operating system.

Multifunction expansion board An add-on circuit board which contains the electronic circuitry for two or more supplemental capabilities (for example, a serial port and a fax modem).

Multimedia upgrade kit A kit containing the necessary hardware and software to upgrade a PC to run multimedia applications (CD-ROM, sound card, and so on).

Multimedia application Computer applications that involve the integration of text, sound, graphics, motion video, and animation.

Multiplatform environment A computing environment which supports more than one platform.

Multiplexer A computer that collects data from a number of low-speed devices, then transmits "concentrated" data over a single communications channel.

Multiplexing The simultaneous transmission of multiple transmissions of data over a single communications channel.

Multitasking The concurrent execution of more than one program at a time.

Multiuser microcomputer A microcomputer that can serve more than one user at any given time.

Nanosecond One billionth of a second.

National Information Infrastructure (NII) Refers to a futuristic network of high-speed data communications links that eventually will connect virtually every facet of our society. See also *information superhighway.*

Natural language A programming language in which the programmer writes specifications without regard to the computer's instruction format or syntax—essentially, using everyday human language to program.

Navigation Movement within and between a software application's work areas.

Network, computer See *computer network.*

Network address An electronic identifier assigned to each computer system and terminal/PC in a computer network.

Network administrator A data communications specialist who designs and maintains local area network (LANs) and wide area networks (WANs).

Network bus A common cable in a bus topology which permits the connection of terminals, peripheral devices, and microcomputers to create a computer network.

Network interface card (NIC) A PC expansion card or PCMCIA card that facilitates and controls the exchange of data between the PC and its network.

Network topology The configuration of the interconnections between the nodes in a communications network.

Neural network Millions of interconnected chips that are designed to enable computers to perform human-type tasks.

Node An endpoint in a computer network.

Non-Windows application A computer application that will run under Windows but does not conform to the Common User Access (CUA) standards.

Nondestructive read A read operation in which the program and/or data that are loaded to RAM from secondary storage reside in both RAM (temporarily) and secondary storage (permanently).

Nonimpact printer A printer that uses chemicals, lasers, or heat to form the images on the paper.

Nonprogrammed decision A decision that involves an ill-defined and unstructured problem (also called *information-based decision*).

Nonvolatile memory Solid-state RAM that retains its contents after an electrical interruption. (Contrast with *volatile memory*.)

Notebook PC A notebook-size laptop PC.

NuBus The architecture of high-end Apple Macintosh computers.

Numeric A reference to any of the digits 0–9. (Compare with *alpha* and *alphanumeric*.)

Numeric key pad An input device that permits rapid numeric data entry.

Object A result of any Windows application, such as a block of text, all or part of a graphic image, or a sound clip.

Object linking and embedding See *OLE*.

Object program A machine-level program that results from the compilation of a source program. (Compare with *source program*.)

Object-oriented language A programming language structured to enable the interaction between user-defined concepts that contain data and operations to be performed on the data.

Object-oriented programming (OOP) A form of software development in which programs are built with entities called objects, which model any physical or conceptual item. Objects are linked together in a top-down hierarchy.

OCR See *optical character recognition*.

OCR scanner A light-sensitive input device that bounces a beam of light off an image to interpret printed characters or symbols.

Offline Pertaining to data that are not accessible by, or hardware devices that are not connected to, a computer system. (Contrast with *online*.)

OLE [*object linking and embedding*] The software capability that enables the creation a compound document that contains one or more objects from other applications. Objects can be linked or embedded.

Online Pertaining to data and/or hardware devices accessible to and under the control of a computer system. (Contrast with *offline*.)

Online service An commercial information network that provides remote users with access to a variety of information services.

Online thesaurus Software that enables a user to request synonyms interactively during a word processing session.

Open application A running application.

Open architecture Refers to micros that give users the flexibility to configure the system with a variety of peripheral devices.

Operating system The software that controls the execution of all applications and system software programs.

Optical character recognition (OCR) A data entry technique that permits original-source data entry. Coded symbols or characters are scanned to retrieve the data.

Optical laser disk A secondary storage medium that uses laser technology to score the surface of a disk to represent a bit.

OS/2 A multitasking PC operating system.

Output Data transferred from RAM to an output device for processing.

P6 Intel's successor to the Pentium processor.

Page printer A printer that prints a page at a time.

Paint software Software that enables users to "paint" electronic images. Resultant images are stored as raster graphics images.

Palmtop PC See *pocket PC*.

Parallel transmission Pertaining to the transmission of data in groups of bits versus one bit at a time. (Contrast with *serial transmission*.)

Parallel conversion An approach to system conversion whereby the existing system and the new system operate simultaneously prior to conversion.

Parallel port A direct link with the microcomputer's bus that facilitates the parallel transmission of data, usually one byte at a time.

Parallel processing A processing procedure in which one main processor examines the programming problem and determines what portions, if any, of the problem can be solved in pieces by other subordinate processors.

Parameter A descriptor that can take on different values.

Parity checking A built-in checking procedure in a computer system to help ensure that the transmission of data is complete and accurate. (Related to *parity error*.)

Parity error Occurs when a bit is dropped in the transmission of data from one hardware device to another. (Related to *parity checking*.)

Password A word or phrase known only to the user. When entered, it permits the user to gain access to the system.

Patch A modification of a program or an information system.

PC card Same as *PCMCIA card*.

PC [*Personal Computer*] A small computer design for use by an individual. See also *microcomputer*.

PC specialist A person trained in the function and operation of PCs and related hardware and software.

PCI local bus [*Peripheral Component Interconnect*] Intel's local bus. (See *local bus*.)

PCMCIA card A credit-card–sized module that is inserted into a PCMCIA-compliant interface to offer add-on capabilities such as expanded memory, fax modem, and so on. Also called *PC card*.

Peer-to-peer LAN A local area network in which all PCs on the network are functionally equal.

Pen-based computing Computer applications that rely on the pen-based PCs for processing capability.

Pen-based PC A personal computer whose primary input device is a stylus or an electronic pen.

Pentium An Intel microprocessor.

Peripheral device Any hardware device other than the processor.

Personal computer (PC) See *PC*.

Personal computing A computing environment in which individuals use personal computers for domestic and/or business applications.

Personal digital assistant (PDA) Hand-held personal computers that support a variety of personal information systems.

Personal identification number (PIN) A code or number that is used in conjunction with a password to permit the user to gain access to a computer system.

Phased conversion An approach to system conversion whereby an information system is implemented one module.

Photo illustration software Software that enables the creation of original images and the modification of existing digitized images.

Physical security That aspect of computer-center security that deals with access to computers and peripheral devices.

Picosecond One trillionth of a second.

Picture element See *pixel*.

Pie graph A circular graph that illustrates each "piece" of datum in its proper relationship to the whole "pie."

Pilferage A special case of software piracy whereby a company purchases a software product without a site-usage license agreement, then copies and distributes it throughout the company.

Pilot conversion An approach to system conversion whereby the new system is implemented first in only one of the several areas for which it is targeted.

Pixel [*picture element*] An addressable point on a display screen to which light can be directed under program control.

Platform A definition of the standards by which software is developed and hardware is designed.

Plotter A device that produces high-precision hard-copy graphic output.

Plug-and-play Refers to making a peripheral device or an expansion board immediately operational by simply plugging it into a port or an expansion slot.

Pocket PC A hand-held personal computer (also called *palmtop PC*).

Pointer The highlighted area in a spreadsheet display that indicates the current cell.

Polling A line-control procedure in which each terminal is "polled" in rotation to determine whether a message is ready to be sent.

Pop-out menu A menu displayed next to the menu option selected in a higher-level pull-down or pop-up menu.

Pop-up menu A menu that is superimposed in a window over whatever is currently being displayed on the monitor.

Port An access point in a computer system that permits communication between the computer and a peripheral device.

Portrait Referring to the orientation of the print on the page. Printed lines run parallel to the shorter side of the page. (Contrast with *landscape*.)

Post-implementation review A critical examination of a computer-based system after it has been put into production.

Power up To turn on the electrical power to a computer system.

PowerPC A microprocessor created by an alliance between Motorola, Apple, and IBM.

Presentation graphics Business graphics that are used to present information in a graphic format in meetings, reports, and oral presentations.

Presentation graphics software User-friendly software that allows users to create a variety of visually appealing and informative presentation graphics.

Prespecification An approach to system development in which users relate their information processing needs to the project team during the early stages of the project.

Primary storage See *RAM*.

Print server A LAN-based PC that handles LAN user print jobs and controls at least one printer.

Printer A device used to prepare hard-copy output.

Private line A dedicated communications channel provided by a common carrier between any two points in a computer network (same as *leased line*.)

Procedure-oriented language A high-level language whose general-purpose instruction set can be used to produce a sequence of instructions to model scientific and business procedures.

Process and device control Using the computer to control an ongoing process or device in a continuous feedback loop.

Processor The logical component of a computer system that interprets and executes program instructions.

Processor-bound operation The amount of work that can be performed by the computer system is limited primarily by the speed of the computer.

Program-item icon A pictograph used in Windows to represent an application.

Program (1) Computer instructions structured and ordered in a manner that, when executed, causes a computer to perform a particular function. (2) The act of producing computer software. (Related to *software*.)

Program register The register that contains the address of the next instruction to be executed.

Programmed decision Decisions that address well-defined problems with easily identifiable solutions.

Programmer One who writes computer programs.

Programmer/analyst The title of one who performs both the programming and systems analysis function.

Programming The act of writing a computer program.

Programming language A language programmers use to communicate instructions to a computer.

PROM [*P*rogrammable *R*ead-*O*nly *M*emory] ROM in which the user can load read-only programs and data.

Prompt A program-generated message describing what should be entered.

Proprietary software package Vendor-developed software that is marketed to the public.

Protocols See *communications protocols*.

Prototype system A model of a full-scale system.

Prototyping An approach to systems development that results in a prototype system.

Pseudocode Nonexecutable program code used as an aid to develop and document structured programs.

Pull-down menu A menu that is "pulled down" from an option in a higher-level menu.

Quality assurance specialist A person assigned the task of monitoring the quality of every aspect of the design and operation of information systems.

Query by example A method of database inquiry in which the user sets conditions for the selection of records by composing one or more example relational expressions.

Radio signals Signals which enable data communication between radio transmitters and receivers.

RAM disk That area of RAM that facilitates disk caching. (See also *disk caching*.)

Random-access memory See *RAM*

RAM [*R*andom-*A*ccess *M*emory] The memory area in which all programs and data must reside before programs can be executed or data manipulated. (Same as *primary storage*; compare with *secondary storage*.)

Random access Direct access to records, regardless of their physical location on the storage medium. (Contrast with *sequential access*.)

Random file A collection of records that can be processed randomly. (Same as *direct-access file*.)

Random processing Processing data and records randomly. (Same as *direct-access processing*; contrast with *sequential processing*.)

Range A cell or a rectangular group of adjacent cells in a spreadsheet.

Rapid prototyping Creating a nonfunctional prototype system.

Raster graphics A method for maintaining a screen image as patterns of dots. (See also *bit-mapped*.)

Read The process by which a record or a portion of a record is accessed from the secondary storage medium and transferred to primary storage for processing. (Contrast with *write*.)

Read/write head That component of a disk drive or tape drive that reads from and writes to its respective secondary storage medium.

Read-only memory (ROM) A memory chip with contents permanently loaded by the manufacturer for read-only applications.

Record A collection of related fields (such as an employee record) describing an event or an item.

Register A small high-speed storage area in which data pertaining to the execution of a particular instruction are stored.

Relational database A database, made up of logically linked tables, in which data are accessed by content rather than by address.

Relational operators Used in formulas to show the equality relationship between two expressions (= [equal to], < [less than], > [greater than], <= [less than or equal to], >= [greater than or equal to], <> [not equal to]). (See also *logical operators*.)

Relative cell address Refers to a cell's position in a spreadsheet in relation to the cell containing the formula in which the address is used.

Report generator Software that automatically produces reports based on user specifications.

Resident font A font that is accessed directly from the printer's built-in read-only memory.

Resolution Referring to the number of addressable points on a monitor's screen or the number of dots per unit area on printed output.

Responsibility matrix A matrix that graphically illustrates when and to what extent individuals and groups are involved in each activity of a systems development process.

Rewritable optical disk A secondary storage medium that integrates optical and magnetic disk technology to enable read-*and*-write storage.

RGB monitor Color monitors that mix red, green, and blue to achieve a spectrum of colors.

Ring topology A computer network that involves computer systems connected in a closed loop, with no one computer system the focal point of the network.

RISC [*R*educed *I*nstruction *S*et *C*omputer] A computer design architecture based on a limited instruction set machine language. (Contrast with *CISC*.)

Robot A computer-controlled manipulator capable of locomotion and/or moving items through a variety of spatial motions.

Robotics The integration of computers and industrial robots.

ROM [*R*ead-*O*nly *M*emory] RAM that can be read only, not written to.

Root directory The directory at the highest level of a hierarchy of directories.

Routers Communications hardware that enables communications links between LANs and WANs by performing the necessary protocol conversions.

RS-232C connector A 9-pin or 25-pin plug that is used for the electronic interconnection of computers modems, and other peripheral devices.

Run To open and execute a program.

Scalable typeface An outline-based typeface from which fonts of any point size can be created.

Scanner A device that scans hard copy and digitizes the text and/or images to a format that can be interpreted by a computer.

Scheduler Someone who schedules the use of hardware resources to optimize system efficiency.

Screen image projector An output device that can project a computer-generated image onto a large screen.

Screen-capture programs Memory-resident programs that enable users to transfer all or part of the current screen image to a disk file.

Screen saver A utility program used to change static screens on idle monitors to interesting dynamic displays.

Screen generator A systems design tool that enables a systems analyst to produce a mockup of a display while in direct consultation with the user.

Scroll arrow Small box containing an arrow at each end of a scroll bar that is used to navigate in small increments within a document or list.

Scroll box A square object that is that is dragged along a scroll bar to navigate within a document or list.

Scrolling Using the cursor keys to view parts of a document that extends past the bottom or top or sides of the screen.

SCSI bus [*Small Computer System Interface*] This hardware interface allows the connection of several peripheral devices to a single SCSI expansion board (or adapter).

Secondary storage Permanent data storage on magnetic disk, CD-R, and/or magnetic tape. (Compare with *primary storage* and *RAM*.)

Sector A disk storage concept of a pie-shaped portion of a disk or diskette in which records are stored and subsequently retrieved. (Contrast with *cylinder*.)

Sector organization Magnetic disk organization in which the recording surface is divided into pie-shaped sectors.

Select Highlighting an object on a windows screen or a menu option.

Sequential access Accessing records in the order in which they are stored. (Contrast with *random access*.)

Sequential files Files containing records that are ordered according to a key field.

Sequential processing Processing of files that are ordered numerically or alphabetically by a key field. (Contrast with *direct-access processing* or *random processing*.)

Serial transmission Pertaining to processing data one bit at a time. (Contrast with *parallel transmission*.)

Serial port A direct link with the microcomputer's bus that facilitates the serial transmission of data.

Serial representation The storing of bits one after another on a secondary storage medium.

Serpentine A magnetic tape storage scheme in which data are recorded serially in tracks.

Server A LAN component that can be shared by users on a LAN.

Server application (1) An application running on a network server that works in tandem with a client workstation or PC application. (See also *client application*.) (2) In object linking an embedding, the application in which the linked object originates.

Server computer Any type of computer, from a PC to a supercomputer, which performs a variety of functions for its client computers, including the storage of data and applications software. See also *client computer*.

Shell Software that provides a graphical user interface alternative to command-driven software.

Shortcut key A key combination that chooses a menu option without the need to display a menu.

Shut down The processes of exiting all applications and shutting off the power to a computer system.

Simultaneous click Tapping both buttons on a point-and-draw device at the same time.

SIMM [*Single In-line Memory Module*] Memory packaged on a circuit board that can be easily connected to a PC's system board.

Smalltalk An object-oriented language.

Smart card A card or badge with an embedded microprocessor.

Soft copy Temporary output that can be interpreted visually, as on a monitor. (Contrast with *hard copy*.)

Soft font An electronic description of a font that is retrieved from disk storage and downloaded to the printer's memory.

Software The programs used to direct the functions of a computer system. (Contrast with *hardware*; related to *program*.)

Software agent Artificial intelligence-based software that has the authority to act on a person or thing's behalf.

Software engineer A person who develops software products to bridge the gap between design and executable program code.

Software engineering A term coined to emphasize an approach to software development that embodies the rigors of the engineering discipline.

Software installation The process of copying the program and data files from a vendor-supplied master disk(s) to a PC's hard disk.

Software package One or more programs designed to perform a particular processing task.

Software piracy The unlawful duplication of proprietary software. (Related to *pilferage*.)

Software suite An integrated collection of software tools that may include a variety of business applications packages.

Sort The rearrangement of fields or records in an ordered sequence by a key field.

Source application, clipboard The software application from which the clipboard contents originated. (Contrast with *destination application*).

Source data Original data that usually involve the recording of a transaction or the documenting of an event or an item.

Source data automation Entering data directly to a computer system at the source without the need for key entry transcription.

Source document The original hard copy from which data are entered.

Source program The code of the original program. (Also called *source code*; compare with *object program.*)

Source program file This file contains high-level instructions to the computer which must be compiled prior to program execution.

Speech synthesis Converting raw data into electronically produced speech.

Speech synthesizers Devices that convert raw data into electronically produced speech.

Speech-recognition system A device that permits voice input to a computer system.

Spelling checker A software feature that checks the spelling of every word in a document against an electronic dictionary.

Spreadsheet file A file containing data and formulas in tabular format.

Spreadsheet software Refers to software that permits users to work with rows and columns of data.

Star topology A computer network that involves a centralized host computer connected to a number of smaller computer systems.

Static RAM (SRAM) A RAM technology whose chips do not require a refresh cycle. (Contrast with *DRAM.*)

Stop bits A data communications parameter that refers to the number of bits in the character or byte.

Structure chart A chart that graphically illustrates the conceptualization of an information system as a hierarchy of modules.

Structured system design A systems design technique that encourages top-down design.

Subroutine A group or sequence of instructions for a specific programming task that is called by another program.

Supercomputer The category that includes the largest and most powerful computers.

Switched line A telephone line used as a regular data communications channel (also called *dial-up line*).

Synchronous transmission A communications protocol in which the source and destination points operate in timed alignment to enable high-speed data transfer.

Syntax The rules that govern the formulation of the instructions in a computer program.

Syntax error An invalid format for a program instruction.

Sysop [*system operator*] The sponsor who provides the hardware and software support for an electronic bulletin-board system.

System Any group of components (functions, people, events, and so on) that interface with and complement one another to achieve one or more predefined goals.

System board A microcomputer circuit board that contains the microprocessor, electronic circuitry for handling such tasks as input/output signals from peripheral devices, and memory chips (same as *motherboard*).

System check An internal verification of the operational capabilities of a computer's electronic components.

System life cycle A reference to the four stages of a computer-based information system—birth, development, production, and death.

System maintenance The process of modifying an information system to meet changing needs.

System operator See *sysop*.

System prompt A visual prompt to the user to enter a system command.

System software Software that is independent of any specific applications area.

System specifications (specs) Information system details that include everything from the functionality of the system to the format of the system's output screens and reports.

Systems analysis The examination of an existing system to determine input, processing, and output requirements for the target system.

Systems analyst A person who does systems analysis.

Systems development methodology Written standardized procedures that depict the activities in the systems development process and define individual and group responsibilities.

Systems programmer A programmer who develops and maintains system software.

Systems testing A phase of testing where all programs in a system are tested together.

Tape backup unit (TBU) A magnetic tape drive design to provide backup for data and programs.

Tape drive, magnetic The hardware device that contains the read/write mechanism for the magnetic tape storage medium. (Compare with *disk drive, magnetic.*)

Tape, magnetic A secondary storage medium for sequential data storage and back up.

Target system A proposed information system that is the object of a systems development effort.

Task The basic unit of work for a processor.

TCP/IP [*Transmission Control Protocol/Internet Protocol*] A set of communications protocols developed by the Department of Defense to link dissimilar computers across many kinds of networks.

Telecommunications The collection and distribution of the electronic representation of information between two points.

Telecommuting "Commuting" via a communications link between home and office.

Telemedicine Describes any type of health care administered remotely over communication links.

Telephone Access Server (TAS) A system that permits users to access their electronic mailboxes remotely via a touch-tone telephone.

Telephony The integration of computers and telephones.

Template A model for a particular microcomputer software application.

Terabyte (TB) About one trillion bytes.

Terminal Any device capable of sending and receiving data over a communications channel.

Terminal emulation mode The software transformation of a PC so that its keyboard, monitor, and data interface emulate that of a terminal.

Text mode One of two modes of operation for PC monitors. (Contrast with *graphics mode*.)

Thesaurus, online See *online thesaurus*.

Third-generation language (3GL) A procedure-oriented programming language that can be used to model almost any scientific or business procedure. (Related to *procedure-oriented language*.)

Throughput A measure of computer system efficiency; the rate at which work can be performed by a computer system.

Throwaway system An information system developed to support information for a one-time decision, then discarded.

Tiled windows Two or more windows displayed on the screen in a non-overlapping manner.

Tiny area network (TAN) A term coined to refer to very small local area networks, typically installed in the home or small office.

Title bar A narrow Windows screen object at the top of each window that runs the width of the window.

Toggle The action of pressing a single key on a keyboard to switch between two or more modes of operation, such as insert and replace.

Total connectivity The networking of all hardware, software, and databases in an organization.

Touch-screen monitors Monitors with touch-sensitive screens that enable users to choose from available options by simply touching the desired icon or menu item with their finger.

Tower PC A PC that includes a system unit that is design to rest vertically. (Contrast with *laptop PC* and *desktop PC*.)

Track, disk That portion of a magnetic disk-face surface that can be accessed in any given setting of a single read/write head. Tracks are configured in concentric circles.

Track, tape That portion of a magnetic tape that can be accessed by any one of the tape drives read/write heads. A track runs the length of the tape.

Trackball A ball mounted in a box that, when moved, results in a similar movement of the cursor on a display screen.

Trackpad A point-and-draw device with no moving parts that includes a touch-sensitive pad to move the graphics cursor.

Tracks per inch (TPI) A measure of the recording density, or spacing, of tracks on a magnetic disk.

Transaction A procedural event in a system that prompts manual or computer-based activity.

Transaction file A file containing records of data activity (transactions); used to update the master file.

Transaction-oriented processing Transactions are recorded and entered as they occur.

Transmission medium The central cable along which terminals, peripheral devices, and microcomputers are connected in a bus topology.

Transparent A reference to a procedure or activity that occurs automatically and does not have to be considered by the user.

TSR [*terminate-and-stay-resident*] Programs that remain in memory so they can be instantly popped up over the current application by pressing a hotkey.

Turnaround document A computer-produced output that is ultimately returned to a computer system as a machine-readable input.

Typeface A set of characters that are of the same type style.

Typeover mode A data entry mode in which the character entered overstrikes the character at the cursor position.

Unicode A 16-bit encoding system.

Uninterruptible power source (UPS) A buffer between an external power source and a computer system that supplies clean, continuous power.

Unit testing That phase of testing in which the programs that make up an information system are tested individually.

Universal product code (UPC) A 10-digit machine-readable bar code placed on consumer products.

UNIX A multiuser operating system.

Upload The transmission of data from a local computer to a remote computer.

Uptime That time when the computer system is in operation.

User The individual providing input to the computer or using computer output.

User-friendly Pertaining to an online system that permits a person with relatively little experience to interact successfully with the system.

User interface A reference to the software, method, or displays that enable interaction between the user and the software being used.

User liaison A person who serves as the technical interface between the information services department and the user group.

User sign-off A procedure whereby the user manager is asked to "sign off," or commit, to the specifications defined by the systems development project team.

Utility program An often-used service routine, such as a program to sort records.

Vaccine An antiviral program.

VDT [*Video Display Terminal*] A terminal on which printed and graphic information is displayed on a televisionlike monitor and into which data are entered on a typewriterlike keyboard.

Vector graphics A method for maintaining a screen image as patterns of lines, points, and other geometric shapes.

Vertical scroll bar   A narrow screen object located along the right edge of a window that is used to navigate up and down through a document or list.

VGA   [*Video Graphics Array*] A circuit board that enables the interfacing of very high-resolution monitors to microcomputers.

Video display terminal   See *VDT*.

Video file   This file contains digitized video frames that when played rapidly produce motion video.

Video RAM (VRAM)   RAM on the graphics adapter.

Video display terminal   See *VDT*.

Virtual machine   The processing capabilities of one computer system created through software (and sometimes hardware) in a different computer system.

Virus   A program written with malicious intent and loaded to the computer system of an unsuspecting victim. Ultimately, the program destroys or introduces errors in programs and databases.

Vision-input systems   A device that enables limited visual input to a computer system.

Visual Basic   A visual programming language.

Visual C++   A visual programming language.

Visual programming   An approach to program development that relies more on visual association with tools and menus than with syntax-based instructions.

VL-bus   [*VESA Local-BUS*] A local bus based on the Video Electronics Standards Association's recommendations.

Voice message switching   Using computers, the telephone system, and other electronic means to store and forward voice messages. (Contrast with *electronic mail*.)

Voice-response system   A device that enables output from a computer system in the form of user-recorded words, phrases, music, alarms, and so on.

Volatile memory   Solid-state semiconductor RAM in which the data are lost when the electrical current is turned off or interrupted. (Contrast with *nonvolatile memory*.)

WAIS   [*wide area information server*] A database on the Internet that contains indexes to documents that reside on the Internet.

Wand scanner   Hand-held OCR scanner.

Wave file   A windows sound file.

Wide area network (WAN)   A computer network that connects nodes in widely dispersed geographic areas. (Contrast with *local area network*.)

Window   A rectangular section of a display screen that is dedicated to a specific document, activity, or application.

Window panes   Simultaneous display of subareas of a particular window.

Windows   A software product by Microsoft Corporation that provides a graphical user interface and multitasking capabilities for the MS-DOS environment.

Windows 95   An operating system by Microsoft Corporation.

Windows application   An application that conforms to the Microsoft Common User Access (CUA) standards and operates under the Microsoft Windows platform.

Windows for Workgroups   Version of Microsoft Windows that includes built-in peer-to-peer networking and e-mail.

Windows NT   A high-end operating system by Microsoft Corporation.

Word   For a given computer, an established number of bits that are handled as a unit.

Word processing   Using the computer to enter, store, manipulate, and print text.

Word wrap   A word processing feature that automatically moves, or "wraps," text to the next line when that text would otherwise exceed the right margin limit.

Work space   The area in a window below the title bar or menu bar containing everything that relates to the application noted in the title bar.

Workgroup computing   Computer applications that involve cooperation among people linked by a computer network. (Related to *groupware*.)

Workstation   A high-performance single-user computer system with sophisticated input/output devices that can be easily networked with other workstations or computers.

World Wide Web (the Web, WWW, W3)   An Internet server that offers multimedia and hypertext links.

Worm   A program that erases data and/or programs from a computer system's memory, usually with malicious intent.

WORM disk   [*Write-Once Read-Many disk*] An optical laser disk that can be read many times after the data are written to it, but the data cannot be changed or erased.

WORM disk cartridge   The medium for WORM disk drives.

Write   To record data on the output medium of a particular I/O device (tape, hard copy, PC display). (Contrast with *read*.)

WYSIWYG   [*What You See Is What You Get*] A software package in which what is displayed on the screen is very similar in appearance to what you get when the document is printed.

X terminal   A terminal that enables the user to interact via a graphical user interface (GUI).

Zoom   An integrated software command that expands a window to fill the entire screen.

INDEX

The fifth edition of *Computers and Information Systems*, is a modular book that is custom published to meet curriculum needs. This book may contain only the Core (C) module or it may also include the Additional Topics (AT) module. Entries in the index are prefaced by a C or an AT, depending on which module is referenced. When several page references are noted for a single entry, boldface denotes the page(s) on which the term is defined or discussed in some depth